W9-DCN-033

THE NATURE OF SYNTACTIC REPRESENTATION

SYNTHESE LANGUAGE LIBRARY

TEXTS AND STUDIES IN
LINGUISTICS AND PHILOSOPHY

Managing Editors:
JAAKKO HINTIKKA, *Florida State University*
STANLEY PETERS, *The University of Texas at Austin*

Editorial Board:
EMMON BACH, *University of Massachusetts at Amherst*
JOAN BRESNAN, *Massachusetts Institute of Technology*
JOHN LYONS, *University of Sussex*
JULIUS M. E. MORAVCSIK, *Stanford University*
PATRICK SUPPES, *Stanford University*
DANA SCOTT, *Oxford University*

VOLUME 15

THE NATURE OF SYNTACTIC REPRESENTATION

Edited by

PAULINE JACOBSON

Dept. of Linguistics, Brown University, Providence

and

GEOFFREY K. PULLUM

Cowell College, University of California, Santa Cruz

D. REIDEL PUBLISHING COMPANY

DORDRECHT : HOLLAND / BOSTON : U.S.A.
LONDON : ENGLAND

Library of Congress Cataloging in Publication Data
Main Entry under title:

The Nature of syntactic representation.

    (Synthese language library; v. 15)
    Rev. papers from a conference held at Brown University in May 1979.
    Includes bibliographies and index.
    1. Grammar, Comparative and general—Syntax—Addresses, essays,
lectures. 2. Generative   grammar—Addresses,   essays,   lectures.
I. Jacobson, Pauline I., 1947–   II. Pullum, Geoffrey K. III. Series.
P291.N3   415   81–15753
ISBN 90–277–1289–1   AACR2
ISBN 90–277–1290–5 (pbk.)

Published by D. Reidel Publishing Company,
P.O. Box 17, 3300 AA Dordrecht, Holland.

Sold and distributed in the U.S.A. and Canada
by Kluwer Boston Inc.,
190 Old Derby Street, Hingham, MA 02043, U.S.A.

In all other countries, sold and distributed
by Kluwer Academic Publishers Group,
P.O. Box 322, 3300 AH Dordrecht, Holland.

D. Reidel Publishing Company is a member of the Kluwer Group.

All Rights Reserved
Copyright © 1982 by D. Reidel Publishing Company, Dordrecht, Holland
No part of the material protected by this copyright notice may be reproduced or
utilized in any form or by any means, electronic or mechanical,
including photocopying, recording or by any informational storage and
retrieval system, without written permission from the copyright owner.

Printed in The Netherlands

TABLE OF CONTENTS

PREFACE

The work collected in this book represents the results of some intensive recent work on the syntax of natural languages. The authors' differing viewpoints have in common the program of revising current conceptions of syntactic representation so that the role of transformational derivations is reduced or eliminated. The fact that the papers cross-refer to each other a good deal, and that authors assuming quite different frameworks are aware of each other's results and address themselves to shared problems, is partly the result of a conference on the nature of syntactic representation that was held at Brown University in May 1979 with the express purpose of bringing together different lines of research in syntax. The papers in this volume mostly arise out of work that was presented in preliminary form at that conference, though much rewriting and further research has been done in the interim period.

Two papers are included because although they were not given even in preliminary form at the conference, it has become clear since then that they interrelate with the work of the conference so much that they cannot reasonably be left out: Gerald Gazdar's statement of his program for phrase structure description of natural language forms the theoretical basis that is assumed by Maling and Zaenen and by Sag, and David Dowty's paper represents a bridge between the relational grammar exemplified here in the papers by Perlmutter and Postal on the one hand and the Montague-influenced description to be found in the contributions of Bach, Cooper, Sag, and others. These connections might be kept in mind when determining an order in which to read the papers, which are arranged in alphabetical order of author's surname rather than in any attempt at a logically determined ordering. The logical connections among the papers are brought out in our Editorial Introduction.

We wish to thank the National Science Foundation for the grant that made the conference possible; Brown University and its linguistics students for hosting the conference and helping to make it a success; and all the participants at the conference – not only those whose work is included in this volume, but all those whose presentations or discussant sessions enriched the conference, including Judith Aissen, Peter Cole, Leland

George, Jane Grimshaw, Gabriella Hermon, David Johnson, Jaklin Kornfilt, Jerry Morgan, Frederick Newmeyer, Edwin Williams, and Arnold Zwicky.

December 1980   PAULINE JACOBSON
                                              GEOFFREY K. PULLUM

EDITORIAL INTRODUCTION

The work collected in this book represents a sampling of recent research in syntax that challenges a position that we will call the *classical theory* of transformational-generative grammar (a term that we define below). This position has dominated syntactic research during much of the last twenty years. The studies in this book are for the most part concerned with developing alternatives to it. Without abandoning the goals or methods of generative grammar, they strike out in directions that depart radically from the classical theory in at least certain respects, and in several cases they reject transformational grammar completely.

The claim that defines what we call the classical theory (on which the definitive source is Chomsky (1965)) is that the syntactic representation of a sentence is (nothing more than) an ordered set of constituent structure trees called a *derivation*, where the first member of a derivation is by definition a *deep structure* and the last is by definition a *surface structure*. Each tree consists of a set of labelled nodes associated with a pair of relations (*dominates* and *precedes*). The sequence of trees that constitute well-formed derivations are those licensed by a set of *transformations*.

Much of the research within the classical theory focussed on claims about properties of derivations and on constraints on the transformational operations that defined them. For example, proposals concerning rule ordering and the cycle assumed the existence of transformational derivations, and sought to characterize them more precisely.

In the classical theory there is no limit set on the number of distinct structures a derivation may contain, and the descriptive latitude that arises out of this property of the model has been exploited to the full in transformational work. In countless transformational studies, descriptive problems were tackled by postulating extra stages in the derivation of some class of sentences, or, in some modifications of the basic theory, by allowing "global derivational constraints" that refer to non-adjacent stages within a derivation.

Starting in about the mid 1970's, two main lines of research arose which led away from the assumptions of the classical theory. The studies in this volume exemplify both of these lines, carrying them in some cases to their

ix

logical conclusions. One such line challenges the role of step-by-step derivations and the roles of the various intermediate levels which are defined by derivations. Research along this line has shown that many of the generalizations classically captured in terms of derivations can instead be captured by components of the grammar other than the transformational one. For example, Brame (1978) and Bresnan (1978) have both argued that the lexicon is the component that accounts for most of what is classically accounted for by transformations. Others have suggested that an enriched notion of semantics can capture many of these generalizations; a good deal of the research within the tradition known as Montague grammar has been in this direction. Work within what has come to be known as trace theory has also suggested that the role of derivations can be reduced by positing an enriched level of surface structure; this is the position taken in, for example, Chomsky (1977, 1980).

The second line of research questions the importance of constituent structure in syntactic description and challenges the claim that precedence and dominance are the right, or the only, primitive relations in syntactic representation. For example, research within the tradition of relational grammar has suggested that notions like *subject* and *object* are primitives of linguistic theory. (These notions are now also used in the lexically-based theory of Bresnan (1978, 1981).)

These two lines of inquiry are logically independent; one could readily envisage a theory in which derivations are completely abandoned but constituent structure is not. One could also envisage a theory in which constituent structure trees are replaced by some other way of representing syntactic form, but derivations are still assumed. And of course, one might consider rejecting both constituent structure and derivations in favor of something else. Although there is no consensus among the contributors to this book concerning which of these directions to take, there is broad agreement about the strategy of departing significantly from the reliance on derivational description that characterizes the classical theory.

The first paper in this book, by Andrews, adopts a framework being developed by Bresnan and Kaplan (see Bresnan (1981)) in which the lexicon assumes a very large part of the burden borne by transformational rules in the classical theory. Andrews discusses the "long-distance agreement" facts of Icelandic, a language in which (as in classical Greek) predicative adjectives and participles agree in morphological features with their subjects, and continue to display this agreement even in sentences where they are widely separated from their subjects in constructions that would be analyzed transformationally in terms of movement.

In the classical theory, such facts were not readily accounted for. An NP might be raised out of its clause into a position where it was a matrix object (perhaps several clauses up from its deep structure position), and would receive accusative case marking on the basis of its derived position. However, a predicative adjective or participle in the clause in which the NP originated would then show accusative case in agreement with this NP, despite the fact that the NP was no longer in the same clause as this predicate (nor even within some fixed distance from it). Global rules were proposed to expand the descriptive power of the classical theory so that it could deal with such facts (Lakoff (1970), Andrews (1971)), and the question of long-distance agreement sparked much controversy concerning, the expressive power necessary in a linguistic theory.

What Andrews shows in the paper presented here is that a much more restricted theory than the classical theory can in fact deal with long-distance agreement. He first discusses how various phenomena classically accounted for by transformations like Passive and Raising can be treated without the use of transformations, and goes on to exhibit a way of stating agreement dependencies. He then shows that the absence of "NP-movement" transformations becomes an asset rather than a liability; crudely, predicative adjectives and participles can only agree with the case that their subjects have in virtue of their "derived" positions, because the "derived" positions of NP's are the only positions they ever have.

The fact that rather recalcitrant syntactic facts sometimes submit to description and explanation more readily without the use of transformations than with raises a significant issue. Andrews is presupposing that natural languages can be adequately described without transformations. But until quite recently most generative grammarians have assumed that phrase structure grammars without transformations simply do not have the expressive power needed to describe natural languages at all. Gerald Gazdar's contribution to this volume sets out to refute this assumption by showing that natural languages can in fact be adequately characterized by phrase structure grammars – indeed, probably by context-free grammars.

Gazdar begins by making a number of points concerning the generative capacity of grammars and the relations between generative capacity and issues like parasability and learnability. He introduces a number of elaborations and extensions of phrase structure rules which allow for the capturing of various linguistic generalizations without increasing the generative capacity of the grammar. He develops and illustrates a set of context-free rules to describe the central aspects of English verb phrases and adjective phrases, covering much of the data that is classically accounted for with transformations like Raising and Equi-NP Deletion, and treating both the syntax and the semantics of the constructions involved. Next, he proposes a non-transformational analysis of coordination, and introduces the concept of a *metarule*. A metarule determines the presence of one set of phrase structure rules in the grammar on the basis of another such set, capturing generalizations by factoring out similarities between rule sets. Gazdar employs metarules in his analysis of the passive construction.

Gazdar's most striking result is his demonstration that the phenomena classically described by means of unbounded movement transformations and constraints on movement can be elegantly captured in terms of context-free phrase structure rules. The operation of such prima facie unbounded movement rules as Topicalization, *Wh*-movement and the like have often been taken to be the best possible illustration of what transformations are and why they have been postulated. Gazdar shows that a principled augmentation of the set of basic node labels and the set of basic phrase structure rules of a language allows a simple account of such constructions, and that the existence of unbounded dependencies is not, as has often been assumed, a counterexample to the claim that natural languages can be described by context-free grammars.

Two different aspects of the line of research initiated by Gazdar are pursued in more detail by other contributors to this book: Sag investigates the program of treating "NP-movement" dependencies (Passivization, Raising, and so on) in a purely semantic way without the use of transformations, while Maling and Zaenen examine the implications of Gazdar's treatment of unbounded dependencies for other languages, specifically the Scandinavian languages.

Sag's paper is concerned primarily with an account of "dummies", i.e., NP's that have traditionally been taken to have a syntactic role but no semantic role, such as the *it* of *It is clear that you don't love me* and the *there* of *There is a spider in the bath*. He shows first in some detail how the classical theory of transformational grammar and the more recent "Revised Extended Standard Theory" (REST) would handle the distribution of dummies, and also extends the discussion to the treatment of idiom chunks like *tabs* in the expression *keep tabs on*. Then, accepting the arguments that have been given over the past few years in favor of moving away from transformational treatments, he tackles the problem of giving a fully explicit alternative in terms of phrase structure grammar.

The approach that Sag advocates involves crucial reference to the semantic properties of sentences, and to meanings of smaller constituents. His solution is based on rejecting the classical assumption that dummies play no semantic role. Thus Sag assigns meanings to the dummies *it* and *there* in such a way that only (and all) VP's of the right sort can combine with these elements to form propositions. Sentences such as *Seven lizards are obvious that you don't love me* (with a dummy-requiring VP but a non-dummy subject NP) and *There gave the prize to Daryl* (with a dummy subject but a non-dummy-requiring VP) are both treated as *semantically* deviant: the meanings of their VP's simply cannot combine with their subjects in such a way as to form propositions.

The unbounded dependencies of the classical theory, which are handled by Gazdar by means of the system of derived categories he develops in section 9 of his paper, are the focus of attention for Maling and Zaenen. They provide a schematic overview of the increasingly important domain of facts concerning "extraction" (unbounded displacement) and island constraints in the Scandinavian languages (they concentrate on Swedish, Norwegian, and Icelandic). An island is a construction in which (or out of which) certain dependencies, normally unbounded in their domain, fail to hold. The definition of "island" has generally always been given in terms of transformations and restrictions on the contexts in which they can apply (the definitive work here is Ross (1967)), but the basic phenomena still have to be explained, of course, in an entirely nontransformational framework.

Maling and Zaenen examine the problem of describing those facts in terms of Gazdar's system of phrase structure grammar. In doing so, they expose a descriptive problem whose solution may turn out to necessitate a change in Gazdar's theory that increases its weak generative capacity. Gazdar's augmentation of the basic categories allows for the existence of node labels having the form A/B where A and B are basic node labels. The intuitive interpretation of a label like S/NP is that it is the label of a constituent that is just like an S except that at one point in it there is a "gap" where an NP would ordinarily have been. The problem posed by a language like Swedish is that it allows multiple extractions of phrases from a single constituent (which English for the most part does not), so that constituents with more than one gap are encountered. This suggests a need for derived categories of the form α/B, where α itself may be a derived category; for example, node labels of the type S/NP/NP might be postulated. But, depending on the exact character of the rules and definitions employed, it is not necessarily the case that a grammar with an open-ended set of categories of this sort will generate a context-free language. Maling and Zaenan explore some of the evidence that bears on this point, and also relate their discussion to questions of parsing and linguistic perception.

The "gaps" in constituents just referred to are the topic to which Jacobson's paper is devoted. Both the approach taken by Gazdar and recent work within trace theory (see e.g. Chomsky (1977, 1981)) assume representations containing empty nodes or gaps in what are classically just positions from which a moved phrase was detached earlier in the derivation. Both approaches use this device to minimize or eliminate the role of transformational derivations. Jacobson is concerned with the question of whether positive evidence can be found to select theories postulating empty nodes over other theories. She develops positive arguments for the existence of empty nodes, and shows that various phenomena can be described in a unitary way if there are representations containing empty nodes, but cannot be captured in a simple way in the classical theory, even given its multiplicity of derivational levels.

Jacobson also argues that it is only certain types of construction that contain empty nodes – broadly speaking, the ones involving unbounded dependencies in the sense discussed by Maling and Zaenen. The "NP-movement" dependencies like Passive and Raising cannot be associated with evidence for gaps.

Finally, Jacobson considers the question of whether there are phenomena in language which indicate a need for reference to the classical theory's level of underlying structure, or whether a single level of representation with gaps is sufficient (a topic which Perlmutter also examines in his contribution below). As an example, she considers the distribution of case-marking of *wh*-words in certain English dialects, and offers some speculations on how this could be handled in a theory with a single level of syntactic representation.

The device of allowing syntactic representations to contain phonetically null elements like "gaps" and permitting semantic rules to refer to them is criticized in the paper by Cooper. Cooper's allusion in his title to "wholewheat syntax" is to the goal of defining a syntax that is unenriched with additives like phonetically silent nodes playing a semantic role as bound variables. Transformational derivations are not abandoned in Cooper's approach. Instead, the application of transformations is associated directly with certain aspects of the semantic interpretation of the constituents they define.

Thus, Cooper holds that neither the deep structure (as in the classical theory) nor the surface structure (as in recent work by Chomsky) should be the basis for translation into "logical form", or for the process of semantic interpretation itself. Instead, the operation of each specific transformation has a semantic correlate. For example, the *wh*-movement operation of taking an S like *you will keep which one* and constructing from it an S like *which one will you keep* is interpreted semantically in a way that involves quantification (with a special *wh* quantifier that Cooper defines) over a domain defined by the S node, and with a variable position defined by the original position of the *wh*-phrase in S.

Cooper's study deals with a further issue, namely the question of how to formulate island constraints (cf. the papers by Gazdar and by Maling and Zaenen). Cooper suggests an approach quite different from that of the classical theory, in which island constraints are constraints on the application of syntactic transformations, and from the approach explored by Gazdar and by Maling and Zaenen, in which island constraints are restrictions on permissible node labels and/or phrase structure rules. In Cooper's view, certain island constraints can be reformulated as constraints on building up *interpretations* of sentences. Like Sag's proposed account of the distribution of dummies, Cooper's paper reanalyzes in semantic terms a phenomenon that has classically been treated as purely syntactic.

The issue of what needs a syntactic account and what needs a semantic one has, of course, been a matter of serious debate since the beginning of the 1970's. More recently, there has been some discussion of the separate issue of what should be treated in the semantic description and what should be accounted for in purely extragrammatical terms (e.g. as a matter of pragmatics). These questions both arise in Bach's paper, which is concerned with an analysis of purpose clauses. Bach considers the question of whether it should be stipulated grammatically that a sentence like *I've brought this to read* is most naturally (or perhaps only) understood as indicating that the speaker will read the thing to which *this* refers. He argues convincingly that this is not something that should be syntactically stipulated.

Bach then goes on to take a closer look at the semantic properties of purpose clauses, coming to the conclusion that the semantics does not fix the identity of the subject of the main verb either. That is, the purpose clause in the above example does say that the book is for reading, but it does not specify a reader. The information that when one says *I've brought this to read* one intends to do the reading oneself is inferred by the hearer under normal circumstances, and not contained in the syntactic or semantic makeup of the sentence. The same is true with regard to the information that when one says *I've brought you this to read* one expects the hearer to do the reading. In his thorough examination of the structure and meaning of purpose clauses, couched in terms of a Montague-like theory for the most part (but containing some comments on the limitations of model-theoretic semantics), Bach sheds light on a number of their peculiar properties and offers some stimulating speculations concerning how we might attempt to achieve an understanding of the rest.

One thing that all the diverse contributions so far discussed have in common is their reliance on syntactic representation in terms of constituent structure of the sort familiar from classical transformational grammar. These works accept the claim that syntactic representations either are, or at least contain, constituent structure trees. A tree is a set of labelled nodes connected by a network of dominance and precedence relations meeting certain conditions. The papers by Perlmutter and Postal reject completely the use of this sort of tree. Both of these authors hold that syntactic representations have to be richer than constituent structure tree representations, and both employ a fair-sized inventory of primitive relations among linguistic elements. This inventory does not include the relation "dominates", but, crucially, does include the relations *is the subject of, is the direct object of,* and *is the indirect object of.* (Andrews also makes use of a level of representation which includes notions of this sort; however, he assumes the existence of ordinary constituent structure as well).

Concentrating on the first of these three central grammatical relations, Perlmutter sets out to illustrate the application of the notion "subject" in linguistic description, and proceeds to challenge theories which posit only a single level, or only two levels, of syntactic representation. He defines five different notions of subject which play a role in the grammars of natural languages. The definitions of these notions crucially rely on positing more than one level of syntactic representation. Perlmutter illustrates the application of these notions to descriptive problems from a wide range of languages.

The heart of Perlmutter's paper lies in his claim that these five notions of subjecthood need to be referred to in grammars. Perlmutter claims that because these notions can be shown to play a role in the syntax of some languages, a framework defining grammatical relations at only a single level of representation cannot be adequate. Perlmutter lays down a challenge to the proponents of single-level syntactic theories like the ones defended in this volume by Gazdar, Maling and Zaenen, and Sag, and two-level theories like the one assumed by Andrews. The challenge is to show how such theories can revealingly analyze the facts from Achenese, Georgian, Italian, Maasai, Russian, and numerous other languages claimed to give evidence of grammatical rules whose statement necessitates more than one representational level – and, in some cases, more than two levels.

The paper by Postal also contains a challenge to single-level and two-level syntactic theories. His paper contains some detailed analysis of a cluster of related problems in French grammar, and uses this analysis as the basis for a number of claims about the nature of syntactic representation. He assumes the theoretical framework of arc pair grammar as set out in Johnson and Postal (1980). This framework can be regarded as a further elaboration of the relational grammar that Perlmutter and Postal have been developing jointly.

Postal is primarily concerned with accounting for the distribution of extraposed indefinite NP's in French. His proposed account of this phenomenon crucially relies on allowing an NP to bear different grammatical relations at different levels of syntactic representation. His paper contains a substantial discussion of the construction type in which a "deep" indirect object (i.e. a 3 in Postal's terminology) is a direct object (i.e. a 2) at a more superficial level. This construction type, henceforth 3-to-2 advancement, is essentially the analog of the Dative Movement transformation in the classical theory. Postal stresses that there can be languages in which 3-to-2 advancement is virtually always in evidence in any clause that has a 3 (he cites Mohawk as one example), and languages in which there is only limited 3-to-2 advancement with certain predicates (e.g. English), as well as languages in which 3-to-2 advancement is very limited indeed, occurring only with one or two predicates, which is what Postal claims is the case in French.

Postal's claims crucially depend on a novel proposal concerning the representation of what is usually called "coreference". Very roughly, his proposal treats (at least certain instances of) "coreference" as being representable in terms of a single NP bearing more than one grammatical relation (not necessarily to the same clause in each case) at the initial or semantically relevant level of representation. Using this idea, and taking into account the evidence for 3-to-2 advancement noted above, Postal conducts an extended examination of a large set of facts not previously assembled in one place, and proposes a unitary explanation for these facts. The crucial feature of his account vis a vis the nature of syntactic representation is that this unitary principle seems unstatable in a theory of grammar that only provides for one level (or even for two levels) of syntactic description.

Dowty's paper in this volume is also concerned with the role of grammatical relations in syntax, but he departs from the positions taken by Perlmutter and Postal in two important respects. First, Dowty rejects the premise that grammatical relations are primitives, and proposes a way of defining them in terms of the way phrases combine with other phrases in a syntax of the Montague type (see e.g. Montague (1974), chapters 6, 7, and 8) and the way meanings for expressions are concomitantly built up. Second, Dowty defends essentially the kind of single-level grammatical theory that Perlmutter and Postal reject, and he attempts to reply to some of the challenges exemplified in their papers.

Dowty begins with a summary of the relevant features of Montague grammar, and then proceeds to define the three grammatical relations mentioned above. A subject, for example, is defined by Dowty as an NP that combine with an expression having the type of meaning that an intransitive verb has, making a sentence. Thus *John* is the subject of *John ate his dinner* because *John* combines with *ate his dinner* to yield a sentence, and *ate his dinner* is, like *dined*, an intransitive verb (for no distinction is made in Montague grammar between single lexical items like *dined* and phrases of the same semantic effect like *ate his dinner*; both belong to the same category, syntactically and semantically).

Using the notions he has defined, Dowty then proposes an account of a number of phenomena which are classically accounted for by transformational operations on constituent structure and which in relational grammar are treated in terms of NP's bearing different grammatical relations at different levels. In Dowty's account, processes like Dative Movement, Unspecified Object Deletion, etc. do not in any way operate on the NP's involved. Rather, they are rules which change the category of the phrases that combine with the NP's, where each such rule is associated with a semantic effect as well as a syntactic one. Dowty gives a number of arguments for preferring his treatment of grammatical relations over other accounts; among them is the claim that a number of the laws stipulated in relational grammar are theorems derivable from more basic properties of his theory.

Dowty's paper marks the beginning of a serious debate between defenders of relational theories which preserve the multi-level characteristics of the classical theory (while abandoning its central features, namely constituent-structure and transformations) and advocates of far more concrete "surface" theories that seek to incorporate the semantic rigor of the work Montague has inspired without giving up the attempt to capture syntactic generalizations. We believe that the basic elements of the debate can be fairly well appreciated on the basis of a reading of the papers assembled in this book. We also believe that as it becomes clearer what the syntactic representations of natural languages are like, it will be seen that much has been learned from the exploration and development of theories that turn out to be wrong, as well as from those that turn out to be closer to being correct. The fact that a number of incompatible viewpoints are argued for in the different contributions to this book should be seen, therefore, as a positive sign. The next significant steps forward in the study of the syntax of human languages will have to involve resolution of some of the issues that emerge as a result of the work presented in this book.

P. J.

G. K. P.

REFERENCES

Andrews, Avery D. (1971) 'Case agreement of predicate modifiers in Ancient Greek,' *Linquistic Inquiry* 2, 127–152.

Brame, Michael K. (1978) *Base Generated Syntax*, Noit Amrofer, Seattle.

Bresnan, Joan W. (1978) 'A realistic transformational grammar,' in M. Halle, J. W. Bresnan and G. Miller, eds., *Linquistic Theory and Psychological Reality*, MIT Press, Cambridge, Massachusetts.

Bresnan, Joan W. (ed.) (1981) The Mental Representation of Grammatical Relations, MIT Press, Cambridge, Massachusetts.

Chomsky, Noam (1965) *Aspects of the Theory of Syntax*, MIT Press, Cambridge, Massachusetts.

Chomsky, Noam (1977) 'On *wh*-movement,' in P. Culicover, T Wasow and A. Akmajian, eds., *Formal Syntax*, Academic Press, New York.

Chomsky, Noam (1980) 'On binding,' *Linquistic Inquiry* 11, 1–46.

Johnson, David E. and P. M. Postal (1980) *Arc Pair Grammar*, Princeton University Press, Princeton, New Jersey.

Lakoff, George (1970) 'Global rules,' *Language* 46, 627–639.

Montague, Richard (1974) *Formal Philosophy: Selected Papers of Richard Montague*, edited by Richmond Thomason, Yale University Press, New Haven, Connecticut.

Ross, John R. (1967) *Constraints on Variables in Syntax*, Doctoral dissertation, MIT, Cambridge, Massachusetts. Published in 1968 by Indian University Linquistics Club.

AVERY D. ANDREWS

LONG DISTANCE AGREEMENT IN MODERN ICELANDIC*

0. The 'long-distance' agreement of predicate modifiers in languages such as Ancient Greek and Modern Icelandic has been a puzzle for the last decade. Various novel mechanisms have been postulated to account for it, such as the global rules of Lakoff (1970), Andrews (1971), the indexing schemes of Baker and Brame (1972), Quicoli (1972) and Fauconnier (1971), the restructuring rule of Emonds (1973), and the system of control relations in Andrews (1973). Yet the basic phenomenon seems quite simple intuitively: predicate modifiers agree with what they modify.[1]

In this paper I will show that the theory of functional interpretation being developed by Joan Bresnan, Ron Kaplan and others[2] provides an account of long-distance agreement that captures this basic simplicity. Most of the facts will follow directly from the lexical representations of the agreeing forms together with the theory of sentence structure. The remainder will be accounted for with a convention for the 'misapplication' of agreement restrictions under certain conditions. Although I shall analyse only Icelandic, it will be evident that the 'global agreement' of Ancient Greek fits the same pattern.

1. The central notion in the theory is 'grammatical function.' A grammatical function is a (mathematical) function that takes as argument part of a sentence-structure and returns as value another part, considered to be a substructure of the first. Grammatical functions may be partial, but not multiple-valued.

The theory postulates that sentences have two levels of structure: constituent structure, which is basically surface structure in some version of the X-bar theory,[3] and functional structure, in which the linguistically significant grammatical functions are represented directly. Functional structure is itself quite simple, being essentially a representation of 'end-of-cycle' grammatical relations together with inflectional features, and the mapping between constituent and functional structures is likewise straightforward.

1

P. Jacobson and G. K. Pullum (eds.), The Nature of Syntactic Representation, 1–33.
Copyright © 1982 by D. Reidel Publishing Company.

1.1 The basic properties of functional structure may be most easily presented by discussing a simple example. (1) gives the functional structure for *I saw you in Cambridge*:

(1)

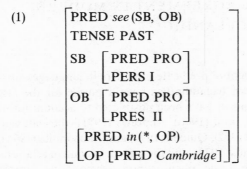

A functional structure may be naturally represented as an unlabelled bracketing. At each level, the structure consists of an unordered set of function name-function value pairs, together with a possibly empty set of adjuncts. For each pair, the second member, the fvalue, is the value of the function named by the first member, the fname. Hence the value of PRED on (1) is 'see (SB, OB).' The formally inclined may take the arguments and values of the grammatical functions to be occurrences of substrings in bracketings.

There are various kinds of grammatical functions. A special function is PRED. The value of PRED is always a representation of the lexical head of the phrase corresponding to the sub-bracketing immediately containing PRED. So in (1) 'see (SB, OB)' is a representation of *saw*, the lexical head of the sentence.

A second class of grammatical functions are the grammatical features. These take as values symbols representating inflectional and other grammatically significant categories. The grammatical features appearing in (1) are TENSE, with value PAST, and PERS, with values I and II (in the subject and object substructures). Grammatical gender, number and case will also be represented and controlled with grammatical feature functions.

Finally there are the relational functions, which represent the linguistically significant grammatical relations. The relational functions in (1) are SB (subject) and OB (object) and OP (object of preposition). The values of PRED and of the grammatical features are functionally atomic in that one cannot apply further grammatical functions to them. Relational functions on the other hand have functionally molecular values, to which further grammatical functions can be applied. Thus we can speak of the PRED of the SB of (1), which is PRO, or the PERS of the OB, which is II.

Composition of functions is represented by juxtaposition of names. Hence the value of the composite function SB PERS on (1) is I, while OB PRED has value PRO. Such two part composites frequently appear in the statement of grammatical constraints such as agreement restrictions, but tripartite or larger composites do not seem to be necessary in linguistic descriptions.

There are furthermore various types of relational functions. The main division is between 'open' functions and 'closed' functions. The closed functions are the usual surface grammatical relations, such as SB, OB and OB2 (second object), together with certain others such as the prepositional functions WITH, BY, etc., that are sometimes borne by objects of prepositions. The open functions on the other hand figure in the analysis of 'subject-raising' constructions, and will be discussed in section 2.

There is more than this to the universal typology of grammatical functions. SB, OB and OB2 for example have generally different behavior than the prepositional functions. I assume that individual grammatical relations are language-particular constructs.

There is an intimate connection between the value of the PRED function and the occurrence of relational functions in a structure. Semantically, the values of the relational functions represent the arguments of the value of the PRED function. Hence in (1), the values of SB and OB represent the two arguments of 'see (SB, OB).' PRED values, also called lexical forms, contain an argument-frame, which is ordered list of relational function names. Each position on the list corresponds to a thematic relation of the lexical item. In our representation for *see*, first position corresponds to the seer, second position to the seen. The function name filling the position determines what grammatical relation the NP filling the thematic relation bears. So 'see (SB, OB)' says that the seer is SB, the seen OB. The thematic relations may be considered to be relativized to the lexical item: although one might seek to identify a small number of universal thematic relations such as Agent, Goal, etc., there is no need to within the theory of sentence-structure (though such a theory might have considerable value in explaining the assignments of grammatical functions to thematic relations).

In addition to their involvement in semantic interpretation, argument-frames constrain the distribution of relational functions through the constraints of Completeness and Coherence. The Completeness Condition requires that the grammatical function filling each argument-position return a value that has a semantic representation. In particular the value must not be undefined. Hence given that the PRED of (1) is 'see (SB, OB),' Completeness requires that the structure provide meaningful values for SB and OB.

The Coherence Condition requires that every substructure with a meaning serve as a argument of some PRED. Some substructures, such as those associated with expletive *there*, have no meaning, and therefore cannot serve as arguments. These will not concern us here. Coherence prevents any relational functions other than SB and OB from being manifested in (1).

The Completeness and Coherence Conditions thus do the work of strict subcategorization in the *Aspects* framework. They are essentially semantic well-formedness conditions, as first urged by Brame (1978).

Not all complements are amenable to the sort of lexical government that seems appropriate for subjects and objects. Some complements seem to have an invariant way of contributing to the meaning of the sentence, and appear whenever they are semantically appropriate. Such complements include (outer) locatives, temporals, and perhaps instrumentals, benefactives and others. One indication that these are not grammatical functions in the sense that SB and OB are is that their names are merely indications of their semantics. While there are processes, such as Passive, which may be stated in terms of the formal notions subject and object, but not in terms of semantically coherent classes of arguments, processes involving these 'peripheral' complements are always stateable in terms of semantically coherent classes rather than merely formal ones.

These complements are called adjuncts. They contribute to the meaning of the sentence in a way determined by their own intrinsic meaning and by general principles of interpretation. Thus there is a principle that if an adjunct denotes a place, it says where the event or state of affairs reported by the sentence takes place or holds true.

Adjuncts may be written into the structure as sub-bracketings not bearing a specific grammatical function to the containing structure. [PRED in (OP), OP [PRED Cambridge]] is thus an adjunct in (1). Although adjuncts have interesting agreement properties (Neidle 1981), they do not figure prominently in the long-distance aspect of agreement, so will not be further discussed here.

1.2. Functional structures are generated simultaneously with their associated constituent structures by phrase-structure rules and the lexicon.

We may think of the PS rules as being annotated with instructions on how to build the associated functional structure.

(2) represents a preliminary version of the PS rules we will need for both Icelandic and English:[4]

(2)   a. $S \rightarrow NP_{SB}\ VP$

        b. $VP \rightarrow V\ (NP_{OB})\ \left(\left\{ \begin{matrix} PP \\ AP \end{matrix} \right\}_{Adjt} \right)^{*}$

        c. $PP \rightarrow P\ NP_{OP}$

        d. $NP \rightarrow N$

A right subscript represents the grammatical function that the bearer holds to its mother, or, more precisely, that the functional structure correspondent of the bearer holds to the functional structure correspondent of the mother of the bearer. Hence (2a) tells us that the functional substructure corresponding to the NP will be the SB of the functional structure corresponding to the dominating S. The VP on the other hand is unsubscripted. This means that the functional structure correspondent of the VP is the *same* as that of the S. Hence material introduced under the VP, such as the OB function, will be functionally a sister to SB rather than a niece, as may be seen in (1). 'Adjt' in (2b) serves not as a grammatical function, but rather to indicate that the functional structure correspondent of what it is subscripted to is to serve as an adjunct. It should be intuitively clear how the annotations in (2) determine the functional structure (1). A formal algorithm for deriving functional structures is provided in Kaplan and Bresnan (1981).

A useful representation of the effects of annotated constituent structure rules is the combined constituent-functional structure diagram of (3):

(3)

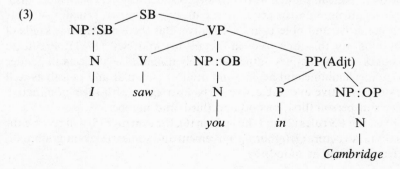

The imitation of Tagmemic notation is deliberate. Such representations are currently held to lack theoretical significance, since constituent and functional structure are supposed to be autonomous levels of structure, connected only by the 'local' statements present in annotated PS rules and lexical items.

The other contributor to functional structure is the lexicon. Lexical items are specified for the material they deposit into the functional structure. The relevant items for (1) for example might be briefly represented as in (4):

(4)   a. [I, N, PRED = PRO, PERS = I, ...]
        b. [you, N, PRED = PRO, PERS = II, ...]
        c. [Cambridge, N, PRED = *Cambridge*, ...]
        d. [saw, V, PRED = *see* (SB, OB), TENSE = PAST, ...]
        e. [in, P, PRED = *in*(OP), ...]

It should be intuitively obvious how these lexical entries induce the grammatical and PRED features in (1). Note especially that the lexicon contains fully inflected forms, such as *saw*.

2. With this brief introduction, we may turn to the analysis of some of the Icelandic constructions that are relevant to long-distance agreement. After some general remarks about Icelandic, I will examine passives, 'subject-raising' constructions, and 'subject-deletion' constructions. The treatment will be informal and incomplete, the data being thoroughly presented and analysed transformationally in Thráinsson (1980), and treated more fully and formally in the present framework in Andrews (1981).

2.1. Modern Icelandic is an SVO language with case-marking of NP. The basic order is clear, though word order is considerably freer than in English. The cases are nominative, accusative, dative and genitive. Usually, subjects are nominative and objects are accusative. But there are various kinds of exceptions to this analysed in detail in Andrews (1981). Predicate adjectives and participles agree with their nominative subjects in gender (masculine, feminine and neuter) and number (singular and plural) as well as case. Indicative and subjective verbs also agree with their nominative subjects in person (first, second and third) and number.

Given the PS rules (2) and the lexicon (6), the sentence (5) will receive the functional structure (7) (ignoring agreement and some irrelevant grammatical features such as mood):

(5)   stúlkurnar kysstu drengina
         the-girls kissed the-boys

(6)   a. [stúlkurnar, N, PRED = *stúlka*, CASE = NOM, GND =
            FEM, NUM = PL, DEF +, ...]

         b. [drengina, N, PRED = *drengur*, CASE = ACC, GND =
            MASC, NUM = PL, DEF +, ...]

         c. [kysstu, V, PRED = *kyssa* (SB, OB), TENSE = PAST, ...]

(7)
$$
\begin{bmatrix}
\text{SB} & \begin{bmatrix} \text{PRED } stulka \\ \text{CASE NOM} \\ \text{GND FEM} \\ \text{NUM PL} \\ \text{DEF +} \end{bmatrix} \\
\text{PRED } kyssa \text{ (SB, OB)} \\
\text{TENSE PAST} \\
\text{OB} & \begin{bmatrix} \text{PRED } drengur \\ \text{CASE ACC} \\ \text{GND MASC} \\ \text{NUM PL} \\ \text{DEF +} \end{bmatrix}
\end{bmatrix}
$$

For PRED values I will use the infinitive of verbs, and the nominative singular of nouns. CASE, GND and NUM represent case, gender and number. DEF represents the suffixed definite article, which I treat as an inflection. Our rules do not explain the distribution of CASE, sufficing merely to determine (7) on the basis of (5).

2.2 The passive in Icelandic is similar to that of English, except for complications ensuing from Icelandic's richer system of case-marking and agreement, and the existence of 'impersonal' passives for intransitive verbs. The passive of (5) is (8):

(8)   drengirnir   voru/urðu   kysstir   (af stúlkunum)
         nom.m.pl.   3.pl.   nom.m.pl.   dat.f.pl.
         the-boys   were/became   kissed   (by the-girls)

The accusative object becomes a nominative subject, and the subject becomes the dative object of the preposition *af*, the derived agent phrase being optional (and generally less preferred than in English). The main verb becomes a passive participle agreeing with its new subject in gender, number and case. There also appears an auxiliary, which may be a form of *vera* 'be' or *verða* 'become,' which agrees with the new subject in person and number like an ordinary finite verb. The basis for the choice of auxiliary is obscure.

Any theory of grammar must have some mechanism whereby the grammatical relations borne by the NP appearing together with the verb get linked with the thematic relations (i.e. 'deep cases') of the verb. Since passivization is essentially a systematic disruption of the usual associations, the linking mechanism is the natural place to describe passivization. In the present theory the linking mechanism is the argument frame, and passivization can be elegantly described as an operation on argument frames. The argument frame of *kyssa* 'kiss,' for example, is (SB, OB), saying that the first (kisser) thematic relation is borne by the SB, and the second (kissed) is borne by the (OB). In the passive on the other hand, the 'kissed' relation is borne by the OB, and the 'kisser' by the dative object of *af*, a relation symbolized by AF DAT, in accord with mechanisms explained and justified in Andrews (1981). The corresponding relation in English is BY OP, as explained in Bresnan (1981b). So the passive argument frame could be represented as (AF DAT, SB). To indicate that the AF DAT relation is optional, we may enclose it in angle-brackets, which will be interpreted as preventing Completeness from ruling the sentence out if an AF DAT does not in fact appear in the functional structure.

A partial representation of the lexical form of the passive participle *kysstir* will then by (9):

(9)   [kysstir, V, PRED = *kyssa* ($\langle$ AF DAT $\rangle$, SB),...]

Ignoring the auxiliary, a gross representation of the functional structure of (8) would be (10):

(10)

$$
\begin{bmatrix}
\text{SB} & \begin{bmatrix} \text{PRED } drengur \\ \text{CASE NOM} \\ \text{GND MASC} \\ \text{NUM PL} \\ \text{DEF } + \end{bmatrix} \\
\textit{kyssa} (\langle \text{AF DAT} \rangle, \text{SB}) \\
\text{AF} \begin{bmatrix} \text{DAT} \begin{bmatrix} \text{PRED } stulka \\ \text{CASE DAT} \\ \text{GND FEM} \\ \text{NUM PL} \\ \text{DEF } + \end{bmatrix} \end{bmatrix}
\end{bmatrix}
$$

In the next subsection I will suggest that the passive auxiliaries are complement-taking verbs, and will give a complete functional structure for passives. The production of the AF DAT substructure is explained in Andrews (1981).

Lexical entries for passive participles may be derived from those for active verbs by a rule whose principal effect is to rewrite the relational functions in an argument frame as follows:

(11)   SB → ⟨AF DAT⟩
         OB → SB

The other effects of the passive rule involve inflectional features, and needn't concern us here.

A convincing lexical analysis of the passive must be able to account for all the various phenomena which have lead people to believe that the passive is transformational. This task is undertaken for English in Bresnan (1981b). Here I will examine one phenomenon that is often used to argue that passive is a transformation, the passivization of 'idiom chunks.'

There are certain noun-verb combinations in English whose meanings are not compositionally determined from those of their parts. Standard examples are *make headway* and *keep tabs on*. In fact it is frequently said that *headway* appears only as object to *make*, although there are in fact a number of meanings of the word, such as 'space under an arch,' for which there is no such restriction. But in normal speech *headway* is only used to mean something like 'progress' in the expression *make headway*. Likewise, in *keep tabs on*, *tabs* means something like 'surveillance'. In no other context does it have this meaning. But *headway* and *tabs* may appear with their idiomatic senses in subject position, providing they have been transformationally moved from a deep structure position that is object of the appropriate verb. Hence (12) are well-formed:

(12)   a. headway was made
         b. tabs were kept on ASIO agents.

If passive is transformational, (12) provides no problem. Otherwise, we have a *prima facie* difficulty.

Icelandic has similar verb-noun combinations. One such is *gjalda torfalögin*, meaning roughly 'to do one's duty.' *torfalögin* appears only as the 'underlying' object of *gjalda*, which normally means 'to pay.' In particular, the expression can be passivized:

(13)   torfalögin voru goldin
         'duty was done'

How can the lexical theory accommodate this?

First, we need a basic analysis of these idiomatic NP. The predicate argument relationships induced by the argument-frames and the functional structures are assumed to be semantically real. The idiom chunk NP's do not serve as genuine arguments of their associated verbs, since other items do not substitute freely for them. Rather the verb-noun combination as a whole has a reading. Hence the PRED feature associated with *gjalda* in this expression will have a one-place argument frame: *gjalda*(SB). What of *torfalögin*? It is treated as one of the elements, alluded to above, which have no meaning. These lack a PRED function and have instead a FORM function, whose value is just a formal marker to distinguish them from everything else that has a FORM function. We shall say that the FORM associated with *torfalögin* is just TORFALÖGIN. The lexical entry for *gjalda*(SB) 'do one's duty' will contain a so-called 'constraint equation' saying that the OB's FORM must be TORFALÖGIN.

So far all the functional structure specifications we have proposed in lexical entries may be interpreted as instructions to put things in functional structure. These may be called 'defining specifications.' Constraint equations on the other hand are restrictions that the thus-assembled functional structures must satisfy in order to be grammatical. Constraint equations are written with '$=_c$,' so that *gjalda*'s may be written 'OB FORM $=_c$ TORFALÖGIN.' The resulting lexical entry for *gjalda* is partially specified in (14):

(14)   [gjalda, V, PRED = GJALDA(SB), OB FORM $=_c$.
        TORFALÖGIN, ...]

A sentence such as *hann galt torfalögin* 'he did his duty' will then get a functional structure like (15) (assuming the lexical entry [torfalögin, N, FORM = TORFALÖGIN, ...]):

(15) $$\begin{bmatrix} \text{SB} \begin{bmatrix} \text{PRED PRO} \\ \text{PERS III} \end{bmatrix} \\ \text{PRED } gjalda\text{(SB)} \\ \text{TENSE PAST} \\ \text{OB [FORM TORFALÖGIN]} \end{bmatrix}$$

The constraint equation on (this sense of) *gjalda* requires *torfalögin* to be present as object, otherwise the constraint equation would not be satisfied.

Note that if we simply put OB FORM = TORFALÖGIN in the lexical entry of *gjalda*, this substructure would be dumped into the functional structure without the necessity of *torfalogin* appearing in the constituent structure. A 'constraining' rather than 'defining' interpretation of the specification is therefore necessary. Constraint equations figure elsewhere in the theory, particularly in the analysis of agreement. It would be nice if a metatheoretical principle could be found to determine when a given specification is defining and when constraining, but as yet none is known.

How can *torfalögin* be prevented from occurring elsewhere, say, as object of any intransitive verb? We need an additional principle, the principle of Formal Coherence, stating that FORM features cannot appear in a functional structure unless they are *required* to satisfy a constraint equation. *Torfalögin* will now appear only as object of *gjalda*, because only here will its presence lead to the satisfaction of a constraint equation.

Given this analysis of idiom-chunks, their passivizability becomes trivial. All we need is for the passivization rule (11) to be able to rewrite symbols in constraint equations as well as in the argument frame. This is reasonable, since the constraint equation is filling on the formal level the function that the argument-frame in serving on the semantic. Under this interpretation, passive will turn the lexical entry (14) into (16):

(16)   [goldin, V, *gjalda* ($\langle$ AF DAT $\rangle$), SB FORM $=_c$
         TORFALÖGIN, . . .]

This lexical entry will call for *torfalögin* in subject position, explaining (13). It is also worth mentioning that *torfalögin* is morphologically neuter plural, and evokes the appropriate agreement morphology on the passive participle of *gjalda*.

There is considerably more to Icelandic passives than we have indicated. There is passivization of verbs taking irregularly case-marked (genitive and dative) objects, with ditransitive verbs, and with intransitives. These are all discussed in Thráinsson (1980) and Andrews (1981). There is also the interaction of passive with 'subject-raising,' which will be discussed below. We have finally not dealt at all with agreement, which will concern us in section 3.

2.3. Icelandic has a 'subject-to-object raising' construction, traditionally known as the *accusativum cum infinitivo* (ACI for short), that is quite similar to the 'subject-to-object raising' construction in English. Examples are (17):

(17)   a. ég tel drenginn(A) elska stúlkuna
       I believe the-boy to-love the-girl
      b. ég tel torfalögin(A) hafa verið goldin
       I believe duty to-have been done

The matrix verb, almost always one of thinking, saying or perceiving, is followed by an accusative NP which is understood as the subject of the complement proposition, followed by an infinitive VP representing the rest of the complement proposition. That an idiom chunk can appear in the accusative position, as in (17b), is a typical argument that the NP and the VP make an S in underlying structure. Thráinsson (1980) produces all the usual sorts of arguments to this effect.

More challenging is to show that the accusative and following VP do *not* constitute a clause in surface structure, but that the accusative is the superficial object of the matrix verb. Here again Thráinsson provides an overwhelming mass of evidence, including even a click-location experiment. For our purposes we need only cite the fact that passivization can apply to the matrix clauses in (17):

(18)   a. drengurinn(N) er talinn elska stúlkuna
       the-boy is thought to-love the-girl
      b. torfalögin(N) eru talin hafa verið goldin
       duty is thought to-have been done

There is also a 'subject-to-subject raising' construction, exemplified in (19):

(19)   a. drengurinn virðist elska stúlkuna
       the-boy seems to-love the-girl
      b. torfalögin virðast hafa verið goldin
       duty seems to-have been done

The argument for subject-raising here is obvious. For the sake of completeness, I also mention that there is a 'subject-raising into nominative object' construction exemplified in (20):

(20)   a. mér(D) virðist drengurinn(N) elska stúlkuna
       to-me seems the-boy to-love the-girl
      b. mér(D) virðist torfalögin(N) hafa verið goldin
       to-me seems duty to-have been done

This construction, discussed in Thráinsson (1980, 426–427) and Andrews

(1981), is actually commoner than that of (19), though of no relevance to our present purposes.

What will our theory need to generate these constructions and explain their properties without transformations? Consider (19a), an especially simple example of 'subject-to-subject raising.' *Drengurinn* is presumably the matrix SB, while *elska stúlkuna* is a VP (or perhaps subjectless S) bearing some grammatical function, let's say, VCOMP. Given an expansion V + VP$_{\text{VCOMP}}$ for VP in the PS rules, (19a) will have the simplified functional structure (21):

(21)
$$
\begin{bmatrix}
\text{SB} \begin{bmatrix} \text{PRED } drengur \\ \text{DEF} + \end{bmatrix} \\
\begin{bmatrix}
\text{PRED } vir\eth ast(\text{VCOMP}) \\
\text{VCOMP } \begin{matrix} \text{PRED } elska(\text{SB, OB}) \\ \text{OB} \begin{bmatrix} \text{PRED } st\acute{u}lka \\ \text{DEF} + \end{bmatrix} \end{matrix}
\end{bmatrix}
\end{bmatrix}
$$

virðast 'seem' does not take the SB as its argument, since if it did, (19b) would be ruled out by Completeness (since *torfalögin*, being meaningless, cannot serve as an argument). So (21) appears to be incoherent. Furthermore it is incomplete, since there is no SB for *elska* 'love' in the VCOMP.

We amend this situation, of course, by arranging matters so that the matrix SB winds up being interpreted as the VCOMP SB as well: then the structure will be both complete and coherent. What I shall do is have the infinitive phrase bear a grammatical function VCOMP(SB/SB) instead of just VCOMP. The intended interpretation of this 'F1(F2/F3)' notation is that whatever bears the function F2 is also taken to bear the function F1 F3. In the present case, the SB will also be the VCOMP SB. (21) may thus be revised to (22):

(22)
$$
\begin{bmatrix}
\text{SB} \begin{bmatrix} \text{PRED } drengur \\ \text{DEF} + \end{bmatrix} \\
\text{PRED } vir\eth ast(\text{VCOMP(SB/SB)}) \\
\text{VCOMP(SB/SB)} \begin{bmatrix} \text{PRED } elska(\text{SB, OB}) \\ \text{OB} \begin{bmatrix} \text{PRED } st\acute{u}lka \\ \text{DEF} + \end{bmatrix} \end{bmatrix}
\end{bmatrix}
$$

It should be quite obvious how the theory explains the 'raisability' of *torfalögin* in (19b). By the F1(F2/F3) notation, *torfalögin* will be both the SB and the VCOMP SB, so the constraint equation of *gjalda* will be satisfied.

A similar functional structure may be proposed for the 'subject-to-object raising' case, but with the infinitive phrase bearing the function VCOMP(OB/SB). For (17a) we would then get the functional structure (23):

$$(23) \quad \begin{bmatrix} \text{SB} \begin{bmatrix} \text{PRO} \\ \text{PERS I} \end{bmatrix} \\ \text{PRED } telja(\text{SB, VCOMP(OB/SB)}) \\ \text{OB} \begin{bmatrix} \text{PRED } drengur \\ \text{DEF} + \end{bmatrix} \\ \text{VCOMP(OB/SB)} \begin{bmatrix} \text{PRED } elska(\text{SB, OB}) \\ \text{OB} \begin{bmatrix} \text{PRED } st\acute{u}lka \\ \text{DEF} + \end{bmatrix} \end{bmatrix} \end{bmatrix}$$

This structure is complete and coherent because *drenginn* in both OB and VCOMP SB, satisfying the argument frame of *elska*.

In order to generate these structures, we propose the following revision of PS rule (2b):

$$(24) \qquad \text{VP} \rightarrow \text{V}(\text{NP}_{\text{OB}})(\text{VP}_{\text{VCOMP}}) \left(\left\{ \begin{matrix} \text{PP} \\ \text{AP} \end{matrix} \right\}_{\text{Adjt}} \right)^{*}$$

VCOMP belongs to the universally-defined category of 'open' grammatical functions. They are by convention always introduced into functional structures followed by '(F2/F3)' for some choice of F2 and F3. The choice of F2 and F3 is determined by the argument frame of the matrix verb. Hence for *virðast* we would have the lexical entry (25a), and for *telja* (25b):

(25)   a. [virðast, V, PRED *virðast*(VCOMP(SB/SB)), ...]
         b. [telja, V, PRED *telja*(SB, VCOMP(OB/SB)), ...]

The F1(F2/F3) notation is thus a complex symbol. We refer to the grammatical function either as F1 or more specifically as F1(F2/F3), as is convenient.

This treatment is notationally different from that in Kaplan and Bresnan (1981). It is however essentially the same, but more convenient within a bracketing formalism for functional structure. The distinction between closed and open grammatical functions receives an especially simple interpretation within this system: open grammatical functions are those that must be followed by (F2/F3), while closed functions, such as SB and

OB, cannot be. Our discussion of agreement in section 3 will provide substantial confirmation for this division of grammatical functions.

With this apparatus we can analyse the passive auxiliaries *vera* 'be' and *verða* 'become' as matrix verbs taking a VCOMP(SB/SB) complement. Extending the same treatment to the perfect auxiliary *hafa*, (19b) receives the functional structure (26):

(26)
$$
\begin{bmatrix}
\text{SB [FORM TORFALÖGIN]} \\
\text{PRED } vir\eth ast(\text{VCOMP(SB/SB)}) \\
\text{VCOMP}
\begin{bmatrix}
\text{PRED } hafa(\text{VCOMP(SB/SB)}) \\
\text{VCOMP}
\begin{bmatrix}
\text{PRED } vera(\text{VCOMP(SB/SB)}) \\
\text{VCOMP [PRED } gjalda(\langle\text{AF DAT}\rangle)]
\end{bmatrix}
\end{bmatrix}
\end{bmatrix}
$$

We will henceforth omit the '(F2/F3)' from functional structure, since the relevant information is provided by the '(F2/F3)' symbol in the associated argument frame. (26) illustrates recursive application of the convention.

There is also the problem of controlling the grammatical features of the nonfinite complements. The passive auxiliaries, for example, require a passive VP, rejecting the bare infinitive of (19). Passive VP can appear freely, however, in the complements to verbs like *virðast* and *telja*, which take the bare infinitive. Hence the subsequence *hafa verið* is in fact optional in (17b–20b). The machinery for controlling whether a VP may or must be passive is developed in Andrews (1981). Since it has no relevance to agreement phenomena, I won't go into it here.

We account for the passivizability of 'raised' NP by having the OB → SB component of Passive rewrite F2 in the F1(F2/F3) notation. Hence Passive will derive the argument-frame *telja*(⟨AF DAT⟩, VCOMP(SB/SB)) from *telja*(SB, VCOMP(OB/SB)). Passive does not get to rewrite F3 in the F1(F2/F3) notation. (18a) will then receive the functional structure (27):

(27)
$$
\begin{bmatrix}
\text{SB}
\begin{bmatrix}
\text{PRED } drengur \\
\text{DEF +}
\end{bmatrix} \\
\text{PRED } vera(\text{VCOMP(SB/SB)}) \\
\text{VCOMP}
\begin{bmatrix}
\text{PRED } telja(\langle\text{AF DAT}\rangle, \text{VCOMP(SB/SB)}) \\
\text{VCOMP}
\begin{bmatrix}
\text{PRED } elska(\text{SB, OB}) \\
\text{OB}
\begin{bmatrix}
\text{PRED } st\acute{u}lka \\
\text{DEF +}
\end{bmatrix}
\end{bmatrix}
\end{bmatrix}
\end{bmatrix}
$$

Passive 'subject-to-object raising' verbs are thus treated as derived 'subject-to-subject raising' verbs.

2.4. The bare infinitives of the previous subsection are one of the two major nonfinite complement types of Icelandic. The other is the infinitive marked with *að*. While bare infinitives represent for the most part 'subject raising' constructions, *að*-marked infinitives generally represent 'subject deletion' or 'Equi' constructions. An assortment of marked infinitive constructions is (28):

    (28)   a. ég(N) aetla að fara til Íslands
                 I intend to to-go to Iceland
            b. ég vonast til að fara til Islands
                 I hope toward to to-go to Iceland
            c. ég bað hana(A) (að) kyssa hann
                 I requested her (to) to-kiss him
            d. ég skipaði honum(D) að kyssa hana
                 I ordered him to to-kiss her

In (28a, b) it is the matrix subject that is the controller of the infinitive, in (28c, d) it is the object. In (28b) the infinitive appears the object of the preposition *til* 'to, towards.' In (28c) the controller is an accusative matrix object; in (28d) a dative matrix object. That the constructions are 'Equi' constructions in a transformational framework follows from the fact that idiom chunks like *torfalögin* are quite impossible in controller position: **torfalögin vonast til að vera goldin*, for example. Much more evidence to this point is provided by Thráinsson (1980).

A crucial property of these infinitives is that they give every indication of being NP, bearing the usual NP grammatical functions such as SB, OB, etc. Observe for example (27b), in which the infinitive appears as object of a preposition. Thráinsson (1980) provides a great deal more evidence that *að*-infinitive phrases, and also subordinate clauses introduced by *að*, are NP. Particularly striking is the fact that *að*-infinitives and *að*-clauses appear in focus position in a clefting construction that is otherwise restricted to uncontroversial NP:

    (29)   a. það sem ég aetla er að fara til Íslands
                 that which I intend is to to-go to Icelandc
            b. það sem ég skipaði honum var að kyssa hana
                 that which I ordered him was to to-kiss her

Unmarked infinitives on the other hand fail this and all other NP tests:

    (30)   a. *það sem drengurinn virðist er (að) elska stúlkuna
            b. *það sem ég tel drenginn er (að) elska stúlkuna

It is worth emphasizing that the facts which suggest that infinitive phrases and clauses are not NP in English simply don't exist in Icelandic. Hence, for example, clauses or infinitives appear with virtually all verbs for which their semantics are reasonable.

There are a few exceptions to the generalization that infinitives with *að* are NP-like 'Equi' constructions and those without are 'raising' constructions. The verb *biðja* 'ask' may appear with a bare infinitive, but keeps its 'Equi' sense. The *að* is obligatory with *biðja* in the Clefting construction of (28), however. There are also various aspectual verbs which take *að*-infinitives but seem to have 'raising' semantics. These verbs, such as *fara að* 'begin,' present various problems which have not been solved.

Supposing that in general *að*-infinitives are NP, what do we do about their understood subjects? Since the infinitives bear closed grammatical functions such as SB or OB, we cannot use the F1(F2/F3) mechanism. Inasmuch as functional structure is a level distinct from constituent structure (rather than, say, merely a system of relations subsisting between items in overt structure), the possibility arises that infinitives might have functional structure subjects that do not correspond to anything in constituent structure. In an investigation of English infinitives conducted preceding the present work, Bresnan (1918c) concludes that English infinitives had two kinds of control: 'grammatical,' or 'functional' control, which is the mechanism developed in 2.3. above, and 'anaphoric control,' in which the rules of functional interpretation produce a functional structure subject that corresponds to nothing in the constituent structure, but is often coreferential to some NP in functional structure (hence the term 'anaphoric').

To formalize this in Icelandic, we might suppose that *að* is a complementizer with both clauses and infinitives, introduced under an S rule formulated as follows:

(31) $S \rightarrow a\partial$ (SB PRED = PRO) S

If the (defining) condition 'SB PRED = PRO' in the parentheses is taken, a 'functional structure pronoun' serving as SB will be put in the functional structure. This will ultimately lead to the generation of an infinitive. If 'SB PRED = PRO' is not taken, the functional SB will have to be provided under S, and a finite clause will result. To get these results, we want the subject NP to be optional under S. A further observation is that in Icelandic there is no evidence for a VP node. Hence we reformulate (2a, b) as (32):

(32) $S \rightarrow (NP_{SB}) V (NP_{OB}) (S_{VCOMP}) \left(\left\{ \begin{matrix} PP \\ AP \end{matrix} \right\}_{Adjt} \right)^{*}$

Given (31) and (32), (28d) will get the functional structure (33), where OB2 is the 'second object' function (Icelandic, like English, has ditransitive verbs with two bare NP objects):

(33)

$$
\begin{bmatrix}
\text{SB} \begin{bmatrix} \text{PRED PRO} \\ \text{PERS I} \end{bmatrix}^i \\[2mm]
\text{PRED } skipa(\text{SB, OB DAT, OB2}) \\
\text{TENSE PAST} \\
\text{OB} \begin{bmatrix} \text{DAT} \begin{bmatrix} \text{PRED PRO} \\ \text{PERS III} \end{bmatrix}^j \end{bmatrix} \\[2mm]
\text{OB2} \begin{bmatrix} \text{SB } [\text{PRED PRO}]^j \\ \text{PRED } elska \text{ (SB, OB)} \\ \text{OB} \begin{bmatrix} \text{PRED PRO} \\ \text{PERS III} \end{bmatrix}^k \end{bmatrix}
\end{bmatrix}
$$

Right superscripts represent referential indices.

If this treatment of $a\eth$-infinitive control is on the right track, we should expect that the relation between $a\eth$-infinitives and their controllers should share properties with the relation between overt pronouns and their antecedents. Fortunately, Thráinsson (1980, 114–116) argues that this is indeed the case.

The assignment of the two types of control to infinitives is determined by the theory in conjunction with elementary properties of the constructions involved. The bare infinitives must be treated with functional control, because an anaphoric control structure requires that the controller be a matrix argument, lest the structure be incoherent. On the other hand, since the marked infinitives behave like NP bearing ordinary grammatical functions like SB and OB, they must be analysed as having anaphoric control. This difference will turn out to be precisely what is needed to explain the way the two kinds of infinitives interact with agreement. The greater variety of possible surface relationships between an anaphoric controller and its infinitive, shown by the possibility of these constructions being clefted, is also a natural consequence of the theory.

Many verbs taking $a\eth$-infinitives, such as *vonast til*, also take finite $a\eth$-clauses, with or without coreference between matrix and complement subjects. Others, such as *biðja* and *skipa*, can take finite clauses with somewhat diminished acceptability. A few, such as *aetla*, absolutely reject finite clauses, requiring the infinitive. These matters are discussed by Thráinsson (1981, 271–273). $a\eth$-infinitives behave alike with regard to NPhood tests and agreement phenomena, regardless of whether they alternate with clauses or not.

There are lexical constraints on what NP the functional subject of an *að*-infinitive can or must be coreferential with. *skipa* 'order' demands coreferentiality with the object, *lofa* 'promise' with the subject, while *bjóða* 'offer' can have coreferentiality with either the subject or the object. Bresnan (1918c) argues that such restrictions should be implemented by conditions involving the thematic relations in a sentence, as originally proposed by Jackendoff (1972). I shall not pursue this 'control problem' further here.

2.5. In order to complete the formalization of the analysis, we must control the distribution of the various finite and nonfinite verb-forms, and also the introduction of an SB by rule (32). The former task may be straightforwardly accomplished by the use of grammatical features and the appropriate defining and constraining specifications on the PS rules and lexical items. Since this is done in Andrews (1981), I will not burden the present exposition with the details.

The second task is more central, and worth discussing here. Consider first ordinary finite clauses, which aren't under functional control, and where rule (31) does not produce a functional SB. If (32) does not generate an SB, nothing will, and the resulting structure will be incomplete.

Consider on the other hand VCOMP structures, and those where (31) does produce a functional structure subject. Here we must prevent (32) from introducing an SB. A simple solution goes as follows. Revise (32) to introduce by defining equation 'FIN + ' along with NP$_{SB}$. 'FIN + ' will then appear in the structure when and only when there is a constituent structure SB introduced under S. We now amend the rules introducing nonfinite complements so that they impose the requirement that FIN be −. The required revisions of (31) and (32) are given below:

$$(34) \qquad S \rightarrow a\eth \begin{pmatrix} SB\ PRED = PRO \\ FIN = - \end{pmatrix} S$$

$$(35) \qquad S \rightarrow \begin{pmatrix} NP_{SP} \\ FIN = + \end{pmatrix} V \begin{pmatrix} NP_{OB} \end{pmatrix} \left(\begin{Bmatrix} NP_{OB2} \\ S_{VCOMP} \\ FIN = - \end{Bmatrix} \right) \left(\begin{Bmatrix} PP \\ AP \end{Bmatrix}_{Adjt} \right)^{*}$$

By writing 'FIN = − ' directly under 'VCOMP' in (35) we indicate that it is the VCOMP whose FIN value is to be defined as ' − .'

Now if rule (35) generates an SB in an anaphoric or functional control structure, the 'FIN +' specification introduced along with the SB will conflict with the 'FIN −' specification introduced by the complement rules, and the structure will be ruled out by the condition that grammatical functions be single-valued.

The FIN feature is also useful in controlling the distribution of verb forms. Finite verbs (those inflected for SB person and number) only appear when (35) introduces an SB. Hence they may be provided with a constraint equation 'FIN $=_c +$.' Likewise, nonfinite forms may be specified 'FIN $=_c -$.'

A final issue we should mention is case-marking of NP. Normally, subjects are nominative and objects are accusative. If this were always true, we could easily deal with case-marking by adding the appropriate conditions to rule (35). In Andrews (1981) it is shown that things are in fact considerably more complicated: subjects and objects can both appear in each of the four cases. Since case marking is fairly complicated, and a theory of it is presented in Andrews (1981), we will leave it unformulated here.

With this treatment of the complement system in hand, we may take up agreement.

3. There are three kinds of agreement in Icelandic: agreement of finite verbs with their subjects in person and number; agreement of predicate adjectives, nominals and participles with their subjects in gender, number and case; and agreement of attributive (i.e., NP-internal) adjectives with their heads in gender, number, case and definiteness (via a strong-weak declensional opposition similar to that of German). It is only the agreements between subject and predicate that will concern us here. I will begin by treating finite verb agreement, and then consider participle and adjective agreement in various structures.

3.1 The properties involved in agreement are treated as grammatical features of NP. For finite verb agreement we will need features PERS for person and NUM for number. There are two basic ways to associate the morphological distinctions with the functional structures. First, one might have a distinct grammatical function value for each morphological one. In this approach NUM would take values SG and PL, and PERS would take I, II and III. But there are many structures, adverbs and prepositional phrases, for example, that we would want to consider to be unspecified for NUM and PERS. If adverbs and prepositions are unspecified for these properties, why not some nominals?

We are thus led naturally to a treatment in terms of markedness, whereby one of the morphological values is taken to correspond to an 'undefined' value in the functional structure. For reasons expounded by Jakobson (1932, 1935), it is appropriate to treat singular number (in Indo-European languages, at least) and third person as the unmarked values of NUM and PERS. The classical argument for this is of course that finite verbs in various 'subjectless' constructions typically take third person singular morphology.

We suppose then that plural nominals have a defining specification NUM = PL, and that first and second person pronouns have defining specifications PERS = I and PERS = II, respectively. Singular nominals have no specification for NUM, and third person pronouns and nouns have no specification for PERS. Singular NP will then be unspecified for number, third person NP unspecified for person.

Finite verb forms will then have constraining equations such as SB PERS = $_c$I and SB NUM = $_c$PL for the first person plural. It should be clear why verb forms have constraining rather than defining specifications. Suppose the first person plural verb form *kysstum* had a defining condition SB PERS = I. It could then be used in a sentence like (5) (with functional structure (7)). *Kysstum*'s defining specification would simply impose PERS I on the SB, regardless of the syntactic form of the constituent structure subject. But under the constraining interpretation, since *stúlkurnar* has no defining specification for PERS, SB PERS is undefined (as opposed to SB NUM, which is PL), so *kysstum* cannot be used.

There are two possible treatments for third person and singular forms. One possibility would be to give them constraining equations to the effect that NUM or PERS are undefined. More natural, however, would be to have these forms bear *no* specifications for PERS or NUM. *Kysstum* and *kysstu* would then have lexical entries like (36):

(36)   a. [*kysstum*, V, PRED = *kyssa* (SB, OB), TENSE = PAST, FIN = $_c$ +, SB PERS = $_c$I, SB NUM = $_c$PL,...]

    b. [*kysstu*, V, PRED = *kyssa* (SB, OB), TENSE = PAST, FIN = $_c$ +, SB NUM = $_c$PL,...]

Kysstu but not *kysstum* will now be usable in (5). But why couldn't the unconstrained form be used when the subject was first person plural, as in the ungrammatical *við kysstu drengina* 'we kissed the boys?.' A blocking convention due essentially to Panini via Kiparsky (1973) provides an answer:

(37)   *Blocking Convention*: If the constraint equations of a form A are
         a proper subset of those of a form B from the same paradigm,
         and the equations of B are satisfied at a position X, then A
         cannot be inserted at X.

(37) will also help account for the distribution of nonfinite forms, if we treat
them as unmarked for FIN. Convention (37) and the morphological theory
which must surround it need more development, but I shall not provide that
here.

   We have not adopted the full Jakobsonian theory of markedness. For
Jakobson, the values of multi-valued features are themselves bundles of
marks. Hence 'first person' would consist of a mark for 'person,' and one for
'ego,' while second person would have only a mark for 'person.' This sort of
treatment does not fit naturally into the present formalism, and, more
significantly, the arguments for the decomposition of feature values into
marks seem considerably shakier (and the particular decompositions more
difficult to motivate) than those for considering one value of a grammatical
feature as unmarked.

3.2. We may now turn to predicate adjectives and participles. Here we have
two new grammatical functions, CASE and GND (gender) to deal with.
Traditionally, nominative is the unmarked case, neuter the unmarked
gender. Both of these assignments are supported in Andrews (1981). Neuter
is the gender of adjectival and participial forms in 'impersonal' constructions where one would want to say that the adjective or participle was
not agreeing with anything. Nominative likewise appears under various
circumstances in which it would be most natural to say that no case-
marking rule was applying. We shall thus postulate for nouns CASE with
values ACC, DAT and GEN; and GND with values MASC and FEM.
   Consider now simple copulative sentences with an adjective:

(38)   a. þeir (N.m.pl) eru (pl) ríkir (N.m.pl)
            they (masculine) are rich
         b. hún (N.f.sg) verður rík (N.f.sg)
            she will-be rich

The adjective is agreeing with the subject in gender, number and case. The
verbs are *vera* 'be' and *verĉa* 'become,' the latter functioning, as it often does,
as a future for the copula.
   There are three kinds of analysis we might propose for these structures.

First, it could be that the predicate adjective provides the PRED, with the copula serving merely as a tense-carrier. Alternatively, we can treat the adjective as a complement to the copula. Since the adjective predicates wealth of the surface subject, and predicational relations must be represented in functional structure, the subject must be the controller of the adjective in a complement analysis. It could be a functional or an anaphoric controller.

This latter analysis seems unlikely, for a variety of reasons. We would be claiming that adjective phrases bore a closed grammatical function, and contained in functional structure their own SB. (38b) would thus have a structure like (39):

$$(39) \quad \begin{bmatrix} SB & \begin{bmatrix} PRED & PRO \\ GND & FEM \end{bmatrix} \\ PRED\ vera\ (SB, A) \\ A & \begin{bmatrix} SB & \begin{bmatrix} PRED & PRO \\ GND & FEM \end{bmatrix} \\ PRED\ rik\ (SB) \end{bmatrix} \end{bmatrix}$$

But adjective phrases are not intimately related to any sort of structure in which the SB appears overtly (as að-infinitives are related to að-clauses, for example). Furthermore an argument frame such as *vera* (SB, A) entails that *vera* designates a relation between the subject and some entity of roughly propositional type (since the value of A is a predication). Hence either a functional control or a non-complement analysis seems more plausible.

In a functional control analysis, we would set up an open grammatical function ACOMP, with copulas having argument frames such as *vera* (ACOMP (SB/SB)). Instead of (39) we would have (40):

$$(40) \quad \begin{bmatrix} SB & \begin{bmatrix} PRED & PRO \\ GND & FEM \end{bmatrix} \\ PRED\ vera\ (ACOMP\,(SB/SB)) \\ ACOMP\ [PRED\ rik\,(SB)] \end{bmatrix}$$

Although the first form of analysis, in which the adjective provides the top-level PRED, would be worth thinking about, I won't pursue it here. As far as agreement is concerned, it is equivalent to the treatment of (40).

It is obvious that the copulative construction of (38) shows gender and number agreement. It is not so obvious that there is case agreement. Even though the subject and adjective are both nominative in form, how do we

know that this is agreement, rather than the result of independent principles
governing the case of subjects and predicate adjectives?

What shows that there is case agreement is, of course, what happens in
the ACI. If we embed (38b) in this construction, we get a sentence like (41):

(41)   ég tel hana (A) (vera) ríka (A)
         I believe her to-be rich

Both *hana*, the 'logical subject' of the adjective *ríka*, and the adjective itself
are in the accusative. This follows quite naturally under the functional
control hypothesis for adjectives. The functional structure of (41) would be
(42):

(42)
$$
\begin{bmatrix}
\text{SB} \begin{bmatrix} \text{PRED} & \text{PRO} \\ \text{PERS} & \text{I} \end{bmatrix} \\
\text{PRED } \textit{telja} \text{ (SB, VCOMP (OB/SB))} \\
\text{FIN} + \\
\text{OB} \begin{bmatrix} \text{PRED} & \text{PRO} \\ \text{GND} & \text{FEM} \\ \text{CASE} & \text{ACC} \end{bmatrix} \\
\text{VCOMP} \begin{bmatrix} \text{PRED } \textit{vera} \text{ (ACOMP(SB/SB))} \\ \text{ACOMP [PRED } \textit{rík} \text{(SB)]} \end{bmatrix}
\end{bmatrix}
$$

All we need to do to get the case-agreement is to have *ríka* bear a
constraining equation SB CASE = $_c$ACC, and the nominative *rík* unmarked. Assuming rules to appropriately case-mark the NP, only the
nominative adjective will be usable in (38b), and only to accusative in (41)
(via the lexical entries and (37)). The anaphoric control hypothesis of (39)
does not fare so well: just because the SB of *vera* becomes accusative, why
should anything happen to the functionally distinct SB of *rík*? A further
mark against the anaphoric control hypothesis emerges from the fact that
the copula is optional in (38) and in all VCOMP structures generally. The
functional control analysis can account for this by allowing AP as well as
VP to be introduced bearing the grammatical function VCOMP. I know of
no sensible treatment within the anaphoric control hypothesis.

Passive participles submit to a similar analysis. Putting (8) in the ACI, we
get (43):

(43)   ég tel drengina (A) (hafa verið) kyssta (A) (af stúlkunum)
         I believe the-boys (to-have been) kissed (by the-girls)

The nominative participle *kysstir* of (8) has been changed to the accusative *kyssta* in (43). Given the structure for passives motivated in 2.2 and 2.3, all we need to do is have passive participles submitted to the same part of the morpology as produces inflected forms of adjectives. *kyssta*, with an SB CASE $=_c$ ACC constraint equation, will be usable in (43) but not (8). *kysstir*, with no CASE constraint, will be usable in (8) but not, thanks to (37), in (43).

The reader familiar with long-distance agreement phenomena may already have realized that our sentence structures and lexical representations predict one of the basic cases of these phenomena: agreement in constructions with multiple occurrences of passive and 'subject-raising' constructions. Suppose we passivize in the matrix of (41) and (43). The result is (44):

(44) a. hún(N) er talin(N) (vera) rík(N)
          she is believed (to-be) rich
      b. drengirnir(N) eru taldir(N) (hafa verið) kysstir(N)
          the-boys are believed (to-have been) kissed

The complement participles and adjectives switch to nominative, exactly as they should, given the sentence structures motivated in section 2.4.

If the structures of (44) are again embedded as ACI, the agreements all switch into the accusative, as obviously required by the theory:

(45) a. þeir segja hana(A) (vera) talda(A) (vera) ríka(A)
          they say her (to-be) believed (to-be) rich
      b. þeir segja drengina(A) (vera) talda(A) (hafa verið) kyssta(A)

In structures of this sort, the adjectives and participles do all and only what the theory says they should do: agree with whatever the F1(F2/F3) convention characterizes as their functional SB. 'Subject-to-subject raising' constructions also behave in the expected way:

(46) a. þeir segja hana(A) virðast (vera) ríka (A)
          they say her to-seem (to-be) rich
      b. hún(N) er sögð(N) virðast (vera) rík(N)
          she is said to-seem (to-be) rich

Long distance agreement with 'subject raising' constructions is thus explained away.

3.3. We now turn to agreement in anaphoric control structures. Some of the basic phenomena are illustrated in (47, 48):

(47)   a. hún(N) vonast til að vera vinsael(N)
            she hopes toward to to-be popular
        b. ég tel hana(A) vonast til að vera vinsaela(A)/vinsael(N)
            I believe her to-hope toward to to-be popular

(48)   a. ég bað hann(A) að vera góðan (A)/góður (N)
            I requested him to to-be good
        b. hann(N) skipaði honum(D) að vera góður(N)/góðum(D)
            he ordered him to to-be good
        c. hann (N) lofaði honum (D) að vera góður (N)/*góðum (D)
            he promised him to to-be good
        d. hana(A) langar til að vera vinsael(N)/vinsaela(A)
            she longs towards to to-be popular
            'she longs to be popular.'

The agreements indicated are the only ones possible. They are given in order of preference.

Our theory predicts that predicate adjectives modifying the SB of anaphorically controlled complements will appear in the nominative case, regardless of the case of the controller. This is because the SB of the adjective is the functional pronoun introduced by rule (34). Since að-infinitives never have overt subjects, there is no evidence for any special case-marking rule applying to such SB (Andrews (1981) and Mohanan (1981) argue that case-marking is for the most part implemented by conditions on functional structure). Therefore they will be unmarked in case, eliciting nominative agreement.

The predicted nominatives are almost always possible, as evident from (47–48). There is only one real exception of which I am aware: að is optional with biðja, and if it is omitted, an adjective such as that in (48a) has to be accusative.

Unfortunately, it is often also possible for the adjective to agree with the anaphoric controller of its SB. This is preferable in (47b) and (48a), and required by some informants.[6] Some informants allow it in examples like (48b) and (48d), with dative object and accusative subject controllers (see Andrews (1976, 1981), Thráinsson (1980) for discussion), while others don't. (48c), where only the nominative is possible, shows that an NP that is not a controller cannot condition agreement.[7]

Although formally unexpected, this phenomenon is not at all unnatural. Consider the functional structure for (48a):

(49)

$$
\begin{bmatrix}
\text{SB} \begin{bmatrix} \text{PRED} & \text{PRO} \\ \text{GND} & \text{MASC} \end{bmatrix}^{i} \\
\text{PRED } bi\eth ja\,(\text{SB, OB, OB2}) \\
\text{TENSE PAST} \\
\text{OB} \begin{bmatrix} \text{PRED} & \text{PRO} \\ \text{GND} & \text{MASC} \\ \text{CASE} & \text{ACC} \end{bmatrix}^{j} \\
\text{OB2} \begin{bmatrix} \text{SB} \begin{bmatrix} \text{PRED PRO} \\ \text{GND MASC} \end{bmatrix}^{j} \\ \text{PRED } vera\,(\text{ACOMP(SB/SB)}) \\ \text{ACOMP [PRED } g\acute{o}\eth\,(\text{SB})] \end{bmatrix}
\end{bmatrix}
$$

Rather than agreeing with its invisible functional SB, the adjective is agreeing with the latter's nearby and visible coreferent.

What I propose is that there is a convention for the systematic 'misapplication' of agreement restrictions to the functional controllers of nonlexicalized SB. The convention is variable, subject to complex 'squishy' conditions. The conditioning factors have been discussed in considerable detail in Friðjónsson (1977), Thráinsson (1980, esp. 361–363) and Andrews (1981). I will therefore merely list some of them:

(50) a. omission of $a\eth$ (when possible) favours misapplication.

   b. accusative controllers elicit misapplication more strongly than do datives (genitive NP are never anaphoric controllers).

   c. an intervening NP prevents misapplication (were (48c) embedded as an ACI, nominative would still be the only possibility on the adjective).

   d. adjective agreement is more likely to misapply than that of predicate nominals or passive participles.

In general, the variable, uncertain nature of agreement under anaphoric control is in marked contrast to its regular character under functional control.

I think there is some plausibility to the idea that this misapplication is in fact a performance phenomenon rather than an actual rule of Icelandic grammar. One indication of this is the fact that examples relevant to the characterization of misapplication are extremely rare in normal perform-

ance, according to Friðjónsson (1977). They are certainly quite rare in
literature. Given this, how could the complex conditioning factors in (50) be
learned?

The force of this observation is strengthened by the fact that some of
these conditions seem also to apply to the very similar phenomena in
Ancient Greek described by Andrews (1971) and Quicoli (1972). Consider a
Greek example parallel to (48b):

(51)   Kűrou (G) edéonto hòs prothumotátou (G)/prothūmótaton (A)
        genésthai of-Cyrus
        they-begged as most-devoted to-be
        'They begged Cyrus to be as devoted to them as possible.'

The adjective (hōs prothūmotátou means 'as devoted as possible') can be
genitive, in agreement with the presumably anaphoric controller of the
infinitival complement, or accusative. Since accusative is the normal case of
the subject of an infinitive, the adjective is presumably here in agreement
with its SB or the SB's controller.

In Greek, nominative and accusative controllers seem to favour misapplication more than do genitive and dative ones, and predicate adjectives
are more prone to it than are predicate nominals and participles. These
resemblances to the conditioning factors of (50) suggest that misapplication
is an essentially universal tendency, conditioned by certain features of
sentence structure and the grammatical patterning of a language.

The presently available evidence on misapplication does not support any
particular formulation. Furthermore the phenonenon is essentially quite
marginal. I will therefore leave it unformalized. Our basic theory successfully predicts the necessity of agreement with a functional controller, and
the phenomenon of nonagreement with an anaphoric controller.
Agreement with anaphoric controllers requires an extra, although not at all
unnatural, device of uncertain character.

· A final matter that demands attention is the fact that predicate adjectives
modifying anaphorically controlled SB do always agree in gender and
number with their controllers. This is presumably a result of the general
convention requiring anaphoric elements to agree in gender and number
with their antecedents. It is a straightforward matter to amend (34) to
optionally place GND MASC/FEM and NUM PL on the functional SB.
The gender-number agreement restriction on anaphora would then filter
the outputs of (34).

3.4. We have explained the obligatoriness of the agreements in 3.2 as opposed to the optionality of those in 3.3 in terms of the distinction between functional and anaphoric control. There is however another possibility consistent with what we have seen so far. In all our functional control structures till now, the controller has not been a matrix argument. In anaphoric control structures, the controller is of course always a matrix argument.

There are various way in which this difference might be exploited to produce a theory of agreement. In the system of Chomsky (1980), for example, the functional control structures would have an empty NP coindexed with its controller by the rule Move NP, while the anaphoric control structures would have an empty NP bound to its controller by a rule of construal (all að-infinitives being structures of obligatory control). Functional control would thus be represented by coindexing at surface structure, while anaphoric control would not be. The differences in agreement could well follow from this.

There is, however, no requirement in the theory that functional controllers not be matrix arguments. In fact, such controllers play a substantial role in Bresnan (1981c) and in Neidle's (1981) account of agreement in Russian. Under the present theory, agreement with such a controller would be obligatory, with no chance of agreement with the 'missing' NP. Under a theory in which the agreement differences were ultimately determined by predicate-argument structure, agreement with the 'missing' NP would be predicted to be possible.

Fortunately, Icelandic has a construction with matrix argument functional controllers. It involves the so-called middle-voice conjugation, whose forms end in -st, diachronically the accusative (third person) reflexive pronoun sik. Middle forms have a variety of uses, being reflexives, reciprocals, simple intransitives, and various other things. A general survey of the uses of the form may be found in Valfells (1970).

The middles that concern us are those derived from ordinary ACI verbs. As an alternative to an ACI in which the SB and matrix OB are coreferential, one may use the middle form of the verb and omit the accusative. Predicate modifiers that would normally agree with the accusative then obligatorily revert to the nominative. Therefore as optional variants of (52) one finds (53):

(52)   a. hún(N) telur sig(A) (vera) ríka(A)
           she believes herself (to-be) rich
        b. ég(N) sagði mig(A) (vera) ríkan(A)
           I said myself (to-be) rich (male speaker)

(53)   a. hún telst (vera) rík(N)
        b. ég sagðist (vera) ríkur(N)

Even though the controllers in (53) are matrix arguments, there is no possibility of the adjectives being accusative in presumed agreement with the 'missing' NP.

If the construction of (53) is itself embedded in the ACI so that the matrix subject becomes accusative, then accusative is necessary on the predicate adjective:

(54)   a. þeir segja hana(A) teljast vera ríka(A)
           they say her to believe-self to-be rich
        b. þeir telja mig(A) hafa sagzt vera ríkan(A)
           they believe me to-have said-self to-be rich

We cannot thus regard the nominative in (53) as a failure of agreement.

Within our theory of functional structure, the optimal analysis of this construction will have the middle verbs derived from the active ones by a rule similar to the Passive, which rewrites OB as SB. This rule's effect on the syntactic aspect of a lexical item may be characterized as follows:

(55)   Middle Rule:
        OB → SB

An argument frame such as *telja*(SB, VCOMP(OB/SB)) will thus be converted into *telja*(SB, VCOMP(SB/SB)). But now the agreement phenomena in (53, 54) are immediately predicted by the functional structures that would be assigned to these examples.

For example, (54a) would get the functional structure (56) (some irrelevant details omitted):

(56)
$$
\begin{bmatrix}
SB \begin{bmatrix} PRED\ PRO \\ NUM\ PL \end{bmatrix} \\
PRED\ segja(SB, VCOMP(OB/SB)) \\
OB \begin{bmatrix} PRED\ PRO \\ CASE\ ACC \end{bmatrix} \\
VCOMP \begin{bmatrix} PRED\ telja(SB, VCOMP(SB/SB)) \\ VCOMP \begin{bmatrix} PRED\ vera(ACOMP(SB/SB)) \\ ACOMP\ [PRED\ rik(SB)] \end{bmatrix} \end{bmatrix}
\end{bmatrix}
$$

Since the accusative *hana* winds up specified as the SB of *rík*, this is what the adjective must agree with. It is the distinction between functional and anaphoric control, rather than any difference in predicate-argument structure, that seems to count in agreement.

4. The theory of functional interpretation thus attains a substantial measure of explanatory adequacy with respect to long distance agreement in Icelandic. Since the various 'subject raising' constructions require functional control, the obligatory agreement of predicate modifiers with the functional controllers is predicted. Since the middle voice construction of 3.4 is best analysed as having a matrix verb lexically derived from an ACI verb, it too must have functional control and obligatory agreement with the controller is predicted. On the other hand, the nominal behavior of að-infinitives shows that they bear closed rather than open grammatical functions, and must therefore have anaphoric rather than functional control. This predicts that predicate modifiers can appear in the nominative in these constructions. The optional, and often marginal, agreement with the anaphoric controllers in these constructions calls for a rather natural convention for misapplication of agreement restrictions, which may well be a performance phenomenon.

The workings of agreement thus fall out from the theory with virtually no work. While many current linguistic theories could probably provide a reasonably sensible account of this data, none known to me provides one so effortlessly.[8]

The same approach holds considerable promise, I believe, for explaining 'global' agreement in Ancient Greek. The careful reader of Andrews (1971) and Quicoli (1972) will realize, however, that considerable work needs to be done on Greek syntax before the theory can be applied in detail. In particular, something comparable to Thráinsson's study of the Icelandic complement system is needed.

When global and long distance agreement phenomena were first noticed, they seemed to require some kind of extension of the descriptive apparatus of transformational grammar, with consequent weakening of its content. But the theory of functional interpretation is more restrictive than transformational grammar (Kaplan and Bresnan 1981). And it is precisely the provisions which allow it to dispense with transformations in the complement system that provide an explanation of long-distance agreement.

The Australian National University
Canberra

NOTES

* My major acknowledgements are to Joan Bresnan, who talked over many aspects of this analysis with me and commented on an earlier version of this paper, and to Höskuldur Thráinsson, who has answered innumerable hard questions about Icelandic. I have also received assistance with the language from Inga Black, Inga Cott, Jón Bjarnason, Guðmundur Ágústsson, Sveinn Ólafson, Vigúss Jakobson, Sigurður Helgason, Jóhann Jóhansson, Baldur Jónsson and Valgi Gould. All errors are of course my own.

This work was made possible by the Outside Studies Program of the Australian National University, and pleasant by the hospitality of the Department of Linguistics and Philosophy at MIT.

[1] Ostler (1976) was as far as I know the first person in the generative literature to insist on this as the basic principle in the theory of agreement.

[2] This theory is a substantially revised version of that presented in Bresnan (1978). It is developed in considerable detail, with exemplification from a variety of languages, in Bresnan (1981a).

[3] At least in languages in which the notion of constituent structure is relevant. See Hale (1979) for an interesting treatment of non-phrase structure languages.

[4] The notation here is an informal version of that of Kaplan and Bresnan (1981).

[5] More accurately, VCOMP(SB/SB) SB. But I will generally use the shorter form for convenience.

[6] Andrews (1973, 1976) erroneously claimed that the adjective in structures like (47b) and (48a) must be accusative, since my informants up to that time had seemed to require it.

[7] This result is preserved even where the subject and the object are coreferential:

   (i) hann lofaði sjálfum ser að vera góður(N)/*góðum(D)
      he promised himself to to-be good

Both (i) and (48c) are acceptable on a different sense of *lofa*, in which it means 'allow,' and takes object control.

The contrast in agreement between (48b) and (48c) also destroys the prospects for an agreement rule that simply applies mindlessly across a variable between an adjective and the nearest NP to the left.

[8] For example, in the framework of phrase-structure grammar developed by Gazdar (this volume), it is an accident that the feature-propagation principles that enforce agreement restrictions always wind up making predicate modifiers agree with what they modify. The sortal theory of long-distance dependencies developed by Sag (this volume) to overcome this defect seems inappropriate for case-agreement, since it would require sorting the universe into different types for each morphological case, an ontologically bizarre move. The situation for phrase-structure grammar gets much worse when one considers the phenomena of long-distance government of irregular case discussed in Andrews (1981).

REFERENCES

Andrews, A. D. (1971) 'Case Agreement of Predicate Modifiers in Ancient Greek,' *Linguistic Inquiry* **2**, 127–152.

Andrews, A. D. (1973) 'Agreement and Deletion,' *Papers from the Ninth Regional Meeting of the Chicago Linguistic Society*, pp. 23–33.

Andrews, A. D. (1976) 'The VP Complement Analysis in Modern Icelandic,' in *Papers from the Sixth Meeting of the North Eastern Linguistic Society, Recherches Linguistiques à Montréal*, **6**.

Andrews, A. D. (1981) 'The Representation of Case in Modern Icelandic,' in Bresnan (1981a).

Baker, C. L. and M. K. Brame (1972) 'Global Rules: A Rejoinder,' *Language* **48**, 51–76.

Brame, M. K. (1978) *Base Generated Syntax*, Noit Amrofer Press, Seattle.

Bresnan, J. W. (1978) 'A Realistic Transformational Grammar,' in Halle, M., J. W. Bresnan and G. A. Miller, eds., *Linguistic Theory and Psychological Reality*, MIT Press, Cambridge, Mass.

Bresnan, J. W. (1981a), ed., *The Mental Representation of Grammatical Relations*, MIT Press, Cambridge, Mass.

Bresnan, J. W. (1981b) 'The Passive in Lexical Theory,' in Bresnan (1981a).

Bresnan, J. W. (1981c) 'Control and Complementation in English,' in Bresnan (1981a).

Chomsky, N. A. (1980) 'On Binding,' *Linguistic Inquiry* **11**, 1–46.

Emonds, J. E. (1973) 'Alternatives to Global Constraints,' *Glossa* **7**, 39–62.

Fauconnier, G. R. (1971) *Implications of Global Phenomena in Syntax*, PhD dissertation, University of California at Los Angeles.

Friðjónsson, Jon (1977) 'Um Sagnfyllinga með Nafnhaetti,' *Gripla* **2**, 132–150.

Gazdar, G. (this volume) 'Phrase Stucture Grammar.'

Hale, Kenneth (1979) 'The Position of Walbiri in a Typology of the Base,' MIT ditto.

Hamp, E. P., F. W. Householder and R. Austerlitz, eds. (1966) *Readings in Linguistics II*, University of Chicago Press, Chicago.

Jackendoff, R. S. (1972) *Semantic Interpretation in Generative Grammar*, MIT Press, Cambridge, Mass.

Jakobson, Roman (1932) 'Zur Struktur des Russischen Verbums,' in Hamp, et al. (1966).

Jakobson, Roman (1935) 'Beitrag zur allgemeinen Kasuslehre,' in Hamp, et. al. (1966).

Kaplan, Ronald and J. W. Bresnan (1981) 'A Formal System for Grammatical Representation,' in Bresnan (1981a).

Kiparsky, Paul (1973) 'Elsewhere in Phonology,' in Anderson, S. R., and P. Kiparsky, eds., *A Festschrift for Morris Halle*, Holt, Rinehart and Winston, New York.

Lakoff, G. P. (1970) 'Global Rules,' *Language* **46**, 627–639.

Mohanan, K. P. (1981) 'Grammatical Relations and Clause Structure in Malayalam,' in Bresnan (1981a).

Neidle, Carol (1981) 'Case Agreement in Russian,' in Bresnan (1981a).

Ostler, N. D. M. (1976) 'Aspects of Case Agreement in Ancient Greek,' MIT ditto.

Quicoli, A. C. (1972) *Aspects of Portuguese Complementation*. PhD dissertation, SUNY Buffalo.

Sag, I. A. (this volume). 'A Semantic Theory of "NP-Movement" Dependencies.'

Thráinsson, Höskuldur (1980) *On Complementation in Icelandic*, Garland, New York.

Valfells, Sigríður (1970) 'Middle Voice in Icelandic,' in Benediktsson, Hreinn, ed. *The Nordic Languages and Modern Linguistics*, Visindafelag Íslendigna, Reykjavík.

EMMON BACH

PURPOSE CLAUSES AND CONTROL

0. INTRODUCTION

My concern in this paper is the syntax and semantics of purpose-clauses in English. The relation of this problem to the question of the nature of syntactic representation is that the topics I will discuss raise interesting questions about what one might *not* want to include as explicit parts of either a syntactic or a semantic representation.

I will first isolate the kind of clause to be considered and note a number of its properties which must be explained in any adequate analysis. I will then present an analysis of purpose clauses. Finally, I will argue that many aspects of the distribution and interpretation of purpose-clauses require for their explanation theories about our understanding of situations in the world, the nature of human action, and a theory about how speakers and hearers build partial models in discourse.

1. PURPOSE CLAUSES

By purpose-clauses I mean a phrase of the sort illustrated by the capitalized portions of the following sentences:

(1)   I bought *War and Peace* TO READ TO THE CHILDREN.
(2)   She brought it over FOR MY BROTHER TO REVIEW.
(3)   They hired him TO GO OVER THE REPORTS.

They are to be distinguished from the superficially similar *in-order-to* clauses of (4) and (5):

(4)   He bought a piano (in order) to please his grandmother.
(5)   She hired a nurse in order for her daughter to learn Swedish.

(Cf. Faraci (1974) for a detailed account of purpose-clauses and a number of similar phrasal types.)

Purpose-clauses contrast with the other type in a number of respects:
(i) Purpose clauses always exhibit a gap:

(6)   *She gave it to me for my brother to review it.

35

P. Jacobson and G. K. Pullum (eds.), The Nature of Syntactic Representation, 35–57.
Copyright © 1982 by D. Reidel Publishing Company.

The gap can occur in subject (3) or non-subject position ((2), (1)). (6) contrasts with (7):

(7)   She gave it to me in order for my brother to review $\left\{ \begin{array}{c} \text{it} \\ *\varnothing \end{array} \right\}$.

In-order-to clauses cannot have non-subject gaps.

   (ii) Purpose clauses cannot be preposed:

(8)   *For my brother to review she brought it over.
(9)   (In order) to please his grandmother, he bought a piano.

   (iii) The purpose clause is always future-oriented with respect to the time of the matrix clause. This is not necessarily the case with *in-order-to* clauses:

(10)   I bought it in order to use up my money.
(11)   I brought it to give to my sister.

In (10) the time of buying and the time of using up my money may be identical. In (11) we must suppose that the time of (potential) giving is at least a little while after the time of buying.

   (iv) There are very heavy restrictions on the choice of matrix verb with purpose clauses, not so in the other case:

(12)   *I read it to review.
(13)   I read it (in order) to review it.
(14)   *The Dean came in to talk to.
(15)   The Dean came in to talk to us.

There is another superficially similar pattern involving an infinitival relative (either immediately after the noun phrase or extraposed). In considering examples it is important to make sure that we are dealing with genuine purpose clauses. Thus, (16) exhibits an infinitival relative and not a purpose clause:

(16)   I saw the book to give to your sister.

We can check that this can't be a purpose-clause by substituting a pronoun for the NP:

(17)   *I saw it to give to your sister.

(Many examples are ambiguous: *I bought a ledger to keep accounts in.*)

   I want here to give an explicit account of the syntax and semantics of purpose-clauses. The above properties and others will follow from various aspects of the analysis. The greater part of the discussion will be concerned with two problems: the problem of control and the problem of limitations on the nature of the matrix sentence (mentioned in (iv) above). Let us consider these two problems in a preliminary way.

1.1. *Control.* The control problem comes in when we have a purpose clause with two gaps, as in (1) above, repeated here:

(1)   I bought *War and Peace* to read to the children.

One gap (in object position in this sentence) must be controlled by the object of the main verb, *War and Peace*. This obligatory control will be accounted for by associating in the semantics a bound variable with the gap, in a manner to be explained. The control of the other gap, in subject position, is more problematical. There has been considerable discussion in the literature of this and related topics.[1] The question is this: Given a sentence like (1), what, if anything, is to be understood as the subject of the infinitival clause, that is, who is supposed to be or intended to be the one who reads the book to the children? It seems pretty clear in (1) that I am the intended reader. But compare the following:

(18)   I bought you *War and Peace* to read to the children.
(19)   I bought it from Bill to read to the children.
(20)   ?I sold *War and Peace* to read to the children.
(21)   I sold you *War and Peace* to read to the children.

In (18) and (21), the understood reader is you, in (19) again me, (20) sounds odd on the intended reading (there's a good *in-order-to* reading with no obligatory gap).

Jackendoff (1972) proposed that the interpretation of sentences containing subjectless infinitivals ($\overline{\text{VP}}$) was determined in large part by a hierarchy of thematic relations such as Agent, Source, Goal, Theme. Using these notions we might say this: In each example given above the obligatory gap is associated with the Theme (this raises problems to which we'll return). In (1) and (19) I am the (Agent and?) Goal; in (18) and (21) you are the Goal; (20) has no overt Goal. Solan (1978) has discussed some of the difficulties that arise in a purely thematic explanation for these and similar constructions. In this paper I want to take the discussion one step further, provide some analysis for the notions that lie beneath the thematic hierarchy, and, as mentioned, raise some questions about the theoretical status of these notions.

1.2. *Restrictions on Matrix.* In (iv) above, I noted that there are heavy restrictions on the nature of the matrix within which a purpose clause can occur. We can single out three sorts of contexts within which purpose clauses confortably occur (cf. again, Faraci, 1974, for discussion):

I. *have, be* (in a place, on hand, available, at one's disposal, in existence...)
II. Transitive verbs which involve continuance or change in the states of affairs indicated in (I) and are of a "positive" sort (see below).
III. Verbs of choice and use.

Here are some more examples to give a bit of intuitive content to the above:

Re I.

(22)   Mary has her mother to consider.
(23)   *War and Peace* is available to read to the students.

Re II.

(24)   We always keep a fire-extinguisher in the kitchen to use in case of fire.
(25)   I got it to prop up the porch with.

The "positive" condition mentioned above can be illustrated by contrasts like these:

(26)   I brought him in for us to talk to.
(27)   ?I sent him out for us to talk to.
(28)   I keep it in my office to amuse my students with.
(29)   ?I keep it out of my office to amuse my students with.

Re III.

(30)   I chose *War and Peace* to read to the students.
(31)   I used it to slice the salami with.

Some examples of unacceptable sentences that result when we choose expressions not fitting the above types are the following:

(32)   ?I read *War and Peace* to impress my friends with.
(33)   ?He came in to talk to.

1.3. *Resultant states.* One of the ingredients of our account of the interpretation of purpose clauses is the notion of a "resultant state". I would like to introduce this notion by digressing from purpose clauses for a moment and considering a simpler but related class of modifiers where the notion of resultant state plays a crucial role. Consider sentence (34):

(34)   Mary got up for an hour.

Excluding an irrelevant and unlikely reading, (34) means something like this: Mary got up and it was someone's intention that she *be* up for an hour. Note that this sentence could be true even if she did not stay up for an hour, as we can see from a continuation like this:

(35)   Mary got up for an hour but had to lie down again after fifteen minutes.

Preposing the *for*-adverbial is impossible, given this reading:

(36)   For an hour, Mary got up.

This sentence has only the unlikely, iterative reading.
    Here are a few more examples of this construction:

(37)   John went to New York for three days.
(38)   I sent the children to their father's for three weeks.
(39)   The exhibition was in New York for three months.

As with purpose clauses it's clear that these sentences crucially involve intentionality (with a *t*). To show this we need only compare sentences where intentionality is inappropriate:

(40)   Dinosaurs appeared on the earth for three million years.

(40) lacks the reading in question and can only be interpreted as something like this: dinosaurs kept on appearing on the earth for three million years. Note that preposing the *for*-phrase does not change the possibility for interpreting this sentence, and a contradiction emerges if we continue thus: *but they became extinct after two million years.* Again this contrasts with (37)–(39), which can have perfectly acceptable continuations like these:

(37′)   . . . but he had to leave after two days.
(38′)   . . . but they came back on the next bus.
(39′)   . . . but it had to close after two.

Whose intention is involved in the interpretation of such sentences? Examples like (39) or the following show that it need not be the intention of the subject:

(41)   The prisoner went to Sing Sing for 99 years.

On the other hand, it seems that if we do interpret the subject as Agent, then it is necessarily the subject's intention that is required.

To get the truth conditions right for sentences of the sort we've been considering, we need to invoke the notion of a resultant state. The resultant states for examples (34), (37), and (38) are respectively:

> Mary got up: Mary's being up.
> John went to New York: John's being in New York.
> I sent the children to their father's: their being with their father.

These examples involve verbs of change. In an analysis of the sort proposed by Von Wright (1963) (cf. Dowty, 1972), they all involve an event of the form $p|\neg p$ or $\neg p|p$. Getting up is a change from not being up to being up, and so on. The second state of affairs is the resultant state. An example like (39), on the other hand, is about a state directly, and implies that there was some act (setting up the exhibition, bringing it to New York) of which the state in question is the result.

Suppose it is true at a world w and time t that Mary gets up. Then it is necessarily true at w and some time t' ($t \leq t'$) that Mary is up. Suppose *John goes to New York* is true at a world w and time t, then it is necessarily true at w and some t' ($t \leq t'$) that John is in New York.

Suppose it is true at a world w and time t that I send the children to their father. Here there is no entailment of the sort just noted. Rather there is only a kind of modal entailment. What is true is that there is a world w' and a time t' ($t \leq t'$) such that the children are with their father at w' and t', and w' is related to w in a certain special way.

Let's call the state which comes about as the result of a verb of change the *resultant state*. Some verbs directly entail the existence of the resultant state (e.g. *get up, go to, bring*). Some, however, do not have such a direct entailment. Rather they involve some sort of modal relation to the resultant state (*send to Bill, give to Bill, leave for Chicago*). The difference can be brought out by suitable continuations.

(40)   ?John went to Chicago but he never got there.
(41)   John left for Chicago but he never got there.
(42)   I sent the letter to Bill but he never received it.

Interestingly, the two verbs *give* differ in this way (Martha Wright pointed this out to me).

(43)   ?I gave Bill the ticket but he never got it.
(44)   I gave the ticket to Bill but he never got it.

(Cf. *I give all my belongings to my great-great grandchildren.*)
Now consider sentence (1) again:

(1)   I bought *War and Peace* to read to the children.

If I buy something, then necessarily I *have* it. In each case involving a verb of exchange like *buy* there is a change of state with respect to ownership or control. In each case the most natural candidate for the intended subject of a subjectless purpose clause is the person who ends up owning or having in his/her control the object in question. For the sentences in question, mention of Sources and Goals serves to pin down more explicitly the previous and resultant states. If I buy a book *from* Mary *for* Bill, then there is a change from a state in which Mary has the book to one in which I have it and intend to bring about a state in which Bill has it.

By using a locution like "the most natural candidate", I want to underline what I take to be a fact: that the relationship between controller and subject position is not obligatory, we have rather to do with a case of "free" control. It certainly is very difficult not to interpret *John* as the understood subject in a sentence like this:

(40)   John bought *Bambi* to read to the children.

Nevertheless, I want to argue that we do not want to treat this as a case of obligatory control (cf. Williams (1980), who reaches similar conclusions within a different framework). The main reason is that if there is no possible controller in the sentence, then there can be control from context.

(41)   A hole is to dig.
(42)   This book is to read to the class.
(43)   *War and Peace* was bought to read to the children.
(44)   Here's *Bambi* to read to your children.

I believe that this is even the case in sentences where a possible overt controller is mentioned. For example, consider the sentence *I brought 'The Wind in the Willows' to read to the children.* Suppose I say this just as I enter a house (my own or someone else's). It seems to me possible to interpret the sentence in such a way that it is simply unspecified who is to do the reading. Or suppose I hand my host a bottle of wine and say *I brought this miserable Morgon to enjoy with our dinner*; I'm surely not suggesting that I alone enjoy the wine.

To summarize, I want the analysis of purpose clauses to show the following:

A. The purpose clause contains exactly one obligatory NP gap, which may occur at any place in the clause.
B. If there are two gaps, one of them must be in subject position and will be subject to principles of "free control".
C. The determination of the most natural controller of the missing subject in case B is given by the answer to the question: who is or will be in a position to "verb" the relevant thing which "corresponds" to the obligatory gap at the time of the resultant state of the matrix.

2. A MINIMAL ANALYSIS

In this section I propose an analysis of purpose clauses. The analysis is minimal in two ways: first, it says very little about what purpose clauses mean and is confined mainly to proposals about the logical structures of sentences containing them; second, it is minimal in the sense that a great deal is left out of these structures. The point is to get us off the ground so that we can then take up the main questions of this paper in Section 3.

I assume that purpose clauses are built out of predefined structures of the form (45) or (46):

(45)   *for NP to VP*: for John to read (it)
(46)   *to VP*: to read (it) to the children

The precise way in which you get the gaps indicated by the parenthesized *it*'s is largely a function of what your general theory is like. I have in mind a framework of the sort sketched in Bach and Partee (1980) and Partee and Bach (1980). But the analysis can for the most part be readily reproduced in a number of other frameworks.

The system makes use of context-free phrase structure rules using features of various sorts.[2] There are no transformations and no indexed elements in the syntax. The semantics is given by a rule-by-rule translation into an intensional logic of the sort used by Montague in PTQ (i.e. paper 8 in Montague, 1974). NP-gaps and pronouns are given translations involving indexed variables. For example, *he* is translated as $\hat{P} \ P\{x_i\}$, $i = 0, 1, 2 \ldots$ Features are to be thought of as functions from expressions to values chosen either from a finite set specified by the grammar (e.g. "masculine", "nominative", PAST, PRESENT) or from several infinite sets.

The latter can be thought of for convenience as special "stores" which keep track of indices on pronouns, including pronoun meanings corresponding to syntactic gaps, pronoun meanings that are free in a local domain, or free period, or pairs of elements (e.g. quantified NP's with indices of the pronoun meanings "left behind" as in Cooper's treatment of quantification in "wh-movement", Cooper, 1975).

The general format for a rule is this:

$$A := B \; C \qquad \text{condition:} \; G(F_i(0), F_k(1), F_l(2))$$

$$0' = F_0(1', 2')$$

The syntactic part of the rule may be interpreted in several ways:

(i) as short for a skeletal Montague rule of the form: if $\alpha \in P_B$, $\beta \in P_C$, then $\alpha\beta \in P_A$.

(ii) As a context free phrase structure rule: $A \to B \; C$

(iii) As a tree-checking rule: $[_A B \; C]$

The semantic part $(0' = F_0(1', 2'))$ specifies that the translation of the result $(0')$ is the result of applying some semantic function (F_0) to the translation of the first $(1')$ and second $(2')$ items to the right of ": = ". The conditions are some operations or statement (G) on the values of features F_i, F_k, F_l, etc. applied to the resultant (0) phrase or its first (1) and second (2) immediate constituents.

Of crucial interest here are two "stores", LPST ("local pronoun store") and QST ("quantifier store"). When a pronoun is put into a structure, the translation gives an arbitrary pronoun translation, and the index chosen is put into LPST. When a gap is generated, an arbitrary pronoun translation is entered into the appropriate place in the translation, a special pair $\langle WH, i \rangle$ is put onto QST, and i is put into LPST. Indices for pronouns remain in LPST until we pass a bounding node (say NP or S), then they are removed, but for any item $\langle WH, i \rangle$ (as well as for other pairs such as quantified NP's) i remains in LPST until specifically removed by a rule that binds the variable. A general condition on all rules that put together two or more constituents is that LPST be disjoint for the two or more constituents.[3]

For the purposes of the present paper, we need to add several things to the set of rules given in Bach and Partee (1980) and Partee and Bach (1980). In that fragment the only kinds of S̄'s were *that*-clauses (interpreted as S's, i.e. of type t, relative clauses were treated as syntactically distinct). Here we want to add the other kind of S̄.

In the papers mentioned we did not treat tenses and auxiliary elements at all. When we include tenses and auxiliaries, the simplest thing to do is to include *to* as an element of TNS.[4] The values for the feature TNS are {Past, Pres, Subjunctive, *to*, NIL}. To introduce the two kinds of $\bar{S}$'s we can adopt the following rules:

$$\text{R1.} \quad \bar{S}: = \text{COMP S}$$
$$0' = 2'$$

Conditions
(i) $\text{Gap}(2) \neq \text{subject}$
(ii) $\text{TNS}(2) = \text{TNS}(1)$
(iii) $\text{COMP}(0) = +$
(iv) $\text{CONTROL}(0) = \text{CONTROL}(2)$

We give the complementizer *that* the value {Past, Pres, Subjunctive} for TNS and the complementizer *for* the value {to}. The reason for the other conditions will emerge below.

$$\text{R2.} \quad \bar{S}: = \text{NP VP}$$
$$0' = 2'(\hat{\ }1')$$

Conditions
(i) $\langle \text{WH}, i \rangle \in \text{QST}(1) \supset \text{Gap}(0) = \text{subject}$
(ii) $\langle \text{WH}, i \rangle \in \text{QST}(2) \supset \text{Gap}(0) = \text{non-subject}$
(iii) $\text{LPST}(0) = \text{QST}_I(0)$
(iv) $\text{QST}(0) = \text{QST}(1) \cup \text{QST}(2)$
(v) $\text{LPST}(1) \cap \text{LPST}(2) = \emptyset$
(vi) $\text{CONTROL}(0) = \text{FREE}$

These two rules will generate S's of the following sorts:

(47)   for John to read it
(48)   that John reads it

The effect of condition (i) on R1 and (i) and (ii) on R2 is to ensure that the grammar generates no structures of the sort **for to read it* or **that reads it* (note that we treat relative clauses as syntactically distinct from ordinary $\bar{S}$'s.) I will not deal further with COMPless $\bar{S}$'s for tensed sentences here, but we do need a further rule for purpose clauses with missing subjects. The following rule will do:

$$\text{R3.} \quad \bar{S}: = \text{VP}$$
$$0' = 1'(\hat{P}P\{x_i\})$$

Conditions
$\text{TNS}(0) = \text{TNS}(1) = to$
$i \notin \text{LPST}(1)$
$\text{CONTROL}(0) = \text{FREE}$

This rule supplies an arbitrary pronoun meaning to make an $\bar{S}$ of the syntactic form *to VP*, but with the meaning of a sentence. (This rule constitutes a reworking of part of our rule for infinitives in the papers alluded to above. The constituent $\overline{\text{VP}}$ of earlier analyses is represented simply as VP with TNS value *to* and *to* itself is a function taking VP's with NIL TNS value to VP's with TNS = *to*.)

The new rules with the treatment of WH-gaps set up to account for *that* relatives will together generate structures like these:

(49)   for John to read $\in \bar{\text{S}}$

   TO $[\text{read}'(\hat{P}P\{x_3\})(\dot{j}^*)], \langle \text{WH}, 3 \rangle \in \text{QST}$

(50)   to read $\in \bar{\text{S}}$

   TO $[\text{read}'(\hat{P}P\{x_4\})(\hat{P}P\{x_5\})], \langle \text{WH}, 4 \rangle \in \text{QST}$

I have made the simplest assumption about the meaning of $\bar{\text{S}}$'s, that is, that they are of type *t* (like *S*). This is necessary in order to get the right meaning for them in the next rule, which is the first step toward purpose clauses. (I am sidestepping the issue of the exact meaning of the operator TO for the time being, except to assume it is a sentence operator.)

R4. PredS: = $\bar{\text{S}}$ TNS(1) = *to*
$0' = \lambda x_i 1'$ $\langle \text{WH}, i \rangle \in \text{QST}(1)$
$\quad\quad\quad\quad\quad$ QST(0) = QST(1) $- \{\langle \text{WH}, i \rangle\}$
$\quad\quad\quad\quad\quad$ LPST(0) = LSPT(1) $- \{i\}$
$\quad\quad\quad\quad\quad$ (SPST(0) = SPST(1) $- \{i\}$)

(SPST keeps track of all free variable indices.)

The result of these rules is to create expressions which denote sets (of individual concepts, in the simplest case), i.e. they are predicates. They are available for a variety of constructions (infinitival relatives, for example).

As I suggested in Section I, I'm going to assume that purpose clauses can be introduced into sentences in two ways (at least), either as arguments of certain verbs or as optional modifiers of certain verbal constructions. The intuition behind this distinction can be seen in the following pair:

(51)   I bought it to give to you.
(52)   I chose it to give to you.

(51) is true just in case I bought it and the purpose of my buying it was to give it to you. If we try to say the same thing about (52) it feels wrong: (52) is true just in case I chose it and the purpose of my choosing it was to give it to

you. I take *choose* (in most uses) to denote a relation between two individuals and a purpose, while I take the purpose clause in sentences like (51) to specify a relation between an individual and an action of buying.

Instances of the second kind are handled by simple subcategorization, i.e. choose is of a category like TVP/PredS or TVP/PurpCl. Instances of the first kind I get by allowing PredS to function as an element in the category of TVP modifiers TVP/TVP. So the function argument structure of the two examples will be like this:

(51') F(to give to you') (buy') (it') (I')
(52')   choose' (F to give to you') (it') (I')

where F is some semantic function giving TVP/TVP meaning to predicates. We now need to say something more about what this function is.

Purpose clauses seem to be related to a variety of prepositional phrases constructed with *for*:

(53)   The chicken is for dinner.
(54)   I bought it for dinner.
(55)   I went to Chicago for the convention.
(56)   She chose it for lunch.

Early transformational analysis (Lees (1960)) assumed that many sentences had two *for*'s in underlying structure and that there was a *for*-deletion transformation; thus (58) might have been derived from a structure like (57):

(57)   I bought it for [for you to read it].
(58)   I bought it for you to read.

There is a difficulty here. The *for* in examples like (53)–(56) is a preposition, i.e. it denotes a function from intensions of NP interpretations to, let's say, IV/IV and TV/TV type meanings. But we've made PredS's predicates, i.e. they denote functions from individual concepts (for example) to truth values. The difficulties are confounded when we consider sentences like these:

(59)   What I hope for is $\begin{cases} \text{for you to go.} \\ \text{a promotion and raise.} \end{cases}$

S̄'s are of type t. The issues raised by these facts are huge and complex and cannot, I believe, be resolved without a richer semantics than that provided by the set-theoretically based possible worlds semantics of Montague. Since

I can't possibly resolve these issues here, I am going to bypass them completely by using ad hoc constants in the logic. I will try to say a little more about their meaning in Section 3. I should point out that there is a general problem here of a different sort. Many prepositional phrases can function in the four positions illustrated in the above examples:

(60)   Mary is in the garden. (t/e?)
(61)   I saw Mary in the garden. (TV/TV?)
(62)   She walked in the garden. (IV/IV?)
(63)   I keep it in the garden. (?)

So here goes:
Purpose clause: = PredS

$$0' = \text{for}' \, (\,\hat{}\,1')$$

Here *for'* is a constant of type $\langle\langle s, \langle\langle s, e\rangle, t\rangle\rangle, \langle\langle s, F(\text{TV})\rangle, F(\text{TV})\rangle\rangle$, that is a function that maps properties into TV/TV modifiers. Now we can classify *choose* and *have* and *be* as verbs that take purpose clauses (and phrases, which we'll leave out of discussion henceforth). Examples of the sort given above will now have the following official translations:

(64)   Mary bought it to read

$$\text{for}' \, (\hat{x}[\text{read}'(\hat{P}P\{x\})(\hat{P}P\{x_4\})])(\,\hat{}\,\text{buy}')(\hat{P}P\{x_5\})(\,\hat{}\,m^*)$$

(65)   Mary chooses it for John to read.

$$\text{choose}' \, (\,\hat{}\,\text{for}'(\hat{x}_3[\text{read}'(\hat{P}P\{x_3\})(\,\hat{}\,j^*)]])(\hat{P}P\{x_5\})(\,\hat{}\,m^*)$$

Note that (64) has a free variable pronoun (with x_4) in subject position in the purpose clause. (The other free pronoun meanings in the above translations correspond to *it*.)

3. THE MEANING OF PURPOSE CLAUSES

I have given a pretty spare, some might feel uninformative, account of the structure of the interpretation of sentences with purpose clauses. I am not at all confident that it is anywhere near correct. But I now want to take up the main point of the paper: Given *some* such explicit account, how much more might we want to say and how and where might we say it.

We can imagine two extreme positions: one is a decompositional treatment in which we actually give an explicit definition of the constants we've used on the basis of more primitive components. Examples of such analyses in other domains abound in the literature, early and late, ranging from the syntactic decompositions of generative semantics through the lexical decompositions of some interpretivists to the decompositional translations into intensional logic of some Montague grammarians.[5] The other extreme is to say nothing more at all; this is perhaps the view expounded by Cresswell (1978). In discussing the meaning of the word *walk*, Cresswell writes (p. 4):

In V(*walk*) we spoke of a time t as being an interval of walking, but made no attempt to say what walking is. This is because the aim of the paper is not intended [sic] to teach people about walking. That knowledge is assumed. The aim of the paper is to show how a knowledge of what walking is is used by speakers of a language containing the symbol *walks*. Nor is the point of the paper to decompose *walks* or any other words into a number of 'semantic primitives' so that its meaning can be explained... It is of course a fact that both running and walking involve movement. It is also a fact that those who know what running and walking are know this. One could therefore have *runs* and *walks* as complex items of which the feature MOVEMENT is a component. The point about model-theoretical semantics is that this feature of V(*walks*) and V(*runs*) need not be put into the symbols. For it is our knowledge of walking and running, represented in the structure by functions from things to world-time pairs, which enables us to see that they have this in common. To put the point in another way, if a speaker has the ability to tell whether, for any a, a is running at $\langle w, t \rangle$ [i.e. at world w and time t, E.B] and whether a is *walking* at $\langle w, t \rangle$ then *by that alone* he has the ability to tell that both these involve movement.

Following Cresswell's line for the cases at hand, we might say something like this: To the extent that we need to invoke notions like Agent or Goal or Resultant State we can appeal directly to what the native speaker knows if she knows the functions denoted by words like *bring*, *sell*, *give*, and so on. (There are, of course, problems involved in the assumption that speakers can "know" the functions presupposed in the model-theory; see Partee (1979).)

   Let's see what it would be like to take these two extreme positions. First, I will try to show some of the difficulties of giving a more specific account of the semantics of purpose clauses. Then, I will lay out the consequences of taking the other, more Cresswellian position.

3.1. *Spelling out the meaning.*   Henceforth, I'll concentrate on the meaning of purpose clauses as TVP modifiers, as in (66):

(66)   John bought *War and Peace* to read.

We've given this a translation composed out of these ingredients: (1) the property denoted by $\hat{x}$ TO [read' $(\hat{P}P\{x\})(\hat{P}P\{x_3\})$] where x_3 is free, (2) the property of properties (NP-intension) corresponding to *John* (i.e. $\hat{P}P\{j\}$), (3) the intension of the transitive verb meaning of *buy*: '*buy'*, (4) the past tense operator, (5) a mysterious tense or modal TO, and (6) a mysterious function *for'* which is supposed to take (1) and make from it a function from (3) to a new transitive verb meaning that corresponds to the English phrase *buy-to-read*.

How might we try to spell out the meaning of *for'*? We might give an explicit meaning rule for *for'* (or, equivalently, give it a more elaborate translation into the intensional logic using either constants corresponding to the English words we use in our meaning rule or semantic primitives of some sort, which usually seem to boil down to the former unless we give explicit meaning rules for *them*). Let's try this on the basis of some of the informal observations we made in Section 1.

I: *for'* denotes that function h from properties of individual concepts to functions from TV-type intensions to TV denotations such that for all NP intensions $\mathscr{P}_1, \mathscr{P}_2$ properties P, and intensions of TV meanings R, $h(P)(R)(\mathscr{P}_1)(\mathscr{P}_2) = 1$ at w, t, g (g an assignment of values to variables) iff what?

Difficulties arise when we try to fill out this meaning rule. Take sentence (66): Suppose we say (66) is true just in case John bought *War and Peace* and intended that *War and Peace* have the property of being such that some (contextually specified) individual (presumably John) read it (presumably sometime later). If this is correct, then we can continue the meaning rule I as follows:

I: (iff) $R(\mathscr{P}_1)(\mathscr{P}_2) = 1$ at w, t, g, and the extension of $\mathscr{P}_2$ at w, t, g includes the property of being an x such that x intends that the extension of $\mathscr{P}_1$ at w, t', g include P at w, t', g for some t' later than t.

for' might then be translated as:

$$\lambda P[\lambda R[\lambda \mathscr{P}_1[\lambda \mathscr{P}_2[R(\mathscr{P}_1)(\mathscr{P}_2) \wedge \mathscr{P}_2\{\hat{x}[\text{intend}'(\,\check{}\mathscr{P}_1\{P\})(\hat{P}P\{x\})]\}]]]]$$

Unfortunately, this meaning rule is not very much more helpful than our previous translation as a means of helping us to understand the special properties of purpose clauses. Suppose John reads *War and Peace* while intending to start a fire with it when he's through. Then the following sentence would incorrectly be predicted to be true (at some later time).

(67)   John read *War and Peace* to start a fire with.

Suppose I have *War and Peace* and intend to get John to destroy it. Then (68) would incorrectly by predicted to be true.

(68)   I hate *War and Peace* for John to destroy.

Moreover, it's not at all clear just what the intention is or that it is always the intention that the object *have* the property represented in the purpose clause. For example, suppose (69) is true:

(69)   John bought *The Golden Notebook* for his children to read.

Can't this be true in a situation where after months of clamoring, John finally gave in? Here he is merely making it possible for his children to read the book in question.

Things become even worse when we take into account the question of agentivity. We saw in Section I that when the matrix verb is not agentive it's not the subject whose intention is involved but rather the agent or cause of the change to or existence of the resultant state. This agent may be explicitly mentioned or simply implicit.

(70)   I received *War and Peace* (from my publisher) to proofread.

In order to make this explicit we would have to introduce some way of representing agentivity in our semantics. Our meaning rule might then be continued like this:

I (iff) $R(\mathscr{P}_1)(\mathscr{P}_2) = 1$ at w, t, g, and there is an individual x such that x did something intentionally to cause $R(\mathscr{P}_1)(\mathscr{P}_2)$ and x intended that. . .

Such an amendment, however, does nothing to circumvent the earlier objections (I leave it to the reader to construct examples like (67) and (68).)

I won't try to pursue this line any further. I believe that if we continue to push it we will end up having to incorporate into out semantics an entire theory of human actions, purposes, and means and ends. So let's turn for a while to a different, more agnostic approach.

3.2. *Not spelling out the meaning.*   How might we defend an approach more in line with the quotation from Cresswell given above?

If we apply Cresswell's reasoning we might say something like this. If a speaker of English knows the functions that will allow her to know the truth conditions for sentences about buying, giving, and so on, she will know that these actions require agents, and that this isn't true for verbs like *receive*. No one is denying the value or validity of the kinds of distinctions that are discussed by writers like Jackendoff. The issue is rather the theoretical status of such notions as agent, source, and goal. In order to focus more closely on the issue, let's consider a somewhat simpler case.

The verb *roll* has been offered as an instance of a verb which can be used in two different ways. When we say *The stone rolled down the hill* we are said to understand *the stone* as being the Theme (with verbs of motion, the thing that moves) but in *John rolled down the hill* we may understand the sentence not only as completely parallel to the previous case, but also in another sense. John may be not only the Theme but also the Agent. The theory of thematic relations says that we need to have two different representations for these two situations. The alternative I'm pursuing here says this: there is only one sense of *roll*. But because of certain things that we know about the world and people we may understand that the sentence could be true not only in a situation where John is inadvertently rolling down the hill but also in situations where John is intentionally rolling down the hill. There are two reasons (at least) to think that the latter way of looking at the situation is better than the first. One is that we can fix the way we understand the sentence by stipulating a context. Suppose the sentence occurs in a story where we have just learned that John has been knocked unconscious. Then we will naturally understand the sentence in the way that would be represented in Jackendoff's theory by saying that John was just the theme and not the agent. (Although even in this case we can cancel that interpretation by subsequent sentences.) The second reason is that there are perfectly good sentences like these: *John rolled down the hill faster than the stone did*. Under various ideas about VP anaphora we should get identical readings for the two parts of the sentence, but I think the sentence is fine even when we understand the first one agentively and with no connotations of animacy in the second part.

Some kinds of verbs naturally require agents just because of what they mean. To buy something is to carry out a socially defined voluntary act involving exchange of currency for goods. Hence it can only be done by agents or their instruments. Others exclude interpreting the subject as the agent. To receive something is of the latter sort. If I receive sixteen grant proposals that means that a result has been achieved that has its origin in an action by some other agent than myself (normally, it is possible that I send things to myself). We can tease out our intuitions about these things, for example, in sentences with modal *will*, as complements to *try*, *decide*, and so on. But, again, we don't have to mark such distinctions formally in our grammars or lexicons. Such features of the meaning of verbs are entirely predictable on the basis of our understanding the truth conditions for the verbs. This is not to say that such distinctions are irrelevant to understanding language or uninteresting or unimportant. But the proper place to discuss them in is some theory about how we understand the world, the nature of human actions, causation, and so on.

So might a Cresswellian argument run. Some linguists (e.g. Chomsky 1975, if I understand him correctly) take the view that since knowledge and belief must be taken into account to give a full interpretation to expressions of natural language, linguistic semantics should stop short of trying to give any such full interpretation. This position seems to me to be untenable, if we really believe that one of the major goals of linguistics is to provide a "window into the mind".

3.3. *Consequences and conclusions.* The consequences of the two extreme positions sketched above seem rather uncomfortable. In the first way of going it seems as if we were driven into incorporating an entire theory of human action into our semantics. In the second way of going we seem to be ending up unable to say anything at all in our linguistic theory about some of the most interesting properties of purpose clauses.

I believe that some of our difficulties arise in inadequacies in the semantic apparatus made available by the possible-worlds approach as it stands.[6] But even if we can extend or modify this apparatus I believe that there is another way of avoiding the uncomfortable conclusions above: that is to recognize that there are at least two other domains of linguistic inquiry beyond syntax and semantics. One is what I have called elsewhere (Bach 1981) *natural language metaphysics.* In such an endeavor we try to understand the conceptual underpinnings of natural languages and natural language. This study has to deal with the place where there is the most immediate and rich interplay between language, the world, and our conceptualization of the world: lexical semantics. The other domain is the theory of *discourse*, where we study how speakers and hearers construct partial models based on texts in contexts (it thus impinges on pragmatics, in several senses of the word).

I am unable at this point to say anything that is not extremely programmatic about either of these domains. I'll conclude by sketching what I expect to be the kinds of answers we might seek in these domains of linguistic theory to some of the questions raised in Section 1. But first let me summarize what we have captured already in our analysis.

I. The fact that there is only one obligatory gap in a purpose clause follows from the fact that we have interpreted PredS's as predicates.[7]

II. The fact that if there are two gaps in the subject one must be a case of free control follows from the special nature of the rule that makes S̄'s out of VP's.[8]

III. The fact that purpose clauses (with obligatory gaps) are associated with the object does not follow from the syntax as such nor from the rather colorless semantic structure we have assigned to sentences with purpose clauses. It does fall into a general pattern noted for TVP modifiers by Keenan and Faltz (1978) and presumably we'll find an explanation when this general pattern is satisfactorily accounted for (cf. Bach 1979 for discussion of the relationship between transitivity and control for other constructions).[9]

These are the only facts that can be explained on the basis of the syntax and semantics I've offered. The remaining properties of purpose clauses might be accounted for as follows:

Suppose we have a good account of what it means to do a certain action with a certain end in mind, or for a certain purpose. This will require knowing something about the difference between voluntary and involuntary actions, and about necessary and sufficient causes and people's beliefs about them. We might expect implications for sentences *about* such purposive actions to flow out of such an analysis. For example, it should be odd to say that a has a property P for a purpose Q if P is the sort of property that is beyond anyone's control, including a's.[10] Among the general patterns available to us to talk about purposes in English are *in-order-to* clauses. Why is the following sentence odd?

(71)   John hates *War and Peace* in order to annoy his brother.

It is odd, because we don't think of hating something as a property under voluntary control. Similarly, if we have a sentence about purposes where the purpose doesn't seem to be one that can be effected by our actions the results are odd:

(72)   They opened the window (in order) to get the sun to shine.

(Note that the oddity of this sentence is a direct function of our beliefs.) But if we have a sentence about a state-of-affairs that can be thought of as the result of some agent's action, then we have no trouble:

(73)   The exhibition is here in order to satisfy the people.

I assume that the meaning of purpose clauses in the narrower sense is to be explicated within a general account of purposeful activity and our language about it. One domain of purposeful activity is that in which we use instruments as means to some end.[11] A paradigm case is represented in a sentence like this:

(74)   I used it to open the door with.

Things can't be used unless they are used as means to an end. (I've suggested that this fact is to be reflected by subcategorizing *use* to take the purpose clauses as arguments.)[12]

A necessary condition for you to do something with an object, or use it as an instrument to some end (cf. footnote 11), is that you have it available, or in your control, or that it be in your "control space". I can't use a screwdriver to open the door with if I don't have a screwdriver. I can't read *War and Peace* to my children if I don't have it. The paradigm cases we've been looking at here all involve such "availability" states. It is here that the notions tagged by the labels of the theory of thematic relations play their role.

Fortunately, linguistics can draw on a rich tradition for help in fleshing out a theory about human actions, causations, purposes and the like, since we are touching here on questions that have preoccupied philosophers for millenia.[13] But as linguists we need not concern ourselves so much with the question of what human actions are as with what we seem to think they are when we talk. (Ultimately, I do not think we can keep these questions entirely separate: the world is the world, and we are in it, and it isn't neatly divided into autonomous subsystems or separate domains.)

So much for ethnometaphysics. What about the theory of discourse? I believe we must invoke such a theory in order to be able to say anything about the question of "control" in purpose clauses. Consider a complex case:

(75)   I bought *Bambi* to give to Mary to pass on to John to take along on the camping trip to read to the children.

To understand this sentence and compute the most likely value for the free variables that our syntax/semantics has put into subject position for the purpose clauses, we need to track the succession of "availability states" through the clause. I buy *Bambi*; I have *Bambi*; I'm going to give it to *Mary*; then Mary will have it; she's supposed to pass it on to John; then he'll have it and will be able to take it along on the camping trip and it will be on hand (for John or anyone else on the trip) to read to the children.[14]

I have just worked out the most likely controllers of the purpose clauses in (75). How did I do it? By understanding what it means to give, pass on, take along, and so on. But then I know English. How much of this can we or should we put into our theories of linguistic competence, into our theories of syntactic and semantic representations? I don't think we'll have a satisfying answer to this question until we've done a lot more work.

Finally, then, let us ask the question most relevant to questions of syntactic and semantic representations. If neither a decompositional treatment nor a completely say-nothing approach seems feasible, how can we proceed?

There is a way. It is to study the structure of admissible models for "standard" interpretations of natural languages. Technically, this can be done in two ways: by tinkering with basic properties and relations in the domains of elements in the model (e.g. time structures, ontological alternatives), or by the use of so-called meaning postulates which place particular constraints on the interpretation of words and constructions. Note that we can avoid many of the difficulties of definitional or decompositional analyses simply by allowing one way implications rather than biconditionals. (For arguments for such an approach, see Fodor, Fodor, and Garrett (1975), Fodor and Fodor (1980). I believe that the best interpretation for notions like those offered by the theory of thematic relations is to think of them as short for meaning postulates of this sort.) Moreover, since we are dealing with the structure of and constraints on *interpretations* what we say need not enter into representations, syntactic or semantic at all. And we can appeal to such meaning postulates when we construct a theory of discourse and make formal models of the kind of inferences that speakers and hearers make when they understand each other.[15]

University of Massachusetts
Amherst

NOTES

[1] See, for example, Jackendoff (1972), Solan (1978), Williams (1980).

[2] The basic framework goes back to proposals of Rick Saenz and Ken Ross (see Ross, 1980), and is quite similar to other non-transformational frameworks currently under development, e.g. those of Brame, (1978); Bresnan (1978); Dowty (this volume); Gazdar (this volume).

[3] This condition accomplishes several things: (1) it accounts for "non-coindexing" in local domains; (2) it ensures that quantified NP's cannot bind pronouns that are locally free in clauses higher than the actual site of the quantified NP. For an explicit recursive definition of "locally free" and the more general notion "free" (SPST), see Bach and Partee (1980).

[4] This account is simplified for present purposes. A more complete treatment must include "governing" and "governed" features for perfect participles and *ing*-forms. For a preliminary statement of the treatment of tense and auxiliaries in a Montague grammar, see Bach (1980). Rick Saenz has a detailed treatment in an unpublished work (to be reported on in the Final Report of the NSF Grant mentioned in footnote 15.)

[5] Dowty (1979) reviews various approaches to the decomposition of meanings in a variety of frameworks.

[6] The well-known difficulties of possible-world semantics should not be taken as cause for despair nor for the abandonment of model-theoretic techniques in semantics. I believe any advances in what is called (curiously) "formal semantics" of natural languages will be built upon the solid achievements of the last ten years of work on possible-world semantics.

[7] I am ignoring across-the-board and other multiple gaps bound by the same lambda operator and assuming that general island constraints will come into play to exclude illicit multiple gaps.

[8] I do not mean to imply that we should rest simply cataloguing this as a brute fact about English. One would want to give some general account that would do justice to the unity and variety of such facts across languages, as in current work within "extended standard theory" and other approaches.

[9] Work of Williams (1980) and others is devoted to giving structural conditions governing the interpretations of such predicative structures. For an alternative approach to such questions (but not this particular one), see Bach and Partee (1980).

[10] Not all uses of purpose clauses fit this paradigm. In particular, examples like the following seems to make reference to some kind of inherent teleology:

   i. Eyes are to see with.
   ii. Little brothers are to take care of.

[11] Barbara H. Partee has suggested to me that purpose clauses in general should be thought of as "instrument-for-a-purpose" clauses, that they always involve "doing something with something". It is certainly true that many of the examples here fit this view.

[12] The verb *use* seems to provide a counterexample to the claim that there can be only one obligatory gap, since even the most plausible examples with overt subjects seem bad: ?*We used this old piano for our children to practice on.* They would also be counterexamples to the theory of predication in Williams, 1980. I suspect that this restriction could be explained on the basis of a good theory of agency, purposes, and instruments, but have no good clues as to how.

[13] I have profited, for example, from the discussions of actions and purposes in Aune (1977).

[14] It should be noted that an example like this must be derived by iteration of the rule for constructing purpose clauses rather than from iteration of the rule for putting purpose clauses together with TVP's. Only in this way can the temporal relations come out right. The analysis of intentionality (cf. Aune, 1977) provides a basis for explaining the observation about futurity in Section 1 above.

[15] Thanks to Edwin Williams, Debbie Nanni, and especially to Barbara Partee for good discussion and criticism. The research reported on here was supported in part by NSF Grant BNS 78–19309. The opportunity to begin thinking about the kind of issues dealt with here was provided by the Centre for Advanced Study in the Behavioral Sciences and the National Endowment for the Humanities, for which grateful acknowledgement is made.

BIBLIOGRAPHY

Aune, Bruce (1977) *Reason and Action*, D. Reidel, Dordrecht.
Bach, Emmon (1979) 'Control in Montague Grammar', *Linguistic Inquiry* **10**, 515–531.
Bach, Emmon (1980) 'Tenses and Aspects as Functions on Verb-Phrases', in C. Rohrer, ed., *Time, Tense, and Quantifiers*, Tübingen: Niemeyer, pp. 19–37.

Bach, Emmon (1981) 'Time, Tense, and Aspect: An Essay in English Metaphysics,' in P. Cole, ed., *Radical Pragmatics*, Academic Press, New York, pp. 63–81.

Bach, Emmon and Barbara H. Partee (1980) 'Anaphora and Semantic Structure', Proceedings of the Chicago Linguistic Society, Vol. 16.

Brame, Michael (1978) *Base-generated Syntax*, Noit Amrofer Press, Seattle.

Bresnan, Joan (1978) 'A Realistic Transformational Grammar', in Morris Halle, Joan Bresnan, and George A. Miller, eds., *Linguistic Theory and Psychological Reality*, Cambridge: MIT Press.

Chomsky, Noam (1975) *Reflections on Language*, Pantheon, New York.

Cresswell, Max J. (1978) 'Prepositions and Points of View', *Linguistics and Philosophy* 2, 1–41.

Dowty, David R. (1972) *Studies in the Logic of Verb Aspect and Time Reference in English*, unpublished doctoral dissertation, the University of Texas, Austin.

Dowty, David R. (1979) *Word Meaning and Montague Grammar*, D. Reidel, Dordrecht.

Dowty, David R. (this volume) 'Grammatical relations and Montague grammar.'

Faraci, Robert A. (1974) *Aspects of the Grammar of Infinitives and FOR-phrases*, unpublished doctoral dissertation, M. I. T.

Fodor, J. D., J. A. Fodor, and M. Garrett (1975) 'The Psychological Unreality of Semantic Representations', *Linguistic Inquiry* 6, 515–531.

Fodor, J. A. and J. D. Fodor (1980) 'Functional Structure, Quantifiers, and Meaning Postulates', *Linguistic Inquiry* 11, 759–770.

Gazdar, Gerald (this volume) 'Phrase structure grammar.'

Jackendoff, Ray S. (1972) *Semantic Interpretation in Generative Grammar*, MIT Press, Cambridge, Massachusetts.

Keenan, Edward L. and Leonard M. Faltz (1978) 'Logical Types for Natural Language,' *U. C. L. A. Occasional Papers in Linguistics* 3.

Lees, Robert B. (1960) *The Grammar of English Nominalizations*, Bloomington, Indiana.

Montague, Richard (1974) *Formal Philosophy*, ed. by Richmond Thomason, New Haven.

Partee, Barbara H. (1979) 'Montague Grammar, Mental Representations, and Reality', in P. French, T. Uehling, and H. Wettstein, eds., *Contemporary Perspectives in the Philosophy of Language* (University of Minnesota Press, Minneapolis) pp. 195–208. (Reprinted in *Philosophy and Grammar*, S. Öhman and S. Kanger, eds., D. Reidel, Dordrecht.)

Partee, Barbara H. and Emmon Bach (1980) 'Quantification, Pronouns, and VP Anaphora', in J. Groenendijk, T. Janssen, and M. Stokhof, eds., *Formal Methods in the Study of Language: Proceedings of the Third Amsterdam Colloquium*.

Ross, Kenneth (1980) *Parsing English Phrase Structure*, unpublished doctoral dissertation, University of Massachusetts, Amherst.

Solan, Lawrence (1978) 'On the Interpretation of Missing Complement NP's', *University of Massachusetts Occasional Papers in Linguistics* 3.

von Wright, George (1963) *Norm and Action*, Humanities Press, New York.

Williams, Edwin (1980) 'Predication', *Linguistic Inquiry* 11, 203–238.

ROBIN COOPER

BINDING IN WHOLEWHEAT* SYNTAX

(*unenriched with inaudibilia)

0. INTRODUCTION

In this paper I shall explore one way of stating constraints on movement as constraints on binding without enriching the syntax with representations of unpronounced bound variables (as, for example, has been proposed by proponents of trace theory). While the only kind of movement that I will talk about here is wh-movement, I believe that the kind of techniques discussed may be extended to other kinds of movement which might be treated as corresponding to the binding of a variable.

There are two parts to the paper. The first will discuss the techniques which make it possible to eliminate representations of silent variables from the syntax and yet still state constraints on movement as constraints on binding. The second speculates on the nature of such constraints, suggesting that a semantic version of George Horn's NP-constraint might be appropriate. I will show how this kind of semantic constraint might yield a solution to certain problems for the NP-constraint and interact with the approach to the lexicon developed by Dowty to provide a new alternative analysis for recalcitrant examples such as *Who did you see a picture of?*

1. THE TECHNIQUES[1]

There are three aspects of the treatment that I am proposing which facilitate the statement of constraints on binding without requiring inaudible representations of variables in the syntax. The first has to do with the nature of the syntax. The second and the third have to do with the connection between syntax and semantics. I shall take them in turn.

1.1. *'Bottom-up' syntax.* I have taken from Montague the idea that syntactic rules should combine phrases into larger phrases, except that I regard the phrases as being represented by labelled bracketings or trees which may be put together (see Bach 1979 for the first precise formulation of this idea). Thus many of the rules may be thought of a backwards phrase structure rules. A stage in the derivation of the sentence *John runs* is represented in (1).

59

P. Jacobson and G. K. Pullum (eds.), The Nature of Syntactic Representation, 59–77.
Copyright © 1982 by D. Reidel Publishing Company.

(1)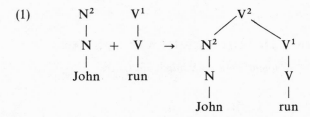

The rule states that a tree rooted by N^2 and another rooted by V^1 may be adjoined under a V^2 node. In addition to such backwards phrase-structure rules, there are transformations which may change structure at the same time as building structure. The effect of *wh*-question movement is illustrated in (2) which represents a stage in the derivation of *Who did John see*?

(2)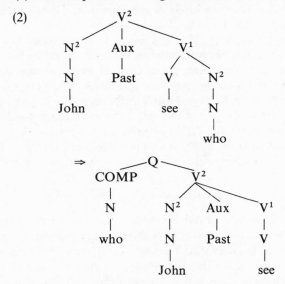

Here the freely generated *wh*-phrase has been moved to the left into the COMP position built for it by the transformation and adjoined to the remaining sentence fragment under the node Q, for question. All this is achieved by a single transformation. (Again I am following Bach 1979 in allowing this kind of rule.) The output represented in (2) may be turned into a direct question by a subsequent application of subject-aux inversion. It may also, however, serve as the input to further phrase-structure-like rules. For example, it may combine with a verb like *wonder*, subcategorized for Q, to form the phrase *wonder who John Past see*. In this case, of course, the Q will function as an embedded question. (Note that the transformation removed the N^2 node which was dominating *who*; this will mean that the *who* will not satisfy the structural description of the *wh*-movement transformation again and thus cannot be moved out of the COMP position of the embedded question.) All of the rules in this grammar are optional and unordered, and there is no division of phrase-structure-like rules and transformations into separate components as in a standard transformational grammar. Any rule of whatever kind may apply when the structure derived so far allows it to. The fact that an embedded question will be derived in its *wh*-moved form before it is combined with a verb like *wonder* will be an important factor in eliminating silent variables from the syntax. The analysis of relative clauses is similar in that a relative clause is derived in its *wh*-moved form before it is combined by phrase-structure-like rules with a noun and a determiner. This general feature of the syntax, that transformations may apply before phrase-structure rules, plays a crucial role in eliminating silent variables.

1.2. *Rule-by-rule semantic interpretation.* The reason that this lack of ordering is so important has to do with the connection between syntax and semantics. Following Montague, we adopt the Fregean compositionality idea and allow each rule in the syntax to correspond to a semantic interpretation rule. Thus the semantics does not interpret structures, as in a standard transformational grammar, but rather the applications of rules. For example, the interpretation rule corresponding to the syntactic rule at work in (1), would simply take the interpretation of the NP *John* (which we will represent here as *John'*) and the interpretation of the VP *run* (represented as *run'*) and combine them in the way specified by the rule, in this case functional application. The semantic process corresponding to the syntactic process in (1) is represented in (3).

(3) $John' + run' \Rightarrow John'(run')$

In this kind of framework it does not make sense to ask which level or levels of syntax should provide input to the semantic component. Firstly, this is true because there are no levels of syntax in the traditional sense. This is a result of the transformations and phrase-structure rules not being divided into separate components. Secondly, it is true because each rule has its corresponding semantic interpretation. This enables us to interpret the rule of *wh*-movement. In a standard transformational grammar one must

interpret a structure preceding the application of *wh*-movement or a
structure resulting after the application of *wh*-movement or one might have
both pre- and post-*wh*-movement structures giving input to the semantic
component, but one may not interpret the actual rule as is possible in this
framework.

This difference becomes important when we consider possible ways in
which one might state constraints on movement as constraints on binding.
Such a statement must treat a *wh*-NP as a quantifier which binds a variable
occurring in the deep structure position of the *wh*-phrase. The constraint
restricts the kind of structure which can occur between the surface structure
position of the *wh*-quantifier and its deep structure site. Clearly such a
constraint cannot be stated before *wh*-movement has applied, since we do
not know where the *wh*-phrase is going to end up. If it is to be stated on a
structure occurring after *wh*-movement has applied, then we must know
where the *wh*-phrase was moved from in order to be able to state the
constraint. Thus we must either encode this position (e.g. with a trace) in the
post-*wh*-movement structure or we must look at more than one level of
structure. However, if we interpret the rule of *wh*-movement itself we can see
that it might be possible to devise an interpretation rule where the origin of
the *wh*-phrase is represented in the semantics by something corresponding
to a variable which is bound by the *wh*-quantifier having the scope of the
whole phrase that has just been built up. Thus the output of the semantic
interpretation rule working on the particular instance of *wh*-movement
given in (2) might be something like (4), where we represent the *wh*-
quantifier as WH^2.

(4) WHx John' (see'([x]))

Clearly, if we can devise such a rule we will be able to characterize the dual
role of the *wh*-phrase in the semantics: as a variable whose role in the
semantic interpretation is determined by the original position of the *wh*-
phrase and as a quantifier whose role is determined by the derived position
of the *wh*-phrase. Because we are interpreting the movement rule itself we
are not obliged to mark the variable position in the syntax and constraints
might be stated as constraints on possible binding relationships in semantic
interpretation.

We have specified approximately what the output to such a semantic rule
should be, but how may we represent its input? Unfortunately, there is no
obvious well-defined semantic operation which would perform the kind of

change represented in (5) which exactly mirrors the *wh*-movement transformation.

(5)   John' (see'(WH)) $\Rightarrow$ WHx John' (see'([x]))

One way to state the difficulty represented by (5) is as follows: suppose that what you see on the left-hand-side of the arrow were well-formed and expressed a proposition. In many theories a proposition is thought of as a set of possible worlds. What exactly would you do to that set in order to get to the interpretation represented on the right-hand-side of the arrow? There is no obvious semantic operation defined on a set of possible worlds which would correspond to syntactic transformations on logical notation represented in (5). Thus a model-theoretic semantics, one in which sentences correspond to things like sets of possible worlds rather than expressions of logical form, naturally restricts options which are available in other theories.[3] The solution to this problem brings me to the third technique involved in eliminating silent variables.

1.3. *Storage.* Clearly if we are to have 100% all natural wholewheat syntax without any artificial additives, then the compositionality principle as it is normally understood cannot be preserved. Consider the sentence (6).

(6)   One of my representatives will visit each customer.

Most people, I think, would agree that *each customer* may be given wider scope than *one of my representatives*. Representing scope ambiguity in the syntax has been determined to cause cases of unnatural syntactic rules and silent variables. Such syntactic representation of semantic scope ambiguities does not even make the syntax more palatable. It merely acts as a preservative, allowing the grammar to preserve a rather strict notion of semantic compositionality where each bit of syntactic structure corresponds to exactly one interpretation. In Cooper (1975, 1978) I have been developing a technique for allowing each phrase to correspond to a set of interpretations. In order to achieve wide scope interpretations while preserving a version of the compositionality principle I have introduced a technique called storage. This simply involves taking an NP interpretation and putting it on ice for a while until you have built up enough of the syntactic tree to represent the scope you want to give the NP. At that point you may take the NP-interpretation out of storage and quantify it in. I will illustrate the mechanism with *wh*-phrases which are special in that they always receive wide scope interpretation. Normally the point at which they are quantified in is represented in the syntax by the COMP position which they end up in. The way that this works for the sentence *who did John see?* is illustrated in (7). The syntactic phrase is represented on the left and its interpretation on the right.

(7)

	INTERPRETATION	STORE
who	$[x]$	WHx
see who	$see'([x])$	WHx
John see who	$John'(see'([x]))$	WHx
who John see	$WHx\ John'(see'([x]))$	

To each phrase we assign now not simply an interpretation but an interpretation together with a store. The store remains empty for interpretations of sentences which do not involve wide scope quantification. The store may contain NP-interpretations if we wish to build up wide scope readings. The NP-interpretation remains in the store, carried along each time we build a new phrase until we have gotten the phrase over which we want the NP to have scope. At this point the NP-interpretation may be retrieved from the store and quantified in. *wh*-NP's must be given wide scope and therefore their interpretations must be entered in the store when they are first encountered in the syntax. The interpretation of the rule of *wh*-movement consists of retrieving the *wh*-interpretation from the store and quantifying it in. Thus we are assigning to each phrase compositionally an ordered pair consisting of an interpretation and a store. The store may be empty and it is only when the store is empty that we have a bona fide meaning of the phrase. Ambiguous phrases are assigned a set of such interpretation/store pairs. These sets are assigned to the syntax compositionally.

2. THE CONSTRAINTS

This kind of treatment makes it very simple to state constraints on *wh*-movement as constraints on binding. Suppose, for example, that we wanted to state the complex NP constraint. We would simply say that complex NP's may not have a *wh*-interpretation in the store. The occurrence of something in the store means that it will eventually get assigned wider scope than the phrase being interpreted. If we wished to state the propositional island condition, we would simply state that propositional islands, however they are to be defined, would not allow a *wh*-interpretation to be in the store. These might be regarded as corresponding to natural processing strategies used by human beings to build up the interpretation of phrases while parsing them. When we have parsed a phrase of a certain kind of complexity it no longer becomes feasible to hold the meaning of part of that phrase for later use in the parse. We must either choose an interpretation for the phrase in which the store is empty or, failing that, we must reject the phrase as unacceptable.

It is interesting to note that the mechanism I am suggesting seems to select among various constraints that have been proposed. Constraints such as the Complex NP Constraint of Ross (1967) and the Propositional Island Condition of Chomsky (1977) are allowed because they can be cast in the form given in (8).

(8)   Structures of kind X (e.g. complex NP, propositional island) may not have WH in the store.

However, a constraint such as the Nominative Island Condition of Chomsky (1980: 13)[4] cannot obviously be stated in this model-theoretic framework. It cannot be cast in the form (8), and it is not at all clear how one might go about looking for a "free nominative anaphor" in the interpretation of an $\bar{S}$ if the interpretation of that $\bar{S}$ is something like a set of possible words. Chomsky's (1980) Opacity Condition[5] too, seems difficult or impossible to state since it too may set us hunting for a "free anaphor" among possible worlds. Note also that subjacency is indirectly ruled out by the treatment proposed here since hopping wh-words from COMP-to-COMP does not make any sense. Whenever a wh-word is moved into COMP position the variable gets bound and the scope of the wh-quantifier is fixed in the semantics. You cannot bind the same variable twice by moving the wh-phrase a second time. I think it is interesting and important that in an attempt to keep the syntax strictly wholewheat and interpret it with a model theoretic semantics we have in a rather natural manner restricted the class of available constraints. I think this is interesting even if some of our favourite constraints have fallen by the wayside, since it may make it possible to determine exactly what additives are needed for the syntax and the semantics in order to make precisely the right class of constraints stateable.

A constraint that is very natural in this kind of system is one that blocks an NP from having wider scope than an NP in which it is embedded, i.e. in movement terms prevents extraction out of an NP. This, of course, would be a semantic version of George Horn's NP-constraint. One reason that the NP constraint seems natural is because it is mainly, and perhaps entirely, NP-interpretations which must be stored by the semantics to be given wide-scope interpretation. We might expect that natural language would find some way of avoiding the situation that would arise if you attempt to store the interpretation of some NP whose interpretation already contains a non-empty store. The resulting situation, according to one way of formalizing things at least, is indicated in (9).

(9)   a. NP_1

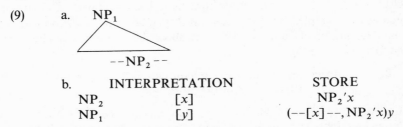

$--NP_2--$

b.   INTERPRETATION   STORE
      NP_2 $[x]$ $NP_2'x$
      NP_1 $[y]$ $(--[x]--, NP_2'x)y$

In storing the interpretation of the superordinate NP_1 to give it wider scope we have had to take into account that NP_1 already has a non-empty store associated with it and so we have stored the ordered pair of interpretation and store corresponding to NP_1. So what we have now is something similar to a self-embedding. We have a store within a store corresponding to the fact that syntactically we have an NP within an NP. This ordered pair which we have stored is somehow supposed to bind the variable y at a later stage of the semantic interpretation. It does not make sense to think of ordered pairs of interpretations as things which can correspond to variable binding operators. But there is not just a technical reason for wanting to avoid the kind of self-embedding represented in (9). If this storage mechanism corresponds in any way to a psychologically real parsing strategy which speakers of the language use in order to interpret sentences, then the situation represented in (9) may be one that we would reasonably expect the human mind to avoid. The mental process which the parsing which the formalism that I have used suggests requires may be similar to that involved in center-embedded relative clauses. We seem to avoid situations where we must store more and more bits of interlocking interpretation without having an opportunity to plug them back in again. There is more than one technical way to solve the problem posed by the situation represented in (9). One of them is to impose the NP-constraint. This may be stated in our terms as in (10).

(10)   The store of an NP interpretation must be empty before it can be further processed.

Given Montague's semantic treatment of NP's, (10) can be stated in purely semantic terms without making reference to the syntactic notion of NP. NP's are given a distinctive kind of model-theoretic interpretation. An NP corresponds to a set of properties. This kind of interpretation is what some logicians regard as the model-theoretic interpretation of quantifiers. Thus Montague's treatment might be seen as making the claim that NP's are natural language quantifiers, rather than treating the determiner as the quantifier as linguists normally have (See Barwise and Cooper, 1981, for discussion of this.) Thus (10) might be recast in purely semantic terms, taking a quantifier now to be a set of properties in model-theoretic terms. This is done in (11).

(11)   If the interpretation is a quantifier (i.e. NP-interpretation), then the store must be empty before the derivation can continue.

Thus we might propose some kind of semantic autonomy condition on possible constraints on binding, e.g. something along the lines of (12).

(12)   No semantic constraint may make reference to syntactic notions.

Note that this would be such a restrictive theory that it would rule out the kinds of constraints represented in (8). For example, consider the complex NP constraint. In the semantics all NP's are interpreted as quantifiers, i.e. sets of properties, and there is no way to draw the distinction between complex and non-complex NP's in the semantics. Hence the complex NP constraint would not be stateable in such a restrictive theory. PIC may also be ruled out if all sentences, whether tensed or not, are thought of as corresponding to propositions. It would presumably depend on one's semantic theory. For example, if propositions are sets of possible worlds or world-time pairs, one has to ask the question whether it is possible to distinguish these sets on the basis of whether they correspond to a propositional island in the relevant language or not.

We have moved towards a very restrictive view of what the possible constraints on binding could be and we have seen that a semantic version of Horn's NP constraint is consistent with this view in a way in which some more syntactically oriented constraints on binding are not. This, of course, is not of much interest if it turns out that the NP constraint is hopelessly wrong. In what follows I shall discuss two apparent problems that arise for the syntactic NP-constraint and discuss how they might be handled.

2.1 *Extraposition rules.* In his dissertation, Horn (1974) notes that examples involving extraposition rules seem to violate a strict version of the NP-constraint on movement. He illustrates this with an example of extraposition-from-NP which I repeat in (13).

(13)   [The man ____] arrived yesterday [who had been am-
        bassador to India]

In Horn (1974) this problem is avoided by requiring that the only movement rules which obey the NP-constraint are those which move a constituent to a node position already present in the tree. Thus extrapositions, which he formulates as rules moving over a variable to the end of the phrase being cycled on, will not be blocked by the constraint, whereas *wh*-movement which moves a constituent to an empty COMP position will be blocked by the constraint. In his most recent statement of the NP-constraint, Horn (1979), offers two alternatives to this solution. One is simply to say that extraposition phenomena should not be handled by extraposition transformations but should be generated directly and undergo an interpretive rule. The other possibility he suggests is to keep the classical extraposition rules but formulate them so that they do not leave a trace. As his latest version of the NP-constraint simply stars any surface structure of the form given in (14), the NP-constraint would not apply to extraposition rules.

(14)   ... [... t ...]$_{NP}$ ...

This last solution corresponds to the intuitive account that is possible if we use the semantic NP-constraint. If extraposition rules as such exist, there seems to be no semantic evidence that they involve wide-scope interpretation of any constituent. Thus extraposition rules would simply not be the kind of rule that is linked to the storage mechanism in the semantics. As the NP constraint is stated on the storage mechanism and not on the syntax the question of extraposition rules obeying the NP-constraint would never arise. Note that we can draw this distinction between *wh*-movement and extraposition purely on the basis of their semantic interpretation. We do not need to distinguish syntactically between rules that do and do not leave traces, a difference which simply encodes their difference in semantic interpretation.

2.2. *Who did you see a picture of*? Sentences like those in (15) represent a problem for the NP-constraint.

(15)   a. What did John eat a loaf of?
          b. What did Harry drink five bottles of?
          c. What does Bill see movies about?
          d. What does Fred collect pictures of?
          e. Which car do you like the gears in?
          f. Which car did John destroy the gears in?
          g. Which book do you like the pictures in?
          h. Which doors do you have the keys to?
          i. Which plans did they get Nixon's approval of?
          j. How many classes do you like all the students in?

Examples (15a–d) are from Horn (1979) and seem to me to be of impeccable grammaticality. (15e–g) are from Cattell (1979) and are for me acceptable if not impeccable. (15h) I find acceptable, (15i) and (15j) I find somewhat dubious although not obviously ungrammatical.[6] One main problem with these examples, as pointed out first, I think, by Chomsky (1977), is that they are not susceptible to the analysis which Horn suggests for examples such as (16).

(16)   Who did John write a book about?

Horn claims that (16) does not violate the NP-constraint because its VP has the structure represented in (17)

(17)

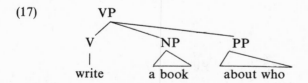

One piece of evidence for this structure is the fact that (18) is grammatical.

(18)   John wrote it about Nixon

The NP in (17) may be independently pronominalized. This is not the case if the PP occurs inside the NP. Thus *destroy* according to his analysis is subcategorized for NP but not for NP PP. This predicts the facts represented in (19).

(19)   a. John destroyed a book about Nixon.
         b. *Who did John destroy a book about?
         c. *John destroyed it about Nixon.

When the NP corresponding to *a book* in these examples is not independently pronominalizable, the PP must be part of the object NP and thus
one cannot extract from behind the preposition. However, all of the
sentences in (15) allow the extraction but do not allow the pronominali-
zation. Thus all the sentences in (20) are ungrammatical.

(20)   a. *John ate it of bread.
         b. *John drank them of milk.
         c. *Bill saw them about Vietnam.
         d. *Fred collects them of landscapes.
         e. *You like them in Fords.
         f. *John destroyed them in my car.
         g. *You like them in *Syntactic Structures*.
         h. *John has them to my office.
         i. *They got it of the burglary plans.
         j. *You like them in three classes.

(Some of these are actually grammatical sentences but not on the
intended reading.)

Horn (1979) avoids this problem by adopting a version of Chomsky's
(1977) PP-extraposition rule which he calls PP-readjustment. According to
Horn's formulation this rule changes the structure (21a) to (21b).

(21)   a.

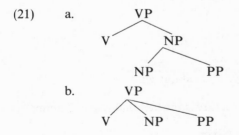

This gives us the best of both worlds. Before PP-readjustment applies we
have the structure (21a) and this on Horn's analysis somehow prevents
lexical insertion of a pronoun under the head NP[7]. PP-readjustment
applies before extraction from the PP and provides a structure which allows
extraction without violation of the NP-constraint.

This rule of PP-readjustment does not seem strictly wholewheat. Firstly, it rearranges structure without re-arranging the terminal string and thus may be susceptible to the kind of criticism that Chomsky originally had against raising-to-object.[8] But there is a second much deeper problem that casts suspicion on this process as a syntactic rule. It is tremendously irregular. Its application not only varies from speaker to speaker but from time to time for a single speaker depending very often on what kind of context we can cook up for the sentence. In this respect the situation seems to be close to that found in nominal compounding as discussed by Zimmer (1971, 1972, 1975 and Downing 1977). Most speakers will reject something like *pumpkin-bus* until you explain to them that it is the bus on the school-trip that is going home by way of the pumpkin fields (so anybody who wants to buy pumpkins should get on the pumpkin-bus). Similarly, many speakers might tend to reject (22) initially.

(22)   Which proposals did you get Jimmy's approval of?

However, it becomes much more acceptable, though perhaps not for all speakers, when you explain that Jimmy is really Jimmy Carter and that part of the regular daily routine at the White House involves getting Jimmy's approval. You might except a White House aide close to the President to be more likely to find (22) acceptable than other speakers of the language. Linguists, on the other hand are more likely to accept (23).

(23)   Which theories did you get Noam's word on?

These kinds of examples suggest that the situation is much more complex than a simple marking of [± PP-adjustment] on certain verbs in the lexicon, as Chomsky (1977) has suggested. Cattell (1979) has made a similar point citing examples such as (15f) which contrasts with (19b) even though the same verb *destroy* is involved. Horn (1978) has also made a similar point citing examples such as (24).

(24)   a. Which cars do you like the motors in?
          b. *Which cars do you like the hubcaps on?
          c. Which women did you like the bikinis on?
          d. *Which women did you like the earrings on?

(24b) is ungrammatical, according to Horn, because it is not easy to imagine judging cars by their hubcaps, whereas it is easy to imagine judging them by their motors. He claims that similar facts hold for the difference between (24c) and (24d). Actually there may be a sex difference here. Certain men are much more likely to judge women by their bikinis than by their earrings. Certain women, however, might be quite likely to judge other women by their earrings, particularly for example, if they are attending a party where all the women have been asked to wear their favourite pair of earrings, what one might call an earring-party. There seems to be a definite connection between the acceptability of (24d) and that of the compound *earring-party.*

Now, it seems to me, that a bona fide wholewheat syntax should not allow its rules to be governed by such peculiar pragmatic factors (though Horn (1979) has a way of linking the syntactic readjustment to a readjustment in functional structure which makes it not too unpalatable.) Therefore, I am not unhappy to report that the PP-readjustment analysis is in principle excluded by the restrictive theory that I am proposing. The main reason is this: suppose we build up an NP such as *a picture of who* with the PP inside it. Its structure and its interpretation, together with the stored WH-quantifier, is represented in (25).

(25)

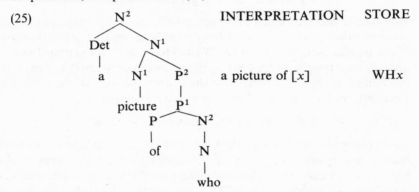

The semantic NP-constraint will stop the derivation from continuing since we have an NP-interpretation with a non-empty store and we cannot retrieve the WH and give it scope within the NP. Hence the derivation will never proceed to a stage where PP-readjustment may apply. (Even if we could figure out a way to build a large enough tree for PP-readjustment, it is doubtful that the natural constraints placed on the system by the model-theoretic semantics would allow a coherent semantic interpretation of such a rule. For example, what would the appropriate function defined on sets of possible worlds be?)

If PP-readjustment does not give us a solution as a syntactic rule, what else can we do with it? The answer, I think, is that we should create a lexical analogue to PP-readjustment. We say that *see a picture, eat a loaf, get*

Jimmy's approval, get Noam's word are all verbs strictly subcategorized for appropriate PP's. Thus we say that the pre-*wh*-movement structure for *Who did you see a picture of?* is as represented in (26).

(26)

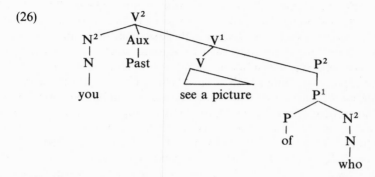

The semantic interpretation involved as this structure is built up will not violate the semantic NP-constraint since the *wh*-NP is not embedded within a larger NP. What we have is a structure very like the result of PP-readjustment. But we have not created it by using a syntactic transformation. Instead we created a complex verb *see a picture*. The framework I am presenting selects this lexical treatment over the syntactic treatment. The question that remains is: is it feasible to treat so many complex expressions such as *drink a bottle, drink two bottles, drink three bottles*, etc. as lexical items? There not only seem to be infinitely many of them but they also seem to obey certain rules of syntax at least in as far as they all have syntactically well-formed NP's inside them. In order to answer this I borrow from Dowty's recent work on the lexicon.

Dowty (1978) and elsewhere argues that the traditional division of syntactic and morphological operations between and syntax and lexicon is too restrictive. For example, polysynthetic languages seem to use morphological operations productively in the syntax and not just in the lexicon. Syntactic operations seem to be at work in the lexicon to obtain, for example, syntactically well-formed idioms and verbs such as *hammer_____flat* which allow infixation of the direct object. There seems to be no way of accounting for the idiosyncracy of the adjectives that may follow *hammer NP* in this construction except by entering the whole verb *hammer_____flat* in the lexicon. If we accept Dowty's theory it does not come as a surprise that lexical items make use of syntactic operations. This would explain one particular peculiarity of complex verbs like *see a picture*.

Now to the productivity problem. We have noted that these complex verbs seem to be created ad hoc under strange conditions in a similar way to the creation of novel compounds. Dowty suggests that native speakers of a language internalize rules of lexical extension – rules which allow us to create new lexical items. These rules can be used in two ways: they can be used to analyze items already existing in the lexicon or they can be used to create new lexical items not previously to be found in the lexicon. It seems that we may use these rules to meet a given situation on an entirely ad hoc basis and create compounds such as *pumpkin-bus* or *earring-party* without ever thinking of them as going into the language or even being permanently entered in our own mental lexicon. It seems that complex verbs such as *see a picture* have much the same kind of status. Some of them are used often enough to warrant entry into the lexicon. Some of them are created ad hoc for a given situation. The fact that there are infinitely many such as *drink a bottle, drink two bottles* etc. should not worry us any more than the fact that we can say *one-seater, two-seater,* etc.

The peculiar pragmatic constraints are presumably due to what kinds of concepts human beings deem worthy of symbolizing by a lexical unit. An example of how subtle this can be is given in my judgments represented in (27).

(27)   a. *Which class do you like the girl in?
          b. Which class do you like the girls in?

(27a), which is taken from Cattell (1979), is bad for me whereas (27b), which differs only in that we have plural *girls*, is fine – reflecting perhaps a non-professional way of judging the quality of classes. (27a) would become okay if all classes contained at most one girl, due to some fiendish administrative quirk. (Cattell, 1979, discusses similar examples involving books and picture(s).) The investigation of this problem is one that will need a lot more input from psychologists working on the nature of concepts and I am happy to be able to push the problem out to the fringes of a linguistic theory of the lexicon rather than having pragmatic notions restricting the application of a syntactic rule of PP-readjustment. One thing that seems fairly clear, though, is that we do not normally form phrasal lexical entries or idioms with deictic pronouns. There are phrasal lexical entries which contain pronouns such as *eat it* as in this *argument eats it* (see Bach (1980) for discussion of *eat it* as an intransitive verb) and *do it* strictly subcategorized for *to NP* as in *Leslie did it to Chris*. But these pronouns are not deictic. The reason that the sentences in (20) such as *John ate it of bread* are so bad is presumably because we are trying to force a lexical unit to contain a deictic pronoun.

3. CONCLUSION

I have suggested that a strictly wholewheat syntax interpreted by a model-theoretic semantics places restrictions on the kinds of constraints on binding that we may state. We may, by adopting a semantic version of the NP-constraint, claim further that constraints on binding make reference only to semantic information and not syntactic information. A set of problem data that arise for the NP-constraint (and other constraints as well) and that have so far involved a somewhat quixotic rule of PP-readjustment may be explained by using a rich theory of the lexicon as has been developed by Dowty. In conclusion, I should like to point out that this raises the question of the degree to which we should allow sentences to have two derivations depending on whether a lexically derived structure is involved or not. It is clear that not all derivations of sentences like (28) should involve the complex verb *see a picture*.

(28)   John saw a picture of Mary.

We must also allow, and in fact we would not be able to prevent, the structure where a *picture of Mary* is an NP. If we allowed only the derivation with a complex verb we would not be able to obtain in passive for this sentences. Perhaps this is related to the recent claim by Wasow (1977) that there is both a lexical and a syntactic rule of passive which allow two derivations for sentences such as (29) and (30).

(29)   Your family was respected.
(30)   Your family was frightened.

University of Wisconsin, Madison

NOTES

1 The techniques discussed here are made explicit and complete in Cooper (1978).
2 For readers interested in details: We take $[x]$ to be what would be represented in something closer to Montague's notation as $\hat{P}P(x)$ (i.e. that sense which picks out at any index the family of sets which contain x). In order to make this abbreviatory notation correspond to Karttunen's (1977) treatment of questions we would need to guarantee

$$WHx\varphi = \lambda p[\exists x\check{\ }p \wedge p = \hat{\ }\varphi].$$

WHx is actually a rather special kind of variable binding operator, although we shall continue to talk of *WH* as a quantifier in the text.

[3] It is important to distinguish between logical *form* (as used in generative semantics and trace theory) and the logical *notation* referred to here. Logical form is part of the output of a grammar and hence its syntactic properties may be referred to by linguistic rules. Logical notation is a system for representing model theoretic objects (e.g. sets of possible worlds) on paper. Hence if we are using a logical notation to represent a model theoretic semantics, linguistic rules may only refer to properties of the model theoretic objects but not to properties of the notation.

[4] The Nominative Island Condition (NIC) says: "A nominative anaphor in S cannot be free in S̄ containing S."

[5] The Opacity Condition says: "If α is in the domain of the subject of β, β minimal, then α cannot be free in β."

[6] Kuno (1979) discusses examples similar to (15i) as problems for the specified subject condition.

[7] This consequence is automatic if the object NP has the semantically preferable structure:

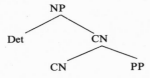

[8] A possible claim that it is because this extraposition is a readjustment rule that it is allowed to rearrange structure without changing the terminal string is certainly a reasonable reply. But then raising-to-object might be viewed as such a readjustment rule.

BIBLIOGRAPHY

Bach, Emmon (1979) 'Montague Grammar and Classical Transformational Grammar,' In *Linguistics, Philosophy, and Montague Grammar*, ed. Steven Davis and Marianne Mithun. University of Texa's Press.

Bach, Emmon (1980) 'In defense of Passive,' *Linguistics and Philosophy* 3, 297–341.

Barwise, Jon and Robin Cooper (1981), 'Generalized quantifiers and natural language,' *Linguistics and Philosophy*, 4, pp. 159–219.

Cattell, Ray (1979) 'On Extractability from Quasi-NP's,' *Linguistic Inquiry* 10, 168–172.

Chomsky, Noam (1977) 'On *wh*-movement,' in *Formal Syntax*, ed. by Peter Culicover, Thomas Wasow and Adrian Akmajian. Academic Press, New York.

Chomsky, Noam (1980) 'On binding,' *Linguistic Inquiry* 11, 1–46.

Cooper, Robin (1975) *Montague's Semantic Theory and Transformational Syntax*, Unpublished Ph. D. dissertation. University of Massachusetts, Amherst.

Cooper, Robin (1978) *A Fragment of English with Questions and Relative Clauses*, University of Wisconsin, ditto.

Downing, Pamela (1977) 'On the Creation and Use of English Compound Nouns' *Language* 53, 810–842.

Dowty, David (1978) 'Applying Montague's Views on Linguistic Metatheory to the Lexicon,' in D. Farkas, W. M. Jacobsan, and K. W. Todrys, eds., *Papers from the Parasession on the Lexicon*, Chicago Linguist Society, Chicago, Illinois.

Horn, George (1974) *The NP Constraint*, Indian University Linguistics Club, Bloomington.

Horn, George (1979) *A Lexical Interpretive Approach to some Problems in Syntax*, Indiana University Linguistics Club, Bloomington.

Karttunen, Lauri (1977) 'Syntax and semantics of questions,' *Linguistics and Philosophy* 1, 3–44.

Kuno, Susumu (1979) 'Functional Syntax,' Paper presented at the Milwaukee Syntax Conference.

Ross, John (1967) *Constraints on Variables in Syntax*, unpublished Ph. D. dissertation, MIT, Cambridge, Massachusetts.

Wasow, Thomas (1977) 'Transformations and the Lexicon', in *Formal Syntax*, ed. by Peter Culicover, Thomas Wasow, and Adrian Akmajian, Academic Press, New York.

Zimmer, Karl (1971) 'Some General Observations about Nominal Compounds,' *Working Papers on Language Universals*, (Stanford University) 5, C1–C21.

Zimmer, Karl (1972) 'Appropriateness Conditions for Nominal Compounds, *Working Papers on Language Universals* (Stanford University) 8, 3–20.

Zimmer, Karl (1975) 'Review of *The Function of the Lexicon in Transformational Grammar* by Rudolf Botha,' *Language* 51, 170–178.

DAVID DOWTY

GRAMMATICAL RELATIONS AND MONTAGUE GRAMMAR

0. INTRODUCTION

In this paper I want to describe a universal theory of "grammatical relations" that arises naturally within the formal theory of syntax and semantics of natural language developed originally by Richard Montague (1970, 1973) and subsequently extended in a certain series of treatments of Montague's ideas that begins with Thomason 1976 (first written in 1972) and includes Thomason 1974, Dowty 1979a (written in 1975), Dowty 1975, Dowty 1978, Bach 1979 (written in 1977), Bach 1980, and Schmerling 1979. I believe this analysis of grammatical relations is supported by some of the same observations as are the related theories of Relational Grammar and Arc Pair Grammar developed by Perlmutter, Postal, and others (Perlmutter and Postal 1977, Johnson and Postal forthcoming, Perlmutter and Postal to appear, Perlmutter this volume, Postal this volume).

Relational Grammar was motivated by the observation that Chomsky's original definition of grammatical relations (Chomsky 1965), which is stated in terms of linear order of constituents and domination by the nodes S and VP, seems inadequate for languages in which the order of constituents is different from English, especially for VSO languages like Breton or Welsh in which there can be no VP node, and perhaps most inappropriate of all for free word-order languages. Nevertheless, these grammatical relations seem to have consistent properties across all these types of languages. In particular, it seems that rules like Passive, Dative Shift and the Raising rules behave in the same way in most languages with respect to their effect on these grammatical relations, though the word orders that result from these processes are quite different from language to language.

Relational Grammar approaches this problem by taking the notions *Subject, Object* and *Indirect Object* (the *term relations*) to be primitives of the theory of grammar, not defined in terms of any more basic concepts. The language-universal rules that 'change' grammatical relations – Passive, Raising, etc. – are defined directly in terms of these relations.

It is not necessary here to describe Relational or Arc Pair grammatical

P. Jacobson and G. K. Pullum (eds.), The Nature of Syntactic Representation, 79–130.
Copyright © 1982 by D. Reidel Publishing Company.

theory in detail, for, I must emphasize, I am *not* attempting to simply reconstruct their theory in terms of Montague's framework, and many of the ideas of Relational Grammar will have no counterpart in the present analysis. For example, there will be no notion of a *chômeur* in the present account. (A chômeur in relational grammar is a noun phrase that has been "displaced" by a relation-assigning rule and is therefore stripped of its term relation; see Perlmutter, this volume.) But I do believe that Relational Grammarians have produced a large body of research on a wide variety of languages showing the need for a universal definition of grammatical relations and relation changing rules, and it is these two fundamental ideas that I would like to account for in Montague's framework.

One essential difference between Relational Grammar and what I am proposing is that I will not take grammatical relations to be primitives but will rather define and motivate them in terms of the way syntax relates to semantics.

In §1., I survey briefly, for the benefit of those with no prior acquaintance with Montague Grammar, those features of Montague's approach which are most relevant for this paper. Those readers already familiar with Montague Grammar should skip this section. The means of defining grammatical relations in a language-independent way is introduced in §2., the fundamental distinction between arguments and modifiers in §3., and the treatment of relation-changing rules (the "category shift" method) in §4. Ten reasons for preferring this account of relation changing rules over the transformational account (TG) and Relational Grammar account (RG) are presented in §5. The next two sections briefly survey the syntactic counterarguments to the category-shift approach and the problem of ergative languages. The paper closes with two general questions raised by this approach to grammatical relations: the distinction between relation-changing and variable-binding rules (§8) and (for me the most provocative question raised by this whole enterprise) the possible reasons for the elusiveness of the distinction between arguments and modifiers (§9).

1. SOME ESSENTIAL FEATURES OF MONTAGUE'S
SYNTAX AND SEMANTICS

Rather than use a phrase structure-grammar to define syntactic structure, Montague used recursive definitions which build up a sentence from the inside out – starting with words, putting them together to form phrases, and putting these together to form sentences. A typical syntactic rule says, for example, if you take a term phrase ("term phrase" is Montague's term for a Noun Phrase; there is no connection with the Relational Grammar use of "term") and combine it with an intransitive verb, you get a sentence. So, since *John* is a term phrase and since *walk* is an intransitive verb, the combination *John walks* is a sentence by this rule. (I am going to ignore verb agreement and case marking for a moment and come back to them shortly.) A diagram of how a sentence is put together is called an *analysis tree* of that sentence, and (1) gives an analysis tree of this example sentence (Little t stands for sentence, since sentences have truth values; big T is term phrase, and IV is intransitive verb.)

(1)   [John walk(s)]$_t$

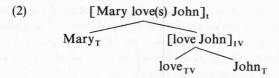

There is no distinction between lexical and non-lexical categories in Montague's syntax, so IV does double duty as the (linguist's) category VP. Moreover, there is a rule which takes a transitive verb (TV) and combines it with a T to give an IV; for example if *love* is a TV and *John* is a T, then by this rule *love John* is an IV. We can now take this IV *love John* and use the first syntactic rule I mentioned to combine it with another T *Mary* to give the sentence *Mary loves John*; its analysis tree is (2):

(2)   [Mary love(s) John]$_t$

Mary$_T$ [love John]$_{IV}$

love$_{TV}$ John$_T$

Before going more deeply into syntax, I need to say something about semantics in Montague Grammar and how it relates to syntax. For the purposes of this paper, fortunately, it is not necessary to delve deeply into Montague's rather complex semantic theory, and I won't need to say anything at all about some aspects of it that Montague considered the most interesting – how quantifiers are treated, for example, and how de dicto and de re ambiguities are handled. Thus I systematically simplify what I say about the interpretation of NPs.

Montague's semantic theory takes as its goal the systematic description of the relationship between expressions of a language and the things they denote or the situations they describe. As such a theory has the essential task of relating linguistic expressions to non-linguistic entities, its basic semantic notions are *truth* and *denotation*. (For more discussion, see Dowty, Wall and Peters (1980) Chapter 1 and Dowty (1979b) Chapter 9.) The theory thus associates with each name an individual that that name denotes in each possible situation. With an intransitive verb such as *walk*, it associates a function that picks out, in any possible situation, the set of things that have the property of walking. The semantic rule for a subject-predicate sentence says that a sentence is true in a situation just in case the individual denoted by the subject is among the set of things denoted by the predicate. Montague's semantics actually represents the denotation of an intransitive verb as a function which maps every individual in the domain into the value *true* or *false* (i.e., the ones mapped onto *true* are the ones "in" the denotation). Thus in a subject-predicate sentence, we apply the function denoted by the predicate to the individual denoted by the subject to get the appropriate truth value of the sentence in any given situation.

It is a fundamental assumption of Montague's approach that there is a semantic rule for each syntactic rule: to get the meaning of a sentence we start with the meanings of the words in it and, for each syntactic rule we used, we apply the corresponding semantic rule to the meanings of the inputs to get the meaning of the output; moreover, we must do this in a completely uniform way: no matter how these inputs were formed syntactically, we must be able to apply the very same semantic rule in exactly the same way.

Now this requirement immediately gives us an apparent problem with the interpretation of transitive verbs. In most systems of logic, a transitive verb is treated as denoting a relation, that is, a set of ordered pairs. For example, the meaning of the verb *love* would be a function that gives, in any possible situation, the set of all pairs of individuals $\langle x, y \rangle$ such that x loves y. A syntactic rule combines such a verb with two names to give a sentence, and the truth value is found by determining whether the pair denoted by the two names is among the set denoted by the verb. However, this won't quite work for Montague's syntactic analysis of transitive verbs: while a TV does in effect combine with the names of two individuals, the verb combines with these Term phrases in two separate rules for the sentence, not one, and moreover the second semantic rule we use has to be the same as the rule for intransitive verbs. Montague resolves this problem by letting a transitive verb denote a function that in any situation, applies to *one* individual to give a new function – this new function is one that will in turn apply to another individual to give a truth value; the best way to explain how this can work is by a diagram. In (3) is the kind of function that would be the denotation that a one-place predicate might have if the domain of discourse consisted of three individuals; it singles out the set $\{a, b\}$.

(3)   (Assume domain of discourse $= \{a, b, c\}$.)

$$\text{Denotation of } walk(x) = \begin{bmatrix} a \to 1 \\ b \to 1 \\ c \to 0 \end{bmatrix}$$

In (4) is an example of the kind of denotation a transitive verb would have for a logician – i.e. this is the situation in which the individual a loves b, b loves c, c loves himself, and no one loves anyone except for these three cases.

(4) $$\text{Denotation of } love(x, y) = \begin{bmatrix} \langle a,a \rangle \to 0 \\ \langle a,b \rangle \to 1 \\ \langle a,c \rangle \to 0 \\ \langle b,a \rangle \to 0 \\ \langle b,b \rangle \to 0 \\ \langle b,c \rangle \to 1 \\ \langle c,a \rangle \to 0 \\ \langle c,b \rangle \to 0 \\ \langle c,c \rangle \to 1 \end{bmatrix}$$

(5) represents an equivalent denotation for a verb *love* under Montague's approach: note that it is a function which applies to the individual named by the object of the verb to give a new function which will then be applied to the individual named by the subject.

(5) $$\text{Denotation of } (love(y))(x) = \begin{bmatrix} a & \to & \begin{bmatrix} a \to 0 \\ b \to 0 \\ c \to 0 \end{bmatrix} \\ b & \to & \begin{bmatrix} a \to 1 \\ b \to 0 \\ c \to 0 \end{bmatrix} \\ c & \to & \begin{bmatrix} a \to 0 \\ b \to 1 \\ c \to 1 \end{bmatrix} \end{bmatrix}$$

Suppose the name *John* denotes individual c; then the meaning of the phrase *love John* would be gotten by applying the function (5) to c, giving the new function on the lower right in the diagram; if the name *Mary* denotes the individual b, then the denotation of *Mary loves John* would be gotten by applying this function to *b*, which gives the value 1, or true, in this case. One can easily inspect the diagram (5) and see that it represent exactly the same information as to who loves who that the diagram (4) represents. Of course, the two diagrams in a sense single out the pairs in reverse order: in (4) the individual denoted by the subject is listed *first* in each pair, while in (5) the function applies to the *object* first.

I have gone over this point in some detail because this idea forms the basis of the theory of grammatical relations I am going to propose. Note that this same method could be extended to verbs with three or more arguments as well: instead of letting a three-place verb (i.e. a ditransitive verb such as *give*) denote a set of ordered triples, we can let it denote a function which applies to one individual and gives as value a second function which then applies to a second individual to give them a third function which applies to the third individual to give a truth value. In other words, the meaning of any verb, no matter how many arguments it has, can always be treated as a function which applies to one thing at a time.

2. DEFINING "GRAMMATICAL RELATIONS"

As I have explained in the previous section, Montague's "one argument at a time" approach to the syntax of intransitive, transitive and (potentially) ditransitive verbs leads to a viable semantic treatment of these verbs as well: the reason for this is, as Schoenfinkel (1924) first observed, that a function of *n* arguments can always be equivalently represented as a function of one argument that yields a function of $n - 1$ arguments as its value. This simple idea is the germ of the account of grammatical relations that I am proposing, for this idea implies a certain interrelationship among the syntactic categories involved in sentences with multi-place verbs (and likewise the syntactic rules used to form sentences with these verbs) as a consequence of the one-to-one relation between semantic rules and syntactic rules that Montague requires. The "principle of grammatical relations" we shall need is thus (6):

(6)   A verb that ultimately takes *n* arguments is always treated as combining by a syntactic rule with exactly one argument to produce a phrase of the same category as a verb of $n - 1$ arguments.

In describing syntactic rules, Montague made a systematic distinction between the *operation* that a syntactic rule performs on an expression, i.e., how it manipulates words or phrases in combining them, and the syntactic *rule* itself. A syntactic rule specifies what *categories* of expressions are inputs to the rule and what category of expression results from the rule, as well as specifying what operation is to be used in putting them together; also, the same syntactic operation might be used in more than one rule.

What I would like to suggest is that the syntactic *operations* used by rules will vary greatly from language to language, but that the syntactic *rules*, aside from the nature of the operation, may be to a large degree the same in all natural languages, as are the semantic operations that correspond to these rules. (In putting together words and phrases to form larger constituents, syntactic operations in MG are not limited to simple concatenation – as are, in effect, phrase structure grammars – but may rearrange or add morphological marking to these phrases as they are combined; in short, syntactic operations may perform any of the manipulations that transformations perform in a TG.) Let me illustrate what I mean by this with a concrete example.

In one of his papers, 'Universal Grammar' (Montague 1970), Montague specified the format of a syntactic rule as an ordered triple: the first member of the triple names a syntactic operation (these are named by a capital "F" with a subscript), the second member is the sequence of categories that are the inputs to the rule, the third member is the category of the output of the rule. Thus the subject-predicate rule and the verb-object rule I used in (1) and (2) would be formalized as in (7); (in addition to these, of course, we have to specify somewhere just what the two operations F_1 and F_2 do).

(7)   S1: $\langle F_1, \langle IV, T \rangle, t \rangle$ (Subject-Predicate Rule)
         S2: $\langle F_2, \langle TV, T \rangle, IV \rangle$ (Verb-Direct Object Rule)

Now I'd like to suggest that these two rules S1 and S2 are used in essentially the same form in languages as diverse as English, Japanese, Breton, and Latin, and moreover that the semantic operations corresponding to these two rules are the same in all of these languages; it is merely in the way the operations F_1 and F_2 are defined that the languages differ.

In English, an SVO language, the operations F_1 and F_2 don't just concatenate expressions but also perform the number agreement and case marking: the exact descriptions of F_1 and F_2 for English are given in (8), along with a corrected sample analysis tree.

(8)   English (SVO):
         $F_1(\alpha, \beta) = \beta^\frown \alpha'$, where α' is the result of marking the verb in α to agree with β.

$F_2(\alpha, \beta) = \alpha^\frown\beta'$, where β' is the result of marking β with accusative case.

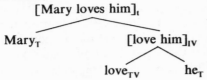

[Mary loves him]$_t$

Mary$_T$ [love him]$_{IV}$

love$_{TV}$ he$_T$

In Japanese, an SOV language, the two operations involve suffixing the markers *-ga* to the subject and *-o* to the object term, but F_2 also differs from English in concatenating its 2nd argument to the left of the first, instead of to the right.

(9)   Japanese (SOV):
$F_1(\alpha, \beta) = \beta + ga^\frown\alpha$
$F_2(\alpha, \beta) = \beta + o^\frown\alpha$

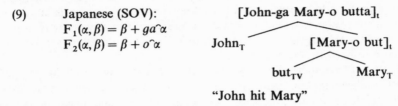

[John-ga Mary-o butta]$_t$

John$_T$ [Mary-o but]$_t$

but$_{TV}$ Mary$_T$

"John hit Mary"

In Breton, a VSO language, something slightly different is called for: the subject-predicate operation will not simply concatenate subject and predicate but will rather insert the subject term phrase after the first word of the verb phrase, i.e. after the verb. This kind of operation, called *right wrap* by Bach (1979), is of course just what *cannot* be done with a PS grammar, and I believe it is one that is found in SVO languages like English as well (though not for the Subject-Predicate operation F_1):

(10)   Breton (VSO):
$F_1(\alpha, \beta)$ = the result of inserting β after the first word in α.
$F_2(\alpha, \beta) = \alpha^\frown\beta$.

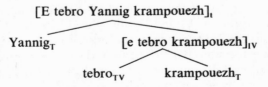

[E tebro Yannig krampouezh]$_t$

Yannig$_T$ [e tebro krampouezh]$_{IV}$

tebro$_{TV}$ krampouezh$_T$

"Johnny will eat crepes"

As the fourth example I have chosen Latin as an example of a so-called "Free word order" language. Now Latin may not be the clearest example of a free word order language and it may be true that no language is completely free in its word order. But for purposes of illustration, let us suppose that the order of S, V and O is completely undetermined by syntactic rules in Latin. Nothing in Montague's general theory requires that sentences of a language be (ordered) strings of symbols, or phrase markers either, so we might regard a grammar for at least certain parts of Latin as producing an unordered set of words as a sentence. The operation F_1 and F_2 then might be defined as in (11): that is, the subject and object are marked by case endings, but the derived expressions are otherwise simply the unions of two unordered sets.[1]

(11)   Latin (free[?]):
$F_1(\alpha, \beta) = \alpha' \cup \beta'$, where β' is the result of marking β nominative and α' is α marked to agree with β.
$F_2(\alpha, \beta) = \alpha \cup \beta'$, where β' is β marked with accusative case.

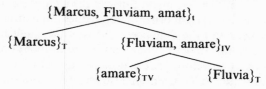

"Marcus loves Fluvia"

What I want to claim about grammatical relations should now become clear: it is syntactic rules such as S1 and S2 – minus the specification of how the operations F_1 and F_2 work – that give us the universal definitions of relations like *Subject-of* and *Object-of*. That is, we will define any term phrase in any language that is combined with an IV via S1 as a subject term, and any term phrase that is combined with a TV via S2 as a direct object; moreover, these are language independent semantic definitions as well, since the semantic rules corresponding to S1 and S2 will be the same in each language. The manifestation of these relationships in the morphology and word order of a language is what differs from language to language.

It turns out that I am not the first (nor was Montague) to suggest that this kind of distinction between syntactic operation and syntactic rule is an important one. Östen Dahl has pointed out (Dahl 1977) that in 1963 H. B. Curry argued for a similar way of viewing the grammar of a language. Curry (1963) noted that the logician's algebraic way of viewing a language – as consisting of a finite set of elementary expressions, that is words, plus a set of operations which can be performed recursively on these to form new, larger expressions – suggested that the most fundamental aspect of grammatical structure is the series of steps by which an expression is put together, the sequence in which expressions and operations are employed in producing a full sentence, not the way this structure is actually represented in terms of linear order or morphological markings. He wrote, "we may conceive of the grammatical structure of a language as something independent of the way it is represented in terms of expressions... This gives us two levels of grammar, the study of grammatical structure in itself and a second level which has much the same relation to the first that morphophonemics does to morphology. In order to have terms for immediate use I shall call these two levels *tectogrammatics* and *phenogrammatics*." (Curry 1963 :65).

In (approximately) Curry's terms, the tectogrammatical structure of a sentence is what would be represented by a Montague Grammar analysis tree, minus the specification of what the expressions at the non-terminal nodes look like. Thus we might think of the tectogrammatical structure of (2) as (12) (the left-to-right order of nodes does not matter); the phenogrammatical structure of the sentence is the way the English operations fill in these non-terminal nodes.[2] What I am claiming about universal grammatical relations, is, therefore, that they are an aspect of tectogrammatics, not phenogrammatics. (Curry himself also observed (1963 :66) that tectogrammatical structure would be more invariant across languages than phenogrammatical structure.)

(12)

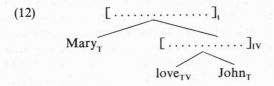

At this point, let me introduce a few more grammatical relations. As I suggested earlier, a three-place verb can be given the same relationship to a transitive verb as a transitive verb has to an intransitive verb. That is, a three-place verb will be treated semantically as a function that applied to an individual to give as value the kind of function a transitive verb denotes; thus syntactically, a three-place verb will be combined with a term phrase to give a transitive verb (or, transitive verb *phrase* we might want to call it, since the category TV, like IV, now has syntactically complex as well as lexical members). The rule defining the Indirect Object relation is S3:

(13) S3: $\langle F_3, \langle TV/T, T \rangle, TV \rangle$ (Verb-Indirect Object Rule)
English: $F_3(\alpha, \beta) = \alpha \widehat{\ } to \widehat{\ } \beta'$, where β' is the accusative form of β.[3]

In English, this rule inserts the preposition *to* before the term phrase, in other languages, it marks it with Dative case. I will call the category of ditransitive verbs "TV/T". This means that the English Verb-Direct Object operation will have to be modified to a "Right Wrap" operation – that is, when combining a verb with a direct object, the direct object will be placed after the first word of the transitive verb phrase; thus English sentences with such verbs will be produced as in the example (14). Fortunately, there is independent motivation for this Right Wrap operation in English, as has been shown by Partee (1975), myself (1979b: ch. 4), and Bach (1980).[4]

(14) [John gives a book to Mary]$_t$

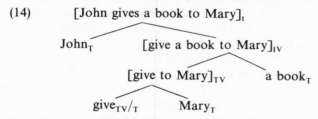

The list of grammatical relations does not stop here. IV-complements, for example, sentence complements or adjective complements, will all be treated as arguments of verbs, just as noun phrases will; these are just "other" grammatical relations like subject and object.

3. ARGUMENTS VERSUS MODIFIERS

Relational Grammarians do talk about some other noun phrase grammatical relations besides Subject, Object, and Indirect Object, namely the (so-called) *Oblique* relations *Benefactive, Instrumental* and *Locative*. Under the present analysis, the latter three kinds of noun phrases have quite a different status from Subject, Object and Indirect Object (called *term relations* by Perlmutter and Postal). While the "term relation" noun phrases are arguments inherently needed for the meaning of a verb, Benefactives, Instrumentals and Locatives, on the other hand, are best treated as modifiers of IVs. That is, a Benefactive rule is a rule that takes a term phrase β and an IV α and turns them into a new IV denoting the property of doing α so as to benefit the individual named by the term β. That is, it might map the set of individuals that walk into the set of individuals that walk for Mary. Such a rule is given in (15):

(15)   S4: $\langle F_4, \langle IV, T \rangle, IV \rangle$ (Benefactive Rule)
Semantic Operation: maps the property denoted by an IV α
into the property of doing α for benefit of individual devoted by
a T β, i.e. $[for'(\beta')](\alpha')$.
English: $F_5(\alpha, \beta) = \alpha^\frown for\ ^\frown\beta$.

There are two reasons why benefactives, etc. are treated this way rather
than as arguments of verbs. First, one can add a benefactive to virtually any
IV whatsoever, regardless of whether it is an intransitive verb, or a verb with
an object, or a verb with other complement(s). For example, you can add
for Mary to the IV *smile*, or the IV *catch a fish* or the IV *try to walk* etc. By
contrast, one cannot add a direct object or an indirect object to just any
verb, but only to one that is subcategorized for an object. One cannot say
**John caught a fish to Mary*, or **An hour elapsed John*, because *catch* and
elapse are not that sort of verb.

Second, the meaning of an IV can be complete without a benefactive (or
instrumental or locative): if I baked a cake, it might be true that I baked it
for someone, but on the other hand, I might simply be a compulsive cake
baker and baked the cake for no one at all. By contrast, the second and/or
third arguments of an inherently two or three-place verb are always implicit
in the meaning of the verb, even if they are unmentioned in the sentence – if
it's true that I sold the house, then simply because of the meaning of *sell*, it
follows that there must be someone to whom I sold the house, whether I say
so or not. This entailment test and the subcategorization test, then, are
proposed as criteria for distinguishing modifiers from arguments.[5]

4. RELATION-CHANGING RULES

Now, I turn to relation changing rules. Just as Relational Grammar
describes Passive, Raising, etc. in a language-universal way, so in the
analysis I am discussing, it will be possible to characterize these so-called
"relation-changing" rules in terms of the universal characterization of
grammatical relations I have described, i.e. in terms of tectogrammatical
structure alone. This method will be quite different from the account of
relation changing rules in either TG or that in RG, however. In contrast to
these theories, it is not the status of a *noun phrase* which is changed by a
relation-changing rule, but rather it is only the *verb* or *verb phrase* which
undergoes any change. I will discuss relation changing rules in three
categories: first, relation-reducing rules, then relation-rearranging rules,
then relation-expanding rules. Since all such rules change the *category* (or

perhaps preferably the subcategory) of a verb in this analysis, I'll call this the *category-changing* analysis of relation-changing verbs.

4.1 Relation-Reducing Rules

In many situations, it may be relevant to assert that one individual stands in a two-place relation to something, a relation such as *eat* or *hunt* or *cook*, but it may not be relevant to the addressee just what other individual that first individual stands in the relation to. Or, the speaker may not know or care what second individual the first stands in the relation to. That is, I may want to say John ate something, but it may be of no interest to say what he ate. Natural language responds to this need, under the present account, by taking a transitive verb, denoting a relation, and turning it into a intransitive verb, denoting a set. There are two ways one can turn a relation – speaking of a relation extensionally now as a set of ordered pairs – into a set of individuals. One can extract the set of individuals that are first members of all the pairs in the relation, or one can take the set of individuals that are second members of pairs in the relation. The first case is treated in classical TG by a transformation which deletes *someone* or *something* from object position. Under the present theory, this can simply be accomplished by a rule which converts a transitive verb into an intransitive verb; the associated semantic rule affects the meaning in the appropriate way. The rule for this is given in (16) and illustrated in (17).

(16)   S5: $\langle F_5, \langle TV \rangle, IV \rangle$ ("Unspecified Object Deletion")
Semantic Operation: $\lambda x(\exists y)[\alpha'(y)(x)]$
English: $F_5(\alpha) = \alpha$

(17)   [John eats]$_t$

John$_T$ [eat]$_{IV}$ (by S5)

          |

          eat$_{TV}$

Here also I give the semantic rule roughly as it is formalized in Montague's system, i.e. via a translation rule into intensional logic, though I have simplified the semantics of noun phrases in these rules for expository purposes. In English, as in most languages, the syntactic operation here is simply the identity operation: it leaves the form of the verb unaltered.

The other kind of relation-reduction – from which a set is formed from the second members of pairs in the relation – is the so-called agentless passive. In this case also the TV is converted to an IV, but here the verb is marked with passive morphology; the rule is given and illustrated below. The semantic operation is similar to that of S5, but the rule here yields "the set of all y such that for some x, x stands in the α'-relation to y."

(18)   S6: $\langle F_6, \langle TV \rangle, IV \rangle$ (Agentless Passive)
Semantic Operation: $\lambda y(\exists x)[(\alpha'(y))(x)]$
English: $F_6(\alpha) = be^\frown\alpha'$, where α' is the passive form of α.

(19)

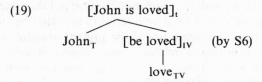

$[\text{John is loved}]_t$

John_T $[\text{be loved}]_{IV}$ (by S6)

love_{TV}

An alternative way that languages have of performing this second kind of reduction is by an impersonal construction. I think the best way of treating this case is by a rule which leaves the verb as a transitive verb but interprets the verb in much the same way as before – the object of the derived verb is still interpreted as the object of the original verb would have been, but the subject now makes a "vacuous" contribution to the meaning of the sentence. The syntax must now be arranged so as to insert a dummy NP into subject position; cf. section 6.

4.2. Relation-Rearranging Rules

By "Relation-Rearranging Rule" I mean a rule which takes one of the hierarchical, multi-argument functions that a verb denotes and converts it into a new function with the same number of arguments but with the arguments interpreted in a different order. One such rule is the agentive passive construction (or "full passive"). The semantic operation that goes with this rule has the ultimate effect of mapping a relation into its converse. As I write the rule here, this "reversing" of the relation and the combination of the function with the argument denoted by the agent phrase are accomplished in one step:

(20)   S7: $\langle F_7, \langle TV, T \rangle, IV \rangle$ (Agentive Passive)
Semantic Operation: $\lambda x[(\alpha'(x))(\beta')]$
English: $F_7(\alpha, \beta) = be^\frown\alpha'^\frown by^\frown\beta'$, where α' is the passive form of α and β' is the accusative form of β.

Syntactically, the rule takes a transitive verb α and a term β and gives in effect "be α-ed by β," as is illustrated in (21).

(21)

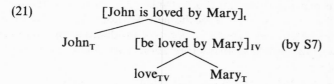

The interpretation of this sentence – *John is loved by Mary* – comes out equivalent to that of the sentence *Mary loves John*. However, the two sentences will have no common syntactic source.

A second relation-rearranging rule in English will be Dative Shift, given and illustrated in (22) and (24) respectively.

(22)   S8: $\langle F_8, \langle TV/T \rangle, TV//T \rangle$ (Dative Shift)
Semantic Operation: $\lambda z \lambda y \lambda x [\alpha'(y)(z)(x)]$
English: $F_8(\alpha) = \alpha$

(23)   S9: $\langle F_9, \langle TV//T, T \rangle, TV \rangle$ (Verb-Oblique Object Rule)
Semantic operation: Functional application
English: $F_9(\alpha, \beta) = F_5(\alpha, \beta)$

(24)

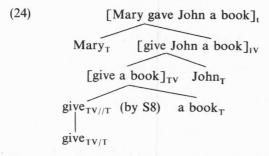

Syntactically, S8 takes a three-place verb, such as *give*, and converts it into a new three-place verb having the same form as the original verb; the resulting verb must be put in a syntactic category distinct from that of the original *give*, however, because the rule combining verbs in TV/T with their object inserts the preposition *to* and we don't want a *to* to appear in this case. Following Montague, I use the double-slash notation TV//T here, to designate this new category; we will need to add a new verb-plus-argument rule S9 (in (23)) to combine the new verb with its first object, but this rule introduces no preposition. The semantic operation for Dative Shift (S8) maps a three-place relation, that is, a set of ordered triples $\langle x, y, z \rangle$, into a new three-place relation such that if any triple $\langle x, y, z \rangle$ was in the first relation, then the triple $\langle x, z, y \rangle$ is in the new relation. Thus a "Dative Shift" sentence like *Mary gives John a book* will be produced as the analysis tree in (24) shows, but it will have an interpretation equivalent to *Mary gives a book to John*.

Note also that we can use the Dative Shift rule and the Passive rule in the same derivation; this automatically gives rise to examples like *John was given a book by Mary*, as illustrated in (25), with the proper interpretation. Of course, we can also get *A book was given to John by Mary* as illustrated in (26) by using Passive but not Dative Shift.

(25)

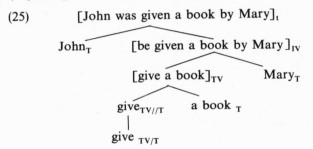

(26)

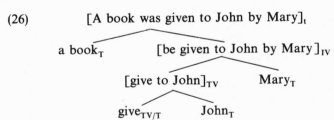

A final example of a relation-rearranging rule is Raising to Object Position. This rule, given in (27), will take as input a verb subcategorized for a sentential object: that is, a verb of the category IV/t (recall that t is the category of sentences).

(27)   S10: $\langle F_{10}, \langle IV/t \rangle, TV/IV \rangle$ (Raising to Object Rule)
        Semantic Operation: $\lambda P \lambda y \lambda x [\alpha'(^\frown P(y))(x)]$
        English: $F_{10}(\alpha) = \alpha$

The rule converts the verb into a verb of category TV/IV – that is, the resulting verb will take first an IV as argument, then a term as direct object, then a term as subject. The syntactic operation leaves the form of the verb unaffected. Semantically, the new verb will have two arguments in place of the propositional argument of the old verb; the new verb will take these two arguments and, in effect, combine them to form a proposition that will be "plugged into" the original verb's meaning. Thus *Mary believes John to love Sue*, as produced in the tree in (28), will be interpreted in the same way as *Mary believes that John loves Sue*. Finally, the combination of Raising and Passive rules can be shown to automatically produce and correctly interpret a so-called "bagel sentence" such as (29), interpreting it as equivalent (modulo tense) to (30).

(28)

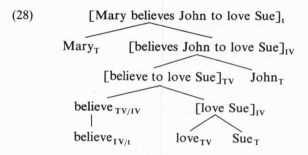

(29)   The bagel was believed by Max to have been claimed by Sam to have been eaten by Seymour.

(30)   Max believed that Sam claimed that Seymour ate the bagel.

4.3. *Relation Expanding Rules*

I have called the third class of relation-changing rules "Relation-expanding rules". These are like the cases of modifier rules I discussed earlier, which effectively map an n-place relation into a $n+1$-place relation. The difference here is that the "added" noun phrase is represented in the syntax as one of the primary grammatical relations, i.e. as a subject or an object. A very familiar example of this sort is the causative rule, in which the new noun phrase, the agent of the causation, appears as the subject of the new verb. The syntactic rule for making a transitive causative verb from an intransitive is given in (31); in English, though not in most other languages, the operation of this rule leaves the form of the verb unaltered.

(31)   S11: $\langle F_{11}, \langle IV \rangle, TV \rangle$ (Causative Rule for Intransitives)
        Semantic Operation: $\lambda y \lambda x (\exists P)[P(x) \text{ CAUSE}[\alpha'(y)]]$
        English: $F_{11}(\alpha) = \alpha$

The semantic operation must be responsible for introducing the causative relationship. This semantic interpretation rule is borrowed from other work (Dowty 1975, 1979), and I won't discuss it here. The meaning of a sentence produced by this rule is like that of a two-clause structure, e.g. "John causes the glass to break" in the case of the example (32), but syntactically there is only one clause.

(32)   [John break the glass]$_t$

        John$_T$ [break the glass]$_{IV}$

            [break]$_{TV}$ (S11) the glass$_T$
                |
            break$_{IV}$

        (Interpretation $= (\exists P)[P(\textit{John}') \text{ CAUSE } [\textit{break}'(\textit{the-glass}')]]$)

Other languages also have a causative rule for turning a transitive verb into a ditransitive causative verb – this is S12 in (33) – and some even have a rule for converting a ditransitive verb into a four-place causative (cf. Dowty 1979).

(33)   S12: $\langle F_{12}, \langle TV \rangle, TV//T \rangle$ (Causative Rule for Transitives)
        Semantic Operation: $\lambda z \lambda y \lambda x (\exists P)[P(x) \text{ CAUSE } [\alpha'(z)(y)]]$

There is a construction in a number of Bantu languages in which a noun phrase with locative, benefactive, or instrumental meaning appears in the syntactic position of the direct object and behaves, with respect to other syntactic rules, as if it were a direct object; this will be a case of a relation-expanding rule in which the added NP appears as the direct object argument of the new verb. The syntactic rule for the benefactive construction of this group, given in (34), will simply convert a transitive verb to a kind of ditransitive verb; the syntactic operation adds a suffix to the verb stem (this kind of suffix is called an applied affix by Bantuists), e.g. the suffix -r- in Chichewa.

(34)   S13: $\langle F_{13}, \langle TV \rangle, TV/T \rangle$ (Bantu Benefactive Construction)

Semantic Operation: $\lambda z \lambda y \lambda x[(\text{ben}'(y))(\alpha'(z))(x)]$
Chichewa: $F_{13}(\alpha) = \alpha + (e/i)r$

The semantic operation corresponding to this, however, specifies that the meaning of the direct-object argument of the verb will be used semantically as a benefactive IV-modifier would be used in English in the way I illustrated earlier, and that the right-most object term of the new verb will be used semantically as the direct-object argument of the original verb. The analysis tree in (35) is based on Chichewa data from Trithart (1979).[6]

(35)

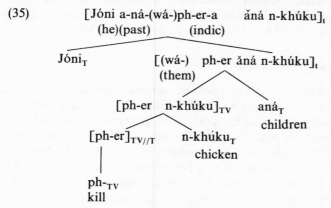

"John killed the chicken for the children"

5. ARGUMENTS FOR THIS TREATMENT OF GRAMMATICAL RELATIONS AND RELATION-CHANGING RULES

Now, having given a brief idea of how the syntax of grammatical relations works under this proposal and how syntax is related to semantic interpretation, I will turn to some reasons why this approach might be preferable to either the TG or RG accounts of the same phenomena. §5.1 and §5.2 provide reasons for preferring the definitions of grammatical relations themselves, the remaining arguments pertain to relation-changing rules.

5.1. *Universal Tendencies in Word Order*

Since Greenberg's (1963) groundbreaking work on word order, linguists have tried to give theoretical accounts of the correlations in ordering of certain constituents across languages that he observed. Under the present analysis, many of these correlations can be described by saying that a VO language is one in which functors tend to be ordered to the left of their arguments, while an OV language is one in which functors tend to come to the right of their arguments. The attempt to account for these word order universals in terms of functor and argument relations is of course not new (cf. Vennemann 1973), but what Montague's semantic framework brings to this enterprise is a semantics formulated explicitly enough that one can justify on semantic grounds alone which constituent is "functor" and which is "argument"; such independent justification is of course necessary if alleged explanations of word order have any true explanatory power.

5.2. *Discontinuous Constituents*

Second, this approach to syntax offers an account of certain discontinuous constituents that is superior to the PS grammar-plus-transformational component theory; this arises from the use of operations like Right Wrap in the structure building rules, as in the Breton case (cf. (10)). Anderson and Chung (1977) have observed, for example, that in Breton, there is no evidence that the VSO word order arises either from an underlying SVO order or an underlying VOS order. Nevertheless, they observe that from the point of view of several syntactic rules, the combination of verb and object seems to behave as a constituent – that is, like a VP constituent in English. This is paradoxical under the transformational theory, since if VSO were the underlying word order, there could be no such underlying constituent. But in the analysis I suggested for Breton, Verb and Object do form a constituent as they do in all languages but only a constituent in the tectogrammatical sense, not (in Breton) in the phenogrammatical structure of the whole sentence where word order is explicitly determined.[7]

5.3. *"Structure-Preserving" Rules*

From my discussion of relation-changing rules, it will be quite clear that the main things that distinguish the category-changing analysis of relation-changing rules from TG and RG are that grammatical relations are here essentially defined in terms of verbs and that relation-changing rules are rules applying to verbs, or to various kinds of verb phrases, not to sentences. Because of this, the category-changing analysis predicts three extremely commonplace observations about these rules in natural language, observations which TG and RG have certainly described adequately but in no way predict; these are discussed in this and the two following sections. Because these observations are so commonplace, I must urge the reader to approach them with as much objectivity as he can muster, to see that they really do provide arguments.

The first of these is the "structure-preserving" nature of rules like Passive, Raising and Dative Shift. That is, the results of applying these transformations are syntactic structures almost exactly like those structures produced independently by PS rules. Joseph Emonds, of course, has even proposed that these belong to a class of transformations that must in principle produce outputs that are of the same form as the PS rules produce – the so-called structure preserving hypothesis (Emonds 1976), but note that there is nothing in the theory of transformations, aside from the structure preserving hypothesis itself, that predicts that this should be so.

Under the category-changing analysis of these rules, however, it does follow that sentences in which grammatical relations have been changed should have the same general form as those in which they have not been changed, for if a relation-changing rule applies to a verb before it combines with its arguments, then the rules which add the noun phrase arguments to a verb after it has had its grammatical relations changed will be (in the simplest grammar) the very same rules that add these arguments to an unchanged verb, namely rules like S1 and S2.[8] Whatever the syntactic operations assigned to these rules in a specific language look like, they will produce the same form of sentence, whether relation-changing rules were involved or not.

5.4. "Relation-Changing" Morphology is Marked on Verbs

The second commonplace observation is that when the application of a relation-changing rule is signified in surface structure by morphological marking, that marking appears on the verb of the sentence, not, for example, on the noun phrases that are allegedly moved by the transformation (or have their relations changed in RG) or on other constituents. This is predicted by the category-changing analysis, since the only constituent the relation-changing rules have to operate on at the time they apply is the verb, hence there is nothing else that a morphological marker could be attached to by the relation-changing rule.[9] Examples of such marking are the passive morphology, the applied suffixes in Bantu, causative affixes and the Dative Shift Affix in Bahasa Indonesian.[10] In both RG and in the TG account, by contrast, a whole sentence is operated on by the rules in question, so there is no obvious reason why the passive marker has to go on the verb rather than on any other constituent in the sentence.

Let me be quick to anticipate a possible objection to this point: it might be objected that the operation of the passive is in fact marked on the Object NP that appears as surface subject, since that NP appears in Subject position and/or in nominative case, rather than in the accusative case or post-verbal position it would have appeared in if the rule had not applied. But this is a question-begging objection, since subject position and/or nominative case is what any subject of a sentence would receive, whether or not a relation-changing rule had applied, so this is not a marking specific to the Passive or other such rule. In other words, what I am predicting does not occur in natural language is a passive rule whose application is marked by a special morpheme on the subject NP in addition to whatever normally marks subjects in that language, but with no morphological marking on the verb.

5.5. Relation-Changing Rules are Lexically Governed by Verbs

The third "commonplace" observation has to do with lexical government. It's well-known that operations like Dative Shift, Raising and Causative are lexically governed in many languages, and that the lexical item which governs them is invariably the verb of the sentence. As in the previous cases, nothing in the TG analysis of these constructions nor in the RG account predicts that it should be the verb (rather than, say, the NP to be moved) that should govern this rule, nor is there any obvious reason why relation-changing rules should be governed lexically while other rules, such as Relativization, Question formation and other unbounded rules, are never lexically governed in any language. Under the category-changing analysis, it's already obvious that it should be the verb, if anything, which governs the rule, since it is the verb which the rules apply to. But we can say more than this.

5.6. Category-Changing Rules as Either Lexical or Syntactic

In a couple of papers (Dowty 1975, 1978), I have proposed a theory of lexical rules for a Montague Grammar framework, and I have argued that Dative Shift, Raising and other such alleged "lexically governed" transformations are lexical rules. According to this proposal, the form of lexical rules and the manner of their semantic interpretation is in general exactly the same as that of true syntactic rules, the only difference being in the status of the outputs of the rule in the grammar: in the case of the syntactic rules, the outputs are all grammatically derived expressions of the language, but in the case of lexical rules, the outputs are merely possible derived lexical items of the language; some of these are actual words, which are listed independently in the lexicon, and some are not. Of the meanings of actual derived words, some meanings conform exactly to the meaning produced by the lexical rule, meanings of other words do not. It follows from this point of view that the only criterion for distinguishing a lexical from a syntactic rule should be the questions of (1) whether the forms produced by the rule are all acceptable or whether there are random lexical exceptions to the rule, and (2) whether the outputs of the rules are all completely predictable in meaning or not.

It also follows, crucially, in this approach that a putative syntactic rule can be treated as a lexical rule instead only if the expressions to which the rule applies are finite in number. Note for example that this will be the case for Dative Shift and some of the other relation changing rules as I have formulated them because they in effect apply only to single verbs, not to more complex expressions. While this is feasible under the category-changing analysis of relation-changing rules, it would not be under the TG or RG accounts, because the rules in these frameworks apply to an infinite number of sentences, not to a finite list of verbs. But even under the category-changing approach it would not be possible to reanalyze rules such as Relative Clause Formation (in English, at least) as category-changing rules applying to a finite number of cases. Hence it is predicted by this approach that such rules are syntactic rather than lexical and cannot have lexical exceptions, as indeed they do not.

I should point out that Joan Bresnan has recently proposed a view of a grammar in which rules such as Passive, Dative Shift, etc. are replaced by lexical rules; these rules she calls *function-dependent* rules (Bresnan 1978). Obviously, such a treatment predicts most of the same observations about these rules as the ones I have just described. But besides the fact that Bresnan is not seeking a language universal definition of these rules as I am via the distinction between tectogrammatical structure and pheno-grammatical structures, and the fact that she is not interpreting these rules in the same theory as I am, there is a further important difference in the claims she and I are making. Whereas she regards all function-dependent rules as lexical rules in principle, I am only claiming that category-changing rules *can* be lexical rules in some circumstances, not that they always *are* lexical rules in all languages. In particular, Bresnan would consider the English passive rule to be a lexical rule, but I do not. Under the present framework, two sets of arguments can be given for treating Passive as a syntactic rule. First, whereas Passive does apply to single lexical transitive verbs in many cases, there are also cases in which the TV expression that undergoes Passive is a syntactically derived phrase instead. For example, all of the italicized phrases in (36) are syntactically complex phrases of the category TV, though the basic verb occurring within them would be put in some other category.

(36) a. Mary *kissed* John/John was kissed by Mary
      b. John *gave* a book *to Mary*/A book was given to Mary by John
      c. John *gave* Mary *a book*/Mary was given a book by John
      d. Mary *persuaded* John *to leave*/John was persuaded to leave by Mary
      e. Mary *painted* the house *red*/The house was painted red by Mary
      f. Mary *appointed* John *chairman*/John was appointed chairman by Mary

Second, Emmon Bach has argued persuasively in his chapter in this volume that under the assumptions of the approach taken by this paper, purpose clauses such as *to deliver groceries in* in (37) must be analyzed as modifiers of transitive verbs, not as modifiers of verb phrases.

(37) Mary bought the truck (for Bill) to deliver groceries in——.
      Max brought in the dean for us to talk to——.

This is necessary, first of all, to account for the interpretation of "missing" object NP in the purpose clause and, secondly, to predict correctly that purpose clauses do not occur with intransitive verbs; that is, we do not get sentences like (38).[11]

(38) *It arrived (for Bill) to deliver groceries in——.
      *The dean came in for us to talk to——.

But such clauses occur in passive sentences as well as active ones, as (39) illustrates.

(39) The truck was bought (for Bill) to deliver groceries in——.
      The dean was brought in for us to talk to——.

Thus the TV expressions that are passivized in (39) must be *buy for Bill to deliver groceries in* and *bring in for us to talk to* respectively; these again are syntactically complex expressions which have a potentially infinite variety of forms, so the Passive rule I have given cannot apply to them unless it is a syntactic rule, not a lexical rule.

The view of category changing rules as potentially *either* lexical *or* syntactic rules is, I think, significant. It means we can recognize a single language-universal characterization of these rules, even though we at the same time recognize that the rules are lexical rules in some languages and syntactic rules in others. (Causative, for example, is clearly a lexical rule in English, but I know of no reasons not to consider it a syntactic rule in Turkish). Since the rules have the same form in either case, it also makes it plausible that a language might have one of these rules as a lexical rule at one historical stage of its development and easily reanalyze it as a syntactic rule at a later stage (or vice versa) without any significant change in the form or interpretation of the rule. Also, this view can more naturally describe the possibility that in the course of language acquisition, children may temporarily acquire as a syntactic rule a rule that is lexical in their parents' speech, since no change in the form of the rule need be postulated when the child later reanalyzes the rule as a lexical rule and starts memorizing its outputs individually. For example, there is some evidence that English-speaking children use the causative rule S11 as a freely productive syntactic rule at some stage of language acquisition (Bowerman 1974), though it is a lexical rule for adult speakers.

5.7. *Object-Controlled vs. Subject-Controlled Verbal Complements*

Bach (1980) has pointed out that, under the category-changing analysis of rules like Passive, we can take advantage of the possibility of the novel way of treating discontinuous constituents I mentioned earlier to systematically exclude on syntactic grounds what had been thought to be lexical exceptions to the passive rule. Excluding such apparent exceptions syntactically is of course critical for this approach, if we are to be able to maintain the claim that Passive is a syntactic rule and that syntactic rules have no lexical exceptions. Bach suggests that it is a systematic principle that when an infinitive complement of a verb is syntactically controlled by a NP outside the infinitive – i.e. when this NP triggers reflexive agreement or number agreement within the infinitive – and when this NP is involved in semantic entailments with respect to the infinitive, then this NP must be the next higher argument of the verb after the infinitive. To see more clearly what this means, compare verbs like *persuade* with verbs like *promise*. In the sentence *Mary persuaded John to wash himself*, the infinitive is controlled by the NP *John*, and it is this NP that will trigger reflexivization in the infinitive. Also *John* is the "understood subject" of *wash himself*. Given Bach's principle, it follows that (40) should be the correct analysis tree for this sentence, since the NP *John* is the next higher argument of the verb after the infinitive.

(40)

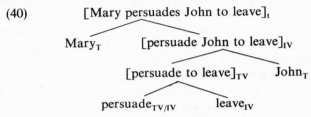

But with verbs like *promise*, the NP that controls reflexivization and is semantically interpreted as the understood subject of the infinitive is the matrix subject NP *Mary*, not the object NP *John*. Thus the proper syntactic analysis for *promise* should be that illustrated in (41), in which the object NP is the argument added before the infinitive, so that the next NP to be added after the infinitive is the subject NP. Thus *persuade* should be put in the same syntactic category TV/IV, while *promise* is put in the category (IV/IV)/T – a verb that combines with a term to give a phrase that then combines with an infinitive to form an IV. In other words, the two sentences have different tectogrammatical structures, in spite of the fact that their phenogrammatical forms would appear to be parallel.

(41)

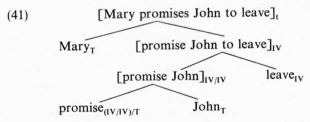

Now I should be careful to point out that Bach's principle does not follow automatically from the assumptions I have developed up to this point, and it is unclear exactly why a principle like this ought to hold (though it does slightly simplify the syntactic treatment of reflexivization and other agreement within infinitive complements, without resorting to an Equi analysis of infinitives). But the interesting thing about Bach's principle is that it predicts that verbs like *promise* can never undergo passive. This is so for the straightforward reason that in the analysis tree of (4.1), no phrase of the category TV is ever produced, yet the category TV is the only input to the passive rule. Likewise, Bach's tests indicate that examples (42a)–(42d) do not contain a phrase of the category TV – instead, the underlined sequence of words will be a tectogrammatical constituent parallel to *promise John* above – so the lack of passives here is also predicted.

(42) a. She *made us* a good chairperson
      b. Mary *promised John* to leave
      c. John *appeared to Mary* to be stupid. (Cf. John appealed to Bill to go to the store)
      d. John *struck Mary* as honest

      a′. *We were made a good chairperson by her
      b′. *John was promised by Mary to leave
      c′. *Mary was appeared to to be stupid by John (Cf. Bill was appealed to by Bill to go to the store.)
      d′. *Mary was struck by John as honest

This correlation between subject control and lack of passives if of course well-known (Visser and other traditional grammarians have noted it), but I know of nothing in any transformational theory that connects the lack of passives with subject control.

5.8   *The Interaction of Causativization with Other Rules*

Judith Aissen (1974) and others have observed that a problem arises with the usual "two-clause" analyses of causative sentences, the analysis sketched in (43):

(43)

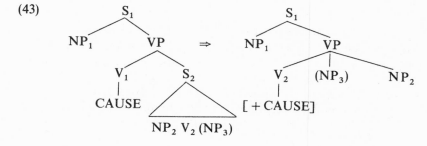

The problem is that cyclic transformations must (in at least many cases, in various languages) be prohibited from applying in the lower clause before causative formation converts the two-clause structure to one clause. But if causative rules are relation-expanding rules applying to verbs, as suggested in §4.3, then there is no lower clause involved in the derivation of causative sentences. (The arguments for the presence of the underlying two-clause-structure are almost entirely semantic in nature and thus not pertinent to syntactic analysis in the present approach.) It might seem at first that the predictions of the relation-expanding analysis are thus the same as those of the hypothesis that causative formation (or "Verb Raising") is pre-cyclic (Aissen 1974).

In fact, the situation is much more complicated than this. If causative formation is treated as a lexical rule in a given language while Passive, Reflexivization, etc. are handled by syntactic rules in that language, then indeed the effect of a "lower clause" application of any such syntactic rule is predicted not to occur, given the theory of lexical rules advanced in Dowty (1978, 1979b). If causative is a syntactic rule or rules, taking as input verb phrases of category IV, TV, etc., it is still predicted that no "lower clause" applications of rules involving the "embedded subject" can be observed (e.g. subject-verb agreement), but since rules such as Passive will give as output expressions of category IV, it is now possible for such rules to "feed" causative formation. Reflexivization, likewise, is best treated in the present approach as giving outputs of category IV (cf. Gazdar and Sag, to appear; Bach and Partee, 1980) and thus giving a potential input to causativization. But in fact, causatives of passives do appear in some languages, ones which can be assumed to have syntactic causative rules (cf. Newmeyer (1976, note 10) on Eskimo; Zimmer (1976) on Turkish). And reflexive pronouns sometimes appear in complements of causatives in various Romance languages (Taraldsen 1976), in positions controlled by the "embedded subject" in a traditional analysis (but compatible with the IV-treatment of reflexivization just mentioned). Though I have not made investigations of all the relevant languages, there seems to me to be a reasonable hope that the remaining failures of syntactic rules to feed causativization (in languages where causativization is syntactic) may be explainable in various language-particular ways: There may be morphological incompatibilities between reflexive and passive affixes (cf. Zimmer (1976, 403ff)); given the rich system of verbal subcategories needed in the present approach, causative can perhaps be excluded from applying to certain motivated subcategories of verb phrases; conditions on Reflexivization will vary from language to

language, causing Reflexivization to interact differently with causativization in different languages.[12]

5.9 *"Wanna" Contraction*

Another argument involves the much-discussed phonological data in (44).

(44) a. Teddy is the man I wanna succeed.
　　　 b. Teddy is the man I want to succeed.

It is known that phonological contraction cannot apply across the
"extraction site" of a transformation like WH-movement, though contraction apparently can apply across the gap left by Passive, Raising, or
Equi (on the movement/deletion analysis of such rules). But in the analysis
being considered here, no deletion or movement of a NP is involved in these
latter rules, though the production of WH-movement constructions requires
a "gap" (subscripted pronoun, trace, etc.) to be put in place of the "missing"
NP, at least temporarily. Hence the distribution of the contraction data is
predicted, given the assumption that gaps uniformly block contraction.
Jacobson (in this volume) surveys the accounts that have been proposed of
the contraction data in RG and in the Extended Standard Theory, arguing
that an account like that advocated here is the most preferable; I refer the
reader to her article for further details.

5.10 *Theoretical Simplicity*

Finally, let me emphasize two differences between RG and the enterprise I
am engaged in. First, RG takes grammatical relations as primitives, while in
the approach I have sketched, grammatical relations play an important role
in the way syntax relates to compositional semantics. Second, the theory of
RG is presently stated as a large body of axioms, or laws, most of which are
entirely independent of one another. Though the approach I have described
is so far much less detailed than their theory, what I have proposed all
results from Montague's general approach to syntax and semantics, plus
only two principles: the 'single argument' principle in (6) and the
assumption that relation-changing rules are operations on verbs, not on full
sentences. All the rest follows as a consequence of these assumptions. Thus
it is interesting that certain of the "Laws" of relational grammar – for
example the Stratal Uniqueness law, the Oblique Law, the Final 1 Law
and perhaps others – arise automatically in this account and cannot be

rescinded except on pain of causing the whole analysis to collapse (cf. footnote 2); this approach is thus inherently *more* falsifiable than Relational Grammar or Arc Pair Grammar with their large numbers of logically independent laws; the proponents of these theories are at liberty to delete some of these laws but still retain the rest of their theory intact.

6. SYNTACTIC COUNTEREVIDENCE TO THE CATEGORY-CHANGING ANALYSIS

There is of course certain counterevidence to the proposal that relation-changing rules do not involve any movement or change in the grammatical status of the noun phrases of a sentence, evidence that is now quite familiar from TG and RG. As I think it is premature to propose the adoption of any specific way of dealing with this counterevidence in the category-changing approach, I will only briefly review the kinds of counterevidence and sketch proposed solutions that I know of.

The most familiar counterevidence is the case of "dummy NPs" that have apparently been raised or passivized, such as the NP *there* in *John believes there to be a unicorn in the garden, There appears to be a unicorn in the garden, There is believed to be a unicorn in the garden*, etc. One kind of solution to the problem presented by "dummy NPs", given in Thomason (ms), is to produce these examples via "long distance" syntactic operations such as are used in Montague's treatment of relative clauses and wide-scope quantification. Thus Thomason produces *There is certain to be a man here* by a special rule that combines *a man* with *be certain to be *there here*, where **there* is a special "non-surfacing" abstract NP that is replaced with a real NP by this rule alone. This approach has certain syntactic inelegances, one of which is the postulation of the abstract element **there*. This is particularly unwelcome in the present context, since one of the virtues of the category-changing method is that it allows one to avoid syntactic abstractness almost entirely.

Another family of solutions has been dubbed by Lauri Karttunen as the "ugly object" analysis. Here one treats the word *there* syntactically as a NP like any other and assigns it a genuine denotation. But this denotation is an abstract and unique semantical object (the "Ugly object") which leads to an incoherent semantic interpretation in most sentences (such as *John found there*, or *There walks*). But certain verb phrases like *be a unicorn in the garden* are given a special interpretation that accepts the "ugly object" as a subject denotation, giving rise to a coherent proposition when and only when this subject is chosen for them; the proposition expressed by *There is a unicorn in the garden* is then approximately the same as that expressed by *A unicorn is in the garden*. Given the semantic rules for Passive and Raising presented in this paper, it follows automatically that *There is believed to be a unicorn in the garden* is semantically coherent, while *There is believed to have found a unicorn in the garden* is incoherent. A particularly clever version of an "ugly object" analysis is given by Sag (this volume), taking advantage of the strict type stratification imposed by Montague to effect the semantic coherence/incoherence of the interpretations in just the right way. Ingenious though Sag's solution is, I feel that it is ultimately no less ad hoc than any other "ugly object" analysis, as Sag exploits the type stratification for purposes which are otherwise unprecedented in MG.

A third kind of solution has been explored by Gazdar in unpublished work. Here, *there* is also given a denotation which has (virtually) no effect on the meaning, but the filtering of inappropriate sentences with *there* is handled by syntactic features rather as verb agreement is treated, and not by "semantic filtering." See Cooper (ms., 1979) for yet another kind of solution.

The second kind of counterargument to the category-changing approach comes from cases where the relational grammarians have claimed that one needs to make reference to the underlying grammatical status of a NP, rather than its "derived" status, to describe some other grammatical facts correctly. For example, Perlmutter (this volume) claims that certain cases of control of reflexivization by an NP in Russian depend on whether that NP was an underlying subject ("initial 1") or not. While a reply to this kind of argument will depend on a thorough examination of the syntax of the language in question, the tack that a defender of the category-changing method would take is to try to show that some other way of identifying the correct class of NPs is possible other than by reference to their "underlying" grammatical status. This may be a somewhat more practical option in the category-changing analysis than in RG, for the class of "chômeurs" of RG would here be divided up into several distinct kinds of grammatical relations.

Perhaps the most puzzling phenomena for the category-changing approach arise in Icelandic (Andrews, this volume), where the case-marking on "Raised" NPs may be one of several cases but seems to depend systematically on the "underlying" grammatical role of the NP (from the point of view of a TG movement analysis). I have no particular proposal to make about such problems at this time but refer the reader to Andrews for some suggestions.

While all these problems must eventually be dealt with successfully if the category-changing approach is to be unequivocally defended, I think it is also important to note a striking asymmetry in the data that argues for the category changing method versus the data that argues against it, if these arguments are to be seen in proper perspective. Much of the evidence that argues for the category-changing method and against the movement analysis (namely, the fact that morphological marking appears on verbs, the structure-preserving nature of relation-changing rules, the fact that verbs govern the rules) appears in all (or most, in the case of lexical government) of the sentences of the language in which a relation-changing rule has applied. On the other hand, the evidence that argues against the category-changing method – namely the behavior of "moved" dummy NPs – appears in relatively few sentences (at least in English-like languages). This asymmetry is all the more striking when considered from the point of view of language acquisition. Sentences with raised or passivized dummy NPs are relatively rare and no doubt confined primarily to learned discourse, hence children learning their native language would be exposed to these sentences rather late, long after the Raising and Passive constructions themselves had been mastered. Unless it could be successfully argued that a child is innately predisposed to acquire a movement analysis of relation-changing rules rather than a non-movement analysis, it seems that a child should in any case acquire a non-movement analysis long *before* the data supporting a movement analysis is encountered.

7. ERGATIVE LANGUAGES

Following Dixon (1979), we may say that a language has *ergative* characteristics to the extent that the "notional object" of a transitive verb (i.e. that NP that would be the object if the sentence were translated into English) is treated syntactically in the same way as the subject of an intransitive IV, while the "notional subject" of a transitive verb is treated differently. (The most frequent manifestation of ergativity is case marking: here the case marking of the notional object of a TV is the same as the subject of an IV, in which instance this marking is known as *absolutive* case, the contrasting case marking of the notional subject of a TV being called the *ergative* case. The terms *nominative* and *accusative* are then reserved for the more familiar case-marking system of non-ergative languages.) I will briefly sketch the way some kinds of ergative languages can be treated under the approach to grammatical relations sketched in this paper. For convenience, I will divide my discussion among three (idealized) types of ergative languages: *deep ergative languages* (in which not only case marking but also all other syntactic properties that distinguish subjects from objects follow an ergative pattern), *surface ergative languages* (in which relatively few characteristics follow an ergative pattern), and *split ergative* languages in which ergative patterning appears consistently in some tenses but never in others.

It may have come as a surprise to some readers that I have not even mentioned semantic notions like "agent" and "patient" in my proposals for universal definitions of subject and object. But in fact such notions need not be invoked in such definitions, and I will argue that they should not be invoked. With a referential theory of semantics and our compositional principles for connecting syntax with meaning, it suffices to identify, e.g., a transitive verb's meaning with a set of ordered pairs at each index; for example, *find* denotes the set of pairs of things such that the first finds the second, and it is only in the domain of lexical semantics that notions like agentivity must be employed in specifying what principles enable one to determine whether an arbitrary pair $\langle x, y \rangle$ is a member of this set (cf. Dowty 1979 for extensive discussion of lexical semantics).

Now note that for any relation R denoted by a transitive verb, a verb denoting the converse of R (denoted R^{-1}) would indicate the same "information" as the original verb – for example, imagine a hypothetical verb *$*dnif$* whose meaning is paraphrasable as "be found by" (yet *$*dnif$* is a basic verb, not a passive of *find*). However, our intuitions are that any English-like language is unlikely to have such a verb, and I believe this is a correct intuition. And in any case, it would be somehow redundant for both *find* and *$*dnif$* to coexist. Rather, languages seem to follow a set of systematic principles that determine, for any relation R, which of R and R^{-1} is denoted by a verb. These principles would be something like the following:

(i) If for any $\langle x, y \rangle \in R$, x is an entity that causes something to happen to y, R is "lexicalized", not R^{-1} (cf. *build, kill, ignite, move*)

(ii) If for any $\langle x, y \rangle \in R$, x is a sentient being that perceives something about y or has an emotion or attitude toward y, R is lexicalized not R^{-1} (cf. *see, hear, love, believe*)

(iii) If for any $\langle x, y \rangle \in R$, x is moving and y is stationary, R is lexicalized, not R^{-1} (cf. *enter, overtake, pierce, collide with*)

This is only a rough statement of these principles; perhaps others are necessary as well, and perhaps a different formulation is preferable.[13] However, I think it would be a mistake to try to conflate all three into a single definition of "agency", for the interesting reason that there is a class of verbs for which principles (i) and (ii) give conflicting results, and it is in this class and only in this class that one finds *both* a relation and its converse lexicalized. This is the infamous class of "psychological" verbs, the class including verbs like *seem, surprise, disappoint, frighten, anger, please*, etc. For example, principle (i) suggests that for x *surprises* y, x should be the "subject," for x can be viewed as causing some emotion in y, while principle (ii) implies at the same time that y should be the subject, for y perceives an emotion toward x. Here one finds (1) pairs of independent lexemes, one the converse of the other (cf. *I like it* vs. *It pleases me*, German *mögen* vs. *gefallen*, *I suppose it is true* vs. *it seems true to me*), and (2) various constructions systematically related to their converses by operations other than the usual passive rules, e.g. the "Psych Movement" construction in English (*I am surprised at it, it surprise me*), "reflexive verbs" or "middle verbs" in other languages. Here also a verb may "reverse" its subject and object historically over time, as was the case with English *think*.

Since these principles (i)–(iii) are essentially independent of the system of grammatical relations as outlined in section 2 of this paper, it is possible and I believe quite reasonable to maintain that a "deep ergative" language[14] like Dyirbal (Dixon 1972, 1979) conforms to the same universal principles of grammatical relations as non-ergative languages and differs from English only in that the *converses* of principles (i)–(iii) are employed in its lexical semantics. In other words, (i)–(iii) are criteria for determining the grammatical direct objects of transitive verbs in Dyirbal, so that the absolutive NPs of that language are actually its grammatical subjects while the ergative NPs are its grammatical direct objects. Moreover, the relation-changing rules of Dyribal are on this view essentially the same as those adumbrated in section 4 – that is, the so-called "antipassive" rule of Dyirbal is simply the Passive in (18) and its semantic interpretation is the same as is given in (18). A complete Montague fragment of this kind for Dyirbal is given in Schmerling (1978), and the reader is invited to consult this to see how straightforward this treatment turns out to be.

A "surface ergative language", one in which ergative characteristics are relatively few by comparison with non-ergative characteristics, will have a less elegant syntax than a consistently ergative or consistently non-ergative language. If for example the case marking of NPs is the only ergative characteristic in a language, the best treatment is probably to make the syntactic operation of the subject-predicate rule sensitive to the form of the IV: if the IV consists of a TV plus object, the subject will be marked with ergative case, but if the IV is intransitive, the subject will be marked with absolutive case. (The object of a TV is in such languages to be uniformly marked with absolutive case).

Note also that when a language is analyzed as "deep ergative" but still has a few non-ergative characteristics, the non-ergative characteristics will have to be treated in a way parallel to the ergative characteristics of a "surface ergative" language. Dyirbal, for example, is a fairly consistently ergative language, but the case marking on first and second person pronouns follows a nominative/accusative pattern. Consequently, the subject-predicate rule for Dyirbal will specify that the subject is marked absolutive when it is not a first or second person pronoun, nominative when it is such a pronoun and the IV is intransitive, and accusative when the subject is such a pronoun and the IV is transitive. The verb-object operation marks the object ergative when it is not such a pronoun but nominative when it is.

On this view, therefore, the choice of whether to analyze a language as deep ergative or surface ergative should probably depend on whether the overall number of ergative syntactic characteristics outweighs the number of non-ergative characteristics. I so far have nothing to propose about puzzling cases like Eskimo, where the ergative and non-ergative characteristics seem about equal in number. (See Johnson (1980) for a Montague grammar analysis of Eskimo as a surface ergative language, though it seems to me from Johnson's data that a deep ergative analysis would be no more complicated.) If any one criterion should be regarded as decisive for this choice, it will perhaps be the way the language treats coordination: when an intransitive IV is conjoined with a transitive IV, the NP which the transitive IV "shares" with the intransitive IV is the "notional subject" of the transitive verb in a non-ergative language but the "notional object" of the transitive IV in a deep ergative language. This of course follows straightforwardly from Montague's treatment of IV-conjunction in the system of this paper for both non-ergative and deep ergative languages, but I see no easy way to analyze the ergative pattern of IV-conjunction as a matter of "surface ergativity".

Finally, I will sketch a theoretical option that presents itself in this approach for treating those cases of "split ergativity" by tense where the ergative pattern appears consistently (i.e. as deep ergativity) in some tenses. It is known (Dixon 1980) that a number of languages follow an ergative pattern in past tense but a non-ergative pattern elsewhere. (This method would only be helpful if the past tense ergativity is "deep", not "surface", though I do not know if any such cases actually exist.) As Bach (ms.) points out, assigning the syntactic category IV to the semantic category of functions from NP denotations to sentence denotations (i.e. treating IV as t/T, as in Montague's "Universal Grammar," rather than as t/e, as in PTQ) permits one to treat tenses as functors that combine with verbs, rather than as operations on full sentences, yet still permit the semantics of tense to be treated adequately. If one adopts this approach and also treats tenses as always combining with a lexical verb (i.e. a verb that has not yet been combined with its objects, if any), it would be possible to give the semantics of the tensing operation in such a way as to "reverse" by semantic means the interpretation of subject and object, in effect turning a non-ergative transitive verb into a "deep ergative" verb. Thus the past tense rule for (basic) IVs would translate $\lambda \mathscr{P}[\text{PAST } \alpha'(\mathscr{P})]$ for verb α but for TVs the rule would translate as $\lambda \mathscr{P} \lambda \mathscr{Q}[\text{PAST } \alpha'(\mathscr{Q})(\mathscr{P})]$ for TV α. These rules would also place the verbs in a new syntactic subcategory, which would trigger ergative/absolutive case marking.

8. RELATION-CHANGING VERSUS VARIABLE-BINDING RULES

In the last two sections, I would like to turn to two questions about the nature of grammatical relations and syntactic rules that this approach raises, questions which further research will have to answer.

Within this approach to syntax, the most fundamental division among syntactic rules traditionally treated as movement rules is between category-changing rules on the one hand, and unbounded movement rules on the other hand, such as Relative Clause formation. An inescapable characteristic of category-changing rules in this analysis is that they can describe apparent "movement" of an NP *from* only one syntactic position and *to* only one syntactic position; this follows from a general constraint in Montague's theory that each syntactic rule must have a unique interpretation, and from the fact that these rules are operations on verbs. For rules like relativization that seem to extract NPs from various positions, a different strategy is called for. These rules must work like variable binding in logic: a noun phrase within the relative clause (perhaps an "empty" one) plays the semantic role of a variable in logic, and the semantic interpretation of the relative clause is that the variable within the clause is bound. For this kind of rule it does not matter where the variable occurs within the clause, it may even be embedded in a subordinate clause within the relative clause. Thus the hierarchy Subject/Direct Object/Indirect Object plays no role whatsoever in the syntax and interpretation of relative clauses, as far as the present theory is concerned. This analysis thus offers no explanation at all for Keenan and Comrie's observation (Keenan and Comrie 1977) that relativization, across languages, seemed to be governed by this hierarchy – that is, that there are some languages in which only subjects may be relativized, others in which both subject and DO can be relativized, others in which subjects, DO and IO can be relativized, and so on, but no languages in which, say, objects but not subjects can be relativized. I have no firm explanation to offer, but I can make the following speculation. Perhaps languages that only allow relativization on subjects actually do not use variable binding at all in forming relative clauses but rather combine an IV – i.e. a sentence lacking a subject – with the head noun to form a relative clause; for example, *man who walks* would come from *man* plus the IV *walks*. It would certainly be possible to write such a rule in Montague's system in such a way as to get the meaning right. A language which allows relativization on both subjects and objects (but no other positions) would then have a second relative clause rule that forms a relative clause out of a TV phrase (along with another NP to serve as its subject), and so on. At some point a language would, as it were, get tired of adding more and more relative clause rules to get new kinds of relative clauses and switch to a variable binding strategy in order to form all kinds of relative clauses by a single rule. Under this hypothesis, there are fundamentally two kinds of strategies for forming relative clauses, with a discrete distinction between the two.[16]

Thus I am suggesting that some languages may use categorial rules for syntactic processes that, in English, are variable-binding processes. The converse may obtain as well: there may be languages that use variable-binding strategies for what in English are category-changing rules. The case I have in mind is a dialect of Shona studied by Kathryn Hodges of the University of Illinois (personal communication). She tells me that in this dialect one can passivize not only the DO, the IO and objects of prepositions within the verb phrase, but even, in some circumstances, a NP from a lower clause within the VP. Thus in effect one might passivize a Shona sentence on the order of *John believes that Mary loves that man* in such a way as to produce *That man is believed by John thatMary loves (him)*. The only way I can imagine writing a non-transformational rule to do this is by a rule that "passivizes" an IV by binding a variable within the

IV and interpreting the IV in such a way as to let the variable be identified with the eventual subject of the IV. If this is correct, the distinction between category-changing and variable-binding rules may vary across languages more often than we would expect from examining only English-like languages.

9. THE ELUSIVE BOUNDARY BETWEEN ARGUMENTS AND MODIFIERS

The second question raised by this approach involves cases where the roles of *arguments* of a verb and of *modifiers* of a verb seem to overlap suspiciously. I'll discuss three such cases. The first case is the roles of benefactive NPs versus Indirect Objects. In a great many languages the case marking for benefactives and for indirect objects is the same. I suspect that this is not really an accident. If one examines the meaning of the most common three-place verbs in various languages – verbs such as *give, sell, show, take, promise, award, offer, say*, etc. – one is struck by the fact that the indirect object in almost all cases names a person who also benefits, in some way or other, by the action of the subject – If I give a book to Mary, then she is a person who benefits from my action. This raises the question whether some languages might conceivably get by without really having any verbs that denote three-place relations but rather make do with only two-place verbs plus benefactive modifiers (of category IV/IV), to express roughly the same ideas we express in English with three-place verbs. Perhaps such languages later change into languages that distinguish between datives – as arguments of verbs – and mere benefactives, and thus this earlier stage explains the convergence of case marking between benefactives and datives. A perhaps even more compelling interpretation of this correlation is that children, in the early stages of language acquisition at which they do not really understand three-place verbs, may have a grammar with only two-place verbs plus benefactives, but the concurrence between benefactive and indirect object case forms in their parents' speech allows them to understand roughly what is being said by their parents anyway.

A second such convergence between arguments and modifiers occurs with the genitive case, this convergence being one that occurs *very* widely in natural languages. This instance involves nouns, rather than verbs. It has long been recognized that many nouns are inherently relational – that is they denote two-place relations just as transitive verbs do. If one is a father or a mother, or a friend, for example, then there must necessarily be at least one person or other *of whom* one is the father, or mother, or friend. Now for such nouns, the genitive case serves to mark the second argument place of the noun; *John's father* denotes the individual that stands in the *father*-relation to John: in other words, the genitive serves much the same role for relational nouns as the accusative case does for transitive verbs. But the genitive case can play another role as well, in all or almost all languages: it serves to form a highly context-dependent modifier, indicating that there is some very salient relation that the genitive NP bears to the individual denoted by the head noun, but it is up to the hearer of the sentence to determine what it is. Thus *John's chair* might mean the chair that John owns, the chair that John built, the chair that John is sitting in or standing near, and so on depending on the context in which it is used. Rich Thomason (personal communication) has pointed out to me that even Plato was aware of this double role that genitives play, for Plato is said to have cited the following fallacious argument which turns on this double use of the genitive: "That dog is John's dog; that dog is a mother, therefore, that dog is John's mother." Once again, I would raise the question whether in some languages, or at some stages of language acquisition, it might always be the case that the genitive is interpreted as indicating a context-determined relation, rather than sometimes as denoting the argument of a relational noun. For example, the noun *mother* might be analyzed as merely denoting a set, and the phrase *John's mother* might be analyzed as denoting an individual that is a mother and stands in some important relation to John, it being up to the speaker's intelligence, rather than his knowledge of semantics of the language, to guess the correct nature of the relation.

The third such case of suspicious convergence would be the agent phrase of a passive. It has been observed that in many languages there is no agentive passive, only an agentless passive, and also that children acquire agentless passives before agentive passives; these observations suggest that in some sense, the agentless passive is more basic. And in a great many languages, the agent of a passive is marked by the instrumental case or by a preposition that elsewhere expresses instrumentality – for example, in the history of English, the agent of a passive has been expressed, at various times, not only with the preposition *by* but also by the prepositions *from*, *with*, *through*, and the dative case alone, all devices elsewhere used to express instrumentality (cf. Visser 1963, 2176–2189). What I would therefore suggest is that some languages with apparent full passives really have only agentless passives as category-changing rules and that the agent phrase in such a passive is really functioning as an instrumental.[18] That is, a sentence such as *John was kissed by Mary* might really be analyzed as saying that John was kissed (by someone or other) and that this came about by means of Mary. This of course doesn't quite mean the same thing as the sentence *Mary kissed John* actually means, but it's close.

If my hypothesis about these cases[18] is correct, then we are faced with the problem of finding a criterion for determining, in any particular case, whether a dative, a genitive, or an agentive phrase in a passive is playing the role of an argument of a verb (or noun) or the role of a modifier. While I feel certain that both kinds of roles are taken by these cases in natural languages at one time or another, I have no idea at present what such a criterion for particular cases might be. Perhaps one useful point which such cases do suggest, however, is that the number of grammatical roles played by noun phrases may greatly exceed the number of distinct morphological case forms employed by the language; hence there should be no embarrassment in principle to postulating two or more distinct rules which use the same case marking for NPs, nor an attempt in a theory such as Montague's to try to determine "the meaning" of the dative, or genitive, or instrumental case.

As I have suggested in discussing all three of these examples, it is tempting to speculate that this convergence between the case marking of a modifier and the case marking of an argument has its ultimate explanation in the stepwise nature of language acquisition. To make the assumptions behind these explanations explicit, we must suppose that at an early stage of language acquisition, there are certain graspable relations such as "x is the agent of an event y", "x is the instrument of event y", "x is an object connected with y in some salient way" and that these relations can be understood by the child at an early age when relations denoted by arbitrary two-place verbs and three-place verbs cannot be readily understood by the child. (I believe that the language-acquisition literature suggests that in general, learning of relational verbs comes later than that of non-relational verbs.) Thus, because the case marking of the arguments of verbs and nouns in the adult's speech corresponds with the case marking for these graspable relations between events and participants, the child is able to understand roughly what the adult says, even though his grammar is not isomorphic to the adult's grammar. Later, the child replaces this grammar with a more sophisticated one having the same overt syntactic form as before but a different semantics. The earlier simpler grammar was nevertheless an important bridge to this adult grammar.[19]

Note also that there is a parallel here between my suggestion about the two-step acquisition of certain datives, genitives and passive agent phrases, and my suggestion that lexical rules are first acquired as syntactic rules by children. In both cases, children are hypothesized to "outgrow" a syntactic analysis of certain constructions, replacing it with one that is more lexically complicated. In both cases, what is accomplished in the second step is greater expressive power. On the one hand, lexically derived words need not be limited in meaning to exactly what a lexical rule predicts for them, but can range over a variety of more specific meanings, which are individually learned. And in the case of three-place verbs, an arbitrary three-place relation can have a greater variety of meanings than can the combination of a two-place verb with a benefactive (instrumental, etc.) modifier of constant meaning. In both cases, this greater expressiveness would be achieved at the expense of a greater burden on lexical memory. Since I take it that there is evidence from language acquisition studies that children do at first use lexical rules like causative (Bowerman 1974) and noun compounding (Clark and Clark 1979) as if they were syntactic rules, I hope this parallel gives us further reason to hope that a like process is happening in the case of benefactives/datives, genitives, and passive agent phrases as well.[20]

This hypothesizing of a two-stage process of language acquisition to explain the apparent "confusion" of arguments and modifiers is of course highly speculative. If correct, however, it may explain why natural language has properties that have given rise to some long-standing problems in both linguistics and philosophy. In linguistics, the choice of analyzing certain NPs as modifiers versus arguments has appeared in the rivalry of case-grammar analyses (where relations like "agent", "experiencer", "goal", etc. are taken as primitives of the semantic interpretation of a sentence, apart from the meaning of its verb – a kind of "modifier" analysis) and the analyses of Generative Semantics and other theories (in which the correspondings NPs have these semantic associations in virtue of the meaning of the verb of the sentence). In the philosophy of language, this same question has arisen (albeit with slightly different examples) as the choice between treating adverbials as predicates of events (cf. Davidson's 1967 analysis of *with a knife* as such a predicate) or as additional argument places of verbs. (This latter dispute may of course be broader than the range of cases under discussion in this paper.)

The Ohio State University
Columbus

ACKNOWLEDGEMENT

I would like to thank Gerald Gazdar, Brian Joseph and Geoff Pullum for their very helpful comments on an earlier version of this paper; this is not to imply that they agree with all its conclusions.

NOTES

[1] As far as I can see, nothing prevents us from writing a grammar in this framework in which some constituents are ordered with respect to others, though their parts are not. This is of course what is needed for Latin, since clause boundaries cannot be violated by the "free" word order of Latin.

[2] A question which now arises is, just what does the phenogrammatical structure of an English-like language consist of? The obvious answer is of course that these structures are phrase-markers of the familiar sort, and it is easy enough to modify Montague's syntactic operations so that they produce such phrase markers instead of the strings which are produced by the operations in PTQ (cf. Partee 1975, 1979). However, once the distinction between tectogrammatical structure and phenogrammatical structure is countenanced, it seems to me to be a non-trivial task to demonstrate that phenogrammatical structures of English actually need to be anything other than, say, strings of morphemes interspersed with word boundaries and (perhaps various kinds of) morpheme boundaries. Note that most of the purposes for which reference to phrase structure is needed (e.g. behavior of conjunction, semantic intuitions about constituent structure, association of an appropriate constituent structure with each reading of an ambiguous sentence) would seem to be satisfied by tectogrammatical structure alone. Also, agreement phenomena can be handled in a rich system of syntactic subcategories such as Gazdar's (in this volume) without rules that make reference to the internal structure of phrases.

[3] This simple description of the English operation F_3 is for illustrative purpose only and, as it stands, gives an apparently inadequate treatment of the constituent structure of the to-phrase (though cf. note 2). One way of remedying this deficiency is to allow syntactic operations to "build" phrase structures, following the suggestions of Partee (1975, 1979). The operation F_3 would then produce $[_{IV}\alpha[_{PP}[_P to]\beta']]$, where β' is the accusative form of β. Another attractive alternative is Gazdar's proposal (in this volume) to treat prepositional phrases as syntactically subcategorized by the "case marking" prepositions that occur as their heads, e.g., there would be categories $PP_{[+to]}$, $PP_{[+for]}$, etc., the syntactic rules assuring that only the appropriate preposition to, for, etc. could be inserted in each such phrase. Though technically basic expressions, such prepositions would be semantically vacuous (i.e. translating in each case as $\lambda \mathscr{P}[\mathscr{P}]$). In other words, the meanings of these prepositional phrases are simply the meanings of their constituent noun phrases. The syntactic rule S3 for English would then simply combine, via simple concatenation, a $TV/PP_{[+to]}$ with a $PP_{[+to]}$ to give a TV, thereby deviating in a trivial way from the official universal syntactic form (though not from the universal semantic form).

[4] A system of grammatical relations such as I have described here is an "optimal" and maximally simple one. In many languages, further syntactic complexity is introduced in that not all verbs of the same logical type are treated syntactically alike. For example, in some languages (German) there are some two-place predicates that take an object in the accusative

case while other two-place predicates take an object in the dative case. In such instances, distinct syntactic subcategories will have to be introduced that correspond to the same logical type. For German, transitive verbs might be split into a category IV/T for accusative-object verbs, a category IV//T for dative-object verbs, and a category IV///T for genitive-object verbs. Distinct syntactic rules having the same interpretation would combine these with their objects, the corresponding operations introducing the appropriate case for each subcategory. (For reasons why dative-object transitive verbs might tend to form a semantically unified class and why the "semantic role" played by such dative objects might tend to be similar to that played by the indirect objects of three-place verbs, see section 9.)

[5] Though I have here given specific criteria for the argument/modifier distinction, primarily for the sake of concreteness at this point in the paper, I definitely believe that further consideration and perhaps revision of these is in order. For example, the entailment test will tell us that *buy* and *sell* are in fact four-place verbs, for the truth of *x bought y* entails not only the existence of a specific buyer *x* and purchased object *y* but also a seller *z* and a sum of money (or other item bartered) *w*. Yet this is a somewhat suspicious result, as it seems hard to justify the existence of a syntactic paradigm of four-place verbs in English on any other grounds. More importantly, the general problem which is the subject of §9 is a major barrier to the establishment of a once-and-for-all criterion for distinguishing arguments from modifiers.

[6] Incidentally, this construction has been viewed by a number of linguists, including Trithart, as a problem for the theory of RG for two reasons. First, it is supposed to follow in RG that if a benefactive NP appears as a direct object, then it must have been promoted to that position by a relation-changing rule and must have displaced the original direct object. The trouble is, there is no grammatical sentence in most Bantu languages in which this putative original structure surfaces – that is, a surface structure in which the benefactive NP appears after some preposition and the "semantic" direct object appears as surface direct object. To see more clearly what this putative source would look like, compare this situation with that of the promotion of indirect object to direct object in Bantu, in which the putative source structure does surface. That is, the supposedly most basic form of IO sentences in Chichewa is exemplified by (i)–where the IO appears at the end of the sentence preceded by the preposition *kwa*, and the "promoted" form of the sentence is shown in (ii);

(i)	Jóni	a-	ná-	(zí)	pats-	a	n-thóchí	kwa	mái	wá-ké
	John	he	past	(them)	give	indic	bananas	to	mother	his

"John gave the bananas to his mother"

(ii)	Jóni	a-	ná	pats-	a	a-mái	á-ke	n-thóchí
	John	he	past	give	indic	mother	his	bananas

"John gave his mother the bananas"

here the original IO appears as DO, the other NP is at the end of the sentence and the verb has no applied affix in Chichewa in this case (though it does, say, in the exact translation of this example in Shona, another Bantu language). The problem is, for benefactive sentences, that there is no example corresponding to the form of (i). Under the proposal I am making, these facts can be described simply by allowing rule S13 to be the only rule which introduces NPs with benefactive meaning into a sentence; there is no separate rule such as S4 (in (15)) for English that introduces them synatactically as modifiers of IVs.

A second problem for RG in these languages is that in the "applied" forms of sentences with benefactives, indirect objects, locatives, and instrumental – that is, the forms of sentences in which these NPs have allegedly been promoted to DO – it is possible to passivize not only the "new" DO but the original DO as well. Thus corresponding to the example in (iii), there are the two passive forms in (iv) and (v).

(iii)   Catherine a-   ná-   (wa-) phik- in-   a   ǎ-ná   n-síma
         Catherine she past them   cook   apl indic children nsima
         "Catherine cooked nsima for the children"

(iv)   á-ná   a-   ná   (yi) phik- ir- idw- a   n-síme
         children they past (it) cook   apl. pass indic nsíma
         "The children were cooked nsima"

(v)   n-síma yi-ná   (yi) phik- ir- idw- a   ǎ-na
         nsima it past (it) cook   apl. pass indic children
         "Nsima was cooked (for) the children"

In RG, this situation conflicts with either the Stratal Uniqueness Law or the Chômage Condition. If we try to maintain in relational grammar that both NPs are DOs at the time passive applies, the Stratal Uniqueness Condition, which states that only one NP can occupy a single grammatical relation at a given stage of the derivation, is violated. If on the other hand we maintain that the second NP after the verb is a demoted DO, then the Chômage Condition is violated in examples like (v), since a NP that is "en chômage" is not supposed to be advanceable by Passive or by another advancement rule. But as I mentioned at the beginning of this paper, there does not seem to be any place for the notion of a chômeur in the theory I am trying to develop; rather, the NPs that are treated as "en chômage" in RG are here treated as NPs which bear grammatical relations to the verb other than Subject, DO or IO. This is an advantage in the present case, because it seems that under the assumptions I am working with the most natural way to account for these additional forms of passive sentences in Bantu languages is to suppose that there is a second passive rule here, a rule that passivizes a TV/T and turns it into a TV:

(vi)   S14: $\langle F_{14}, \langle TV/T \rangle, IV//T \rangle$ (2nd passive rule)
         Semantic Operation: $\lambda z \lambda y (\exists x)[\alpha'(y)(z)(x)]$
         Chichewa: $F_{14}(\alpha) = \alpha + idw$

The derivation is illustrated by the tree in (vii).

(vii)

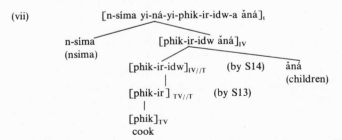

"Nsima was cooked (for) the children"

Semantically, this rule is interpreted by a semantic operation which interprets the NP following *ni* as the subject of the original verb, the noun phrase which will be added immediately after the new verb as the direct object of the original verb, and the subject NP as the benefactive, locative or instrumental, depending on the kind of "applied" verb that is being passivized.

Note that the framework I am discussing will not permit us to adopt an alternative solution sometimes suggested for this situation by critics of relational grammar – namely, to analyze sentences such as (iii) as having two direct objects. Rather, it follows from the fundamental assumption with which I began this paper, namely that multi-argument verbs always combine with their arguments one at a time, that only one term can be a direct object. Thus the Stratal Uniqueness law of RG is an automatic consequence of the approach I am taking (as are some other laws of RG, such as the Oblique Law and the Final I Law). However, there is some independent evidence in Chichewa (though not apparently in Kinyarwanda) that the two NPs are not treated exactly alike by the grammar. Only the first NP after the verb, i.e. the one I am treating as the true direct object, can be reflexivized by the subject NP in Chichewa (cf. Trithart (1979, 7)). Interestingly enough, Postal and Perlmutter (to appear) have responded to the challenge presented by this kind of data by relaxing the conditions on chômeurs; in sentences like that in (iii) they analyze the displaced DO as an IO rather than as a chômeur; then the passive form (v) is accounted for by postulating a rule advancing a III to I; note that this is quite parallel to what I have suggested for this case. Weakening the notion of chômeur in this way of course reduces the role played by this concept significantly in their theory, but, as will already be clear, I think this is a step in the right direction.

[7] What at first blush appears to be a distinct alternative to a "Right Wrap" analysis for the Verb-plus-Object cases in English is presented in Gazdar and Sag (to appear). Their approach uses only phrase-structure rules (i.e. rules of simple concatenation) and thus cannot treat Right Wrap as a syntactic operation. However, theirs is in fact an instance of a Right Wrap analysis nevertheless, for it in effect treats Right Wrap as a syntactic "metarule." Gazdar foresees a possible goal of stating universal constraints on meta-rules by limiting them to a few operations such as Right Wrap. Thus there is apparently no real conflict between my approach and Gazdar's on this point, and his program in general seems to be compatible with the proposals of this paper.

[8] This claim must be carefully hedged in certain ways. If the claim that category-changing rules are structure preserving is to have content, we must suppose that in general, a category-changing rule places a verb into a category that already exists independently in the grammar. Consider for example the rule of Raising to Object Position and suppose that as a category-changing rule this is formulated as a rule which shifts a verb from IV/t into TV/IV. If the category TV/IV is already employed in the grammar and has lexical members (in this case, the so-called "Equi" verbs like *force* and *persuade*), it follows from the fact the syntactic rules are set up to give sentences containing basic TV/IV verbs a certain form (e.g. *John persuades Bill to be careful*) that sentences with verbs "raised" into the category TV/IV will have a parallel form (e.g. *John believes Bill to be careful*), i.e. it follows that Raising to Object position is "structure-preserving." If on the other hand we allowed this rule to shift verbs not into TV/IV but rather into an entirely new category TV//IV, then no parallelism whatsoever would follow automatically, for we could write new rules for the category TV//IV that led to an entirely different form from those existing for the category TV/IV.

It should also be noted that the "full passive" verb phrases produced by the rule S7 in this paper are not predicted to have a "structure preserving" internal structure, i.e. the elsewhere attested form of verb phrase plus pre-positional phrase. (It would have been possible, for example, to write this rule in such a way as to place the agent NP before the verb). As explained in §9, I would attribute the form of these passive phrases not to any general constraint of grammatical theory but to the hypothesis that English full passives are a historical reanalysis of an agentless passive combined with an instrumental prepositional phrase (a reanalysis that is probably recapitulated "ontogenetically" in the course of language acquisition). On the other hand, passive verb phrases are predicted to be "structure-preserving" with respect to external constituents (e.g. placement and marking of the subject NP, verb agreement, etc.), simply because both passive rules give output expressions of category IV.

[9] It is apparently not the case that all languages mark passives by an affix on the verb, however. Permutter and Postal (1977) cite full passive sentences from Mandarin and Achenese with no passive affix on the verb, it being rather the presence of a morpheme (glossed as "by") accompanying the agent NP that distinguishes these sentences from actives. While the full implications of such cases cannot be assessed without examination of a wider range of data, it is perhaps pertinent to note that the cases cited are compatible with the particular formulation of the full passive rule given in (20), which takes a TV and an NP (to serve as agent) to form a passive verb phrase. That is, this rule merely predicts that the application of Passive will be indicated (by affix, word order, etc.) somewhere within the verb phrase, not necessarily on the verb itself. The fact that the verb is the most common locus of the passive marker within the VP is, in any case, probably best accounted for by a theory of the "head of " a phrase, the head being that word within a constituent to which bound morphemes are attached to signal the application of a rule to the phrase as a whole. (However, it is not clear to me that the full passive rule as stated in (20) is correct for all languages; cf. the discussion of agent phrases in §9.)

[10] An interesting question which this observation raises is why some relation-changing operations are accompanied by morphological marking on the verb and others are not. Passive seems always to be morphologically marked, for example, while Raising is not marked in any language I know. But I think there is a fairly clear explanation for this in terms of avoidance of ambiguity. That a verb has undergone Raising to Object Position will always be apparent from the appearance of the complement or complements that follow: if it hasn't undergone raising there will follow a full sentence with subject NP in nominative case and inflected verb; if Raising has taken place, there will instead be an NP in accusative case and an infinitive. (These comments are intended to apply only to Raising to Object as it is found in English and similar languages, not "Copy-Raising" as occurs in Greek – cf. Joseph (1980).)

Passive is a different situation. Let me now restrict attention to the agentless passive since (as explained in section 9) I regard it as a more basic relation-changing rule than the agentive passive. As far as I know, every language that has this relation-reducing operation also has the other relation-reducing operation as well – that is, Object "Deletion". If one of these two operations were not marked morphologically, then a sentence like "John hunted" would be ambiguous between the reading "John hunted someone or something" and "Someone or something hunted John", a rather intolerable ambiguity. Now it seems to be a universal (though *not* one predicted by this analysis) that the relation-reducing operation that omits the object NP is the "unmarked" case and the relation-reducing operation that omits the (underlying) subject is the marked case. Dative shift, on the other hand, is morphologically marked on the verb in some languages – such as Bahasa Indonesia (Chung, 1976) – but not in others, like English. Because of the way this construction arose historically in English, the dative sentence where Dative Shift has not taken place is distinguished by the preposition *to* before the indirect object, while the shifted sentence is not, so no ambiguity results. An ambiguity introduced by a Dative Shift rule is a relatively tolerable one, in any case, because of the "animacy asymmetry" between direct and indirect objects (cf. Hawkinson and Hyman, 1974). The meanings of most three-place verbs in most languages is such that the "semantic" indirect object will always be animate and usually human, while the "semantic" direct object will usually be non-human, often inanimate.

[11] In assessing the validity of this prediction, it is important to distinguish between the purpose clauses Bach is discussing and other superficially similar infinitival constructions. e.g. extraposed infinitival relative clauses; cf. Bach (this volume) for these distinctions.

[12] It may be noted that the relation-expanding analysis makes many of the same predictions as the Clause Reduction/Clause Union analysis of Perlmutter and Aissen (1976) and Aissen (1977); since a causative verb is formed before any arguments are added, this analysis treats all "surface" NPs as *dependent on* (in their terms) the matrix verb. For those familiar with their articles, it may help to sketch the treatment of Clause Reduction and Union in the present approach. A Spanish example in which no clause reduction applies would be built up as in (i):

(i)

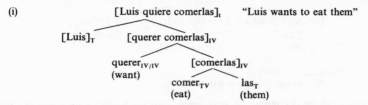

Clause Reduction would be a rule that combines an infinitive complement verb directly with a transitive verb to form a compound transitive verb, i.e. it combines α of IV/IV with β of TV to form $\alpha\beta$ of TV, translating as $\lambda\mathscr{P}[\alpha'(\beta'(\mathscr{P}))]$ Since some but not all IV/IV verbs in Spanish participate in Clause Reduction, it should be assumed that this is a lexical rule. The derivation of the Clause Reduction example corresponding to (i) is then (ii)

(ii)

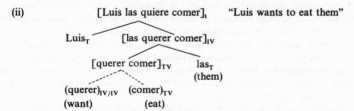

Here, the dotted lines indicate the part of the derivation that is lexical; note that here the object pronoun *las* cliticizes to the compound verb *querer comer*, not the complement verb *comer* as before.

Similarly, the ordinary "Subject-to Object Raising" derivation with *dejar* ("let") is illustrated in (iii)

(iii)

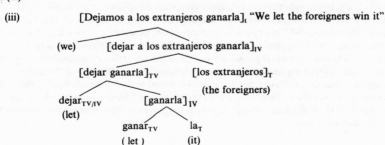

Clause union is now treated as a (lexical) rule compounding (in this case) a verb α, such as *dejar*, of category TV/IV with a transitive verb β to give a derived three-place verb, i.e. a verb of category TV/T; the translation rule $\lambda\mathcal{P}\lambda\mathcal{Q}[\alpha'(\hat{\ }[\beta'(\mathcal{P})])(\mathcal{Q})]$ insures that the indirect object of the new verb will be interpreted as the semantic "subject" of the complement TV, while the object of the new verb is interpreted as the complement verb's semantic "object."

(iv)

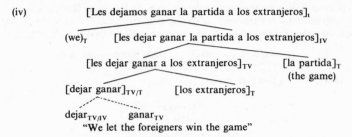

"We let the foreigners win the game"

The proclitic *les* in the TV-phrase *les dejar ganar a los extranjeros* is the result of Clitic Doubling, i.e. a pronominal "copy" of the NP *los extranjeros*; its form is *les* (Dative 3rd person plural) rather than *los* (Accusative 3rd person plural) because it copies the grammatical indirect object of the compound verb *dejar ganar*. Though many details of Clause Reduction and Clause Union remain to be described, I expect that the method sketched here can be extended to treat them in a reasonably natural way.

[13] Discussions of principles like (i)–(iii) can be found in the early literature on Case Grammar (Fillmore 1968), where the problem is viewed as one of deciding which of the underlying case roles (Agent, Experiencer, Goal, etc.) will appear as surface subject.

[14] While I believe that Dixon has shown beyond reasonable doubt that Dyirbal really is a "deep ergative" language in the sense defined in this paper, I am aware that there are those who are skeptical of Dixon's claim that there are "deep ergative" languages. To them, I would point out that nothing in the general account of grammatical relations presented in this paper hinges on the existence of "deep ergative" languages.

[15] My use of "subject" thus turns out to be almost exactly what Dixon (1979) refers to as "syntactic pivot". What I am calling "deep ergative" languages are what Dixon calls languages with "S/O syntactic pivot", and what I am calling non-ergative and "surface ergative" languages are those that Dixon classifies as having a "S/A syntactic pivot." By "subject", Dixon refers to those NPs selected by (i)–(iii) (in non-ergative languages). I do not mean to suggest that Dixon's notion of subject (i.e. "agent") plays no role in syntax, but simply that it plays less of a role in syntax than the relational grammarians assume; in particular, it plays no role in the universal statement of relation-changing rules. As an example of the role that agent does play, the "missing NP" in imperative sentences must necessarily be an agent; this means that the syntax and semantics of the imperative rule must be different in deep ergative languages and in non-ergative languages, as must the semantics of the complements of verbs like *try* and *intend* (cf. Schmerling 1979). Dixon's "subject" may indeed have the status of a language universal in some sense, but it is quite a different sort of universal from "subject" in my sense (= Dixon's pivot). Dixon provides a thorough and I believe insightful discussion of all the manifestations that ergativity has in various languages, and I believe his conclusions are not in conflict with mine.

[16] Rather tantalizing indirect evidence that this scenario might be correct for English comes from Gazdar's (1980) arguments that even "adult" English possesses a relative clause formation rule that forms 'subject' relatives (e.g. *man who loves Mary*) directly from an IV *love Mary*) without variable binding, in addition to the variable binding relative clause rule that forms relatives on non-subject position (*man who Mary loves*); parallel evidence for the two sorts of rules can be found in French and in Swedish (Gazdar 1980, note 22).

[17] The suggestion that agentless passives are more syntactically basic than agentive passives and that agent phrases are instrumental modifiers has been made for various languages on various grounds, of course; see for example Hoard (1979) for evidence for this analysis in Quileute, a Northwest American Indian language.

[18] There may be other instances of case convergence besides these three. For example, the Dative case converges with the locative or directional case in some languages, and indeed, there is some sense or other in which the indirect object of a verb of giving (*John gave the book to Mary*) represents a "location" at which the object given ends up. So-called "localist" case theories of semantics (Anderson 1971) exploit this kind of convergence by attempting to reduce all non-locative case relations to "abstract" locative cases. It should be clear by now why I think this is only a partially correct interpretation of such case convergences.

[19] There may be other cases where certain properties of natural language are ultimately explained by the need for children to be able to acquire it via simpler stages. One such case, suggested by Dowty (1975a) and noticed independently by William Ladusaw (personal communication) may involve the semantics of noun phrases. When one compares first-order predicate logic with the treatment of NPs in Montague's PTQ, the semantics of English NPs seems an unnecessary complication – wouldn't English have been a simpler language if it had merely a category of names (of type e), a category of predicates, and the familiar quantifiers of first-order predicate logic? But note that children first acquire names and definite NPs and that the phenomena that demand the higher-order analysis of NPs (indefinites, relative clauses, and pronouns as bound variables) appear rather late in the language acquisition process. Perhaps children first acquire a grammar of English in which the category NP uniformly has denotations of type e, only later replacing this with a higher-order analysis of NPs of the same superficial syntactic form. Thus the unified (if clumsy) category NP of adult English has the virtue of serving as a satisfactory model for a first-order child's grammar, enabling adult and child to communicate effectively over a limited range of sentences.

[20] I should be careful to add that I am not to be construed as saying that a formal syntax and semantics for natural languages has to account for the psychological processes of language, nor that, in general, formal semantics should take language acquisition data into account before proceeding. I am anxious to keep the two tasks of formal semantics and of psycholinguistics separate. All I am suggesting is that in the formal theory of natural languages, there may arise certain details of the form of grammars that are never entirely explained in the formal theory itself, but are only explained by certain features of language acquisition situations.

REFERENCES

Aissen, Judith (1974) 'Verb Raising' *Linguistic Inquiry* 5, 325–366.

Aissen, Judith (1977) 'The Interaction of Clause Reduction and Causative Clause Union in Spanish,' *NELS* 7, 1–18.

Aissen, Judith and David M. Perlmutter (1976) 'Clause Reduction in Spanish,' *BLS* 2, 1–30.

Anderson, John M. (1971) *The Grammar of Case: Towards a Localist Theory*, Cambridge University Press.

Anderson, S. and S. Chung (1977) 'On Grammatical Relations and Clause Structure in Verb-Initial Languages,' *Syntax and Semantics* 8, ed. Sadock and Cole, Academic Press.

Andrews, Avery (this volume) 'A Lexically-Based Analysis of Case Marking and the Complement S Stem in Icelandic.'

Bach, Emmon (1979) 'Control in Montague Grammar,' *Linguistic Inquiry* 10, 515–533.

Bach, Emmon (1980) 'In Defense of Passive,' *Linguistics and Philosophy* 3, 297–342.

Bach, Emmon (ms.) 'Tenses and Aspects as Functions on Verb Phrases,' to appear in the proceedings of the 1979 Stuttgart Conference on Tense and Aspect.

Bach, Emmon (this volume) 'Purpose Clauses and Control.'

Bach, Emmon and Barbara Partee (1980) 'Anaphora and Semantic Structure,' *Papers from the Parasession on Anaphora*, CLS 16.

Bowerman, Melissa (1974) 'Learning the Structure of Causative Verbs: A Study in the Relationship of Cognitive, Semantic and Syntactic Development,' *Papers and Reports on Child Language Development* 8, Stanford University.

Bresnan, Joan (1978) 'A Realistic Transformational Grammar,' in Halle, Bresnan, and Miller, eds., *Linguistic Theory and Psychological Reality*, MIT Press.

Chomsky, Noam (1965) *Aspects of the Theory of Syntax*, MIT Press.

Chung, Sandra (1976) 'An Object-Creating Rule in Bahasa Indonesia,' *Linguistic Inquiry* 7, 41–89.

Clark, Eve and Herbert Clark (1979) 'When Nouns Surface as Verbs,' *Language* 55, 767–811.

Cooper, Robin (ms.) 'Montague's Syntax,' Paper presented at the 1979 Milwaukee Conference on theories of Syntax.

Curry, H. B. (1963) 'Some Logical Aspects of Grammatical Structure,' *Structure of Language and Its Mathematical Aspects: Proceedings of the Twelfth Symposium in Applied Mathematics*, ed. Jakobson, American Mathematical Society, pp. 56–68.

Dahl, Östen (1977) 'Operational Grammars,' *Logic, Pragmatics and Grammar*, ed. Dahl, Dept. of Linguistics, University of Göteborg, pp. 71–116.

Davidson, Donald (1967) 'The Logical Form of Action Sentences,' *The Logic of Decision and Action*, ed. Rescher, University of Pittsburgh Press.

Dixon, R. M. W. (1972) *The Dyirbal Language of North Queensland, Cambridge Studies in Linguistics* 9, Cambridge University Press.

Dixon, R. M. W. (1979) 'Ergativity,' *Language* 55, 59–138.

Dowty, David R. (1975a) 'Toward a Theory of Word formation for Montague Grammar,' *Texas Linguistic Forum* 2, ed. Schmerling, University of Texas Department of Linguistics, 69–96.

Dowty, David R. (1975b) 'The Montague-Adjukiewicz System of Syntactic-Semantic Categories as a Linguistic Theory of Syntactic Category and Grammatical Relation,' paper presented at the 1975 annual meeting of the Linguistic Society of America.

Dowty, David R. (1978) 'Governed Transformations as Lexical Rules in a Montague Grammar,' *Linguistic Inquiry* 9, 393–426.

Dowty, David R. (1979a) 'Dative "Movement" and Thomason's Extensions of Montague Grammar,' *Linguistics, Philosophy and Montague Grammar*, ed. Davis and Mithun. 152–223.

Dowty, David R. (1979b) *Word Meaning and Montague Grammar*, D. Reidel, Dordrecht.

Dowty, David R., Robert Wall, and Stanley Peters (1980) *Introduction to Montague Semantics*, D. Reidel, Dordrecht.

Emonds, Joseph (1976) *A Transformational Approach to English Syntax*, Academic Press.

Fillmore, Charles (1968) 'The Case for Case,' *Universals in Linguistic Theory*, ed. Bach and Harms, Holt, Rinehart and Winston.

Gazdar, Gerald (1980) 'Unbounded Dependencies and Coordinate Structure,' to appear in *Linguistic Inquiry*.

Gazdar, Gerald, and Ivan Sag (to appear) 'Phantom Categories in Phrase Structure Grammar,' to appear in the proceedings of the 1980 Amsterdam Conference on Formal Methods in Linguistics.

Gazdar, Gerald (this volume) 'Phrase Structure Grammar.'

Greenberg, Joseph (1963) 'Some Universals of Grammar with Particular Reference to the Order of Elements,' *Universals of Language*, ed. Greenberg, MIT Press, 58–80.

Hawkinson, Annie and Larry Hyman (1974) 'Hierarchies of Natural Topic in Shona,' *Studies in African Linguistics* **5**, 147–170.

Hoard, James E. (1979) 'On the Semantic Representation of Oblique Complements,' *Language* **55**, 319–332.

Jacobson, Pauline (this volume), 'Evidence for Gaps.'

Johnson, David E. and Paul M. Postal (forthcoming) *Arc Pair Grammar*, Princeton University Press, Princeton, NJ.

Johnson, Marion (1980) 'Ergativity in Inuktitut (Eskimo), in Montague Grammar, and in Relational Grammar,' Indiana University Linguistics Club.

Joseph, Brian D. (1980) 'Linguistic Universals and Syntactic Change,' *Language* **56**, 345–370.

Keenan, Edward, and Bernard Comrie (1977) 'Noun Phrase Accessibility and Universal Grammar,' *Linguistic Inquiry* **8**, 62–100.

Montague, Richard (1970) 'Universal Grammar,' *Theoria* **36**, 373–398.

Montague, Richard (1973) 'On the Proper Treatment of Quantification in Ordinary English,' *Approaches to Natural Language*, ed. Hintikka et. al. D. Reidel, Dordrecht.

Partee, Barbara (1975) 'Montague Grammar and Transformational Grammar,' *Linguistic Inquiry* **6**, 203–300.

Partee, Barbara (1979) 'Montague Grammar and the Well-Formedness Constraint,' in F. Heny and H. Schnelle, eds., *Syntax and Semantics* **10**: *Papers from the Third Groningen Round Table*, New York, Academic Press.

Perlmutter, David M. (this volume) 'Syntactic representation, syntactic levels, and the notion of subject.'

Perlmutter, David and Paul Postal (1977) 'Toward a Universal Characterization of Passivization,' *Proceedings of the Third Annual Meeting of the Berkeley Linguistic Society*, ed. Whistler et al., Berkeley Linguistics Society, pp. 393–417.

Perlmutter, David and Paul Postal (to appear) 'Some Proposed Laws of Basic Clause Structure,' to appear in *Studies in Relational Grammar* **1**, ed. Perlmutter.

Postal, P. M. (this volume) 'Some Arc Pair Grammar Descriptions.'

Sag, Ivan (this volume) 'A Semantic Theory of "NP Movement" Dependencies.'

Schmerling, Susan (1979) 'A Categorial Analysis of Dyirbal Ergativity,' *Texas Linguistic Forum* **13**, ed. Smith and Schmerling, 96–112.

Schoenfinkel, Moses (1924) 'Über die Bausteine der Mathematischen Logik,' *Mathematische Annalen* **92**, 305–316.

Taraldsen, Knut Tarald (1976) 'On the Cyclicity of Verb Raising,' *Proceedings of the Twelfth Regional Meeting of the Chicago Linguistic Society*, pp. 617–627.

Thomason, Richmond (1974) 'Some Complement Constructions in Montague Grammar,' *Proceedings of the Tenth Regional Meeting of the Chicago Linguistic Society*, pp. 712–722.

Thomason, Richmond (1976) 'Some Extensions of Montague Grammar', *Montague Grammar*, ed. Partee, Academic Press, pp. 77–117.

Thomason, Richmond (ms.) 'Montague Grammar and Some Transformations,' University of Pittsburgh ms., dated May 1976.

Trithart, Lee (1979) 'Topicality: An Alternative to the Relational View of Bantu Passive,' *Studies in African Linguistics* 10, 1–30.

Vennemann, Theo (1972) 'Explanation in Syntax,' *Syntax and Semantics* 2, ed. Kimball, Academic Press, 1–50.

Zimmer, Karl (1976) 'Some Constraints on Turkish Causativization,' in M. Shibatani, ed., *Syntax and Semantics* 6: *The Grammar of Causative Constructions*, pp. 399–412.

GERALD GAZDAR

PHRASE STRUCTURE GRAMMAR*

1. INTRODUCTION

> As far as the alleged "return to structuralism" is concerned: first of all, suppose that were true – fine! It often happens that hypotheses in the natural sciences are abandoned at a certain period because they are inadequate, but are then reconstructed later when a higher level of comprehension has been attained.
>
> Chomsky (1979: p. 197)

Transformational grammars for natural languages, as currently envisaged, deploy a large number of devices: complex symbols, base rules, rule schemata, lexical insertion rules, lexical redundancy rules, movement rules, coindexing procedures, binding conventions, local and nonlocal filters, case marking conventions, feature percolation, constraints on movement, and so on. The mathematical properties of the resulting baroque systems are almost entirely unknown: we are ignorant, for example, as to whether ungrammaticality with respect to such grammars is decidable, i.e. given an arbitrary string on the terminal vocabulary, no way is known of proving that that string is not generated by the grammar. In this situation, claims by grammarians to the effect that such and such a string of words cannot be generated by their grammar merely reflect their intuitions about the apparatus they are using. These intuitions cannot be verified at present and may indeed by unverifiable in principle (i.e. if the class of grammars permitted under universal grammar generate nonrecursive sets).

Much work has been devoted in recent years to the question of constraining the class of available grammars for natural languages. But, with honourable exceptions (e.g. Janssen, Kok, and Meertens 1977, Lapointe 1977, Pelletier 1980, Wasow 1978), this work has been free of serious mathematical content. In view of this fact, claims in the current literature implying that one variant of TG (say one with filters but no obligatory rules) is more restrictive than another (say one with obligatory rules but no filters) are about as sensible as claims to the effect that Turing machines which employ narrow grey tape are less powerful than ones employing wide orange tape.

131

P. Jacobson and G. K. Pullum (eds.), The Nature of Syntactic Representation, 131–186.
Copyright © 1982 by D. Reidel Publishing Company.

The strongest way to constraint a component is to eliminate it. In this paper I shall outline a type of generative grammar that exploits several of the resources of transformational grammar (e.g. phrase structure rules, rule schemata, complex symbols, feature conventions) but which, crucially, does not employ either transformations or coindexing devices. This type of generative grammar is provably capable of generating only the context-free (CF) languages and is, to all intents and purposes, simply a variant of CF phrase structure grammar.

One of the metatheoretical motivations for adopting the present approach is that the formal properties of the languages that can be generated, and of the grammars doing the generating, are relatively well understood given the considerable body of mathematical work that now exists on CF languages and grammars (see Book 1973 for a concise survey). Another motivation is that if we only allow ourselves to employ apparatus restricted to CF generative capacity, then we are making a very strong universal claim about the properties of natural languages, one which is presently unfalsified (see Pullum & Gazdar (1981) for discussion).[1] Whereas, if we continue to use movement and deletion rules, non-local filters, and/or coindexing devices, then we will be working within a relatively unconstrained theoretical framework or at best one about whose constrainedness we know very little, and we would consequently only be committed to relatively weak universal claims.

In a recent paper, Levelt makes the following observation: 'if it is the Aspects-formalism that constitutes the child's innate knowledge of natural languages, then given the Peters and Ritchie results (1973) and Gold's (1967) technical definition of learnability, natural languages are unlearnable, since the class is r.e.' (1979: 6). He points out that, given the unacceptability of this conclusion, there are only two routes out of the dilemma it poses: either one considers alternative technical definitions of learnability or else one reduces the class of grammars permitted. He distinguishes two potential ways of doing the latter: 'the intensional way consists of defining "possible grammar" in such a way that the class is small. Going from r.e. languages to decidable to context-free would be such a step' (1979: 8). The extensional way consists simply of stipulating the class of r.e. set-inducing grammars permitted by universal grammar, for example by giving a finite list of such permissible grammars. Levelt then shows that, given Gold's learnability definition, the extensional way provides no solution to the dilemma posed above: 'reducing the cardinality of the class, or using some evaluation measure, are in themselves insufficient to guarantee learnability as long as the grammars generate r.e. languages: the child will never know how to exclude a grammar' (1979: 11). In particular, Levelt is able to prove that the finiteness, or otherwise, of the cardinality of the set of possible natural language grammars is irrelevant to learnability if the languages they characterize are nonrecursive. He shows that even in the limiting case of there being only two possible grammars for the learner to choose between, the choice cannot be made on the basis of some finite set of well-formed strings of the language unless the two languages are completely disjoint.

Gold (1967) defined "informant presentation" learnability in terms of the possibility of defining an algorithm that could map finite sets of ⟨ string, grammaticality judgement⟩ pairs into grammars. He showed, inter alia, that it was in principle possible to construct such algorithms for CF languages. A corollary of his result is that is is possible, in principle, to construct algorithms to map finite sets of ⟨ tree, grammaticality judgement⟩ pairs into grammars when the trees involved are induced by CF-PSGs (this follows since the dendro language of a CF-PSG is itself a CF language).[2] As it happens, the computer science literature now contains usable algorithms that, in effect, achieve such a mapping. These algorithms (see Fu and Booth (1975) and Levine (1979) for discussion and references) map into frontier-to-root finite state tree automata, rather than CF-PSGs as such. However, for every CF-PSG there exists a finite tree automaton that admits exactly the tree set induced by the grammar (Thatcher 1973). And given the tree automaton for a CF tree set, it is straightforward to construct the CF-PSG for that tree set. These algorithms cannot be applied to non-CF languages because non-CF languages cannot be analysed by a frontier-to-root finite state tree automaton.[3]

The sentences of a natural language can be parsed. We do it all the time. Furthermore, we do it very fast (see Marslen–Wilson 1973, for relevant psycholinguistic evidence). But 'for transformational grammars, it is not known that processing time can be any less than a doubly exponential function of sentence length' (Peters 1979). Transformational grammars thus fail to provide even the beginnings of an explanation for one of the most important, and most neglected, facts about natural languages: parsing is easy and quick. Sentences of a context-free language are provably parsable in a time which is, at worst, proportional to less than the cube of the sentence length (Valiant 1975, Graham 1976). Many context free languages, even ambiguous ones, are provably parsable in *linear* time (Earley 1970: 99). These parsability results, and the avenues of research that they open up, provide a significant computational motivation for constraining natural language grammars to CF generative capacity (see Sheil 1976, Kaplan 1978, for more detailed discussion).

Nevertheless, as Joshi, Levy and Yueh (forthcoming) pertinently remark, 'context-freeness should not be used as a justification for poor style'. If to do things exclusively by direct phrase structure generation was to lead inevitably to aesthetic disaster (re. simplicity, economy, generality, empirical motivation, etc), whilst competing transformational analyses were paragons of elegance and enlightenment, then one might reasonably feel inclined to reject the former in favour of the latter. However, in latter sections of this paper I shall be arguing implicitly that phrase structure analyses can be at least as elegant, general, etc., and no more prone to counterexamples, than the alternative transformational accounts of the same phenomena.

2. COMPLEX SYMBOLS

Harman (1963) deserves the credit for first seeing the potential of PSGs incorporating complex symbols.[4] The use of a finite set of complex symbols (however constructed) in a PSG, in place of the traditional finite set of monadic symbols, leaves weak generative capacity unchanged: a CF-PSG employing complex symbols will only be able to generate CFLs. Furthermore, if we take grammars that induce isomorphic structural descriptions to be strongly equivalent, then the use of complex symbols has no effect on strong generative capacity either: every grammar employing complex symbols generates a tree-set that is isomorphic to the tree-set generated by some CF-PSG not employing complex symbols, and conversely.

In the light of these self-evident and trivial observations, it is surprising that Chomsky once saw fit to claim that 'a system...that makes use of complex symbols is no longer a phrase structure grammar..., but rather is more properly regarded as a kind of transformational grammar' (1965:98). Transformational grammars can move arbitrarily large constituents about, delete constituents under identity, substitute one morpheme for another, restructure trees, allow one to make a deep structure/surface distinction, and generate any recursively enumerable set you care to think of. Phrase structure grammars which employ complex symbols can do none of these things, so it is hard to see why one would want to refer to such grammars as 'transformational'.

For the most part, the complex symbol system adopted in this paper is simply a variant of the type that has become standard in recent TG. I assume a two-bar $\bar{X}$ system[5] that distinguishes between $\bar{\bar{X}}, \bar{X}$, and X (lexical) categories, and so one component of a complex symbol must provide an indication of this distinction. The exact manner of this indication is immaterial; I shall stipulate that it takes the form of an integer as the first member of an ordered pair (following Bresnan 1976b). The other component of a complex symbol will be a feature bundle encoding syntactic category, subcategorization, and morphosyntactic and morphological information.[6] I shall use a familiar notation for such familiar objects. For example, $\bar{\bar{N}}[+ \text{PRO}, - \text{SNG}]$ represents the phrasal $[+ N, - V]$ plural pronominal complex symbol for which a pedantic representation might be $\langle 2, [+ N, - V, + \text{PRO}, - \text{SNG}, \dots] \rangle$. Where features are left unspecified, then in general the symbol stands as a variable ranging over permissible feature combinations.

I assume certain general, putatively universal, conventions of feature distribution. The most important of these is what I shall call the Head Feature Convention (HFC, hereafter):

(2.1)   HFC: In a rule of the form $D \to \dots \delta \dots$ where δ is the head of D,
δ carries all the features associated with D.

We may define "head of", at least for the purposes of this paper, as follows:

(2.2)   In a rule of the form $D \to \dots \delta \dots$, δ is the head of D
if and only if
(i) $D = \langle i, [\alpha N, \beta V] \rangle$
(ii) $\delta = \langle j, [\alpha N, \beta V] \rangle$
(iii) $j \leq i$
(iv) there is no δ' ($\delta' \neq \delta$) introduced by this rule such that
$\delta' = \langle k, [\alpha N, \beta V] \rangle$ where $k \leq j$

Something rather similar to HFC is implicit or explicit in a lot of recent transformational grammar (see, e.g. Baker 1978: 336 ff. Hellan 1977: 90–91) but it has not often been fully appreciated just how much follows from such a convention.[7] For example, take English subject-verb agreement. Suppose that the tensed S expansion rule is this:[8]

(2.3) $\bar{\bar{V}}_{[+\text{FIN}]} \to \bar{\bar{N}}_{[\alpha]}\ \bar{V}_{[\alpha]}$, where α range over permissible combinations of agreement features.

Note that I am following Jackendoff (1977) here in taking S to be the maximal projection of V. Now the HFC, taken together with (2.3) and the other phrase structure rules we would need in any case, suffices to capture all the straightforward facts about subject-verb agreement in English. The following tree will make it clear how this is so:

(2.4)

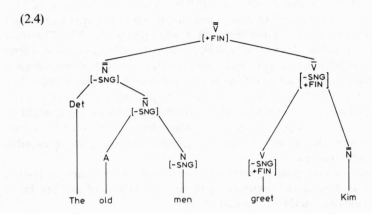

It is not necessary to locate the subject noun, look up what agreement features it is carrying, then locate the first tensed verb in the $\bar{\bar{V}}$ and copy the noun's agreement features across. Instead (2.3) ensures that both $\bar{N}$ and $\bar{V}$ carry the same agreement features, and the HFC ensures that these find their way onto the relevant head noun and head verb.[9]

The rule given in (2.3) is, in fact, a finite rule schema which collapses n phrase structure rules where n is the number of permissible combinations of agreement features. Most of the rules to be given in this paper are, implicitly or explicitly, finite rule schemata of this general type. Employing such finite rule schemata does not affect the type of grammar we are using: each rule schema can always be expanded into some finite set of non-schematic CF-PSG rules and the resulting grammar will simply be a CF-PSG. However, finite rule schemata do provide an elegant way of capturing syntactic generalizations.

We make two additions to the orthodox feature system outlined above, one minor, the other major. The minor modification allows the feature bundle component to include *as features* the names of certain coordinating morphemes, complementizers and prepositions. The major modification consists in allowing ordered pairs of complex symbols, as so far characterized, also to count as part of the nonterminal vocabulary of the grammar. This innovation will be discussed in detail in section 8, below.

3. THE INTERPRETATION OF PHRASE STRUCTURE RULES

There are many ways of interpreting the formalism of a phrase structure grammar but only two of these ways need concern us here. One way, adopted in *The Logical Structure of Linguistic Theory* (Chomsky 1975), interprets a phrase structure rule as a rewriting rule, a rule which maps strings into strings. Thus the rule in (3.1):

(3.1),   S → NP   VP

is a function which maps strings of the form X-S-Y into strings of the form X-NP-VP-Y. The derivation of some terminal string is the set of all the strings that arise in the mapping from the initial symbol to that terminal string. Given certain restrictions, which we shall return to, a tree may than be defined on the basis of the derivation.

The second way of interpreting PS rules, due originally to Richard Stanley (see McCawley 1968: 39), is to treat them as node admissibility conditions. A node labelled S in a tree is admitted by the rule in (3.1) if and only if that node immediately and exhaustively dominates two nodes, the left one labelled NP and the right one labelled VP. A tree is analysed by the grammar if and only if every non-terminal node is admitted by a rule of the grammar. Under this interpretation, then, phrase structure rules are well-formedness conditions on trees. There is no notion of a derivation and it makes no sense to order the rules.

Chomsky has stated that 'obviously it makes no difference whether ... we consider the rules to be rewriting rules or "tree conditions"' (1975:48). This is incorrect. To begin with, Sampson has pointed out, in a review of *LSLT*, that 'one thing at stake is that Chomsky's approach forces him to impose two quite arbitrary restrictions on phrase structure rules, namely that no rule may rewrite any symbol A as either the null string or as a sequence including A; both of these forbidden types of rule frequently seem appropriate in the description of real languages, and under the alternative view of phrase-structure grammars there is no objection to them' (1979: 368). Among the familiar rules that these arbitrary restrictions prohibit are the following:

(3.2)	a.	NOM	→	NOM	S	
	b.	NP	→	NP	S	
(3.3)	a.	VP	→	V	VP	
	b.	VP	→	V	NP	VP

(3.4) $NP[+PRO, +NOM] \to e$

(3.5) $COMP \to e$

Both competing analyses of relative clauses (3.2), a common treatment of auxiliary verbs (3.3a), the rule that a verb like *make* needs (3.3b), subject pronoun drop in Romance languages (3.4), and null COMP expansion (3.5) are all eliminated.

There is a second way in which the interpretation of PS rules makes a difference. Chomsky has claimed that 'phrase structure grammars have the weak generative capacity of unrestricted rewriting systems (arbitrary Turing Machines) if one symbol is taken to be "blank" [i.e. the empty string *e*]' (1977: 132). And in a standard transformational textbook we find the following: 'it is possible to prove that the class of languages generable by phrase-structure grammars with free deletion rules is exactly the same as the class of languages generable by unrestricted rewriting systems. We are looking for restrictions on grammars that will narrow down the class of possible languages. But by including deletion rules in our phrase structure grammars, we would open the back door after carefully closing the front door. This argument must be taken on faith at this point' (Bach 1974: 42). The claim being made by Bach and Chomsky is misleading to say the least: it is *only* true of context-sensitive (CS) PSG's under a rewriting interpretation of the rules, and there is *no* interpretation of CF-PSG's under which it is true (Bar-Hillel, Perles & Shamir 1961: 85). It is not true of CS-PSGs grammars under a node admissibility interpretation. The only effect on weak generative capacity of allowing *e*-productions in PSGs (whether CF or CS) under a node admissibility condition interpretation, is that the language consisting solely of the empty string can then be generated.

The third and perhaps the most important mathematical difference between the alternative interpretations of PSGs only emerges when we consider CS rules like that shown in (3.6):

(3.6) $A \to \omega/\varphi \text{------} \psi$

In a surprising and neglected paper, Peters and Ritchie (1969, 1973) showed that CS-PSGs under a node admissibility interpretation can only analyze CF languages. However, as is well known, such grammars under a rewriting interpretation can generate any CS language. There is thus a well-defined algebraic sense in which the node admissibility interpretation of PSGs is more restrictive than the rewriting interpretation. Since there is, at present, no reason for believing that any natural languages are strictly CS (i.e. CS but not CF), it is proper to assume the more restrictive interpretation of

PSGs, namely the node admissibility interpretation.

Joshi and his associates (Joshi and Levy 1977, Joshi, Levy, and Yueh, 1978, forthcoming) have recently generalized the Peters and Ritchie result to phrase structure grammars which are allowed to make reference not just to left-right tree contexts but also to top-bottom tree contexts. Thus the contextual conditions can include both proper analysis predicates of the form $\varphi\underline{\quad}\psi$, as in (3.6) above, and domination predicates of the form $\delta(A, \varphi\underline{\quad}\psi)$ which holds of a node labelled A just in case there exists a path from the root of the tree to some terminal symbol which contains as a substring the string $\varphi A\psi$. They then define a class of phrase structure rules called "Local constraints" that have the form shown in (3.7)

(3.7) $A \rightarrow \omega/C_A$

where C_A is any Boolean combination of proper analysis and domination predicates.

For example, a grammar of English might include the following pair of rules:

(3.8)   a. $\bar{S} \rightarrow \mathit{that}$ S
         b. $\bar{S} \rightarrow S/\neg\delta(\bar{S}, S\underline{\quad}S)$

The local constraint in (3.8b) will ensure that no $\bar{S}$ which is immediately dominated by S will appear without the complementizer *that*.

Phrase structure grammars which employ local constraints can only analyze CF languages.

Any local filter, in the sense of Chomsky and Lasnik (1977), can be mapped into local constraint type contextual conditions on phrase structure rules. It follows that augmenting a phrase structure grammar (under a node admissibility condition interpretation) with a local filter component will have no effect on the weak generative capacity of the overall grammar – it will still only be able to generate CF languages.[10]

It is worth noting, since it is by no means intuitively obvious, that the n^3 parsability result for CF languages holds also when the PSG defining the set of parse trees employs e-productions (see Aho and Ullman 1972: 320ff) and when it incorporates local constraints (see Joshi, Levy, and Yueh, forthcoming, for proof).

I will not in fact employ CS rules, local constraints or local filters anywhere in the present paper. My purpose in the preceding digression was to establish (i) that the interpretation of phrase structure rules affects their properties in an important way, and (ii) that the class of CF-language-inducing PSGs is much more interesting formally than most linguists currently appear to believe.

4. RULE FORMAT AND STRICT SUBCATEGORIZATION

Since phrase structure rules are interpreted here as node admissibility conditions rather than as string-to-string mapping rules, the familiar rewrite arrow notation for PS rules will not be used, but instead a notation which reflects more directly the relation such rules bear to the (sub)trees that they admit. Instead of (4.1)

(4.1) $\bar{V} \to \bar{N} \quad \bar{V}$

then, we have

(4.2) $[_{\bar{V}} \bar{N} \bar{V}]$

and analogously for all other rules.

Each syntactic rule in the grammar will be associated with a semantic translation rule which gives the translation of the constituent created by the syntactic rule as a function of the translations of the latter's parts. This stipulation instantiates what Bach (1976:2) has called the *rule-to-rule* hypothesis concerning the semantic translation relation. The semantic translation rules themselves will take the form of a mapping into intensional logic.

It is worth emphasising that the intensional logic representations do not constitute a linguistic level in the sense in which the Generative Semanticist's "Semantic Representation" did, or recent REST's misleadingly named "Logical Form" does. As in Montague (1973), the intensional logic is invoked here purely as an expository device. In principle, the translation procedure and the intensional logic representations can be eliminated in favor of defining the "real semantics", i.e. the model theory, directly on the (surface) syntactic representations induced by the grammar. Thus the present proposals constitute a single-level linguistic theory in the sense of Perlmutter (this volume) in that it makes no use of abstract levels of grammatical description.

Although very little will be said in this paper about matters semantic, the fact that an algorithm for translation into intensional logic is given taken together with the fact that a model theory is available for intensional logic (in Montague 1973) ensures that the syntactic theory developed below can be associated with a genuine semantic theory, and not merely with an ill-specified mapping into an uninterpreted pseudo-logic.

A rule of grammar will be taken to be a triple of which the first member is an arbitrary integer – the number of the rule (the role of which will become apparent shortly) – the second member is a PS rule, and the third is a semantic translation rule showing how the intensional logic representation of the expression created by the PS rule is built up from the intensional logic representations of its immediate constituents. A Montague-like prime convention will be used in the semantic rules: $\bar{N}'$ stands for the (complex) expression of intensional logic which is the translation of the subtree dominated by $\bar{N}$; run' is the constant of intensional logic which translates the word *run* in English; and so on. And we adopt a further prime convention for intensions: we let α'' stand for the intension of α', thus $\alpha'' = \hat{\ }\alpha'$. Within this framework the celebrated S → NP VP rule of English would be stated thus:

(4.3) $\langle 1, [\ _{\bar{V}}\ \bar{N}\ \bar{V}], \bar{V}'(\bar{N}'')\rangle$

"Rule" will be used to refer both to the triple and to its second and third members (the latter sometimes qualified with "syntactic" and "semantic", respectively) but this should not cause confusion. Notice that the semantic translation rule in (4.3) is not the one adopted by Montague (1973) in PTQ in which the NP is a function taking the VP as argument. Instead we are taking VPs to denote functions from NP intensions to truth values, following Montague's (1970) earlier treatment in his 'Universal Grammar' (see Thomason (1976), Keenan and Faltz (1978), Keenan (1979a), and Bach (1980b) for motivation).

Let us turn now to rules for PP:[11]

(4.4) $\langle 2, [\ _{\bar{P}}\ \bar{P}], \bar{P}'\rangle$

(4.5) $\langle 3, [\ _{\bar{P}}\ P\ \bar{N}], P'(\bar{N}')\rangle$

Many languages mark NP's which stand as indirect object, passive agents, etc., with morphological case-marking as dative, ablative, etc. In English one finds a class of PP's where such languages would have NP's and these PP's are distinguished, not by casemarking but by choice of preposition (cf. Jackendoff 1977: 80–81, Fodor 1978: 444 n 12, McCloskey 1979: 208–210). Suppose them that such PP's carry the name of the particular preposition as a feature so that the grammar employs complex symbols of the form $\bar{P}[to], \bar{P}[of], \bar{P}[for]$ and $\bar{P}[by]$. These PP's can nevertheless still be expanded by means of the regular PP rules as given in (4.4) and (4.5). The Head Feature Convention will carry the feature down onto the prepositions that are the heads of such PP's, and then the following rule can realize the feature as the relevant preposition:

(4.6) $\langle 4, [_P \mathscr{F}], \lambda\tau[\tau] \rangle$
$\qquad\quad [\mathscr{F}]$

where $\mathscr{F} \in \{to, for, by, of, \ldots\}$ and τ is of type $\langle\langle e, t \rangle, t \rangle$.

The semantic rule here is an identity function mapping NP extensions into themselves. Thus this kind of PP will end up having exactly the same meaning as the NP it dominates. This analysis makes the claim then that in such PPs the preposition does not carry any independent meaning but serves merely to indicate the argument place occupied by the NP. This is in marked distinction to other PPs which we would want to get assigned an adverbial-type meaning that varied in a regular way depending on the particular preposition involved. There is some evidence for the semantics given in (4.6), consider the following pairs of sentences:

(4.7) a. Kim gave a book only to Sandy.
　　　 b. Kim gave a book to only Sandy.

(4.8) a. Kim bought a book only for Sandy.
　　　 b. Kim bought a book for only Sandy.

(4.9) a. Sandy was given a book only by Kim.
　　　 b. Sandy was given a book by only Kim.

These pairs are truth-conditionally synonymous as (4.6) predicts they will be. But now consider similar minimal pairs where a "real" preposition is involved:

(4.10) a. Kim put books only on the boxes.
　　　　b. Kim put books on only the boxes.

(4.11) a. Kim left only after two days.
　　　　b. Kim left after only two days.

Clearly these pairs are not truth-conditionally synonymous, nor would we expect them to be. There is a related bit of evidence for the semantics in (4.6): in Spanish "real" PP's can be modified by *como* (*how*) and *casi* (*almost*) whereas subcategorization PP's cannot be so modified (I am indebted to Paloma Garcia-Bellido for this observation). This would be predictable if subcategorization PPs had NP-like meanings rather than PP-like meanings.

Any grammar for a natural language has to provide some way of capturing the fact that different lexical items of the same (gross) syntactic category can have different distributions. In a transformational grammar of a traditional kind this fact is described using the devices of strict subcategorization rules and selectional restrictions. I assume without argument that all the work done by the latter should be done by the semantics or pragmatics. One obvious way to do strict subcategorization in a phrase structure grammar is by means of CS rules like that in (4.12):

(4.12) $V \rightarrow throw/\text{——}NP$ *out*

As noted in section 3, above, the use of CS-PSG rules, interpreted as node admissibility conditions, would not allow any non-CF languages to be generated. However, the approach to strict subcategorization implicit in rules like (4.12) would be to all intents and purposes equivalent to the *Aspects* positions on strict subcategorization. Heny has recently pointed out that the latter succeeds in missing a rather significant generalization:

The internal structure of every strict subcategorization feature, including those that have to be included in the lexical specification of an item (such as + [——NP – Manner] on *frighten*), precisely mirror the order and optionality of the elements in the PS rule expanding the node immediately dominating the item in question. Thus, the lexicon will necessarily repeat information, time and time again, which is at least in part already extractable from the PS rules. No verb can have the feature + [——Manner – NP] in English, because no PS rule or combination of PS rules introduces the elements V, NP and Manner in the relevant order. This problem can be viewed entirely from within the lexicon or from the point of view of the interaction of the lexicon and the PS rules. Looked at either way something is amiss. Heny 1979: 339–340.

And Carlson and Roeper draw attention to:

A potential difficulty with the phrase structure rules for the English VP. Attempts to write detailed VP PS rules, such as we find in Jackendoff (1977), invariably allow for expansions that do not occur. Carlson and Roeper 1980: 162.

Jackendoff's VP expansion rule looks like this:

(4.13) $\bar{V} \rightarrow V \quad (NP)(Prt)(\{ {NP \atop AP} \})(\{ {AdvP \atop QP} \})(PP)(PP)(\bar{S})$

(Jackendoff 1977: 64)

Assuming this rule, and assuming that *throw* is subcategorized as in (4.12), our grammar will generate the following string:

(4.14)   * Kim threw the meal out Sandy quite slowly to Lee in the woods that Robin loved Pat.

Example (4.14) is not a sentence of English. Two solutions present themselves, neither being very attractive. The syntactic solution is to augment (possibly by convention, see Chomsky 1965: 111) the rule in (4.12) and every other subcategorization rule with a whole list of negative contextual conditions to rule out most of the possibilities introduced by (4.13). This seems an ungainly way to circumvent the problem that (4.13) creates. The semantic solution is to argue that (4.14) is, in fact, grammatical, but that it cannot be interpreted by the semantic component of the grammar. The logic of this line of argument leads one to abandon syntactic restrictions on subcategorization altogether, otherwise one ends up in the peculiar position of claiming that whilst (4.14) is bad for semantic reasons, (4.15) is bad for syntactic reasons:

(4.15)   * Kim threw.

A serious problem with a purely semantic approach to subcategorization emerges when we consider minimal pairs such as those shown in (4.16)–(4.20):[12]

(4.16)   a. Kim is likely to throw up.
          b. * Kim is probable to throw up.
(4.17)   a. Sandy made Kim throw up.
          b. * Sandy forced Kim throw up.
(4.18)   a. Sandy forced Kim to throw up.
          b. * Sandy made Kim to throw up.
(4.19)   a. Sandy spared Kim a second helping.
          b. * Sandy deprived Kim a second helping.
(4.20)   a. Sandy deprived Kim of a second helping.
          b. * Sandy spared Kim of a second helping.

There does not seem to be any way in which the clear differences in acceptability of these examples can be made to follow from the meaning differences, if any, between the lexical items involved.

Coordination interacts with CS subcategorization in a technically problematic manner. Assume that both *throw* and *hand* have [___ NP PP] among their subcategorization frames. Now consider how one might generate example (4.21):

(4.21)   Kim threw and handed things to those outside.

Clearly, *handed* meets the subcategorization requirement, being left-adjacent, as it is, to an NP followed by a PP. Equally clearly, *threw* does not meet the subcategorization requirement since it is left-adjacent to *and-V-NP-PP*. A transformational grammar which is prepared to employ a rule of coordination reduction will not run into this problem, of course. In a phrase structure grammar using CS subcategorization the only way to handle coordination of lexical categories seems to be to introduce a special convention for interpreting the context condition in such cases. Such a convention will itself lead to problems. Thus presumably both *prefer* and *promise* will have [____NP $\overline{\text{VP}}$] among their subcategorization frames. If so, the convention just alluded to will ensure that our grammar generates the string in (4.22):

(4.22)   *Kim preferred and promised Sandy to go.

It is quite possible that the problems with CS lexical insertion discussed above are amenable to more or less satisfactory solutions. However, rather than pursue that here, I propose to develop an alternative approach to strict subcategorization, one which only employs context-free rules. The format for rules, as outlined at the beginning of this section, enables us to capture the unruly and idiosyncratic syntactic facts of subcategorization in a fairly elegant way. Suppose we have a rule of grammar *n* that introduces a lexical category *C* and that only a proper subset of lexical items of category *C* can appear under *C* in the environment created by the syntactic component of rule *n*. Then we can allow *n* to be a feature on *C*, and interpret rule *n* as shown in (4.23) to be an abbreviation-by-convention of (4.24):

(4.23) $\langle n, [\ldots C \ldots], \ldots \rangle$

(4.24) $\langle n, [\ldots C \ldots], \ldots \rangle$
                     $[n]$

This use of rule numbers as subcategorization features eliminates the need for context-sensitive rules of lexical insertion. A context-free PS rule can allow $C[n]$ to dominate only those lexical items permitted in the context defined by rule *n*. A direct consequence of this is that the proposals regarding subcategorization stipulated by Chomsky (1965: 96ff) fall out as theorems in the present system. Chomsky stipulates that a category *C* can be subcategorized only for material α and β such that *C* is introduced by a rule $\sigma \rightarrow \alpha C \beta$ (1965: 99). Consider an example:

(4.25) $\langle 9, [\,_{\overline{V}}\ V\ \overline{N}\ \overline{P}\,], \ldots \rangle$
                        $[to]$

where $V[9] \rightarrow \{hand, sing, throw, give, \ldots\}$

Rule 9 says that a VP can consist of a V[9] followed by an NP followed by a dative PP. And among the lexical items that can be dominated by V[9] are *hand, sing, throw, give,* etc. Nothing outside $\bar{V}$ could be relevant to deciding whether or not *hand,* say, can be inserted. This is what is guaranteed by Chomsky's rule "$V \rightarrow CS/\_\_\alpha$, where α is a string such that $V\alpha$ is a VP" (1965: 96). Note that the use of complex symbols enables us to avoid the charge usually levelled against such context-free phrase structure proposals for lexical insertion, namely that by distinguishing V_i from V_j, say, we lose generalizations about verbs (e.g. that they all take tense). We do not lose the generalization since $V[i]$ and $V[j]$ have at least two features in common (namely $[+ V, - N]$) and it is this fact which accounts for the generalizations that can be made.

Before ending this section, I need to say something about the assumptions I am making with respect to inflectional morphology. Lexical categories may bear morphosyntactic features, thus a tree may, for example, contain a node labelled V[9, + PRP], where + PRP indicates a present participle, immediately dominating *handing.* Following Brame (1978b) and Lapointe (1980), I assume that such forms are given by the lexicon directly and not constructed by affixation of -*ing* to *hand* by some syntactic rule such as Affix Hopping or the syntagmatically triggered morphological rules of Pullum and Wilson (1977). In the case of a feature like + PRP the phonological shape of the word form will be fully predictable by a general lexical redundancy rule, whereas in the case of a feature like + NEG the lexicon will need to specify the idiosyncratic forms (e.g. *won't/*willn't*) and the accidental gaps (*e.g. *amn't*). See Gazdar, Pullum, and Sag (forthcoming) for detailed proposals concerning the role of morphosyntactic features in stating the regularities of the English auxiliary system.

5. ENGLISH VP AND AP RULES

The rules to be given in this section combine the approach to subcategorization developed above with (i) Bresnan-style claims (e.g., Bresnan 1978) about syntactic categories and constituent structure, and (ii) a Montague-based approach to semantics. A similar Bresnan-Montague marriage has already been exploited very successfully by Klein (1978), Ladusaw (1980), and by McCloskey (1979) in his grammar of Modern Irish, and the present proposals are indebted to those works. In this kind of approach, all the semantic work done in a classical transformational grammar by lexically governed syntactic rules like Equi and Raising is done by a combination of lambda abstraction and meaning postulates. Since the syntactic proposals which are the main focus of this paper are almost entirely independent of the details of the semantics adopted, I shall hardly go into the latter at all, and instead simply refer the reader to Thomason (1976) and Dowty (1978) where the relevant issues are given serious consideration.[13]

Following Hust and Brame (1976: 251), I shall assume that all verbs are marked with a feature indicating whether or not they are transitive (we will use $[\pm \text{TRN}]$ for this purpose). Crosslinguistically, there are compelling reasons for rejecting Chomsky's claim that such a feature 'can be regarded merely as a notation indicating occurrence in the environment ___ NP' (1965: 93). One obvious problem is that his claim will lead us to define transitivity in four different ways in order to accommodate (i) SVO and VOS, (ii) OVS and SOV, (iii) OSV, and (iv) VSO languages. If there are crosslinguistic generalizations to make about transitive verbs then they will certainly by missed by treating transitivity merely as a contextual condition on lexical insertion. Another problem is that in certain Micronesian languages, e.g. Kusaiean, verbs may appear in both transitive and intransitive forms in the environment ___ NP, and it is their transitivity, not their adjacency to NP, that determines the applicability of passive, the possibility of adding NP modifiers, and the position of verb suffixes (Comrie 1979: 1064–1065). And in Hindi-Urdu both transitive and intransitive verbs can occur in the environment NP___ # but the subject will only take ergative case if the verb that appears in this environment is a transitive one. Amritavalli (1979) argues at length that it is impossible to capture the relevant generalizations about ergative case marking and passivization in Hindi-Urdu if transitivity is identified with [NP___ #]. He concludes 'that verbs should be marked both for transitivity and for strict subcategorization features, and that these features are independent of each other' (ibid: 91). Arguments suggesting that this conclusion carries over to English are developed at some length in Bach (1980a) and I shall henceforth assume its correctness without further discussion. In addition, I shall adopt a version of Amritavalli's markedness convention (ibid: 92). In the present framework something like the following would have the desired results:

> In a rule introducing V and $\bar{\text{N}}$ under $\bar{\text{V}}$, the value of V for [TRN] will be + unless otherwise specified. Elsewhere it will be −.

Brame's "$\overline{\text{VP}}$" category is analysed here as an infinitive verb phrase whose head verb is the untensed, uninflected auxiliary verb *to*.[14] The expansion rule is given in (5.1); feature specifications are omitted by convention in the semantic part of a rule.

$$(5.1) \qquad \langle 5, [_{\bar{V}} \quad V \quad \underset{[BSE]}{\bar{V}}], \lambda \mathscr{P} V'(\hat{} \bar{V}'(\mathscr{P})) \rangle$$
$\underset{[INF]}{}$

where *to* is the only item of category V[5].

Here the feature BSE on the embedded $\bar{V}$ ensures that the head of that $\bar{V}$ appears in the bare infinitive form (via the HFC); see Gazdar, Pullum and Sag (ibid) for detailed discussion of this rule which is, in fact, merely an instance of a much more general rule schema for the introduction of auxiliary verbs.

As in Gazdar (1981), I take the familiar "S" category to be a sentence optionally marked by the feature + C(omplementizer), hence $\bar{S} = \bar{V}[\pm C]$. Here $\bar{V}[- C]$ is an ordinary tensed sentence, and $\bar{V}[+ C]$ expands in virtue of the following rule:

$$(5.2) \qquad \langle 6, [_{\underset{[+C]}{\bar{V}}} \quad that \quad \underset{[-C]}{\bar{V}}], \quad \bar{V}' \rangle$$

Most verbs and adjectives that take sentential complements subcategorize for $\bar{V}[\pm C]$, but a few require $\bar{V}[+ C]$ and consequently the *that* is obligatory in their complements (see Shir 1977: 62–3 for relevant data). In the rules that follow in this section, I shall abbreviate $\bar{V}[\pm C]$ as $\bar{V}$.

In the examples that follow, the *a*-line defines a rule of number *n*, the *b*-line lists example lexical items of category V[*n*] (or A[*n*]), and the *c*-line gives an example of a constituent admitted by the rule.

(5.3)   a. $\langle 7, [_{V} \quad V], V' \rangle$

b. run, die, eat, sing, . . .

c. runs.

(5.4)[15]   a. $\langle 8, [_{V} \quad V \quad \bar{N}], V'(\bar{N}'') \rangle$

b. eat, sing, love, give, close, . . .

c. eats Fido.

(5.5)   a. $\langle 9, [_{V} \quad V \quad \bar{N} \quad \underset{[to]}{\bar{P}}], V'(\bar{P}'')(\bar{N}'') \rangle$

b. hand, give, sing, throw, . . .

c. hands Fido to Kim.

(5.6)   a. $\langle 10, [_{\bar{V}} \quad V \quad \bar{N} \quad \underset{[for]}{\bar{P}}], V'(\bar{P}'')(\bar{N}'')\rangle$

     b. buy, cook, reserve,...
     c. buys Fido for Kim.

(5.7)[16]   a. $\langle 11, [_{\bar{V}} \quad V \quad \bar{N} \quad \bar{N}], V'(\bar{N}'')(\bar{N}'')\rangle$

     b. spare, hand, give, buy,...
     c. spares Fido a bath.

(5.8)   a. $\langle 12, [_{\bar{V}} \quad V \quad \bar{V}], V'(\bar{V}'')\rangle$

     b. know, believe, expect,...
     c. knows that Fido runs

(5.9)   a. $\langle 13, [_{\bar{V}} \quad V \quad \bar{N} \quad \bar{V}], V'(\bar{N}'')(\bar{V}'')\rangle$

     b. promise,...
     c. promises Kim that Fido runs.

(5.10)   a. $\langle 14, [_{\bar{V}} \quad V \quad \bar{N} \quad \bar{V}], V'(\bar{V}'')(\bar{N}'')\rangle$

     b. persuade, tell,...
     c. persuades Kim that Fido runs.

(5.11)   a. $\langle 15, [_{\bar{V}} \quad V \quad \underset{[INF]}{\bar{V}}], V'(\bar{V}'')\rangle$

     b. try,...
     c. tries to run.

(5.12)   a. $\langle 16, [_{\bar{V}} \quad V \quad \underset{[INF]}{\bar{V}}], \lambda\mathscr{P}[V'(\hat{\ }\bar{V}'(\mathscr{P}))]\rangle$

     b. tend, happen,...
     c. tends to run.

(5.13)   a. $\langle 17, [_{\bar{V}} \quad V \quad \underset{[INF]}{\bar{V}}], \lambda\mathscr{P}\mathscr{P}\{\lambda x[V'(\hat{\ }\bar{V}'(\hat{P}P(x)))(\hat{P}P(x))]\}\rangle$

     b. want, prefer, expect,...
     c. wants to run.

(5.14)   a. $\langle 18, [_{\bar{V}} \quad \underset{[-TRN]}{V} \quad \bar{N} \quad \underset{[INF]}{\bar{V}}], V'(\bar{N}'')(\bar{V}'')\rangle$

     b. want, prefer,...
     c. wants Fido to run.

(5.15)   a. $\langle 19, [_{\bar{V}} \quad V \quad \bar{N} \quad \underset{[INF]}{\bar{V}}], V'(\hat{\ } \bar{V}'(\bar{N}'')) \rangle$

b. expect, believe, ...
c. expects Fido to run.

(5.16)   a. $\langle 20, [_{\bar{V}} \quad V \quad \bar{N} \quad \underset{[INF]}{\bar{V}}], V'(\bar{V}'')(\bar{N}'') \rangle$

b. persuade, ask, force, ...
c. persuades Fido to run.

(5.17)   a. $\langle 21, [_{\bar{V}} \quad \underset{[-TRN]}{V} \quad \bar{N} \quad \underset{[BSE]}{\bar{V}}], V'(\bar{V}'')(\bar{N}'') \rangle$

b. make, ...
c. makes Fido run.

(5.18)   a. $\langle 22, [_{\bar{V}} \quad \underset{[-TRN]}{V} \quad (\bar{N}) \quad \underset{[INF]}{\bar{V}}], \lambda \mathscr{P} \mathscr{P} \{ \lambda x [V'(\bar{N}'')$

$(\hat{\ } \bar{V}'(\hat{P}P(x))) (\hat{P}P(x))] \} \rangle$

b. promise, ...
c. promises Kim to run.

(5.19)[17] a. $\langle 23, [_{\bar{V}} \quad V \quad \underset{[to]}{(\bar{P})} \quad \underset{[INF]}{\bar{V}}], \lambda \mathscr{P} [V'(\bar{P}'')(\hat{\ } \bar{V}'(\mathscr{P}))] \rangle$

b. seem, appear, ...
c. seems to Kim to run.

(5.20)[18] a. $\langle 24, [_{\bar{V}} \quad V \quad \bar{A}], V'(\bar{A}'') \rangle$

b. be.
c. is stupid.

(5.21)   a. $\langle 25, [_{\bar{V}} \quad V \quad \bar{A}], \lambda \mathscr{P} [V'(\hat{\ } \bar{A}'(\mathscr{P}))] \rangle$

b. seem, appear, ...
c. seems stupid.

(5.22)[19] $\langle 26, [_{\bar{A}} \quad \bar{A}], \bar{A}' \rangle$

(5.23)[20] a. $\langle 27, [_{\bar{A}} \quad A], A' \rangle$

b. stupid, open, closed, ...
c. stupid.

(5.24)   a. $\langle 28, [_{\bar{A}} \quad A \quad \underset{[to]}{\bar{P}}], \lambda \mathscr{P} [A'(\mathscr{P})(\bar{P}'')] \rangle$

b. known, attracted, drawn, ...
c. attracted to Fido.

(5.25) a. $\langle 29, [_{\bar{A}} \quad A \quad (\bar{P})], A'(\bar{P}'')\rangle$
$\qquad\qquad\qquad\quad {}_{[by]}$

b. uninhabited, unloved, ...
c. uninhabited by man.

(5.26) a. $\langle 30, [_{\bar{A}} \quad A \quad \bar{V} \;], \lambda \mathscr{P}[A'(\,\hat{}\, \bar{V}'(\mathscr{P}))]\rangle$
$\qquad\qquad\qquad\quad {}_{[INF]}$

b. likely, ...
c. likely to run.

(5.27) a. $\langle 31, [_{\bar{A}} \quad A \quad \bar{V} \;], \lambda \mathscr{P}\mathscr{P}\{\lambda x[A'(\,\hat{}\,\bar{V}'(\hat{P}P(x))) \; (\hat{P}P(x))]\}\rangle$
$\qquad\qquad\qquad\quad {}_{[INF]}$

b. eager,
c. eager to run.

(5.28) a. $\langle 32, [_{\bar{A}} \quad A \quad \bar{P} \quad \bar{V} \;], A'(\,\hat{}\,\bar{V}'(\bar{P}''))\rangle$
$\qquad\qquad\qquad\quad {}_{[for]} \quad {}_{[INF]}$

b. eager, ...
c. eager for Fido to run.

In the rules in (5.18), (5.19), and (5.25) above, I am assuming the following convention for the semantics of optional arguments:

(5.29)   Optional Argument Convention:
           If $\beta' = \ldots(\alpha'')\ldots$, where β immediately dominates an optional constituent α and α'' is of type $\langle s, \langle\langle e, t\rangle, t\rangle\rangle$, then when α is omitted, $\beta' = \ldots(\hat{P}[\exists x P(x)])\ldots$

This has the effect of ensuring existential quantifications into missing argument positions. This convention is exploited in the treatment of agentless passives given in section 8, below.

The rules given above combine together to admit trees like the following:

GERALD GAZDAR

(5.30)

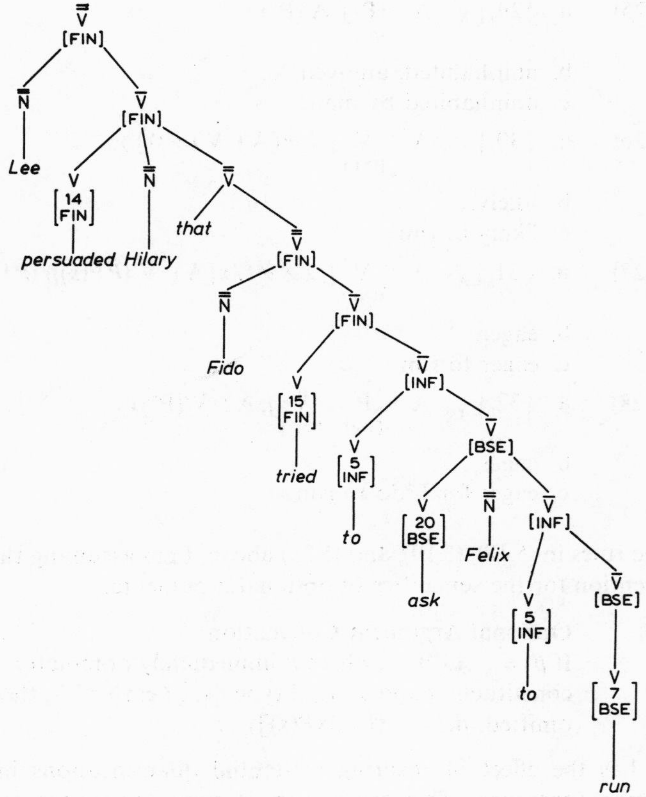

V̿
[FIN]

N̄
Lee

V̄
[FIN]

V
[14
FIN]
persuaded

N̄
Hilary

V̿
[FIN]

that

V̿
[FIN]

N̄
Fido

V̄
[FIN]

V
[15
FIN]
tried

V̄
[FIN]

V̄
[INF]

V
[5
INF]
to

V̄
[INF]

V̄
[BSE]

V
[20
BSE]
ask

N̄
Felix

V̄
[INF]

V
[5
INF]
to

V̄
[BSE]

V̄
[BSE]

V
[7
BSE]
run

(5.31)

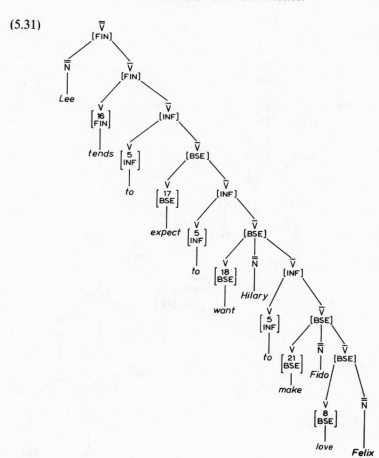

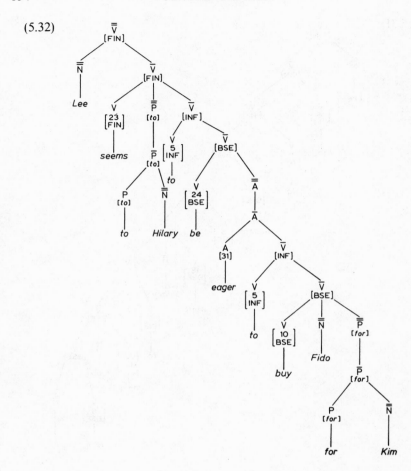

154   GERALD GAZDAR

(5.32)

(5.33)

6. COORDINATION

CF-PSGs, as standardly defined, are subject to the restriction noted in (6.1):

> (6.1)   A grammar contains finitely many rules of the form $A \rightarrow \omega$ where $A \in V_N$ and $\omega \in (V_N \cup V_T)^*$.

This restriction can be seen to pose a technical problem when one recalls that natural language coordinate structures are (i) flat rather than nested, and (ii) indefinitely extensible. Linguists typically provide for these facts by proposing rules of the general form shown in (6.2):

> (6.2) $\alpha \rightarrow \alpha \ldots \alpha$ where $\alpha \in V_N$

This is at odds with the restriction noted above since, on the intended interpretation, (6.2) is neither a well-formed CF-PSG rule, nor does it stand for a finite set of such rules.

This problem is entirely an artefact of the restriction in (6.1). Suppose we consider a class of grammars, identical to the CF-PSGs as standardly defined except insofar as they are subject to the restriction given in (6.3) rather than that of (6.1):[21]

> (6.3)   A grammar contains finitely many rules of the form $A \rightarrow \omega$ where $A \in V_N$ and ω is a regular expression over $V_N \cup V_T$.

This class of grammars will generate all and only the languages generated by CF-PSGs as restricted by (6.1).[22]

I henceforth adopt the restriction of (6.3) in preference to that of (6.1), and I shall refer to the rules so characterized as *regular CF-PSG rules*.

Natural languages appear to exhibit only two types of regular CF-PSG rule for coordination. These are shown in (6.4):[23]

> (6.4)   a. $\alpha \rightarrow \underset{[\mathscr{C}_1]}{\alpha^+} \quad \underset{[\mathscr{C}_2]}{\alpha}$
>
> b. $\alpha \rightarrow \underset{[\mathscr{C}_1]}{\alpha} \quad \underset{[\mathscr{C}_2]}{\alpha}$

Here α^+ is the positive closure of $\{\alpha\}$ (i.e. $\{\alpha, \alpha\alpha, \alpha\alpha\alpha, \ldots\}$). There are three parameters of language variation: (i) the range of permissible values of α, (ii) the ways in which the coordinate features $\mathscr{C}_1$ and $\mathscr{C}_2$ are spelt out, and (iii) which of (6.4a-b) are employed. Thus, in English α can stand for any syntactic category, $\mathscr{C}_1$ has no realization but $\mathscr{C}_2$ is always spelt out as *and* or *or* as the left daughter of $\alpha[\mathscr{C}_2]$, and both (6.4a) and (6.4b) are to be found in the grammar. Thus:

(6.5)   a. (*And) Kim, and Sandy, and Hilary.
         b. Kim, Sandy, *(and) Hilary.

In Latin, $\mathscr{C}_2$ can be spelt out as *et* as the left daughter of $\alpha[\mathscr{C}_2]$ or as *que* as the right sister of the first word in $\alpha[\mathscr{C}_2]$. $\mathscr{C}_1$ also has these possible realizations. We find such examples as the following attested (from Lewis and Short 1879: 1509):[24]

(6.6)   a. Quod mihique eraeque filiaeque erili est.
         b. Romanique et Macedones et socii.
         c. Et singulis universisque honori fuisse.

We are now in a position to define the rules needed to handle constituent coordination in English:

(6.7) $\langle 34, [_\alpha \ \alpha^+ \ \underset{[\mathscr{C}]}{\alpha} \ ], \mathscr{C}'(\alpha',\ldots,\alpha') \rangle$

(6.8) $\langle 35, [_\alpha \ \alpha \ \underset{[\mathscr{C}]}{\alpha^+}], \mathscr{C}'(\alpha',\ldots,\alpha') \rangle$

(6.9) $\langle 33, [_\alpha \ \underset{[\mathscr{C}]}{\mathscr{C}} \ \alpha], \alpha' \rangle$

where α is any syntactic category and $\mathscr{C} \in \{and, or\}$.
For the semantic interpretation of cross-categorial co-ordination see Cooper (forthcoming), Keenan and Faltz (1978), and Gazdar (1980a).
These rules will induce trees such as those shown in (6.10).

(6.10)   a.   b.

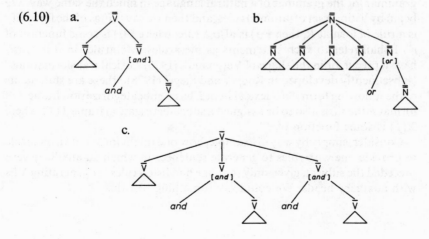

         c.

As can be seen from (6.10), the rules correctly provide for the facts about English coordinate surface structure noted by Ross (1967: pp. 90–91), namely that the coordinating word always forms a constituent with the immediately following conjunct and is not simply a sister of all the conjuncts. Indeed, given the universal characterization of possible coordination rules in (6.4) above, there is no way it could be a sister of all the conjuncts.

7. METARULES

A generative grammar typically gives a recursive definition of the sentences (and of their associated structural descriptions) of a language. It does not seem to have occurred to linguists until recently that it might be possible to give an inductive definition of the set of rules in the grammar. Such an inductive definition can be seen as a grammar for the grammar. This "hypergrammar"[25] can express generalizations about the language generated by the grammar that are not themselves expressible in the latter. In this paper, and in Gazdar (1981) and Gazdar, Pullum and Sag (forthcoming), crucial use is made of what we refer to as metarules. These can be seen as clauses in the inductive definition of the grammar. Consider, by way of analogy, how the syntax of propositional calculus is standardly given. One begins by listing or enumerating a set of (atomic) sentences, and then one says "if A is a sentence, then $\neg$A is a sentence" and "if A and B are sentences then A $\wedge$ B is also a sentence" and so on. We can formulate a grammar for the grammar of a natural language in much the same way. We begin by listing a set of (atomic) rules, and then we say things of the form "if r is a rule of format R, then F(r) is also a rule, where F(r) is some function of r". I shall refer to such statements as metarules. Metarules in this sense, have a precursor in the shape of Vergnaud's (1973) "lexical transformations" (subsequently developed in Roeper and Siegel (1978)): these are statements of the following form: "if a lexical item L has a subcategorization frame f of format F then L is also to be assigned a subcategorization frame T(f), where T(f) is some function of f".

Consider, simply by way of example, how one might formulate a metarule to provide one with rules to generate sentences in which an auxiliary verb preceded the subject, given only that one had listed rules for generating VPs with auxiliary heads. We could say something like this:[26]

(7.1)   For every rule in the grammar of the form:

$$\left[\begin{smallmatrix} \bar{V} \\ \left[\begin{smallmatrix} AUX \\ FIN \end{smallmatrix}\right] \end{smallmatrix} \quad V \quad \begin{smallmatrix} \bar{V} \\ [\alpha] \end{smallmatrix}\right]$$

add a rule of the form:

$$\left[\begin{smallmatrix} \bar{\bar{V}} \\ \left[\begin{smallmatrix} INV \\ AUX \\ FIN \end{smallmatrix}\right] \end{smallmatrix} \quad V \quad \begin{smallmatrix} \bar{V} \\ [\alpha] \end{smallmatrix}\right]$$

Thus for every phrase structure rule that can expand a tensed auxiliary $\bar{V}$ as a tensed auxiliary V followed by a $\bar{V}$, there is a corresponding rule expanding $\bar{V}$ as V followed by a complement $\bar{V}$ which carries exactly the features carried by the complement $\bar{V}$ in the input rule. This embedded $\bar{V}$ will itself be expanded by the normal sentence expansion rule given at (4.3) above, but repeated here for convenience:

(7.2) $\langle 1, [_{\bar{V}} \quad \bar{N} \quad \bar{V}], \bar{V}'(\bar{N}'') \rangle$

The HFC ensures, of course, that any features on $\bar{V}$ in rule 1 get carried onto the daughter $\bar{V}$.

The metarule in (7.1) can be expressed more succinctly using the following notation:

(7.3) $\left[\begin{smallmatrix} \bar{V} \\ \left[\begin{smallmatrix} AUX \\ FIN \end{smallmatrix}\right] \end{smallmatrix} \quad V \quad \bar{V}\right] \Rightarrow \left[\begin{smallmatrix} \bar{\bar{V}} \\ [INV] \end{smallmatrix} \quad V \quad \bar{V}\right]$

This notation suppresses certain conventions. The output rule of a metarule is identical to the input rule except in respect of those items specifically changed by the metarule and changes consequent upon those changes. In particular the rule number of the input remains unchanged, consequently subcategorization gets carried over from input to output. Feature specifications also will be carried over unchanged (unless the metarule itself changes them). Thus the metarule in (7.3) will map the rule shown in (7.4a) into the rule shown in (7.4b) and the latter will allow us to generate the auxiliary initial sentence shown in (7.5):

(7.4)   a. $\langle 36, [_{\begin{smallmatrix} \bar{V} \\ \left[\begin{smallmatrix} AUX \\ FIN \end{smallmatrix}\right] \end{smallmatrix}} \quad V \quad \begin{smallmatrix} \bar{V} \\ [BSE] \end{smallmatrix}], ... \rangle$

b. $\langle 36, [_{\begin{smallmatrix} \bar{\bar{V}} \\ \left[\begin{smallmatrix} INV \\ AUX \\ FIN \end{smallmatrix}\right] \end{smallmatrix}} \quad V \quad \begin{smallmatrix} \bar{V} \\ [BSE] \end{smallmatrix}], ... \rangle$

where $V[36] \rightarrow \{can, may, must, will, ...\}$

(7.5)

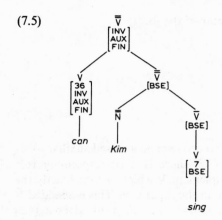

The notation employed in (7.3) makes metarules look suspiciously like transformations but appearances here are deceptive: a transformation maps trees into trees whereas a metarule maps rules into rules. If one adds transformations to a CF-PSG then (i) one is employing two quite distinct rule types, (ii) one completely changes the expressive power of one's theory, and (iii) one ends up with a grammar that assigns at least a pair of structural descriptions to each string generated. By contrast, if one adds metarules to a PS grammar then one merely enlarges, in a rule-governed way, the set of PS rules one is employing, but the overall grammar itself remains PS.

Of course, it is not sufficient merely to list syntactic metarules like (7.3). One has also to say something about the semantics of the rules that result. Each syntactic metarule needs to be given a semantic counterpart showing how the semantics for the new rule can be arrived at as a function of the semantics of the input rule and/or the constituents of the output rule. Thus the full version of (7.3) ought to look something like this:

(7.6) $\langle [\ _{\bar{V}} \ V \ \bar{V}], \ \lambda \mathscr{P}[V'(^\frown \bar{V}'(\mathscr{P}))]\rangle \Rightarrow$
         $\begin{bmatrix} AUX \\ FIN \end{bmatrix}$

         $\langle [\ _{\bar{V}} \ V \ \bar{V}], \ V'(\bar{V}'')\rangle$
         $_{[INV]}$

We require that metarules be finitely specifiable. The only variables permitted in the structural analysis (to borrow the transformational terminology in an obvious manner) are abbreviatory ones, that is a variables which range over a finite subset of $(V_N \cup V_T)^{*27}$. Adherence to this requirement ensures that closing the grammar under some set of metarules will not result in an infinite set of rules being produced.[28]

A metarule can replace the transformation known as "particle movement":

(7.7) $\langle [_{\bar{v}}\ \ V\ \ \bar{N}\ \ Pt\ \ X],\mathscr{F}\rangle \Rightarrow$

$\langle [_{\bar{v}}\ \ V\ \ Pt\ \ \underset{[-PRO]}{\bar{N}}\ \ X],\mathscr{F}\rangle$

Likewise the clause-bounded "clitic preposing" transformation standardly invoked for Romance languages:[29]

(7.8) $\langle [_{\bar{v}}\ \ V\ \ \underset{[-PRO]}{\bar{N}}\ \ X],\mathscr{F}\rangle \Rightarrow$

$\langle [_{\bar{v}}\ \ \underset{[+PRO]}{\bar{N}}\ \ V\ \ X],\mathscr{F}\rangle$

And metarules will allow the grammars of VSO languages to employ the category VP (cf. Dowty 1978a: 112):

(7.9) $\langle [_{\bar{v}}\ \ V\ \ X],\mathscr{F}\rangle \Rightarrow$

$\langle [_{\bar{v}}\ \ V\ \ \bar{N}\ \ X],\mathscr{F}(\bar{N}'')\rangle$

Anderson and Chung (1977: 22–24) provide clear evidence for the existence of a VP constituent in the surface structure of certain Breton sentences, and a case can also be made for the reality of VP-like constituents in Modern Irish (McCloskey, 1980).

In the next section we consider how metarules can provide an analysis of the passive construction.

8. PASSIVE

Following the arguments of Keenan (1980)[30], we take passive to be a phrasal rather than a sentential or lexical operation. A passive VP differs syntactically from the corresponding English active VP in at least two and at most three ways: (i) the verb is morphologically marked, (ii) the direct object NP is not present in the VP, and (iii) there may be a *by*-PP present. Everything else remains the same. Such a construction is readily susceptible of analysis by metarule:

(8.1) $\langle [_{\bar{v}}\ \ \underset{[TRN]}{V}\ \ \bar{N}\ \ X],\ \ \mathscr{F}(\bar{N}'')\rangle \Rightarrow$

$\langle [_{\ \bar{v}\ \atop [PAS]}\ \ V\ \ X\ \ \underset{[by]}{(\bar{P})}],\lambda\mathscr{P}[\mathscr{F}(\mathscr{P})(\bar{P}'')]\rangle$

In words: for every active VP rule which expands VP as a transitive verb followed by NP, there is to be a passive VP rule which expands VP as V followed by what, if anything, followed the NP in the active VP rule, followed optionally by a *by*-PP. As discussed in the preceding section, the rule number is held constant by convention so the subcategorization feature on V will be the same for both the input and the output rule. The PAS feature will get carried onto the V in the passive VP in virtue of the Head Feature Convention discussed in section 2 above, and it will determine the passive morphology on the expansion of V. Bach provides a number of arguments for $\bar{V}[PAS]$, that is 'a syntactic category of passive verb phrases, distinct from any other category in English' (1980a: 315).

The semantic manipulation in (8.1) substitutes an NP intension type variable for $\bar{N}''$ in the VP translation, applies the resulting function to the agent $\bar{P}''$, and abstracts into the resulting open sentence to produce a function with the sort of VP-type meaning we require. In the absence of a *by*-PP, the Optional Argument Convention discussed in section 5 above ensures that we get the existential quantification appropriate to agentless passives. Recall that the semantics of *by* proposed in (4.7) above ensures that the $\bar{P}[by]$ has an NP-type meaning.

Passive VPs are introduced by the following phrase structure rules:

(8.2) $\quad \langle 37, [\ _{\bar{V}\atop [AUX]}\quad V\quad \underset{[PAS]}{\bar{V}}\ ], \lambda \mathscr{P}[V'(\,\hat{}\,\bar{V}'(\mathscr{P}))] \rangle$

where V[37] can only be *be*.

(8.3) $\quad \langle 38, [_{\bar{V}}\quad V\quad \underset{[PAS]}{\bar{V}}\ ],\quad V'(\bar{V}'') \rangle$

where V[38] can only be *get*.

(8.4) $\quad \langle 39, [_{\bar{V}}\quad V\quad \bar{N}\quad \underset{[PAS]}{\bar{V}}\ ], V'(\,\hat{}\,\bar{V}'(\bar{N}'')) \rangle$

where V[39] $\rightarrow \{get, have, see, hear, ...\}$

To see how (8.1) works out in practice, I exhibit its output with respect to three of the VP rules given in section 5 above.

(8.5) $\quad \langle 8, [\ _{\bar{V}\atop [PAS]}\quad V\quad \underset{[by]}{(\bar{P})}], \lambda \mathscr{P}[V'(\mathscr{P})(\bar{P}'')] \rangle$

(8.6) $\quad \langle 14, [\ _{\bar{V}\atop [PAS]}\quad V\quad \bar{V}\quad \underset{[by]}{(\bar{P})}], \lambda \mathscr{P}[V'(\bar{V}'')(\mathscr{P})(\bar{P}'')] \rangle$

(8.7) $\quad \langle 20, [\ _{\bar{V}\atop [PAS]}\quad V\quad \underset{[INF]}{\bar{V}}\quad \underset{[by]}{(\bar{P})}], \lambda \mathscr{P}[V'(\bar{V}'')(\mathscr{P})(\bar{P}'')] \rangle$

These rules then admit such trees as the following:

(8.8)

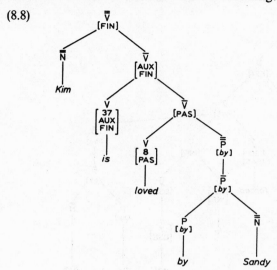

(8.9)

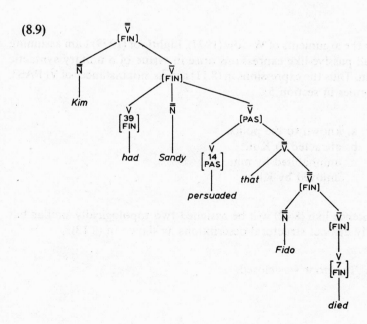

(8.10)

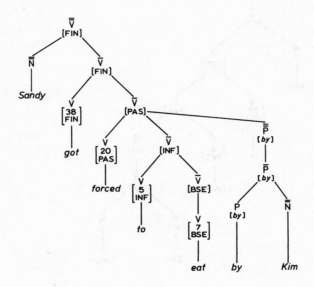

Following the arguments of Wasow (1977), Lightfoot (1979) I am assuming that not all passive-like expressions arise in virtue of a unitary syntactic mechanism. Thus the expressions in (8.11) are Ās, not instances of V̄[PAS], given the rules in section 5:

(8.11)   a. known to the police.
          b. attracted to Kim.
          c. uninhabited by man.
          d. unloved by Kim.

And a sentence like (8.12) will be assigned two topologically similar but categorially distinct structural descriptions as shown in (8.13):

(8.12)   The door was closed.

(8.13)   a.

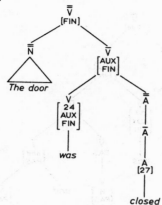

b.

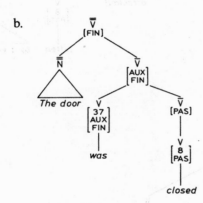

The structure in (8.13a) will be assigned the meaning of *the door was not open* and (8.13b) will be assigned the meaning of *the door was closed by some entity.*

This analysis, taken together with the rule schema for coordination given in section 6 above, predicts that the following sentence (from Bach 1980a: 321) has two structural descriptions.

(8.14)   John was attacked and bitten by a vicious dog.

It is assigned these structures:

(8.15)   a.

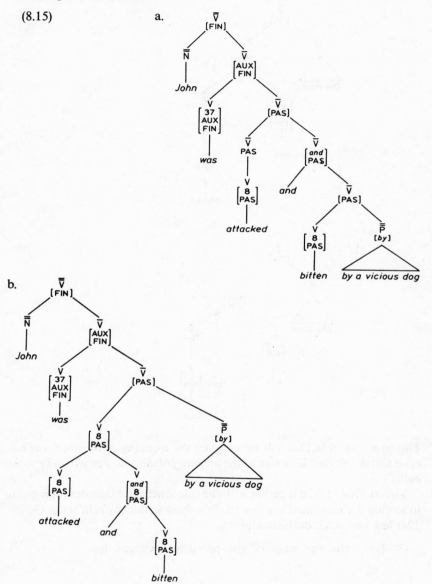

The second structure induces the reading where the dog both bites and attacks, whereas the first structure induces a reading which is noncommittal with respect to the agency of the attack.[31]

The phrasal treatment of passive given above is similar in certain respects to the lexical analysis, given by Bresnan (1978). However, as Keenan (1979b) has pointed out, her analysis incorrectly requires the presence of the copula before the passive VP, her semantics becomes incoherent when there is a quantified NP in the *by*-PP, and she does not allow for coordinate structures like those shown in (8.15b).

Not all passive VP rules arise as the product of the metarule in (8.1). The grammar of English will need to list at least the following rule:

(8.16) $\langle 40, [_{\bar{V} \atop [PAS]}\ V\ \underset{[INF]}{\bar{V}}\ ], \lambda \mathscr{P}[V'(\overset{\frown}{V'}(\mathscr{P}))] \rangle$

where $V[40] \to \{repute, rumor, see, say, make, \ldots\}$

in order to generate examples like the following, taken from Bach (1980a: 328):

(8.17)   a. John was said to be in Rome.
          b. Mary is reputed to be a genius.
          c. John was seen to have left.

9. UNBOUNDED DEPENDENCIES

Bresnan has claimed that unbounded syntactic dependencies 'cannot be adequately described even by context-sensitive phrase structure rules, for the possible context is not correctly describable as a finite string of phrases' (1978: 38). Despite accurately reflecting the metagrammatical intuitions of a significant body of linguists, this claim is a non-sequitur. The fact that natural languages allow dependencies whose domain is not describable as a finite string of phrases has no bearing on the descriptive adequacy of any familiar class of grammars. Even finite state grammars allow for the description of certain kinds of unbounded dependency.[32]

And phrase structure grammars can handle unbounded dependencies in an elegant and general way provided that we exploit the resources offered by a complex symbol system and by the possibility of making statements about the set of rules that the grammar may employ.

Let V_N be the set of *basic* category symbols (i.e. the set of all nonterminal symbols standardly used). Then we define a set $D(V_N)$ of *derived* categories as follows:

$$(9.1) \qquad D(V_N) = \{\alpha/\beta : \alpha, \beta \in V_N\}$$

Suppose counterfactually that S and NP were the only basic categories; then the set of derived categories would consist of S/S, S/NP, NP/NP, and NP/S. This notation is reminiscent of categorial grammar but, despite a tenuous conceptual link, these derived categories are not to be interpreted in the way categorial grammar prescribes.[33] The intended interpretation is as follows: a node labelled α/β will dominate sub-trees identical to those that can be dominated by α, except that somewhere in every subtree of the α/β type there will occur a node labelled β/β dominating a resumptive pronoun, a phonologically null dummy element or the empty string, and every node linking α/β and β/β will be of the form σ/β for some category σ. Intuitively then, α/β labels a node of type α which dominates material containing a hole of type β (i.e. an extraction site on a movement analysis). So, for example, S/NP is a sentence which has an NP missing somewhere.[34]

Defining a new set of syntactic categories is not of itself sufficient, of course, to ensure that the trees in which they figure have the property just described: we need, in addition, a set of rules to employ them.

What we have to do is define a set of rules each of which expands a derived category just as the corresponding basic rule would have done for the basic category, except that exactly one of the dominated categories is now paired with the same hole-indicating category as is the dominating category. The set of such rules will consequently allow the hole information to be "carried down" the tree.

Let G be the set of *basic* rules (i.e. the set of rules that a grammar not handling unbounded dependencies would require). For any syntactic category β, there will be some subset of the set of the nonterminal symbols V_N each of which can dominate β according to the rules in G. Let us call this set $V_\beta(V_\beta \subseteq V_N)$. Now, for any category $\beta(\beta \in V_N)$ we can define a (finite) set of derived rules $D(\beta, G)$ as follows:[35]

$$(9.2) \qquad D(\beta, G) = \{ [_{\alpha/\beta} \ \sigma_1 \ldots \sigma_i/\beta \ldots \sigma_n] : [_\alpha \sigma_1 \ldots \sigma_i \ldots \sigma_n] \in G \ \& \\ 1 \le i \le n \ \& \ \sigma_i \in V_\beta \}$$

An example of the application of (9.2) should make this clearer. Suppose that the set G of basic rules looks like this:

(9.3)   a. {[$_{\bar{\bar{V}}}$ Ñ V̄],
          b. [$_{\bar{V}}$ V V̄].
          c. [$_{\bar{V}}$ V V̄],
          d. [$_{\bar{V}}$ V P̄],
          e. [$_{\bar{V}}$ V Ñ],
          f. [$_{\bar{V}}$ V Ñ P̄],
          g. [$_{\bar{\bar{N}}}$ Ñ P̄],
          h. [$_{\bar{P}}$ P̄],
          i. [$_{P}$ P Ñ]}

Then the set D(Ñ, G) will look like this:

(9.4)   a. {[$_{\bar{V}/\bar{N}}$ Ñ/Ñ V̄], [$_{\bar{\bar{V}}/\bar{N}}$ Ñ V̄/Ñ],
          b. [$_{\bar{V}/\bar{N}}$ V V̄/Ñ],
          c. [$_{\bar{V}/\bar{N}}$ V V̄/Ñ],
          d. [$_{\bar{V}/\bar{N}}$ V P̄/Ñ,
          e. [$_{\bar{V}/\bar{N}}$ V Ñ/Ñ],
          f. [$_{\bar{V}/\bar{N}}$ V Ñ/Ñ P̄], [$_{\bar{V}/\bar{N}}$ V Ñ P̄/Ñ],
          g. [$_{\bar{N}/\bar{N}}$ Ñ/Ñ P̄], [$_{\bar{N}/\bar{N}}$ Ñ P̄/Ñ],
          h. [$_{\bar{P}/\bar{N}}$ P̄/Ñ],
          i. [$_{\bar{P}/\bar{N}}$ P Ñ/Ñ]}

and the set D(P̄, G) will look like this:

(9.5)   a. {[$_{\bar{V}/\bar{P}}$ Ñ/P̄ V̄], [$_{\bar{\bar{V}}/\bar{P}}$ Ñ V̄/P̄],
          b. [$_{\bar{V}/\bar{P}}$ V V̄/P̄],
          c. [$_{\bar{V}/\bar{P}}$ V V̄/P̄],
          d. [$_{V\bar{P}}$ V P̄/P̄],
          e. [$_{\bar{V}/\bar{P}}$ V Ñ/P̄],
          f. [$_{\bar{V}/\bar{P}}$ V Ñ/P̄ P̄], [$_{\bar{V}/\bar{P}}$ V Ñ P̄/P̄]
          g. [$_{\bar{N}/\bar{P}}$ Ñ/P̄ P̄], [$_{\bar{N}/\bar{P}}$ Ñ P̄/P̄],
          h. [$_{\bar{P}/\bar{P}}$ P̄/P̄],
          i. [$_{\bar{P}/\bar{P}}$ P Ñ/P̄]}

Derived rules have no special lexical or semantic properties. Thus, all derived rules will have the same rule-numbers, the same subcategorization properties and the same semantic translations as the basic rules from which they derive. Consequently they do not need to be separately listed or separately specified since everything about them is predictable from (9.2) taken together with the basic rules.

In addition to derived rules, we also need *linking* rules (these will be a subset of the basic rules) to introduce and eliminate derived categories. For the majority dialect of English (British or American) we need only the following rule schema to eliminate derived categories:

$$(9.6) \qquad \langle 41, [_{\alpha/\alpha} \quad t], \quad h_\alpha \rangle \text{ where } \alpha \in V_N$$

Here h_α (mnemonic for 'hole') is a distinguished variable ranging over denotations of type α (i.e. NP denotations if $\alpha = $ NP, PP denotations if $\alpha = $ PP, etc.). And t is a dummy element postulated solely for phonological reasons (i.e. it will serve to block contraction), it serves no semantic function (h_α is the variable, not t), and for other dialects or languages we could replace t with the empty string–(which would have no phonological effects) or with a proform. The rules ensure that t is placed in precisely those locations where contraction-inhibiting phonological effects have been noted, and consequently the analysis faces none of the difficulties faced by the analyses criticised in Postal and Pullum (1978).

The apparatus developed above can be used to handle all constructions involving an unbounded dependency.[36] However, since exactly the same principle is involved in every case, it will suffice here to illustrate its application by reference to just two constructions, namely topicalization and English free relatives.

At least one recent linguistics textbook (Perlmutter and Soames, 1979: 230–231) argues that the facts of English topicalization are beyond the descriptive powers of a phrase structure grammar.[37] But the phrase structure rule schema in (9.7), taken together with the apparatus developed above, exactly captures these facts:

$$(9.7) \qquad \langle 42, [_{\bar{\bar{V}}} \quad \alpha \quad \bar{\bar{V}}/\alpha], \quad \lambda h_\alpha [(\bar{\bar{V}}/\alpha)'](\alpha') \rangle$$
$$\text{where } \alpha = \bar{\bar{X}}.$$

This schema will induce structure like those shown in (9.8)–(9.11):

(9.8) a.

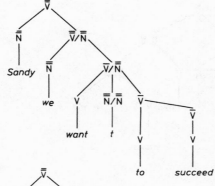

b.

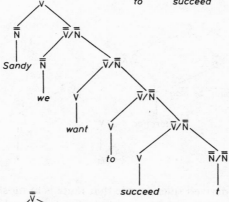

(9.9)

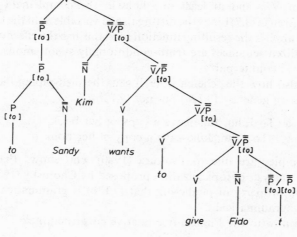

(9.10)

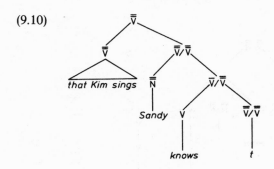

(9.11)

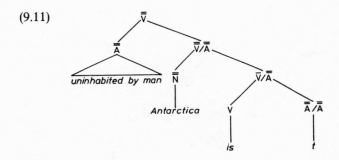

Note how the derived rules ensure that there is at most one hole in the complement $\bar{V}/\alpha$ and at least one hole in the complement $\bar{\bar{V}}/\alpha$. The semantics given in (9.7) binds the distinguished variable h_α in the translation of $\bar{\bar{V}}/\alpha$ and applies the resulting function to α: this has the effect of ensuring that topicalized sentences are truth-conditionally synonymous with their untopicalized counterparts.

Notice also how the schema in (9.7) gets the pied-piping facts exactly right. Thus we generate (9.12a) but not (9.12b):

(9.12)   a. To John, Julie gave a copy of her book.
          b. *To John, Julie gave a copy of her book to.

These examples are due to Iwakura (1980) who shows that the *wh-*movement analysis of topicalization proposed by Chomsky (1977) has the unfortunate property of predicting that (9.12b) is grammatical and that (9.12a) is ungrammatical.

We turn now to the English free relative construction:[38]

(9.13) $\langle 43, [_\alpha \quad \alpha \quad \bar{\bar{V}}/\alpha], \ldots \rangle$, where $\alpha = \bar{X}$.
$\begin{bmatrix} WH \\ ever \end{bmatrix}$

This analysis of free relatives is due, in effect, to Bresnan and Grimshaw (1978), and the structures induced by (9.12) will by virtually isomorphic to those proposed by them. The difference lies in the fact that the present framework can dispense with their rule of Controlled Pro Deletion (ibid: 370) and the coindexing convention associated with it. In (9.14) and (9.15) below we exhibit the structures that (9.13) will assign to Bresnan and Grimshaw's examples (119) and (120) (ibid: 357).

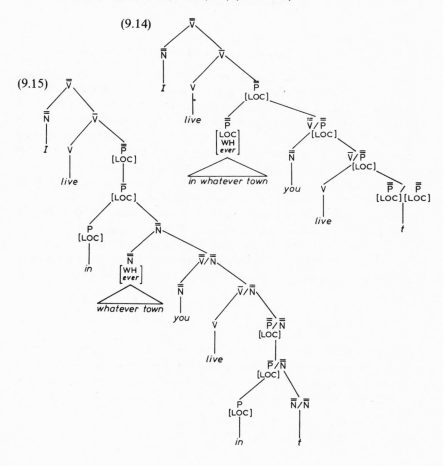

Note that our rule for topicalization given at (9.7) above, taken together with (9.13) makes exactly the same predictions as Bresnan and Grimshaw's analysis. I repeat their examples (their (121), ibid: 358) below:

(9.16)　　a. Whatever town you live in I'll live in.
　　　　　b. *Whatever town you live, I'll live in.
　　　　　c. In whatever town you live, I'll live.

The major advantage of the present analysis over that proposed by Bresnan and Grimshaw, apart from its basis in a more constrained linguistic metatheory, is that it automatically predicts the badness of examples like (9.17):

(9.17)　　a. *I will live in whatever town you live near the sea.
　　　　　b. *I will live in whatever town you live in Brighton.

The only ways Bresnan and Grimshaw could account for such examples are (i) appeal to as yet unspecified interpretive rules, or (ii) ordering Controlled Pro Deletion before lexical insertion, or (iii) introducing a filter to block strings containing certain types of unindexed WH phrase. But the facts follow from (9.13) since derived categories must, of necessity, dominate "holes". This is a quite general advantage of the present framework over analyses employing controlled deletion for unbounded dependencies.

Note also that the familiar c-command condition on the relation between the controlling expression and the controlled "hole" simply follows from the use of context-free phrase structure rules to generate this kind of construction: in a rule of the form $[_y \ \alpha \ \beta/\alpha]$ or $[_y \ \beta/\alpha \ \alpha]$, α cannot help but c-command the hole in β/α. But the c-command condition on binding has to be separately stipulated in theories which employ transformations like Controlled Pro Deletion or *wh*-movement to handle unbounded dependencies.

10. ISLANDS

As Brame (1978a: 100ff) has pointed out, some island constraints account for data whose problematic status is merely an artefact of the postulation of movement rules. He considers the following examples (from Chomsky 1973: 88):

(10.1)　　a. I believe the dog is hungry.
　　　　　b. I believe the dog to be hungry.

(10.2) a. *The dog is believed is hungry by me.
       b. The dog is believed to be hungry by me.

If passives derived via NP-movement, then both (10.2a) and (10.2b) will be generated in the absence of any constraints. Imposition of the Tensed S condition will block (10.2a). But, in frameworks such as Brame's or that of the present paper, which abjure all movement rules, there is no problem with this data, and consequently no need to invoke a Tensed S condition to account for it.[39]

Another example of an artefactual island constraint is Ross's (1967) Coordinate Structure Constraint (CSC). Gazdar (1981) shows in detail how all the phenomena covered by the CSC, together with the across-the-board violations of it, simply follow from the analysis of unbounded dependencies developed in section 9 above, and the rule schemata for coordination given in section 6 above. Briefly: α cannot be coordinated with α/β since α and α/β are not the same syntactic category. But α can be coordinated with α, and α/β can be coordinated with α/β. Thus:

(10.3) a. *The person that Kim loves and Lee hates Kim irritates me.
          ($\bar{V}/\bar{N}$ & $\bar{V}$)
       b. The fact that Kim loves Lee and Lee hates Kim irritates me.
          ($\bar{V}$ & $\bar{V}$)
       c. The person that Kim loves and Lee hates irritates me.
          ($\bar{V}/\bar{N}$ & $\bar{V}/\bar{N}$)

Numerous island constraints other than the CSC have been proposed in recent years. Unfortunately, few if any of them are as resilient to counterexample as the CSC is. Nevertheless, it is perhaps worth pausing to consider how one might formalize constraints once thought only applicable to movement rules in the framework of a theory in which no movement at all takes place.[40] It will be helpful to repeat the definition of the derived rule set at this point:

(10.4) $D(\beta, G) = \{ [_{\alpha/\beta}\, \sigma_1 \ldots \sigma_i/\beta \ldots \sigma_n] : [_\alpha \sigma_1 \ldots \sigma_i \ldots \sigma_n] \in G\, \&$
        $1 \leq i \leq n\, \& \sigma_i \in V_\beta \}$

We can formalize certain island constraints, if we wish, simply by stipulating that certain types of definable derived rule are not employed by a language (or by any language, if the constraint suggested is intended as a universal). Suppose we wanted to impose the A-over-A constraint. Then we could add a condition that $\alpha \neq \beta$ to (10.4). This would have the effect of preventing the creation of any derived rules of the form shown in (10.5):[41]

(10.5)　　$*[_{\alpha/\alpha}\ldots]$

Ross's (1967: 114) Left Branch Condition would involve prohibiting rules of the form shown in (10.6):[42]

(10.6)　　$*[_{\bar{N}/\bar{N}}\quad \bar{N}/\bar{N}\ldots]$

And his Complex NP Constraint (CNPC) would look like this:

(10.7)　　$*[_{\bar{N}/\alpha}\quad \bar{N}\ldots\Sigma/\alpha\ldots]$

Bresnan's (1976a) generalization of CNPC, the Complex Phrase Constraint, would look something like this:

(10.8)　　$*[_{\beta/\alpha}\quad \beta\ldots\Sigma/\alpha\ldots]$

And Horn's (1974) NP Constraint like this:

(10.9)　　$*[_{\bar{N}/\alpha}\ldots]$

The island constraints mentioned in (10.5)–(10.9) have in common their locality: that is to say that they can all be stated by reference to a particular class of rules. Equivalently, they could be formulated as filters on tree sets which ban all trees exhibiting certain local mother-daughter relationships. But some island constraints discussed in the recent literature (e.g. Subjacency) have not had this local character. Fodor (1980), developing an idea due to Koster (1978), proposes that nonlocal constraints on unbounded dependencies be stated on projection paths, where the latter are defined to be maximal subpaths of paths from root to terminal such that every node-label in the subpath is of the form α/β where β is a constant and α varies.[43]

Thus Maling and Zaenen (1980a) have proposed that the complex island facts in Italian discussed by Rizzi (1978) can be elegantly captured by the tree filter on projection paths shown in (10.10):

(10.10)　　Throw out all trees containing a projection path of the form
　　　　　　$\ldots\bar{Q}/\beta\ldots\bar{\Sigma}/\beta\ldots$

It is worth remarking that imposition of tree filters of the type shown in (10.10) has no effect on the generative capacity of the class of grammars employing them: the output of a CF-PSG filtered by a finite list of such tree filters will be a CFL. This can be simply proved by reference to finite state tree automata.

The definition of derived category as given in the previous section only allows for categories of the form α/β where $\alpha, \beta \in V_N$ and V_N simply consists of familiar complex symbols like, $\bar{N}, \bar{V}, \bar{\bar{V}}$, etc. A consequence of this definition is that the formalism has the effect of imposing the wh-island constraint: there can be no more than one unbounded dependency into a constituent.

This is arguably correct for English although there are a number of problematic examples even here. But it is clearly incorrect for such languages as Hebrew (Reinhart 1980), Italian (Rizzi 1978), Modern Irish (McCloskey 1979), and the Scandinavian languages (see Engdahl (1980a, 1980b) and Maling and Zaenen (this volume, 1980a) for extensive discussion).

Suppose we generalize the definitions of derived category (and derived rules) to permit categories of the form shown in (10.11):

(10.11) $\quad \alpha/\beta_1, \ldots \beta_n$

Two possibilities then present themselves. We could restrict n to be some small finite number the exact value of which would constitute a parameter of permissible language variation. Thus, arguably, for Palauan, Polish and Russian we have $n = 0$ (i.e. no unbounded dependencies whatsoever are permitted), for English $n \leq 1$, for Icelandic $n \leq 2$ (Maling and Zaenen 1980), while for Swedish the upperbound value for n must be at least 3 (see the data in Engdahl 1980a). For any finite value for n the resulting grammar will be CF. Engdahl (1980b) has, however, developed an argument against adopting any finite bound on n by analogy with the argument of Miller and Chomsky (1963) against restricting multiple centre embedding.

Suppose we put no restriction on n for a language like Swedish. This has the effect of taking us out of the class of CF-PSG's and into the class of *indexed grammars* (Aho 1968). Unrestricted indexed grammars generate the *indexed languages*. These are a proper superset of the CFLs (e.g. they include $\{a^n b^n c^n\}$) and a proper subset of the context-sensitive languages. In a recent textbook on formal languages, Hopcroft and Ullman remark that 'of the many generalizations of the context-free grammars that have been proposed, a class called "indexed" appears to be most natural, in that it arises in a wide variety of contexts' (1979: 398).

However, there is, as yet, no linguistic evidence to suggest that we need the full power of the indexed grammars. Thus, even assuming that Swedish permits arbitrarily many unbounded dependencies into a single constituent, there is no reason to believe that the stringset consisting of all and only the grammatical sentences of Swedish is anything other than a CFL.

Consequently, a move towards the adoption of indexed grammars needs to be accompanied by specific proposals for constraining the expressive power of such devices in linguistically relevant ways.

University of Sussex
Brighton

NOTES

* This paper owes a special debt to Geoff Pullum whose manifold contributions have gone well beyond the call of editorial duty. I am also very grateful to the following rather long list of people for their comments and criticism: Emmon Bach, Lee Baker, Mike Brame, Ken Butcher, Richard Coates, David Dowty, Steve Draper, Elisabet Engdahl, Janet Fodor, Paloma Garcia-Bellido, Steve Harlow, Frank Heny, Polly Jacobson, Theo Janssen, Aravind Joshi, Ewan Klein, Bill Ladusaw, John Lyons, Joan Maling, Peter Matthews, Andrew Mill, Barbara Partee, Stan Peters, Paul Postal, Andrew Radford, Ivan Sag, Aaron Sloman, Neil Smith, Arnim von Stechow, Anthony Warner, Tom Wasow, and Annie Zaenen. This research was supported by grant HR 5767 from the SSRC (UK).

[1] As Wasow has pointed out, the goal of constraining the class of languages generated by permissible grammars is 'inherently more ambitious' (1978: p. 82) than the goal of constraining the class of permissible grammars: 'although the class of grammars may be restricted without changing the class of languages, the converse is, of course, not true; that is, it is not possible to limit the class of languages without limiting the class of grammars' (ibid: p. 82).

[2] The implicit learnability idealization made here, namely that the algorithm has access to surface structures, is no more implausible than that made in Hamburger and Wexler (1973) where the learner is assumed to have access to deep structures.

[3] However, I would not want to go as far as to claim that 'if all of English could be given in a context free (sensitive) form the learnability problem would be solved' (Keenan, 1979a).

[4] Unfortunately, Chomsky's discussions (1965: 210–211, 1966: 40–50) of Harman's proposals are spoilt by an irritating terminological imperialism. Consequently, he never responds to Harman's fundamental point, which I take to be this: 'The critique of phrase structure consists in the construction of a formal model of phrase-structure theory and the demonstration that this is inadequate as a complete theory of grammar. The defense of phrase structure consists in ... repudiating the model of constituent structure, as Chomsky defines it, and for replacing it with a model which obviates the original criticisms' (1963: pp. 610–611).

[5] See Harris (1951), Chomsky (1970), Selkirk (1972), Bresnan (1976b), Emonds (1976), and Jackendoff (1977) for various proposals.

[6] E.g. WH, PRO (as in Chomsky 1977), LOC, TEMP, DIR (Bresnan and Grimshaw 1978), agreement features (e.g. Wasow 1975: p. 374), etc.

[7] But see Kratzer, Pause and Stechow (1973).

[8] For arguments that agreement is phrasal rather than lexical see Keenan (1979a).

[9] The preceding discussion constitutes a refutation of the claim that verb agreement instances a 'grammatical process that is beyond the generative capacity of ... the CF-PSG' (Grinder and Elgin 1973: p. 65.)

[10] Stan Peters has pointed out to me that this result can be proved directly, and more elegantly, by defining local filters in terms of tree automata, but I shall not do that here. See Thatcher (1973) and Levy (forthcoming) for an introduction to tree automata.

These remarks about local filters are included purely for their technical interest and do not constitute an implicit endorsement of their putative status as a component in natural language grammars. Following Brame (1979, 1980), I regard filters of the Chomsky and Lasnik type as inadequate and generalization-missing attempts to recapitulate lexical restrictions. They may be necessary to patch up the output of a transformational grammar, but they should have no role to play in a grammar of the kind proposed here.

[11] We will ignore other possible expansions of $\bar{\bar{P}}$ and $\bar{P}$ here.

[12] I am grateful to John Lyons for reminding me of the relevance of these facts.

[13] I am indebted to Ewan Klein and Barbara Partee for some painstaking advice on the semantic components of the rules given.

[14] The idea that *to* is a kind of verb, suggested in unpublished work by Dick Hudson and by Paul Postal, is adopted in Gazdar, Pullum and Sag (forthcoming).

[15] Note that lexical items can be multiply listed, thus *eat* is a V[7] as well as a V[8]. But $([_V eat])'$ is a one-place predicate, whereas $([_V eat])'$ is a two-place predicate. The meanings of
[7] [8]
such contextual variants of the same word can be captured by meaning postulate schemata such as the following one:

For all α such that $V[7] \to \alpha$ and $V[8] \to \alpha$,

$$\Box \forall \mathscr{P}[([_V \alpha])'(\mathscr{P}) \leftrightarrow ([_V \alpha])'(\hat{P}\exists x P(x))(\mathscr{P})]$$
[7]   [8]

This is a notational variant of the approach proposed by Dowty (1978b).

[16] Following Oehrle (1975), Dowty (1978b), and Hoekstra (1980), we treat the dative alternation in English as a purely lexical matter.

[17] This rule only deals with the construction where *seem* and *appear* have full lexical subjects rather than dummy *it* or *there*. For a treatment of dummy subject dependencies, see Sag (this volume).

[18] This rule is included only for the sake of completeness. See Gazdar, Pullum and Sag (forthcoming) for a more general analysis of the complements of copular *be*.

[19] We will ignore other possible expansions of $\bar{A}$ here.

[20] Following Wasow (1977), we assume that passive adjectives like *closed* are arrived at by lexical rule. Non-adjectival passives are discussed in section 8, below.

[21] On regular expressions, and the notation used to characterize them, see, e.g. Hopcroft and Ullman 1979: pp. 28–29.

[22] This is trivial to prove, and it follows in any case as a corollary of a more general theorem proved by Langendoen (1976).

[23] Although the strings generated by these regular CF-PSG rules can be generated by ordinary CF-PSG rules, the trees that they induce cannot. So one can reasonably ask whether employing rules like those in (6.4) is going to making parsing of CFLs harder (assuming, that is, that the parse tree we want is the one that would be assigned by (6.4)). The answer is no: Earley points out that his algorithm 'has the useful property that it can be modified to handle an extension of context-free grammars which makes use of the Kleene Star notation' (1970: p. 101) [Note that $\alpha^+ = \alpha\alpha^*$].

²⁴ I am grateful to Peter Matthews and Richard Coates for enabling me to discover exactly what the Latin coordination facts were.

²⁵ This terminology is due to Langendoen (1976). The idea of using a grammar to generate one's grammar originates with van Wijngaarden (1969) who used the technique to give a perspicuous syntax for the computer language ALGOL68. A good introduction to his work can be found in Cleaveland and Uzgalis (1975). Janssen (1980) employs a van Wijngaarden-style two-level grammar to define a generalization of Montague's PTQ syntax.

²⁶ This metarule, and the auxiliary $\bar{V}$ rules assumed below, are taken from Gazdar, Pullum and Sag (forthcoming) from which further details should be sought.

²⁷ A desirable consequence of this requirement is that coordination rules can never feed metarules.

²⁸ I am grateful to Tom Wasow for making me aware that some such restriction on grammar and metarule systems was required. Aravind Joshi has pointed out to me that allowing a single non-abbreviatory variable in the structural analysis of metarules would open the way to PS grammars with infinite sets of rules, but would not result in any of those grammars inducing non-context-free languages. Non-context-free languages can only result when two or more non-abbreviatory variables are permitted.

²⁹ Cf. Brame 1978a: 110–112. Also Monzon 1979.

³⁰ Keenan's paper mysteriously ascribes various properties to the analysis of passives proposed in Gazdar (1981). This is mysterious since the closest thing to an analysis of passives in Gazdar (1981) is the following tautology: 'if there are no transformations then there is no passive transformation'. Pace Keenan, it does not follow from this, or from anything else in that paper, that 'there are two passive operations in English' (ibid: 212) or that 'adjective phrases are derived from TVPs and the passive VPs are formed by an independent rule which adjoins copular verbs like *be* with adjective phrases' (ibid: 213).

³¹ Note that the present analysis, like Bach's, predicts that a sentence like (i) is also ambiguous:

    (i)   John was attacked and bitten.

The putative readings are one in which the same agent is responsible for both the attacking and the biting, and one in which it is left open as to whether the same agent was responsible. This ambiguity prediction is not obviously correct. Thus Paul Postal points out that example (ii) is predicted to have a necessarily false reading as well as a banal reading, but intuitively it appears only to have the latter:

    (ii)   Seven is preceded and followed.

³² Thus, for example, it is trivial to arrange for all the sentences generated by some finite state grammar to end with the same terminal symbol that they began with, even when there is no upper bound on the length of sentence generable by the grammar.

³³ At least, not in general. In the case of the rule for topicalization at (9.7) below, it happens that S/α combines with an α to form an S, exactly as they would on a categorial interpretation of the notation.

³⁴ Aravind Joshi has pointed out to me that a notation having the same interpretation as derived category symbols is to be found in Zellig Harris's work, thus: 'S-N or "S excising N" indicates an S string from which one N has been cut out' (1962: p. 11n). However, Harris appears to use such labels simply as a descriptive device for the analysis of texts, rather than as an essential component of an explicit generative grammar for English. More recently, c.f. Baker (1978: p. 113), and Hellan (1977: p. 128).

[35] The definition in (9.2) is a metarule, albeit a very general one, and could just as well be stated in the abbreviatory notation for metarules introduced in section 7 above. Thus:

$$\langle [_\alpha \ X \ \sigma \ Y], \ \mathscr{F} \rangle \Rightarrow$$

$$\langle [_{\alpha/\beta} \ X \ \sigma/\beta \ Y], \ \mathscr{F} \rangle \qquad \text{where } \sigma \in V_\beta \subseteq V_N.$$

[36] See Gazdar (1980b) for comparative "deletion" and "subdeletion" dependencies, and Gazdar (1981) on relative clauses and constituent questions.

[37] I am grateful to Geoff Pullum for drawing this passage to my attention.

[38] The generality of α here is slightly spurious: as Bresnan and Grimshaw demonstrate, when $\alpha = $ PP we have to restrict it to locative and temporal PPs. Note also that the use of the *ever* feature on the head is simply to get the morphology of free relatives right (see Bresnan and Grimshaw 1978: 338–339). Its presence does not amount to the obviously false claim that the *ever* suffix has to appear in free relative heads.

[39] *Believe* is introduced by the V rules $[_{\bar{V}} \ V \ \bar{V}]$ and $[_{\bar{V}} \ V \ \bar{N} \ \underset{[\text{INF}]}{V}]$ (see (5.8) and (5.15), above). Only the latter can be input to the passive metarule (8.1) since the former does not mention a post-verbal $\bar{N}$. Consequently, the only passive rule for *believe* will be $[_{\bar{V}} \ \underset{[\text{PAS}]}{V} \ \underset{[\text{INF}]}{V} \ \underset{(\text{by})}{(\bar{P})}]$. This will admit (10.2b) but not (10.2a).

[40] The question of how one formalizes island constraints is, of course, distinct from the question of how one motivates them. The remarks made here only address the question of formalization, a question that is rarely addressed in the literature.

[41] Remember that $[_{\alpha/\alpha} \ t]$ is not itself a derived rule and so it will not be forbidden by the addition of a $\alpha \neq \beta$ clause to (10.4).

[42] See Gazdar (1981) for detailed discussion of a generalization of (10.6) referred to there as Generalized Left Branch Condition.

[43] Definition is not quite this simple, however, since we need to ignore pseudo-paths caused by the contiguity of two genuine projection paths. For example, in a case like that shown in (i):

(i)

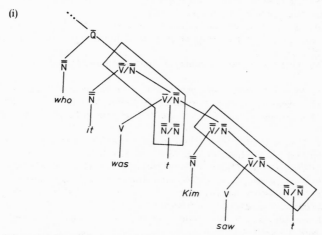

It is straightforward, though tedious, to define the notion of projection path so as to exclude the path from the highest $\bar{V}/\bar{N}$ to the lowest $\bar{N}/\bar{N}$ in (i).

BIBLIOGRAPHY

Aho, A. V. (1968) 'Indexed grammars – an extension of context-free grammars,' *Journal of the Association for Computing Machinery* **15**, 647–671.

Aho, A. V. and J. D. Ullman (1972) *The Theory of Parsing, Translation, and Compiling*, Prentice-Hall, Englewood Cliffs.

Amritavalli, R. (1979) 'The representation of transitivity in the lexicon,' *Linguistic Analysis* **5**, 71–92.

Anderson, S. R. and S. Chung (1977) 'On grammatical relations and clause structure in verb-initial languages,' In P. Cole and J. M. Sadock (eds.), *Syntax and Semantics 8: Grammatical Relations*, Academic Press, New York, 1–25.

Bach, E. (1974) *Syntactic Theory*, Holt, Rinehart & Winston, New York.

Bach, E. (1976) 'An extension of classical transformational grammar,' Mimeo, University of Massachusetts, Amherst, Massachusetts.

Bach, E. (1980a) 'In defense of Passive.' *Linguistics and Philosophy* **3**, 297–341.

Bach, E. (1980b) 'Tenses and aspects as functions on verb-phrases,' In C. Rohrer (ed.) *Time, Tense and Quantifiers*, Max Niemeyer, Tübingen.

Baker, C. L. (1978) *Introduction to Generative-Transformational Syntax*, Prentice Hall, Englewood Cliffs, New Jersey.

Bar-Hillel, Y., M. Perles, and E. Shamir (1961) 'On formal properties of simple phrase structure grammars,' *Zeitschrift für Phonetik, Sprachwissenschaft und Kommunikationsforschung* **14**, 143–172. Reprinted in R. D. Luce et al. (eds.) (1965) *Readings in Mathematical Psychology*, Wiley, New York, 75–105.

Book, R. V. (1973) 'Topics in formal language theory,' in A. V. Aho (ed.) *Currents in the theory of computing*. Prentice Hall, Englewood Cliffs, New Jersey, 1–34.

Brame, M. K. (1978a) *Base Generated Syntax*, Noit Amrofer, Seattle.

Brame, M. K. (1978b) 'The Base Hypothesis and the Spelling Prohibition,' *Linguistic Analysis* **4**, 1–30.

Brame, M. K. (1979) 'Chomsky/Lasnik filters are special cases of functional deviance,' in *Realistic Grammar*, Noit Amrofer, Seattle, pp. 67–107.

Brame, M. K. (1980) 'Lexicon vs filters,' in T. Hoekstra et al. (eds.), pp. 73–95.

Bresnan, J. W. (1976a) 'Evidence for a theory of unbounded transformations,' *Linguistic Analysis* **2**, 353–393.

Bresnan, J. W. (1976b) 'On the form and functioning of transformations,' *Linguistic Inquiry* **7**, 3–40.

Bresnan, J. W. (1978) 'A realistic transformational grammar,' in M. Halle, J. Bresnan, and G. A. Miller (eds.), *Linguistic Theory and Psychological Reality*, MIT Press, Cambridge.

Bresnan, J. W. and J. Grimshaw (1978) 'The syntax of free relatives in English,' *Linguistic Inquiry* **9**, 331–391.

Carlson, G. and T. Roeper (1980) 'Morphology and subcategorization: Case and the unmarked complex verb,' in T. Hoekstra et al. (eds.), pp. 123–164.

Chomsky, N. (1965) *Aspects of the Theory of Syntax*, MIT Press, Cambridge, Ma. .

Chomsky, N. (1966) *Topics in the Theory of Generative Grammar*, The Hague, Mouton.

Chomsky, N. (1970) 'Remarks on nominalization,' in R. A. Jacobs and P. S. Rosenbaum (eds.) *Readings in English Transformational Grammar*, Ginn, Waltham.

Chomsky, N. (1973) 'Conditions on transformations,' in *Essays on Form and Interpretation*, North Holland, New York, 81–160.

Chomsky, N. (1975) *The Logical Structure of Linguistic Theory*. Plenum, New York.

Chomsky, N. (1977) 'On Wh-movement,' in Culicover et al. pp. 71–132.

Chomsky, N. (1979) *Language and Responsibility*, Harvester Press, Hassocks.

Chomsky, N. & H. Lasnik (1977) 'Filters and control,' *Linguistic Inquiry* 8, 425–504.

Cleaveland, J. and R. Uzgalis (1975) *Grammars for Programming Languages: What Every Programmer Should Know About Grammar*, American Elsevier, New York.

Comrie, B. (1979) 'The languages of Micronesia,' *Linguistics* 17, 1057–1071.

Cooper, R. (forthcoming) *Quantification and Syntactic Theory*, D. Reidel, Dordrecht.

Culicover, P. W., T. Wasow, and A. Akmajian (1977) *Formal Syntax*, Academic Press, New York.

Dowty, D. (1978a) 'Applying Montague's views on linguistic metatheory to the structure of the lexicon,' *Papers from the Parasession on the Lexicon*, Chicago Linguistic Society, Chicago, Illinois, pp. 97–137.

Dowty, D. (1978b) 'Governed transformations as lexical rules in a Montague Grammar,' *Linguistic Inquiry* 9, 393–426.

Earley, J. (1970) 'An efficient context-free parsing algorithm,' *Communications of the ACM* 13, 94–102.

Emonds, J. E. (1976) *A Transformational Approach to English Syntax: Root, Structure-Preserving, and Local Transformations*, Academic Press, New York.

Engdahl, E. (1980a) 'Unbounded dependencies in Swedish,' Paper presented to the Sloan workshop on alternatives to transformational gramars, Stanford.

Engdahl, E. (1980b) 'WH constructions in Swedish and the relevance of subjacency,' to appear in *Papers from the Tenth Regional Meeting of the North Eastern Linguistic Society*.

Fodor, J. D. (1978) 'Parsing strategies and constraints on transformations,' *Linguistic Inquiry* 9, 427–473.

Fodor, J. D. (1980) 'Parsing, constraints and the freedom of expression,' Mimeo, University of Connecticut.

Fu, K-S., and T. L. Booth (1975) 'Grammatical inference: Introduction and survey,' *IEEE Transactions on Systems, Man, and Cybernetics* 5, 95–111, 409–423.

Gazdar, G. J. M. (1980a) 'A cross-categorial semantics for coordination,' *Linguistics & Philosophy* 3, 407–409.

Gazdar, G. J. M. (1980b) 'A phrase structure syntax for comparative clauses,' in T. Hoekstra et al. (eds.), pp. 165–179.

Gazdar, G. J. M. (1981) 'Unbounded dependencies and coordinate structure,' *Linguistic Inquiry* 12, 155–184.

Gazdar, G. J. M., G. K. Pullum, and I. Sag (forthcoming) 'Auxiliaries and related phenomena in a restrictive theory of grammar', to appear in *Language*.

Gold, E. M. (1967) 'Language identification in the limit,' *Information and Control* 10, 447–474.

Graham, S. L. (1976) 'On-line context-free language recognition in less than cubic time,' *Proceedings of the Eighth Annual ACM Symposium on the Theory of Computing*, pp. 112–120.

Grinder, J. T. and S. H. Elgin (1973) *Guide to Transformational Grammar: History, Theory, Practice*, Holt, Rinehart and Winston, New York.

Hamburger, H. and K. Wexler (1973) 'Identifiability of a class of transformational grammars,' in J. Hintikka, J. M. E. Moravcsik and P. Suppes (eds.), *Approaches to Natural Language*, D. Reidel, Dordrecht.

184   GERALD GAZDAR

Harman, G. H. (1963) 'Generative grammars without transformation rules: a defense of phrase structure,' *Language* 39, 597–616.
Harris, Z. S. (1951) *Methods in Structural Linguistics*, University of Chicago Press, Chicago, Illinois.
Harris, Z. S. (1962) *String Analysis of Language Structure*, Mouton, The Hague.
Hellan, L. (1977) 'X̄-syntax, categorial syntax and logical form,' in T. Fretheim & L. Hellan (eds.) *Papers from the Trondheim Syntax Symposium*, Trondheim, pp. 83–135.
Heny, F. (1979) Review of Chomsky (1975), *Synthese* 40, 317–352.
Hoekstra, T. (1980) 'The status of the indirect object,' in W. Zonneveld and F. Weerman (eds.), *Linguistics in the Netherlands 1977–1979*, Foris, Dordrecht, pp. 152–169.
Hoekstra, T., H. v. d. Hulst and M. Moortgat (1980) *Lexical Grammar*, Foris Publications, Dordrecht.
Hopcroft, J. E. & J. D. Ullman (1979) *Introduction to Automata Theory, Languages, and Computation*, Addison-Wesley, Reading, Massachusetts.
Hust, J. R. and M. K. Brame (1976) 'Jackendoff on interpretive semantics,' *Linguistic Analysis* 2, 243–277.
Iwakura, K. (1980) 'On WH-movement and constraints on rules,' *Linguistic Analysis* 6, 53–95.
Jackendoff, R. (1977) *X̄ syntax: a Study of Phrase Structure*, MIT Press, Cambridge, Massachusetts.
Janssen, T. M. V. (1980) 'On problems concerning the quantification rules in Montague grammar', in C. Rohrer (ed.) *Time, Tense, and Quantifiers*, Max Niemeyer, Tübingen, pp. 113–134.
Janssen, T. M. V., G. Kok and L. Meertens (1977) 'On restrictions on transformational grammars reducing the generative power,' *Linguistics and Philosophy* 1, 111–118.
Joshi, A. K. and L. S. Levy (1977) 'Constraints on structural descriptions: Local transformations,' *SIAM Journal of Computing* 6, 272–284.
Joshi, A. K., L. S. Levy, and K. Yueh (1978) 'Local constraints in the syntax and semantics of programming languages,' In *Proceedings of the 5th Annual Symposium on Principles of Programming Languages*.
Joshi, A. K., L. S. Levy, and K. Yueh (forthcoming) 'Local constraints in the syntax and semantics of programming languages,' to appear in *Journal of Theoretical Computer Science*.
Kaplan, R. M. (1978) 'Computational resources and linguistic theory,' Paper presented to TINLAP 2.
Keenan, E. L. (1979a) 'On surface form and logical form,' *Studies in the Linguistic Sciences* 8.2.
Keenan, E. L. (1979b) 'Passive: A case study in markedness,' Paper presented at the GLOW Colloquium on Markedness, Scuola Normale Superiore, Pisa.
Keenan, E. L. (1980) 'Passive is phrasal (not sentential or lexical),' in T. Hoekstra et al. (eds.), pp. 181–213.
Keenan, E. L. and L. Faltz (1978) *Logical types for natural language*, UCLA Occasional Papers in Linguistics 3.
Klein, E. H. (1978) *On Sentences Which Report Beliefs, Desires and other Mental Attitudes*, PhD dissertation, University of Cambridge.
Koster, J. (1978) 'Conditions, empty nodes, and markedness,' *Linguistic Inquiry* 9, 551–593.

Kratzer, A., E. Pause, and A. von Stechow (1973) *Einführung in Theorie und Anwendung der generativen Syntax*, Athenaum, Frankfurt.

Ladusaw, W. (1980) *Polarity Sensitivity as Inherent Scope Relations*, Garland, New York.

Langendoen, D. T. (1976) 'On the weak generative capacity of infinite grammars,' *CUNYForum* **1**, 13–24, City University of New York.

Lapointe, S. G. (1977) 'Recursiveness and deletion,' *Linguistic Analysis* **3**, 227–265.

Lapointe, S. G. (1980) 'A lexical analysis of the English auxiliary verb system,' in T. Hoekstra et al. (eds.), 215–254.

Levelt, W. J. M. (1979) 'On learnability: a reply to Lasnik and Chomsky,' Mimeo, Nijmegen.

Levine, B. A. (1979) *The automated inference of tree systems*, PhD dissertation, Oregon State University.

Levy, L. S. (forthcoming) 'Automata on trees: a tutorial survey,' To appear in *Egyptian Computer Journal*.

Lewis, C. T. and C. Short (1879) *A Latin Dictionary*, Oxford: Clarendon Press..

Lightfoot, D. (1979) 'Rule classes and syntactic change,' *Linguistic Inquiry* **10**, 83–108.

Maling, J. and A. Zaenen (1980) 'Notes on base-generation and unbounded dependencies,' Paper presented to the Sloan workshop on alternatives to transformational grammar, Stanford.

Maling, J. and A. Zaenen (this volume) 'A base-generated account of Scandinavian extraction phenomena.'

Marslen-Wilson, W. D. (1973) *Speech Shadowing and Speech Perception*, unpublished PhD dissertation, MIT.

McCawley, J. D. (1968) 'Concerning the base component of a transformational grammar,' *Foundations of Language* **4**, 243–269. Reprinted in *Grammar and Meaning*, Academic Press, New York, 35–58.

McCloskey, J. (1979) *Transformational syntax and model theoretic semantics*, D. Reidel, Dordrecht.

McCloskey, J. (1980) 'Is there Raising in Modern Irish?' *Eriu* **31**, 59–99.

Miller, G. A. & N. Chomsky (1963) 'Finitary models of language users,' in *Handbook of Mathematical Psychology* II, chapter 13, Wiley, New York.

Montague, R. (1970) 'Universal grammar,' In Montague (1974).

Montague, R. (1973) 'The proper treatment of quantification in ordinary English,' In Montague (1974).

Montague, R. (1974) *Formal philosophy* (ed. by R. H. Thomason), Yale University Press, New Haven.

Monzon, M. C. (1979) *A Constituent Structure Rule Grammar of the Spanish Clitic Positioning in Complex and Simple Sentences*, MA dissertation, Austin.

Oehrle, R. (1975) *The Grammatical Status of the Dative Alternation*, PhD dissertation, MIT.

Pelletier, F. J. (1980) 'The generative power of rule orderings in formal grammars,' *Linguistics* **18**, 17–72.

Perlmutter, D. M. and S. Soames (1979) *Syntactic Argumentation and the Structure of English*, University of California Press, Berkeley.

Peters, P. S. (1979) 'How semantics keeps syntax psychologically computable,' paper presented to the Cognitive Studies Seminar, University of Sussex.

Peters, P. S. and R. W. Ritchie (1969, 1973) 'Context-sensitive immediate constituent analysis: context-free languages revisited.' In (1969) *ACM Symposium on Theory of*

Computing, ACM, New York, 1–8. And in (1973) *Mathematical Systems Theory* **6**, 324–333.

Peters, P. S. and R. W. Ritchie (1973) 'On the generative power of transformational grammars,' *Information Sciences* **6**, 49–83.

Postal, P. M. and G. K. Pullum (1978) 'Traces and the description of English complementizer contraction,' *Linguistic Inquiry* **9**, 1–29.

Pullum, G. K. and G. J. M. Gazdar (1981) 'Natural languages and context-free languages,' Stanford Cognitive Science Group working paper.

Pullum, G. K. and D. Wilson (1977) 'Autonomous syntax and the analysis of auxiliaries,' *Language* **53**, 1–37.

Reinhart, T. (1980) 'A second COMP position,' to appear in the proceedings of the Pisa Colloquium on Markedness, Annali della Scuola Normale Superiore, Pisa.

Rizzi, L. (1978) 'Violations of the WH-island constraint in Italian and the subjacency condition,' *Montreal Working Papers in Linguistics* **11**, 155–190.

Roeper, T. and M. E. A. Siegel (1978) 'A lexical transformation for verbal compounds,' *Linguistic Inquiry* **9**, 199–260.

Ross, J. R. (1967) *Constraints on Variables in Syntax*, PhD thesis, MIT. Published by Indiana University Linguistics Club, Bloomington, Indiana.

Sag, I. (this volume) 'A semantic theory of "NP-movement" dependencies.'

Sampson, G. (1979) 'What was transformational grammar?' [Review article on Chomsky (1975)], *Lingua* **48**, 355–378.

Selkirk, E. (1972) *The Phrase Phonology of English and French*, PhD dissertation, MIT, Published by Garland, New York, 1979.

Sheil, B. (1976) 'Observations on context free parsing,' *Statistical Methods in Linguistics* **7**, 71–109.

Shir, N. E. (1977) *On the Nature of Island Constraints*, (PhD thesis, MIT.) Indiana University Linguistics Club, Bloomington, Indiana.

Thatcher, J. W. (1973) 'Tree automata: an informal survey,' in A. V. Aho (ed.) *Currents in the Theory of Computing*, Prentice Hall, Englewood Cliffs, New Jersey.

Thomason, R. H. (1976) 'On the semantic interpretation of the Thomason 1972 fragment,' Mimeo, Pittsburgh.

Valiant, L. G. (1975) 'General context-free recognition in less than cubic time,' *Journal of Computer and System Sciences* **10**, 308–315.

van Wijngaarden, A. (1969) 'Report on the algorithmic language ALGOL 68,' *Numerische Mathematik* **14**, 79–218.

Vergnaud, J-R. (1973) 'Formal properties of lexical derivations,' *Quarterly Progress Report of the Research Laboratory in Electronics* **108**, 280–287, MIT.

Wasow, T. (1975) 'Anaphoric pronouns and bound variables,' *Language* **51**, 368–383.

Wasow, T. (1977) 'Transformations and the Lexicon,' in Culicover et al., pp. 327–360.

Wasow, T. (1978) 'On constraining the class of transformational languages,' *Synthese* **39**, 81–104.

PAULINE JACOBSON

EVIDENCE FOR GAPS

1. INTRODUCTION*

1.1. *Goals*

In what I will refer to as the classical theory of transformational grammar, it is assumed that there is no single level of representation for a sentence like (1) at which the NP *which table* is the leftmost constituent and at which there is an NP following *under*:

(1)   Which table is the book under?

Yet it is generally agreed that such a sentence behaves in certain respects as though there is an NP following *under* (for example, *under* does not normally occur without a following NP); such behavior is classically accounted for by positing an abstract derivational level at which *which table* follows *under*.

Recently there have been a number of proposals to the effect that the syntactic representation of a sentence includes a level which is richer than any single level in the classical theory. A consequence of such proposals is that the role played by distinct derivational levels can be greatly diminished or even entirely eliminated. So, for example, it·is claimed in trace theory (see, e.g., Fiengo (1974); Chomsky (1977)) that the surface structure of (1) contains an empty NP node after *under* (where this node is co-indexed with the NP *which table*). While most work within this theory still assumes the existence of derivations, a variety of phenomena which are classically accounted for at earlier derivational levels are instead taken to be properties of surface structure. Others have suggested that a level of representation containing empty nodes can, along with some other devices, be used ˈto eliminate derivations entirely; such a proposal is made, for example, in Gazdar (this volume). (Gazdar's representations differ from those in trace theory in that the empty nodes are not co-indexed with any other node.) A slightly different view of an enriched structure is one in which the NP *which table* is both in the leftmost position and in the position following *under*. I will refer to this as a multi-dominational theory, since it allows a node to be directly dominated by more than one node simultaneously.[1] Again, some pro-

187

P. Jacobson and G. K. Pullum (eds.), The Nature of Syntactic Representation, 187–228.
Copyright © 1982 by D. Reidel Publishing Company.

ponents of this view have pointed out that a single multi-dominational structure can capture many or all of the generalizations classically captured by derivations.

There are three main purposes to this paper. The first is to provide new motivation for the existence of an enriched level of representation. While it has often been shown that phenomena classically accounted for by derivations can instead be accounted for by positing an enriched level of representation, the approach here is to show that there are phenomena which simply can't be accounted for in a non ad hoc way in the classical theory. On the other hand, these phenomena can be handled quite simply with an enriched representation.

Second, I will argue that the relevant level contains empty nodes rather than multi-domination. (I will not specifically address the question of whether or not these nodes are co-indexed with other nodes; for the phenomena discussed here no such co-indexing is necessary so I will assume that it does not exist.) Thus the results here argue against a theory which posits a single multi-dominational representation for a sentence. As will be discussed, such a theory has essentially the same problems as the classical theory with respect to the facts developed here.

The third purpose of this paper is to provide evidence as to the range of constructions containing empty nodes. This evidence supports the distinction made in, e.g., Bresnan (1978) and Dowty (1978; this volume) between constructions like Passive, Equi and Raising on the one hand and constructions like wh-questions, relative clauses, Tough-movement and Gapping constructions on the other. Bresnan, Dowty and others have shown that Passive, for example, can be accounted for without positing any level of syntactic representation in which there is some NP in what is classically analyzed as the extraction site. In this view, Passive is treated not as a process mapping structures into other structures, but rather as a process mapping phrases of one category – in this case transitive verbs – into phrases of another category – here, intransitive verbs. Dowty shows that Raising and Equi can be treated in a similar fashion. Raising to Object, for example, can be formulated as a process which maps verbs that combine with sentential complements to form intransitive verbs into verbs which take VP complements to form transitive verbs. The fact that the "derived" object of the Raising verb is the "logical" subject of the embedded VP can be accounted for purely in the semantics by an appropriate translation of the Raising construction; no level of syntactic representation is needed at which the NP is the subject of the lower clause. The results here are consistent with such a treatment of these constructions in that these constructions will be shown to contain no empty node in the position classically analyzed as the extraction site position. The absence of such a node here follows under the category-changing approach.

Raising, Equi and Passive contrast with constructions like wh-questions and relative clauses. As discussed in Dowty, the latter type could not be treated as involving category-changing rules. First, there is no single constituent that can be analyzed as the "derived" phrase, since the domain of these constructions is unbounded. Even if this were not the case, a category-changing analysis does not account for the fact that any NP can be missing in these constructions; it is not some fixed argument of the verb which is missing. In other words, even if these constructions had only a single clause as their domain, they could be treated as involving category-changing rules only by positing as many separate rules as there are possible NP positions in a clause.

Gapping is an interesting construction in this regard. While it is not unbounded, it could not be treated as a process mapping phrases of one category into those of another. Not only is it unclear which constituent could be analyzed as undergoing the category change, but here too the missing constituents can be any of a number of different constituents:

(2)   a. I gave the book to Mary and the record to Sue.
            (Subject and Verb missing)
        b. John ate bananas quickly and Sam slowly.
            (Verb and Object missing)
        c. Sam put a book on the table and Bill a record.
            (Verb and PP missing)

Thus it is not surprising that, as will be shown in Section 3, Gapping behaves like relative clauses and wh-questions in containing an empty node (or nodes) in the position(s) of the missing material.

The discussion here is not meant to imply that constructions like relative clauses could not also be base-generated, where an empty node is generated in the position of the missing constituent. I will return to this directly below; the main point here is simply that these constructions contrast with constructions like Passive in that there is a level of representation for these with some node in what is classically treated as the extraction site.

Before continuing, it will be useful to clarify some terminology. In what follows, I will refer to empty nodes as gaps, and will designate them with the symbol $\emptyset$. As in the discussion above, I will be using the term "extraction site" without meaning to imply that some node has necessarily been moved or deleted from the position in question. The term "extracted node" is similarly used simply for convenience, without any particular theoretical significance. In fact, I will often use terminology of the classical theory which suggests movement or deletion analyses of various constructions. This terminology is adopted simply because of its familiarity; the results in this paper will hold in a theory in which gaps are base-generated and in which (with one possible exception) there are no movement or deletion rules. (The exception here involves cliticization rules; my discussion of these in Section 3 presupposes that structures with cliticized items are derived from more abstract structures. It may well be, though, that the same results would obtain given a base-generated account of clitics; I will leave this question open.)

1.2. *Implications of Gaps*

Before turning to the evidence for a level of representation with gaps, let us briefly consider the significance of such a level for the organization of the grammar and, in particular, for the role of derivations. A transformational analysis of extraction constructions like wh-questions, topicalized sentences, etc., has traditionally been motivated by two kinds of facts. First, there are ways in which these constructions behave as though there is a node of the appropriate type in the position of the extraction site. One case like this was noted above; prepositions cannot, in general, occur without a following NP,[2] but they can in these constructions. The classical way to account for such a "missing" NP is to posit that at some level there is an NP in this position, that the relevant restrictions (such as the above restriction on prepositions) are properties of this level, and that the NP is moved into its surface position, or, in the case of some constructions, is deleted. Clearly, though, a representation with gaps can account for such behavior without positing an abstract derivational level. A single level of representation is sufficient here because this representation does contain a node of the appropriate type in the extraction site position. (For a proposal as to how to capture the dependency between a missing node and the extracted node without movement or deletion rules, see Gazdar (this volume)).

However, there are also cases by which the extracted item itself behaves as though it is in the position of the extraction site. A classical example of this type is case-marking in the dialect which makes the distinctions in (3); here the case marking on the fronted wh-word is determined by the position of the extraction site:

(3)   a. $\left\{\begin{array}{c}\text{*Who} \\ \text{Whom}\end{array}\right\}$ did John see?

     b. $\left\{\begin{array}{c}\text{Who} \\ \text{*Whom}\end{array}\right\}$ did John say was coming?

I will refer to phenomena of this sort, where properties of material dominated by the extracted node are determined by the position of the extraction site, as phenomena exhibiting *strong connectivity*. (Note that the existence of strong connectivity can be captured in the classical theory only given a movement analysis of those constructions in which it occurs, and its existence is typically used to motivate movement rather than deletion analyses of those constructions.)

Strong connectivity appears problematic for a theory in which the only level of syntactic representation in one where the extracted node is in its fronted position and where there is an empty node in the position of the extraction site. Since the main purpose of this paper is to motivate the existence of such a level, we should briefly consider what kind of theory could both include such a representation and account for the existence of strong connectivity.

One possibility would be only a slight modification of the classical treatment of the relevant extraction constructions. That is, it could be that these constructions are derived by movement rules, but that these rules leave empty nodes in the position of the extraction sites. This is essentially the approach taken in trace theory. Thus those phenomena exhibiting strong connectivity would be properties of a pre-movement derivational level, whereas phenomena which do not would be properties of surface structure.

However, there are at least two problematic aspects of this theory. First, this predicts not only the existence of the two levels under discussion here, but of any number of intermediate levels as well. At these intermediate levels, some constituents have been moved, and some haven't. Yet there is no known motivation for these additional levels. Second, no principled way has been discovered to predict which phenomena will hold at which level. To put this differently, there is no prediction here as to what will exhibit strong connectivity and what won't.

Another account of strong connectivity is possible within a theory along the lines of Bresnan (1978, 1981). Here there are two and only two levels of syntactic representation – a level of constituent structure and a level of functional structure. The latter includes information concerning the grammatical function of each item, but does not include constituent structure notions such as precedence. (The distinction between the grammatical function or relation of an item and constituent structure is not novel in this approach; this is one of the fundamental ideas of Relational Grammar (Perlmutter and Postal (1977); Johnson and Postal (to appear). In relational grammar, however, constituent structure plays much less of a role.) So, for example, the constituent structure of (3a) in this approach would contain only an empty node after *see*, but in the functional structure the *wh*-NP would be stipulated as the object of *see*. Thus, while in this theory there is no level of representation at which the *wh*-NP follows *see*, strong connectivity can be accounted for at functional structure.

This theory is attractive in that it does not posit the additional levels posited in the classical theory. Moreover, it provides at least some predictions as to what will and what won't exhibit strong connectivity. Any phenomena which is a property of constituent structure rather than functional structure cannot have strong connectivity, whereas processes sensitive to the grammatical function of an item will. So, for example, the fact that a fronted *wh*-word is case-marked according to the position of the gap is easily accounted for here. While there is no level of representation at which this is in the constituent structure position of the gap, case-marking can easily be formulated as a functional structure process – subjects receive nominative case, while NP's with other grammatical relations receive accusative case.

A third account of strong connectivity is possible within the framework proposed in Gazdar (this volume). Here there is only a single level of syntactic representation, which includes base-generated gaps in the position of extraction sites. However, strong connectivity can be accounted for by treating certain phenomena as being features on nodes, and by ensuring that the "extracted" node in the relevant constructions will have the same features as the node dominating the gap. So, for example, if case is a feature on nodes, then the distribution of case-marking in (3) is accounted for provided that the *wh*-node must have the same features as the node in the position of the extraction site. One of the major motivations for Gazdar's approach – in which there is only one level of syntactic representation – is that the proposed mechanisms provably generate only context-free languages.

The main purpose of the present paper is simply to argue for a level of representation containing gaps; a detailed consideration of how to account for strong connectivity is beyond the scope of this paper. However, since the question arises as to why the phenomena discussed in Secs. 2 and 3 do *not* exhibit strong connectivity, I will return to this briefly in Sec. 4. In particular, since Gazdar's approach offers a more constrained theory of grammar than past approaches, I will discuss this question with respect to this approach.

2. THE OBJECT PRONOUN CONSTRAINT

The first piece of evidence for the existence of gaps that I will consider concerns the constraint first noted in Ross (1967) which blocks the (b)-sentences below:

(4)   a.   I gave Mary the book for Christmas.
        b.   *I gave Mary it for Christmas.
(5)   a.   I looked up the information in the almanac.
        b.   *I looked up it in the almanac.

It will be shown below that this constraint cannot be formulated in any simple way either in the classical theory, or in a theory with a single multi-dominational structure; it can, however, be stated quite simply if there is a representation containing gaps. Moreover, this constraint indicates that not all constructions classically analyzed as involving movement contain gaps. In particular, it can be shown that there is no gap after the verb in a Passive sentence.

2.1. *The Constraint within the Classical Theory*

Following Ross, we will assume for now that there is a constraint blocking structures in which an object pronoun is separated from the verb. (Some other accounts are discussed in 2.3). That is, we will assume that the constraint blocks structures of the form in (6):[3]

(6)   *$[_{VP}$ V X A $[_{NP}$ pro] Y] where the NP is directly
                              dominated by VP
        (A here is a variable ranging over nodes)

I will refer to (6) as the Object Pronoun Constraint.

In the classical theory, the question arises as to the level at which this constraint holds. Ross claimed that this was a constraint on surface structure; but it is also conceivable in this theory that the constraint holds cycle-finally. A cycle-final constraint would block a structure which met the description in (6) at the end of the cycle containing the VP. Notice that, given the assumption that there is a rule of Dative Movement, this cannot be a constraint on deep structures since, while (4b) is bad, the structure which underlies it in this account is not:

(7)   I gave it to Mary for Christmas.

Wasow (1975) argued that the constraint cannot, in fact, be a surface constraint, and that it must hold cyclically.[4] His evidence for this is based on the contrast between (8b) and (9b):

(8)   a.   It's hard to tell those children the stories.
          b. ?*Those children are hard to tell the stories.
(9)   a.   *It's hard to tell those children them.
          b.   *Those children are hard to tell them.

Note that (8b) is itself somewhat bad, but I agree with Wasow's judgement that (9b) is significantly worse. This indicates that the constraint must hold prior to the application of Tough-Movement, since this rule removes the NP which intervenes between the verb and the pronoun. A surface constraint in the classical theory predicts that (9b) should be no worse than (8b). However, given the assumption that *hard* takes a sentential comple-ment, and the consequent assumption that the *tell*-cycle is distinct from the cycle on which Tough-Movement applies, (9b) would be blocked by a cycle-final constraint. Here the structure at the end of the *tell*-cycle is:

(10)   [$_S$ NP [$_{VP}$ to tell the children them]]

where (10) violates the constraint in (6).
The same point can be illustrated with wh-Fronting:

(11)   a.   John gave someone the book.
          b. ?*Who did John give the book?
(12)   a.   *John gave someone it.
          b.   *Who did John give it?

Again (12b) is worse than (11b), and a surface constraint in the classical theory will not account for this contrast. However, a cycle-final constraint would block (12b) given the assumption that wh-Fronting applies after the *give*-cycle (this would follows if S and S̄ are separate cycles). Here (12b) would have the same structure as (12a) at the end of the *give*-cycle.
Yet, as discussed in Jacobson (1977), the interaction of Tough-Movement with this constraint also shows that in the classical theory the constraint

cannot be cyclic. If it were, then it is predicted that the violation will remain when the pronoun in (9a) rather than the intervening NP is removed on a higher cycle. But this prediction is incorrect:

(13)   a.   It's hard to tell the children the stories.

         b.   The stories are hard to tell the children.

(14)   a.   *It's hard to tell the children them.

         b.   They're hard to tell the children.

Here (14b) is grammatical, despite the fact that (10) is its structure at the end of the *tell*-cycle.[5]

Notice that the problem for the classical theory is independent of the assumption that the *tell*-cycle is distinct from the *hard*-cycle. The same problem arises if tough-predicates take VP rather than sentential complements and the embedded VP does not form a separate cycle. Regardless of whether one or two cycles are involved here, the constraint must hold prior to the application of Tough-Movement in order to correctly block (9b), but it cannot hold before Tough-Movement without also incorrectly blocking (14b). Thus, there is no single level in the classical theory at which the constraint can be stated.[6]

2.2. *Accounting for the Constraint with Gaps*

Consider now a theory with a representation in which wh- and Tough-Movement constructions contain empty nodes in the extraction site positions. The facts discussed above are automatically accounted for if the constraint holds for this representation. The structure of (9b) will be (15).

(15)   the children are hard [$_{VP}$ to tell $\emptyset$ them]

This is blocked because a gap intervenes between the verb and the pronoun. (14b), on the other hand, does not violate the constraint. Here there is no pronoun which is separated from the verb, but rather a gap:

(16)   they are hard [$_{VP}$ to tell the children $\emptyset$]

This constraint illustrates an important consequence of the claim that certain extraction sites are empty nodes. Note that the constraint blocks sentences which have two properties. First, there must be some node between the verb and the pronoun. But what the node dominates is irrelevant; it can, for example, dominate a full NP, a pronoun, or even be a non-NP:[7]

(17)   a. *I gave Mary it.
         b. *I gave her it.
         c. *I gave away it.

Secondly, it is crucial that what is separated from the verb is a *pronoun*; full NP's can of course be separated from the verb. Thus, the lexical properties of the intervening material are not crucial, but the lexical properties of the NP which is separated from the verb are.

In the classical theory, there is no single level at which the constraint holds because an NP removed by Tough-Movement continues to behave as though it is in the lower VP in terms of its intervening between the verb and the pronoun. But when the pronoun is removed, the sentence does not act as though a pronoun remained in the lower VP. This situation is exactly what is predicted to be the case if the constraint holds for a representation containing gaps. That is, it is predicted that an extraction site will behave as though there is some node in that position, but the lexical material dominated by the extracted node will be irrelevant.

To illustrate this further, it is worth comparing this to a global account in the classical theory, and to a formulation of the constraint on a multi-dominational structure. Looking first at a global formulation, the constraint would essentially have to block sentences whose cycle-final structure is as in (6) only if the relevant pronoun is in the same VP in surface structure. That is, the constraint would block derivations containing the following two structures:

(18)   cycle-final structure: $[_{VP_x} \; V \; X \; A \; [_{NP_y} \; pro] \; Y]$

         surface structure: $[_{VP_x} \; V \; X \; [_{NP_y} \; pro] \; Y]$

Aside from certain formal difficulties with this constraint (for example, each node would have to be indexed to ensure that it is the same VP and the same pronoun at the two derivational levels), a theory permitting a constraint like (18) provides no explanation as to why the facts should be as they are. The crucial cases, along with their putative source (9a), are repeated here:

(9)   a. *It's hard to tell the children them.
(9)   b. *The children are hard to tell them.
(14)   b. They are hard to tell the children.

The problem here is that in a theory which allows constraints like (18), it is just as easy to formulate a constraint which has the opposite effect. Thus a constraint which blocks derivations containing the two structures in (19) is no more complicated than (18), but this constraint makes the incorrect prediction that (9b) is grammatical and (14b) is not:

(19)   cycle-final structure: $[_{VP_x} \text{ V } \text{ X } \text{ A } [_{NP} \text{ pro}] \text{ Y}]$

surface structure: $[_{VP} \text{ V } \text{ X } \text{ A } \text{ Y}]$

And a much simpler constraint would be one blocking both (9b) and (14b) (a simple cycle-final constraint would have this effect), or one predicting that both are grammatical (a surface constraint would do this).

A multi-dominational account of the constraint has essentially the same problem. Consider a representation for *tough*-constructions in which the extracted NP is both in the subject position of the upper clause and in the position of the extraction site. If the constraint holds for such a representation, then it is correctly predicted that (9b) along with (9a) is ungrammatical. But this has exactly the same effect as a cyclic constraint in the classical theory; (14b) is incorrectly predicted to be ungrammatical because the pronoun *they* is in the lower VP and is separated from the verb.

There are ways that a multi-dominational representation could be elaborated to accommodate this constraint. Suppose that we distinguish between the "real" position of an extracted node and its other positions, which we will refer to as "pseudo" positions. A theory incorporating such a distinction has been proposed by Peters in unpublished work, and is independently needed if a multi-dominational structure is the only representation for a sentence since it is necessary to specify where the NP is actually pronounced. Let us assume a convention whereby a node referred to in a constraint like (6) is, unless otherwise specified, either a real or a pseudo node. However, nodes which are only real nodes can also be specified; these will be designated by double underlines.

Given this, the constraint could be formulated as follows:

(20) $*[_{VP} \text{ V } \text{ X } \text{ A } \underline{[_{NP} \text{ pro}]} \text{ Y}]$

Again, though, the other three logically possible situations are equally simple to describe; there is no reason why the constraint should be (20) rather than any of the following:

(21)   a. $*[_{VP} \text{ V } \text{ X } \underline{\underline{A}} \text{ } [_{NP} \text{ pro}] \text{ Y}]$
         b. $*[_{VP} \text{ V } \text{ X } \underline{A} \text{ } [_{NP} \text{ pro}] \text{ Y}]$
         c. $*[_{VP} \text{ V } \text{ X } \underline{\underline{A}} \text{ } [_{NP} \text{ pro}\underline{]} \text{ Y}]$

(21a) blocks (14b) while allowing (9b); (21b), like a classical cyclic constraint,

blocks both sentences; and (21c), like a classical surface constraint, blocks
neither. Thus there is no reason why that part of the constraint which refers
to lexical properties should refer only to the "real" position of an NP; but
this follows automatically if there is only an empty node in the position of
the extraction site.

At this point, I should forestall a possible objection to the claim that a
representation with gaps allows for a more explanatory account of these
facts. As noted in the Introduction, there are cases of strong connectivity;
for certain phenomena, an extracted node behaves as though it is in the
position of the extraction site with respect to material that it dominates.
Thus some provision must be made for such cases; as discussed in Section 1,
these can be accounted for either by positing another level of representation
(either an earlier derivational level, as in the classical theory, or a level of
functional structure), or with the use of features on nodes. Let us assume for
the moment that there is another level of representation in addition to a
representation with gaps; I will return to the latter solution below.
   As long as there is some other representation to account for strong
connectivity, it might be argued that a theory including a representation
with gaps is, in the end, no more explanatory than either the classical theory
or a theory with a single multi-dominational structure. That is, I have
said nothing so far to rule out the possibility that the Object Pronoun
Constraint holds at this other level. Without some principled distinction
between phenomena exhibiting strong connectivity and those which don't,
it is not in fact predicted that the facts here could be no other way. To put
this slightly differently, since there are some processes exhibiting strong
connectivity, it remains to be explained why this constraint does not.
   Yet even in the absence of a way to predict that this constraint does not
hold at the level with strong connectivity, the view that I am advocating still
offers more limited possibilities than either of the two accounts discussed
above. At worst, there are two ways that the facts could be, rather than four.
Thus, suppose that there is a level of representation at which the extracted
NP is in the position of the extraction site as well as a level of representation
including gaps, and suppose further that nothing precludes the possibility
that the Object Pronoun Constraint holds at the former level. This means
that (9b) and (14b) could both be ungrammatical, or the facts could be as
they are. It would, however, be impossible for both sentences to be
grammatical (unless there was yet another level of representation where

there is no gap in the extraction site position, but there is no motivation for positing such a level.) Moreover, there is no way to formulate a constraint which would block (14b) and allow (9b). Note that the classical theory without global constraints like those in (18) and (19) also allows only two possibilities; the problem here is simply that neither is the correct one.

While it might seem like a small savings to reduce the possibilities from four to two, this becomes more significant when we consider that the actual situation can be inferred on the basis of positive data alone. The grammaticality of (14b) is sufficient to rule out the possibility that this constraint holds for the level at which the NP is in the extraction site. The ungrammaticality of (9b), which could not be inferred by positive evidence, is automatic in this theory.[8]

The same remarks hold if strong connectivity is accounted for with a single level of representation by the use of features on nodes. Thus consider a theory which does not preclude the possibility that there is a feature [Pro] on NP's dominating pronouns (that is, the set of features on nodes could vary from language to language). Moreover, suppose that *tough*-constructions could be accounted for in such a way as to require that the subject of the *tough*-predicate has the same features as the gap.

Given this, nothing precludes the possibility that the the Object Pronoun Constraint will exhibit strong connectivity in *tough*-constructions, and thus it could be that (14b) as well as (9b) is ungrammatical. This would follow if *tough*-constructions do have the above requirement, and if English does include the feature [Pro]. Since the subject of *hard* in (14b) is the node NP, the gap would have to be the same node, and so (14b) should violate
[Pro]
the constraint.

Again, though, this is the only other possible way that the facts could be, and the actual distribution can be inferred by positive evidence. Thus the grammaticality of (14b) is sufficient to show that either [Pro] is not a feature in English, or that there is no requirement that the subject of *tough*-predicates have the same feature as the gap. I will return to this in Sec. 4, and will show that the second is actually correct. (Moreover, it will be shown that this follows simply from the formulation of the rules introducing *tough*-constructions within this framework; it is not actually necessary to learn that (14b) is grammatical in order to infer that connectivity does not hold here.) For now, though, we can note simply that the ungrammaticality of (9b) is automatic in this theory since there is no level of representation without a gap in the extraction site position.

2.3. *Other Accounts of the Object Pronoun Constraint*

Because the above discussion crucially assumes that sentences like (4b) and (5b) are blocked by a constraint on structure like (6), it is worth considering two alternative accounts of the constraint. The first proposal which I will consider is framed within the classical theory, and is discussed in some detail in Wasow (1975); this proposal is that these sentences violate a condition on the application of an obligatory cliticization rule. While I am not disputing the claim that an object pronoun can cliticize onto a verb which immediately precedes it[9] (I will, in fact, make crucial use of this in Section 3), I will show here that these facts cannot be accounted for by an obligatory rule.

Wasow assumed a transformational account of Dative Movement, and suggested that there is an obligatory rule to the effect that a pronoun can cliticize onto an immediately preceeding verb. He further proposed that this rule is ordered before Dative Movement. (The same effect would be achieved if obligatory rules must apply as soon as their structural description is met.) Given the classical account of Dative Movement, in which sentences like (4a) are derived from structures of the form:

(22)   V   NP   *to*   NP   X

this proposal correctly blocks (4b):

(4)   b. *I gave Mary it for Christmas.

In this account, the structure underlying (4b) is (7), and cliticization must apply first to (7) to give (23):

(7)   I gave it to Mary for Christmas.

(23)   I [$_V$ gave it] to Mary for Christmas.

A crucial assumption here is that a cliticized pronoun is no longer dominated by NP; hence (23) does not meet the structural description for Dative Movement, and (4b) cannot be derived.

(5b) is blocked in a similar fashion given Emonds' formulation of Particle Movement (Emonds, 1976), and given the assumption that cliticization is also ordered before Particle Movement. Here the underlying structure would be (24):

(5)   b. *I gave away it.

(24)   I gave it away.

Again cliticization will first apply to (24), bleeding the application of Particle Movement.

There are, however, several problems with this proposal. First, it incorrectly predicts that a sentence like (25) is ungrammatical:

(25)   Mary was given it for Christmas by John.

(25) would be blocked in the same way that (26) is:

(26)   *John gave Mary it for Christmas.

Both would underlyingly have the structure:

(27)   John gave it to Mary for Christmas.

and cliticization would have to first apply, blocking not only the Dative Movement sentence (26), but also the Dative-Passive (25).[10]

Second, this proposal has the same problem as a cycle-final constraint with respect to the contrast in (14):

(14)   a. *It's hard to tell the children them.
        b. They are hard to tell the children.

As in the case of (25), this account provides no derivation for (14b). Obligatory cliticiation would have to apply before Dative Movement, blocking not only the intermediate structure (14a) but also (14b). In other words, this proposal makes the wrong predictions in cases where, in the classical theory, there is some intermediate structure exhibiting the violation but where this violation is redeemed by the later application of rules.

Perhaps the most obvious problem with this account is that it also blocks sentences like:

(28)   It was seen by Bill.

If cliticization must apply before Dative Movement then it must also apply before Passive. Thus given an underlying structure like (29), cliticization would have to first apply to give (30), to which Passive could no longer apply:

(29)   Bill saw it.
(30)   Bill [$_V$ saw it]

Of course this problem would not arise in a theory in which Passives are base-generated, but the proposed account of the ungrammaticality of (4b) assumes a transformational account of Dative Movement, and therefore must also assume that Passives are derived transformationally.

However, given the assumption that pronouns which immediately follow a verb can optionally cliticize onto the verb, it is possible to formulate a slightly simpler constraint than the one in (6); the constraint could block structures of the form in (31):

(31)   *[$_{VP}$ V X [$_{NP}$ pro] Y] (where the NP is directly

dominated by VP)

The variable X here is to be interpreted in the usual fashion, as a variable ranging over any string, including nothing. This constraint, then, simply blocks any VP containing an uncliticized pronoun, even if nothing intervenes between the verb and the pronoun. Consider then a sentence like:

(32)   I saw him.

(32) does not violate the constraint because *him* can be a clitic. On the other hand, cliticization could not apply in (4b):

(4)   b. *I gave Mary it for Christmas.

since *it* does not immediately follow *give*; (4b) therefore violates (31).[11] (An account like this is suggested in Baker (1979)).

The choice between (6) and (31) does not affect the conclusions reached earlier in this section. (9b) must still contain some node between *tell* and *them*, in order to block the cliticization of *them* onto *tell*. However, the extracted NP itself cannot be in this position, as it would, for example, in a multi-dominational representation. If it were, then (14b) would also be ungrammatical; this sentence violates the constraint in (31) just as it does (6).

2.4. *Passives*

Consider again the contrast between (25) and (26):

(25)   Mary was given it for Christmas by John.
(26)   *John gave Mary it for Christmas.

In contrast to wh-questions and Tough-Movement constructions, the grammaticality of (25) shows that Passives do not contain gaps in what is classically treated as the extraction site position. If they did, then (25) should violate the constraint, as its structure would be:

(33)   Mary was given $\emptyset$ it for Christmas.

As discussed in Section 1, the non-occurrence of a gap here is predicted if Passive is treated as a category-changing process. In this account, there is no level of representation for (25) with an NP in object position. Further evidence that there is no gap in a Passive construction will be given in the next section; there I will discuss another phenomena which motivates the existence of gaps, and which can be tested with a much greater range of constructions.

3. VP DELETION, STRESS AND TO-CLITICIZATION

3.1. *Wanna-Reduction*

Because much of what will be discussed in this section is closely connected to the phenomenon which I will refer to as "*wanna*-reduction", it will be useful to first review some proposals which have been made as to when this reduction can occur. Most accounts of this assume that there is a series of processes by which *want to* in (34a) reduces to give *wanna* in (34b), and that this reduction first involves the cliticization of *to* onto *want*:

(34)   a. I want to leave.
         b. I wanna leave.

It is also usually assumed that *to* can only cliticize onto certain verbs, since there are only a small number of verbs which allow this extreme reduction. Thus compare (34b) with (35b):[12]

(35)   a. I tend to sleep late in the morning.
         b. *I tenna sleep late in the morning.

While I will assume that *wanna* reduction involves leftward cliticization of *to*, I will give evidence in 3.4 that *to* can actually cliticize leftward onto any verb or adjective of which the VP beginning with *to* is the complement. What is special about *want* is not that it governs cliticization, but rather that it governs additional phonological (or perhaps morphological) reductions which *tend*, for example, does not.

The major problem in characterizing the conditions under which *wanna*-reduction can occur is that, at first noticed by L. Horn (cited in Lakoff

(1970)), this is not always possible when *want* and *to* are adjacent in surface structure (as surface structure is characterized in the classical theory):

(36)   a.   Who do you want to die?
         b. *Who do you wanna die?

Since this observation was first made, there have been a variety of proposals to account for the difference in grammaticality between (34b) and (36b).

Bresnan (1971a) shows that this contrast is predicted in the classical theory if *to*-cliticization applies cyclically, where *to* can cliticize leftward onto *want* if they are adjacent during the *want* cycle. Given the standard account of Equi, the subject of the lower clause in (34) is removed on the *want*-cycle, and hence *want* and *to* are adjacent during this cycle. Assuming that wh-Fronting applies on a higher cycle (as it would, for example, if S̄ and S are both cyclic nodes), *wanna*-reduction cannot apply in (35), since *who* intervenes between *want* and *to* at all points during the *want*-cycle.

Another account of the contrast here is one in which (36a) contains a gap in surface structure between *want* and *to*, and where *to* can cliticize onto *want* only if the two are adjacent in surface structure. If this is correct, the question arises as to just what constructions contain gaps. Obviously, (34) cannot contain a gap in surface structure despite the fact that, in traditional terms, there is a deletion site between *want* and *to*.

Lightfoot (1976) has argued that what have traditionally been analyzed as Equi constructions like (34) do in fact contain empty nodes in surface structure, but that these are formally distinct from the empty nodes left by movement rules (i.e., traces). The latter are co-indexed with the moved NP, while the former are unindexed. Thus he suggests that unindexed empty nodes (PRO's) are "invisible" to the structural description of a rule; the presence of a PRO between *want* and *to* in (34a) will therefore not block *to*-cliticization.[13]

In this account, the crucial difference between (34) and (36) corresponds, roughly, to the classical distinction between movement and deletion constructions. Thus Lightfoot claims that Passive and Raising constructions both contain indexed gaps, and that these would also block processes like *to*-cliticization.[14] In Section 2 I have provided evidence against this position; there it was shown that the Object Pronoun Constraint does not block sentences like (25):

(25)   Mary was given it for Christmas by John.

indicating that there is no gap in the object position in a Passive sentence.

Additional evidence against Lightfoot's generalization will be presented below.

Postal and Pullum (1977) claim that the crucial distinction between (34) and (36) is not that one involves movement and the other deletion (or, interpretation of PRO's). Rather, they suggest that *wanna*-reduction can apply only if the cycle-final subject of *want* is, in classical terms, the same as or coreferential to the cycle-final subject of the complement clause. (This is not the terminology they use, since they are assuming quite a different framework, but this characterizes the predictions made by their proposal.) Reduction can apply in (34) because the cycle-final subject of *want* is coreferential to that of *to leave*. In (36), on the other hand, *you* is the cycle-final subject of *want*, whereas *who* is the cycle-final subject of the complement clause. This account, then, predicts that there could be a Raising verb which allows the extreme reduction; in support of this Postal and Pullum cite the behavior of *have* in (37):

(37)   There hasta be a tornado on Monday.

This might be answered by claiming that the *hasta/hafta* construction does not involve Raising. The matter is debated by Chomsky and Lasnik (1978) and Pullum and Postal (1979).

A fourth account, similar to a suggestion in Bresnan (1978), is one which claims, with Lightfoot, that it is the presence of a gap in surface structure which blocks *to*-cliticization in (36), but that the crucial difference between (34) and (36) is not a matter of "movement" vs. "deletion" constructions. Instead, constructions like Equi, Passive and Raising do not contain gaps.[15] As discussed above, this is consistent with an analysis of these constructions in which they involved category-changing rules. This is the account which I will argue for.

Note that the cyclic account of Bresnan (1971a), the "subject-sharing" account of Postal and Pullum, and the "category-changing" account all make the same predictions concerning the possibility of reduction in Equi, Raising and Passive constructions. It is, therefore, difficult to find evidence to distinguish these positions. And, even though Lightfoot's proposal makes different predictions from these three with respect to Passive and Raising constructions, previous discussion of this has been somewhat inconclusive because there are so few verbs which allow the extreme reduction exhibited by *wanna*.

My evidence for the last account, then, will be based not simply on the distribution of reduction, but on its interaction with another phenomenon.

In 3.2 and 3.3 I will consider a constraint which affects the co-occurrence of VP Deletion sites and other extraction sites. This constraint provides evidence for the existence of gaps in constructions like (36), and it further shows that there are no gaps in Equi, Raising or Passive constructions. In 3.4 and 3.5 I will return to the question of *to*-cliticization, and will discuss its interaction with this constraint.

3.2. *Extraction and VP Deletion*

Consider first the following contrasts:

(38)   a.   The Red Sox are the team that I want to win.
         b. ?*The Red Sox are the team that I want to.
         c.   Tim is the man that I asked to leave.
         d. ?*Tim is the man that I asked to.

While (38b) and (38d) are perhaps not fully ungrammatical, they are certainly quite odd, and contrast with (38a) and (38c). (For convenience, I will use the term ungrammatical in referring to sentences of this form despite the fact that this is slightly misleading.) I will later suggest that the oddness of these sentences is a consequence of principles concerning stress combined with the nature of gaps. If this is correct, it is not surprising that the judgements here are somewhat delicate, as judgements concerning stress facts often are. Note, incidentally, that the oddness of (38b) and (38d) is not attributable solely to the fact that these involve VP Deletion with no context supplied; even without any context (39), which also involves VP Deletion, is much better:

(39)   I want to.

Topicalization constructions and wh-questions show the same behavior as relative clauses here:

(40)   a.   Tim, I asked to leave.
         b. ?*Tim, I asked to.
(41)   a.   Who do you want to win?
         b. ?*Who do you want to?
         c.   Who did you ask to leave?
         d. ?*Who did you ask to?

It appears, then, that some principle prohibits sentences in which the constituent immediately preceding *to* is extracted, and where *to* is followed by a VP Deletion site.

As a first approximation of this principle, we might suppose that there is a constraint blocking structures in which *to* is flanked by gaps; we will tentatively formulate this constraint as in (42):[16]

(42)   *X $\emptyset$ to $\emptyset$ Y

(Although this formulation assumes that a VP Deletion site is also a gap in surface structure, I will show in 3.5 that this assumption is not actually crucial.)

The constraint as formulated in (42) refers explicitly to gaps. It will, however, be shown later that the effects of (42) follow from the fact that gaps do not contain lexical items in conjunction with principles concerning stress and cliticization, where these principles do not refer to gaps. In view of this, I would like to suggest that no constraint in grammar can explicitly mention gaps. I make this suggestion somewhat tentatively, because there are a number of phenomena which have been argued to be sensitive to the presence of gaps. Among these are several of the filters discussed in Chomsky and Lasnik (1977)[17] and the failure of Auxiliaries to reduce before gaps. A detailed consideration of all of these cases is beyond the scope of this paper, but it seems quite possible that some of these cases could be reanalyzed in ways similar to the analysis which will be proposed for (42).

Thus, we will take (42) as a description of the situation, rather than as an actual constraint in English grammar. Before continuing, let us consider an alternative description of the situation, which is that the subject of *to* followed by a VP Deletion site cannot be extracted. This, in fact, might initially appear more attractive in that it could perhaps be shown to follow from pragmatic principles interacting with VP Deletion. Nevertheless, this generalization is incorrect. The following, in which the subject has been extracted, is grammatical:

(43)   Who did you ask not to?

There are, moreover, cases like (45d) below whose ungrammaticality does not fall within the scope of this generalization, but is subsumed under the generalization expressed in (42).

Assuming that there is some principle which has the effect of blocking sentences in which *to* is flanked by gaps, it is possible to test the presence of gaps in a range of constructions. In addition to wh- and topicalized constructions, there are other extraction sites which cannot immediately precede *to* $\emptyset$. For example, Tough-Movement is impossible here; this is not surprising in view of the evidence in Section 2 that Tough-Movement constructions contain gaps:

(44)   a.   John would be hard to ask to leave.
         b.   ?*John would be hard to ask to.

Another phenomenon showing this behavior is Gapping. Thus, consider first the sentence:

(45)   a.   John tried to leave on Sunday, and Mary tried to leave on Monday.

VP Deletion alone can occur in the second conjunct:

(45)   b.   John tried to leave on Sunday, and Mary tried to on Monday.

Gapping can also occur alone here:

(45)   c.   John tried to leave on Sunday, and Mary to leave on Monday.

But it is impossible for both to occur:

(45)   d.   ?*John tried to leave on Sunday, and Mary to on Monday.

Note that there is in general no restriction against the occurrence of both processes in a single conjunct:

(46)   a.   John is likely to try to leave on Sunday, and Mary is likely to try to leave on Monday.
         b.   John is likely to try to leave on Sunday, and Mary to try to on Monday.

The violation occurs only when the Gapping site immediately precedes *to* $\emptyset$.

Yet not all constructions classically analyzed as involving movement or deletion show this behavior; Raising, Equi and Passive constructions can occur here. So, for example, if there were a gap in Raising to Object constructions, then the grammaticality of (47) is unexplained, since the gap would immediately precede *to* $\emptyset$:[18]

(47)   I want Tim to.

Moreover, Equi constructions also cannot contain a gap in the position of the "deleted" NP; both (48) and (49) are grammatical:

(48)   I want to.
(49)   I asked Sam to.

In other words, the surface structures of these cannot be (50) and (51), since these would fit the description in (42):

(50)   I want [∅ to ∅]
(51)   I asked Sam [∅ to ∅]

The grammaticality of (48) and (49) is, of course, compatible with the notion of gaps argued for by Lightfoot, in which the gaps produced by the application of movement rules (traces) are distinct from base-generated gaps (PRO's) which would occur in (48) and (49). Thus, just as this account posits that the process reducing *want to* to *wanna* is sensitive to this distinction, so it would be expected that the constraint here only blocks sentences in which a trace (and not a PRO) precedes a *to* which is followed by a VP Deletion site. (It is unclear, though, how this can account for the ungrammaticality of (45d), the example involving Gapping.)

However, the constraint in (42) can also be tested with Raising to Subject and with Passive constructions. So, consider:

(52)   John seems to

This is grammatical, despite the fact that, in the classical theory, an NP has been extracted from the position immediately preceding *to*. If Raising constructions contained gaps, the structure here would be (53), which would violate the constraint:

(53)   John seems [∅ to ∅]

Similarly, as evidenced in the last section, Passive constructions cannot contain gaps; (54) is grammatical, indicating that its structure is not (55):

(54)   John is expected to.
(55)   John is expected ∅ to ∅

The evidence above shows that there is some essential difference between extraction constructions like wh-questions on the one hand and Raising constructions on the other. However, the conclusion that the former constructions contain gaps and the latter do not crucially assumes that the generalization expressed in (42) is the correct account of these facts. It could be that gaps are irrelevant here, and that the different behavior of these two types of constructions follows from some other difference between them. After all, both the cyclic account of *wanna*-reduction and the subject-sharing proposal predict that Equi, Passive and Raising will behave differently from wh-questions with respect to this phenomenon. Yet neither of these proposals assumes gaps; the predicted difference is based on other properties of these constructions. It is therefore worth considering whether the distinctions here can be expressed by some generalization along the lines of these proposals.

Let us first consider Postal and Pullum's proposal concerning *wanna*-reduction. Their prediction that Equi, Passive and Raising constructions will behave differently from wh-Fronting crucially hinges on the nature of the subject of the *to*-VP in the two constructions. But there is no obvious analogue to this proposal for the constraint under discussion here. In both (41d) and (43) it is the subject of the *to*-VP which is extracted, yet there is a contrast between these two sentences. This contrast indicates that what is crucial is simply the position of the extraction site with respect to *to*. Moreover, sentences like (45d) show that the constraint holds even when the extraction site is not a subject.

Turning to a cyclic account within the classical theory, we might suppose that some principle predicts that nothing can be extracted if it immediately precedes *to* at the end of the cycle of the verb whose complement is the *to*-clause. (I am ignoring here the additional complication of restricting this to *to*'s which are followed by VP Deletion sites.) In other words, there would be a constraint with the effect of allowing extractions to apply on the cycle immediately above *to*. Hence Passive, Equi and Raising could apply; but the application of rules like wh-Fronting and Gapping on higher cycles would be blocked. Obviously, this account is extremely implausible; it is difficult to imagine just what the relevant principle could be. In particular, it seems unlikely that the cycle above *to* would be the crucial one, rather than the *to*-cycle itself. But aside from its implausibility, this description does not, in fact, account for all of the facts. It too fails to distinguish between the ungrammatical (41d) and the grammatical (43). This contrast shows that the cycle on which the extraction applies is irrelevant.

3.3. *The Stress Principle*

As noted in Note 18, a sentence like (56) is quite strange with stress on *want*; the stress here must be on *Tim*:

(56)   a.   I want Tím to.
        b.   ??I wánt Tim to.

Again it might appear at first that the oddness of (56b) is attributable to pragmatic principles interacting with VP Deletion. For example, it could be that there is some pragmatic reason why the subject of a deleted VP must be stressed; or, that it is simply difficult to imagine a context in which the subject would not be stressed. But the following sentences, in which the subject is not stressed, all sound far more natural, even out of context:

(57)   a. Tim is expécted to.
       b. Tim wánts to.
       c. I asked Tim nót to.

Another sentence in which the subject need not be stressed is one in which it is a pronoun; thus compare (56b) and (58):

(56)   b. ??I wánt Tim to.
(58)   I wánt him to.

Moreover, a sentence like (56b) is odd even given appropriate context. Thus, in the discourse below, the (b)-answer is worse than (a), yet there is no obvious explanation for this in terms of the inappropriateness of the (b)-sentence in this context:

(59)   Q: Do you think that Tim will leave?
       A: a. Well, I wánt Tim to leave, but I don't think he will.
          b. ??Well, I wánt Tim to, but I don't think he will.

Rather, I will assume that there is a principle by which stress must fall on the constituent immediately preceding an occurrence of *to* which is followed by a VP Deletion site; I will refer to this as the stress principle.[19] (Again, this is intended as a description of the generalization rather than as a formulation of the constraint.) Note that the grammaticality of (58) as opposed to (56b) would appear to be problematic for this generalization also, since *him* in (58) is not stressed. However, given the assumption that object pronouns cliticize onto a verb which immediately precedes them, this sentence is in fact consistent with the stress principle. Here the constituent immediately preceding *to* $\emptyset$ is *want him*, and this is stressed.

Given the stress principle, combined with the assumption that certain constructions contain gaps, it follows that the extraction site in these constructions cannot immediately precede *to* $\emptyset$. Consider a sentence like (41b), whose structure would be (60):

(41b)   ?*Who do you want to
(60)   who do you want $\emptyset$ to $\emptyset$

Since the constituent immediately preceding *to* here is a gap, it is impossible for stress to be on this constituent; (41b) therefore violates the stress principle.[20]

The essential claim here is, first, that a sentence like (41b) is bad for the same reason that (56b) is, and, secondly, that what these two sentences have in common is that the constituent immediately preceding *to* is unstressed. Note that (56b) is slightly better than (41b), which might cast some doubt on the claim that the two violate the same constraint. Actually, though, the difference here is compatible with this analysis. In (56b), *Tim* can receive some stress, even though the primary stress is on *want*. In (41b), the constituent before *to* is a gap, and obviously a gap can receive no stress at all. It is therefore not surprising that this sentence is worse.

This means, then, that there need not be a constraint like (42) which refers to the gap before *to*; the inability of a gap to occur here is simply an instance of the more general principle that a constituent without stress cannot precede *to* $\emptyset$. Of course, the statement of the stress principle as given here still refers to gaps in that it refers to the gap following *to*. Thus, as it stands, the stress principle remains a counterexample to the suggestion made earlier that no constraint explicitly mentions gaps. In the next two sections I will discuss the interaction of this principle with *to*-cliticization, and will arrive at a reformulation which does not refer to a gap to the right of *to*.

Before turning to this, however, it is worth pointing out that the stress principle behaves in much the same way as the Object Pronoun Constraint with respect to extraction sites. Therefore, it provides a similar kind of motivation for a level of representation with gaps as opposed to an account within either the classical theory or a theory with a single multi-dominational structure. In the classical theory, there is no single level of representation at which the stress principle can be stated to account for the extraction cases. Suppose, for example, that stress is assigned cyclically (as argued for in Bresnan (1971b)), and that the stress principle could be formulated to predict that, at the end of the cycle of the verb immediately above the *to*-clause, the constituent preceding *to* must be stressed. (Again, I am ignoring the problem of restricting this to cases in which *to* is followed by VP Deletion.) Since question pronouns are generally unstressed, this predicts the ungrammaticality of (41b); the structure for this sentence at the end of the *want*-cycle is:

(61)   you want who to . . .

Yet there are cases where the extracted NP is stressed which are nevertheless ungrammatical:

(62) a. ?*Which mán do you want to?
      b. ?*Tím, I asked to.

If the stress principle holds cyclically, then these should be grammatical. (62a), for example, will have the following structure at the end of the *want*-cycle:

(63) I asked which mán to.

Nor can the classical theory account for these with a surface constraint. While a theory without gaps correctly predicts that (62) violates the stress principle at surface structure, it does not account for the ungrammaticality of (64):

(64) ?*Who do you wánt to.

Thus (64) behaves as though there is an NP in the position of the extraction site and therefore the stressed constituent *want* does not immediately precede *to*. But the extracted NP itself does not behave as though it is in this position; even though the extracted NP is stressed in (62), the stress principle is violated.

These facts are equally problematic for a theory with a single multi-dominational structure. Such a theory accounts for the violation in (41b) since the stressless NP *who* immediately precedes *to*, but it does not account for (62), since here a stressed NP immediately precedes *to*. Here, unlike in the case of the Object Pronoun constraint, the problem cannot even be solved by allowing for a distinction between "real" and "pseudo" nodes. In order to block (62), the constraint must *only* block structures in which a real stressless constituent precedes *to*. But this fails to block (41b), since while (41b) contains a stressless constituent before *to*, this is not a real node. Hence this theory would need two separate constraints. If, on the other hand, extraction sites are empty nodes and consequently unstressed, a single principle will account for all of these cases.

3.4. *To-Cliticization*

To summarize so far, there is a principle which predicts that stress must fall on the constituent immediately preceding a *to* which is followed by a VP Deletion site. The ungrammaticality of (41b) follows from this principle if it contains a gap in the extraction site position. Moreover, Equi, Passive and Raising constructions cannot contain gaps, as indicated by the grammaticality of (47)–(49), (52) and (54).

But now consider the following, in which the subject of the matrix clause is stressed:

(65)   Í want to.
(66)   Jóhn seems to.
(67)   Jóhn is expected to.

These sentences are quite natural, despite the fact that the constituent immediately preceding *to* ∅ is not stressed. Regardless of whether or not a gap precedes *to*, these should violate the stress principle.

Suppose, though, that *to* cliticize leftward onto any verb or adjective which immediately precedes it.[21] If this is correct, then *to* in (65)–(67) can be a clitic, which would mean that the stress principle can be violated in just those cases where cliticization has applied. We could therefore assume that the stress principle affects only a *to* which is an independent word. As will be shown in the next section, this assumption actually leads to a very simple statement of this principle.

There is, in fact, independent motivation for the claim that *to* can cliticize in these sentences. First, many speakers allow reduction of *to* to *tə* here:[22]

(68)   a. I want tə.
        b. He wants tə.
(69)   John seems tə.
(70)   John is expected tə.

Even for speakers who find these bad or questionable, there is a sharp contrast between these and sentences with reduced *to* where the item preceding *to* is not a verb or adjective:

(71)   *I want Sam tə.
(72)   *I persuaded Sam tə.
(73)   *I want very much tə.

Note that the inability of *to* to cliticize leftward in cases where it is preceded by something other than a verb or adjective can only be demonstrated by considering sentences with VP Deletion. When *to* is followed by a full VP, it can reduce regardless of what precedes it:

(74)   a. I want Sam tə leave
        b. I persuaded Sam tə stay
        c. I want very much tə win

The reduction of *to* in these sentences is discussed in detail by Selkirk (1972), who argues that this is part of a general process by which monosyllabic grammatical morphemes can reduce when they precede their heads. That this reduction occurs when leftward cliticization could not be involved can be shown by sentences like:

(75)   Tə run is no fun.

In 3.5 I will return to the reduction of *to* in sentences like (74) and (75); for now we can assume Selkirk's account of this.

This second piece of evidence for leftwards cliticization in (65)–(67) concerns the process of *wanna*-reduction. As noted in 3.1, most accounts of this posit a rule cliticizing *to* onto *want*, but it has generally been assumed that *to* can cliticize only onto a few verbs. This means positing a lexically governed cliticization rule, where the rule is governed by the item hosting the clitic. In general, though, cliticization rules are not governed in this way. While the cliticizing item is generally lexically specified, the host is not. The claim here, then, is that *to*-cliticization can apply onto any verb or adjective; the lexical item involved is irrelevant.

Of course the fact that *want* behaves differently from, for example, *tend* must be captured somehow; clearly one of the processes involved in *wanna*-reduction is lexically governed. But if one of the other processes involved in the derivation of *wanna* is of a type which can in general be lexically governed, it is far more likely that this is what distinguishes *want* from other verbs. John McCarthy (personal communication) has suggested that the governed process in *wanna*-reduction is a further weakening of the boundary between *want* and the clitic *to*, and that this process is similar to the process discussed in Chomsky and Halle (1968) whereby the boundary between a verb like *keep* and the past tense ending is weakened, giving the past tense form [kɛpt]. Obviously this process is governed, since the past tense of *reap* is [ript].

Whether or not this is exactly the correct characterization, there is evidence that certain kinds of reductions which don't involve clitics are governed and that, moreover, *want* governs such a reduction. Thus, in my dialect, *want* rhymes with *taunt*; these are pronounced [wɔnʔ] and [tɔnʔ]. However, the two have different past tense form. The past of *want* is either [wɔ̃təd] or, more normally, [wɔnəd]. *Taunt* has only [tɔ̃təd] as its past form; *[tɔnəd] is impossible, The same holds for the progressive; [wɔ̃tɪŋ] and [wɔnɪŋ] are both possible (again, the second is far more natural), whereas the only progressive form for *taunt* is [tɔ̃tɪŋ], not *[tɔnɪŋ]. It is also worth noting that just as [wɔ̃təd] and [wɔ̃tɪŋ] are quite unnatural in this dialect, so is [wɔ́tə]; [wɔnə] is far more natural. It is likely, then, that whatever process is involved in the derivation of the past tense form [wɔnəd] is also involved in *wanna*-reduction. Since *taunt* does not permit deletion of the final *t* in these forms, it is clear that the relevant process is lexically governed.[23] Note too that just as *tend to* does not reduce to *tenna*, so the past tense form of tend is [tɛ̃dəd], not *[tɛnəd].

Given the assumptions that the stress principle affects only uncliticized *to*'s and that *to* can cliticize in (65)–(67), let us return to the claim that there are no gaps in Passive, Equi and Raising constructions. It was argued earlier that the fact that (48), (52) and (54) do not violate the stress principle shows that they do not contain a gap before *to*. But since *to* can be a clitic in these as well, the stress principle is irrelevant.

Nevertheless, it must still be concluded that these contain no gap, for consider the conditions under which cliticization can apply. If there is a gap in these constructions, then *to* can cliticize across a gap:

(76)   a. I want ∅ to

        b. John seems ∅ to

        c. John is expected ∅ to

But then nothing would prevent cliticization in the extraction constructions discussed earlier. So for example, the ungrammaticality of (41b) is unexplained, since *to* could cliticize across the gap here:

(41)   b. ?*Who do you want to?
(77)   who do you want ∅ to

If *to* is a clitic, then (41b) should not violate the stress principle.

The question of where *to* can cliticize leftward is, of course, basically the same as the question of where *wanna*-reduction can occur. If cliticization is generalized as suggested above, the subject-sharing account and the cyclic account will also predict that *to* can cliticize in (48), (52) and (54), but not in (41b). However, as discussed earlier, there is nothing analogous to these proposals which predicts the ungrammaticality of (41b). The fact that *to* cannot cliticize here is insufficient to account for this, since *to* also cannot cliticize in the grammatical (56a):

(56)   a. I want Tím to.

If, on the other hand, (41b) contains a gap, then both the violation of the stress principle and the failure of *to* to cliticize are explained, and so there is no reason to posit either cyclic cliticization or a subject-sharing constraint on cliticization.

Since the stress principle and cliticization interact in a rather complex way, let me summarize to this point. I am assuming two principles particular to English grammar:

i.   When *to* is an independent word and is followed by a VP Deletion site, stress must fall on the constituent preceding it. (This principle will be simplified in the next section.)
ii.   *To* can cliticize leftward onto an adjacent verb or adjective.

These two principles will account for all of the facts discussed above when taken in conjunction with the assumption that Gapping, wh-questions, Tough-Movement and Topicalization constructions contain empty nodes (while Passive, Raising and Equi constructions do not.)

It follows from (i) that (56b) is bad, whereas (56a) does not violate this principle. Sentences like (65)–(67), on the other hand, are grammatical because *to* is a clitic, and therefore unaffected by the stress principle (i). The ungrammaticality of (41b) follows from the interaction of these principles. *To* cannot be a clitic because it is not adjacent to *want*; a gap intervenes between *want* and *to*. Since *to* is not a clitic here, (41b) violates the stress principle as the constituent immediately preceding *to* is a gap and therefore unstressed.

What remains to be explained is why the stress principle affects only *to*'s which are followed by VP Deletion sites. Related to this is the question of how to formulate this principle without reference to a gap after *to*. We will now turn to these questions to arrive at a reformulation of the stress principle as stated in (i).

3.5. Rightwards Cliticization

In light of the claim in 3.4 that the stress principle affects only uncliticized *to*'s, consider again (45d) in which the constituent preceding *to* is Gapped:

(45)   d. *John tried to leave on Sunday, and Mary to on Monday

Given the view of gaps that I have been arguing for, the structure of the second conjunct of (45d) contains an empty V-node to the left of *to*. Assuming that the VP Deletion site is also an empty node (I will return to this directly), the structure is, very roughly:

(77)

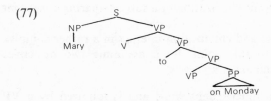

(There are several questions concerning the exact structure, such as where the PP is attached, which are irrelevant to the discussion here.) If this is essentially the correct structure, then it follows that (45d) violates the stress principle; here *to* is preceded by an empty, and therefore stressless, constituent.

Note, though, that *to* is preceded by a V; yet it must be that *to* has not cliticized onto the empty V-node. (If it were a clitic here, then the stress principle whould not apply.) The inability of *to* to cliticize leftward here is, in fact, hardly surprising. Assuming that cliticization involves an erasure of word boundaries, then it follows that only lexical items and not empty nodes can host cliticization. In other words, the failure of *to* to cliticize leftwards here does not indicate that the cliticization rule must specifically exempt gaps. Rather, given that cliticization affects adjacent lexical items, it will not apply when one of the two items is non-lexical.

We can now turn to the sentences discussed earlier in which *to* reduces even though it could not have cliticized leftward:

(78)   a. Tə run is no fun.
         b. I want very much tə win.

Suppose that in these sentences *to* has cliticized rightward onto the following verb.[24] This would not only account for the ability of *to* to reduce here, but it allows for a much simpler formulation of the stress principle. Roughly, this principle could be stated as follows:

(79)   When *to* is an independent word, it must be preceded by a stressed constituent.

Undoubtedly, (79) could be simplified even further; it seems likely that this too follows from more general principles. Suppose, for example, that there is a principle in English by which every other constituent is stressed. *To*, in general, cannot be stressed, and so it would have to be preceded by a stressed constituent. The clitic *to* is unaffected as it is not an independent word. This account is admittedly quite vague, but it does not seem implausible that (79) would follow from some more general principle like this.

If this is correct, then no constraint referring to *to* followed by a VP Deletion site is necessary. In sentence like:

(80)   a. I wánt Tim to win.
        b. Who do you want ∅ to win?

to can be preceded by a stressless constituent because it has cliticized onto *win*. It is just where it is followed by a VP Deletion site that it cannot be a clitic. Assuming that VP Deletion sites are also gaps, *to* cannot cliticize rightward because there is no lexical item to host the cliticization. Note, though, that it is not actually necessary to assume that there are empty nodes in a VP Deletion site, it could be that there is no node here at all. If rightwards cliticization of *to* applies only onto V's, cliticization will be impossible regardless of whether or not there is a gap here.

By way of summary, let us return to the constraint in (42), which was formulated to block structures in which *to* is flanked by gaps:

(42)   *X ∅ to ∅ Y

The discussion above shows that no separate constraint like (42) needs to be included in the grammar of English; the effects of this constraint follow from the stress principle, the cliticization rules, and the fact that gaps do not contain lexical items. Since gaps are not lexical, they cannot host cliticization, nor can they be stressed. Consequently, any *to* flanked by gaps must be an independent word. But it will also be preceded by a constituent which has no stress on it, and so the stress principle will be violated. What is crucial in this account is the existence of a level of representation in which there are nodes in the extraction site positions, but where such nodes do not dominate lexical items.

4. *On Strong Connectivity*

This paper has been concerned with showing that there are phenomena by which a sentence behaves as though there is a node in the position of an extraction site, but where the material dominated by the extracted node does not behave as though it is in this position. The existence of phenomena of this sort is problematic both for the classical theory and for a theory with a single multi-dominational representation; the problem for these theories is that at the level of representation at which there is a node in the extraction site position, everything dominated by this node is also in that position. Moreover, there are no known phenomena which require a representation at which there is no node at all in an extraction site position. This too is not explained in the classical theory since this theory does include a level of representation without such a node. Moreover, a multi-dominational theory which is elaborated in such a way as to account for the type of phenomena discussed earlier also fails to account for the fact that constraints of this type do not exist.

On the other hand, there do appear to be phenomena by which an extracted node behaves as though it is in the position of the extraction site with respect to material that it dominates; that is, there are cases of what I have been calling strong connectivity. Given the existence of a representation with gaps, there still remains the question of how to account for phenomena of this type. As discussed earlier, one way to account for these cases is to posit another level of representation at which the extracted node is in the position of the extraction site. But these cases can also be accounted for within a theory like that proposed in Gazdar (this volume) in which there is only a single level of syntactic representation. The basic idea of this account is to treat phenomena like case-marking not as being only properties of material dominated by the extracted node, but as being properties of the extracted node itself. Before closing this paper, I would like to very briefly explore this type of account of strong connectivity and discuss the implications of this for the processes discussed in this paper.

The approach to strong connectivity within the kind of framework outlined in Gazdar relies on two kinds of devices. First, nodes can be marked with features and, crucially, nodes whose features differ are not nodes of the same type. Second, extraction constructions such as wh-questions, Topicalization, etc. are base-generated with gaps in the position of the extraction site. The dependence between the "extracted" node and the extraction site is captured by the introduction of slash-categories; for an explication of this I refer the reader to Gazdar's paper in this volume (section 9).

Let us consider, then, how this approach can account for case-marking in wh-questions, as exemplified by the following sentences:

(3)   a. $\left\{\begin{array}{l} \text{*Who} \\ \text{Whom} \end{array}\right\}$ did John see?

         b. $\left\{\begin{array}{l} \text{Who} \\ \text{*Whom} \end{array}\right\}$ did John say was coming?

The distribution of *who* and *whom* here is accounted for if NP's are marked with the feature $[\pm \text{NOM}]$, and if wh-questions are introduced by the following rule (from Gazdar (1979):

(81) $[_Q \underset{[\text{WH}]}{\alpha} \quad S/\alpha]$

(81) is a rule schema, where α ranges over node labels. (Further restrictions need to be placed on the set of nodes which can occur here, but this is irrelevant here.) What is crucial is that the node $\underset{[+\text{NOM}]}{\text{NP}}$ is not the same as the node $\underset{[-\text{NOM}]}{\text{NP}}$. Thus if one of these occurs as the leftmost daughter of Q, then the "slashed" node (i.e., the missing node) will be a node of the same type. Further phrase structure rules will ensure that the node $\underset{[+\text{NOM}]}{\text{NP}}$ cannot occur in the position of the gap in (3a) (while $\underset{[-\text{NOM}]}{\text{NP}}$ is impossible in the gap position in (3b).) It is, therefore, predicted that the case-marking of the wh-NP is determined by the position of the gap, though there is no level of representation at which the wh-NP is in this position.

Note that there are two conditions necessary in order for connectivity to hold. First, it will hold only for processes which are properties of node labels. Second, it can only hold between a node and a gap which are introduced by the same phrase structure rule. Consider, for example, the following two rules for wh-relative clauses proposed in Gazdar (1979) (I ignore here and in the discussion which follows the semantics associated with these syntactic rules):

(82) $[_{NP} \quad NP \quad R]$

$[_R \underset{[\text{WH}]}{\alpha} \quad S/\alpha]$

If something like these rules is correct, it is predicted that there will be connectivity between a relative pronoun and the gap position, but not between the head noun and this position.[25] So, for example, in a language with relative clauses like English relatives but where full NP's are case-marked, the head noun of a relative clause should not be case-marked according to the position of the gap, while the relative pronoun should.

Similarly, the simplest account of Tough-Movement constructions would be one which introduced VP/NP's as the complement of *tough*-predicates; in other words, these can be accounted for by roughly the following rule:

(83) $[_{AP}$ A VP/ NP $]$
                          [− NOM]

Since the subject of the Tough-Movement predicate is not introduced in the same rule as the rule introducing the slash category, there will not be connectivity between this NP and the position of the gap. What is especially interesting about this theory, then, is that a gap need not be connected in the syntax with any other node. If (83) is correct, then the gap in a Tough-Movement construction is an example of just such a gap. This analysis correctly predicts, then, that even though the gap is in object position, the subject of the *tough*-construction will not receive object case-marking:

(84)   a.   He is hard to please

            b.   *Him is hard to please

Let us return, then, to the interaction of the Object Pronoun constraint with Tough-Movement constructions, as exemplified by the following:

(9)   a.   *It's hard to tell the children them
            b.   *The children are hard to tell them
(14)   b.   They are hard to tell the children

The theory under discussion here accounts for these facts in the way discussed earlier. (9b) is ungrammatical because there is a gap in the position of the extraction site; (14b) is grammatical because the subject of *hard* is not itself in this position. What is interesting here is that even if the distinction between pronouns and full NP's is a feature on nodes (and hence a property of the dominating node, rather than simply a property of the lexical items dominated by this node), the lack of connectivity here is predicted since the subject of a *tough*-predicate need not have the same features as the gap. Thus while the subject of (14b) would be the node NP
                                                                         [Pro]
the gap will not be this node. Note that there is no analogous solution in a multi-dominational theory. Connectivity cannot be blocked between the subject of the *tough*-predicate and the gap; since some NP must be in the position of the extraction site it would have to be the subject of the *tough*-predicate. Thus, a multi-dominational account provides nothing corresponding to a gap which has no syntactic connectivity to some other

node. Note too that no extra mechanisms are needed to ensure the lack of strong connectivity here; this follows simply from the formulation of *tough*-constructions in (83).

However, this does not mean that all questions concerning which phenomena and which constructions will exhibit connectivity are automatically answered within this framework. It remains to be explained, for example, why the stress principle does not exhibit connectivity even in constructions like wh-questions and Topicalization (the lack of connectivity in these constructions is evidenced by (62)). To clarify the problem, it will be useful to show how the relevant principles could be formulated so as to incorrectly predict connectivity here; I will then briefly speculate on a possible solution.

Suppose, first, that stress is a feature on nodes, and that if some node is marked with this feature then the feature is "passed down" in such a way as to ensure that one of the lexical items dominated by this node is stressed. (This can easily be done in essentially the same way that slashed categories are "passed down".) The stress principle, then, will be formulated to ensure that the node immediately preceding *to* has the feature [Stress]. Moreover, let us assume that the gap in a wh-question must have all of the same features as the wh-word (with, perhaps, the exception of the feature [WH]). Given this, it is incorrectly predicted that the stress principle will show connectivity in wh-questions, thus (62a) should be grammatical in this account:

(62)   a. ?*Which mán do you want to?

The wh-NP here is a node with the feature [Stress]; consequently the gap preceding *to* would also have this feature even though this node contains no lexical item which is actually stressed.

Assuming that stress is a node feature, two things are needed to avoid this incorrect prediction. First, the rules introducing extracted NP's and gaps must be permitted to allow certain specified features to differ; in particular, the feature [Stress] must be allowed to differ. (This will have no effect on the power of the grammar.) Second, there must be some principle ensuring that empty nodes never contain the feature [Stress]; this would follow, if there were a principle ensuring that any node with the feature [Stress] must dominate a stressed lexical item; such a principle does not appear unreasonable. Given these mechanisms, a wh-NP could be stressed even though the node at the extraction site would not contain this feature. (62a) will thus correctly be blocked since *to* is necessarily preceded by a stressless constituent.

What is needed, though, is some principled way of predicting which features are permitted to differ, and a principled way of predicting that a feature like [Stress] must be absent on an empty node. As suggested above, it is not unreasonable to assume that features with phonological consequences cannot occur on these nodes, but a more precise account of this is needed.

While I have no definitive solutions to these questions, I would like to point out again in closing that even without a way to predict what processes will exhibit connectivity, a theory containing a level of representation with gaps still allows for a better account of the phenomena discussed here than does the classical theory or a multi-dominational theory. As discussed above, these theories cannot account for the stress principle and the extraction cases with a single constraint, while these can be collapsed if there are gaps. More importantly, perhaps, the hypothesis that there are gaps means that there is no reason to posit a representation where no node occurs in the extraction site position, nor is there any reason to posit that certain constraints can "ignore" the nodes in extraction site (i.e., no distinction is necessary between real and pseudo nodes). Thus it is predicted that no processes will behave as though there is no node at all in these positions, and this prediction appears to be correct.

Brown University,
Providence

NOTES

* For conversation, criticisms and comments on the material in this paper, I am grateful to Jane Grimshaw, Lauri Karttunen, John McCarthy, Fritz Newmeyer, Stan Peters, Geoff Pullum, Sue Schmerling and Annie Zaenen.
[1] This idea has been proposed in a variety of works, including Morin and O'Malley (1969) and Sampson (1975). More recently, it is explored in Jacobson (1977) and in unpublished work by Peters. A similar kind of suggestion is also made in Hudson (1976) and in Johnson and Postal (to appear); however the above terminology is a bit misleading for their proposals in that they allow a node to bear more than one grammatical relation simultaneously, but it is not in two distinct places in terms of constituent structure.
[2] Emonds (1976) proposes that there are actually intransitive prepositions; he analyzes what are traditionally treated as particles in "verb-particle" constructions in this way. This, however, does not affect the point here, since even if some prepositions can occur without NP's, *under* generally does not (it does not occur in the verb-particle construction).

[3] There are certain complications in the formulation of this constraint which I am ignoring. For example, if has often been noted that only definite, anaphoric pronouns are subject to this restriction; note the grammaticality of the following:

    i.   I gave John one.
    ii.   I gave John that.

Also, Ross (1967) and others have pointed out that stress on the pronoun improves it; I have found a good deal of idiosyncratic variation with regards to the acceptability of sentences like (iii) (where *her* is to be taken anaphorically, not dictically):

    iii.   I looked up hér.

(My own judgment is that (iii) is better than (5b), but not fully grammatical.)

    While I am glossing over these complications, I do not think that they will substantially affect the conclusions arrived at here.

[4] Wasow does not actually argue for a cycle-final constraint as discussed above; rather he suggests that the effects of the constraint would follow from an obligatory cyclic cliticization rule. This suggestion is discussed in 2.3.

[5] It might be thought that this difficulty could be avoided by a minor revision of the constraint so that it only blocked VP's with accusative pronouns in this position. However, such a revision is of no help, since (i) is also grammatical:

    i.   I expected them to be hard to tell the children.

[6] Similar evidence that the constraint cannot be cyclic is not available from wh-questions, since question pronouns are in any case not subject to the constraint. In other words, while (i) (which is parallel to (14b)) is grammatical:

    i.   What did you tell the children?

it cannot be concluded from this that the constraint must apply before the fronting of *what*. Question pronouns (like other non-anaphoric pronouns) can in general be separated from the verb, as indicated by the following:

    ii.   Who told the children what?

[7] Some speakers do in fact find (17b) grammatical, to which I will return in fns. 9 and 11.

[8] This of course still leaves unanswered the question as to how the constraint itself can be learned, but this question is independent of the issues being considered here. For some discussion of this, see Baker (1979).

[9] This would, in fact, provide an account of the dialect in which (17b) is grammatical:

    17b.   I gave her it.

Here *it* is not separated from the verb, since *give her* is the verb. Unfortunately, though, it is then difficult to account for the dialect in which (17b) is not grammatical (though see fn. 11).

[10] Wasow does, in fact, note this problem; his discussion is somewhat inconclusive on this point since he notes that sentences like (25) are questionable. While sentences of this form might be slightly awkard, all of the speakers that I have consulted find a strong contrast between (25) and (26).

¹¹ An account like this provides a fairly simple way to describe the dialect difference noted in fns. 7 and 9. For the dialect in which (17b) is grammatical, cliticization can apply twice; that is, *her* can cliticize onto *give*, and *it* onto *give her*. For the dialect in which this is ungrammatical, double cliticization is impossible.

¹² Rapid speech is being excluded here; the reduction in (35b) probably is possible in rapid speech.

¹³ This suggestion is made more explicit in Chomsky (1977); Chomsky suggests that there is a level at which unindexed empty nodes are deleted but indexed empty nodes are not, and that *wanna* reduction applies after this level. It follows from this that PRO's will not block reduction.

¹⁴ Lightfoot does, in fact, argue that there is evidence that a Passive trace blocks reduction, since reduction is impossible in (ib):

i.   a.   The knife was used to slice the salami.
       b. *The knife was usta slice the salami.

However, as has been noted in a number of replies to Lightfoot, there is no reason to think that the lexical item use in (i) governs the relevant processes for reduction. For further discussion, see Postal and Pullum (1977), Andrews (1978) and Pullum and Postal (1979).

¹⁵ Claims of this sort can be found in Selkirk (1972) and Baker and Brame (1972).

¹⁶ This needs to be more precise; the only constructions which are blocked is one where the gap preceding [*to* ∅] is a sister of [*to* ∅]. A gap can precede this when it is contained within the sister constituent:

i.   I want [the man Mary likes ∅] to ∅

¹⁷ One such filter discussed in Chomsky and Lasnik is the impossibility of an extraction site immediately after *that*. For an account of this constraint which does not require reference to gaps and which also does not require the existence of movement rules, see Gazdar (1981).

¹⁸ (47) requires the main stress to be on *Tim*; the following is somewhat odd:

i.   ?I wánt Tim to.

I return to this in the next section.

¹⁹ Again, this must be refined in the same way as the refinement of (42) discussed in fn. (16). Stress must be somewhere on the constituent which is a sister of [*to* ∅].

²⁰ For some reason, (i) is somewhat better than (ii):

i.   ?Who do yóu want to.
ii.   ?*Who do you wánt to.

While I have no explanation for this, the same holds true in the parallel cases without gaps; (iii) is better than (iv):

iii.   ?Í want Tim to.
iv   ?I wánt Tim to.

²¹ This needs to be restricted further; *to* can cliticize only onto a verb or adjective of which the VP introduced by *to* is the complement.

²² Some speakers do not allow sentences like (68)–(70); Bresnan (1971), in fact, cites sentences

of this type as ungrammatical. I have no explanation for why these are impossible for some speakers; perhaps this has to do with phonological principles.

[23] Of course it could be argued that the difference in the past tense forms of *want* and *taunt* does not have to do with what rules they govern, but rather is due to some difference in their underlying forms. But if this is correct, then this could also be what accounts for the fact that *want to* has [wɔnə] as its surface form.

[24] Rightwards cliticization of certain morphemes is also proposed in Bresnan (1971a).

[25] It has often been noted that there are in fact certain processes by which the head noun of a relative clause behaves as though it is in the position of the gap. One such example concerns the distribution of Picture Noun Reflexives (see Jackendoff (1972) and Jacobson (1977) for discussion); another is the distribution of idiom chunks, as in (i):

i.   The attention that we paid to that proposal was miniscule.

If the remarks above are correct, then cases of this sort would have to be accounted for in some other way. See Sag (this volume) for some discussion of idiom-chunk arguments for movement.

REFERENCES

Andrews, A. (1978) 'Remarks on *to*-adjunction,' *Linguistic Inquiry* 9, 261–268.
Baker, C. L. (1979) 'Syntactic theory and the projection problem,' *Linguistic Inquiry* 10, 533–581.
Baker, C. L. and M. K. Brame (1972) 'Global rules: a rejoinder,' *Language* 48, 51–75.
Bresnan, J. (1971a) 'Contraction and the transformational cycle in English'. Reproduced by Indiana University Linguistics Club, 1978.
Bresnan, J. (1971b) 'Sentence stress and syntactic transformations,' *Language* 47, 257–281.
Bresnan, J. (1978) 'Towards a realistic theory of transformational grammar' in J. Bresnan, M. Halle and A. Miller (eds.). *Linguistic Theory and Psychological Reality*, M. I. T. Press, Cambridge, Masschusetts.
Bresnan, J. (ed.) (1981) *The Mental Representation of Grammatical Relations*, M. I. T. Press, Cambridge, Massachusetts.
Chomsky, N. (1977) 'On wh movement' in P. Culicover, T. Wasow and A. Akmajian (eds.), *Formal Syntax*, Academic Press, New York.
Chomsky, N. and M. Halle (1968) *The Sound Pattern of English*, Harper and Row, New York.
Chomsky, N. and H. Lasnik (1977) 'Filters and control,' *Linguistic Inquiry* 8, 425–504.
Chomsky, N. and H. Lasnik (1978) 'A remark on contraction,' *Linguistic Inquiry* 9, 268–274.
Dowty, D. (1978) 'Governed transformations as lexical rules in a Montague Grammar,' *Linguistic Inquiry* 9, 393–426.
Dowty, D. (this volume) 'Grammatical relations and Montague Grammar.'
Emonds, J. (1976) *A Transformational Approach to English Syntax*, Academic Press, New York.
Fiengo, R. (1974) *Semantic Conditions on Surface Structure*, unpublished dissertation, M. I. T.
Gazdar, G. (1979) 'English as a context-free language,' unpublished ms.
Gazdar, G. (this volume) 'Phrase structure grammar'.
Gazdar, G. (1981) 'Unbounded dependencies and coordinate structure,' *Linguistic Inquiry* 12.

Hudson, R. (1976) *Arguments for a Nontransformational Grammar*, University of Chicago Press, Chicago, Illinois.

Jackendoff, R. (1972) *Semantic Interpretation in Generative Grammar*, M. I. T. Press.

Jacobson, P. (1977) 'Some aspects of movement and deletion,' in *Proceedings of the Third Annual Meeting of the Berkeley Linguistic Society*, 347–359.

Johnson, D. and P. Postal (to appear) *Arc Pair Grammar*, Princeton University Press, Princeton, New Jersey.

Lakoff, G. (1970) 'Global rules,' *Language* **46**, 627–639.

Lightfoot, D. (1976) 'Trace theory and twice moved NP's,' *Linguistic Inquiry* **7**, 559–582.

Morin, Y. C. and M. O'Malley (1969) 'Multi-rooted vines in semantic representation,' in R. I. Binnick et al., eds., *Papers from the Fifth Regional Meeting*, Chicago Lingusitic Society, Chicago, Illinois.

Perlmutter, D. M. and P. M. Postal (1977) 'Some universals of passive' in *Preceedings from the Third Annual Meeting of the Berkeley Linguistic Society*, 347–359.

Postal, P. M. and G. K. Pullum (1978) 'Traces and the description of English complementizer contraction,' *Linguistic Inquiry* **9**, 1–29.

Pullum, G. K. and P. M. Postal (1978) 'On an inadequate defense of "trace theory",' *Linguistic Inquiry* **10**, 689–706.

Ross, J. R. (1967) *Constraints on Variables in Syntax*, unpublished dissertation, M. I. T.

Sag, I. A. (this volume) 'A semantic theory of "NP-Movement" dependencies.'

Sampson, G. (1975) 'The single mother condition,' *Journal of Linguistics* **11**, 1–11.

Selkirk, E. (1972) *The Phrase Phonology of English and French*, unpublished dissertation, M. I. T., Cambridge, Massachusetts.

Wasow, T. (1975) 'Anaphoric pronouns and bound variables,' *Language* **51**, 368–383.

JOAN MALING AND ANNIE ZAENEN

A PHRASE STRUCTURE ACCOUNT OF SCANDINAVIAN EXTRACTION PHENOMENA*

0.0 The aim of this paper is threefold: (i) to present data from Scandinavian languages that any general theory of island constraints must account for; (ii) to describe these data in the framework being developed in Gazdar (this volume), Sag (this volume), Gazdar, Pullum and Sag (1980), and to show that while a straightforward extension of the framework to cover the Scandinavian data is possible, it leads to an increase in generative capacity of the theory so that it no longer provides grammars only for context-free languages; and (iii) to sketch a theory of island constraints that transfers some of the burden of explanation from the syntax to processing mechanisms on the one hand and to discourse organization on the other.

The problems encountered by transformational grammars have recently led to the exploration of alternatives. One such alternative is relational grammar, represented in this volume by Perlmutter and Postal; another alternative is the return to "base-generation" of some or all of the constructions previously thought to involve transformations. Our paper takes the latter approach. By the mid seventies, several linguists had presented arguments that cyclic transformations be eliminated in favour of base-generation of both the underlying and the derived forms, e.g. Freidin (1975) for Passive, Brame (1976) for Equi, and Oehrle (1976) for Dative Movement. More recently, serious attempts have been made to develop grammars that eliminate either entire classes of transformations, or all of them. For example, Bresnan (1978) and Dowty (1978) propose to eliminate the class of "cyclic" transformations, and the "lexical-functional" grammar developed in Bresnan (1980b), Andrews (this volume), and the proposals in Brame (1978), Gazdar (this volume) and Peters (1979) do away with all transformations. The more explicit of these proposals are attractive because they present frameworks that are tightly constrained in generative power and thus make more realistic claims about parsability and learnability than most transformational grammars (see Gazdar, this volume). However the work done within this perspective does not yet have the scope of work done in the transformational framework; it is not obvious that the formal constraints of these frameworks can be maintained when more data are taken into consideration.

229

P. Jacobson and G. K. Pullum (eds.), The Nature of Syntactic Representation, 229–282.
Copyright © 1982 by D. Reidel Publishing Company.

In this paper we propose to widen the data base of the theory by giving an account for a new set of data within the framework developed by Gazdar and others. As we will show, some of the multiple extraction facts actually present a problem for one of the strongest claims made in Gazdar (1980), namely that natural languages are context-free languages.

Not all the problems presented by the data are related to the power of the grammar, however. We will discuss two other issues in some detail, namely the status of a nested dependency constraint as proposed in Fodor (1978) and the relation between resumptive pronouns and "traces."

Although the analysis we present seems to be descriptively adequate, it certainly raises problems of explanatory adequacy. We think these problems cannot be addressed insightfully without a model of the interaction between syntax, processing and discourse organization. We have adopted here the view that the syntax must capture all the generalizations that can be defined structurally, even if one must look outside the syntax for an insightful explanation for certain of them. As a result, our syntax contains some rather ad hoc constraints. We will sketch a model of the interaction between the syntax and processing mechanisms that gives a non-syntactic motivation for these constraints.

The general outline of the paper is as follows. In Section 1 we present the salient facts about Scandinavian extraction that must be accounted for and then discuss briefly their relevance for some of the recent accounts of island constraints.[1] In Section 2 we present the essential features of the phrase structure framework that we will use, and illustrate it with English data. Section 3 contains an account of the Scandinavian data in the framework insofar as they are statable in structural terms, and in Section 4 we discuss some nonstructural factors and sketch a model of the interaction between syntax, processing, and discourse organization.

The work presented here is in many respects inconclusive, but it raises interesting problems that a phrase structure framework must be able to deal with in order to be an attractive option among approaches to syntax.

1. EXTRACTION IN SCANDINAVIAN LANGUAGES: FACTS AND PREVIOUS ACCOUNTS

Ross' (1967) constraints on extraction in English have been found to have parallels in many languages. However, the fact that languages are intriguingly similar in exhibiting such constraints should not lead us to ignore the differences in extractibility that can be found even among languages as closely related as English and the Scandinavian languages. Some of these differences have been documented before in the transformational literature. Extractions out of complex NP's in Danish are studied in detail in Erteschik (1973);[2] Allwood (1976) presents an overview of the problems encountered in Swedish with respect to the complex NP constraint and extractions out of NP's in general. Extractions out of *wh*-islands in the various Scandinavian languages are documented in Maling (1978)[3] and for Swedish and Norwegian in Engdahl (1979), who also studies "crossing" dependencies. Violations of the Fixed Subject Constraint in Icelandic (as well as Dutch) are documented in Maling & Zaenen (1978).

However a comprehensive overview of the data is lacking. In this section we will attempt to give a systematic overview of two phenomena:

(1)   the extraction possibilities in Swedish, Norwegian and Icelandic out of the main structures whose English analogues are islands;

(2)   the distribution of resumptive pronouns in these constructions.

In the last subsection we will point out some of the problems that these data pose for several theories of island constraints.

1.1 In this section we will document the extraction possibilities out of the various constructions one by one for Icelandic, Norwegian and Swedish.[4]

1.1.1 *Extractions out of Wh-Clauses*

As in English, extractions out of *that*-clauses are allowed in all Scandinavian languages, as illustrated in (1).

(1)   a. Vem   sa   Kari   att   Jan   hade
        b. Hvem   sa   Kari   at   Jon   hadde
        c. Hvern   sagði   Kari   að   Jón   hefði
           Who   said   Kari   that   John   had

           sett   pa   bio?   (Swedish, henceforth S)
           sett   pa   kino?   (Norwegian, henceforth N)
           séð   í   bíó?   (Icelandic, henceforth I)
           seen   at   cinema?

           'Who did Kari say that John had seen at the movies?'

The Scandinavian languages differ from English, however, in also allowing extraction out of *wh*-clauses, as illustrated below:

(2)   a. Vilka   böcker   frågade Jan   vem
        b. Hvilke   bøker   spurte   Jon   hvem
        c. Hvaða   bækur   spurði   Jón   hverjir
           what   books   asked   John who

        som   skrev? (S)
        (som)   hadde   skrevet? (N)
                 hefði   skrifað? (I)
        (that)   (had)   written
        'What books did the teacher ask who had written?'

(3)   a. Vem   vet du inte   om   Jan såg
        b. Hvem   vet du ikke   om   Jon sa
        c. Hvern   veistu ekki   hvort Jón sá
           who   do-you-not-know   whether John saw

        på   bio? (S)
        på   kino? (N)
        í   bíó? (I)
        at   movies
        'Who don't you know whether John saw at the movies?'

As (2) shows, extraction is not limited to *whether/if*-clauses but can also apply to clauses to which *wh*-movement has already applied. Further examples of such double extractions are given in Engdahl (1979) for Swedish. She shows that extraction is equally possible by questioning, relativization, and topicalization. The same holds for Norwegian and Icelandic, with the complicating factor that in Norwegian some speakers prefer cleffed versions over topicalizations quite generally.[5] These data are of course a potential problem for the account of the *wh*-island constraint given in Chomsky (1977); this will be discussed below in Section 1.3.

1.1.2 *Extraction Out of Relative Clauses*

In Swedish and Norwegian, extraction out of relative clauses is often possible whereas in Icelandic such extractions seem to be impossible.[6] The following example from Allwood (1976) was accepted by all our Norwegian informants but by none of the Icelandic ones:

(4)   a. De   blommorna   känner jag   en   man   som säljer. (S)
        b. De   blomstene   kjenner jeg en   mann   som selger. (N)
        c. * Þessi blóm   þekki ég   mann, sem selur. (I)
           these   flowers know   I   a   man   that sells
        'These flowers, I know a man who sells.'

However extraction out of a relative clause does not always result in an acceptable sentence. Moreover in the cases where these extractions are bad, the use of resumptive pronouns[7] does not improve the sentence. As we will see, this is different from other cases in which a constituent is extracted out of a structure that in English is an island. An example of an unacceptable extraction is given in (5):

(5) a. * Lisa   talar   jag med den poiken
     b. * Lisa   snakker jeg med den gutten
     c. * Lisu   talaði   ég   við   strákinn,
          Lisa   talked   I   with the boy

     som kysst   (henne). (S)
     som kysset (henne). (N)
     sem kyssti (hana). (I)
     that kissed (her)
     'Lisa, I talked with the boy who kissed (her).

It seems clear that the constraint on extraction out of relative clauses is not a structural one. The contrast between (4) and (5) seems rather to have to do with what the sentence is "about": in (5) the sentence is more about *the boy* than about *Lisa* and hence the topicalization is ungrammatical. In (4) on the other hand, the sentence can be interpreted as being about *those flowers*, and hence topicalization is possible.

One might think that one of the constraints is that extraction is only possible out of indefinite CNP's, but this seems too strong, if *definite* means "having a definite article." Taraldsen (1979) gives the following contrast:

(6)   Marit finner vi aldri den gutten som
        Mary   find   we never the boy   who

        kan hamle opp med   (T(62))
        can handle

but

(7)   * Marit har vi endelig funnet den gutten som
          Mary   have we finally found   the boy   who

        kan hàmle opp med   (T(61))
        can handle

In the negative version, (6), *the boy* is non-referential, whereas in (7) it must be referential; again it is much easier to interpret (6) as a statement about Mary than (7).

Some discussion of such functional constraints on extractability can be found in Kuno (1976), Erteschik (1973) and Allwood (1976).

In Section 4 we will come back to the role of functional factors in an account of island constraints.

1.1.3 *Extractions Out of Nonrelative NP's*

As is pointed out in Allwood (1976), extraction out of nonrelative complex NP's is quite common in Swedish; the same holds for Norwegian and Icelandic; as illustrated below:

(8)   a. Vilket fangelse finns det föga hopp att man kommer helskinnad fram? (Engdahl (1979)) (S)

         b. Hvilket fengsel er det lite håp (om) at man kommer helskinnet fra? (N)

         c. Úr hvaða fangelsi er lítil von til að maður komi heill?
'Which prison is there little hope (for) that one comes unhurt from'? (I)

Further examples can be found in Allwood (1976) and Engdahl (1979).

Extraction out of simple (non-sentential) NP's lead to problems of the same type as found in English (see Horn (1975) for a discussion of the English data): extractions like those in (9) are good, just as they are in English, but the examples in (10) are judged much less acceptable. The acceptability depends on the context (see Allwood (1976) for discussion); however extraction seems to be more readily accepted in such cases in the Scandinavian languages than in English.

(9)   a. Vem skrev Pelle en bok om?

         b. Hvem skrev Pelle en bok om?

         c. Um hvern skrifaði Palli bók?
'Who did Pelle write a book about?'

(10)   a. *Vem forstörde Pelle en bok om?

         b. *Hvem ødela Pelle en bok om?

         c. *Um hvern eyðilagði Palli bók?
'Who did Pelle destroy a book about?'

As argued in Horn (1975), (9) might not be a case of extraction out of NP at all, but may be derived from a source where the NP 'a book' and the PP 'about who(m)' do not form one constituent. Although the problems with this approach have never been worked out totally satisfactorily for English, it is tempting to apply it to the Scandinavian languages too, especially since we have been unable to find any clear examples of extractions out of subject NP's, the only case where such a reanalysis would be impossible.

This concludes the overview of the extractions that are possible in Scandinavian languages but not in English, and that do not lead to the insertion of resumptive pronouns in any of the Scandinavian languages. In the next subsection, we will illustrate the cases where in Swedish, and to a lesser degree in Norwegian, resumptive pronouns are used to "save" otherwise unacceptable extractions.

1.2 The Distribution of Resumptive Pronouns

In several cases where extraction is impossible in Standard English, extraction is possible in Swedish and Norwegian when a resumptive pronoun is left behind in the extraction site. This strategy does not seem to be used in modern Icelandic, in contrast with older stages of that language, where one finds resumptive pronouns with a distribution that is however essentially different from that found in the other modern Scandinavian languages (Maling (1976)).

1.2.1 Sentential Subjects

In none of the Scandinavian languages is extraction possible out of a sentential subject without leaving a resumptive pronoun; in Swedish and Norwegian however, it is possible to extract when such a pronoun is left behind. We have been unable to construct such examples for Icelandic. The Swedish and Norwegian contrasts are illustrated in (11) and (12). As can be deduced from these examples, the "internal NP-over-S" constraint is less strong in these languages than in English. As in English, the embedded sentential subjects are better when the complementizer that introduces them is different from the complementizer that introduces the matrix clause.[8]

(11)   a. Det här är en sorts problem som Kalle påstår att hurivida Pelle klarer att lösa $\left\{ \begin{array}{c} \text{det} \\ *\varnothing \end{array} \right\}$ eller ei kommer att visa om han är intelligent. (S)

    b. Dette er en type oppgave som Kalle hevder at om Pelle greidde a løse $\left\{ \begin{array}{c} \text{den} \\ *\varnothing \end{array} \right\}$ vil vise om han er intelligent. (N)

'This is the kind of problem that Kalle says that whether Pelle succeeds in solving it will show if he is intelligent.'

(12)   a. De talade om den skrivning som Pelle undrade om det att Kalle redan läst $\left\{ \begin{array}{c} \text{den} \\ *\varnothing \end{array} \right\}$ kunde göra någon skillnad. (S)

b. De snakket om den prøven som Pelle lurte på om det at Kalle allerede hadde lest $\left\{ \begin{array}{c} \text{den} \\ *\varnothing \end{array} \right\}$ ville ha noen innvirking på resultatet. (N)

'They talked about the exam that Pelle wondered whether (it) that Kalle had already read it would make no difference in the result.'

1.2.2 Crossing Dependencies

Another place where resumptive pronouns can occur is in the crossing pattern of double extractions (see (14b)). However, this only happens in Swedish; in both Icelandic and Norwegian, we can find double crossing extractions without resumptive pronouns as shown in (13). In Icelandic a resumptive pronoun is totally impossible, whereas in Norwegian it is optional. In cases with triple (crossing) extractions, however, a resumptive pronoun is obligatory even in Norwegian.

(13)   a. Den här presenten kan du säkert aldrig komma på vem jag fick $\left\{ \begin{array}{c} \text{den} \\ *\varnothing \end{array} \right\}$ av____. (S)

b. Denne gaven her vil du ikke gjette hvem jeg fikk (den) fra____. (N)
'This gift can you not guess who I got (it) from____.'

c. Þessum krakka hérna$_i$ geturðu aldrei imyndað þér hvaða gjöf$_j$ ég gaf t$_i$ t$_j$. (I)
'This boy here can you never guess what gift I gave.'

(The Icelandic example is slightly different here; gefa 'to give' in Icelandic is a verb that takes a dative and an accusative, obligatorily in that order.)

What distinguishes these examples from those of double extractions given earlier is the pattern of filler-gap dependencies. Whereas in the earlier examples we had the pattern illustrated in (14)a, we now have the pattern illustrated in (14)b.

(14)   a. F$_1$ F$_2$ G$_2$ G$_1$ b. F$_1$ F$_2$ G$_1$ G$_2$

As the example shows, in Swedish a pronoun is required in the first extraction site in this case; in Norwegian however this is not necessary, and in Icelandic a pronoun is ungrammatical.

As we will see, whereas triple extractions are impossible in Icelandic, they are possible in Swedish and Norwegian. If the extractions intersect, we need a resumptive pronoun even in Norwegian in those cases. A Norwegian example is given in (15).

(15)　　Det er politimannen som jeg lurer på hvilke piker dommeren

vill vita hvilke droger $\left\{ \begin{matrix} \text{han} \\ *\varnothing \end{matrix} \right\}$ trodde $\left\{ \begin{matrix} \text{de} \\ *\varnothing \end{matrix} \right\}$ hadde solgt

$\left\{ \begin{matrix} \varnothing \\ *\text{den} \end{matrix} \right\}$ till barne. (N)

'This is the policeman$_i$ that I wonder which girls$_j$ the judge will want to know which drugs$_k$ he$_i$ thought they$_j$ had sold ___$_k$ to the children.'

As the pattern in (15) and (13) shows, the pronoun appears in the first extraction site of a crossing pair, not in the last. We will come back to the significance of this distribution.

1.2.3 *The Fixed Subject Constraint*

As is well-known, it is impossible in English to extract a subject NP immediately following a complementizer. This phenomenon, which we will refer to as the Fixed Subject Constraint (Bresnan (1972)), is illustrated by the contrast between (16a) and (16b), and by the ungrammaticality of (17):

(16)　　a. *Who do you think that saw Mary?
　　　　b.　Who do you think saw Mary?

(17)　　　*Who do you wonder if saw Mary?

Such extractions are perfectly acceptable, however, in Icelandic, as is amply documented in Maling & Zaenen (1978 henceforth M & Z). Two examples are given here:

(18)　　Hver sagðir þú að__vaeri kominn til Reykjavíkur? (I)
　　　　'Who (nom.) said you that was come to Reykjavik?' (M & Z, (6))

(19)　　þetta er maðurinn, sem þeir segja að__hafi framið glæpinn. (I)
　　　　this is the-man, that they say that has committed the-crime
　　　　(M & Z, (18))

In Swedish, unlike Icelandic, the Fixed Subject Constraint holds, as illustrated by the following contrast:

(20) a. *Vem tror   du   att __ skulle komma i tid? (S)
        Who believe   you   that   will   come   on time?

    b. Vem tror   du skulle komma i   tid?
        Who believe you will   come   on   time

As in English, deletion of the complementizer results in a grammatical sentence. However Swedish has a second strategy for avoiding violations of the FSC: the use of a resumptive pronoun. This is illustrated by the contrast between (21a) and (b):

(21)   a. *Vem undrade alla om skulle komma i tid?   (S)
         b. Vem undrade alla om *han* skulle komma i tid? (S)
            'Who$_i$ did everybody wonder if (he$_i$) would come on time?'
            (Engdahl (1979), (22))

Whenever available, COMP-deletion is the preferred strategy. The use of resumptive pronouns after *om* and *wh*-words follows from the fact that these are not deletable. When *att* is not deletable, as is the case with clausal objects of prepositions, a resumptive pronoun is again possible:

(22)   Vem$_i$ är det svårt att bortse från $\begin{Bmatrix} att \\ *\emptyset \end{Bmatrix} \begin{Bmatrix} han_i \\ *\emptyset \end{Bmatrix}$ snarter? (S)
         'Who is it hard to ignore that he snores?'

After a deletable *att*, a resumptive pronoun is used only when embedded several clauses down from its antecedent (where it would be optional in any case, as we will see), as shown by the following contrast:

(23)   a. *Vem$_i$ tror Inge att han$_i$ skulle komma? (S)
         b. Vem$_i$ sa du att Jan är säker på att Inge tror att han$_i$ skulle
            vinna? (S)
            'Who did you say that Jan is sure that Inge believes that he
            will win?'

The Norwegian data concerning the FSC is much less clear. Some speakers do not accept subject extractions after *at* but others do. So for some speakers the following is grammatical, whereas for others it is not:[9]

(24)   (*) Hvem tror du at skulle vinne? (N)
             'Who do you think that will win?'

Subject extractions out of *om* or *wh*-clauses seem to be much better. The following sentences were accepted even by the speakers who reject (24):

(25) Montague kan jeg ikke huske hvor $\left\{ \begin{array}{c} \emptyset \\ \text{*han} \end{array} \right\}$ kommer fra. (N)

'Montague I can't remember where (*he) comes from.'

(26) Montague kan jeg ikke huske om $\left\{ \begin{array}{c} \text{*han} \\ \emptyset \end{array} \right\}$ døde i Kalifornia
(N)

'Montague I can't remember if (*he) died in California.'

After non-deletable *at*, extractions are also accepted, as in the following examples:

(27) Hvem er du sikker på at $\left\{ \begin{array}{c} \emptyset \\ \text{* han} \end{array} \right\}$ skulle vinne? (N)

'Who are you sure that (*he) will win?'

Resumptive pronouns cannot generally be used in Norwegian to fix up violations of the FSC: those speakers who reject (24), also reject

(28) *Hvem tror du at han skulle vinne? (N)
Who$_i$ do you think that he$_i$ will win?

If the extraction site is more deeply embedded, a resumptive pronoun is more acceptable, but as in Swedish, it would be optional in these cases anyhow.

1.2.4. *Optional Resumptive Pronouns*

The final cases in which resumptive pronouns can appear in Norwegian and Swedish is when the extraction site is embedded more than two clauses down from its antecedent. The use of resumptive pronouns is optional in that case, even in Swedish, unlike the other cases we have discussed. A Norwegian example is given in (29).

(29) Dette er filmen som jeg ikke vet om noen husker hvem (som) har spilte i (den). (N)
'This is the film$_i$ that I don't know if anyone remembers who played in (it$_i$).'

Further documentation of the phenomenon can be found for Swedish in Engdahl (1979). Erteschik (1973, 122) notes that Danish is less likely to use resumptive pronouns than Swedish; Maling (1978) gives examples where pronouns are used in Swedish and Danish but not in Norwegian. Here, as elsewhere, Icelandic avoids resumptive pronouns altogether.

1.3 Theoretical Problems

Subsections 1.1 and 1.2 provide a succinct overview of the extraction facts that have to be accounted for. Before presenting our treatment of the data, we will briefly review some recent accounts of extraction constraints for which these data present problems. We will first consider accounts based on subjacency: Chomsky's (1977) proposal as adapted by Rizzi (1978), then as adapted by Reinhart (1979), and finally Taraldsen's (1979) reanalysis of relative clauses in Norwegian, designed to fit the Norwegian data into the Chomsky-Rizzi model. We will show that none of these proposals can deal with the Scandinavian data.

We will then briefly discuss the constraint on crossing extractions proposed in Fodor (1978), and finally point out that the violations of the FSC in Norwegian are a problem for the correlation proposed in Maling and Zaenen (1978).

1.3.1 Island Constraints and Subjacency

Since Chomsky (1973), several attempts have been made to give a unitary account of major island constraints in which the notion of subjacency plays a central role. The basic idea is that a grammatical rule can involve A and B only if they are not separated by more than one cyclic node. Successive cyclic movement from COMP to COMP, where the COMP-position is an 'escape hatch,' explains the apparent violations of this principle.

1.3.1.1 *Rizzi's account of wh-island violations in Italian.* In Chomsky (1973) not only subjacency but also the Tensed-S Condition and the Specified Subject Condition played a role in the account of island constraints. Rizzi's (1978) main innovation is to propose that these conditions are not relevant for Italian, and that it is the subjacency condition, together with the assumption that NP and S̄ are binding nodes In Italian, that explains the extraction facts in that language. The way in which these assumptions would allow for some violations of the *wh*-island constraint is illustrated in (30) (= Rizzi (6b)); the relevant portion of the sentence is diagrammed in (30b).

(30)   a. Tuo fratello, a cui mi domando che storie abbiano rac-
               contato, era molto preoccupato

'Your brother, to whom I wonder which stories they told, was very troubled.'

b. tuo fratello, $[_{\bar{s}}$ *a cui$_i$* $[_s$ mi domando $[_{\bar{s}}$ *che storie$_j$* $[_s$ abbiamo raccontato $t_j\,t_i$]]]]

Wh-movement of *a cui* 'to whom' directly into the higher COMP from its base position, crosses two S-nodes but only one S̄-node. Hence such extractions will not violate subjacency if S̄ rather than S counts as the binding node. Rizzi (1978) shows that these assumptions make the right predictions for the pattern of allowable extractions in Italian.

The Scandinavian cases, however, cannot be reanalyzed in the same way, as shown for Swedish in Engdahl (1979). This can be seen by considering the following Icelandic example from Maling (1978); extraction in this case should proceed as shown in diagram (31b).

(31)   a. Þetta eru kvæðin, sem kennarinn spurði hverjir við héldum að hefði skrifað.
        'These are the poems that the-teacher asked who we thought that had written.'

b. kvæðin $[_{\bar{s}_1}$ sem $[_{s_1}$ kennarinn spurði $[_{\bar{s}_2}$ hverjir$_j$ $[_{s_2}$ við héldum $[_{\bar{s}_3}$ að $[_{s_3}\,t_j$ hefði skrifað t_i]]]]]]]

Example (31b) shows clearly that subjacency is violated no matter what sentential node is taken as binding: *wh*-movement of the relative pronoun from S̄$_3$ to S̄$_1$ crosses two S̄-nodes. Similar sentences are ungrammatical in Italian and are ruled out under Rizzi's account; but they are grammatical in all the Scandinavian languages under consideration, as illustrated in Maling (1978) and Engdahl (1979); the Norwegian equivalent of (31) is given in (32):

(32)   Dette er de diktene som laererin spurte oss hvem vi trodde hadde skrevet. (N)

So Rizzi's parametrization of Chomsky's proposal does not take care of the Scandinavian extraction facts.

1.3.1.2 *Reinhart's (1979) double COMP-hypothesis.* Another modification of Chomsky's framework can be found in Reinhart's analysis of Hebrew violations of the *wh*-island constraint. Reinhart assumes that in Hebrew there are two complementizer positions available to which *wh*-constituents can be moved. This proposal is however not particularly attractive for Scandinavian. First, of course, there should be independent motivation for a second COMP-position. While this might be available in Swedish and

Norwegian, where one finds sequences of the form *wh*-word + complementizer,[10] such evidence is totally lacking in Icelandic; yet the extraction patterns for Icelandic are the same.

Even worse for the double-COMP hypothesis, however, is the fact that in Swedish and Norwegian, extractions are not limited to two. The following example of a triple extraction seems to be acceptable to native speakers of Swedish, given enough context; its Norwegian counterpart (33b) was acceptable to some of our informants, but not all. The sentence is diagrammed in (33c).

(33) a.

Sådana här	känsliga	politiska	frågor	har
such	touchy	political	questions	have
jag	flera	studenter	som	det
I	many	students	that	there
inte	finns	någon	som	jag
not	is-found	anyone	that	I
tror	skulle	våga	prata	med
believe	should	dare	talk	with
∅	om	∅		
∅	about	∅		

b. Slike foelsomme politiska fragor har jeg flere studenter som det ikke finnes noen som jeg tror ville våge å prata med om.

c.

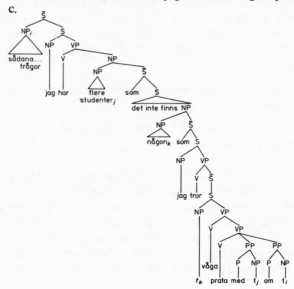

Another example from Engdahl (1979) is:

(34) a. Var det Södersjukhuset som hälsovärdsmyndigheterna lät
undersöka vilka färskvaror det var oklart vilken grossist som
hade levererat till?
'Was it the South hospital $\emptyset_i$ that the Health Department
investigated which produce$_j$ it was unclear which caterer$_k$
that t_k had delivered t$_j$ to t_i?

The diagram for the maximal *som*-clause is:

b.

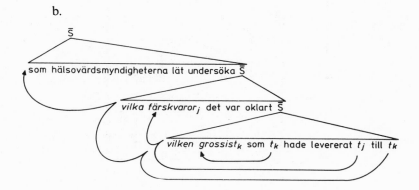

It seems obvious that allowing two, three (or even more?) COMP positions
seriously undermines the explanatory value of successive-cyclic *wh*-
movement.

1.3.1.3 *Taraldsen's reanalysis of relative clauses in Norwegian.* The last
relevant proposal made in the framework of Chomsky (1977) that we are
aware of is Taraldsen (1979). It was designed specifically to take care of the
problem posed by the existence of extractions out of relative clauses in
Norwegian. We will address only the question of extraposition analysis of
extractions from relative clauses, and not the other theoretical points that
Taraldsen considers. The basic idea is quite simple: the extractions
exemplified in Section 1.1.2 will be only apparent violations of the CNPC if
in fact S̄ is assumed to be the binding node (together with NP), as in Italian,
and if the relative clause is extraposed before extraction takes place.
Extraposition is sometimes vacuous, as illustrated in (35):

(35) Per   kjenner jeg [$_{NP}$ ingen] [$_{\bar{S}}$ som——liker——] (N)(Taraldsen (2))
      Peter know   I   nobody   who   likes

The derivation of (35) would run as follows: the underlying structure is given in (35a); extraposition of S̄ yields (35b), and then *wh*-movement out of the extraposed clause yields (35c).[11]

(35) a.
    [Per] [s̄ COMP[s jeg kjenner [NP[NP ingen] [s̄ som[s *t* l iker WH]]]]].

    b. [Per] [s̄ COMP[s jeg kjenner [NP ingen] [s̄ som [s *t* liker WH]]]].

    c.

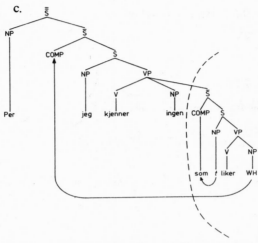

After extraposition, *wh*-movement directly from the base position to the highest COMP crosses only one S̄-node.

There are several problems with the extraposition analysis. First, as Taraldsen notes himself, the analysis requires a reordering of extraposition with respect to *wh*-movement such that extraposition is part of the transformational component rather than the stylistic component. A large part of Taraldsen's paper is devoted to the defense of this move, which we will not discuss here. Second, the extraposition analysis predicts that extraction out of relative clauses on subject NP's will be possible if extraposition has applied. This prediction is wrong, as illustrated in (36)– (37).

(36) a. Ingen som stemte på Nixon ble invitert. (N)
       No one who voted for Nixon was invited.
    b. Ingen ble invitert som stemte på Nixon. (N)
       No one was invited who voted for Nixon.

(37)   a. *Nixon ble ingen som stemte på invitert.   (N)
             Nixon was nobody who voted for invited.
         b. ?*Nixon ble ingen invitert som stemte på   (N)
             Nixon was nobody invited who voted for.

Finally, the extraposition analysis makes the same predictions as Rizzi (1978) with respect to embedded questions, since extraposition from NP cannot be invoked here. Hence it will be falsified by the same examples. A relevant example is repeated here:

(32)   Dette er de diktene som laererin spurte oss hvem vi trodde hadde skrivet.   (N)
         'These are the poems that the teacher asked us who we thought had written.'

For the representation of this sentence, see the tree given with the Icelandic example in (31b).

Of course, similar violations can also be constructed for relative clauses even when they are extraposed. An example is given in (38).

(38)   Det er Chomsky (som) jeg ikke kjenner noen som lurer på om Marit burde ta et kurs hos.
         'It is Chomsky (that) I don't know anybody who wonders whether Marit should take a course with.'

Taraldsen himself gives an example, shown in (39), of the same kind, except that it contains an embedded *at*-clause instead of an *om*-clause.

(39)   a. Per kjenner jeg ingen som tror at du liker.
             Peter know I nobody who thinks that you like.
         b. Per [COMP jeg kjenner [ingen] [$_\bar{s}$ som tror [$_\bar{s}$ at du liker____]]]

As shown by the diagram in (39b), this extraction violates the subjacency constraint even after extraposition with $\bar{S}$ as the binding node. Taraldsen says that he considers this sentence to be ungrammatical; he notes, however, that there are speakers who do accept it. Our own informants were equally divided as to the grammaticality of such sentences.

Taraldsen does not discuss embedded questions, so we do not know if for him (32) is grammatical, as it was for *all* our informants. If it is grammatical, Taraldsen's analysis of relative clauses actually makes the situation for the subjacency theory worse: certain apparent violations of the CNPC are accounted for by extraposition and the choice of $\bar{S}$ as a binding node, whereas the same explanation cannot account for all violations of the *wh*-island constraint.

Under the assumption that extraction is possible out of both CNP's and *wh*-islands, as in Swedish, where the reanalysis proposed by Taraldsen cannot be maintained; (see Engdahl (1979) for examples and discussion), there is a trivial way to account for the situation within the Chomskyan framework,[12] namely by assuming that neither S nor S̄ are binding nodes in these languages. This proposal requires giving up the attempt to account for the sentential subject constraint in terms of subjacency and makes it necessary to go back to a special subject constraint, as was the case in Chomsky (1973).[13]

The assumption that there are no sentential binding nodes seems to account for the Swedish data and some Norwegian dialects that pattern like Swedish. However, regardless of the problems caused by other Norwegian dialects that seem to exhibit an asymmetry with respect to violation of the *wh*-island constraint and the CNPC, the assumption does not extend to Icelandic. In that language, as shown in Sections 1.1.1 and 1.1.2, it is possible to extract out of embedded questions but not out of relative clauses. This situation is not new; for older stages of the language it is documented in Maling (1976).[14] This state of affairs is of course more troublesome for the subjacency account of island constraints, since the predicted relationship between the CNPC and the *wh*-island constraint does not hold. It is clear that to explain the lack of extraction out of relative clauses we need at least one bounding node at the sentential level in addition to NP.

So Taraldsen's account, far from solving a problem for the subjacency account, creates another one by creating an asymmetry between indirect questions and relative clause extractions even in dialects where this asymmetry does not seem to exist. The Icelandic data show that this problem is unavoidable, even if it is assumed that Swedish and (some dialects of) Norwegian can be accounted for by assuming that there are no sentential binding nodes in these languages.

Although the extraposition analysis does not account for the extraction phenomena, it remains to be explained why sentences like (40a) are better than (40b).[15]

(40)   a. Per slipper jeg ikke noen inn som liker
          Peter let I not anybody in who likes
         b. ???Per slipper jeg ikke noen som liker inn.
          Peter let I not anybody who likes in.

We have not investigated this problem, but part of the solution seems to be given by Taraldsen (1979) himself: he notices that extraction and extraposition possibilities both correlate with "non-referentiality": in Norwegian only non-referential NP's seem to be good foci in the sense of Guéron (1976), and only out of foci can extraposition or extraction take place. However, if this is correct, one would not expect (40b) to be as bad as it is since the extraposition out of foci does not seem to be obligatory. The conditions on extraposition of relative clauses in Norwegian and the differences between Swedish and Norwegian in extractibility out of these clauses clearly need more study; however, it seems unlikely that the right solution to these problems will lead to a solution of the problems encountered by the subjacency analysis in Scandinavian languages.[16]

1.3.2 Other Constraints on Extractions

In the previous subsection we discussed the problem posed by the Scandinavian data for the framework developed by Chomsky and his students. In this subsection we will point out some problems for some less far-reaching proposals that have been made: *in casu* the constraint against crossing dependencies (Section 1.3.2.1) and the correlation between the FSC and the obligatoriness of overt subjects proposed in Maling & Zaenen (1978) (Section 1.3.2.2).

1.3.2.1 *The "Nested Dependency Constraint"*. It has been noted several times that when double dependencies between gaps and fillers are allowed in one structure, they get considerably worse when the pattern is as shown in (14b) instead of as in (14a) (repeated here for convenience from Section 1.1).

(14)   a. F_1 F_2 G_2 G_1 b. F_1 F_2 G_1 G_2

In one form or another, several linguists have proposed a constraint against the (b)-pattern (e.g., Kuno & Robinson (1977), Bordelois (1974)), Hankamer (class lectures (1976)), and more recently Fodor (1978) who formulates the constraint as follows:

(41)   If there are two or more filler-gap dependencies in the same sentence, their scopes may not intersect.

Fodor (1978) limits the relevance of this constraint to gaps of the same category. She mainly discusses cases where the dependencies are not "unbounded," since double unbounded dependencies are in general not allowed in English (see Section 2.2).

As a universal constraint, (41) has been attacked on the basis of data in Turkish and Japanese in a recent paper by Kuno, Kornfilt and Sezer (1980). However, these languages differ from English in ways that might be thought relevant for the NDC ("free" word order, "free" pro-drop,[17] and case marking in Turkish and to a lesser degree in Japanese). So it is interesting to see how well the NDC fares in languages that are more similar to English. As the examples in Section 1.1 show, only Swedish bears out the NDC, if, as Fodor assumes, resumptive pronouns are not subject to the constraint. The Norwegian and Icelandic data show that the NDC does not have the same grammatical status in those languages as it has in Swedish and English. If the ultimate explanation of the NDC is that it is a processing strategy, the case of Icelandic might not be that aberrant, since case marking will in that language disambiguate most cases of crossing extractions. But this cannot be said for Norwegian, where most case marking has disappeared. It is interesting to note that both in Icelandic and in Norwegian, crossing extractions without resumptive pronouns seem to be limited to two. In Icelandic this seems to be the general upper limit for unbounded extractions. In Norwegian, as we have noted in Section 1.1 (14), resumptive pronouns are used when three extractions with crossing paths are attempted.

1.3.2.2 *The fixed subject constraint.* Finally the Norwegian data present a problem for the claim made in Maling & Zaenen (1978) that there was a correlation between the non-obligatoriness of subject dummies and the violations of the FSC.[18] We observed that both Dutch and Icelandic, two German languages that allow subject extraction as in (42), also allow sentences like (43), although neither of these languages has a more general "pro-drop" rule:

(42)   a. Hver heldur þú að væri kominn till Reykjavikur? (I)
        b. Wie denk je dat naar Reykjavik gekomen is? (Dutch)
           Who think you that was come to Reykjavik?
(43)   a. Í gaer var dansað. (I)
        b. Gisteren werd gedanst. (Dutch)
           'Yesterday was danced', i.e. 'There was dancing yesterday.'

We postulated that only languages where sentences like (43) are possible would allow cases like (42); languages that do not allow (43) would have a surface constraint prohibiting empty subject positions is tensed clauses; such a surface constraint would then also rule out (42).

In Norwegian, however, we have found the following situation: whereas some speakers accept (24), repeated here for convenience,

(24) Hvem tror du at skulle vinne? (N)
      'Who do you think that will win?'

the same speakers do not accept (44).

(44) I gar regnet $\left\{ \begin{matrix} \text{det} \\ *\varnothing \end{matrix} \right\}$. (N) (Ungrammatical without *det*)

       yesterday rained it
       'Yesterday it rained.'

However, it will have become clear to the reader that dialect variations are very common in Norwegian. It would be not too astonishing, assuming that *some* speakers accept (44), if the correlation between the grammaticality of (24) and (44) did not hold for all speakers, given the interaction between the different dialects. This obviously needs further investigation among a larger group of informants and we have not as yet been able to carry out such investigations.

In Section 1.3 we have shown that the Scandinavian data cannot be handled by the proposed attempts to "parameterize" Chomsky's (1977) framework to account for other languages. While this does of course not show that another "parameterization" would not be possible for those languages, it casts some doubt on the usefulness of the enterprise, since each adaption of the framework according to a *different* parameter weakens the predictive power of the framework.

We have also pointed out some problems the data pose for less far reaching proposals such as Fodor's NDC and our own account of the FSC.

In the next sections we will develop a descriptive account of unbounded extractions in Scandinavian and in Section 4 we will come back to the problem of explanatory adequacy.

2. THE TREATMENT OF ISLAND CONSTRAINTS IN PHRASE STRUCTURE GRAMMAR

2.0. In this section we shall briefly recapitulate the main features of the version of phrase structure grammar presented by Gazdar in this volume, and illustrate from English how island constraints can be handled in that framework. For convenience of reference we shall call Gazdar's framework *generalized phrase structure grammar* (GPSG).

2.1 *Essential Features of Generalized Phrase Structure Grammar*

In a GPSG, rules of grammar are triples consisting of an arbitrary integer (the rule number), a node admissibility condition, and a formula indicating how the constituent defined by the rule can be translated into intensional logic and thus assigned an interpretation in a model. The node admissibility conditions, which we shall mainly be concerned with, are labelled bracketed strings of the form shown in (45).

(45) $[_\alpha \ldots]$
        where α is a nonterminal symbol and . . . is either e (the empty string) or a string of one or more terminal or nonterminal symbols.

A node admissibility condition like (45) admits a portion of a tree that has a root labelled α and has the string '. . .' as its immediate constituents. A set of node admissibility conditions (henceforth syntactic rules, or simply *rules*) can admit a set of trees: a tree is admitted if every node in it is either (a) a terminal node or (b) the root of a subtree that is admitted by one of the rules. The set of terminal strings of a set of trees admitted by a grammar of this sort is always a context-free language. This result continues to hold even if the definition in (45) is extended to allow '. . .' to contain labelled bracketings as well as just symbols from the terminal and nonterminal vocabularies.

We shall refer to five varieties of rules: basic rules, derived rules, linking rules, elimination rules and metarules. *Basic rules* simply use the basic vocabulary of node labels familiar from transformationalist syntax. For English, the basic syntactic rules might include those in (46).

(46) $[_S \text{NP VP}] \ [_{VP} \text{V NP}] \ [_{VP} \text{V NP NP}] \ [_{VP} \text{V NP PP}] \ [_{PP} \text{P NP}]$

Derived rules are automatically added to the stock of basic rules by a universal convention (see (9.2) in Gazdar's chapter). They involve additional node labels called *derived categories*. The set of derived categories for a language with nonterminal vocabulary V_N is defined in (47).

(47) $\{\alpha/\beta : \alpha, \beta \in V_N\}$

Derived categories label "incomplete constituents" and are used for handling unbounded dependencies. Derived rules expand a derived category α/β in a way similar to the way α would be expanded except that one of the immediately dominated nodes has the label γ/β instead of just γ. Examples of derived rules related to the basic rules in (46) are given in (48).

(48) $[_{S/NP}$ NP VP/NP$]$ $[_{VP/NP}$ V NP/NP$]$ $[_{PP/NP}$ P NP/NP$]$

By guaranteeing that a node labelled α/β will immediately dominate a node that is γ/β for some γ, the derived rules in effect pass information about "holes" up or down the tree, because 'α/β' is interpreted as 'an α constituent with a hole of type β in it'. Apart from this special interpretation, derived rules have no peculiar syntactic or semantic properties.

To permit subtrees rooted by basic categories to contain derived categories, *linking rules* are provided in the grammar. A linking rule introduces a derived category *de novo*. Some examples of linking rules for English are given in (49), in their full form as triples.

(49)   a. $\langle 100, [_S \ \alpha \ S/\alpha], \lambda h[(S/\alpha)'](\alpha')\rangle$ where α is NP,
                                                  PP, AP, $\bar{S}$, or $\bar{Q}$

    b. $\langle 101, [_{NP} \ \ NP \ R], \lambda r[NP'](R')\rangle$

    c. $\langle 102, [_{\bar{Q}} \ \ \underset{[+wh]}{\alpha} \ \ S/\alpha], \lambda p[\exists n[p \wedge (p = \lambda h[(S/\alpha)'](\alpha'))]]\rangle$

Rule 100, in (49a), introduces topicalized sentences. Rule 101, in (49b), introduces relative clauses, which are labelled with the category R. Rule 102, in (49c), introduces embedded *wh*-questions, which belong to the category $\bar{Q}$. We will refer to the first term in these constructions as the *head phrase* of the construction, to the category with a "hole" of the same category as the head phrase as the *slashed category*, and to the category of the hole (or the hole itself) as the *missing constituent*.

Elimination rules allow derived categories to dominate strings that do not contain a slashed category. One elimination rule that Gazdar suggests is

(50) $\langle 41, [_{\alpha/\alpha} \ t], h_\alpha\rangle$ where $\alpha \in V_N$

This allows categories like NP/NP to dominate t, a dummy terminal symbol that marks the location of "holes" for phonological purposes. Note that other elimination rules could be postulated.

Some rules in a GPSG are not simply listed, but are generated by higher level statements of the form "if r is a rule, then $F(r)$ is a rule" where F is some function of the form of *r*. These statements are called *metarules*. The notation for metarules is illustrated, and examples given, in Gazdar's chapter.

2.2. *Some English Island Constraints in GPSG*

We now give a few examples of how English extraction constraints might be stated in GPSG. Our aim is not to give either an exhaustive account or a range of new facts. We simply want to draw attention to the fact that many constraints can be stated in a very succinct way in this framework.

As Gazdar points out, an island constraint can be thought of as blocking all *derived* rules of a particular form. For example, the Sentential Subject Constraint might be viewed as a ban on derived rules of the form (51)

(51) $*[_{S/\alpha} \quad \bar{S}/\alpha \dots]$

We might generalize this to block all extraction out of S-dominated subordinate clauses (e.g. adverbial clauses) by stating it as (52).

(52) $*[_{S/\alpha} \dots \bar{S}/\alpha \dots]$

Alternatively, if we assume that sentential subjects are $\bar{S}$'s dominated by NP, we can collapse the Sentential Subject Constraint with the constraint that extraction out of subjects is in general prohibited and restate (51) as (53).

(53) $*[_{S/\alpha} \quad NP/\alpha \dots]$

2.2.1 *The Double Hole Constraint*

A quite general constraint on extraction in English is that it is not possible to extract twice out of the same (tensed?) clause. This constraint has been referred to informally by Jorge Hankamer in class lectures as the "double hole" constraint. In a framework where raising and equi rules are supposed to leave holes, there are, of course, numerous counterexamples to this generalization and the constraint must be limited explicitly to "extraction" rules. But we are not assuming such a framework: raising and equi constructions are instead base-generated without incomplete (derived) constituents. The dichotomy between "extraction" rules and bounded rules is captured in a very straightforward and explicit way in the formalism. The only incomplete constituents are those created by the linking rules.

In fact, given the GPSG framework as we have sketched it thus far, the double hole constraint need not even be stated. The rule schema (47) which creates derived nodes does not define incomplete constituents with more than one hole. Unfortunately, two classes of sentences come readily to mind which suggest that too strong a claim is being made here: (i) sentences involving both *tough*-movement and unbounded leftward movement, and (ii) sentences involving a combination of leftward and rightward movement.

2.2.1.1. *Tough-movement and the double hole constraint.* It is possible to relativize, question and topicalize out of the complement of a *tough*-predicate, as illustrated in (54).

(54)   Tell me what sort of student subjacency is difficult to explain to.

We shall assume that the complements to *tough*-predicates are of the category $\overline{VP}$, as argued in Bresnan (1971, 1978). The structure of the embedded question clause in (54) is shown in (55).

(55)

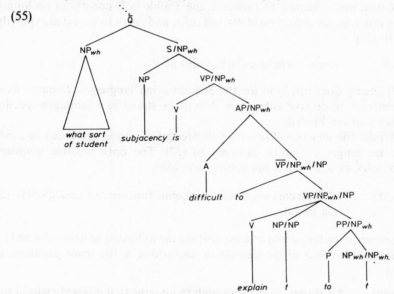

To admit such trees we need to make the definition of derived categories recursive. This can be achieved by dropping "basic" from the characterization of set G in (47). Derived categories will then be characterized as in (56a) and derived rules as in (56b).

(56)   a. Let V_N be the set of basic category symbols, and $D(V_N)$ be defined as follows:
   i. If $\alpha \in V_N$, then $\alpha \in D(V_N)$;
   ii. If $\alpha \in D(V_N)$ and $\beta \in V_N$, then $\alpha/\beta \in D(V_N)$;
   iii. Nothing else is in $D(V_N)$.

   b. Let R be the set of basic rules, and $D(R)$ be defined as follows:
   i.. If $r \in R$, then $r \in D(R)$;
   ii. If $[_\alpha \sigma_1 \ldots \sigma_i \ldots \sigma_n] \in D(R)$, where $1 \leq i \leq n$ and α and all σ_k $(1 \leq k \leq n)$ are in $D(V_N)$, then $[_{\alpha/\beta} \sigma_1 \ldots \sigma_i/\beta \ldots \sigma_n]$ $\in D(R)$, where $\beta \in V_N$;
   iii. Nothing else is in $D(R)$.

Each application of the rule scheme in (56a) defines a finite set of derived categories, but since it is recursive, the set of nonterminal symbols $D(V_N)$ is potentially infinite.

Given rule schema (56), however, the double hole constraint no longer falls out from the definition of derived rules, and needs to be stated explicitly as in (57).

(57)   *$S/\alpha/\beta$ where $\alpha \in D(V_N)$ and $\beta \in V_N$.

(57) clearly does not hold for the Scandinavian languages. If stated as a constraint on derived categories, it must be stated as a language-specific constraint for English.

Under the analysis of *tough*-predicates given above, sentences like (54) are no longer a counter-example to (57). The only possible counter-examples would come from sources like (58):

(58)   ??These cars are tough to imagine that anyone would sell to his best friend.

However, even for people who accept (58), the following sentence derived by *wh*-movement out of the *that*-clause embedded in the *tough*-predicate is bad:

(59)   *Who are these cars tough to imagine that anybody would sell to?

We will assume therefore that the *tough*-movement construction is not a problem for the double-hole constraint as stated in (57).

2.2.1.2 *Advantages of the double hole constraint.* The double hole constraint as stated in (57) captures a certain number of generalizations about English extractions in a very economical way. Note that the constraint precludes extraction out of indirect questions, except those introduced by *if* or *whether* (since these are basic rather than derived categories). For a great number of speakers of English, extractions out of *if* and *whether* clauses are good in contradistinction to extractions out of other embedded questions, and for all speakers, they are significantly better. Although the dialects that do not allow extractions out of *if* and *whether* clauses need an extra constraint, we think that (57) captures a real generalization in this case. Not only does (57) exclude extractions out of embedded questions, it also takes account for the ungrammaticality of extractions out of relative clauses but not out of other complex NP's. Again this seems to be the right result.

It has been noticed several times, beginning with Ross (1967), that extraction out of nonrelative complex NP's is not always bad. It seems likely that the cases in which these extractions are impossible should be taken care of by a better definition of the "bridge" conditions under which extraction is possible in general rather than by a structural constraint. This point is argued at length on the basis of French data in Godard (forthcoming) and the arguments presented there carry over to English (see also Erteschik (1979) and Allwood (1976)).

2.2.1.3 *One remaining problem for the double hole constraint.* In the previous subsections we have shown that (57) would allow us to account for several of the island constraints that hold in English in a very economical way. There is unfortunately one counterexample to the generalization as it stands; it results from the interaction between Right Node Raising or heavy NP shift and leftward movement rules. This interaction creates "doubly slashed" categories, and in some sentences, at least, the double holes seem to be at the S-level. Consider the following examples, which seem fully grammatical:

(60)   a. At what booksale did Hilary discover, and Rob buy, an autographed copy of *Syntactic Structures*?
    b. Into the wastebasket, Hilary put tearfully and Rob dropped sheet by sheet, their autographed copies of *Syntactic Structures*.

Ignoring adverbs and subject-auxiliary inversion, such sentences seem to have the structure shown in (61):

(61)

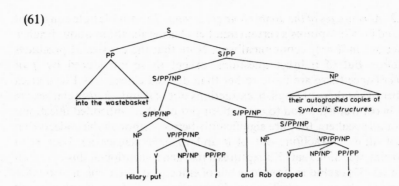

In (60b) both extracted PP's are subcategorized for by the verb so it seems unavoidable that the coordination (and hence the double hole) is at the sentential level.

If no solution to this problem can be found (57) will have to be complicated so as to allow for a distinction between right and leftward movement rules; this however would make it less attractive as an insightful generalization.[19]

2.2.1.4 Double holes and the power of grammar in English.

We have discussed these facts in some detail, not only to show how island constraints might be captured in the framework under consideration, but also because the possible number of holes has to do with the generative capacity of the grammar. If the definitions in (56) are adopted, there is no built-in upper limit anymore to the number of derived categories; if no principled upper bound can be found, the theory will no longer be restricted to providing grammars only for CF languages.

We suspect however that the existence of doubly or even triply slashed categories in English does not pose a real problem for the CF character of the syntax of English since there does seem to be a principled upper bound: no "extraction" rule applies more than once in the same domain, so in English the number of holes is less than or equal to the number of extraction rules. Since that number is finite, there is an upper bound to the number of "slashes" a category can have. However, this does not hold of the Scandinavian languages, which do allow multiple applications of the same rule in the same domain. As a result, the definitions in (56) in conjunction with the linking rules of Scandinavian will allow for non-CF languages (see Section 3.1).

3. THE TREATMENT OF ISLAND CONSTRAINTS IN THE SCANDINAVIAN LANGUAGES

3.1 *Derived Categories and Context-Free Languages*

The grammaticality of extractions out of *wh*-clauses and some relative clauses was noted in Section 1. It is illustrated here with two examples.

(62)   Jag kjenner en melodie som ingen visste hvem skrev. (N)
         'I know a song that nobody remembers who wrote.'

(63)   Vilken film kunde han inte minnas vem som regisserat? (S)
         'Which movie could he not remember who directed?'

As should be clear from the discussion in the preceding section the existence of such sentences forces us to extend the class of derived nodes beyond those allowed in ECFL. A straightforward way to do so was proposed in (56). However, rule schema (56) allows for an indefinite number of derived categories. Since the vocabulary we are using is no longer finite, we seem to get out of the class of CFL, if no other principled constraint is found. This can be proved by showing that our rule schema allows the generation of languages of the type $a^n b^n c^n$, which are not context-free (see Gazdar, this volume, for some further discussion).

Of course, there may well be a de facto upper bound on the number of extractions in Scandinavian languages. It seems unlikely that more than three can be processed. However to build such an arbitrary upper bound into the grammar is as unsatisfying as it would be to impose an arbitrary upper bound on the number of center embeddings which the grammar of English would be allowed to generate.

Of course, our proposal is only one way of handling the Scandinavian data. It is a very natural one but it may be that a more sophisticated treatment can avoid the conclusions that have to be drawn from our analysis.[20] In looking for such a solution one should keep in mind that the main attraction of CFG lies in the fact that some results about parsibility and learnability have been proven about them; but since it is not impossible that interesting results about learnability and parsibility could hold for more powerful grammars, there is no reason to require CFG's per se. We leave these problems to more mathematically inclined linguists and in what follows we will spell out our (non-context free) treatment of Scandinavian multiple extractions.

The rule schema in (56) allows us to get the multiple holes; the remaining problem is to assure the right distribution of resumptive pronouns. We will first argue that resumptive pronouns are of the same syntactic type as holes (Section 3.2), then give the rules that introduce them (Section 3.3), and finally (Section 3.4) we will give a comparative fragment of the grammars of Icelandic, Swedish and Norwegian with respect to long distance dependencies.

3.2 *The States of Resumptive Pronouns*

In this section we want to make the point that there is no reason to assume that resumptive pronouns are of a different syntactic category than t.[21] In Section 4, we will argue that this phonological realization is motivated by processing constraints. In this section we first give arguments for treating resumptive pronouns as being of the same syntactic category as t, and show that they have a different distribution than anaphoric pronouns. We will then illustrate this difference by looking at the different distribution of pronouns in left dislocation constructions, where we assume the pronouns to be "free," as compared to topicalization, where they are "resumptive."

3.2.1 *Resumptive Pronouns as Instances of* α/α

The reasons for treating resumptive pronouns as being of the same syntactic category as t are: (i) their behavior in coordination, (ii) the duplication of linking rules that would be otherwise necessary, (iii) the fact that they are not in free variation with epithets, and (iv) the difference in distance requirements as compared to free pronouns.

3.2.1.1 *Coordination.*[22] Gazdar proposes in this volume that coordination is possible only between constituents of exactly the same syntactic type, where a slashed category is *not* of the same syntactic type as its unslashed counterpart, e.g. S/NP is not of the same type as S. This account predicts that if resumptive pronouns are not of the same syntactic category as t (i.e. if they are not instances of α/α), then coordination between constituents containing a gap and those containing a resumptive pronoun should not be possible. However, this is not the case, as shown by the following grammatical example; the relevant structure is shown in (64b).

(64) a. Där borta går en man som jag ofta   träffar
         there goes   a   man$_i$ that I   often   meet

         ∅   men inte   vet   vad *han* heter. (S)
         t$_i$ but not   know what he   is-called

'There goes a man that I often meet but don't know what he is called.'

b.

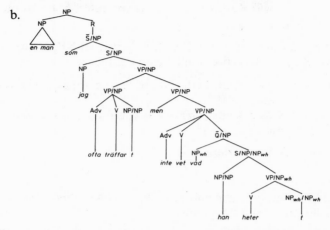

As the tree structure shows, this is a case of a **VP/NP** coordinated with a **VP/NP**. However, if resumptive pronouns are not analyzed as instances of $[_{NP/NP} t]$, then the coordination will be between VP/NP and VP, and the sentence should be ungrammatical.[23]

3.2.1.2 *Duplication of linking rules.* To treat resumptive pronouns as a syntactically different category would force us to duplicate the linking rules for each construction type: relatives, topicalizations, questions, clefts, etc. One linking rule will generate the versions with holes and the other will generate versions without holes. We would have to specify the essentially complementary environments in which these pairs of linking rules apply: holes occur in non-subject position and in subject-position not immediately following a complementizer, whereas resumptive pronouns occur in subject position after an overt complementizer. The situation in the Scandinavian languages is here quite different from that in languages where resumptive pronouns can also occur optionally and one has only to block the form with a *t* in certain environments; here we have to block the form with a pronoun in a number of environments as well, so essentially complementary constraints will have to be stated for these two cases. This seems to miss a generalization.

Another problem is that the second type of rule will have to specify that the NP must be a pronoun and cannot be another full NP. The following is ungrammatical in all Scandinavian languages:

(65)   *Det var Kalle (som) Petter spurte deg om Maria ville komme
tidsnok. (N)
'It was Kalle (that) Peter asked you if Mary would come on
time.'

And the sentence does not get better if there is an NP in the sentence that
can be interpreted as coreferential with e.g. the head of the cleft as in (66).

(66)   *Var det Kalle Petter spurte deg om den personen ville komme
tidsnok? (N)
'Was it Kalle Peter asked you if that person would come on
time?'

This brings us to our third point:

3.2.1.3. *Epithets are not allowed in free variation with resumptive pronouns.*
The following is still ungrammatical:

(67)   *Var det Kalle Petter spurte deg om den tulligen ville komme
tidsnok? (N)
'Was it Kalle Peter asked you if that idiot would come on
time?'

If one wants to say that the problem creating the ungrammaticality of (65)
to (67) is semantic in nature, one will have to develop a quite sophisticated
semantic filter to rule these sentences out; it is clear that an appeal to
coreference will not suffice.

3.2.1.4 *Distance requirements.*[24] A last respect in which we find quite a big
difference in the relation between resumptive pronouns and their "antecedents" and free or "bound" pronouns and their antecedent is in the
distance required between the two.

In Scandinavian languages, as in English, coreference is normally
possible when the pronoun is one clause down from its antecedent as in (68):

(68)   Kalle$_i$, jag påstod att jag skulle lära honom$_j$/honom$_i$
Engelska. (S)
'Kalle, I venture to say that I should teach him English.'

As we have already seen this is not the case for resumptive pronouns; the
following is impossible:

(69)   *Vem$_i$ tycker du att jag skulle lära honom/henne$_i$
        Engelska? (S)
        'Who think you that I should teach him/her English?'

From this example it is clear that the distribution is not only different from
that of "free" pronouns but also from that of so-called bound pronouns
illustrated by the following example:

(70)   Varje lingvist tycker att *han* borde lära sig åtminstone ett annat
        språk. (S)
        'Each linguist thinks that he should learn at least one other
        language.'

3.2.2 Differences Between Resumptive Pronouns and LD Pronouns

The special status of resumptive pronouns in unbounded dependencies can
be further clarified by comparing their behavior to that of pronouns in the
Left Dislocation construction, which we think are bona fide free pronouns.
The constraint on Left Dislocation is not that the pronoun be syntactically
bound in any particular way, but rather that the NP (or PP) in initial
position must be "taken up" by an NP (or PP) in the sentence which follows.

(i) Distance requirement.

In Left Dislocation constructions, the pronoun can be in the clause
immediately following the left dislocated element:

(71)   a. Kalle, han är en trevlig grabb! (S)
        b. Kalle, han er en kjekk kar! (N)
        c. Kalli, hann er ágætur strákur! (I)
        'Kalle, he's a fine fellow!'

Resumptive pronouns can never be this close to their antecedents in these
languages.

(ii) Epithets.

In a Left Dislocation construction the LD element can be taken up by an
epithet instead of a pronoun.

(72)   a. Kalle, jag tycker inte om den idioten! (S)
        b. Kalle, jeg liker inte den tulligen! (N)
        c. Kalli, mér líkar ekki fiflið ! (I)
        'Kalle, I don't like that idiot!'

However, epithets cannot occur in the constructions that resumptive pronouns occur in as shown in the previous section.

(iii) Islands.

Left Dislocation can go into structures that cannot be saved by resumptive pronouns; for example, left-dislocated NP's can be linked up with their pronouns even when these pronouns are inside relative clauses with definite heads. The following topicalization out of a relative clause is bad (as pointed out in Engdahl (1979b)), with or without resumptive pronoun, whereas the corresponding left-dislocated sentence is good.

(73)   a. *Kalle känner jag flickan som gillar (honom). (S)
        Kalle$_i$ know I the-girl that likes (him$_i$).
        b. Kalle, jag känner flickan som gillar honom/*$\emptyset$. (S)

Note the different position of the matrix verb in (73a) and (b); word order serves to distinguish LD from topicalization unambiguously in the Scandinavian languages (as well as in German and Dutch).

Presumably the syntactic binding relation that holds between a topicalized element and its gap or resumptive pronoun is sensitive to the definiteness (or whatever else the right semantic property may be) of the head of the relative clause; but the anaphoric binding relation is not sensitive to the same property. Here again, anaphoric and bound pronouns pattern together, and are distinct from resumptive pronouns:

(74)   Everybody$_i$ knows somebody that he$_i$ doesn't like.

This concludes our discussion of the status of resumptive pronouns. We have shown that their privileges of occurrence are quite different from those of free pronouns and given some reasons to think that they are to be treated syntactically like t. We will now proceed upon that assumption and spell out the syntactic rules that are needed to generate the sentences with resumptive pronouns.

3.3 Rules for Introducing Resumptive Pronouns

Thus far we have no rules to introduce resumptive pronouns where they are needed. We will use specific local constraints to introduce them in their different contexts. For example, the rule shown in (75) will introduce resumptive pronouns to circumvent the Fixed Subject Constraint. (We use context-sensitive rule notation to represent a "local constraint"; see Gazdar's chapter, section 3.)

(75) $S/NP \rightarrow NP/\underline{NP}$ $VP \Big/ \left\{ \begin{array}{l} att \\ om \end{array} \right\}$ ____

The underlining of the slashed category is a simple marking convention which specifies how the slashed category is to be realized; a new elimination rule will be added to spell out NP/$\underline{NP}$ as a pronoun rather than a trace. More generally, the elimination rule is as given in (76).

(76) $[_{\alpha/\underline{\alpha}}$ Pronoun]

The semantic translation of this rule is the same as that for the elimination rule introducing traces. Since derived categories have no special lexical or semantic properties, the resumptive pronoun will automatically acquire all agreement features that an ordinary pronoun in the same position would have.

3.3.1 Sentential Subjects

As shown in Section 1.2.1, extraction out of sentential subjects is possible when a resumptive pronoun is left behind. In this case too, coordination facts show that the sentence containing the sentential subject must be of the category S/NP:

(77)   Dette er den eksamenen som Per sa at hvor godt Lars gjorde det
        på *den* ville bestemme om han kommer inn på medisin og som
        Lars faktisk greide ____ bra. (N).
        'That's the exam that Peter said that how well Lars does on *it*
        would determine whether he gets into med school, and that Lars
        indeed aced ____.'

Resumptive pronouns in this construction can be introduced by the metarule given in (78).

(78) $[_{S/\alpha}$ $\bar{S}/\alpha \ldots] \Rightarrow [_{S/\alpha}$ $\bar{S}/\underline{\alpha} \ldots]$

Again a filter has to be added to rule out the variant with the gap (see (90)).

3.3.2. Crossing Dependencies and Resumptive Pronouns

In Section 1.2 we noted that Swedish makes use of resumptive pronouns in cases of crossing unbounded dependencies. Note that in the Swedish examples in (79), taken from Engdahl (1979), the interpretation changes with the use of resumptive pronoun.

(79)   a. Här är flickorna som jag inte minns vilka pojkar läraren bad
           dem dansa med____. (= Engdahl (45a))
           'Here are the-girls$_i$ that I don't remember which boys$_j$ the
           teacher asked *them$_i$* to dance with t_j'
        b. Här är flickorna som jag inte minns vilka pojkar läraren
           bad____dansa med____. (= Engdahl (46a))
           'Here are the-girls$_i$ that I don't remember which boys$_j$ the
           teacher asked $\emptyset_j$ to dance with [them$_i$]'

The resumptive pronoun always precedes the gap, a situation which can be
represented graphically as in (80).

(80)   a. F_1 F_2 Pro   Gap   b.   *F_1 F_2 Gap   Pro

Moreover, the situation represented in (81a) never occurs, but only the one
shown in (81b):

(81)   a.   *F_1 F_2 Gap   Gap   b. F_1 F_2 Gap   Gap

Rule schema (56) will generate the necessary doubly-slashed constituents,
but to ensure the right interpretation of gaps with fillers, we need to state
how the elimination rules interact. The following principle will guarantee
that in sentences with two gaps, only the nested interpretation will be
available.

(82)   *$[_{A/\alpha/\beta}$ .... B/\alpha ... C/\beta ...]$

According to the convention in (82), node expansions in which the order of
holes leads to nested dependencies will be admitted, whereas expansions
leading to intersecting dependencies will be ruled out. While this stipulation
may seem ad hoc as stated, it makes sense in view of the possible translation
of CF grammars into push-down automata: it encodes the "last-in, first-
out" principle into a left-to-right parser.

A more problematic case is created by the grammaticality of crossing
extractions, such as (79a). For Swedish, where the resumptive pronoun is
obligatory in such cases, we propose the following metarule:

(83) $[_\alpha$ ... $\beta/\gamma/\delta$ ...] $\Rightarrow [_\alpha$ ... $\beta/\delta/\gamma$ ...]$

and a filter to rule out the ungrammatical cases (see (94)). The left-right
ordering convention stated in (82) holds for both underlined and non-
underlined categories. The same elimination rule (76) that creates resumptive pronouns in other contexts will apply here.

This method of creating crossing dependencies can easily be extended to three-hole sentences, without ever having more than two missing constituents on hold in memory (see Section IV). Where the holes are all produced by multiple leftward extractions, the following patterns of gaps and resumptive pronouns are predicted:

(84)   a. F_1 F_2 F_3 G_3 G_2 G_1 $\varnothing$ $\varnothing$ $\varnothing$
        b. F_1 F_2 F_3 G_1 G_3 G_2 pro $\varnothing$ $\varnothing$
        c. F_1 F_2 F_3 G_3 G_1 G_2 $\varnothing$ pro $\varnothing$
        d. F_1 F_2 F_3 G_2 G_3 G_1 pro $\varnothing$ $\varnothing$
        e. F_1 F_2 F_3 G_2 G_1 G_3 pro   pro $\varnothing$
        f. F_1 F_2 F_3 G_1 G_2 G_3 pro   pro $\varnothing$

Some Norwegian examples of three-hole sentences with resumptive pronouns as the result of crossing dependencies are given below:

(85)   a. Det er politimannen som jeg lurer på hvilke piker dommeren

   vill vite hvilke droger $\begin{Bmatrix} *\varnothing \\ han \end{Bmatrix}$ trodde $\begin{Bmatrix} *\varnothing \\ de \end{Bmatrix}$ hadde solgt

   $\begin{Bmatrix} *den \\ \varnothing \end{Bmatrix}$ til barne.   (N)

   'This is the policeman$_1$ that I wonder which girls$_2$ the judge
   will want to know which drugs$_3$ he$_1$ thought they$_2$ had
   sold ____$_3$ to the children.'

   b. Her er pusher som jeg lurer på hvilke piker dommeren vill
   vite hvilka stoffer folk hørte ham snakker med dem om $\varnothing$.
   'Here is the pusher$_1$ that I wonder which girls$_2$ the judge will
   want to know which things$_3$ people heard him$_1$ talk with
   them$_2$ about $\varnothing_3$.'

The fact that there are two-hole crossing dependencies *without* resumptive pronouns in Norwegian and Icelandic evidently presents a problem for our approach. The interpretation of such sentences seems to depend on agreement information and selectional restrictions.

3.3.3 *The Long-distance Principle*

There are certain situations where resumptive pronouns are optional rather than obligatory, even in Swedish. The simplest of these cases is the one in which the extraction site is embedded more than two clauses down from its head, as mentioned in Section 1.2.4.

(86)   a. Dette er filmen som jeg ikke vet om noen husker hvem (som)
             har spiller i (den). (N)
             'This is the film$_i$ that I don't know if anyone remembers who
             played in (it$_i$).'
(86)   b. Här är boken som läraren frågade om vi mindes vem som
             skrivit (den).   (S)
             'Here is the book$_i$ that the teacher asked if we remember who
             wrote (it$_i$).'

In order to describe this use of resumptive pronouns, we need something
more than simple node admissibility conditions, because we need to count
the number of sentential nodes between the filler (antecedent) and the
extraction site. One way to do this was proposed by Gazdar (personal
communication) on the basis of an idea of J. Fodor inspired by Koster
(1978). In order to define the necessary tree admissibility conditions of the
type needed, we must define a notion of "main projection path" (MPP) as
follows:

(87)   The main projection path is any subpath of a path from root to
         terminal having the property that every node label in the
         subpath is of the form α/γ, where γ is constant and α is allowed to
         vary.

The effect of optional resumptive pronouns can be achieved with the
following metarule:

(88) $[_{S/\gamma} \ldots \alpha/\gamma \ldots] \Rightarrow [_{S/\gamma} \ldots \alpha/\underline{\gamma} \ldots]$

         if it occurs in a main projection path of the form
         $\ldots \alpha/\gamma \ldots \beta/\gamma \ldots$, where α and β are sentential categories.

Metarule (88) will allow sentences both with and without resumptive
pronouns; unlike the case of crossing dependencies, no filter of the type (82)
assigns an asterisk to the "source."
    The use of tree admissibility conditions can be shown not to increase the
generative power of the grammar (Joshi, Levy & Yueh (1978)), but it does
allow for a subset of grammars which would not be allowed if node
admissibility conditions were enough. One might well want to restrict the
possible conditions on tree "filters." For the distance principle that we are
concerned with here, the requirement on α and β is that they be sentential
nodes, a category including S, $\bar{S}$, Q, $\bar{Q}$, R and probably $\overline{VP}$. Our impression
is that the α and β relevant to the statement of tree admissibility conditions
will always be sentential nodes. Such a restriction is clearly in the spirit of

subjacency and the original notion of cyclic node. Although proposals can be found in the recent literature for elevating almost every phrasal category to the status of cyclic (or bounding) node, it seems likely that phrasal categories (NP, PP, AP) need never be mentioned in tree-filters. Thus their use can be restricted to node admissibility conditions, where they can be used to prohibit preposition stranding (*PP/NP) or to capture the NP-constraint of Horn (1975) in languages such as Irish (McCloskey, personal communication).

3.4 *Island Constraints in Scandinavian Languages: a Summary*

Icelandic:
Derived categories: extend the rule schema to allow at most double holes, or give a recursive definition as in (56) and a filter for more than two holes, as in (89):

(89) $*S/\alpha/\beta/\gamma$ where α and β are in $D(V_N)$ and γ is in V_N

Sentential Subject Constraint:

(90) $*[_{S/\alpha} \quad \bar{S}/\alpha \ldots]$ for all α

Complex NP Constraint:

(91) $*R/\alpha$ for all α

Genitive Constraint:[25]

(92) $*[_{NP/NP} \ldots NP/NP \ldots]$

Crossing dependencies with two gaps are allowed because there is no convention to rule them out; resumptive pronouns are generally unavailable in Icelandic, hence they are not introduced.

Swedish:
Derived categories: see definition (56).
Elimination Rules: add $[_{\alpha/\alpha}$ Pronoun] as in (76).
Sentential Subject Constraint: see (90).

Left-branch constraint:

(93) $*[_{NP/NP} NP/NP \ldots]$

Crossing convention:

(94) $*[_{A/\alpha/\beta} \ldots B/\alpha \ldots C/\beta \ldots]$ for all α, β, A, B, C.

Devices creating underlined categories:
Fixed Subject Constraint:

(95) $S/NP \rightarrow NP/\underline{NP} \quad VP \Big/ \left\{ \begin{array}{l} \text{att} \\ \text{om} \end{array} \right\}$ _____

Sentential subjects with resumptive pronouns:

(96) $[_{S/\alpha} \quad \bar{S}/\alpha \ldots] \Rightarrow [_{S/\alpha} \quad \bar{S}/\underline{\alpha} \ldots]$

Crossing dependencies:

(97) $[_{\alpha} \ldots \beta/\gamma/\delta \ldots] \Rightarrow [_{\alpha} \ldots \beta/\delta/\underline{\gamma} \ldots]$

Long distance principle:

(98) $[_{S/\gamma} \ldots \alpha/\gamma \ldots] \Rightarrow [_{S/\gamma} \ldots \alpha/\underline{\gamma} \ldots]$

        if it occurs in a main projection path of the form
        $\ldots \alpha/\gamma \ldots \beta/\gamma \ldots$, where α and β are sentential categories.

Norwegian. The Norwegian facts are not as easy to capture in a small list of simple node admissibility conditions. For most speakers the Fixed Subject Constraint does not hold, and resumptive pronouns are not allowed in the site of subject extractions. Unlike Icelandic, however, the resumptive pronoun strategy is available to many Norwegian speakers in the case of crossing dependencies resulting from multiple leftward extractions; unlike Swedish, this strategy is not obligatory.

There is a simple way to look at multiple extractions in such Norwegian dialects: they allow both the sentences generated by the grammar postulated for Icelandic and the sentences generated by the grammar postulated for Swedish. We could hypothesize that some speakers of Norwegian have two grammars for multiple leftward extractions. It is clear that to allow for this type of explanation complicates the relation between theory and fact considerably, and makes it much more difficult to falsify a theory. However this situation should not be ruled out on theoretical grounds; other cases of multiple analyses have been proposed in the literature (e.g. Hankamer (1975)). Our account of the interaction between perceptual and syntactic constraints suggests that this situation is in fact extremely likely.

4. A MIXED MODEL OF ISLAND CONSTRAINTS

In the previous sections we have presented data on extraction in Scandinavian languages, and shown that unitary, purely syntactic accounts of island constraints cannot handle them. We have also developed a base-generated account of the data which is descriptively adequate but which does not, however, seem to lead to any real insight into the extraction phenomena. In this section we will try to isolate some nonsyntactic factors that might play a role in the observed variation.

4.1 Nonstructural Factors

In the previous section we have written a grammar that will generate only those extractions that are admissible on structural grounds. This grammar will still wildly overgenerate as far as the set of acceptable sentences goes, most notably with respect to relative clauses. As the grammar is written, extraction out of relative clauses is freely allowed in Swedish and Norwegian. Certain examples of such extractions are clearly good; an example is repeated here for convenience:

(6)   Marit finner vi aldri den gutten som kan hamle opp med. (N)
        'Mary, we'll never find the boy who can handle'

It seems impossible, therefore, to rule out this type of extraction on structural grounds. However, we have also noted that *most* extractions out of relative clauses are not good in Swedish and Norwegian. For example, the following sentence is not accepted:

(5)   a. *Lisa talar jag med pojken som kysst (henne). (S)
        Lisa, I talked with the boy who kissed (her).

In such cases, the use of a resumptive pronoun does not lead to acceptability.

This situation is not limited to relative clauses. In Swedish and Norwegian, most extractions out of comparative clauses are bad, as illustrated with the following example:

(99)   *Det er mannen som Jon mater flere fugler enn jeg tror bor
        nær——. (N)
        'This is the man$_i$ that John feeds more birds than I think live
        near____$_i$.'

In these cases as well, a resumptive pronoun does not improve matters:

(100)   *Det er mannen som Jon mater flere fugler enn jeg tror bor nær
          ham. (N)

          'This is the man$_i$ that John feeds more birds than I think live
          near him$_i$.'

One can however, find examples of grammatical extractions out of
comparative clauses; an example is given in (101):

(101)   Jeg vet om jobber som du bruker mer tid på bilen enn vil ta å
          utfore____. (N)

          'I know of a-job$_i$ that you spend more time on the-car than will
          take to finish $\emptyset_i$.'

Once again, the difference between (*99) and (101) is not structural. It has
been argued that the difference between good and bad extractions out of
relative clauses should be accounted for on semantic and pragmatic
grounds. The most extensive discussion to date is found in Kuno (1976),
who mainly studied the extractions out of relative clauses embedded within
relative clauses. He argues that it must be possible to construe the higher
relative clause as "about its head." Thus a sentence like the following
Japanese one (from Kuno (1979)) is bad, despite the fact that Japanese
allows extractions out of relative clauses, because it is strange to characterize a book by the circumstance that the publisher that published it burned
down:

(102)   ?? Syuppansita kaisya ga kazi de yakete-simatta   hon o yonda.
          published company   fire by was-burned-down book I-read

However the following sentence, which has the same structure as the
example in (102), is better:

(103)   Syuppansita kaisya ga toosansite-simatta   hon o yonda.
          published company   bankrupted-has been   book I-read

          'I read a book which the company that published [it] went
          bankrupt.'

It is easier to imagine a context in which such a characterization of a book
would be appropriate.

     Kuno (1976) illustrates the point with Japanese examples, and with

English examples as well. While there is some discussion and disagreement about the grammaticality judgments on the following sentences, it is clear that there is indeed a progression from worse to better:

(104)   This is the child who John married a girl who dislikes.

(105)   This is the child who I know a family which is willing to adopt.

(106)   This is the child who there is nobody who is willing to adopt.

(= Kuno 1–20(a–c))

It seems to be the case that some speakers of English find even (106) ungrammatical, even though it can be construed as being about *the child*. Thus in English, at least for some speakers, the prohibition against extraction out of relative clauses is a syntactic constraint. The same is not true in Swedish and Norwegian, however, where the equivalent of (106) is perfectly acceptable. The Swedish version is given below:

(105)   Det här är barnet som det inte finns någon som vill adoptera.

Allwood (1976) makes observations that point in the same direction, and isolates the following factors affecting acceptability of the extraction: extraction is better if (i) the head of the most deeply embedded relative clause is indefinite, and (ii) the verb of the higher clause is of the type called "bridge verbs" (Erteschik (1973)). The verb *know* seems to be the most acceptable "bridge" in any language.

While all this is rather vague, the following picture seems to emerge: *a relative clause serves to characterize its head*. It is rarely the case that this characterization is successful if it involves extraction out of another relative clause; however, if it *is* successful, the sentence is grammatical in languages like Japanese and Swedish (but not in English). As Kuno observes in a footnote, the constraint operates not only in relative clauses, but also with respect to topicalizations and *wh*-questions: the question must be about the questioned constituent, and it must be possible to construe what follows a topic as a predication about it.[26]

If this is the right approach to relative clauses, it stands to reason that the insertion of a resumptive pronoun is not going to help: the pragmatic organization of the discourse will be violated regardless of the presence or absence of a resumptive pronoun.[27] It remains to be explained, then, why the use of a resumptive pronoun does make a difference in certain other constructions. We turn to this question now.

4.2 *Resumptive Pronouns*

In the previous section we observed that some constraints on extraction are motivated by discourse principles. It does not seem plausible that the presence or absence of a resumptive pronoun has anything to do with these principles: the general organization of the sentence in terms of backgrounding and foregrounding, old and new information, grammatical relations, etc., remains the same, whether or not a resumptive pronoun is present. Thus it seems reasonable to look for another type of explanation for the observed differences between other clause types with and without resumptive pronouns.[28]

4.2.1 *Resumptive Pronouns and Surface Constraints*

A first observation that can be made is that while resumptive pronouns do not influence the overall organization of the sentence, they make a clear difference at the local level. If we assume that there are surface constraints on elements that are obligatory in certain types of sentences, resumptive pronouns can make it possible to respect such constraints, whereas a gap might lead to violations.

In Maling & Zaenen (1978) we hypothesized that the fixed subject constraint was such a surface constraint: in certain languages tensed clauses need an overt subject after a complementizer. Whatever the rationale for such a surface constraint may be, the fact that it is a *surface* constraint suggests that if the resumptive pronoun strategy is available in a given language, then it could be used to save extractions out of subject position. As we have seen, this is indeed the case. In Swedish, where the fixed subject constraint holds as in English, a resumptive pronoun is used to allow extractions out of subject position without violating the surface constraint.

However, not all resumptive pronouns seem to play this role: In extractions out of sentential subjects, no clause-internal surface constraint is violated. In such cases, the most promising approach seems to be the hypothesis that resumptive pronouns facilitate processing.

4.2.2 *Resumptive Pronouns and Processing*

The idea that resumptive pronouns facilitate processing is neither new nor counterintuitive. However, it is far from clear why this should be the case. In what follows we will give a broad outline of a model which explicates to a certain degree why pronouns are easier to process than holes. The basic idea is simple: resumptive pronouns are easier to process than gaps because, unlike gaps, processing them does not lead to an interruption in the primary task involved in the processing of a clause, namely the building up of its predicate argument structure.[29]

Let us spell out in a bit more detail how this works. The view that a primary task of the language processor is to figure out the predicate argument structure of each clause can hardly be controversial; without this one would not be able to reconstruct the propositional content of the clause. The view that "gaps" lead to an interruption of that process has been substantiated in work by Wanner & Maratsos (1978), who have shown that a peak in processing load[30] is found in relative clauses when a hearer encounters the first constituent following a gap. Assuming a language with strict word order and without free pro-drop (e.g. English and the Scandinavian languages), this is the moment when the hearer realizes that there is a constituent missing in the clause that he is currently processing. Wanner & Maratsos attribute this increase in processing load to the fact that the hearer has to go back to his memory store, extract a stored constituent, and assign a grammatical function to it, before going on with the processing of the rest of the clause. They call this increase the *assignment load*.

That a resumptive pronoun would not lead to such an increase in processing load in the middle of a clause is something that requires testing; but there is some prima facie plausibility to this view: characteristically resumptive pronouns have the same morphological shape as normal personal pronouns. Accordingly when one hears the sentence they occur in, one does not necessarily treat them as related to constituents on hold. Locally, within the clause itself, there is no argument missing, and hence the hearer can continue the process of determining the predicate argument structure without interruption.

Of course, nonresumptive pronouns must also be linked up with their referents. It is essential to the hypothesis proposed here that the linking of gaps to their antecedents is psychologically different from the linking of free anaphors to their antecedents, and that what free anaphor and resumptive pronoun processing have in common is the fact that the mechanism by which they are linked up to their antecedent does not interrupt the processing of the clause they appear in.

This hypothesis leaves several points unexplained: when is a resumptive pronoun assigned to its antecedent? Why is it commonly the case that resumptive pronouns cannot occur "too close" to their antecedents? etc. We cannot address these questions here; they are the object of our research in progress. But we want to make three points here.

The first one is a defensive one: one rather obvious way of elaborating the hypothesis sketched above is to assume that resumptive pronouns are assigned to their antecedents later than gaps are. If this is the case, one must explain how they can facilitate processing in view of another finding of Wanner & Maratsos (1978), namely the hold load. The hold hypothesis says that the processing load is higher across the interval between the *wh*-constituent and its following bound anaphor than at other moments (ceteris paribus). Under the hypothesis sketched above however, the *wh*-constituent stays on hold longer when the extraction site is filled with a resumptive pronoun than when there is a gap, since the resumptive pronoun is not immediately recognized as filling the place of the *wh*-constituent. Accordingly resumptive pronouns should be more difficult to process than gaps because of the greater hold load.

There are several remarks to be made: first the hold hypothesis has some initial implausibility: it predicts that it would generally be better for gaps to follow their fillers as quickly as possible. However there is no evidence that natural languages are set up to meet such a requirement: for languages in which subjects precede objects, a gap in a subject clause would follow its antecedent more closely than a gap in an object clause; hence extraction out of subject clauses should be preferred. However extraction out of sentential subjects is usually not allowed in these languages.

Another example is the preference noted in Kuno (1973) to have incomplete constituents in clause final rather than in clause initial or clause medial position. These observations are not in accord with the idea that gaps have to follow their fillers as soon as possible to reduce the hold load. More importantly, recent tests have shown that the hold hypothesis is at the very least too simplistic (M. Ford, ·personal communication).

Another factor that might play a role is the following: the hypothesis sketched above does not necessarily imply that resumptive pronouns are overall easier to process than gaps; it may be that they lead to a more even distribution in processing load. The assignment of a gap is hypothesized to cause a peak in processing load at a particular moment; the assignment of a resumptive pronoun might in itself be as difficult or even more difficult but occur at a moment when the overall processing load is lower.

Secondly the hypothesis implies that the structures in which resumptive pronouns are found are in themselves more difficult to process than those out of which extraction is possible without leaving a resumptive pronoun. One place where resumptive pronouns are used and this seems to be true is sentential subjects. It has been found that non-extraposed sentential subjects are more difficult to process than subordinate clauses which follow their main clauses (see e.g. Holmes (1963)).[31] Again further research is needed.

Thirdly, one set of facts the proposed account of resumptive pronouns would handle well is the distribution between the pronouns and gaps in the case of crossing extractions in Swedish, first noticed and described in Engdahl (1979). As we have seen (cf. section 3.3) we find a pronoun instead of a hole in the following configuration:

(106) F_1 F_2 pro G_2 (= 80a)

The *raison d'être* for constraints like the NDC has been hypothesized to be the fact that some aspects of short term memory work like a push-down storage mechanism (Fodor (1978)). Under such a hypothesis the dependency sketched in (106) should not be possible. If however the pronoun is not immediately linked up with its antecedent, we can process such crossing dependencies in a push-down fashion: we bypass the resumptive pronoun, processing it as a normal NP, without assigning it to an antecedent; when we process the "second" gap we assign it to the last filler F_2; then since we have one filler left in push-down storage we assign it to the pronoun. Again this hypothesis depends crucially on when exactly pronouns are hooked up with their antecedents.[32] Since little is known about this, even for "free" pronouns, it will take some further research to confirm this hypothesis.

In this last subsection we have sketched a hypothesis explaining the use of resumptive pronouns in certain contexts. Further work is needed to determine the relation between our processing hypotheses and the organization of the grammar itself: in Section 3.2 we argued that resumptive pronouns behave in several ways like gaps and accordingly we have treated them as such in the syntax; in this section we have stressed the differences between resumptive pronouns and gaps, and hypothesized that resumptive pronouns are processed in some respects like free pronouns of the same morphological shape. Obviously this hybridization calls for further clarification of the relationship between syntax and processing, a problem we leave to the future.

For the moment we have shown that island constraints may exhibit a wide range of variation even among closely related languages and that it seems profitable to look upon them as a less unitary phenomenon than has been traditionally assumed. We have also shown that the formalism developed in Gazdar (1980) can easily be extended to describe a wide range of data it was not designed to handle. Several problems however remain: for instance, in modern Scandinavian languages the appearance of resumptive pronouns does not pattern according to the traditional transformational distinction between movement and deletion rules; but in other languages it does – how will a base-generated framework capture that distinction? Also: if our tentative conclusion that "base-generation" is possible but that context-free grammars are not powerful enough to handle the full range of data is correct, we are again faced with a search for constraints that cannot be reduced to a simple-minded limitation of the mathematical properties of grammars.

Brandeis University
Waltham, Mass.
Harvard University
Cambridge, Mass.

NOTES

* We thank G. N. Clements, E. Engdahl, G. J. M. Gazdar, J. Hankamer, P. I. Jacobson, A. Joshi, L. Karttunen, S. Peters, G. K. Pullum and C. Smith for comments, discussions and criticism; P.-K. Halvorsen, L. Hellan and S. Lie for help with the Norwegian data; Dora Hjártar, Magnús Fjalldal and Höskuldur Thráinsson for help with the Icelandic; and E. Engdahl for the Swedish data. All remaining errors are of course our own. Partial support was provided by NSF grant No. BNS 78–16522 to Brandeis University.
[1] Although the account of extraction phenomena presented here will be in terms of the base-generated framework of Gazdar (this volume), the terminology will make use of the metaphors introduced within transformational grammar, since they will be understood by the largest group of readers.
[2] Given that Erteschik (1973) was the first to point out the differences between English and the Scandinavian languages with respect to extraction constraints, it is a bit ironical that we do not have further data to present on Danish. The lack of readily available informants has prevented us from taking Danish into account here.
[3] Maling (1978) reported an asymmetry with respect to *wh*-islands, namely that extraction is possible by relativization but not by questioning. It seems that this asymmetry does not exist for all speakers (cf. Engdahl (1979), Taraldsen (1978)); and for some speakers who do find such an asymmetry, the reason may well be an overriding preference for clefted versions of both *wh*-questions and topicalizations (cf. Svein Lie (1980)).

Various factors influence the acceptability of questioning out of *wh*-islands, particularly the relative "weight" of the extracted *wh*-phrase. Thus (ii) is much better than (i):

(i)   ?*What don't you know who wrote?
(ii)   Which article don't you remember who wrote?

This factor has been noted by Engdahl (1979), and by Rizzi (1978), who noted a similar asymmetry in Italian. The relative badness of questioning versus relativization out of *wh*-islands cannot be attributed to a general prohibition against multiple *wh*-questions, as suggested by Rizzi for Italian, since multiple *wh*-questions of the type "Who put what where?" are fully acceptable in the Scandinavian languages, as they are in English. In this paper we will assume that extraction out of *wh*-islands is generally allowed, and that any asymmetries with respect to different extraction rules should not be built into the syntax.

It should be noted that even for dialects lacking such asymmetries, the conclusion of Maling (1978) still holds, namely that subjacency does not account for the observed violations of the *wh*-island constraint without relaxing either strict cyclicity or the doubly-filled COMP prohibition. See discussion of Rizzi's hypothesis below.

Moreover, other asymmetries noted in Maling (1978) remain a problem for a uniform *wh*-movement analysis. In particular, the treatment of possessive NP's in Icelandic: possessive NP's can of course be questioned by *wh*-movement, but they are not accessible to relativization by any strategy. There is never any surface evidence of *wh*-movement in relative clauses, even in this case, and deletion of the possessive NP *in situ*, which was possible in Old Icelandic (Maling (1976)), is no longer possible, presumably because it would violate some version of the A-over-A or a Genitive NP constraint.

[4] To talk about Swedish, Norwegian and Icelandic as monolithic entities with no variation among the speakers of each language is of course an oversimplification. As will become clear, the variation among Norwegian speakers is so important that even for an overview like this one, it is not possible to maintain the fiction of one grammar. In Icelandic we found less variation among the different speakers that we consulted; some differences are pointed out at the relevant moments. For Swedish we have relied mostly on data from E. Engdahl; some of the data can be found in her papers, and some were communicated personally.

[5] For some discussion see Lie (1980)

[6] One of our informants accepted one extraction out of a relative clause, namely (i):

(i)   Kaffi   þekki   ég engan   á Íslandi,   sem   ekki   drekkur
        Coffee   know   I no one   in Iceland   that   not   drinks
        'Coffee, I know no one in Iceland who doesn't drink.'

All other informants rejected even this sentence. This situation seems similar to English, where some speakers will also accept an occasional violation of the CNPC.

[7] In Scandinavian languages, the difference between topicalization and Left Dislocation is clearly marked by the difference in word order; even when a resumptive pronoun is present in a topicalized sentence, it is possible to distinguish it from a LD construction because in the former the verb will be in second position, whereas in LD the verb will (superficially) be in third position. See Maling & Zaenen (1978b).

[8] As in English, the extraposed versions are very much preferred, and extraction out of the extraposed clause is possible without leaving a resumptive pronoun behind.

[9] In some nonstandard dialects there seems to be another option: namely to use *som* after *at*

(Mete Markey, personal communication); it is not clear whether *som* is in complementizer or subject position. We have not been able to investigate this further.

[10] The evidence consists of sequences of *wh*-word *som* which occur primarily in case of subject extractions; the status of *som* is not clear, however.

[11] For the sake of the argument, we give the structure assigned under Chomsky's (1977) *wh*-movement analysis of topicalization, in which topicalization is collapsed with left dislocation. For arguments against this analysis see Zaenen & Maling (1977), Maling & Zaenen (1978b), and Zaenen (1980).

[12] This was pointed out independently by E. Williams in a discussion with E. Engdahl and M. A. C. Huybregts after the presentation of some of this material in a workshop at Harvard in November, 1979.

[13] In Scandinavian languages, it is conceivable that the SSC falls under subjacency even if S is the bounding node because sentential subjects can be introduced with a lexical hand, *det* 'it', and could therefore be assigned the structure of a complex NP.

[14] It is not particular to Icelandic, either; see Goldsmith (to appear) for a discussion of a similar case in Igbo.

[15] The following version is also accepted, and in fact, preferred, by our informants:

(i)   Per slipper jeg ikke inn noen som liker.
        Peter let I not in anyone who likes

In (i) the entire NP has been extraposed. Presumably Taraldsen will analyze these sentences as being derived by applying Heavy NP Shift first, followed by extraposition from NP. This implies that Heavy NP Shift cannot be a stylistic rule either.

[16] One can try to combine the features of Reinhart's and Rizzi's analyses by assuming a double-COMP position and S as a binding node, and by abandoning the SSC and the tensed-S conditions as constraints on *wh*-movement. We leave this exercise to the patient reader.

[17] The exact conditions on "pro-drop" in these languages are unknown. To talk about *free* pro-drop is certainly an exaggeration. One needs to investigate the phenomenon further to see if the pro-drop pattern can be used to explain the apparently crossing extractions. The point we want to make is that whereas it is clear that the prohibition against crossing dependencies as such is not a universal, it might be possible to link its existence or nonexistence in a language to other characteristics of the language.

[18] This is essentially the correlation noticed in Perlmutter (1971) as refined in Maling & Zaenen (1978a) to make the distinction between personal pronoun subjects and dummy subjects. For a more detailed discussion of the FSC and some problems with it, see those works and the references cited therein.

[19] Resumptive (or rather *pre*sumptive pronouns) are never possible as "placeholders" for rightward movement rules. This holds also true in Swedish and Norwegian, which might be an indication that the two phenomena (rightward and leftward dependencies) should be distinguished more than they are in this proposal. Note that the term "extraction" rule is traditionally intended to cover only leftward movement.

[20] Another way of looking at the situation was suggested by B. H. Partee in a discussion at the Workshop on Linguistics and Mathematics, Amherst, 1979: we might assume that Swedish speakers have several grammars, one that allows only one extraction, one that allows two extractions, one that allows three extractions, etc. Each of these grammars allows only a finite number of extractions, and hence the union of any finite set of them is still context-free.

[21] Arguments to the same effect are given in McCloskey (1979) for Irish. The arguments given

here are further elaborated in Zaenen and Maling (1980) and Zaenen, Engdahl and Maling (1981).

[22] As far as we can see, the version of across-the-board extraction presented in Williams (1978) in a *wh*-movement framework also necessitates the assumption that resumptive pronouns are the spelled-out traces left after *wh*-movement has applied. This is a problem for the assumptions about the constraints on *wh*-movement made in that framework.

[23] As pointed out in an earlier version of this paper, and independently by McCloskey (personal communication), this account runs into trouble with sentences like (i):

(i)   This is the woman that John said that she and Bill are having an affair.

In (i) we have coordinated an NP/NP and an NP. Similar sentences are good in Scandinavian languages and in Irish. On the other hand, the following combinations have to be excluded: *t and t* or *t and pro*. We assume this latter problem to be of a different nature, but the acceptability of sentences like (i) seems to be an indication that our syntactic treatment of resumptive pronouns might be too simplistic.

[24] The distance requirement of Scandinavian resumptive pronouns is quite different from the requirements found in certain other languages (and even from those of an earlier stage of Icelandic); for a more typical case, see e.g. McCloskey (1979) and Clements (1979).

[25] We refer to this as the Genitive NP Constraint rather than the Left Branch Constraint since the normal position for possessives in Icelandic is postnominal rather than prenominal. Extraction from either position is impossible.

[26] This cannot be the whole story. Extraction out of relative clauses in Swedish seems to be less free than in Japanese. We have no suggestions to offer about what the relevant difference may be, but the possibility of null anaphora in Japanese is an obvious place to look.

[27] This is not contradicted by languages where relativization normally involves a resumptive pronoun, since in these languages the syntactic constraints are obviously different.

[28] This might lead to the view that Topicalization and LD should have the same function too. This is not, however, the case, as argued for English by E. Prince (1980). It also does not follow from our own assumptions; as we have argued elsewhere (Maling & Zaenen (1978b)), the left dislocated constituent is outside of the sentential domain, whereas the topicalized constituent is inside that domain. Thus there are other differences between the two constructions than just the presence or absence of a resumptive pronoun.

[29] Note that resumptive pronouns are *not* used to help locate the gap and so reduce ambiguity. The reader can verify for himself that they could not be used for this purpose given the fact that resumptive pronouns have the same morphological shape as other personal pronouns.

[30] We are simplifying the discussion by calling "processing load" two phenomena that would have to be distinguished in a more adequate model: some instances that are memory load and others that are more clearly processing load itself. The discussion in Wanner & Maratsos is not totally clear. They talk about memory load, but it is not evident that the assignment load is a memory load; however, the task that they gave their subjects was a memory task. We are currently investigating whether the results would be the same if the task were a reaction time task.

[31] The experimental finding that sentential subjects are more difficult to process than their extraposed counterparts does not explain why this should be so. One possible account would be to assume that the difficulty has to do with the fact that in SVO languages the functional role (in the sense of Bresnan 1978) of subjects is not clear until the verb is processed (since this role depends on the nature and the voice of the verb). It seems to be true in general that one cannot

extract out of constituents whose functional role is not yet assigned. This holds for nonsentential subjects too, as shown by the following example:

(i)   *Island constraints, nobody's theory of works.

The following observations might also be relevant: as is well known, it is impossible to extract out of preposed *wh*-constituents as illustrated in (ii) and (iii).

(ii)   *Island constraints, I can imagine which theory about Robin prefers.
(iii)   * Which cars did the insurance adjuster want to know which parts of the fire had damaged?

(Since in GPSG these preposed constituents are not themselves slashed categories, the extraction does not fall under the "double hole" constraint.)

Since *wh*-constituents have no functional role assigned to them no binding inside is possible. The same constraint could also explain the subjectlike behavior of "raised" subjects noted in Chomsky (1973) and illustrated in (iv)

(iv)   *Who did you expect stories about to tempt Mary?

Since the grammatical object of expect has no functional role in the main clause extraction is correctly predicted to be impossible.

A problem for this account is that it predicts (*ceteris paribus*) that extractions out of subjects should be allowed in VSO languages. However that is not generally the case (McCloskey, personal communication).

[32] This model has to be relaxed to account for the limited crossing extractions of Norwegian and Icelandic.

REFERENCES

Allwood, J. (1976) 'The Complex Noun Phrase Constraint as a Non-universal Rule,' *Occasional Papers in Linguistics* 2, University of Massachusetts, Amherst, Massachusetts.

Bordelois, I. (1974) *The Grammar of Spanish Causative Complements*, unpublished doctoral dissertation, MIT.

Brame, M. K. (1976) *Conjectures and Refutations in Syntax and Semantics*, Elsevier, New York.

Brame, M. K. (1978) *Base-Generated Syntax*, Noit Amrofer, Seattle.

Bresnan, J. (1971) 'On Sentence Stress and Syntactic Transformations.' *Language* 47, 257–281.

Bresnan J. (1972) *Theory of Complementation in English Syntax*, doctoral dissertation, MIT. Published (1979), Garland Press, New York.

Bresnan, J. (1978) 'A Realistic Transformational Grammar,' in M. Halle, J. Bresnan & G. A. Miller (eds.) *Linguistic Theory and Psychological Reality*, MIT Press.

Bresnan, J. (1980a) 'Polyadicity,' in T. Hoekstra, H. van der Hulst & M. Moortgat (eds.) *Lexical Grammar*, Foris, Dordrecht.

Bresnan, J. (1980b) ed. *The Mental Representation of Grammatical Relations*, MIT Press.

Chomsky, N. (1973) 'Constraints on Transformations,' in S. Anderson and P. Kiparsky, eds., *A Festschrift for Morris Halle*, Holt, Rinehart & Winston.

Chomsky, N. (1977) 'On *Wh*-movement,' in P. Culicover, T. Wasow and A. Akmajian (eds.) *Formal Syntax*, Academic Press.

Clements, G. N. (1979) 'Binding domains in Kikuyu,' unpublished paper, Harvard University.

Dowty, D. (1978) 'Governed Transformations as Lexical Rules in a Montague Grammar,' *Linguistic Inquiry* 9, 393–426.

Engdahl, E. (1979) 'The Nested Dependency Constraint as a Parsing Principle,' in E. Engdahl and M. Stein (eds.) *Papers presented to Emmon Bach*, University of Massachusetts, Amherst, Massachusetts.

Engdahl, E. (1979) '*Wh*-Constructions in Swedish and the Relevance of Subjacency,' Papers from the Eleventh Regional Meeting, North Eastern Linguistic Society, Ottawa, Ontario.

Erteschik-Shir, N. (1973) 'On the Nature of Island Constraints,' doctoral dissertation, MIT. Published (1977), Indiana University Linguistics Club.

Fodor, J. (1978) 'Parsing Strategies and Constraints on Transformations,' *Linguistic Inquiry* 9, 427–473.

Freidin, R. (1975) 'The Analysis of Passives,' *Language* 51, 384–405.

Gazdar, G. (this volume) 'Phrase Structure Grammar.'

Gazdar, G., G. K., Pullum, and I. Sag (1980) 'A Phrase Structure Grammar for the English Auxiliary System,' unpublished ms.

Godard, D. (forthcoming) *Relative Clauses in French*, Ph.D thesis, University of Pennsylvania.

Goldsmith, J. (1980) 'The Structure of *Wh*-questions in Igbo.' *Linguistic Analysis* 7, 367–393.

Gueron, J. (1976) 'The Interpretation of PP Complements,' in H. van Riemsdijk (ed.) *Green Ideas Blown Up*, Institute for General Linguistics, University of Amsterdam.

Hankamer, J. (1975) 'Multiple Analyses' in C. Li (ed.), *Mechanisms of Syntactic Change*, University of Texas Press, Austin, Texas.

Holmes, V. (1973) 'Order of Main and Subordinate Clauses in Sentences Perception,' *JVLVB* 12, 285–293.

Horn, G. (1975) 'The NP Constraint,' unpublished Ph.D. thesis, University of Massachusetts, Amherst.

Joshi, A., L. Levy & K. Yueh (1978) 'Local Constraints in the Syntax and Semantics of Programming Languages,' *Proceedings of the Fifth Annual Symposium on Principles of Programming Languages*.

Koster, J. (1978) 'Conditions, Empty Nodes and Markedness,' *Linguistic Inquiry* 9, 551–594.

Kuno, S. (1973) 'Constraints on Internal Clauses and Sentential Subjects,' *Linguistic Inquiry* 4, 363–385.

Kuno, S. (1976) 'Subject, Theme and Speaker's Empathy,' in C. Li (ed.), *Subject and Topic*, Academic Press, New York.

Kuno, S. (1979) Colloquium talk, Harvard Workshop in Syntax.

Kuno, S. and J. Robinson (1972) 'Multiple *Wh*-questions,' *Linguistic Inquiry* 3, 463–487.

Kuno, S., J. Kornfilt and E. Sezer (1980) 'The Non-universality of the Nested Dependency Constraint,' *Harvard Studies in Syntax and Semantics* III, Harvard University, Cambridge, Massachusetts.

Lie, Sv. (1980) 'Wh-questions and Subjacency in Norwegian,' unpublished ms., University of Oslo.

Maling, J. (1976) 'Old Icelandic Relative Clauses: An Unbounded Deletion Rule,' in D. Nash,

J. Kegl & A. Zaenen (eds.) *Papers from the Seventh Regional Meeting*, North Eastern Linguistic Society, Harvard University, Cambridge, Massachusetts.

Maling, J. (1978) 'An Asymmetry with respect to *Wh*-islands,' *Linguistic Inquiry* **9**, 75–89.

Maling, J. and A. Zaenen (1978a) 'The Non-universality of a Surface Filter,' *Linguistic Inquiry* **9**, 475–497.

Maling, J. and A. Zaenen (1978b) 'Germanic Word Order and the Format of Surface Filters,' paper read at the Amsterdam Colloquium on Local Constraints, to appear in F. Heny (ed.), *Binding and Filtering*, Croom-Held, London.

McCloskey, J. (1979) *Transformational Syntax and Model Theoretic Semantics*, Reidel, Dorecht.

Oehrle, R. (1976) *The Grammatical Status of the English Dative Alternation*, unpublished Ph.D. thesis, MIT.

Peters, S. (1979) 'Phrase Structure Syntax and the Semantics of Comparatives,' paper presented at the Workshop on Comparatives, University of Sussex, July.

Perlmutter, D. (1971) *Deep and Surface Structure Constraints in Syntax*, Holt, Rinehart and Winston.

Perlmutter, D. (this volume) 'Syntactic Representation, Syntactic levels, and the Notion of Subject.'

Postal, P. (this volume) 'Some Arc Pair Grammar Descriptions.'

Prince, E. (1980) 'A Comparison of Left Dislocation an Topicalization in Discourse,' unpublished ms., University of Pennsylvania.

Reinhart, T. (1979) 'A Second COMP-position,' to appear in *Anali della Scuola Normale Superiore*, Pisa.

Rizzi, L. (1978) 'Violations of the *Wh*-island constraint in Italian and the subjacency condition,' in *Montreal Working Papers in Linguistics* **11**.

Ross, J. R. (1967) *Constraints on Variables in Transformations*, Ph.D. Thesis, MIT. Published (1968), Indiana University Linguistics Club.

Sag, I. (this volume) 'A Semantic Account of "NP-movement" Dependencies.'

Taraldsen, K. T. (1978) 'The Scope of *Wh*-movement in Norwegian," *Linguistic Inquiry* **9**, 623–641.

Taraldsen, K. T. (1979) 'The Theoretical Interpretation of a class of "marked" Extractions,' in *Anali della Scuola Normale Superiore*, Pisa.

Wanner, E. and M. Maratsos (1978) 'An ATN Approach to Comprehension,' in M. Halle, J. Bresnan & G. Miller (eds.) *Linguistic Theory and Psychological Reality*, MIT Press, Cambridge, Massachusetts.

Williams, E. (1978) 'Across-the-board Rule Application,' *Linguistic Inquiry* **9**, 31–43.

Zaenen, A. (1980) *Extraction Rules in Icelandic*, unpublished Ph.D. thesis, Harvard University, Cambridge, Massachusetts.

Zaenen, A. and J. Maling (1980) 'The Status of Resumptive Pronouns in Swedish,' paper read at the Fourth International Conference of Nordic and General Linguistics, Oslo, Norway, June 23.

Zaenen, A., E. Engdahl, and J. Maling (1981) 'Resumptive Pronouns Can Be Syntactically Bound.' *Linguistic Inquiry* **12**, 4

DAVID M. PERLMUTTER

SYNTACTIC REPRESENTATION, SYNTACTIC LEVELS, AND THE NOTION OF SUBJECT*

1. GOALS

This paper addresses two questions:

(1)   What is the nature of syntactic representation?
(2)   What is the notion of 'subject' in linguistic theory?

It is argued that these questions are crucially interrelated, and without a proper answer to the first it is impossible to provide a proper answer to the second.

The recent literature contains considerable discussion of (2) and of how one can "identify" subjects in one language or another. In some cases it is concluded that particular languages do not have subjects or that there is no viable notion of subject, either in linguistic theory or in the grammars of individual languages.[1] The position taken here is that such work is fundamentally misguided because it assumes that the notion of subject is to be defined in terms of other notions – whether phrase structure configurations (Chomsky, 1965), "behavioral properties" (Keenan, 1976), or case (Hale, Jeanne, and Platero, 1977). Some discussion, e.g. that in Chomsky (1977, 75–76) and Bresnan (1978, 14–18), assumes definitions of grammatical relations in terms of different notions in different languages. However, all of this work shares the assumption that grammatical relations are not to be taken as primitive, but rather defined in terms of other notions. The inadequacies of the various attempts to define grammatical relations in terms of other notions need not detain us here; they are discussed in Johnson (1977, 1979), Klokeid (1980), and Perlmutter (to appear c). The position taken here is that of Perlmutter and Postal (1974) – that grammatical relations are primitives of linguistic theory.

Attempts to define grammatical relations in terms of other notions have depended on certain assumptions about the nature of syntactic representation. Chomsky (1965, 68–74) considered representing grammatical relations ("functional notions") in phrase markers directly. He rejected this alternative, claiming that such representation would be superfluous, and that grammatical relations could be defined in terms of structural

283

P. Jacobson and G. K. Pullum (eds.), The Nature of Syntactic Representation, 283–340.
Copyright © 1982 by D. Reidel Publishing Company.

configurations in phrase markers. The realization that grammatical relations cannot be defined in terms of such notions (cf. the references cited above) led to two steps that are essentially the defining characteristics of relational grammar: taking grammatical relations as primitive theoretical notions, and adopting syntactic representations in the form of relational networks (RN's) that represent grammatical relations directly. This paper argues that once grammatical relations are taken as primitive notions and sentence structure is represented in terms of RN's, the result is surprising: there are distinct notions of subject that play a role in the grammars of natural languages. A tentative typology of five such notions is constructed, and examples are provided where each is needed to state some syntactic rule or generalization.

The strategy adopted here is this. The notion 'subject' is taken as a primitive notion of linguistic theory. Syntactic representation is in terms of RN's, which represent, among other things:

(3)   a. the primitive *grammatical relations* that nominals bear to
              clauses
           b. the distinct *linguistic levels* at which nominals bear gram-
              matical relations to clauses

As explained in §2 below, an arc with R-sign '1' and coordinate c_i which has a nominal node *a* at its head and a clause node *b* at its tail has the interpretation that *a* bears the primitive 1-relation (the subject relation) to *b* at the c_i level.

Given syntactic representations in terms of RN's, it is then possible to define *derivative* notions of subject, e.g. 'initial 1,' 'final 1,' etc. In this paper five such derivative notions of subject are defined. Examples are given where these notions of subject are needed in individual grammars.

Thus, on the one hand it is argued here that the different notions of subject needed in the grammars of individual languages provide motivation for the inclusion of (3a-b) in syntactic representation. On the other hand, it is argued that syntactic representation in terms of RN's sheds light on the notion of subject; one reason for earlier confusion with respect to this notion has been the lack of adequate syntactic representation in terms of RN's.

The conclusions reached here also bear on what promises to be one of the most controversial issues in syntactic theory in the 1980's: is it necessary to posit more than one syntactic level? A number of recent proposals assume that one syntactic level is sufficient. Such "surfacist" proposals are typically based on reanalyses of data primarily from English, but they have not yet considered data from a wide range of languages. If "surfacist" proposals adopted syntactic representations in terms of grammatical relations, they would be able to account for the data for which the notion of 'final subject' is used here, but it is not clear how they would account for the data for which the other four notions of subject are proposed, since these notions of subject rely on non-final levels of representation. Such approaches must confront the relevant data and make explicit how they would account for it if they are to have any claims to adequacy.

In brief, the goals of this paper are:

(4)   a. to show that syntactic representation in terms of RN's sheds light on the notion of subject

         b. to construct a tentative typology of notions of subject, with an indication of the types of data that motivate the inclusion of each in the set available to grammars

         c. to show that the data in question provides support for the representation of clause structure in terms of RN's

         d. to indicate some types of phenomena that "surfacist" approaches to syntax must deal with effectively if they are to have claims to adequacy.

Parallel to the notions of subject developed here there are corresponding notions of direct and indirect object. Thus, alongside the notions 'final 1,' 'initial 1,' 'acting 1,' etc. there are 'final 2,' 'initial 2,' 'acting 2,' etc., and similarly for 3s. However, this paper concentrates on the typology of notions of subject.

The goal in (4b) is perhaps premature at this stage. The number of languages investigated from this point of view is still extremely small, and only a few phenomena have been studied in much depth. For this reason, at two points in the exposition it will be pointed out that there is presently insufficient evidence to establish that certain notions of subject *must* be used, to the exclusion of all alternatives. In both of these cases, however, there *is* evidence for the corresponding notions of direct object. It therefore seems likely that evidence for the relevant notions of subject will eventually be forthcoming. These notions are therefore included in the typology, with indication of the inconclusive nature of the evidence presently available to support them.

2. ON TNE NATURE OF SYNTACTIC REPRESENTATION

To represent the types of information in (3), three types of primitive linguistic elements are introduced:[2]

(5)   a. a set of nodes representing linguistic elements

b. a set of R-signs, which are the names of the grammatical relations that elements bear to other elements

c. a set of coordinates, which are numbers used to indicate the level(s) at which elements bear grammatical relations to other elements

As described in Perlmutter and Postal (1977, to appear a), the fact that a certain linguistic element bears a certain grammatical relation to some other element at a certain level can be represented by a formal structure called an *arc*. An arc consists of an ordered pair of nodes, an R-sign, and a sequence of coordinates, and is representable by either of the following equivalent notations:

(6)   a.

$$\text{GR}_x \Big| c_i \quad \begin{array}{c} b \\ \downarrow \\ a \end{array}$$

b. $[\text{GR}_x \ (a, b) \langle c_i \rangle]$

The interpretation of (6) is that the primitive linguistic element a bears the relation whose name is GR_x to the primitive linguistic element b at the c_i level. Thus, if GR_x is '1', the name of the subject relation, and c_i is c_1, then the arc in (7) indicates that a bears the 1-relation to b at the first or c_1 level of b.

(7)   a.

$$1 \Big| c_1 \quad \begin{array}{c} b \\ \downarrow \\ a \end{array}$$

b. $[1 \ (a, b) \ \langle c_1 \rangle]$

Since arcs can be represented pictorially as arrows, as in (6a–7a), a in these arcs is called the *head* of the arc, and b the *tail*. The R-signs '1', '2', '3', and 'Cho' are the names of the subject, direct object, indirect object, and chomeur relations, respectively. A complete account of clause structure in these terms will have to specify the class of possible linguistic elements, the class of primitive grammatical relations, the class of possible linguistic levels, and constraints on the possible combinations of these elements in RN's.

The basic elements of clause structure can be represented in these terms. Consider the Passive clause:

(8)   That possibility was considered by Lobachevsky.

Ignoring such things as verb tense, auxiliary verbs, prepositions, and the linear order of elements, the structure of (8) can be represented as:

(9)

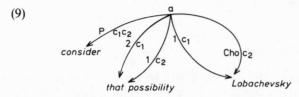

(9) indicates that (8) has two levels of structure. The fact that *Lobachevsky* bears the 1-relation at the first level and the chomeur relation at the second is indicated by the fact that *Lobachevsky* heads a 1-arc with coordinate c_1 and a Cho arc with coordinate c_2. Similarly, the fact that *that possibility* bears the 2-relation at the first level and the 1-relation at the second is indicated by the fact that *that possibility* heads a 2-arc with coordinate c_1 and a 1-arc with coordinate c_2. The fact that *consider* bears the Predicate relation to b at both the first and second levels is indicated by the fact that *consider* heads a P-arc with coordinates $c_1 c_2$.

The notion of linguistic level can now be reconstructed in terms of the notion of *stratum*, which is defined as follows:

(10)   A *stratum* is the maximal set of arcs sharing some tail node and some fixed coordinate.

Thus, the ith stratum of b, where b is a node and c_i is an arbitrary coordinate, is the set of all arcs with tail b and coordinate c_i. The RN in (9) has two strata, the first or c_1 stratum consisting of the arcs in (11) and the second or c_2 stratum consisting of the arcs in (12).

(11)

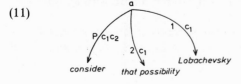

(12)

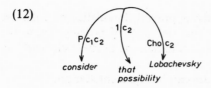

Sometimes it is convenient to represent RN's in the form of *stratal diagrams*, which make the strata stand out more clearly. The stratal diagram in (13) abbreviates the RN in (9).

(13)

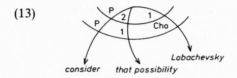

In some stratal diagrams the symbol 'Î' will be used in place of 'Cho' to indicate a 1-*chomeur*, i.e. a nominal which is a 1 in the stratum before the first one in which it is a chomeur. 2-*chomeur* and 3-*chomeur* are defined analogously.

The notions of 'initial stratum' and 'final stratum' have special significance for the concerns of this paper. They can be defined as follows:

(14)   a. A stratum S is the *initial* stratum of b if and only if S is the c_1 stratum of b.

b. A stratum S is the *final* stratum of b if and only if S is the c_k stratum of b and there is no c_{k+1} stratum of b.

These notions are crucial for the definitions of some of the notions of subject discussed in this paper.

Some additional terminology used in this paper can now be introduced.[3] The 1-relation, the 2-relation, and the 3-relation are referred to collectively as the 'term relations'. Thus, '1,' '2,' and '3' are the 'term R-signs,' and an arc with one of these R-signs is a 'term arc.' Similarly, the 1-relation and the 2-relation are referred to collectively as the 'nuclear term relations,' '1' and '2' are the 'nuclear term R-signs,' and an arc with a nuclear term R-sign is a 'nuclear term arc'. Finally, the 2-relation and the 3-relation are the 'object relations,' '2' and '3' are the 'object R-signs,' and an arc with an object R-sign is an 'object arc'.

The representation of clause structure in terms of RN's has a significant consequence: different languages are seen to have the same grammatical constructions, despite language-particular differences of various kinds. Thus, as argued in Perlmutter and Postal (1977), RN's including sub-networks of the form

(15)

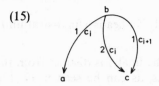

characterize what is common to Passive constructions in all languages, despite language-particular differences in word order, case marking, and verbal morphology. Similarly, it becomes possible to speak in cross-linguistic terms of constructions such as 3–2 Advancement, Benefactive-3 Advancement, Inversion, Antipassive, Clause Union, Possessor Ascension, etc. This approach has two consequences. First, it makes it possible to claim that what at first may appear to be disparate phenomena in various languages are in fact instances of the "same" phenomena, where the sameness can be brought out in terms of grammatical relations. Second, it provides the basis for a characterization of the entire class of grammatical constructions in natural languages.

The representation of clause structure in terms of RN's brings out an important difference between relational grammar, on the one hand, and both structuralist grammar and transformational grammar, on the other. The latter two frameworks are alike in taking the syntactic structure of a clause to consist essentially of linear order and dominance relations among its elements, but they differ in that in transformational grammar the syntactic structure of a sentence is a sequence of representations called a derivation. Each representation in the derivation, however, is a phrase marker showing linear order and dominance relations among elements. In this sense, transformational grammar retains structuralist grammar's conception of the basic nature of clause structure. Both structuralist and transformational frameworks lack cross-linguistically viable notions of grammatical relations. In relational grammar, grammatical relations are used for the construction of grammars of individual languages, for the statement of linguistic universals, and for the characterization of the class of possible grammatical constructions in natural languages.

In this paper, it is argued that an adequate syntactic representation must represent both grammatical relations and distinct syntactic levels in order to state rules and generalizations in the grammars of individual languages.

3. THE NOTION OF FINAL 1

The notion of 'final 1' of a clause can be defined in terms of the notion of 'final stratum' defined in (14b):

(16)   A nominal is a *final* 1 of *b* if and only if it heads a final-stratum 1-arc with tail *b*.

In clauses involving an advancement to 1, the final 1 is distinct from the initial 1. This is the case in Passive clauses, as can be seen in (9–13). Similarly, clauses with an Oblique advancement to 1, clauses with a dummy as final 1, or clauses in which some ascendee as the final 1, are all clauses in which the final 1 is distinct from the initial 1.[4]

The notion of final 1 is needed to state a wide variety of rules and generalizations in many languages. I illustrate with examples from English and French.

First, the rule of Verb Agreement in English and French can be given informally as follows:

(17)   *Verb Agreement*
         A finite verb heading a P-arc with tail *b* agrees in person and number with the final 1 of *b*.

This can be seen most clearly in Passive clauses, where the verb agrees with the final 1 rather than with the initial 1:[5]

(18)   The changes *were* criticized by the press.
(19)   Les changements *ont* été critiqués par la presse.

It can also be seen in Object Raising clauses:

(20)   These books *are* difficult to read.
(21)   Ces livres *sont* difficiles à lire.

Second, the condition on Equi victims in English and French is statable in terms of the notion 'final 1':

(22)   *Condition on Equi Victims*
         Only the final 1 of a clause can be an Equi victim.

This can be seen clearly in the case of Passive clauses:

(23)   The candidates do not want to be criticized by the press.
(24)   *The press does not want (for) the candidates to be criticized (by).

*(24) is ungrammatical on the reading on which it would be synonymous with:

(25)   The press does not want to criticize the candidates.

If the condition on Equi victims in English were stated in terms of the notion 'initial 1', or in terms of the notion 'nominal heading a 1-arc' (without specification of level, cf. §5), then in cases where the complement is a Passive clause, the final chomeur (the initial 1) would qualify as Equi victim, and *(24) would be grammatical on a reading synonymous with (25). The same thing can be seen in French:

(26)   Les candidats ne veulent pas être critiqués par la presse.

There is no way to construct a grammatical sentence of French in which the initial 1 (the final chomeur) of a Passive clause is an Equi victim. Similarly, in Object Raising clauses, the final 1 qualifies as Equi victim:

(27)   The children want to be difficult to convince.
(28)   Les enfants veulent être difficiles à convaincre.

In Perlmutter (1979, to appear b) it is shown that Italian and Russian also have (22) as the condition on Equi victims. Davies (1980, 1981) shows the same thing for Choctaw, a Muskogean language of Oklahoma and Mississippi. These works consider the interaction of (22) with the Inversion construction, in which the "Inversion nominal" is the initial 1 and final 3. It is shown that in these cases, the Inversion nominal cannot be an Equi victim, which follows from the statement of the condition in (22) in terms of the notion 'final 1'.

In similar fashion, the notion of 'final 1' is needed to state a variety of rules and conditions in individual grammars. Thus, in the Subject Raising construction in various languages, only the final 1 of a complement can head an arc in the matrix clause. This is the case in English:

(29)   Those conclusions seem to have been criticized by the critics.
(30)   * The critics seem (for) those conclusions to have been criticized (by).

If an initial 1 could head a matrix clause arc in the Subject Raising construction, regardless of whether or not it is a final 1, then *(30) would be grammatical. But it is not. This supports a formulation of the condition on Subject Raising in English in terms of the notion 'final 1'. The condition is the same in many other languages. Similarly, there are languages in which only a final 1 can "launch" a floating quantifier. Other examples could be cited.

In sum, the notion of 'final 1' is needed in the grammars of many languages. One of the goals of this paper is to indicate some of the motivation for levels of syntactic representation other than the final one, since various recently proposed theories of syntax deny the existence of such levels; some such theories are mentioned briefly in §10. In terms of this goal, the notion of final 1 is likely to be the least controversial of the various notions of subject discussed in this paper. I therefore proceed now to notions of subject that depend on levels of representation other than final.

4. THE NOTION OF INITIAL 1

The notion of 'initial 1' of a clause can be defined in terms of the notion 'initial stratum' defined in (14a):

(31)   A nominal is an *initial* 1 of *b* if and only if it heads an initial-stratum 1-arc with tail *b*.

The need for the notion of initial 1 is illustrated by Verb Agreement in Achenese, an Austronesian language of Sumatra studied by Lawler (1977). The following examples illustrate verb agreement in Achenese:[6]

(32)   Lon *lon*-ja?   u-pikan.
        I   1SG-go   to-market
        'I go to the market'

(33)   Gɔpnyan *gɨ*-ja?   u-pɨkan.
        he$_{older}$ 3_0-go   to-market
        'He goes to the market'

(34)   Gɔpnyan ka   *gɨ*-cɔm   lon.
        she$_{older}$ PERF 3_0-kiss   me
        'She (already) kissed me'

In (32), the verb has the first person singular perfix *lon-* in agreement with the 1 *lon*. In (33) and (34), the verb prefix is *gɨ-*, the form used for agreement with a third-person 1 designating an individual older than the speaker. The interesting feature of Achenese verb agreement can be seen by comparing (34) with the corresponding Passive:

(35)   Lon ka *gɨ*-cɔm   le-gɔpnyan.
        I PERF 3_0-kiss   by-her$_{older}$
        'I have (already) been kissed by her'

The verb in (35) bears the marker *gi-*, in agreement with the *initial-stratum* 1 (*gɔpnyan*), not with *lon*, the final-stratum 1.

The rule of Verb Agreement can be stated informally as follows:[7]

(36)   *Verb Agreement in Achenese*
         The verb of a clause *b* agrees with the *initial* 1 of the clause.

In (32–34) the nominal that determines verb agreement is both initial and final 1 of the clause. The crucial case is (35), which shows that Achenese verb agreement must be stated in terms of the notion 'initial 1' rather than 'final 1.'

(35) would not be evidence for this conclusion if, instead of a Passive clause, it were some kind of topicalization of the 2 (in this case, *lon*). However, there is evidence that such sentences are not examples of topicalization, but rather are Passive clauses as characterized in Perlmutter and Postal (1977) – i.e., evidence that the initial 2 of such clauses is the final 1.

First, only final 1s can be Equi victims in Achenese and, as Lawler shows, the initial 2 of a sentence like (35) can be an Equi victim, thus providing evidence for its final 1hood. For example, there is Equi in complements of *ut^θaha* 'try, make an attempt', as in:

(37)   Dɔʔto   *gi*-ut^θaha (baʔ) *gi*-piret^θa   uring   agam   nyan.
         doctor 3_0-try   IRR 3_0-examine   person male   that
         'The doctor made an attempt to examine that man'

Equi is also possible with a Passive complement:

(38)   Uring   agam   nyan   *ji*-ut^θaha (baʔ) *gi*-piret^θa   le-d ɔʔto.
         person male   that 3_y-try   IRR 3_0-examine   by-doctor
         'That man made an attempt to be examined by the doctor'

In the matrix clause the verb has the agreement prefix *ji-*, used for a third person younger than the speaker, in agreement with *uring agam nyan*. In the Passive complement, however, the verb has the prefix *gi-*, in agreement with *d ɔʔto*, the initial 1 and final chomeur of the complement, which appears marked with the preposition *le* used to mark Passive chomeurs in Achenese. The Equi victim in the complement is the *final* 1 of the complement, not *d ɔʔto*. Since elsewhere in Achenese only 1s can be Equi victims, sentences like (38) provide evidence that we are in fact dealing with Passive clauses, in which a 2 is a final 1, rather than with a topicalization construction.

Second, as Lawler shows, the 2 that advances to 1 in the Passive construction can be the 2 of a higher clause in the Subject-to-Object Raising construction.

(39)   Hakem gi-dawa   jih   ka ji-cu   lïmõ nyan
         judge 3_0-consider him$_y$ PERF 3_y-steal   cow that
         'The judge considers him to have stolen that cow'

The fact that *jih* is a 2 of the matrix clause in (39) can be seen in the fact that it advances to 1 in the corresponding Passive:

(40)   Jih gi-dawa   le-hakem   ka ji-cu   lïmõ nyan.
         he$_y$ 3_0-consider by-judge PERF 3_y-steal   cow that
         'He is considered by the judge to have stolen that cow'

In (40), the complement verb has the prefix *ji*-, in agreement with *jih*, while the matrix verb has the prefix gi-, in agreement with its initial 1 (*hakem*). To see that the clause type under discussion is Passive, in which a 2 advances to 1, consider the correspondent of (39) with a Passive complement:

(41)   Hakem gi-dawa   lïmõ nyan ka ji-cu   le-jih.
         judge 3_0-consider cow that PERF 3_y-steal by-him
         'The judge considers that cow to have been stolen by him'

The complement verb agrees with *jih*, its initial 1. *Lïmõ nyan*, the final 1 of the complement, is raised to 2 of the matrix clause in (41), and as a consequence it can advance to 1 in that clause:

(42)   Lïmõ nyan gi-dawa   le-hakem   ka ji-cu   le-jih.
         cow that 3_0-consider by-judge PERF 3_y-steal by-him
         'That cow is considered by the judge to have been stolen by him'

The complement verb has the prefix *ji*- in agreement with *jih*, the initial 1 of the complement, while the matrix verb has the prefix gi-, in agreement with the matrix clause initial 1 *hakem*, although *lïmõ nyan* is the *final* 1 of both clauses. Since it is the *final* 1 of a clause that can be the 2 of the matrix clause in the subject-to-Object Raising construction, the fact that the initial 2 of a complement Passive clause can be the matrix 2 in this construction provides evidence for its final 1hood in the Passive clause. This supports the view that the clauses in question are indeed Passive clauses, and not topicalization constructions. At the same time, examples like (42) provide evidence for the formulation of Verb Agreement in (36).

The formulation in (36) interacts in an interesting way with the Unaccusative Hypothesis [cf. Perlmutter and Postal (to appear b) and Perlmutter (1978a)], under which the initial stratum of some basic clauses contains a 2-arc but no 1-arc. Such clauses are called 'initially unaccusative'. Clauses whose initial stratum contains a 1-arc but no 2-arc are 'initially unergative'. Taken together with the Unaccusative Hypothesis, the formulation of Verb Agreement in (36) makes an interesting prediction:

(43)   Initially unergative clauses will manifest verb agreement in Achenese; initially unaccusative clauses will not.

The Unaccusative Hypothesis is presented in Perlmutter (1978a) in three distinct versions. Under the strongest, initial unergativity vs. unaccusativity is universally predictable on the basis of the semantics of the clause. Thus, it is possible to test the joint prediction of (36) and the strongest version of the Unaccusative Hypothesis in Achenese, using the semantic characterization of initial unergativity vs. initial unaccusativity in Perlmutter (1978a). For a significant class of cases, the prediction is confirmed. Thus, the examples in (44), which satisfy the semantic characterization of initial unergativity, do manifest verb agreement, while those in (45), which satisfy the semantic characterization of initial unaccusativity, do not:[8]

(44)   a. Gɔpnyan gɨ-mɨlangũə.
           'He swims.'
        b. Gɔpnyan gɨ-mɨnari.
           'They are dancing.'
        c. Gɔpnyan gɨ-pike.
           'He is thinking.'
        d. Gɔpnyan gɨ-ingat.
           'He remembers.'
        e. Gɔpnyan gɨ -pluəng.
           'He runs.'
        f. Gɔpnyan gɨ-dɔng.
           'He stands.'
        g. Gɔpnyan gɨ-duwə?.
           'He sits.'
        h. Anɨ? miet nyan jɨ-mɨlhɔ.
           child that fight
           'Those children fought.'

(45)   a. Gɔpnyan rhɨt.
           'He fell.'
        b. Gɔpnyan lham.
           'He drowned.'

c. Gɔpnyan gadɔh bɨklam.
'He disappeared last night.'
d. Gɔpnyan hanɔt lam iə.
he float in water
'He floated in the water.'
e. Bɔm bɨrɨtoh.
'The bomb exploded.'
f. Jih mate.
'He (younger) died.'
g. Gɔpnyan ka mit.
they PERF less
'They have decreased in numbers.'
h. Gajah na.
elephant exist
'Elephants exist.'

The examples in (44), which the strongest version of the Unaccusative Hypothesis predicts to be initially unergative, require verb agreement prefixes; they would be ungrammatical without them. The examples in (45), which the strongest version of the Unaccusative Hypothesis predicts to be initially unaccusative, cannot have verb agreement prefixes; they would be ungrammatical with them. Comparison of this data with that in Perlmutter (1978a) from Dutch thus shows a striking correspondence: intransitive clauses that form impersonal passives in Dutch require verb agreement in Achenese, while those that cannot form impersonal passives in Dutch cannot have verb agreement in Achenese.

The two phenomena that seem to be correlated would at first appear to have nothing in common. Under the strongest version of the Unaccusative Hypothesis, however, the former clauses are predicted to be initially unergative, while the latter are initially unaccusative. The particular consequences of this in each language then follows from other theoretical constructs: the advancement analysis of impersonal passives and the 1-Advancement Exclusiveness Law [Perlmutter and Postal (to appear b)] in the case of Dutch impersonal passives, and the formulation in (36) in the case of Achenese Verb Agreement. The data in (44–45) thus conforms to the prediction in (43), and seems to support both the strongest form of the Unaccusative Hypothesis and the formulation of Achenese Verb Agreement in (36).

However, (44–45) do not give the entire picture for Achenese Verb

Agreement. First, many additional examples remain to be tested; the data in (44–45) is obviously only a small sample of the class of Achenese intransitive clauses. Second, Lawler (1977) cites the following pair:

(46)   a. Gɔpnyan tɨngəh   *gɨ-ʔeh.*
               he   PROG   sleep
              'He is sleeping.'

      b. Gɔpnyan (tɨngəh) tɨngɨt.
               he   PROG   asleep
              'He is asleep.'

The verb in (46a) requires the agreement prefix, while in (46b) an agreement prefix cannot be used. The pair in (46) provides a clear challenge to the twin claims that: a) the strongest version of the Unaccusative Hypothesis is correct, and b) (36) is the correct formulation of Achenese Verb Agreement. If Achenese initially intransitive clauses *with* verb agreement are initially unergative and those *without* verb agreement are initially unaccusative, and if the distinction between the two is universally predictable from the semantics of the clause, how can (46a) contrast with (46b) as it does? Either there must be a semantic difference between these two clauses that is relevant to the putative universal semantic distinction between initially unergative and initially unaccusative clauses, or else the strongest version of the Unaccusative Hypothesis and (36) cannot both be correct.

Since the required kind of semantic difference between (46a) and (46b) cannot be shown at present, an account of Achenese Verb Agreement in terms of (36) requires giving up the strongest version of the Unaccusative Hypothesis, i.e. the claim that initial unergativity vs. initial unaccusativity is universally predictable from the semantics of the clause. This means that it will be necessary to find evidence internal to each language for distinguishing initially unergative clauses from initially unaccusative ones.[9] A theory incorporating this weaker version of the Unaccusative Hypothesis will thus provide a broader characterization of the class of natural languages, since semantically equivalent clauses will be initially unergative in some languages and initially unaccusative in others. The question is then whether or not natural languages actually differ in this respect.

The evidence bearing on this question that has been assembled so far indicates that languages indeed differ in this respect. Comparison of the data on Dutch in Perlmutter (1978a) with the data in Albanian (Hubbard (1979, 1980)), Choctaw (Davies (1980)), French (Raposo (in preparation)),

Georgian (Harris (1981)), Halkomelem (Gerdts (1980)), Italian (Perlmutter (in preparation) and Rosen (1981)), Lakhota (Williamson (1979)), and Turkish (Özkaragöz (1980)) shows differences from one language to another with respect to the initial unergativity vs. unaccusativity of semantically equivalent clauses. Thus, the available evidence is not consistent with the strongest form of the Unaccusative Hypothesis. It *is* consistent with a weaker position under which initial unergativity vs. unaccusativity is postulated on syntactic grounds but is not universally predictable from the semantics of the clause. On the basis of the languages studied so far, there seems to be a *tendency* for initial unergativity vs. unaccusativity to correspond with the semantics of the clause as sketched in Perlmutter (1978a) and Perlmutter and Postal (to appear b), but the correspondence is not absolute.

If a weaker form of the Unaccusative Hypothesis is adopted, then, the contrast between (44) and (46a), on the one hand, and (45) and (46b), on the other, can be captured by a grammar of Achenese which posits the former to be initially unergative and the latter initially unaccusative, and which formulates Verb Agreement as in (36). Since this formulation uses the notion 'initial 1,' it provides support for including this notion among those available to individual grammars.

However, although the formulation of Achenese Verb Agreement in (36) (in conjunction with the Unaccusative Hypothesis) accounts for the data, it is not the only possible formulation. An alternative account of the contrast in agreement between (44) and (46a), on the one hand, and (45) and (46b), on the other, would be to posit that the predicates in the two classes belong to different grammatical categories, i.e. the former are verbs and the latter are adjectives. Achenese Verb Agreement would then be formulated so that verbs, but not adjectives, agree. Lawler (1977) assumes an account of the contrast between (46a) and (46b) along these lines.

It is clear that there are two contrasting classes of intransitive clauses in Achenese. The question is whether this contrast is to be acounted for in terms of initial unergativity vs. unaccusativity, or in terms of predicates' membership in categorially distinct classes: verbs and adjectives. The issue must be resolved on the basis of evidence internal to Achenese.

Of course, it is conceivable that evidence from Achenese might make it necessary to posit *both* a distinction between initially unergative and initially unaccusative clauses, *and* a distinction between verbs and adjectives. In that case, it is conceivable that the division between initially unergative and unaccusative clauses might not coincide with that between clauses with verbal as opposed to adjectival predicates. That raises the possibility that there could be initially unaccusative clauses that manifest verb agreement. If this should be the case, it would not be possible to formulate Achenese Verb Agreement in terms of the notion 'initial 1,' since there would be clauses with no initial 1 which nevertheless manifest verb agreement. That is, there would be clauses of the form:

(47)

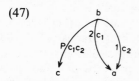

in which the verb would be agreeing with a nominal that is *initial* 2 and *final* 1. An adequate formulation of the agreement rule would have to account for agreement in these cases, while still accounting for the fact that in Passive clauses the verb agrees with the initial 1 rather than the final 1.

This situation could be resolved by defining a notion of *first* 1:

(48)   A nominal *a* is the *first* 1 of *b* if and only if it heads an arc with R-sign '1' and first coordinate c_k and there is no arc $[1(c, b)\langle c_x c_i c_y \rangle]$, where $i < k$ and $a \neq c$.

Thus, in Passive clauses the initial 1 would be the first 1, while in initially unaccusative clauses, the initial 2 that advances to 1 would be the first 1. Verb Agreement could then be formulated as:

(49)   *Verb Agreement in Achenese*
         The verb of a clause *b* agrees with the *first* 1 of the clause.

At present I know of no evidence that the notion 'first 1' is needed, either for the formulation of Achenese Verb Agreement, or for any other rules in natural languages.[10] One source of evidence bearing on this issue would be the interaction with the Unaccusative Hypothesis of phenomena that appear to need the notion 'initial 1.' If nominals that can be shown to be initial 2s and final 1s of initially unaccusative clauses behave like putative 'initial 1s,' then the rules in question cannot be formulated in terms of the notion 'initial 1'; the notion 'first 1' would be needed instead.

Two distinct questions must be answered: 1) Are there any cases where the notion 'first 1' is needed to state some rule or generalization? 2) If so, can the notion 'first 1' replace that of 'initial 1' everywhere the latter seems to be needed, or are both notions necessary? These questions must be answered by future research.

The notion of initial 1 has been used to state various language-particular rules and generalizations. For example, Bell (1974, 1976, to appear) uses it to state the conditions on Equi and reflexives in Cebuano, a Philippine language. Harris (1976, 1981) uses it to state the condition on TAV-Reflexivization in Georgian (cf. §8 below), as well as in a constraint on Inversion. Harris (to appear a) argues that the notion of initial 1 is needed to state Verb Agreement in Udi, a Caucasian language.

Aside from rules using the notion of initial 1, various other rules have been argued to involve reference to the initial level. Harris (1976, 1981) argues that reference to this level is necessary in the rules governing verb stem suppletion and the distribution of the preverbs *da-* and *ga-* in Georgian. Özkaragöz (1980) argues that the constraint governing -*ArAk* adverbial clauses in Turkish must refer to the initial level. Allen and Frantz (1978) and Allen (to appear) argue that the verb agreement rule in Southern Tiwa, a Tanoan language of New Mexico, refers to the initial level. Based on these results and the findings of Allen and Gardiner (1977), Allen, Frantz, Gardiner, and Perlmutter (to appear) argue that initial grammatical relations figure crucially in the rules needed to account for verb agreement, the choice of agreement morphemes, noun incorporation, and the suppletion of certain verb stems in Southern Tiwa. Perlmutter (to appear e) argues that reference to the initial level is also necessary in the grammar of Luiseño, a Uto-Aztecan language of southern California. Future research will have to determine both the range of phenomena that are stated in terms of initial grammatical relations (including the notion of initial 1), and the extent (if any) to which the latter notion must be supplemented or supplanted by the notion of first 1.

5. THE NOTION OF 1

Some rules and generalizations in the grammars of natural languages refer to the notion 'nominal heading a 1-arc', with no specification of the stratum or strata in which the nominal in question heads a 1-arc. I illustrate this type of generalization with the condition governing possible antecedents of reflexives in Russian. This condition governs both antecedents of the reflexive pronouns *sebja* (and its case variants *sebe* and *soboj*) and the reflexive possessive *svoj* where *svoj* requires an antecedent. The reflexive pronouns are inflected only for case; the same forms are used for all genders and both singular and plural number. The reflexive possessive *svoj* is adjectival in form, agreeing with the head it modifies in gender, number, and case.

A necessary (but not sufficient) condition for a nominal to be the antecedent of a reflexive in Russian can be formulated as follows:

(50)   *Necessary condition on antecedents of reflexives in Russian*
       Only a nominal heading a 1-arc can serve as antecedent of a reflexive.

This condition is formulated in Perlmutter (to appear b) and discussed further in Perlmutter (1978b, 1981, to appear d). It builds on the work of Peškovskij (1956), Klenin (1974), Chvany (1975), and Timberlake (1979). Some of the examples cited below are taken from these sources.[11]

The condition in (50) accounts for the fact that the following are unambiguous:

(51)   *Ja* rasskazal Borisu anekdot o   *sebe*
       I   told   DAT   joke   about REFL
       'I told Boris a joke about myself'
(52)   *Ja* rasskazal Borisu anekdot o   *svoej*   žene
       I   told   DAT   joke   about REFL's   wife
       'I told Boris a joke about my wife'

Ja can antecede the reflexive in these cases because it heads a 1-arc in the associated RN's; *Borisu* cannot serve as antecedent because it heads a 3-arc but not a 1-arc. The fact that nominals heading only a 2-arc cannot antecede reflexives can be seen in the following example:

(53)   Poetomu ja otošel ot   temy iskusstva i   stal
       therefore I left   from topic art/GEN and began

       rassprašivat' xudožnika o   *nem* samom
       question   artist/ACC about him   EMPH

       'Therefore I left the topic of art and began to question the artist about himself'

In (53), the nonreflexive pronoun *nem* is used; the reflexive *sebe* could not be used to refer to *xudožnika* 'artist,' for the latter heads a 2-arc but not a 1-arc in the associated RN.

A 2, 3, or nonterm cannot antecede a reflexive in Russian even if there is no overt 1 to serve as antecedent:

(54)   a. Mne   bylo skazano obo   *mne.*
          me/DAT   was told   about   me
          'I was told about myself' (Lit.: 'To me was told about me')
       b. *Mne bylo skazano o *sebe.*

The dative nominal *mne* in (54) heads a 3-arc but not a 1-arc, and therefore does not qualify as an antecedent of a reflexive.

The necessary codition on antecedents of reflexives cannot be stated in terms of linear order, as the following examples show:

(55)   Anekdoty o   *sebe*   nam   rasskazyvali tol'ko *inostrancy.*
       jokes   about REFL us/DAT told   only   foreigners
       'Only foreigners told us jokes about themselves'

(56)   Borisu rasskazyval anekdot o   *sebe*   tol'ko *Sergej.*
       DAT   told   joke   about REFL only
       'Only Sergej$_i$ told Boris$_k$ a joke about himself$_i$'

In (55), both *nam* and *inostrancy* follow the reflexive. Only *inostrancy* can be the antecedent, for it heads a 1-arc; *nam* heads only a 3-arc. In (56), *Borisu* cannot be the antecedent of *sebe* even though it precedes it, because it heads a 3-arc but not a 1-arc in the associated RN. On the other hand, *Sergej* is the antecedent, even though it follows the reflexive, because it heads a 1-arc.

Active-passive pairs provide interesting contrasts:

(57)   a. *Anna* otpravila rebenka   k *svoim* roditeljam.
          sent   child/ACC to REFL's parents
       'Anna set the child to her parents'

       b.

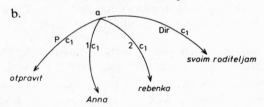

(58)   a. *Rebenok* byl   otpravlen k *svoim*   roditeljam.
          child   was   sent   to REFL's parents
       'The child was sent to his parents'

       b.

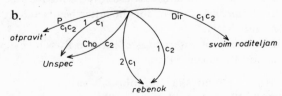

In (57), *rebenka* is not a possible antecedent because it heads a 2-arc but not a 1-arc. In the corresponding Passive (58), however, *rebenok* heads a 1-arc (as well as a 2-arc) and therefore qualifies as an antecedent. Contrasts like that between (57) and (58) show that the condition on antecedents of reflexives cannot be stated in terms of semantic roles, because the semantic roles in (57) and (58) are the same, while the grammatical relations are different.

Since the antecedent of the reflexive heads a 1-arc in all the examples cited so far, these examples are all consistent with the condition in (50). However, they are also consistent with an alternative formulation:

(59)   Only a *final* 1 can serve as antecedent of a reflexive in Russian.

Crucial examples showing that (59) is inadequate and hence that (50) must be adopted are those where the antecedent of a reflexive heads a 1-arc, but *not in the final stratum*. These examples are of (at least) two types.

First, as Klenin (1974) shows, there are examples where what in relational terms is a Passive chomeur is antecedent of a reflexive:

(60)   a. Èta kniga   byla kuplena *Borisom* dlja *sebja*.
            this book   was   bought INSTR   for   REFL
            'This book was bought by Boris for himself'

         b.

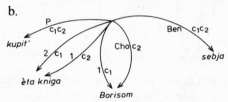

In (60), the antecedent is an initial 1 but not a final 1.[12]

The second type of example comes from Inversion clauses, in which the initial 1 is a final 3. The evidence for Inversion in Russian is given in Perlmutter (to appear b), and will not be repeated here. The following example is relevant:

(61)   a. *Mne*   nužna bolee udobnaja kvartira
            me/DAT needs more   comfortable apartment

            ne   dlja *sebja*   a   dlja *svoej*   sem'i.
            NEG   for   REFL   but for   REFL's family

            'I need a more comfortable apartment not for myself, but for my family'

b.

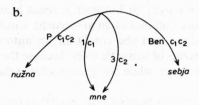

The RN for (61a) includes the subnetwork in (61b).[13] *Mne* qualifies as antecedent of a reflexive because it heads an initial-stratum 1-arc, even though it does not head a final 1-arc.

In many Inversion clauses, the initial 2 advances to 1 and heads a final 1-arc. Advancees to 1 in Inversion clauses can also antecede reflexives:

(62) a. *Boris* ne nužen *svoim* detjam.
      NOM NEG needs REFL's children/DAT
      'Boris's children don't need him'

b.

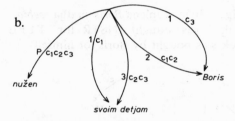

In (62) *Boris*, the initial 2 and final 1, is the antecedent of the reflexive *svoim*.

Reviewing the data on Russian reflexives presented here, we see that there is no single stratum in which a nominal must head a 1-arc in order to qualify as antecedent of a reflexive; it qualifies as long as it heads a 1-arc *in some stratum*. This is captured by the formulation in (50). The necessary condition on antecedents of reflexives in Russian thus provides an example of a condition statable in terms of the notion 'nominal heading a 1-arc,' with no further specification.

Other generalizations of this form exist in natural languages. First, Perlmutter (to appear b) argues that the condition on possible controllers of gerund constructions in Russian also refers to the notion 'nominal heading a 1-arc,' with no further specification. Second, Davies (1980, 1981) argues that this notion is needed to state the rules of Choctaw governing antecedents of reflexives, nominative case marking, nominative agreement markers, and same-subject marking.

There are also generalizations specifying that a nominal must meet *two* conditions, one of which is that it head a 1-arc (with no further specification). In Perlmutter (in preparation) it is argued that the condition for the perfect auxiliary *essere* in Italian is:

(63)   *Perfect Auxiliary Selection in Italian*
         A clause *b* requires the auxiliary *essere* in perfect tenses if and only if there is a nominal *a* which:
         i) heads a 1-arc with tail *b*
         and
         ii) heads an object arc with tail *b*.
         Otherwise clause *b* requires the auxiliary *avere*.

Hubbard (1979, 1980) argues that the condition governing non-active verb morphology in Albanian is similar. It can be stated as follows:[14]

(64)   Non-Active *Morphology in Albanian*
         A clause *b* requires non-active morphology if and only if there is a nominal *a* which:
         i) heads a 1-arc with tail *b*.
         and
         ii) heads a 2-arc with tail *b*.
         Otherwise clause *b* requires active morphology.

The rules in (62) and (63) are of interest here because they both use the notion 'heads a 1-arc' (with no further specification).

Finally, there are cases where rules refer to nominals heading object arcs (with no further specification). (63) and (64) illustrate this. Further, Davies (1980, 1981) argues that Choctaw has rules determining accusative and dative agreement markers that refer to the notions 'nominal heading a 2-arc' and 'nominal heading a 3-arc,' respectively, and that Possessor Ascension to 3 in Choctaw references the notion 'nominal heading an absolutive arc'. Finally, the notion 'nominal heading an object arc' is used by Harris (to appear a) to account for case marking in Udi, and by Williamson (1979) to account for the case of person markers on the verb in Lakhota.

The significance of all these cases is the same. All are examples of rules referring to the notion 'nominal heading an *n*-arc' (for different values of *n*). Taken together, they account for an impressive array of data that any alternative proposal will have to account for.

For most of these cases, however, a caveat is in order. Consider first the necessary conditions on possible antecedents of reflexives and controllers of gerund constructions in Russian. Although the former condition has been stated here in terms of the notion 'nominal heading a 1-arc,' no argument has been given why the condition could not be stated as follows:

(65)   Only a nominal that heads either an initial or a final 1-arc can serve as antecedent of a reflexive in Russian.

(65) would account for all the data cited here. The only argument against the formulation in (65) at present is that there is no reason to state the condition as a disjunction, as in (65), when it can be given as a single statement, as in (50). Note that the statement in (65) offers no explanation of why the two notions in the disjunction are 'initial 1' and 'final 1,' rather than, say, 'initial 1' and 'final 2.' On these grounds, the statement in (50) is preferable to that in (65). The same considerations, *mutatis mutandis*, apply to the various rules stated in terms of the notion 'nominal heading an *n*-arc,' (for different values of *n*) mentioned above.

Still, the case for this notion would be stronger if there were examples that *require* statement in terms of the notion 'nominal heading an *n*-arc,' rather than a disjunction, as in (65). One example of this involves the notion 'nominal heading a 2-arc,' and comes from the Antipassive construction in Choctaw, studied by Davies (to appear). Choctaw has sentence pairs such as the following:

(66)   a. Chi-banna-li.
             2ACC-want-1NOM
             'I want you'
         b. Chi-sa-banna.
             2ACC-1ACC-want
             'I want you'

(66b) exemplifies the Antipassive construction. Davies shows that the first person nominal in (66b) behaves like a final 1 with respect to Equi. With respect to case marking, clefting, reflexives, and same-subject marking, the first person nominal in (66b) behaves like a nominal heading a 1-arc, while the second person nominal behaves like a nominal heading a 2-arc. Crucially, however, the first person nominal in (66b) (unlike that in (66a)) determines an *accusative* agreement marker on the verb. Davies uses this fact to argue that Choctaw provides evidence for Postal's (1977) analysis of Antipassive constructions, in which a 1 is demoted to 2 and then advances back to 1:

(67)

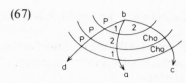

Davies argues that (66b) has the structure in (67), with *a* the first person nominal and *c* the second person nominal. Davies formulates the relevant rule as follows:

(68)   *Accusative Marking in Choctaw*
         A nominal heading a 2-arc determines an accusative agreement marker on the verb.

The fact that the initial 1 (*a* in (67)) determines an accusative agreement marker on the verb then follows from the formulation in (68), although *a* heads *neither an initial nor a final 2-arc*. On the one hand, this provides striking confirmation of Postal's analysis of Antipassive constructions as having the structure in (67). On the other, (68) is a rule that should be formulated in terms of the notion 'nominal heading a 2-arc,' and can not be formulated in terms of the disjunction 'nominal heading an initial or final 2-arc.'[15] Thus, Davies' work on Choctaw provides evidence for allowing rules to refer to the notion 'nominal heading an *n*-arc,' with no further specification.

Since there seems to be no possibility of replacing all such rules by disjunctions stated in terms of initial or final grammatical relations, I include the notion 'nominal heading a 1-arc' among the notions of subject that must be sanctioned by linguistic theory.

6. THE NOTION OF ACTING 1

In Perlmutter and Postal (to appear c), the notion 'acting term$_x$' is defined as follows:

(69)   *Acting Term$_x$* (Definition)
         A nominal node is an *acting term$_x$* of clause *b* if and only if:
         i) it heads a term$_x$ arc, A, with tail *b* whose last coordinate is c_i, and
         ii) it does *not* head an arc B with tail *b* having a *term* R-sign distinct from term$_x$ and having coordinate c_j, where $j > i$.

This definition groups, for example, final 1s and final 1-chomeurs together as acting 1s, because although a final 1-chomeur is not a final 1, it is a 1 in the last stratum in which it is a term.

In Perlmutter and Postal (to appear c, Appendix D), the notion of acting 1 is used to account for case marking in Maasai, a Nilo-Hamitic language of Kenya studied by Tucker and Mpaayei (1955).

In Maasai, case is marked by tone, as in the following examples:

(70)　e-dol embártá
　　　 3-see horse/ACC
　　　 'He sees the horse'
(71)　e-dol embartá
　　　 3-see horse/NOM
　　　 'The horse sees him'

In (70), *embártá* is the final 2 and therefore accusative, while in (71) *embartá* is the final 1 and therefore nominative. Similarly:

(72)　áa-dol　　　　　　(nánú)
　　　 3SgSubj/1SgObj-see　1Sg/ACC
　　　 'He sees me'
(73)　á-dol　　　(nanú)
　　　 1SgSubj-see 1Sg/NOM
　　　 'I see him'

In Passive clauses in Maasai, the initial 2 has accusative tone:

(74)　a-dol　　　Sirónkà
　　　 1SgSubj-see ACC
　　　 'I see Sironka'
(75)　e-isis-i　　　Sirónka
　　　 3-praise-PASS ACC
　　　 'Sironka is praised'

Similarly, the initial 1 in Maasai passives appears to have nominative tone, although Tucker and Mpaayei do not always mark tone:

(76)　e-rik-i　　　nkishu aainei lmurran
　　　 3-lead-PASS cattle　my　young-men
　　　 'My cattle will be led by the young men'

lmurran in (76) apparently has the same tone it would have as subject of an active clause.

The analysis of Maasai passives proposed in Perlmutter and Postal (to appear c) is that they are impersonal passives. Under the universal analysis of impersonal passives proposed there, the RN for (75) would be abbreviated as the stratal diagram in (77), and that for (76) would be abbreviated in (78):

(77)

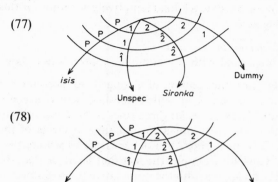

(78)

'Dummy' represents a dummy nominal. Both initial nuclear terms are final chomeurs. Under the definition of 'acting term$_x$' in (69), the initial 2 of an impersonal passive is an acting 2, and the initial 1 is an acting 1. Thus, the fact that the former are accusative and the latter nominative in Maasai can be accounted for by means of the following rules:

(79)   *Case Marking in Maasai*
      a. Acting 2s are accusative.
      b. Acting 1s are nominative.

If (79) is incorporated into the grammar of Maasai, then (79b) provides an example of a rule referring to the notion 'acting 1.'[16]

Other rules referring to the notion 'acting 1' have been proposed by Klokeid (to appear) for Nitinaht, a Wakashan language of Vancouver Island (British Columbia). Nitinaht has active-passive pairs such as the following:

(80)   Tl'itcitl-ibt-'a   (oxw) waaxaats'al (ooyoqw) ba'itlqats- 'aq.
      sting-PST-INDIC NOMbee   ACC   boy   the
      'A bee stung the boy'
(81)   Tl'itcitl't-t-'a   (oxw) ba'itlqats- 'aq (oxw-iit)
      sting/PASS-PST-INDIC NOM boy   the NOM-PASS
      waaxaats'al.
      bee
      'The boy was stung by a bee'

The conditions under which the case morphemes in parentheses or their absence are felicitous need not concern us here. The crucial point is that the nominative marker *oxw* can appear on the 1 of the active, and on both the final 1 and the chomeur in the passive. Klokeid tentatively accounts for this by means of the following rule:

(82)   *Nominative Marking in Nitinaht*
        An acting 1 is marked with the nominative preposition *oxw*.

Klokeid also tentatively uses the notion of acting 1 to account for pronominal encliticization and cases in which question words are not marked with a preposition. Thus, (at least) three rules of Nitinaht refer to this notion. The Nitinaht data rules out a formulation in terms of the notion 'initial 1,' since the advancee from 2 to 1 behaves like a 1 with respect to the rules in question. Thus, for example, the fact that *ba'itlqats-'aq*, the initial 2 and final 1 of (81), can appear with the nominative preposition *oxw* shows that (82) could not be formulated in terms of the notion 'initial 1.' Since advancees from 2 to 1 in Nitinaht passives also behave like 1s with respect to pronominal encliticization and the possibility of question words without a preposition, none of the three Nitinaht rules that Klokeid tentatively formulates in terms of 'acting 1' could be formulated in terms of 'initial 1.'

In the case of Maasai, formulation in terms of *initial* grammatical relations can be ruled out for rules that have been formulated in terms of the notion of acting 2. The first such rule is (79a). The crucial evidence comes from examples in which a nominal heading an initial Oblique arc advances to 2. That is the case, for example, in:

(83)   a. Áá-dung-íé-ki enkálém
            'I am cut with a knife'

        b.

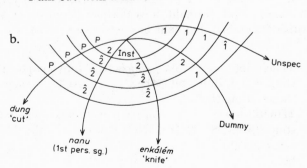

Under the analysis proposed in Perlmutter and Postal (to appear c), (83a) is an impersonal passive of a clause involving advancement of an Instrument to 2, with the structure in (83b). The key fact is that *enkálém* has accusative tone.[17] Since it is not an initial 2, such examples exclude the possibility of stating the accusative case rule in terms of the notion of initial 2, instead of that of acting 2 as in (79a).

Another rule of Maasai is formulated in terms of the notion of acting 2 in Perlmutter and Postal (to appear c):

(84)   *Object Agreement*
        Object agreement on the verb of a clause is determined by a first or second person singular *acting* 2 of the clause.

The agreement morphemes that appear on Maasai verbs show agreement with the final 1 as well as with an acting 2. Here we will consider cases where the final 1 is third person singular and the acting 2 is first person singular. This is the case in (72), where the agreement morpheme is *áa-*. Here the final 1 is third person singular; the first person singular nominal is the final 2, and hence also an acting 2. In (83), the first person singular nominal is the initial 2 put en chômage by the advancement of an Instrument to 2. Hence it is an acting 2. The dummy that is the final 1 of this impersonal passive clause is third person singular, so the agreement morpheme here is *áa-*, as in (72). Finally, consider an example with a first person singular advancee to 2 (and hence not initial 2):

(85)   a. Áa-bol-oki-ní olbéné
           'The bag is opened for me'

        b.

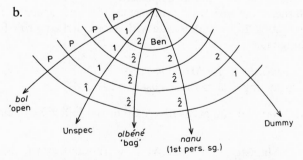

Here, too, the agreement morpheme is *áa-*. Thus, the formulation of Object Agreement in (84) correctly accounts for the presently available data from Maasai.

Unfortunately for the goals of the present paper, I know of no evidence from Maasai and Nitinaht that the rules *must* be formulated as in (79), (82), and (84). The following alternatives would also account for the presently available data:

(86)   *Case Marking in Maasai*
      a. A nominal heading a 2-arc is accusative.
      b. A nominal heading a 1-arc is nominative.

(87)   *Object Agreement in Maasai*
      A first or second person singular nominal heading a 2-arc with tail *b* determines object agreement on the verb of *b*.

(88)   *Nominative Marking in Nitinaht*
      A nominal heading a 1-arc is marked with the nominative preposition *oxw*.

That is, these rules could be stated in terms of the notions discussed in §5. These notions could also be used to state the other rules of Nitinaht for which Klokeid tentatively uses the notion of acting 1.

Rules formulated in terms of the notion 'acting 1' and rules using the notion 'nominal heading a 1-arc' would make different predictions about additional data in both Maasai and Nitinaht. For example, if either of these languages has the Inversion construction (cf. the discussion of (61) in Russian in §5, and that of (108) in Italian in §7), the behavior of Inversion nominals would decide the issue. If they behave like 1s with respect to the relevant phenomena, the rules must refer to the notion 'nominal heading a 1-arc.'[18] If they do not, the notion of acting 1 would be needed. However, no such additional data is available at present.

Although there is presently no evidence for the notion 'acting 1,' there is evidence for 'acting 2.' I will illustrate with a case marking rule found in a variety of languages.

(89)   *Accusative Case Marking*
      An acting 2 is in the accusative case.

This rule accounts for the accusative case in the following example from Latin:

(90)   a. Magister   puerōs   grammaticam   docet.
        teacher/NOM   boys/ACC   grammar/ACC   teaches
        'The teacher teaches the boys grammar'

b.

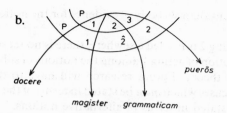

Under the 3-2 Advancement analysis of this example, both *puerōs* and
grammaticam satisfy the definition of 'acting 2.' In accordance with (89),
both are in the accusative case.

The evidence that (89) for Latin cannot be stated in terms of the notion
'nominal heading a 2-arc,' as in (86a), comes from Passive clauses:

(91)   a. Puerī   grammaticam ā magistrō   docentur.
        boys/NOM grammar/ACC by teacher/ABL are-taught
        'The boys are taught grammar by the teacher'

b.

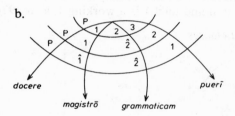

Puerī in (91) heads a 2-arc, but since it is a final 1, it does not satisfy the
definition of 'acting 2' in (69). A formulation of Accusative Case Marking for
Latin like that in (86a) would incorrectly predict *puerī* to be in the
accusative case. In fact, it is in the nominative by virtue of its final 1 status;
this is a consequence of an independently needed rule of Latin. (91) thus
provides evidence for the formulation in (89) for Latin, as opposed to one
like (86a). Note also that *grammaticam* is in the accusative case in (91), since
it satisfies the definition of 'acting 2.'

Klokeid gives an argument exactly parallel to this one for accusative
marking in Nitinaht. Marlett (to appear) gives a parallel argument based on
data from Seri, a Hokan language of northern Mexico. Tohsaku (in
preparation) uses the notion of acting 2 to state certain rules of Ainu, and
Perlmutter and Postal (to appear c) use this notion to account for clitics in

Welsh. Thus, there is a considerable body of evidence for the notion 'acting 2.'

Since the notion of acting 2 is needed elsewhere, there is no reason not to tentatively include the notion of acting 1 among the notions of subject to be sanctioned by linguistic theory. Future research will have to determine whether or not there are cases which *must* be stated in terms of the notion of acting 1 and cannot be stated in terms of alternative notions.

7. THE NOTION OF WORKING 1

The notion 'working 1' is defined in Perlmutter (1979) as follows:

(92)   *Working* 1 (Definition)
        A nominal node is a *working* 1 of clause b if and only if:
        i) it heads a 1-arc with tail b, and
        ii) it heads a final-stratum term arc with tail b.

This definition covers the following cases. First, in monostratal clauses, the nominal that is both initial and final 1 is a working 1, as in (93):

(93)   *Monostratal clauses*

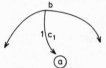

Second, in Passive clauses, the nominal heading a final-stratum 1-arc is a working 1, but the nominal heading a final-stratum Cho arc is not, since it does not satisfy (92–ii). Thus, in (94), a is a working 1, but c is not:

(94)   *Passive clauses*

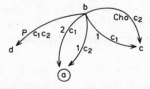

Finally, in Inversion clauses, the Inversion nominal is a working 1, since it heads both a 1-arc and a final 3-arc, thereby satisfying both conditions in (92):

(95)   *Inversion clauses*

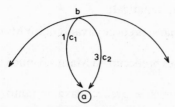

The notion of working 1 is used in Perlmutter (1979) to state various conditions in the grammars of Italian, Japanese, and Quechua. I illustrate its use here with the condition on controllers of the 'consecutive *da* + infinitive' construction in Italian.[19]

'Consecutive *da*' is the name applied to instances of the preposition *da* that introduce infinitival complements of constructions involving forms such as *tanto* 'so much, so many,' *abbastanza* 'enough,' *talmente* 'so,' and several others:

(96)   Giorgio non ha abbastanza soldi *da poter pagare il riscatto.*
         'Giorgio doesn't have enough money to be able to pay the ransom'

(97)   a. Giorgio mi ha rimproverato tante volte che mi ha fatto paura.
         'Giorgio rebuked me so many times that he scared me'
         b. *Giorgio* mi ha rimproverato tante volte *da farmi paura.*
         'Giorgio rebuked me so many times that he scared me'

The key point about the consecutive *da* + infinitive construction for present purposes is that a matrix clause nominal is understood as the subject of the infinitive occurring with consecutive *da*. I will call this nominal the *controller*. In all examples of the construction cited here, the controller will be italicized.

The condition on controllers of this construction can be given informally as follows:

(98)   *Condition on controllers of the consecutive DA + infinitive construction in Italian*
         The controller must be a *working* 1 of the clause in which consecutive *da* + infinitive is embedded.

Since *Giorgio* is both initial and final 1 of the matrix clause in (96) and (97), it qualifies as a working 1 and therefore satisfies (92). The 2 in (99) is not a working 1, and so *(99b) is ungrammatical:

(99)   a. Le difficoltà finanziarie preoccupavano tanto Mario che si è ammalato.
           'Financial difficulties preoccupied Mario so much that he got sick'
        b. *Le difficoltà finanziarie preoccupavano tanto *Mario da amalarsi*.

Similarly, note the contrast between (100b) and *(101b):

(100)   a. La mamma mi ha rimproverato tante volte che si è rotta le scatole.
        b. *La mamma* mi ha rimproverato tante volte *da rompersi le scatole*.
           'My mother reprimanded me so many times that she got fed up'
(101)   a. La mamma mi ha rimproverato tante volte che mi sono rotto le scatole.
           'My mother reprimanded me so many times that I got fed up'
        b. *La mamma *mi* ha rimproverato tante volte *da rompermi le scatole*.

La mamma, the 1 of the matrix clause, can control the consecutive *da* + infinitive construction, but *mi*, the matrix 2, cannot.[20]

A nominal that is both initial and final 3 cannot control the consecutive *da* + infinitive construction:

(102)   a. Ho telefonato a Giorgio tante volte che si è arrabbiato.
           'I telephoned Giorgio so many times that he got angry'
        b. *Ho telefonato a *Giorgio* tante volte *da arrabbiarsi*.

Note also that a 3 cannot control the consecutive *da* + infinitive construction even if it is in initial position and there is no other overt nominal that could serve as controller:

(103)   a. A Giorgio è stata detta la stessa cosa tante volte che è diventato matto.
           'The same thing was said to Giorgio so many times that he went crazy'
        b. *A *Giorgio* è stata detta la stessa cosa tante volte *da diventare matto*.

This eliminates the possibility that the condition on possible controllers might be one of the following:

(104)   a. The highest-ranking nominal in the clause (with respect to its grammatical relation on the hierarchy of grammatical relations) that would be semantically possible as controller is the controller.
        b. The nominal in initial position is the controller.

A condition along the lines of (104b) is also ruled out by examples such as the following:

(105)   a. A queste donne Giorgio ha dato tanti fiori che sono diventate matte.
           'To these ladies Giorgio gave so many flowers that they went crazy'
        b. *A *queste donne* Giorgio ha dato tanti fiori *da diventare matte.*

The ungrammaticality of *(105b) shows that *queste donne* cannot control the consecutive *da* + infinitive construction, although it is in initial position. *Giorgio* cannot be construed as the controller because the predicate adjective in the infinitival clause has the feminine plural ending that would be required if *queste donne* were the controller.

Final 1s in Passive clauses are working 1s by the definition in (92) and therefore qualify as controllers of the *da* + infinitive construction:

(106)   a. Sono stato rimproverato dalla mamma tante volte che mi sono rotto le scatole.
        b. Sono stato rimproverato dalla mamma tante volte *da rompermi le scatole.*
           'I was rebuked by my mother so many times that I got fed up'

Crucially, Passive chomeurs do not head final Term arcs. They therefore do not satisfy condition (ii) in (92). Thus they are not working 1s and cannot control the consecutive *da* + infinitive construction:[21]

(107)   a. Sono stato rimproverato dalla mamma tante volte che si è rotta le scatole.
           'I was rebuked by my mother so many times that she got fed up'
        b. *Sono stato rimproverato dal*la mamma* tante volte *da rompersi* le scatole.

Crucially, again, Inversion nominals, which head final-stratum 3-arcs, satisfy the definition in (92) and therefore qualify as controllers of the consecutive *da* + infinitive construction:

(108)   a. A mio marito è talmente piaciuta una compagna d'ufficio che ci ha lasciati tutti quanti ed è andato a vivere con lei.
         b. A *mio marito* è talmente piaciuta una compagna d'ufficio *da lasciarci tutti quanti e andare a vivere con lei.*
            'My husband took such a liking to a co-worker at the office that he left us all and went to live with her'

Further information on the Inversion construction and the class of Inversion triggers in Italian can be found in Perlmutter (1979). As argued in detail there, the RN associated with (108a-b) includes the following subnetwork:

(109)

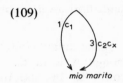

Mio marito in (108) consequently satisfies the definition of 'working 1' and qualifies as controller of the consecutive *da* + infinitive construction.

Significant for the present paper is the fact that the notion 'working 1' is needed to state the condition on controllers of the consecutive *da* + infinitive construction in Italian. Other conditions stated in terms of this notion are discussed in Perlmutter (1979).

8. THE POSSIBILITY OF ADDITIONAL NOTIONS OF SUBJECT

If all rules stated in terms of subjecthood were stated in terms of final subjecthood, there would be no need to define additional notions. Since in fact there are rules that require other notions of subjecthood it has been necessary to define the notions needed for these rules.

There are also cases that cannot be formulated in terms of any of the notions of subjecthood defined in this paper. Such cases give us two options; we can either define additional notions of subjecthood to accommodate them, or we can account for the data by means of language-particular rules. I illustrate this situation with the condition on antecedents of the reflexive *tav* in Georgian.

Harris (1981) shows that only a subject can antecede this reflexive:

(110)   Mxaṭvari   daxaṭavs   Vanos   tavis-tvis.
         painter/NOM   paints   DAT   REFL-for
         'The painter$_i$ will paint Vano$_k$ for himself$_i$.'

(111)   a. Nino ačvenebs paṭara Givis tavis   tavs   sarķeši.
            NOM shows   little DAT EMPH REFL mirror-in
         b. Nino paṭara Givis tavis tavs ačvenebs sarķeši.
         c. Sarķeši paṭara Givis tavis tavs ačvenebs Nino.
            'Nino$_i$ shows little Givi$_k$ herself$_i$ in the mirror.'

(110) and (111) are unambiguous; only the subjects *mxaṭvari* and *Nino* can
be the antecedents of the reflexives. (111) shows that this generalization
holds regardless of possible variations in word order.

Harris also shows that *tav* and its antecedent must be members of the
same clause. Of greater interest here, however, are the interactions of the
condition on antecedents of *tav* with Passive and Inversion constructions.

The final 1 of Passive clauses can *not* be the antecedent of *tav*:

(112)   *Vano daxaṭulia (cnobili mxaṭvris mier) tavis-tvis.
         NOM is-painted famous painter by   REFL-for
         'Vano$_i$ is painted (by a famous painter) for himself$_i$.'

*(112) in Georgian thus contrasts with (58) in Russian, where a Passive
advancee to 1 antecedes a reflexive. Further, a Passive chomeur cannot
antecede a reflexive in Georgian. Thus, *(112) is also ungrammatical on the
reading where *cnobili mxaṭvris* is the antecedent of the reflexive. Further,
consider:

(113)   a. *Es   çigni   naqidia Ninos mier tavis-tvis.
            this book/NOM   was-bought by   REFL-for
            'This book was bought by Nino for herself.'
         b. *Es çigni naqidia tavis-tvis Ninos mier.

*(113) contrasts with (60) in Russian, where a Passive chomeur antecedes a
reflexive.

Harris's condition can be stated as follows:

(114)   *Condition on Antecedents of TAV in Georgian*
         A nominal *a* can be the antecedent of a *tav*-reflexive with tail *b*
         only if *a*:
         i) heads an *initial* 1-arc with tail *b*, and
         ii) heads a *final term arc* with tail *b*.

The condition in (114) correctly accounts for the Georgian data presented so far.

It also accounts for the possible antecedents of *tav* in Inversion constructions. The initial 1 that is the final 3 in the Inversion construction can serve as antecedent:[22]

(115)   a. Turme   Gelas daurçmunebia tavisi   tavi.
             apparently DAT convinced   EMPH REFL/NOM
             'Apparently Gela has convinced himself.'

        b.
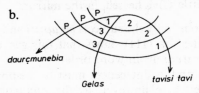

However, the final 1 of the Inversion construction cannot serve as antecedent:

(116) a. *Turme   tavis   tavs   daurcmunebia   Gela.
           apparently   EMPH REFL/DAT convinced   NOM
      b. *Turme Gela daurçmunebia tavis tavs.
         'Apparently Gela has convinced himself.'

The structure of (116) would be like that in (115b), but with *Gela* and the reflexive reversed. But *Gela* cannot be the antecedent because, although it is the final 1, it is not the initial 1. This contrasts with (62) in Russian, where an advancee to 1 in the Inversion construction antecedes a reflexive.

(114) accounts for all this Georgian data. It states two conditions that antecedents of *tav* in Georgian must meet. The first is that the nominal head an initial 1-arc. This condition is like the condition on Verb Agreement in Achenese discussed in §4. If this were the *only* condition on antecedents of *tav* in Georgian, examples like *(113) would be grammatical. The fact that (114) requires that antecedents of *tav* be both subjects and final terms is similar to the notion of working 1 discussed in §7, but with one important difference: it specifies that the 1-arc the nominal heads must be in the *initial* stratum. If the relevant notion were that of working 1, sentences like *(112) and *(116) would be grammatical.

Thus, the condition on antecents of *tav*-reflexives in Georgian is distinct from any of the notions of subjecthood defined in this paper. Of course, it is possible to define an additional notion of subjecthood:

(117)   *Initial Working* 1
         A nominal is an *initial working* 1 of clause *b* if and only if:
         i) it heads an initial 1-arc with tail *b*, and
         ii) it heads a final term arc with tail *b*.

This notion could then be used to state the condition on *tav*-reflexives in Georgian. However, this is the only case presently known to me where this notion is needed. It therefore seems preferable *not* to incorporate (117) in linguistic theory, but rather to state (114) as a language-particular rule in the grammar of Georgian. If future research should show the notion in (117) to be needed in a variety of cases, this definition can be incorporated in linguistic theory and used to state the relevant rules.

The condition on antecedents of *tav*-reflexives in Georgian illustrates several points. First, the typology of notions of subjecthood in this paper is tentative; future research may show additional notions to be necessary. Second, it is *not* claimed that the notions defined here are the only ones that will be needed in individual grammars; language-particular rules must be recognized as well.

The basic orientation of this paper is to argue for a multiplicity of notions of subject and for the recognition of distinct syntactic levels, which are needed for the notions of subjecthood proposed. The development of a theory of the notions to be used in language-particular rules is beyond the scope of this paper.

In this connection, it is interesting that three language-particular rules cited here consist of *conjunctions* of independently needed conditions. Thus, (114) in Georgian requires that a nominal head an *initial* 1-*arc* and a *final term arc*. Both are conditions needed for other rules in other languages. Similarly, (63) in Italian and (64) in Albanian each state conjunctions of two conditions of a type needed independently. This suggests that when a theory of the types of statements allowed in grammatical rules is developed, it should allow conjunctions of such statements in language-particular rules.

9. NOTIONS OF SUBJECT AND LINGUISTIC THEORY

9.1 *The Empirical Basis of Different Notions of Subject*

Linguistic theory needs different notions of subject to account for the data in natural languages. Statements failing to specify which notion of subject is intended are simply uninterpretable. For example, it is often said that only a

subject can antecede a reflexive in a given language. While such a statement
is true of both Russian and Georgian, these languages differ with respect to
reflexive-antecedent pairs, as was pointed out in §8. Similarly, consider
McCawley's (1976, 52) statement that "the subject-antecedent condition is
far from peculiar to Japanese. For example, Modern Greek, Swedish,
Tamil, and Korean exhibit the same characteristic." Without specification
of the relevant notion(s) of subject, we do not know whether the conditions
on antecedents of reflexives in these languages are the same or different.

In stating empirically different conditions, the five notions of subject
defined here provide a partial typology of rules referring to the 1-relation.
Consider the possibilities for a language with the following three clause
types:

(118)   *Monostratal clauses*

(119)   *(Personal) Passive*

(120)   *(Personal) Inversion*

(121) indicates the class of nominals specified by a rule stated in terms of
each of the notions of subject:

(121)   a. Final 1:   a, c, e
         b. Initial 1:   a, b, d
         c. 1:   a, b, c, d, e
         d. Acting 1:   a, b, c, e
         e. Working 1:   a, c, d, e

The thesis of this paper is that rules referring to each of these notions of
subject are found in grammars.

9.2. *Toward a Theory of Language Differences*

The typology of notions of subject defined here is a step toward a theory of language differences. For example, three languages can limit antecedence of reflexives to subjects, but one may limit them to *final* 1s, one to *acting* 1s, and the third to *working* 1s. Taking grammatical relations as theoretical primitives gives us a cross-linguistically viable notion of subject, reconstructed as 'nominal heading a 1-arc' internal to each grammar. Positing distinct syntactic levels means that different nominals can head 1-arcs at different levels, making possible the typology developed here. The characterization of language differences it provides is a positive consequence of the approach. If we did not take grammatical relations as primitives and posit distinct syntactic levels, it would not be possible to characterize language differences in this way. Frameworks that do not take grammatical relations as primitives or posit distinct syntactic levels must make explicit their accounts of the data in each language and the ways languages can differ. This has generally not been done.

The theory of language differences based on the typology of subject notions developed here, like any theory of language differences, provides an element essential to a theory of linguistic change. To continue with the same example, a language might change the specification of the condition on antecedents of reflexives, stating it in terms of "final 1" at one stage, "acting 1" at another, "working 1" at another, and so on. This should interact in interesting ways with the addition or loss of constructions such as Inversion, Passive, etc. Since the successive stages through which a language passes are distinct but closely related languages, linguistic change should offer a particularly good view of the possible minimal differences between languages. For this reason, it offers a fertile ground for the testing and refinement of any theory of language differences.

9.3 *Language Differences and Behavioral Definitions of Subjecthood*

Keenan (1976) attempted to find certain syntactic properties shared by all subjects, and only subjects, in all languages, and to use these properties as the basis of a definition of the notion of subject itself.[23] The thesis of this paper provides an explanation of why Keenan's proposal, or any proposal to define the notion of subject in terms of "behavioral properties" of nominals, is doomed to failure:

(122)   a. A phenomenon stated in terms of one of the notions of
            subject in one language may not be restricted to subjects in
            another language.
         b. Even the phenomena stated in terms of some notion of
            subject in a variety of languages may be stated in terms of
            different notions of subject in different languages.
         c. There is no reason to suppose that those phenomena stated
            in terms of the *same* notion of subject in various languages
            will be found in all languages.

The combined import of (122a-c) is that there is probably no phenomenon
statable in terms of the *same* notion of subject in every language. Certainly
there is no reason to assume any such phenomena to exist.

The alternative that must be taken, as argued here and in Perlmutter and
Postal (1974), Johnson (1977, 1979), Klokeid (1980), and Perlmutter (to
appear c), is to take grammatical relations as theoretical primitives and
construct explicit grammars and grammar fragments. The thesis of this
paper is that when this is done, different notions of subject, definable in
terms of the information represented in RNs, will prove to be necessary.

9.4 *Distinct Subject Notions: Some Unwarranted Conclusions*

Typically, different rules in a grammar are stated in terms of different
notions of subject. Thus Bell (1974, 1976, to appear) proposes an analysis of
Cebuano in which the rules governing reflexives and Equi are stated in
terms of the notion of initial 1, while those governing Relativization and
Quantifier Float are stated in terms of final subjecthood. Davies (1980,
1981) argues that a number of rules of Choctaw use the notion 'nominal
heading a 1-arc,' while the conditions on Equi victims and the omission of
subject pronouns are stated in terms of the notion of final 1. Perlmutter
(1979) argues that in Italian, Verb Agreement, Quantifier Float, and the
conditions on Equi victims and the omission of subject pronouns are stated
in terms of the notion of final 1, while those governing consecutive *da*, Equi
in gerund constructions and the participial absolute, and adverbial
infinitival clauses are stated in terms of the notion of working 1. Perlmutter
(to appear b) argues that in Russian, Verb Agreement, Case Marking, and
the condition on Equi victims reference the notion of final 1, while the
conditions on antecedents of reflexives and controllers of the gerund
construction use the notion 'nominal heading a 1-arc.' Additional examples
could be cited.

The situation in which different rules in a grammar refer to different notions of subjecthood has led some linguists to rather surprising conclusions. For example, Schachter (1976), basing himself in part on Bell's early work on Cebuano, constructed a taxonomy of "subject-like properties" in Tagalog. He found that different classes of nominals were relevant for different "subjectlike properties." This led Schachter to state:

The obvious conclusion, it seems to me, is that there is in fact no single syntactic category in Philippine languages that corresponds to the category identified as the subject in other languages. Rather, there is a division of subject-like properties between the category we have been calling the topic and the category we have been calling the actor, with a few subject-like properties reserved for the intersection of the topic and the actor, the actor-topic.

Relevant here is Schachter's underlying assumption of the existence of "the category identified as the subject in other languages." The underlying assumptions seem to be: 1) that all rules referencing subjects in a given language are stated in terms of the same notion of subjecthood, and 2) that the relevant notion of subjecthood is the same in all languages, or at least in all languages that (in Schachter's terms) have subjects. However, there is no reason to make such assumptions. Indeed, as indicated above, languages in which different rules reference different notions of subjecthood are common, and probably typical. Viewed from this perspective, the situation in Tagalog, where different rules would have to be stated in terms of different notions of subjecthood, is not unusual. Schachter's claim that the Tagalog data leads to the conclusion that there is no notion of subject in Philippine languages is unwarranted.[24]

Foley and Van Valin (1977) also doubt the universality of the notion of subject. They examine so-called "subject properties" in Tagalog, Navajo, and Lakhota and conclude that there are no properties shared by subjects, and no other nominals, in these three languages. They conclude: (p. 315) "the attempt to elevate the notion of subject to a theoretical construct is doomed, because no explicit universal definition can be given, i.e. no set of criteria can be given which will consistently identify the same NPs as subjects not only cross-linguistically but also within some languages."

Foley and Van Valin's approach has something in common with Schachter's: both assume that it is necessary to make explicit a mechanical procedure for "identifying" subjects internal to a given language. Foley and Van Valin expect such a procedure not only internal to each language, but also cross-linguistically. They make their assumption explicit on p. 293:

Obviously, if these theoretical generalizations [stated in terms of subjects] are to have any validity, it is necessary to give a universal characterization of subjecthood. Therefore, one must provide a methodology by which one can identify that noun phrase which functions as a subject within the grammatical system of a language.

In effect, Foley and Van Valin assume that linguistic theory must provide a discovery procedure for grammars – that is, a mechanical procedure for constructing a grammar. Chomsky's (1957, 56) remarks on this requirement are as applicable to Foley and Van Valin's approach as they were to the approaches he was criticizing:

One may arrive at a grammar by intuition, guess-work, all sorts of partial methodological hints, reliance on past experience, etc. It is no doubt possible to give an organized account of many useful procedures of analysis, but it is questionable whether these can be formulated rigorously, exhaustively, and simply enough to qualify as a practical and mechanical discovery procedure. At any rate, this problem is not within the scope of our investigations here... We are... interested in describing the form of grammars (equivalently, the nature of linguistic structure) and investigating the empirical consequences of adopting a certain model for linguistic structure, rather than in showing how, in principle, one might have arrived at the grammar of a language.

Foley and Van Valin (pp. 318–319) conclude:

If one nevertheless wishes to maintain that subject is a viable universal category, then the burden of proof is on him to show that despite the problems we have exhibited, 'subject' can be defined universally in some way and that significant generalizations can be stated in terms of subjects so defined.

But Foley and Van Valin's two basic assumptions are false. First, the notion of subject does not need to be defined in terms of other notions, because it can be taken as one of the primitive notions of linguistic theory. Second, linguistic theory does not need to provide a mechanical discovery procedure for grammars that would tell the linguist which RNs to assign to sentences of a language. The import of this paper is that if grammatical relations are theoretical primitives and RNs adopted as syntactic representations, it is then possible to state generalizations in a variety of languages in terms of different notions of subjecthood definable in terms of the information represented in RNs. Thus, the approach advocated here does provide a cross-linguistically viable notion of subjecthood in terms of which generalizations can be stated – both internal to individual languages and cross-linguistically. Two examples of cross-linguistic generalizations stated in terms of subjecthood are the 1-Advancement Exclusiveness Law of Perlmutter and Postal (to appear b) and the Final 1 Law of Perlmutter and Postal (to appear a).[25]

10. NOTIONS OF SUBJECT AND SINGLE-LEVEL AND TWO-LEVEL THEORIES OF SYNTAX

The different notions of subject defined and exemplified in §3–7 are possible only if syntactic representations represent grammatical relations at different levels. Thus, evidence for these notions of subject is at the same time evidence for the recognition of multiple levels in syntax. This is of interest because a number of current syntactic frameworks fail to posit more than one syntactic level, while others posit two levels, with the notions represented at the two levels drawn from distinct sets. Frameworks of both types fail to represent subjecthood at more than one level, and therefore fail to capture some of the generalizations brought out in this paper.

The current single-level frameworks can be viewed as reactions to the multiplicity of levels (reconstructed as stages in derivations) posited in transformational grammar. These proposals must be viewed in the light of the overall breakdown in the late 1970s of many of the assumptions of transformational grammar. So many things had simply been assumed by transformationalists without empirical justification that it appeared to many that almost everything could be questioned or rejected with a minimum of argument. Reinforcing this point of view was the fact that work in transformational frameworks had concentrated so heavily on English that many considered it sufficient to show some alternative to be viable for English in order to conclude that it was viable as an overall syntactic theory. The result has been a number of proposals recognizing only one syntactic level for a clause, extensionally close to what has been characterized in this paper as the final stratum. Brame's (1978) base-generated syntax and (1980) "realistic" grammar should probably be regarded as falling in this category. The clearest example of an entirely single-level theory is to be found in Gazdar's paper in this volume. Since these frameworks posit a single syntactic level that is similar to the final stratum posited here, it is unclear how they would account for the data accounted for here by means of the notions of initial 1, 1, acting 1, and working 1. If they are to have any claim to adequacy, these frameworks must face and resolve these problems, making explicit the devices they posit to account for the data and the empirical claims they make about the class of natural languages. Otherwise, the phenomena cited here as evidence for syntactic levels other than the final one constitute *prima facie* evidence against what appears to be the basic empirical claim of these frameworks.

Another type of proposal posits two levels – a level of semantic roles

(Agent, Patient, Experiencer, etc.) or some other "deep" relations, and a syntactic level which may or may not be conceived of in terms of grammatical relations. Such proposals include Filmore's (1968, 1977) case grammar, Anderson's (1971, 1977) localist case grammar, Dik's (1978, 1980) functional grammar, and the "role and reference" grammar of Foley and Van Valin (1977) and Van Valin and Foley (1980), following ideas of Schachter (1977). Very similar in their essential claims about levels are Bresnan's (1978) "realistic transformational grammar", the framework assumed by Andrews (this volume), and Kac's (1978, 1980) "corepresentational grammar." While there are differences among these frameworks, with respect to the concerns of this paper they are alike in positing two levels, with the notions represented at the two levels drawn from two disjoint sets. Crucially, they represent subjecthood only at the second level. Thus, if we can translate the structures a framework of this sort might posit into stratal diagrams, their basic approach can be illustrated through the following structures for the active and passive sentences of Achenese in (123) and (124).

(123)   a. Drɔn ni-pajoh bɔh-mamplam.
              you   2₀-eat   fruit-mango
              'You eat the mango.'

         b.
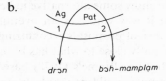

(124)   a. Bɔh-mamplam ni-pajoh le-drɔn.
              fruit-mango   2₀-eat   by-you
              'The mango is eaten by you.'

         b.
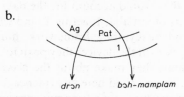

The first level represented in (123) and (124) involves Fillmorean "semantic roles." At this level, *drɔn* is represented as an Agent and *bɔh-mamplam* as a Patient. The roles or relations would be different in some of the frameworks, but the general idea remains the same. The second level in these diagrams is that of grammatical relations. This level represents these frameworks' claim that in (123) *drɔn* is subject and *bɔh-mamplam* direct object, while in (124) *bɔh-mamplam* is subject and *drɔn* is neither subject nor direct object.

The prominence of semantic roles in these frameworks brings out the fact that work in relational grammar has not been explicit about the place of semantic roles in the theory. They have generally been assumed to be an aspect of the semantic representation of sentences, and have therefore not been included in syntactic representations. Thus, (125) would be given as the stratal diagram for (124):

(125)

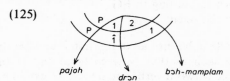

If it were desired to represent semantic roles in syntactic structures, (124) could be represented as the stratal diagram in (126):

(126)

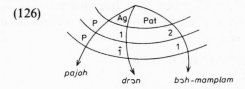

This would require some modifications in the class of R-signs, in the assignment of coordinates, the definition of the notion 'initial,' etc. It therefore seems preferable not to adopt such representations unless there is clear evidence that syntactic rules need to refer to these semantic roles. For comparison with (124), however, the representation in (126) makes the real difference between relational grammar and the frameworks under discussion stand out more clearly:

(127)   Relational grammar posits grammatical relations (1, 2, 3, etc.) *at more than one syntactic level.* The frameworks under discussion do not.

Compare the representation of (124a) in (124b) with that in (125) and (126). The crucial difference for present purposes is that in relational grammar, *drɔn* is represented as an initial 1 and *bɔh-mamplam* as an initial 2, while in the other frameworks under discussion they are not. As a consequence of this basic difference, there are two types of generalizations that are statable in relational grammar, but not in these other frameworks.

The first type are generalizations stated in terms of *initial* grammatical relations. Achenese Verb Agreement, discussed in §4, illustrates this type of generalization. Since these frameworks do not have a notion of initial 1 distinct from final 1, they would have to attempt to state the generalization in terms of semantic roles (Agent, Patient, etc.). Dik (1978, 117) makes this explicit, formulating Achenese Verb Agreement as follows:

> (128)   Agreement in Achenese according to FG:
>   The verb agrees with the Agent.

(128) accounts for most of the data, but not all of it. First, it apparently does not account for contrasts such as that between (46a) and (46b). Presumably a categorial difference between verbs and adjectives would be posited (along the lines discussed in §4) and used to account for such contrasts in agreement. More seriously, (128) does not account for cases where the nominal determining Achenese Verb Agreement is semantically not an Agent, but an Experiencer or Cognizer. Such examples include (39–42), (44c), (44d), and the following, cited by Lawler (1977) (the nominal determining agreement italicized):

> (129)   a. *Gɔpnyan gɨ*-nging anɨ? agam nyan.
>   'He sees the boy.'
>   b. Anɨ? agam nyan *gɨ*-nging le-*gɔpnyan*.
>   'The boy is seen by him.'

Additional examples can be cited:[26]

> (130)   Gɔpnyan gɨ-musulet *gɨ*-rasa le *mahkamah*.
>   'That she lied was felt by the court.'
> (131)   Gɔpnyan *jɨ*-banci le *adɔwə-gɨ*.
>   'She is hated by her younger sibling.'
> (132)   Tɨmpat gɔpnyan *jɨ-pɨ*-rusa? le *pɨkara nyan*.
>   'His position is undermined by that matter.'
> (133)   Bubong nyan *jɨ*-tumpang le *tameh*.
>   'The roof is supported by columns.'
> (134)   Lon *jɨ-pɨ*-ingat gadoh gɔpnyan le *haba*.
>   'I was reminded of his disappearance by a message.'

Thus, frameworks that lack initial grammatical relations distinct from final ones and therefore attempt to state Achenese Verb Agreement in terms of semantic roles cannot use a rule like (128). This rule would have to be replaced by a disjunction of at least three roles:

(135)   The verb agrees with the Agent, Experiencer, or Cognizer.

But even this is not adequate. Additional semantic roles would have to be mentioned to account for examples like (132) and (133). Further, there are contrasts such as the following:

(136)   a. Gɔpnyan gɨ-tɨrɨmon surat.
            'He received a letter.'
         b. Gɔpnyan ka gɨ-bre buku nyan kɨ-kamɔ.
            'He gave the book to us.'

The Recipient gɔpnyan determines agreement in (136a), but in (136b) the Recipient kamɔ does *not* determine agreement. It is not clear how a statement in terms of semantic roles would distinguish between these.

At worst, a statement in terms of semantic roles will not be able to account for the data. At best, it will yield a disjunction of various roles, providing no explanation of why these terms should figure in the disjunction rather than others. The relational grammar formulation in (36), on the other hand, captures the generalization in terms of initial subjecthood.

Language-particular rules such as Achenese Verb Agreement that are stated in terms of initial subjecthood thus illustrate one type of generalization statable in relational grammar but not in frameworks such as Fillmore's, Anderson's, and Dik's, which fail to represent subjecthood at more than one level. The same holds for generalizations in which initial subjecthood is a component part. In this category are generalizations in terms of the notion of working 1 discussed in §7, and the condition on antecedents of Georgian reflexives in (114).

Another type of generalization statable in relational grammar but not in these frameworks are generalizations in terms of the notions 'nominal heading an n-arc' discussed in §5, and those in terms of the notion 'acting term$_x$' discussed in §6. The crucial fact about such generalizations is that they refer to subjecthood, direct objecthood, etc. *at more than one level*. Consider, for example, the condition on antecedents of Russian reflexives in (50). The frameworks in question have a notion extensionally equivalent to the relational grammar notion of final 1, but nominals that are not final 1s are not 1s at any level. Thus, under the analysis these frameworks would provide, there is no generalization uniting the antecedents of reflexives in examples like (60) and (61) with those in the other examples discussed. This matter is discussed in greater detail in Perlmutter (1978b, 1981 to appear d), so it need not detain us here.

In brief, there are two sorts of generalizations statable in relational grammar but not in frameworks that posit two levels with the relations represented at the two levels drawn from disjoint sets.[27] Data such as that cited in this paper shows that grammars must indeed be able to state generalizations of these two types.

This discussion of single-level and two-level theories of syntax has necessarily been brief. Full comparison of these frameworks is a much larger task. In general, one cannot conclude that a given framework cannot state a certain generalization unless one has actually tried to state it in that framework and thereby determined what devices will have to be posited. However, the discussion here, while brief, has focussed on some types of generalizations that are statable under the approach advocated here, and which appear not to be readily statable in frameworks that fail to posit subjecthood at more than one level. In this paper, cases have been cited where levels other than the final stratum are needed to state generalizations in the grammars of twenty different languages. If single-level and two-level theories of syntax are to have any claims to adequacy, their advocates must do two things. First, they must show that these frameworks can state the generalizations in question without loss of generality. Second, they must make explicit the devices they use to do this and the consequences for these frameworks' overall characterization of the class of natural languages.

11. CONCLUSIONS

This paper has argued that linguistic theory needs more than one notion of subject to state rules and generalizations in the grammars of natural languages. The information needed to define the different notions of subject will be present in syntactic representations if they represent at least two things: the primitive grammatical relations that nominals bear to clauses, and the syntactic levels at which they bear them. The entire discussion presupposes two things provided by relational grammar: cross-linguistically viable notions of grammatical relations, and a way of representing distinct syntactic levels. The former are provided by taking grammatical relations as theoretical primitives rather than as notions to be defined in terms of other notions. The latter is provided by the fact that each arc in an RN has a non-null sequence of coordinates, which makes it possible to reconstruct syntactic levels in terms of strata. Thus, the present paper provides motivation for syntactic representation in terms of RNs.[28]

University of California
San Diego

NOTES

* This is a revised version of a paper given at the Conference on the Nature of Syntactic Representation held at Brown University, Providence (Rhode Island) in May 1979. I have benefited from Jane Grimshaw's comments on the paper at the conference and from comments on an earlier draft of this paper by Judith Aissen, Josh Ard, William Davies, Matthew Dryer, Donna Gerdts, Jeanne Gibson, Alice Harris, Terry Klokeid, Stephen Marlett, Paul Postal Eduardo Raposo, Carol Rosen, John Ross, and especially Pauline Jacobson and Geoffrey Pullum. All errors and shortcomings are my own.

This work was supported in part by the National Science Foundation through Grant No. BNS78–17498 to the University of California, San Diego.

[1] For example, see Schachter (1976, 1977), Foley and Van Valin (1977), and Van Valin (1977). See §9.4 below for discussion.

[2] This discussion draws heavily on Perlmutter and Postal (1977, to appear a), and closely follows the presentation in Perlmutter (1980).

[3] Most of the terminology and definitions given here are taken from Perlmutter and Postal (to appear a).

[4] Clause structure can be characterized in terms of four construction types: advancements, ascensions, dummy constructions, and Clause Union.

[5] The treatment here may be an oversimplification in that it ignores the possibility that (18–21) in English and French may be biclausal and involve Raising, with e.g. *the changes* in (18) as final 1 both of the clause whose predicate is *were* and of that whose predicate is *criticized*. For discussion of the periphrastic passives of German and Welsh in these terms, see Perlmutter and Postal (to appear c).

[6] Since the pronoun *gɔpnyan* refers to third persons older than the speaker, it is glossed as 'he,' 'she,' or 'they.' Since many Achenese sentences have no overt indications of tense, the tense varies in English glosses.

[7] Lawler presents a different solution to the problem of Achenese Verb Agreement.

[8] I am indebted to T. Iskandar for this Achenese data.

[9] This also affects some of the conclusions drawn in Perlmutter (1978a) and Perlmutter and Postal (to appear b), where it was assumed that initial unergativity vs. unaccusativity is predictable. If it is not, arguments based on the putative distinction between initially unergative and unaccusative clauses must be supported by language-internal evidence. Needless to say, if initial unergativity vs. unaccusativity cannot be predicted, it is impossible to maintain the broader hypothesis that all initial grammatical relations are predictable.

[10] Harris (1978, 1981) states a rule for Number Agreement determined by third person

nominals in Georgian that at first appears to use the notion 'first 1.' However, closer examination reveals that this is not the case. Harris's rule is:

(i)   The first subject that is a final term determines Number Agreement.

This is empirically distinct from the following:

(ii)   A nominal determines Number Agreement if and only if it:
     a. is the first subject, and
     b. is a final term.

The difference between the two formulations can be seen in Passive constructions, where the advancee from 2 to 1 satisfies (i) but not (ii); (ii) is not satisfied because the initial 1, not the advancee from 2 to 1, is the first 1. And in this construction in Georgian, third person advancees do determine Number Agreement. Thus, given other aspects of Harris's analysis, (i) but not (ii) is the correct formulation.

This is relevant here because (ii) states two conditions, one of which is that the nominal be the 'first 1.' If (ii) were correct, it would thus constitute evidence for the notion 'first 1' in syntax. (i), on the other hand, states a *single condition* in terms of the notion 'first 1 that is a final term.' This is *not* the notion 'first 1.'

Harris (1981, Chapter 15, footnote 7) suggests that the notion 'first 1 that is a final term' may also be needed to state a generalization concerning word order in Georgian.

[11] The condition in (50) does not specify the clause membership of the reflexive or its antecedent. This is left unspecified here because of a class of cases where a reflexive in a complement has its antecedent in the matrix clause. It is not clear at present whether or not a separate rule is needed for such cases. Nonetheless, the condition in (50) holds for both types of cases.

Timberlake (to appear) discusses some cases where the antecedents of Russian reflexives stand in oblique cases, and proposes that "oblique control should be described by hypothesizing one or more axes, each with a set of hierarchized relations, such that the relation of prominence on a secondary axis can, under some circumstances, make up for lack of prominence on the axis of grammatical relations and qualify an oblique to function as the controller." This raises a number of issues which cannot be discussed here. For present purposes, it is sufficient to note that Timberlake does *not* propose abandoning a condition formulated in terms of grammatical relations such as the one in (50).

[12] Speakers' judgments differ with respect to the antecedence of reflexives in Passive clauses in which both the final 1 and the Passive chomeur are plausible antecedents. Compare (58) and (60) with:

(i)   Rebenòk byl otpravlen Annoj k svoim roditeljam.
     'The child was sent by Anna to his/her parents'

For some speakers, such sentences are ambiguous. For others, they are not. The preferred reading is that with the final 1 as antecedent, unless pragmatic factors predispose toward the other reading. The grammars of some speakers will need a statement in addition to (50) to account for such sentences. See Klenin (1974) and Timberlake (to appear) for additional discussion.

Some speakers find sentences with a Passive chomeur as antecedent of a reflexive decidedly worse than other examples. For such speakers, the condition on antecedents of reflexives should perhaps be stated in terms of the notion 'working 1' (cf. §7) instead of the notion in (50).

[13] The RN in (61b) is incomplete, but additional aspects of the structure of this example are beyond the scope of this paper.

[14] The formulation of the condition in Hubbard (1979) is slightly more complex, due to certain assumptions about the analysis of the strong-form reflexive *veten*. The adoption of Rosen's (1981) proposal for the treatment of such forms eliminates this additional complexity.

[15] As Williamson (1979) shows, Lakhota is another language with clauses in which both the notional 1 and notional 2 determine accusative agreement on the verb, e.g.

(i)   i-ni-ma-tą
             2ACC-1ACC-proud
             'I am proud of you'

(The traditional term 'Patient' instead of 'accusative' is misleading because nominals that are not semantically Patients determine this marking on the verb, as in (i).) Williamson further shows that one of these behaves like a subject in that it can be an Equi victim and can determine the third person plural subject clitic *pi*, while the other one behaves like an object in that it can be reflexive and can determine the third person plural object clitic *wička*.

Williamson states: "The analysis for 'double-patient' verbs which is the most satisfactory is one which posits an initial stratum with an initial object and an oblique argument which are obligatorily advanced to subject and object, respectively. This is diagrammed below.

(ii)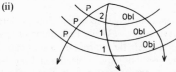

The difficulty of this analysis lies in arguing that the object in these clauses is an initial oblique." (Williamson uses the cover symbol 'Obj' in (ii) because either '2' or '3' would be consistent with her data.)

Alongside (ii), another possible analysis for (i) would be to assign it an Antipassive structure like (67). Under this analysis, the accusative marking rule in Lakhota would be like (68) in Choctaw, using the notion 'nominal heading a 2-arc.' The fact that the first person nominal determines accusative agreement in (i) would be accounted for by virtue of the fact that it heads a 2-arc in the second stratum of a structure like (67). The ability of the second person nominal to be reflexive and to determine the object clitic *wička* would be accounted for by virtue of the fact that it heads a 2-arc in an RN like (67), while the fact that the first person nominal can be an Equi victim and determine the subject clitic *pi* would be accounted for by virtue of the fact that it heads a final 1-arc. This analysis is consistent with all of Williamson's data. If it should prove correct, it would provide another example like that proposed by Davies for Choctaw.

One empirical difference between the analysis suggested by Williamson and the Antipassive analysis concerns the arc headed by the second person nominal in (i) in the final stratum. Under the former analysis, it heads a final 2-arc or 3-arc, while under the Antipassive analysis it heads a final Cho arc. Further reaearch on Lakhota is needed to determine whether there is evidence internal to that language for either of these two analyses.

[16] In this case, the conclusion that (79b) is the correct formulation of the rule is underdetermined by the data. Given only this data, the rule for nominative case marking in Maasai could just as well be stated in terms of the notion 'initial 1' discussed in §4, or that of 'nominal heading a 1-arc' discussed in §5. We return to these alternatives below.

[17] Tucker and Mpaayei (1955, 177) cite *enkalém* as the nominative form and *enkálém* as the accusative form. The accusative form can be seen in:

(i)   á-dúng-í-é enkálém (Tucker and Mpaayei, 142)
        'I cut it with a knife.'

in which *enkálém* has advanced from Instrument to 2 and is consequently a final 2.

[18] Davies (1980) uses data of precisely this kind to argue for rules stated in terms of this notion in the grammar of Choctaw.

[19] This argument was pointed out to me by Carol Rosen.

[20] The expression *rompersi le scatole* 'to get fed up' necessarily includes a reflexive clitic agreeing in person and number with the subject of the clause. Thus, if *la mamma* is controller of the consecutive *da* + infinitive construction and hence subject of the complement, the reflexive clitic is the third person form *si*, while if the first person singular nominal is the controller, the reflexive clitic will have the first person singular (reflexive) form *mi*.

[21] If *la mamma* were controller, the reflexive clitic in the complement would have the third person form *si* (cf. fn. 19).

[22] For evidence for Inversion in Georgian, see Harris (1976, 1981, to appear b).

[23] For a critique of Keenan's approach, see Johnson (1977).

[24] For a more detailed refutation of Schachter's arguments, based on Philippine language data, see Bell (1976, to appear). There is additional discussion in Perlmutter (1978b, to appear d).

[25] It has sometimes been claimed that because some languages have ergative-absolutive morphological systems, these languages do not have subjects. While limitations of space prevent a discussion of ergativity here, the crucial fact is that in the typical case, a grammar has rules referring to both absolutivity/ergativity and subjecthood/direct objecthood. Linguistic theory must therefore provide grammars with the means of stating both types of rules. Syntactic representations in terms of RNs do just that. Ergativity and absolutivity depend on transitivity, and a given clause can be transitive at one level and intransitive at another. Thus, one cannot speak of transitivity or intransitivity of *clauses*, but only of *strata*. The relevant notions can be defined as follows:

(i)   a. A stratum S_i of a clause node is *transitive* if and only if it contains both a 1-arc
           and a 2-arc.
        b. A stratum S_i of a clause node is *intransitive* if and only if it is not transitive.

(ii)   a. An arc A is an Erg arc in stratum S_i if and only if A is a 1-arc and S_i is
           transitive.
        b. An arc A is an Abs arc in stratum S_i if and only if:
           i) A is a nuclear term arc, and
           ii) A is not an Erg arc in S_i.

Just as some rules refer to the notions 'initial 1,' 'final 1,' etc., others refer to 'initial Erg,' 'final Erg,' 'final Abs,' etc. Thus the existence of rules referring to both sets of notions does not invalidate the universality of subjects. On the contrary, RNs including 1-arcs, 2-arcs, etc. make it possible to account for the fact that languages typically have both rules referring to absolutivity and/or ergativity, and rules referring to subjecthood and/or direct objecthood.

[26] These examples are taken from Perlmutter (1981), where it is argued that Achenese Verb Agreement cannot be stated in terms of the semantic functions posited in Dik's (1978) functional grammar. I am indebted to T. Iskandar and T. Hoekstra for the Achenese data.

[27] There are also other types of generalizations statable in relational grammar but not in these frameworks, but such generalizations are beyond the scope of this paper.

Some of these frameworks also rely on definitions of grammatical relations in terms of phrase structure configurations, case marking, or other notions. On the inadequacy of such proposals, cf. Johnson (1979), Klokeid (1980), and Perlmutter (to appear c).

[28] This paper has argued primarily for the representation of distinct syntactic levels, rather than for the representation of grammatical relations. However, none of the cross-linguistic comparison undertaken here would be possible without syntactic representation in terms of grammatical relations. For example, it would not be possible to compare different languages' conditions on the antecedents of reflexives in the way undertaken here. For a summary of arguments that grammatical relations cannot be defined in terms of phrase structure configurations or case, cf. Perlmutter (to appear c).

REFERENCES

Allen, Barbara J. (to appear) 'Goal Advancement in Southern Tiwa.'

Allen, Barbara J. and Donald G. Frantz (1978) 'Verb Agreement in Southern Tiwa.' *Proceedings of the Fourth Annual Meeting of the Berkeley Linguistics Society* (University of California, Berkeley). Revised version in Perlmutter (ed.) (to appear a).

Allen, Barbara J., Donald G. Frantz, Donna B. Gardiner, and David M. Perlmutter (to appear) 'Possessor Ascension and Syntactic Levels in Southern Tiwa.'

Allen, Barbara J. and Donna B. Gardiner (1977) 'Noun Incorporation in Isleta,' *Work Papers of the Summer Institute of Linguistics, University of North Dakota*, Vol. 21.

Anderson, John M. (1971) *The Grammar of Case*, Cambridge University Press, Cambridge, London, New York, and Melbourne.

Anderson, John M. (1977) *On Case Grammar*, Croom Helm, London and Humanities Press, Atlantic Highlands, N.J.

Andrews, Avery D. (1971) 'Case Agreement of Predicate Modifiers in Ancient Greek,' *Linguistic Inquiry* 2, 127–151.

Andrews, Avery D. (this volume) 'Long Distance Agreement in Icelandic.'

Bell, Sarah J. (1974) 'Two Consequences of Advancement Rules in Cebuano,' *Papers from the Fifth Annual Meeting of the North Eastern Linguistic Society* (Harvard University, Cambridge).

Bell, Sarah J. (1976) *Cebuano Subjects in Two Frameworks,* Unpublished doctoral dissertation, MIT. Available from Indiana University Linguistics Club.

Bell, Sarah J. (to appear) 'Advancements and Ascensions in Cebuano,' in Perlmutter (ed.) (to appear a).

Brame, Michael K. (1978) *Base-Generated Syntax*, Noit Amrofer, Seattle.

Brame, Michael K. (1980) 'Realistic Grammar,' in Michael K. Brame, *Essays toward Realistic Syntax*, Noit Amrofer, Seattle.

Bresnan, Joan (1978) 'A Realistic Transformational Grammar,' in Morris Halle, Joan Bresnan, and George A. Miller (eds.) *Linguistic Theory and Psychological Reality*, MIT Press, Cambridge and London.

Chomsky, Noam (1957) *Syntactic Structures*, Mouton and Co., The Hague.

Chomsky, Noam (1965) *Aspects of the Theory of Syntax*, MIT Press, Cambridge and London.

Chomsky, Noam (1977) 'On WH-Movement,' in Culicover, Wasow, and Akmajian (eds.) (1977).

Chvany, Catherine (1975) *On the Syntax of BE-Sentences in Russian*, Slavica Publishers, Cambridge.

Cole, Peter and Jerrold M. Sadock (eds.) (1977) *Syntax and Semantics 8: Grammatical Relations*, Academic Press, New York, San Francisco, and London.

Culicover, Peter W., Thomas Wasow, and Adrian Akmajian (eds.) (1977) *Formal Syntax*, Academic Press, New York, San Francisco, and London.

Davies, William D. (1980) 'Inversion in Choctaw,' Unpublished paper, University of California, San Diego.

Davies, William (1981) 'Choctaw Subjects and Multiple Levels of Syntax,' in Hoekstra, van der Hulst, and Moortgat (eds.) (1981).

Davies, William D. (to appear) 'Antipassive: Choctaw Evidence for a Universal Characterization,' in Perlmutter (ed.) (to appear a).

Dik, Simon (1978) *Functional Grammar*, North-Holland Publishing Co., Amsterdam, New York, and Oxford.

Dik, Simon (1980) 'Seventeen Sentences: Basic Principles and Application of Functional Grammar,' in Moravcsik and Wirth (eds.) (1980).

Fillmore, Charles J. (1968) 'The Case for Case,' in Emmon Bach and Robert T. Harms (eds.) *Universals in Linguistic Theory*, Holt, Rinehart, and Winston, New York.

Fillmore, Charles J. (1977) 'The Case for Case Reopened,' in Cole and Sadock (eds.) (1977).

Foley, William A. and Robert D. Van Valin (1977) 'On the Viability of the Notion of "Subject" in Universal Grammar,' *Proceedings of the Third Annual Meeting of the Berkeley Linguistics Society* (University of California, Berkeley).

Gazdar, Gerald (this volume) 'Phrase Structure Grammar.'

Gerdts, Donna (1980) 'Causal-to-Object Advancement in Halkomelem,' *Papers from the Sixteenth Regional Meeting of the Chicago Linguistic Society* (University of Chicago, Chicago).

Hale, Kenneth, LaVerne Masayesva Jeanne, and Paul Platero (1977) 'Three Cases of Overgeneration,' in Culicover, Wasow, and Akmajian (eds.) (1977).

Harris, Alice C. (1976) *Grammatical Relations in Modern Georgian*, Unpublished doctoral dissertation, Harvard University, Cambridge.

Harris, Alice C. (1978) 'Number Agreement in Modern Georgian,' *International Review of Slavic Linguistics* 3, 75–98 (*The Classification of Grammatical Categories*, ed. by Bernard Comrie).

Harris, Alice C. (1981) *Georgian Syntax: A Study in Relational Grammar*, Cambridge University Press, Cambridge, London, New York, and Melbourne.

Harris, Alice C. (to appear a) 'Case Marking, Verb Agreement, and Inversion in Udi,' in Perlmutter (ed.) (to appear a).

Harris, Alice C. (to appear b) 'Inversion as a Rule of Universal Grammar: Georgian Evidence,' in Perlmutter (ed.) (to appear a).

Hoekstra, Teun, Harry van der Hulst, and Michael Moortgat (eds.) (1981) *Perspectives on Functional Grammar*, Foris Publications, Dordrecht.

Hubbard, Philip L. (1979) 'Albanian Neapolitan Morphology: Passive, Multi-Attachment, and the Unaccusative Hypothesis,' *Linguistic Notes from La Jolla*, No. 6 (University of California, San Diego).

Hubbard, Philip L. (1980) *The Syntax of the Albanian Verb Complex* (Doctoral dissertation, University of California, San Diego).

Johnson, David E. (1977) 'On Keenan's Definition of "Subject of,"' *Linguistic Inquiry* 8, 673–692.

Johnson, David E. (1979) *Toward a Relationally-Based Theory of Grammar*, Garland Publishing Co., New York.

Kac, Michael (1978) *Corepresentation of Grammatical Structure*, University of Minnesota Press, Minneapolis.

Kac, Michael (1980) 'Corepresentational Grammar,' in Moravcsik and Wirth (1980).

Keenan, Edward L. (1976) 'Towards a Universal Definition of "Subject,"' in Li (1976).

Klenin, Emily R. (1974) *Russian Reflexive Pronouns and the Semantic Roles of Noun Phrases in Sentences*, Unpublished doctoral dissertation, Princeton University, Princeton.

Klokeid, Terry J. (1980) 'On Defining Grammatical Relations in Wakashan Languages.' Presented at annual meeting of the Canadian Linguistic Association, Montreal, June 1980.

Klokeid, Terry J. (to appear) 'Multiple Levels in Syntax: Evidence from Nitinaht.'

Lawler, John M. (1977) '*A* Agrees with *B* in Achenese: A Problem for Relational Grammar,' in Cole and Sadock (eds.) (1977).

Li, Charles N. (ed.) (1976) *Subject and Topic*, Academic Press, New York, San Francisco, and London.

Marlett, Stephen A. (to appear) 'Personal and Impersonal Passives in Seri,' in Perlmutter (ed.) (to appear a).

McCawley, Noriko (1976) 'Reflexivization: A Transformational Approach,' in Masayoshi Shibatani (ed.) *Syntax and Semantics 5: Japanese Generative Grammar*, Academic Press, New York.

Moravcsik, Edith and Jessica Wirth (eds.) (1980) *Syntax and Semantics 13; Current Approaches to Syntax*, Academic Press, New York, San Francisco, and London.

Özkaragöz, Inci (1980) 'Evidence from Turkish for the Unaccusative Hypothesis,' *Proceedings of the Sixth Annual Meeting of the Berkeley Linguistics Society* (University of California, Berkeley).

Perlmutter, David M. (1978a) 'Impersonal Passives and the Unaccusative Hypothesis,' *Proceedings of the Fourth Annual Meeting of the Berkeley Linguistics Society* (University of California, Berkeley).

Perlmutter, David M. (1978b) 'Emprical Evidence Distinguishing Some Current Approaches to Syntax,' Colloquium lecture presented at the annual meeting of the Linguistic Society of America, Boston.

Perlmutter, David M. (1979) 'Working 1s and Inversion in Italian, Japanese, and Quechua,' *Proceedings of the Fifth Annual Meeting of the Berkeley Linguistics Society* (University of California, Berkeley),

Perlmutter, David M. (1980) 'Relational Grammar,' in Moravcsik and Wirth (eds.) (1980).

Perlmutter, David M. (1981) 'Functional Grammar and Relational Grammar: Points of Convergence and Divergence,' in Hoekstra, van der Hulst, and Moortgat (eds.) (1981).

Perlmutter, David M. (ed.) (to appear a) *Studies in Relational Grammar*, University of Chicago Press, Chicago.

Perlmutter, David M. (to appear b) 'Evidence for Inversion in Russian and Kannada,' in Perlmutter (ed.) (to appear a).

Perlmutter, David M. (to appear c) 'Grammatical Relations as Primitives of Linguistic Theory.'

Perlmutter, David M. (to appear d) 'The Inadequacy of Some Monostratal Theories of Passivization,' in Perlmutter (ed.) (to appear a).

Perlmutter, David M. (to appear e) 'Possessor Ascension and Some Relational Laws.'

Perlmutter, David M. (in preparation) 'Multiattachment and the Unaccusative Hypothesis: The Perfect Auxiliary in Italian.'

Perlmutter, David M. and Paul M. Postal (1974) Lectures on Relational Grammar, Summer Linguistic Institute of the Linguistic Society of America, University of Massachusetts, Amherst.

Perlmutter, David M. and Paul M. Postal (1977) 'Toward a Universal Characterization of Passivization,' Proceedings of the Third Annual Meeting of the Berkeley Linguistics Society (University of California, Berkeley).

Perlmutter, David M. and Paul M. Postal (to appear a) 'Some Proposed Laws of Basic Clause Structure,' in Perlmutter (ed.) (to appear a).

Perlmutter, David M. and Paul M. Postal (to appear b) 'The 1-Advancement Exclusiveness Law,' in Perlmutter (ed.) (to appear a).

Perlmutter, David M. and Paul M. Postal (to appear c) 'Impersonal Passives and Some Relational Laws,' in Perlmutter (ed.) (to appear a).

Peškovskij, Aleksandr M. (1956) Russkij sintaksis v naučnom osvescěnii,[7] Gosudarstvennoe učebno-pedagogičeskoe izdatel'stvo Ministerstva Prosveščenija RSFSR, Moskva.

Postal, Paul M. (1977) 'Antipassive in French,' Lingvisticæ Investigationes 1, 333–374.

Postal, Paul M. (this volume) 'Some Arc Pair Grammar Descriptions.'

Raposo, Eduardo (in preparation) 'The Interaction of Clause Union and SE-Reflexivization in Romance.'

Rosen, Carol (1981) The Relational Structure of Reflexive Clauses: Evidence from Italian. (Doctoral dissertation, Harvard University).

Schachter, Paul (1976) 'The Subject in Philippine Languages: Topic, Actor, Actor-Topic, or None of the Above?' in Li (ed.) (1976).

Schachter, Paul (1977) 'Reference-Related and Role-Related Properties of Subjects,' in Cole and Sadock (eds.) (1977).

Steele, Susan (1977) 'On Being Possessed,' Proceedings of the Third Annual Meeting of the Berkeley Linguistics Society (University of California, Berkeley).

Timberlake, Alan (1979) 'Reflexivization and the Cycle in Russian,' Linguistic Inquiry 10, 109–141.

Timberlake, Alan (to appear) 'Oblique Control of Russian Reflexivization,' in Catherine Chvany (ed.) Studies in Slavic Syntax.

Tohsaku, Yasu-Hiko (in preparation) 'Impersonal Passives in Ainu.'

Tucker, A. N. and J. Tompo Ole Mpaayei (1955) A Maasai Grammar, Longmans Green and Co., London.

Van Valin, Robert D. (1977) 'Ergativity and the Universality of Subjects,' Papers from the Thirteenth Regional Meeting of the Chicago Linguistic Society (University of Chicago, Chicago).

Van Valin, Robert D. and William A. Foley (1980) 'Role and Reference Grammar,' in Moravcsik and Wirth (eds.) (1980).

Williamson, Janis (1979) 'Patient Marking in Lakhota and the Unaccusative Hypothesis,' Papers from the Fifteenth Regional Meeting of the Chicago Linguistic Society (University of Chicago, Chicago).

PAUL M. POSTAL

SOME ARC PAIR GRAMMAR DESCRIPTIONS

1. BACKGROUND AND GOALS

The goal of this paper[1] is to illustrate something of the approach to grammatical theory and description made possible by the framework of *arc pair grammar* (henceforth: APG) as described in Johnson and Postal (to appear). This framework is not easy to discuss currently because its conceptions of the two basic aspects of grammatical theory, the nature of sentences and the nature of grammars, are novel. The APG conception of *sentence* is an outgrowth of previous ideas in relational grammar. Nonetheless, it contains many unique elements and the previous ideas have been extensively reinterpreted and embedded in a richer and more extensive framework. The APG conception of grammars is entirely novel. It would be misleading to speak about sentences without saying something about grammars, so I shall begin by saying a little about the view of grammar and grammatical rule inherent to the APG framework. Then I illustrate how this conception applies to an actual range of problems. The idea is to show how this framework makes available novel and otherwise unavailable hypotheses about grammatical structure, of a type currently unknown to grammatical discussions.

One can think of a natural language as a pair of a *grammar* and a set of sentences called a *corpus*. The goal of grammatical theory is to characterize the class of natural languages. The theory contains a set of laws, of which we will focus on the major category, namely, *sentence laws*. It also contains a formal definition of its reconstruction of the notion *sentence*, called a *pair network*. Grammars are regarded as sets of statements, that is, formulae with truth values. These statements are the grammatical rules. The logical character of these rules is exactly that of sentence laws except for two differences. Rules, unlike sentence laws, which hold for the sentences of all natural languages, hold only for the sentences of those individual languages whose grammars contain them. Second, rules must be constructed from a fixed theoretical vocabulary (beyond the logical vocabulary), whereas laws are subject to no such constraint (since the theory provides an exhaustive listing of *all* the laws).

341

P. Jacobson and G. K. Pullum (eds.), The Nature of Syntactic Representation, 341–425.
Copyright © 1982 *by D. Reidel Publishing Company.*

Grammaticality in APG can be reduced to the truth of certain statements. Suppose the grammar of some language L consists of a set of statements G(L). Take some arbitrary object, O, a carrot, a sentence-like abstract object, an atom, a symphony, or what not. O is a sentence in L if and only if: (i) O satisfies the definition of 'Pair Network' provided by the theory as its reconstruction of the notion *sentence* and (ii) all of the sentence laws evaluate as true with respect to O (O satisfies all the sentence laws) and (iii) each rule in G(L) evaluates as true with respect to O.

Looked at in this way, every object which satisfies the definition of 'Pair Network' and satisfies all the sentence laws is a sentence of L *unless* there is some rule in the grammar of L which evaluates as false for that object. Thus, the function of the rules of a grammar is to pick a subset from the a priori given class of all natural language sentences, i.e. from the set of objects which satisfy both the definition of 'Pair Network' and all of the sentence laws. In this view, grammatical rules never state that something is well-formed, only that various a priori possibilities are ill-formed.

Thus in APG rules are not, as they seem always to have been in the generative linguistics of the past, operations on, or mappings between, linguistic structures. Rules are just laws with a limited (one language) domain. Rules do not 'apply'; there can then be no question of the order of their application, cycles, etc. There is no contrast between optional and obligatory rules. Rules, being material implications, express necessary conditions on sentencehood. The principles which control the interaction of distinct rules, and between rules and laws, are simply those of logic. There are no components, no lexicon, and none of the kinds of things found in other linguistics: base rules, transformations, interpretive rules, etc. Every rule is a material implication expressing some condition on sentencehood.

One final note. Past generative linguistics has assumed without argument that the way to characterize languages is to state constraints on the nature of rules and grammars. It has had very little to say about sentences *directly*. But the view developed in APG terms is that most of what we know about language can (and should) be expressed in the form of laws about sentences and that it is at least possible that there are no real constraints on rules beyond those manifest in the definition and function of rules I have already sketched. This approach is taken in Johnson and Postal (to appear), where over one hundred laws governing pair networks are formally stated.

There it is shown in a number of cases why it is unnecessary to say anything specific about rules to eliminate impossible situations, given a rich set of laws precluding certain kinds of things as sentences. The only proviso necessary is that there are also probably laws which quantify over corpora. But space preclude any discussion of that here.

To make this account a little more concrete, consider passivization. Whatever this is, it is a possibility for some natural languages and therefore the structure of passives is such as to not violate any sentence laws. Thus passive clauses are a memebr of the set of a priori possible sentences. To the extent that a language has passive structures freely, no rules whatever are then needed to describe them. But limitations on passivization found in one language but not in another must result from language-particular rules. The ultimate limitation in this domain would be a statement blocking all passivization, which may exist in languages like, e.g., Walbiri. All of the rules discussed in the body of this paper are, then, designed to rule out universal possibilities found in some natural languages but not in that whose corpus is described by the grammar containing them.

In what follows, I will apply this framework initially to some facts about indirect objects in English and French and then extend the discussion to propose a hypothesis to explain some mysterious facts about a construction in French. The overall goal is to illustrate how this novel way of looking at sentences and grammars can be applied to the description of some difficult facts into which past linguistics has not been able to provide much insight.

2. RESTRICTIONS ON THE ADVANCEMENT AND NON-ADVANCEMENT OF 3's TO 2

We can begin by considering (1):

(1)   a Melvin gave the tomato to Joanne.
        b. Melvin gave Joanne the tomato.

Such sentences have, of course, been much discussed in the transformational literature under the assumption that (1b) involved application of a transformation called Dative Movement. In the present framework, (1a, b) would have the respective partial representations in (2a, b).

The diagrams in (2) represent objects called *pair networks*, which are the APG reconstruction of sentence. A pair network consists essentially of two

(2)   a.

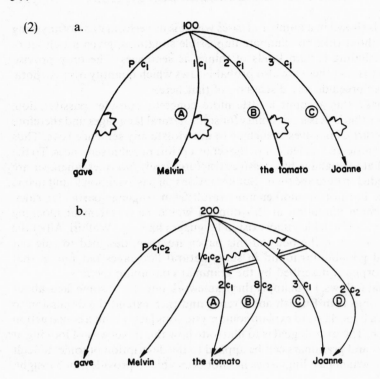

c. Relational Sign (Elements   Grammatical Relation
   of the Formalism)   Names (Elements of Natural
                                     Language)

1	the *subject* relation (holds between nominal nodes and clause nodes)
2	the *direct object* relation (holds between nominal nodes and clause nodes)
3	the *indirect object* relation (holds between nominal nodes and clause nodes).

(Contd.)

(*Contd.*)

c. Relational Sign (Elements of the Formalism)	Grammatical Relation Names (Elements of Natural Language)
8	the *chômeur* relation (holds between nominal nodes and clause nodes)
P	the *predicate* relation
F	the *flag* relation
Marq	the *marquee* relation
L	the *labels* relation
Stem	the *stem* relation
Cli	the *clitic of* relation
U	the *union* relation (holds between predicate of lower clause and a higher clause)

primitive relations *sponsor* and *erase*, holding between defined objects called *arcs*. The sponsor relation is represented by the wavy arrows, the erase relation by the double shafted arrows. Every arc in a pair network must have a sponsor. Arcs, which are in effect enriched, directed lines from ordinary graph-theoretic work, represent grammatical relations holding between the *nodes* which form their heads and tails. The nodes, which are of various types (logical nodes, grammatical category nodes, phonological nodes, non-terminal nodes), represent every type of linguistic element. The *R-(elational) signs* occurring on arcs indicate what relation the arc represents. The *coordinates* (c_n) represent various levels of the tail node of the arc containing them. Coordinates permit a reconstruction of the notion 'level' in terms of the precise concept *stratum*. Roughly, the c_kth stratum of node a consists of all and only the arcs with tail a one of whose coordinates is c_k.

Associated with each pair network are three graphs, which are simply sets of arcs meeting certain conditions. These are the *R-graph*, which consists of all the arcs which are arguments of sponsor and erase; the *L-graph*, which consists of all and only the arcs which sponsor themselves and the *S-graph*, which consists of all and only those arcs which are *not* erased (diagrammatically, those *not* at the heads of double-shafted arrows). It is claimed that L-graphs represent the meaning of sentences; S-graphs represent roughly their superficial forms (ignoring phonology). The erase relation functions essentially to determine S-graphs.

Returning to (2), (2a) is oversimplified in ignoring the structure relevant to the existence of the prepositional phrase; this structure is considered in detail in Johnson and Postal (to appear: Chapter 13). In what follows, I ignore prepositions. The key difference between (2a, b) independent of the preposition is that in the latter the 3 arc has a 2 arc *local successor* D.[2] Informally, I will say in such a case that the 3 (that is, the node which is the head of the 3 arc) *advances* to 2.[3] The various R-signs occurring on the arcs, indicating what relations they represent, in these structures and those to follow, are given in (2c). As can be seen, some are traditional, some derive from work in relational grammar (cf. Perlmutter and Postal (to appear a, to appear b, to appear c)), and several are unique to APG work. Thus, whereas *Joanne* is a 3 at the first level of node 100, it is a 2 at the second level.[4] Concomitantly, A, a 2 arc, has an 8 arc local successor and thus *the tomato* is a chômeur at the second level of 100. The difference in word order between (2a, b) is a function of general principles of clausal ordering *for English*, indicated highly informally by the sequence in (3).

(3) $(1)^\frown P^\frown(2)^\frown(3)^\frown(8)$

This is relevant for *surface arcs*, that is, those without erasers. The order in (2a, b) is thus a function of the fact that surface 2s precede both surface 3s and surface chômeurs in English.[5]

Internal to the APG framework, no English rules are necessary to permit structures like (2b); there is no analogue of the transformation Dative Movement. At the same time, (1b) is assigned the same initial relations as (1a), these relations being those of semantic relevance. Various laws guarantee that all arcs which sponsor themselves have the first coordinate c_1 and conversely; these are *the initial arcs*. Given this, I have simplified all diagrams to omit representation of self-sponsorship, which can be 'read off' from the presence of a c_1. The reason no rule is needed is that neither (2a) nor (2b) violates any sentence laws and hence both will be well formed in any language lacking rules to block them.

On the other hand, if there were verbs occurring in structures like (2a) but not in those like (2b), rules would be necessary, as they would be in the case where verbs occur only in (2b) style structures. Both such situations are, as we will see, known in English, and cross-linguistically.

I make a rather strong, if so far unformalized, claim relevant to this discussion. Namely, I assume that for a verb with fixed meaning, M, the initial clause arcs which can cooccur with a P arc whose head corresponds to M, are universally determined and in a unique way.[6] Thus for a verb meaning, e.g., 'sell', there will always be an initial 1 arc, an initial 2 arc, and an initial 3 arc, and, moreover, the head of the 1 arc will always represent the so-called agent, the head of the 2 arc the object sold and the head of the 3 arc the entities doing the buying.

To see a little more clearly what this informal hypothesis, call it the Principle of Initial Determination (PID), means, consider (4):

(4)   a. Peter told Mary that Jacques would come.
          b. French:
               Pierre a dit à Marie que Jacques viendrait.
               to

Since the occurrences of *tell* and *dire* in the paraphrases in (4) have, as far as can be determined, the same meaning, the hypothesis about initial arcs comes into play. Consider the status of the *semantically* parallel nominals *Mary/Marie*. Factors internal to English leave little doubt that *Mary* in (4a) behaves superficially as a 2 (it passivizes: *Mary was told that Jacques would come*, does not take the preposition *to*, occurs directly post-verbally, etc. On the contrary, considerations internal to French leave little doubt that *Marie* in (4b) behaves superficially as a 3. *Marie* cannot be the 1 of a passive clause corresponding to (4b): **Marie a été dit(e) que Jacques viendrait*; *Marie* is marked with the preposition *à* typical of output 3s in French, and the sentence corresponding to (4b) with the recipient of the telling represented by a pronoun involves a *dative* clitic (italicized):

(5)   Pierre *lui* a dit que Jacques viendrait.

Thus (4a, b) differ at least partly in *superficial* clausal relations. But PID requires that they have isomorphic initial arcs. The nominals *Mary/Marie* must head initial arcs of the same type in both (4a, b).

The possibilities would seem to be that these nominals head initial 3 arcs in both or initial 2 arcs in both. If both nominals are initial 3s, one needs to say for English that (4a) involves advancement of the 3 to 2, while if one took both to be initial 2s, one would have to speak of demotion of a 2 to a 3 in French. Since English allows many cases of advancement of 3s to 2 (cf. (1)) the initial 3 hypothesis is more plausible. Moreover, it is consistent with the fact that in other sentences, like (6), the recipient of an act of telling shows up superficially as a 3; in these cases, French *dire* and English *tell* occur in structures which are even *superficially* parallel:

(6)   a. I told that to John.
          b. J'ai dit ça á Jean.

Further, it is well known that, in French, 3s in general do not advance to 2,[7] so that the absence of an example like (7) with *Marie* a superficial 2 alongside (4b) can be taken as a general fact rather than as an ad hoc limitation on *dire*.

(7)   *J' ai dit Marie que Jacques   viendrait.
           I   told   Marie that Jacques come would.

Finally, taking the 'recipient' to be initial 3 in both cases permits the nominal representing the thing told to be initial 2 in both cases. This type of analysis is independently attested in other sentences with the same verb even in English, e.g., in (6a). Overall then, it seems correct in current terms to assume that both *Marie/Mary* are initial 3s in (4a, b), and hence that (4a) involves advancement of a 3 to a 2.

In APG terms, no rule is needed to permit this advancement, just as none was required to allow (1b). However, rules are necessary to guarantee inter alia both (8a, b):

(8)   a. There is no analogue in French of (4b) with *Marie* head of a local successor 2 arc, e.g., *(7).
          b. There is no analogue in English of (4a) with *Mary* head of an output 3 arc (*Peter told to Mary that Jacques would come.).

Given what is often said about French, one might take it to be a language precluding any advancement of 3s to 2, that is, one having the rule in (9), or some rule that subsumes it. (In this and all following rules and definitions, *universal* quantifiers are suppressed.):

(9)   Local Successor (A, B) → Not (2–3 Local Successor (A, B))
          "If A is a local successor of B, it is not the case that A is a 2 arc and B a 3 arc."

However, while there may be languages having (9), French is not really one of them. A certain number of French verbal elements permit advancement of 3s to 2 (others mentioned below *require* this). Among those permitting such advancement are, for at least some speakers,[8] *fournir* 'to furnish, supply'[9]:

(10)   a. Le gouvernement a   fourni des uniformes aux   troupes.
           the government   has furnished uniforms to the troops

       b. Le gouvernment a fourni les troupes $\begin{cases} \text{d'uniformes} \\ \text{avec des uniformes} \end{cases}$.
                          the troops with   uniformes

Such cases are quite parallel to English (1), except that, as seen below, there is an unusual argument internal to French supporting the conclusion forced by PID that *les troupes* in (10b) cannot be an initial 2.

   The relevant rule for French must thus be less general than (9), and is probably along the lines of (11b):

(11)   a. Informally, we say that *V-Stemmed* (a, b) if and only if the nodes instantiating *a, b* occur in an R-graph configuration of the form (coordinates suppressed):

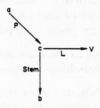

In this case, *a* is a node representing a clause, *c* a node representing a full verb.

       b. French Rule 1

       Tail 2–3 Local Successor (a, A, B) →

          $(\exists b)\left(\text{V-Stemmed (a, b)} \wedge b \in \left\{ \begin{array}{c} \text{fourn (ir)} \\ \vdots \end{array} \right\} \right)$

       "If arc A with tail node *a* is a local successor of B, and A is a 2 arc and B is a 3 arc, then *a* is V-stemmed by *fourn*, or by...."

Under the assumption that *dire*, like most French stems which permit 3s at all, is *not* in the stem set indicated in (11b), (11b) guarantees (8a) while allowing (10b) (with a structure analogous to (2b)).

   The analysis of (10b) as involving advancement of a 3 to 2 is to a significant extent forced by PID. For, given the meaning relations between pairs like (10a, b), that principle requires such clauses to have isomorphic initial relations. It would not allow taking *les troupes* to head an *initial* 2 arc in (10b), given that this is not a plausible analysis for (*à*) + *les troupes*[10] in (10a). Since, in APG terms, there is no such thing as a lexicon, there is no principled difference between rules like (9), which mention no particular lexical items, and less general rules like (11b), which do. A language whose grammar contains (9) blocks all advancement of 3s to 2, or, in other terms, has a completely unproductive 3 to 2 advancement construction. French, having (11b), (more precisely, various versions of (11b) for different speakers depending on the stem-list that governs advancement of 3s for them) has an extremely unproductive construction of this type, limited to just the verbs ultimately to be properly listed in (11b). Other languages may have fully productive constructions of the relevant sort, freely allowing pairs like (1a, b), (10a, b) for all verbs taking 3s. Such languages lack rules limiting 2 arc local successors for 3 arcs to any particular contexts.

English is intermediate between French and such languages, if they exist, allowing more advancement of 3s to 2 than French, but still having many restrictions. For example, it is well-known that such advancement is not possible with verbs like *donate, explain, prove,* and many others:

(12)   a. I donated my diamonds to the local church.
         b. *I donated the local church my diamonds.

Nothing precludes a language which is, in a sense, opposite to one with a rule like (9). A language with (9) in its grammar allows no advancement of 3s to 2. The opposite would be a language requiring all 3s to advance to 2. Such languages probably exist. Although there are typically certain complications involving unspecified 3s and a few others, in the languages I am referring to, earlier 3s (initial or not) will never show up as superficial 3s, which do not exist. 3s will in general advance to 2 and show up as 2s'(barring passivization, etc.). Mohawk, a Northern Iroquoian language, is, I think, a language like this. Without going into details, the considerations suggesting such a treatment are these:[11]

(13)   a. Mohawk verbs object-agree with final stratum 2s.
         b. The noun stems of the heads of *initial* 2 arcs can have doubles ('can be incorporated') in the verbs of their clauses.
         c. Thus the verb in a standard transitive clause with incorporation will object-agree with the nominal whose stem is incorporated (e.g., schematically:

> *I* [*I-it-house-cleaned*] *big house* = 'I cleaned the big
> house';
>
> *I* [*I-him-indian-like*] *big indian* = 'I like the big indian
> (male)'

d. But in ditransitive clauses (those taking initial 3s or those
   taking benefactives, etc., which advance to 3) a Mohawk
   verb object-agrees with the initial 3, benefactive, etc., although only the notional 2 permits incorporation
   (schematically:

> *I* [*I-him(*it)-house-sold*] *John big house* = 'I sold the big
> house to John').

While the facts in (13d) might be described in an ad hoc way unique to
Mohawk, e.g., by stating the agreement rule in such a way that a verb
object-agrees with a 2 only if there is no 3 (at the relevant level)[12] and with a
3 otherwise, they follow naturally from the generalizations in (13a–c) with
no complication of the agreement rule if one assumes Mohawk has a rule
requiring almost[13] all 3s to advance to 2, predicting that these 3s will
behave like superficial 2s (cf. the agreement facts in (13d)) but not like initial
2s (cf. the incorporation facts in (13d)). This same rule will account for the
fact independent of agreement that there is no motivation for recognizing
any *superficial* 3s in Mohawk. Another case of a language where in general a
3 is not permitted to show up as an output 3 has been described by Aissen
(to appear a, to appear b) for the Mayan language Tzotzil.

Return now to the unexplained fact that advancement of 3s to 2 is in some
cases required with *tell*, e.g., that *(8b), repeated as (14), is ill-formed:

(14)   = (8b) *Peter told to Mary that Jacques would come.

This is not an across-the-board requirement on *tell* clauses, since one finds
both (15a, b):

(15)   a. I told that to John.
        b. I told John that.

Rather, it seems connected to the presence of an initial 2 *which is a
complement clause*:

(16)   a. *I told to John to sing.
        b. *I told to John how to dance.
        c. *I told to sing to John.
        d. *I told how to dance to John.

This pattern is by no means universal in English. Verbs like, e.g., *explain*, do occur with complements and superficial 3s; in fact no advancement of 3 to 2 is possible with *explain*:[14]

(17)   a.   Hank explained to John that whales could talk.
        b.   *Hank explained John that whales could talk.

I conclude that there is a rule of limited generality which forces 3 to 2 advancement with certain verbs, including *tell, show* (but not *explain*), when the initial 2 is a complement clause. One might formulate this along the lines of (18):

(18)   English Rule 1
        Tail 3 arc (a, A) $\wedge$ Tail 2 arc (a, B) $\wedge$ Initial(B) $\wedge$ Head Labelled (C1, B) $\wedge$
        V-Stemmed (a, b) $\wedge$ b$\in\{$*tell, show,* ...$\}$
        $\rightarrow (\exists C)(2$–$3$ Local Successor (C, A))
        "If A is a 3 arc with tail node *a* and B is a 2 arc with tail *a* and B is both initial and has a head labelled C1 (thus corresponding to a clause) and *a* is V-stemmed with *tell*, or *show*, or, etc., then there exists a 2 arc C which is a local successor of A."

Thus, in the absence of rules, 3s will freely advance to 2 or fail to advance to 2. Only when one of these possibilities is blocked in some language are rules necessary, to force advancement of a 3 to a 2 in some contexts or to block it in others. Both situations can exist, even in the same language, as illustrated by the blockage of advancement with *explain*, the requirement of advancement with *tell*, etc.

3. A MYSTERIOUSLY LIMITED CONSTRUCTION IN FRENCH

Consider again French Rule 1, which limits advancement of 3s to 2 in French to clauses based on a small class of verb stems. Suppose one includes in this class, beyond elements from footnote 7, the stems for the verbs *obéir* 'to obey', *désobéir* 'to disobey' and *pardonner* 'to pardon'. As is well-known (cf. Grevisse (1969: 563), Kayne (1975: 245)), these are the three verbs in French which, while not occurring with superficial direct objects (2s),[15] unexpectedly do occur in *personal*[16] passive clauses. More precisely, these are the only three verbs which appear to permit a 3 to passivize in French.[17] Compare the regular *téléphoner* 'to telephone':

(19)   a.   Paul $\left\{ \begin{array}{l} \text{obéira} \\ \text{téléphonera} \end{array} \right\}$ à son père.

Paul $\left\{ \begin{array}{l} \text{will obey} \\ \text{will telephone} \end{array} \right\}$ (to) his father

b.   Paul lui $\left\{ \begin{array}{l} \text{obéira} \\ \text{téléphonera} \end{array} \right\}$.

Paul to-him $\left\{ \begin{array}{l} \text{will-obey} \\ \text{will-telephone} \end{array} \right\}$.

c.   *Paul $\left\{ \begin{array}{l} \text{obéira} \\ \text{téléphonera} \end{array} \right\}$ son père.

d.   *Paul $\left\{ \begin{array}{l} \text{l'obéira} \\ \text{le téléphonera} \end{array} \right\}$.

Paul $\left\{ \begin{array}{l} \text{him will-obey} \\ \text{him will-telephone} \end{array} \right\}$

e.   Paul sera $\left\{ \begin{array}{l} \text{obéi} \\ \text{*téléphoné} \end{array} \right\}$ par ses enfants.

Paul will be $\left\{ \begin{array}{l} \text{obeyed} \\ \text{telephoned} \end{array} \right\}$ by his children

By allowing the 3s with *obéir*, etc., but not *téléphoner* to advance to 2, one can account for the possibility of the passive in (19e) in the same way as for other passives.

If it is odd that *obéir, désobéir*, etc., unlike the typical verb occurring with a superficial 3 and no superficial 2 (e.g., *parler* 'to speak', *téléphoner*, etc.), should permit passives, an even odder property of the resulting passives is noted by Kayne (1975:246). These passives *fail* to enter into the *extraposition of indefinite construction* (henceforth *EXI*(construction)[18]), which is typically quite free with passives. EXI is a construction in which an indefinite nominal[19] which would otherwise be the final 1 of a clause shows up postposed to the verb, with the dummy nominal *il* manifesting as the final 1. It can be illustrated by such *non-passive* examples as:

(20)   Martin (1970: 377, 381)
         a. Il   passe   un   train   toutes les   heures.
            it   passes a   train   every   hour
         b. Il   meurt   un   homme   toutes les   minutes.
            dies   a   man   every   minute

These correspond to the *non*-EXI cases with essentially the same meanings:

(21)   a. Un train passe toutes les heures.
         b. Un homme meurt toutes les minutes.

In saying that EXI is normally possible with (personal) passives, I mean that there typically corresponds to a standard French passive like (22a) an EXI variant like (22b) (stylistically rather marked as bureaucratic or journalistic usage, as N. Ruwet informs me).

(22)   a. Beaucoup de   steaks   ont été   manges (par   les   gosses).
            many   steaks   were   eaten by   the   kids
         b. Il a été mangé beaucoup de steaks (par les gosses).

However, the EXI construction is blocked for passives of *obéir, désobéir*, etc.:[20]

(23)   a. (i) Beaucoup de parents sont obeis   (par/de leurs enfants).
                many   parents are   obeyed by   their children

             (ii) Beaucoup de parents sont   désobéis (par/de leurs
                                                disobeyed
                  enfants).
         b. Kayne (1975: 246)
             (i) *Il est obéi beaucoup de parents (par/de leurs enfants).
             (ii) *Il est désobéi beaucoup de parents (par/de leurs
                  enfants).

Noting that the EXI construction is not in general possible with *adjectives*, Kayne (1975: 246) proposes that the apparent personal passives based on *obéir, désobéir, pardonner* are not really passives, but rather adjectival clauses. He gives one argument for this view beyond the fact that it would apparently explain the ban on EXI passives like *(23b). Like clauses based on adjectives, apparent passive clauses like (23a) cannot generally occur as infinitival complements to causative *faire*, although ordinary passives do occur as complements to *faire* under certain circumstances.

But, as observed by Kayne himself (1975: 246, fn.), with *obéir*, etc., apparent passives *do* occur as complement to *faire* given the presence of the reflexive clitic (*se*) on the verb in the main clause. And, as noted by Morin (1977), the limitations on *obéir* passives in these infinitives are like those on other verbs (*respecter* 'to respect') which take ordinary superficial 2s and whose passives are thus not exceptional like those of *obéir*. Morin thus rejects this basis for Kayne's claim that *obéir* passives are adjectival clauses.[21] Indeed, since *faire* complements do not permit adjectival clauses, the fact that *obéir* passives occur in these complements indicates that they are *not* adjectival clauses. Further, Kayne gives no reason to believe that the apparent *obéir*, etc., passives could occur in diagnostic environments permitting adjectives but not passive participles. As shown by Authier (1972: 65–70), these include positions after *devenir* 'become' and *rendre* 'make'.[22] Moreover, Kayne does not indicate how the apparent passives in *obéir*, etc., are to be described as adjectival clauses in such a way as to account generally for the 'agent' character of the nominal in the *par/de* phrase, or the fact that the subject 1s of such clauses are understood exactly as the superficial 3s in active clauses with these verbs. These results are 'automatic' under a passive analysis in the sense that they follow from the same principles relevant for all passive clauses. Thus the apparent generalization which Kayne sought linking *(23b) to the impossibility of EXI with adjectival clauses would not be genuine; it would have to be purchased at the cost of special ad hoc interpretive rules for the apparent *obéir* passives. For these, although not passives in Kayne's terms, would have just the semantic properties to be expected if they were, vis à vis notions like 'agent', etc.

A further problem for the view that the apparent *obéir* passives are adjectival is that such verbal elements can be coordinated with elements that are unquestionably verbal. Grevisse (1969: 564) cites:

(24)   Les rois normands réalisèrent le miracle de se faire accepter et obéir par tous.
         the kings norman achieved the miracle of getting themselves accepted and obeyed by everyone

Such coordination would hardly be expected if *obéir* in these passive complements were not of the same category as *accepter*.

Notice that PID precludes an analysis anything like Kayne's a priori, given the semantic identity between e.g., (23ai) and its English translation, since it requires the English and French clauses to have identical initial relations.

I conclude that Kayne's attempt to explain facts like *(23b) via a claim that apparent passives in *obéir*, etc., are not really passives is untenable.

This leaves Kayne's important observation about the failure of *obéir*, etc., passives to enter into EXI, as well as the brute fact that *obéir*, etc., permit personal passives at all. The goal of most of the rest of this paper is to offer an account of the former which appeals crucially to the fact that the relevant verbs take complement nominals which are not 2s but 3s. I suggest that there is a general constraint on EXI formulable in APG terms which interacts with the earlier[23] 3hood of the nominals passivized with these verbs to predict the nonexistence of the EXI cases. Unlike Kayne's adjectival proposal, the present description of facts like *(23b) is based on an independently motivated restriction of great generality. This will be argued to provide insight into various constriants on EXI having nothing to do with verbs like *obéir*.

In APG terms, EXI is one of a class of constructions inherently involving *dummy nominals*. These are nominals which correspond to the heads of a specified class of arcs called *ghost arcs*[24]. My account of a simple EXI example like (25b) would be as in (25c):

(25)   a. Quelque chose d'extraordinaire arrivera.
          something   extraordinary will happen.
    b. Il arrivera quelque chose d'extraordinaire.
    c.

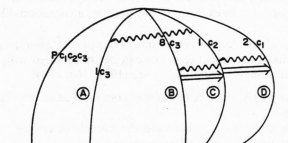

In this pair network, A is the ghost arc, with the nominal (il) corresponding to its head by definition a dummy nominal. D is a 2 arc, in keeping with a hypothesis which Perlmutter and I have referred to as the *Unaccusative Hypothesis*.[25] This claims that, in contrast to standard grammatical tradition, some *intransitive* predicates occur with initial 2 arcs rather than initial 1 arcs.[26] Given PID, the class of such predicates is universally determined, and a verb meaning 'happen', like French *arriver*, is one of them.

In this case, the initial 2 advances to 1, C being the local successor of D.[27] If that were all, one would have the representation of (25a). However, this intransitive verb permits the EXI construction, represented by the fact that arc C sponsors the ghost arc A. This leads to the earlier 1 becoming a final chômeur, indicated by the 8 arc with final coordinate c_3. Note that the order of constituents in (25b), like that in (25a), follows from the sequencing principle in (3), which is roughly as valid for French as for English.

Although examples like (22b) are in a clear sense both impersonal and passives they are *not* impersonal passives in a significant sense worth making technical. In this regard, one should not confuse ill-formed examples like *(23b) with clauses such as (26), first brought to my attention in 1974 by G. Fauconnier:

(26)   Il a   été obéi   au   capitaine.
        it has been obeyed to the   captain = 'The   captain   was
                                              obeyed.'

Unlike (22b) and *(23b), which are EXI variants of the *personal* passive clauses in (22a) and (23a), (26) is a true *impersonal* passive clause. Observe that (26) does *not* meet the 'indefiniteness' conditions of EXI constructions. (26) differs from clauses like (22b) and *(23b) in that the complement 3 nominal, *le capitaine*, is not the head of any 1 arc and thus is at no stage the subject of the clause. In term of Chapter 10 of Johnson and Postal (to appear), (26) would have essentially the structure in (27) (β is a variable over coordinate sequences):

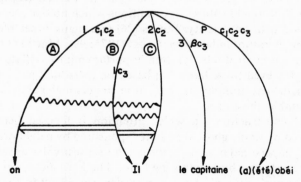

Here C is the ghost arc which determines that *il* in (26) is a dummy nominal and thus that the clause is impersonal. In this sense, (26) shares

properties with both (22b) and *(23b). However, observe that the ghost arc
C in (27) is not a *facsimile* of its sponsor, A. One arc is a facsimile of another
if it is a neighbor (has the same tail node) and has the same R-sign. And
while A and C in (27) are neighbors, their R-signs (1 and 2) are distinct. We
say that a ghost arc is *stable* if it is a facsimile of its sponsor, *unstable*
otherwise. The ghost arc A in (25c) is thus stable. Similarly, an analysis of
the ghost arc in the structure of (22b) would show it to be stable (cf. the
analogous ghost arcs E and E in (48c, d) below). More generally, the ghost
arcs defining EXI constructions are uniformly stable 1 arcs.

The claim of Johnson and Postal (to appear, Chapter 10) is that
impersonal passive clauses in the narrow technical sense are characterized
by *un*stable ghost arcs. These are subject to a law, PN law 84 in Chapter 10,
which requires them to have remote successors which are facsimiles of the
ghost arc sponsors. The consequence of this is that the dummy defining an
impersonal passive clause can never occur in a variant clause not subject to
passivization. Put differently, impersonal passives never have directly
corresponding actives, that is, actives with the dummy. Hence French
*(28a) is impossible and (28c) in English is not an impersonal passive clause
but a personal passive of the corresponding active in (28b), which contains a
dummy heading a stable ghost arc in the complement:

(28)   a. *On   l'   a obei   au   capitaine.
            one   it   obeyed to the   captain = 'One   obeyed   the
                                       captain.'
         b. I believe it to be raining.
         c. It is believed to be raining.

Impersonal passives are relatively marginal in French (compare, e.g.,
German or Welsh) and subject to conditions which no one seems to have
ever specified with any clarity. But as (26) and many other illustrations
found in the literature indicate (cf. Gross (1975: 99); Martin (1970: 387)),
their existence is not in doubt. It is thus important not to conflate them with
EXI examples, even those like (22b) based on (personal) passives.[28] For,
while both involve dummy 1s, only true impersonal passives like (26)
involve *un*stable ghost arcs.

The EXI construction, on which attention is focused here, is thus
characterized by stable ghost arcs, 1 arcs sponsored by neighboring 1 arcs.
In contrast, impersonal passives in the narrow sense involve unstable ghost
arcs, 2 arcs sponsored by neighboring 1 arcs. The 1 arc successors of these 2
arcs are then not 'optional'. Their non-existence will lead to a violation of
the previously mentioned PN law 84.

In describing EXI, involved in current terms are constraints on the class of 1 arcs, like C, which can sponsor stable ghost arcs like A in (25c). We can think of the constraints in this construction as being specified by rules which include one of the form:

(29)   1–1 Local Sponsor (A, B) ∧ Ghost (B) ∧ Not (Head Labelled (Cl, A)) → ...
         "If a 1 arc A locally sponsores a ghost 1 arc B, and the head of A is not labelled Cl, then..."

The third conjunct here simply indicates that we are not concerned with the construction involving so-called extraposition of complement clauses, although French has such a construction rather parallel to that found in English.

In what follows I want then to fill in the dots in (29). Necessary is a condition which will at a minimum represent the basic and traditionally described constraints on this construction but which will also offer insight into other more subtle restrictions, including Kayne's observations about *(23b).

Traditional observations of relevance about EXI include (cf. especially Martin (1970: 380–387)):

(30)   a. It is not possible with ordinary transitive clauses.
         b. It is not possible with most indirect transitive clauses.
         c. It is possible with a class of intransitive clauses (cf. Martinon (1927: 287))
         d. It is possible with ordinary (personal) passive clauses.
         e. It is possible with reflexive passives, the so-called *se*-moyen or middle *se* cases.

The claim in (30a) is illustrated by such facts as:

(31)   Ruwet (1972: 166)
         a. Quelqu'un a mangé ce   gateau.
            someone   ate   that   cake

         b. *Il a mangé $\left\{ \begin{array}{l} \text{ce gateau quelqu'un} \\ \text{quelqu'un ce gateau} \end{array} \right\}$.

It is worth pointing out that the restriction in (30a) is *not* avoided when the 2 defining a transitive clause manifests as an accusative clitic, as in (32a, b) (cf. also Kayne (1975:379–381)), or when it occurs in a non-standard (for out-

put 2s) position due to what is called 'extraction' in transformational
linguistics (cf. 32c, d).[29]

(32)   a. Quelqu'un l'a mangé.
                    it
        b. *Il l'a mangé quelqu'un.
        c. C' est Claude que trois   femmes ont tué
           it is Claude that three women killed
        d. *C'est Claude qu'il a tué trois femmes.

(30b) refers to a traditional analysis of clauses in French grammar
whereby those which contain a 1 and some kind of verbal complement
nominal that is *not* a superficial 2 are referred to as *indirect transitives*. In
our terms, this imprecise account covers a variety of distinct clause types.
These include those where a verb occurs with a superficial 1 and a
superficial 3 (verbs like *obéir*, as well as the more regular *téléphoner*, *parler*,
etc.), and a superficial 1 and nominal (in a prepositional phrase) which is not
a 3 (or a 2). In the former category are clauses like (33a), which, as (33b, c)
illustrate, systematically preclude EXI:

(33)   a. Beaucoup de femmes ont parlé à Max hier   soir.
           many   women spoke   to Max yesterday evening
           *Il a parlé beaucoup de femmes à Max hier soir.
           *Il a parlé à Max beaucoup de femmes hier soir.

In the second category, are examples based on a verb like *resembler*
'to resemble':

(34)   Martin (1970: 382)
        *Il y   ressemblait une chose que j' avais vue et   qui...
         it to it resembled   a   thing that I had seen and which...

On the other hand, some examples of this second category[30] of indirect
transitive clauses permit EXI:

(35)   Martin (1970: 382)
        Il provenait de cet état de fait une telle volonté de changement
        que...
        It resulted from that state of affairs such a will for change that...

We will not have anything to say about indirect transitive clauses until
Section 5.5, where we consider the problems they raise for the account of
EXI developed here.

(30c) has already been illustrated by (20) and (25). However, this statement also covers a variety of reflexive intransitive verbs, such as those in:

(36)   Martin (1970: 382)
      a. Il se produit toutes sortes de modifications.
         it takes place all   sorts of modifications
      b. Il s' y   passe   quelque chose d'étonnant.
         it   there happens something   astonishing

These are cases of what Ruwet (1972: Chapter 3) calls *intrinsic* or *neuter* reflexives. They should not be confused with the quite distinct *se* moyen cases, illustrated in, e.g., (37) below[31]. The latter are reflexive passives of transitive verbs, while the reflexives in (36) correspond to no transitives with the same meaning. Nor should French reflexive marked clauses like (36) be confused with 'coreferential' reflexive clauses (cf. (39, 41, 42) below), which correspond to English clauses with a reflexive (*-self*) object. (30d) is already illustrated by (22). (30e) is illustrated by:

(37)   Gross (1975: 96)
      a. Beaucoup de bonbons se mangeront chez Marie.
         many   candies   will be eaten   at Marie's place.
      b. Il se mangera beaucoup de bonbons chez Marie.

To understand these traditional observations, let us begin with the last two. Since passives and middle clauses can be argued to be intransitive *at later strata*, it may seem at first, given (30c), that the relevant constraint on EXI could simply require intransitivity at the last stratum of the arc which sponsors the ghost arc (the c_2 stratum of C in (25c)). However, unspecified object clauses, like (38a), which both (i) *look* intransitive and (ii) *are* superficially intransitive by the criterion of their behavior in *faire* complements[32] are unequivocally incompatible with EXI:

(38)   Ruwet (1972: 166) citing J.C. Milner
      a. Quelqu'un a mangé.
         Someone ate.
      b. *Il a mangé quelqu'un.

While (38b) is well-formed, it is not under the relevant EXI reading, which would make it an essential paraphrase of (38a). (38b) has only an irrelevant people-eating reading, where *il* is an anaphoric pronoun and *quelqu'un* is both initial and final 2 of what is simply an ordinary transitive clause.

Moreover, indirect transitive clauses like that in *(33a) also both look intransitive and are superficially intransitive by the criterion of behavior in the complement of *faire*.[33] But these also do not permit EXI. Cases like *(33) and *(38b) block EXI for reasons that no one has ever really succeeded in elucidating.[34]

The somewhat mysterious fact (given (30c)) that unspecified object cases fail to 'feed' EXI becomes more mysterious when placed side by side with the explicit observation of Kayne (1975: 381) and less explicit observation of Fauconnier (1974: 213) that EXI is possible, at least for many speakers, in 'coreferential' reflexive clauses.[35]

(39)   Fauconnier (1974: 213)
    a. Une femme s'est offerte (pour mener le combat).
       A woman offered herself (to lead the battle)
    b. Il s'est offert une femme (pour mener le combat).

Notable about clauses like (39a) is that they both *look* intransitive and are superficially intransitive by the criterion of behavior as a complement of *faire*.[36] It is particularly important to observe, as does Kayne (1975: 381), the contrast between clauses like (39) with a *reflexive* clitic corresponding to the 2 of a transitive clause and those clauses like (32a) with a *non-reflexive* accusative clitic.[37] Thus these facts, particularly the contrast between ordinary reflexive clauses and unspecified object cases, offer a challenge to an account of EXI. For there appear to be two types of clauses, both initially transitive, both superficially intransitive-looking and both superficially intransitive by the *faire* criterion. And yet only one permits EXI.

I will suggest that there is a natural APG treatment which not only largely handles the basic facts in (30), and predicts the contrast between ordinary reflexive clauses and unspecified object clauses, but that this same analysis also predicts the failure noted by Kayne of *obéir*, etc., passives to permit EXI, despite (30d). We will then see this same hypothesis has many other correct and surprising consequences.

Before getting to this account, it is necessary to stress the way that most cases of so-called 'coreference' are treated in pair networks. Namely, it is claimed that there is no such relation of relevance to grammar and that pronouns and their antecedents are connected by no semantic relation whatever. The link between antecedent and pronoun is syntactic. Pronouns play no semantic role at all. Rather, 'coreference' is represented by self-sponsoring overlapping arcs. This amounts to saying that 'coreference' is apprehended when a single nominal element bears two or more initial relations.[38] In the formalism, this is represented by a single nominal node heading two or more self-sponsoring arcs. In these terms, the structure of an English clause like (40a) would be essentially (40b):[39]

(40)   a. A woman offered herself.

    b.

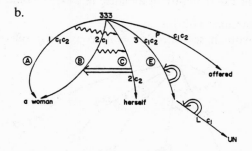

The key elements here are that *a woman* heads two initial arcs, A and B, but only one final stratum and one surface arc, namely A. On the other hand, C, an arc technically called a *replacer*, heads only a final stratum and surface arc, but no initial arc. Therefore, C is *semantically* non-existent, which is consistent with the fact that the semantic properties of relevance about the role of *a woman* in such examples are expressed by arcs A and B. (40b) is transitive at both of its strata, that is, the c_1 and c_2 strata of node 333 each contain both a 1 arc and a 2 arc, although the 2 arcs are different.

French ordinary reflexive clauses have the basic properties of (40) but several additional ones as well, in particular, the fact that the reflexive nominal is not visible and that there is a reflexive verbal clitic, *se/s'* in third person cases:

(41)   Marie s'est   tué.
            self-is   killed = 'Marie killed herself.'

A problem, discussed in Postal (1976), is that these clauses in French behave *intransitively* in causative constructions with *faire*. This is notable since structures like (40b) are superficially transitive, which, under the laws claimed to be valid for clause union constructions like the *faire* construction,[40] would predict that cases like (41) would behave transitively in such cases in spite of the invisibility of their reflexive nominals.[41] In Postal (1976) it was proposed that this feature of French reflexive clauses is a function of the fact, independently attested for other languages like Eskimo, that the relevant clauses are subject to antipassivization, roughly the demotion of a transitive 1 to 2, determining that the original reflexive 2 becomes a chômeur. But I think this was partially incorrect. Although French reflexive clauses are subject to a type of detransitivization, I now hypothesize that this is the direct demotion of the reflexive 2 to 3.[42]

I thus propose that the structure of a clause like (42a) would be (42b):

(42)   a. Une femme s'offrira.
         a   woman self-offer-will = 'A woman will offer herself.'

         b.

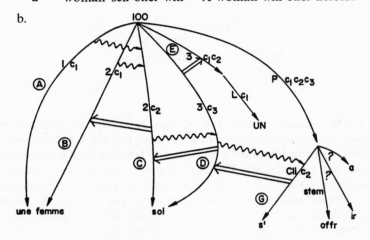

As can be seen, arcs A, B, C and E in (42b) are essentially isomorphic to the identically labelled arcs in the English pair network in (40b). That is, the French and English reflexive clauses share all this structure. However, I claim that the French sentence differs in that the pronominal 2 arc C has a 3 arc local successor, (D), and that this successor sponsors the clitic arc G in the verb, which erases it. In other words, I am claiming that reflexive pronouns which are 2s necessarily demote to 3 in French.[43] This leaves the final stratum of a reflexive clause not containing a 2 arc. Thus, in (42b), no 2 arc has the final (for node 100) coordinate c_3.

The final stratum intransitivity of reflexive clauses accounts, under the general principles of clause union constructions, for the fact that French reflexive clauses behave intransitively in the *faire* construction. It also provides the basis for a natural account of a traditionally well-known fact about French grammar, namely, that although pronominal 3s normally yield a dative clitic, this is *not* possible when the 2 manifests as a reflexive clitic:

(43) a. Pierre lui présentera Marie. = 'Pierre will present
to him/her present-will Marie to him/her'
b. Pierre se présentera à Jacques. = 'Pierre will present
self to himself to Jacques.'
c. *Pierre se lui présentera. = 'Pierre will present himself to
him/her.'
d. *Pierre lui se présentera. = 'Pierre will present himself to
him/her.'
e. Pierre se présentera à lui. = 'Pierre will present himself to
him/her'

Rather, as (43) shows, the underlying 3 shows up as a strong pronoun form
rather than a verbal clitic. This is normally thought of as a constraint on
clitic combinations (cf. Kayne (1975: 173), Perlmutter (1971: 53–66)),
although problems for such a view are noted. But under the proposal made
about the demotion of reflexive 2s to 3s, facts like (43d, e) can be taken to be
a reflex of the fact that the earlier 3 in cases like (43b) cannot be a later 3
(under pain of violating a basic principle. The Stratal Uniqueness
Theorem,[44] which allows only one Term arc of any type *per stratum*).
Hence, under the reflexive demotion account, the structure of (43b) is (44):

(44)

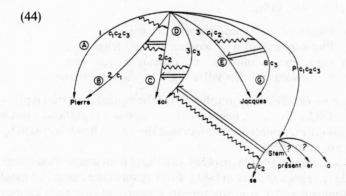

The key point here is that *Jacques* is not an output 3 but an output
chômeur, and thus so would be the pronoun in (43e). Consequently, the
failure of dative cliticization in such cases can be taken to be a result of the
absence of the necessary output 3. That is, 3 chômeurs would not determine
dative cliticization.[45]

With this background, I am now almost ready to return to the conditions on the EXI construction, that is, to filling in the dots in the partial rule in (29). One further observation is in order. In APG terms, cases of 'coreference' fall together in a clear formal respect with successor cases. Both involve *overlapping* arcs. The difference is that in the 'coreference' cases the overlapping arcs are both self-sponsoring and hence have the first coordinate c_1, while in successor cases, the successor is sponsored by its predecessor and never has the coordinate c_1. This formal similarity is used, in Johnson and Postal (to appear: Chapter 11), as the basis for an explanation of the existence of constructions like reflexive passives. For in these terms, passives involve overlapping 1 and 2 arcs in the successor relation (cf. (48c,d) below) while ordinary reflexives involve overlapping self-sponsoring 1 and 2 arcs, as in e.g., (40b) and (42b). It is then not surprising that in some cases passive constructions and ordinary reflexive constructions should have the same morphology.

I claim that this same similarity between successor pairs and overlapping self-sponsoring arc pairs is responsible for the behavior of French 'coreferential' reflexive clauses with respect to the EXI construction. For return to the French clause represented in (42b). The nominal *une femme* corresponds here not only to the head of a 1 arc, but also to the head of an *initial* 2 arc, indicating that it functions logically as the direct object just as it does in a sentence like (45a).

(45)   a. Pierre offrira   une femme à son ami.
           Pierre offer-will a   woman to his friend.
        b. Une femme offrira   un cadeau à son ami.
           a   woman offer-will a gift   to his friend

That is, *une femme* in (42b) plays jointly both of the logical roles that it plays separately in (45a,b). However, *une femme* functions as a superficial 1 not a superficial 2 in (42), represented by the fact that the 2 arc it heads is erased by the replacer arc C in (42b).

Contrast the structure of (42a) in (42b) with that for an unspecified object clause like (38a), represented as in (46a), if one ignores the claim in Postal (1976) and Johnson and Postal (to appear: Chapter 8) that such clauses really involve antipassivization, and represented as in (46b) if one does not ignore this:

(46) a.

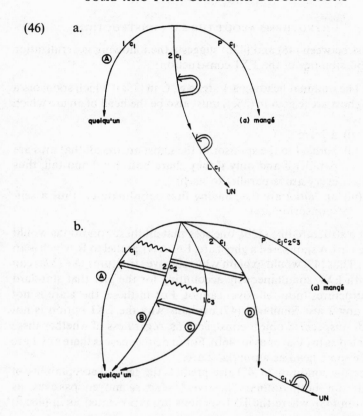

b.

Comparing (46) with (44), the following contrast emerges. While in (44) the nominal heading the 1 arc, A, which is a potential ghost arc sponsor also heads a 2 arc, B, which is initial, the corresponding arcs in (46) do not meet this condition. Thus the head of the 1 arc, A, in (46a), heads no 2 arc at all; the head of the 1 arcs, A and C, in (46b), does also head a 2 arc, B. But this is not an initial arc. In this respect then, under either (46a) or (46b), unspecified object clauses do not differ from ordinary, full unpassivized transitive clauses, which would also not contain a 1 arc whose head also heads an initial 2 arc with the same tail. This is suggestive since unspecified object clauses and ordinary transitive clauses behave alike under the EXI construction.

4. A HYPOTHESIS ABOUT THE EXI CONSTRUCTION

The contrast between (46) and (42b) suggests the following generalization about the possibilities of the EXI construction:

(47)   The nominal heading a 1 arc (e.g., C in (25c)) which sponsors a ghost arc (e.g., A in (25c)) must also be the head of an arc which is:

(i) a 2 arc

(ii) *parallel* to the sponsor of the ghost arc (recall that arcs are parallel if and only if they share both head and tail, thus every arc is parallel to itself)

(iii) an *initial* arc (i.e., having first coordinate c_1, thus a self-sponsoring arc).

Glancing at a structure like (42b), one sees that all these conditions would be met if the 1 arc A sponsored a ghost arc. For A is parallel to B, which is an initial 2 arc. Thus (47) would explain why reflexive structures like (39a) can combine with EXI, simultaneously accounting for the fact that standard transitive structures (non-reflexive) cannot. For in these, the 1 arc is not parallel to any 2 arc. Similarly, (47) explains why the EXI option is not available for unspecified object constructions, regardless of whether these are represented as in (46a) or as in (46b). For in neither case is there any 1 arc with has the same head as an *initial* 2 arc.

Moreover, the condition in (47) also predicts the general acceptability of EXI variants for both ordinary passives[46] and *se* moyen passives, as reillustrated in (48), where the EXI versions are represented as in (48c,d) respectively.

(48)   a. Ruwet (1968: 348)

(i) Des erreurs   ont   été   commises.
   errors   have been committed

(ii) Il a été commis des erreurs.

b. Gaatone (1970: 401)

(i) Beaucoup d'histories sur   les cardinaux se racontaient.
   many   stories   about the cardinals were told

(ii) Il se racontait beaucoup d'histoires sur les cardinaux.

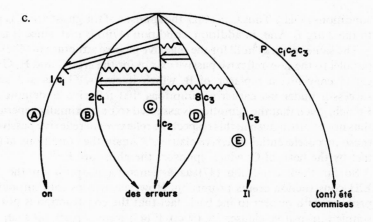

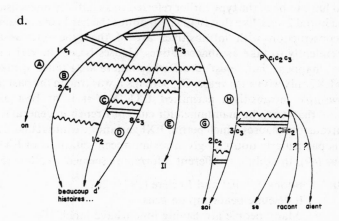

These representations are the reconstructions in APG terms of the standard relational grammar view of passivization. The basic idea is that passivization involves a 2 arc having a 1 arc local successor such that the *first* coordinate index of that 1 arc successor is +1 of the *last* coordinate index of some other 1 arc.[47] In these terms then, observe how the head of the 1 arc local successor in any passive based on an *initial* 2 will always meet conditions (47i,ii). Thus C in (48c), the sponsor of the ghost arc E, is parallel to the 2 arc B. And, in addition, condition (47iii) is met, since B is initial.

The same remarks hold for the reflexive passive structure in (48d). This is parallel to the non-reflexive passive except for the arcs G and H. G is a so-called *copy arc*, a replacer of B, which it erases. G has a 3 arc local successor under my earlier assumptions that reflexive 2s demote to 3 in French, given that the demotion is assumed to be maximally general[48] and thus not to distinguish in this respect the reflexives in reflexive passives from those in 'coreferential' reflexive clauses.[49] Again the conditions of (47) are met by the head of C, which sponsors the ghost arc E.[50]

So far then, condition (47) as a general constraint on the French EXI construction seems promising. However, it runs into an immediate problem with respect to the basic fact that the construction is possible in simple intransitive clauses (cf. (30c)). If (47) were correct, *all* such clauses would have to be of the type earlier referred to as initially unaccusative, i.e., taking initial 2 arcs, like that in (25). No doubt the hard core of examples of this construction with intransitives are of the type one would wish independently to take as unaccusatives, clauses based on verbs meaning 'arrive', 'happen', 'fall', 'exist', etc. Perhaps there are French speakers who allow EXI only with such verbs. Or, perhaps it was true in the past that only *unaccusative* intransitives permitted EXI. But it is at best extremely doubtful that it can be maintained for current French in general that all of the intransitive clauses which permit EXI variants are initial unaccusatives. This is particularly doubtful given certain recent citations of EXI clauses such as (49). In addition, different informants seemed to allow (50a,b):

(49)   Boons, Guillet and Leclère (1973: 201)
         Il dejeune beaucoup de gens.
         'Many people are having lunch/have lunch'[51]

(50)   a. Il travaille beaucoup d'ouvriers dans cette usine.
            'Many workers work in that factory'
         b. ?Il a souri beaucoup de femmes hier soir.
            'Many women smiled yesterday evening'

All of these verbs, which take so-called agent nominals, are among those that one would, on independent grounds, wish to analyze as taking initial 1s. (Cf. Perlmutter (1978). Perlmutter and Postal (to appear b, to appear c), Postal (to appear)).

I conclude that it is not really possible to maintain (47), as is. Fortunately, there is a simple weakening of this condition which has its essential virtues and yet is still consistent with examples like (49) and (50). To state this, one needs the defined notion *absolutive*, a concept known to be relevant for certain phenomena in so-called ergative languages. Basically, a nominal is absolutive at a level if it is a nuclear term (1 or 2) at that level and there is no lower ranking nuclear term at that level, where 1s outrank 2s. Hence absolutivity groups together intransitive 1s, intransitive 2s and transitive 2s and separates them from transitive 1s. Formally, the relevant notion is as in (51b):

(51)   a. *Ergative* $(A, c_k(b)) \leftrightarrow 1$ arc (A) $\wedge$ A$\in c_k$ stratum (b) $\wedge$ ($\exists$B) (2 arc (B) $\wedge$ B$\in c_k$ stratum(b))

"An arc A is ergative at the c_kth stratum of node b if and only if A is a 1 arc in the c_kth stratum of b and there is some 2 arc which is a member of that stratum."

   b. *Absolutive* $(A,\ c_k(b)) \leftrightarrow$ Nuclear Term arc (A) $\wedge$ A$\in c_k$ stratum(b) $\wedge$ Not (Ergative (A, $c_k(b)$))

"An arc A is absolutive at the c_kth stratum of node b if and only if A is a Nuclear Term arc which is a member of that stratum and A is not ergative at that stratum."

Given this notion of absolutivity relative to a stratum of a node, one can restate condition (47) in such a way as to be indifferent to the existence of (49), (50).

(52)   The nominal heading a 1 arc (call it A) which sponsors the ghost arc defining an EXI construction must also be the head of an arc (call it B) such that:
   (i) B is absolutive at the c_1 stratum of its tail node.
   (ii) B is parallel to A.

This condition allows as sponsors of EXI ghost arcs only those 1 arcs which are parallel to either:

(53)   a. initial intransitive 1 arcs
   b. initial intransitive 2 arcs
   c. initial transitive 2 arcs

But it blocks as potential ghost arc sponsors those 1 arcs not parallel to any initial arcs or those which are only parallel to initial ergative arcs, or only to initial 3 arcs, Oblique arcs, etc. Thus, in particular, it blocks as sponsors those 1 arcs whose heads are the 1s of transitive clauses (except for 'coreferential' reflexive clauses). The extensional consequences of (52) are now largely[52] those of (47), except that (52) is compatible with examples like (49), (50).

One can now use (52) to fill out the rule in (29) for the French EXI construction:

(54)   French Rule 2
       Tail 1–1 Local Sponsor $(a, A, B) \wedge$ Ghost $(B) \wedge$ Not (Head
       Labelled $(C1, A)) \rightarrow$
           $(\exists C)(\text{Parallel}(C, A) \wedge \text{Absolutive}(C, c_1(a)))$

       "If a 1 arc, A, with tail node a and whose head node is not a
       clause node locally sponsors a ghost 1 arc, B, then there exists an
       arc C which is parallel to A and which is absolutive at the first
       stratum of a."

I have already shown how this rule predicts that there are no EXI variants of pure transitive clauses or unspecified object clauses and how it allows such variants for ordinary passives, reflexive passives and pure intransitive clauses of either type. Consider how it explains the apparently exceptional failure of the passives based on *obéir*, *désobéir* and *pardonner* to have EXI versions. In particular, recall the ill-formedness of e.g., *(23bii), noted by Kayne. Remembering that *désobéir* occurs with a superficial 3 in nonpassives, the proper structure for *(23bii) (repeated as (55a)) in present terms would seem to be (55b) (cf. footnote 20)[53].

(55)   a. *Il est desobéi beaucoup de parents.
       b.

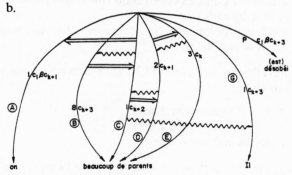

The chief undiscussed assumption illustrated by (55b) is that the passive of a *désobéir* clause is possible because the earlier 3 advances to 2 (yielding arc D in (55b)). This 2 arc can then have a 1 arc local successor like a less exceptional 2 arc cooccurring at a stratum with a 1 arc. The reason I assume that the 3 advances to 2 in cases like (55), rather than advancing directly to 1, is that this accounts in a general way for the fact that the resulting clauses have the properties of standard, non-reflexive passive clauses (past participles, auxiliary *être*, etc.). Moreover, the possibility of a 3 advancing to 2 with verbs like *obéir* in the face of the general impossibility of this (cf. the contrasts with *téléphoner* in (19)), can be easily obtained simply by adding *obéir*, etc., but not *téléphoner*, etc., to the list of stems in the independently necessary French Rule 1 in (11).

I hedge in (55b) with respect to the first coordinate of arc E. If one takes this to be an initial arc, then $c_k = c_1$. But I doubt that this is the proper analysis. The key point is that the head of E is the head of a 2 arc only at c_{k+1}, necessarily $\neq c_1$. Therefore, the 1 arc sponsor of the ghost arc G is not parallel to any arc absolutive at c_1. Given (55b), it is then predictable that no EXI versions of *désobéir*, etc., passives can exist, since the conditions in French Rule 2 cannot be met. In other words, the gross assumption that the *earliest* relation of the non-initial 1 nominal occurring superficially with *obéir*, etc., is *not* the direct object relation interacts properly with French Rule 2 to predict the otherwise mysterious non-existence of EXI variants of *obéir* passives.

Our proposal is to add *obéir*, etc., to the list of stems in French Rule 1 to make them exceptions to the general fact about French that 3s do not advance to 2. This permits one to specify in a simple way how these verbs can have passives at all while most French verbs which only take 3s, e.g., *téléphoner*, *parler*, etc., do not.[54] However, this treatment fails so far to predict that the 'intermediate' forms like *(19c, d) are not well-formed, those in which the 3 advances to 2 *but does not further advance to* 1. Since this is also an ad hoc fact about these verbs,[55] an additional ad hoc rule is required:

(56)   French Rule 3
        Tail 2–3 Local Successor (a, A, B) $\wedge$ V-Stemmed (a, b)

$$\wedge\ b\in \left\{ \begin{array}{c} \text{pardonn (er)} \\ \text{désobé (ir)} \\ \text{obé (ir)} \end{array} \right\} \rightarrow$$

$(\exists C)(1\text{–}2 \text{ Local Successor } (C, A))$

"If A is a 2 arc local successor of a 3 arc, B, with tail *a* and *a* is v-stemmed *b* and *b* is a member of the set containing *pardonn*, *désobé* and *obé*, then there exists a 1 arc, C, which is a local successor of A."

However, this rule only requires the 2 arc local successor of a 3 arc with these verbs to have a 1 arc local successor. It therefore fails to distinguish ordinary passivization with these verbs from the reflexive, *se* moyen type of passivization. As observed by Ruwet (1972: 110), this is inadequate, since in general *se* moyen forms based on these verbs are rejected:

(57)   Ruwet (1972: 110)
?*Un chef   pareil,   ça ne s'obéit   pas.
 a   boss   like that that   self obeys not = 'A boss like that, he is
                                                 not obeyed'

However, Ruwet observes that some speakers, he cites the French linguist Maurice Gross, accept these. Therefore, French Rule 2 might seem correct for speakers like Gross.[56] For those making the judgement in (57), however, its *consequent* must be amended to the less general:

(58)   French Rule 3a
        [Antecedent = Antecedent of (56)] → (∃C)(1–2 Local Successor
        (C, A)) ∧ Not((∃D))(Replace(D, A)))

        "...then there exists a 1 arc C which is a local successor of A and there does not exist an arc D which replaces A."

Given the definition of 'replace' and certain laws in Johnson and Postal (to appear), this rule will preclude the existence of a 2 arc like G in (49) in all *obéir*, etc., passives, thus forcing these to be plain passives rather than *se* moyen type passives.

Return to French Rule 2, and its basic generalization about the EXI construction, namely, that the 1 arc sponsor of the ghost arc must be parallel to an initial absolutive arc. This generalization is stateable in a useful way only because, in APG terms, the relation *parallel* between arcs covers both the case of local predecessor/successor, and the case of neighboring overlapping arcs which are self-sponsoring. Thus when one requires a 1 arc, A, to be parallel to an initial absolutive arc, B, there are the following logically possible cases (given Stratal Uniqueness):

(59)   a. A = B and A is initially absolutive, hence A is initial 2 arc of
           an initially transitive stratum, initial 2 arc of an initially
           intransitive stratum, or initial 1 arc of an initial intransitive
           stratum.
        b. A ≠ B in which case B has the three possibilities stated for A
           in (59a), with these three crosscutting the following
           distinction:

> (i) A and B are both self-sponsoring arcs.
> (ii) A and B are related by the local successor relation

(59bi) is relevant for reflexive clauses like (42) while (59bii) is relevant for plain passive and *se* moyen passive clauses, as well as pure intransitive clauses of the *unaccusative* type (e.g., that in (25)). On the other hand, (59a) is relevant for any cases where EXI is possible in intransitive clauses taking an initial 1, like (49). The point to be stressed is that the overall generalization made possible by (59b) is a function of the particular substantive way in which APG representations handle so-called 'coreference', namely, by overlapping self-sponsoring arcs, thus making such constructions partially formally similar to successor cases.

Recall from footnote 35 the statement by Martin (1970) to the effect that, contrary to what we have assumed so far, EXI is not possible with reflexive clauses. Since there are citations of such clauses by sophisticated French speakers who are also linguists, Martin's claim is clearly not true for *all* French speakers. But it is true for some, who reject examples like (39b) (while still accepting EXI in non- 'coreferential' reflexive cases like (36), (37), etc.). In fact, one speaker I consulted did reject (39b). This variant of French is as easily describable as that covered by French Rule 2. One simply replaces the consequent conjunct involving the predicate *Parallel* with one referring to the less general *Local Successor*, yielding:

(60)   French Rule 2a (for speakers who reject examples like (39b))
         Antecedent = Antecedent of (54) $\rightarrow$ ($\exists$C)(Local Successor (A, C) $\wedge$ Absolutive (C, $c_1(a)$)))

         "...then there exists an arc C which is absolutive at the first stratum of a and of which A is the local successor."

For speakers whose grammar contains French Rule 2a rather than French Rule 2, the only 1 arcs which would be suitable ghost sponsors in this construction would be local successors of initial 2 arcs, thus 1 arcs in unaccusative intransitive clauses and 1 arc local successors in all types of passive clauses. This revised rule predicts a correlation between those speakers who reject the 'coreferential' reflexive cases like (39b) and those who should reject all cases of EXI with pure intransitive clauses based on initial 1s as in (49) and (50). I have had no way of testing such a correlation.

If it does *not* hold, then, for speakers who reject EXI variants of 'coreferential' reflexive clauses but otherwise show no significant difference from those subject to French Rule 2 in allowing EXI with initial 1 intransitives, the following rule could be proposed:[57]

(61)   French Rule 2b
[Antecedent = Antecedent of (54)] → (∃C)(Absolutive $(C, c_1(a))$
∧ (A ≠ C → Local Successor (A, C)))

"...then there exists an arc C which is absolutive at the first stratum of a, and, if A is distinct from C, A is a local successor of C."

The potential dialects of French represented by French Rules 2a and 2b are less interesting than that represented by French Rule 2. Only the latter brings out the crucial similarity between pairs of parallel 1 and 2 arcs which are self-sponsoring and pairs which are in the local successor relation.

Of course, speakers governed by any of French Rules 2, 2a or 2b would be predicted to reject EXI constructions with 1s of pure transitives or unspecified object pure transitives.

Making use of French Rule 2 and the assumption that the verbs *obéir*, etc., are exceptionally allowed to coexist with advancement of 3s to 2, I have provided a hypothesis which explains Kayne's important observation about the impossibility of EXI with the passives of these verbs. The explanation takes this ill-formedness to be a special case of a more general constraint on EXI which also blocks the possibility of this with ordinary transitive clauses, unspecified object transitives, etc. I now want to consider briefly further types of facts which the initial absolutivity hypothesis built into French Rule 2 predicts, facts which have for the most part not, to my knowledge, even been systematically noted still less accounted for.

The failure of *obéir* passives to permit EXI was accounted for by way of the assumption that the nominal which is superficial 1 in such passives is not an initial 2 but rather an earlier 3 which advances to a (necessarily) non-initial 2 status before advancing to 1. It would follow then that if French had verbs parallel to such English cases as (1), only the passives corresponding to (1a) could be possible sources for EXI.

But we already pointed out that, although rarer than in English, French does have such verbs, including, for certain speakers, *fournir* and others noted by Blinkenberg (1960) and cited in footnote 9. Moreover, for speakers who permit both of the patterns in (10) above, passivization seems to be free:

(62)   a. Beaucoup d'uniformes ont été fournies   aux   troupes.
            many   uniforms were   furnished to the troops
        b. Beaucoup de troupes ont été fournis   avec des uniformes.[58]
            many   troups were   furnished with   uniforms

The initial absolutivity condition, combined with the analysis of the variant clauses imposed by PID, determines that EXI should only be possible for cases like (62a). And this seems to be correct:[59]

(63)   a. Il a été fourni beaucoup d'uniformes aux troupes.
          b. *Il a été fourni beaucoup de troupes avec des uniformes.

Moreover, of course the same principles predict that speakers who allow *se moyen* forms corresponding to both (62a, b) will at best permit EXI variants only in the case corresponding to (62a). And this also seems to be correct:

(64)   a. Beaucoup d'uniformes se fournissent aux troupes.
            'Many uniforms are furnished to the troops.'

          b. Beaucoup de troupes se fournissent avec des uniformes.
            'Many troops are furnished with uniforms.'

(65)   a. Il se fournit beaucoup d'uniformes aux troupes.
          b. *Il se fournit beaucoup de troupes avec des uniformes.

While I have not been able to study in detail the verbs cited by Blinkenberg as permitting, in my terms, 'optional' advancement of 3s to 2 in French, the limited cases I have been able to examine with informants who permit the base examples like (10b), (62b) and (64b) have provided no clear instance where the nominal corresponding to an initial 3 (given PID) could appear in an EXI construction after getting to be a 1 by ordinary or *se moyen* passivization. Although this class of verb requires much more intensive study, the preliminary results support the initial absolutivity hypothesis.

Moreover, these results also provide an unusual type of argument for the much more abstract PID, which requires that nominals appearing as superficial 2s in cases like (10b) be taken to correspond to initial 3s.

For French speakers who accept examples like (10b), (62b), etc., verbs like *fournir*, like English *give*, are simply subject to no constraints at all as far as the possibility of 3s advancing to 2. However, logically there could be (and in both English (cf. (18) above) and French there are, I claim) clauses whose 3s must advance to 2. Thus consider the French verb '*munir*' to furnish, 'supply'. Given PID, the meaning parallelisms between, e.g., *munir*, and *fournir*, would demand parallel initial arcs with the recipient of the objects supplied represented in each case by the head of an initial 3 arc. But unlike *fournir*, *munir* can in no case occur with a superficial 3. One finds only examples like:

(66)   a. On a muni *beaucoup d'ouvriers* d'armes.
         One supplied many workers with arms.

         b. Beaucoup d'ouvriers se sont munis d'armes.
         Many workers provided themselves with arms.

In (66a) the italicized nominal represents the superficial 2. But PID, as interpreted here, claims that this superficial 2 must correspond to an earlier 3, while the post *d'* nominal must then be a final chômeur corresponding to an earlier 2. Unlike cases like (10) above, with *fournir*, or (1) above with *give*, there are no pairs of parallel examples to support this view directly. However, it can be supported by French Rule 2.

If the italicized nominal in (66a) corresponds to an initial 2, as the superficial absence of a variant of (66a) with this nominal as superficial 3 might suggest, then, for speakers who permit EXI with 'coreferential' reflexive clauses like (39) and (41), it would be predicted, in default of further rules, that (66b) would have a well-formed EXI variant. However, if, as PID claims, the superficial 2 which occurs in *munir* clauses must be an advancee from 3, then the reflexive in (66b) is not determined by the head of an initial 2 arc but an initial 3 arc and thus the conditions of French Rule 2 cannot be met.

As predicted by the PID analysis and French Rule 2, even speakers who permit EXI with 'coreferential' reflexive clauses seem to reject EXI variants of, e.g., (66b):

(67)   a. *Il s'est muni d'armes beaucoup d'ouvriers.
         b. *Il s'est muni beaucoup d'ouvriers d'armes.

Under PID, *(67) is ill-formed because the structure of (66b) would be:

(68)

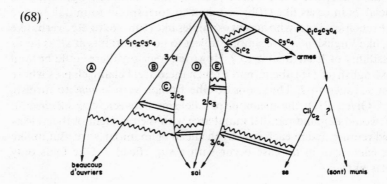

Here D is the 2 arc local successor of C required by the ad hoc constraint on *munir* and similar verbs which does not permit an earlier 3 to manifest as an output 3. Arc E is a function of the rule discussed earlier (cf. footnote 43), which requires a reflexive 2 arc to have a 3 arc local successor.[60] No analogue of E would thus exist in the structure of (66a). Given this structure then, the examples in *(67) are ill-formed because the ghost arc sponsor would correspond to A in (68). But A is not parallel to any arc absolutive at c_1 and French Rule 2 is not satisfied.

*(67) illustrates that even for speakers who permit EXI with 'coreferential' reflexive clauses like (39) and (41), this is only possible when the reflexive corresponds to an initial 2 of the clause. Thus the failure of EXI in *(67) is matched, as expected, by a similar failure even for these speakers with other clauses in which the reflexive corresponds to an initial 3 (which can manifest as a superficial 3).

(69)   a.   Beaucoup de femmes ont parlé à Claude hier soir.
             Many women spoke to Claude yesterday evening.
        b.   Beaucoup de femmes se sont parle hier soir
                            spoke to themselves/each other
        c.   *Il s'est parlé beaucoup de femmes hier soir.

In sections 5.2 and 5.4, we consider other cases not involving 3s where 'coreferential' reflexive clauses also predictably have no EXI variants even for speakers who permit sentences of the type in (39).

Of course, the same principles which block *(67) combine to predict that all speakers governed by French Rules 2, 2a or 2b should reject EXI with either ordinary passives or *se* moyen passives of *munir* clauses, since, given PID, the nominal which can be superficial 1 in a non-EXI passive with *munir* will always correspond to an initial 3, precluding satisfaction of the initial absolutivity condition. Thus the following are correctly predicted:

(70)   a.   Beaucoup d'ouvriers ont été munis d'armes.
             Many workers were supplied with arms.
        b.   *Il a été muni d'armes beaucoup d'ouvriers.

One should also predict a parallel result for *se* moyen type passives. Unfortunately, the example:

(71)   Beaucoup d'ouvriers se   munissent d'armes.
        many   workers self provide   with arms

which is the form to be expected of a *se* moyen passive corresponding to

(66a) in the present tense (*se* moyen precluding a past definite tense specification, as shown by Ruwet (1972:95)) also has the form of a clause in which the superficial 1 is the initial 1, the reflexive a reflex of an initial 3, the clause meaning 'Many workers equip themselves with arms.' The only French speaker I was able to check (71) with only accepted this reading for (71), thus making it impossible to test on this occasion whether *se* moyen permits EXI with *munir*. Possibly further work could permit the construction of genuine *se* moyen clauses with *munir*, permitting the test.

In any event, the evidence from plain passives in (70) is unequivocal and when combined with the behavior of *munir* illustrated in *(67) provides striking evidence for the hypothesis that the nominal which can only occur as an output 2 in non-passives with *munir* is not an initial 2 (but rather, according to PID, an initial 3). At the same time, this evidence supports French Rule 2 and its initial absolutivity condition and PID.

Let us consider one further case where it seems plausible to analyze a French verb as requiring advancement of 3s to 2. Given the parallelism in meaning between 'promise' and 'threaten', I think a proper formulation of PID will require such predicates to occur in initially isomorphic structures, with the individual to whom something is promised or threatened always represented by an initial 3. However, while the French verb *promettre* 'to promise' occurs with a superficial 3, which cannot advance to 2, the verb *menacer* 'to threaten' occurs with a superficial 2, never a superficial 3. Notice that *menacer* permits a richer class of structures than the corresponding English verb:

(72)   a.   Claude a menacé beaucoup de femmes (d'élimination).
             Claude threatened many women (with elimination).
        b.   Beaucoup de femmes ont été menacées (d'élimination) (par Claude).
        c.   *Il a été menacé beaucoup de femmes (d'élimination) (par Claude).

(73)   a.   Beaucoup d'ouvriers ont été menacés d'être mis au chômage.
             Many workers were threatened to be put out of work.
        b.   *Il a été menacé beaucoup d'ouvriers d'être mis au chômage.

Again, the assumption that the nominal designating the individuals 'threatened' must correspond to an initial 3 explains the otherwise unprincipled impossibility of EXI (recall that this is normally free for

passives). There are other verbs in French which occur only with superficial
2s (for fixed meanings) which I think PID would require to be *initial* 3s, e.g.,
prier 'to ask, beg', *aviser* in the sense of 'inform' or 'warn', *renseigner* 'to
inform', etc. In all cases then, the initial absolutivity condition would
predict the impossibility of EXI when the 2s predicted to be advancees from 3
are superficial 1s as the result of ordinary or *se moyen* passivization. The
possible scope for tests of the initial absolutivity condition in these cases is
thus quite large.

So far I have illustrated how the initial absolutivity condition in French
Rules 2, 2a and 2b interacts with postulated advancement of 3s to 2,
blocking EXI constructions for 2s which advance to 1 or which head arcs
parallel to 1 arcs when these 2s *are not initial 2s*. But the same condition
would, naturally, also interact with other types of advancement to 2, e.g., of
locatives, to predict that initial locatives which advance to 2 and then to 1
could never yield EXI variants. I will consider one case to illustrate that the
initial absolutivity condition is also relevant to a domain independent of 3s:

(74) a. On a chargé beaucoup de colis   sur le   cargo.
          one loaded   many   packages on the cargo ship.
      b. On a chargé le cargo   avec des colis.
              the cargo ship with packages
      c. Beaucoup de colis ont été chargés sur le cargo.
      d. Il a été chargé beaucoup de colis sur le cargo.

      e. Beaucoup de cargos ont été chargés$\left\{ \begin{array}{l} \text{de colis} \\ \text{avec des colis} \end{array} \right\}$.
          many cargo ships

      f. *Il a été chargé beaucoup de cargos$\left\{ \begin{array}{l} \text{de colis} \\ \text{avec des colis} \end{array} \right\}$

Strikingly, as predicted, there is a gap in the EXI paradigm when it is a
question of a nominal which, under PID, would bear an initial locative
relation rather than the initial direct object relation. The gap in (74) is even
more striking because it is, as predicted, paralleled by a gap with *se* moyen:

(75) a. Beaucoup de colis   se   chargent sur les cargos.
         many   packages self load   on cargo ships
      b. Il se charge beaucoup de colis sur les cargos.
      c. Beaucoup de cargos se   chargent avec des colis.
         many cargo ships   self load   with packages
      d. *Il se charge beaucoup de cargos avec des colis.

Again, there are no doubt other verbs like *charger* which permit alternative constructions, and all of these offer possible tests of the initial absolutivity condition. This claims that the EXI construction will always show gaps when combined with the passive and *se* moyen paradigms, the gaps existing when the nominal relevant for EXI corresponds to an initial locative rather than the initial 2.

5. SPECIAL CASES AND THEIR INTERACTION WITH EXI AND FRENCH RULE 2

5.1 *Accusative Clitics and 'Extraction'*

It was pointed out earlier (cf. (32)) that the incompatibility of EXI with transitive clauses is *not* eliminated when the 2 yields an accusative clitic or when the 2 is, in transformational terms, 'extracted'. These consequences are straightforward entailments of the predictions made by French Rule 2 for transitive clauses with non-clitic, 'unextracted' 2s, given the way that cliticization and 'extraction' are described in APG terms.

Consider first *(32b), repeated as:

(76)   *Il l'a mangé quelqu'un.

This is the kind of fact one might try to account for transformationally with rule ordering or by saying, e.g., that extraposition is cyclic while cliticization is postcyclic (hence, at the point of extraposition, the clitic 2 would still be in 'direct object position'). In APG terms, the relevant part of the structure of (76) would be as in (77) with E a foreign sponsoree of the 2 arc D.

(77)

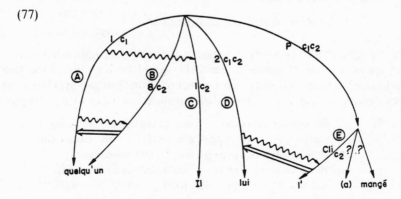

In these terms, the existence of cliticization, i.e., the difference between the real French (78a) and the hypothetical *(78b) with a non-clitic accusative pronoun, is simply the existence of the pair Sponsor (D, E) and the pair Erase (E, D), the former determining the existence of arc E:

(78)   a. Pierre l'a mangé
               it ate
         b. *Pierre a mangé lui.
                          it

But these pairs and arc E in no way contribute to making A meet the initial absolutivity condition in French Rule 2, since they cannot determine that A is parallel to an initial absolutive arc.

Without going into details, the properties of the 'extraction' examples are essentially identical to the clitic cases. So-called 'extraction' of a 2 means, in APG terms, that a 2 arc will have some kind of foreign successor (which typically erases the predecessor 2 arc). Cf. Johnson and Postal (to appear, Chapter 7). Thus these pairs, by their very nature, can also in no way contribute to the satisfaction of the initial absolutivity condition by a 1 arc.

Thus in both the cliticization and 'extraction' cases, the fact that transitive clauses with these additional features behave with respect to EXI just like transitive clauses without them under French Rule 2 is just what is to be expected in APG terms, given the initial absolutivity condition.

5.2 *Reflexive Antipassive Clauses*

French has a number of verbs which (i) are reflexive; (ii) take prepositional phrases, usually in *à* or *de* and (iii) whose clauses correspond to ordinary transitive clauses in other languages. Thus consider the essential paraphrases:

(79)   a. Beaucoup de femmes se sont attaquées au président.
         b. Many women attacked the president.

PID requires these to have isomorphic initial arcs. My hypothesis to accomplish this would be that (79a) has a transitive initial structure, with *le président* corresponding to the head of an initial 2 arc. (79a) is then *superfically* not parallel to (79b) because (i) it is an antipassive clause and (ii) the readvancement of the 2 to 1 typical of antipassive clauses (cf. (46b)) is of the 'copy' variety, yielding a reflexive 2 arc. This interacts with the earlier claim that reflexive 2s must demote to 3s. In these terms, the structure of (79a) would be:

(80)

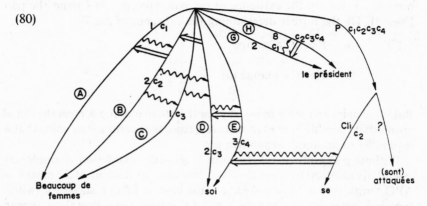

Here D is the copy arc which results from the fact that the kind of re-advancement of 2 to 1 found in the antipassive clauses with *attaquer* must leave a copy.

If something like (80) is the right structure of (79a) and similar clauses, then the prediction is made that all clauses analogous to (79a) are incompatible with EXI, that is, they will behave like ordinary transitive clauses in this regard. This follows since neither of the 1 arcs in (80), A or C, is parallel to any initial absolutive arc. In fact, the only initial arc parallel to either A or C is A itself, which is ergative at c_1. The prediction is correct, since:

(81)   a. Beaucoup de femmes se sont occupées de   ça.
          many   women applied themselves to that
        b. *Il s'est occupé beaucoup de femmes de ça.
        c. Beaucoup de femmes se sont servies des outils.
                                        used   tools
        d. *Il s'est servi beaucoup de femmes des outils.

And alongside of (79a) one finds:

(82)   *Il s'est attaqué beacoup de femmes au président.

Thus both the initial absolutivity condition and the antipassive analysis are supported, in particular, the aspect of the latter which takes clauses like (79a) to be initially transitive. If such clauses were taken to be initially intransitive because they are finally intransitive, the systematic failure of EXI would be unexplained in any known terms.

This discussion brings out how important it is to distinguish among various types of reflexive clauses in French in a principled way. We have found that EXI is basically possible for *all* speakers with *se* moyen reflexives and intransitive inherent reflexive clauses, is possible for *some* speakers with 'coreferential' reflexive clauses *when the reflexive corresponds to an initial 2* (cf. *(67) and *(69b)) and is not possible for any speakers, as far as I know, with what I take to be reflexive antipassive clauses like (79a, 81a, 81c).

5.3 Predicate Nominal Constructions

Another important consequence of the initial absolutivity condition in French Rule 2 is that it properly predicts the impossibility of EXI in predicate nominal constructions, given the analysis of these in Johnson and Postal (to appear: Chapter 7). That work suggests that a predicate nominal clause is an initially transitive clause in which the initial 2 arc has a P arc local successor. Hence the initial 2 is a final predicate, and the clause is intransitive at the final stratum. In these terms, the structure of a French predicate nominal clause like (83) would be (ignoring the auxiliary *sont*) (84):[61]

(83)   Beaucoup de femmes sont actrices.
        many   women are   actresses

(84)

Given this, the initial absolutivity condition in French Rule 2 properly predicts:

(85)   *Il est actrice(s) beacoup de femmes.

For A in (84) is ergative at c_1 and not parallel to any arc absolutive at c_1 (since not parallel to any arc at all except itself), and hence cannot sponsor a ghost arc. Such cases are interesting because, as shown by Kayne (1975: 208–209), though not explained in his terms, predicate nominal clauses behave intransitively in *faire* constructions, as predicted by the clause union laws in Johnson and Postal (to appear: Chapter 8), given the final stratum intransitivity of such clauses. Thus, just as in the case of unspecified object clauses, final stratum intransitivity is not sufficient to permit EXI, as French Rule 2 predicts.

Given other basic, independent assumptions, the analysis of predicate nominal constructions of the form in (84) predicts not only the impossibility of EXI in (85) but a variety of other facts about such clauses in French. These include (cf. Kayne (1975: 208)):

(86)   a. Their failure to have ordinary passive variants.
    b. Their failure to have *se* moyen variants.
    c. Their failure to occur in 'object raising' constructions.
    d. Their intransitive behavior in *faire* complements.

This follows because the constructions in (86a, b) require 2 arcs to have 1 arc local successors, while that in (86c) requires term arc foreign successors for 2 arcs, impossible if the only 2 arc in a clause has a P arc local successor as in (84), since successorhood is unique (cf. Johnson and Postal (to appear: Theorem 19)). Finally, (86d) follows since structures like (84) are intransitive in their final strata. The truth of (86a–d) can be illustrated with the predicate nominal taking verb *devenir* 'become':

(87)   a. Pierre deviendra   un   bon   medecin.
       Pierre become-will a   good   doctor
    b. *Un bon medecin sera   devenu   par/de Pierre.
       be-will   become   by
    c. *Un bon medecin, ça   se   devient très   difficilement.
       that self   becomes very difficulty
    d. *Un bon medecin sera   difficile   à   devenir.
       difficult   to   become
    e. Kayne (1975: 208)

Cela fera   devenir ⎧ son fils un bon   professeur⎫
that make-will become ⎨ his son a   good professor ⎬
       ⎩ *un bon professeur à son fils⎭

= 'That will make his son become a good professor'

The behavior of predicate nominals thus supports French Rule 2 and the proposed analysis of such clauses illustrated in (84).

5.4 The Interaction of EXI and 'Raising' Constructions

In APG terms, arcs which define what are usually called 'raising' constructions will never be c_1 arcs, since they are (foreign) successors and hence not self-sponsoring. Therefore, the initiality part of the absolutivity condition predicts that no French 'raising' construction can ever 'feed' the EXI construction. By this I mean that if the complement clause does not *independently* allow EXI, embedding it under a 'raising' verb is predicted never to allow it either.

Exactly this is pointed out to be the case by Fauconnier (1974: 208–210) for intransitive 'raising' verbs like *commencer* 'to begin'.[62] For example, *répondre* clauses do not permit EXI and embedding them under *commencer* does not either:

(88)   Fauconnier (1974: 209)
     a. Plusieurs hommes   répondent.
           several   men   answer
     b. *Il répond plusieurs hommes.
     c. Plusieurs hommes commencent à   répondre.
                  begin   to   answer
     d. *Il commence à répondre plusieurs hommes.

On the other hand, the following are both possible:

(89)   Fauconnier (1974: 210)
     a. Quelques personnes commencent   à   arriver.
          a few   people   are beginning to   arrive
     b. Il commence à arriver quelques personnes.

But this must be, not because *commencer* permits EXI in the main clause but because it was possible in the complement and it was the dummy that 'raised' (technically, heads the foreign successor arc).

As Fauconnier (1974: 209) states, then:
        "... les mêmes verbes permettent ou interdisent l'extraposition,
        qu'il y ait ou non montée du sujet: ..."

In current terms, the impossible *(88d) viewed on the analysis where the dummy would only be a main clause element (that is, would correspond to the head of *no* complement clause arc) would have the structure in (90), under my (non-crucial for this discussion) assumption that *commencer* is an *unaccusative* type of intransitive verb, and thus takes an initial 2:

(90)

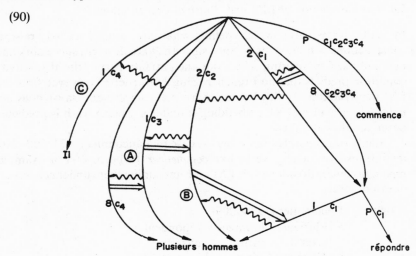

In (90), while A, the sponsor of the ghost arc, is parallel to, and also a local successor of, an absolutive arc, B, that is, one absolutive at c_2, A is not parallel to any *initial* absolutive arc and French Rule 2 is not satisfied. Thus the rule proposed makes the prediction that every intransitive 'raising' verb must be like *commencer* in this respect, the behavior noted by Fauconnier following from exactly the same condition which blocks EXI with transitives, etc.

Obviously, the same condition would function in the same way for *transitive* 'raising' verbs, if any. Here it is only via passivization that the 'raised' nominals could become main clause 1s and thus potential entrants to the EXI construction. Some such sentences exist, although the class of complements susceptible to what I consider this kind of 'raising' is even more limited in French than in English. Thus alongside of examples like: (91a) one finds passives like (91b).[63]

(91)   a. On a jugé beaucoup de femmes coupables.
          one judged many   women guilty
    b. Beaucoup de femmes ont été jugées coupables.
       many   women were judged guilty

A priori one might then expect passives like (91b) to yield EXI variants, especially given the normal compatibility of passives and EXI. But the initial absolutivity condition predicts, when combined with a 'raising' analysis of cases like (91a), that the EXI version must be ill-formed:

(92)   *Il a été jugé coupable beaucoup de femmes.

This then further supports French Rule 2,[64] and in particular, the specification that the absolutivity condition must hold *initially* (for all the other requirements of French Rule 2 are met in *(92) under a 'raising' analysis).[65]

In this regard, consider cases like:

(93)   Beaucoup de femmes se croient intelligentes.

Many women self-believe intelligent = 'Many women believe themselves intelligent.' These involve reflexives of the 'coreferential' sort. Under a 'raising' analysis, the structure of (93) would be:

(94)

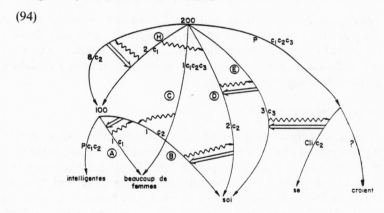

The key point is that (94) contrasts with earlier 'coreferential' reflexive structures like (41). In those, a single node not only headed two self-sponsoring arcs, but these arcs *had the same tail*, and hence were parallel. Here, the nominal node corresponding to *beaucoup de femmes* heads two self-sponsoring arcs. A and C. But, under a 'raising' analysis, these have different tails. That is, the nominal is understood as the semantic 1 of *croient* and the semantic 1 of *intelligentes*. Arc B represents the need for a pronoun, and its head would manifest as a non-reflexive pronoun (*elles*) in the 'unraised' structure corresponding to (93), namely:

(95)   Beaucoup de femmes croient qu'elles   sont intelligentes.
         many   women believe that they   are   intelligent

The fact that the pronoun manifests as a reflexive in (93) is thus a function of 'raising', represented chiefly by the foreign successor D in (94). This has a 3 arc local successor, E, because of the claim that reflexive 2s demote to 3s in French.

Significantly, under these assumptions, crucially under the 'raising' analysis, unlike earlier *non*-'raising', 'coreferential' reflexive structures such as (41), (94) fails the initial absolutivity condition in French Rule 2. That is, C is parallel to no initially absolutive arc. In fact, it is parallel to no arc except itself. And C is initially ergative since the 2 arc H is in the c_1 stratum of node 200. French Rule 2 then predicts, even for those speakers who permit EXI with reflexive structures like (41), that this will not be possible for (93). This is apparently correct:

(96)   *Il se croit intelligent beaucoup de femmes.

This again provides interesting support for French Rule 2, and, in particular, for the initiality part of the absolutivity condition. It also supports a 'raising' analysis of the relevant *croire* clauses, and thus indirectly PID, which would require this, given the semantic parallelism between pairs like, e.g., (93) and (95).

5.5 *Indirect Transitive Cases*

In Section 3, it was observed that what are called indirect transitive verbs in French grammatical studies are, to a significant extent, incompatible with EXI (cf. (30b)), although some do permit EXI. Despite the terminology, indirect transitive verbs are superficially intransitive in several respects. First, they lack any visible superficial 2; second, they behave intransitively as complements of *faire* (if they can occur as such complements); third, except for *obéir*, etc., already discussed, they have no *personal* passives of either the ordinary or *se moyen* varieties, and fourth, they do not permit accusative clitics corresponding to their 'indirect' complement.

If, corresponding to this superficial intransitivity, indirect transitive verbs are analyzed as *initially* intransitive, then French Rules 2, 2a, 2b are compatible with EXI variants of all such clauses. These rules would fail to predict incompatibility of the bulk of such clauses with EXI. While this would not be disconfirmatory for these rules, it is rather suspicious. One would hope that a hypothesis as general as the initial absolutivity condition built into these rules would provide some insight into the behavior of indirect transitives with respect of EXI.

The possibility exists that there is a deeper analysis of the diverse class of indirect transitive verbs which would interact with the initial absolutivity condition to predict the incompatibility of these verbs with EXI. Let us restrict attention to indirect transitives which occur with a superficial 1 and a superficial 3. What we say about these will carry over to cases where the complement is an oblique nominal rather than a 3.

At issue is the difference between pairs like:

(97)   a. Beaucoup de femmes lui   ont parlé.
            many   women to him spoke
        b. Des idées   lui   sont venues
            ideas   to him came

Although both involve a superficial 1 and 3 (manifesting here as the clitic *lui*) and no superficial 2, only the latter type is compatible with EXI:

(98)   a. *Il lui a parlé beaucoup de femmes.
        b. Il lui est venu des idées.

If the initial strata of the clauses in (97) are as similar as their superficial strata, such contrasts can of course not be predicted by the initial absolutivity conditon.

Suppose, however, one hypothesizes that indirect transitives, like *parler*, in which the superficial 1 is an 'agent' are initially transitive verbs, verbs whose initial 2 is necessarily unspecified. This would be consistent with the fact that, e.g., to speak to Sally is to say something to Sally, indicating that semantically there is an argument corresponding to the hypothesized 2 of *parler*. The superficial intransitivity of *parler* clauses would then have to be attributed to antipassivization, just as that of unspecified object clauses without superficial 3s like (38a) above. If such an analysis of clauses like (97a) could be sustained, the failure of EXI in cases like *(98a) would follow from French Rule 2, rather than being left mysterious.

To account for the possibility of EXI in cases like (98b), all that is necessary is that the clause *not* be initially transitive. The most plausible analysis of such clauses is, I suspect, one where the superficial 1 corresponds to an initial unaccusative 2, with the superficial 3 being either an initial 3 or perhaps corresponding to an earlier oblique nominal.

Another example similar to (98b) in involving a verb which takes a superficial 1 and 3 and which yet permits EXI is provided by Y.-C. Morin:

(99)   Il lui   en   a survecu beaucoup.
         it to him of them survived many = 'Many of them sur-
                                           vived him.'

Here also the most plausible analysis is probably one in which the nominal yielding *en . . . beaucoup* is an initial unaccusative,[66] with the superficial 3 corresponding to an earlier oblique nominal. The clause would thus be initially intransitive, and EXI would not be blocked.

As argued in Harris (1976, to appear a, to appear b) and Perlmutter (1979, to appear a), some earlier strata transitive clauses have a structure involving *inversion* without passivization. This means that an ergative 1 demotes to 3 yielding a stratum containing a 2 and a 3, with the 2 then advancing to 1 yielding a superficial 1–3 structure. In many languages, such analyses are limited to particular verbs. Observe that any verbs analyzed in this way would *not* be predicted to be incompatible with EXI. However, it seems that verbs for which an inversion analysis is most plausible in French, e.g., *importer* 'to matter', *appartenir* 'to belong', *plaire* 'to be pleasing', etc. are incompatible with EXI. No French speaker I consulted was happy with EXI examples with such verbs and most rejected them outright. I conclude that there must be some further constraint precluding EXI in a clause with a 3 arc local successor of a 1 arc.

Summing up, my major suggestion is that the bulk of indirect transitives which preclude EXI do so because they are *initially* transitive clauses and thus fail to satisfy the initial absolutivity condition. The superficial intransitivity of such clauses must then be attributed to antipassivization. Under this kind of analysis, a blocked example like *(34), which has no 3, involves an initial 2 which demotes to chômeur as a result of antipassivization (manifesting as the clitic *y* in *(34) since pronominal). On the other hand, and indirect transitive with no 3 permitting EXI, like that in (35), would not be initially transitive but, probably initially unaccusative, with the complement nominal oblique at all strata. Under these conditions, (35) would meet the initial absolutivity condition.

These inconclusive remarks on indirect transitives are not an attempt to save the initial absolutivity condition from counterexamples, for indirect transitives provide none, but rather to consider the possibility that the explanatory scope of this principle extends to this domain, accounting for what would otherwise be unpredicted gaps in the possibilities of the EXI construction.

5.6 *Clause Union Cases*

A further prediction of the initial absolutivity condition is that none of what are called in APG terms *clause union* constructions can permit EXI in French. Thus it is correctly determined that the indefinite nominal in a case like (100) cannot appear extraposed:

(100)   a. Quelqu'un a fait tomber Marie.
            someone   made fall   Marie

        b. *Il a fait tomber $\left\{ \begin{array}{l} \text{quelqu'un Marie} \\ \text{Marie quelqu'un} \end{array} \right\}$

However, *(100b) is not too interesting because it could be argued that such examples, like *(31b) above, are precluded by some independent constraint in French blocking two postverbal nominals. However, unlike such constraints, the initial absolutivity condition on EXI also properly predicts the failure of EXI variants in situations like:

(101)   a. Beaucoup de choses font   rire.
            many   things make   laugh = 'Many things make
                                                 one laugh.'

        b. *Il fait rire beaucoup de choses.[67]

In this case, there is no natural appeal to superficial transitivity. The absolutivity condition would, however, be relevant under the relatively standard clause union analysis in (102), under which the 1 arc headed by an indefinite nominal is parallel to no initially absolutive arc.

(102)

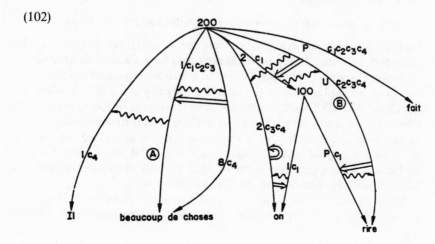

Here A is parallel to no initially absolutive arc. This follows, it should be stressed, only because the complement clause, that corresponding to node 100, is taken to be an initial direct object of the main clause. If, as in many recent transformational analyses, *faire* constructions were analyzed as taking sentential complements which are *not* objects, then A itself would be an initial absolutive arc and the required prediction would not follow. However, in APG terms, it is proposed that there are laws (cf. Johnson and Postal (to appear, Chapter 8, Section 6)) which only permit a U arc like B defining such a construction if the node like 100 heads an initial 2 arc. That view, when combined with the initial absolutivity condition on EXI, gives exactly the right answer for *(101b).

, A class of apparent counterexamples to the interaction of the initial absolutivity condition with an analysis of *faire* constructions along the lines of (102) has been observed by Aissen (1979):

(103)   Il se fait   exécuter beaucoup de prisonniers politiques
         it self makes execute   many   prisoners   political
         = 'A lot of political prisoners get (themselves) executed'

My hypothesis about such clauses is that they are *not* instances of the same construction type illustrated in, e.g., (101a). In the latter, *faire* is a genuine causative verb meaning 'have' or 'make'. But as the translation indicates, this is not the case in (103), which is quite parallel to a so-called *get* passive in English. However, if one considers the sentence obtained by replacing *il* in (103) by the extraposed nominal (changing the verb inflection accordingly), the result is ambiguous:

(104)   Beaucoup de prisonniers politiques se font exécuter.

(104) is not only an essential paraphrase of (103) but has the genuine causative meaning, 'Many political prisoners have themselves executed.' If (103) were genuinely an EXI variant of a structure parallel to (102), there would be no explanation of the lack of ambiguity of (103). Put differently, the claim that EXI is impossible for such structures properly predicts the absence of a reading for (103) parallel to the true causative meaning of (104). Hence one is simply left with the, in any event inevitable, problem of providing a second analysis for clauses like (104) to account for their ambiguity. Given previous remarks, this analysis must interact with the initial absolutivity condition on EXI to allow (103).

My proposal would be as follows. The construction in (103) involves passivization in the complement (even though passive chômeurs marked with *par* seem impossible). EXI is thus possible in the complement as with other passive clauses based on initial 2s. The main verb *faire* then determines 'raising' and occurs in a clause which is itself a reflexive passive. In the case of (103), these hypotheses determine that the final 1 of the complement is the nominal heading the ghost arc which is a complement arc. This has a successor 2 arc in the main clause, which is the basis for the reflexive passivization in the main clause.

Of course, a great deal of work would be required to validate an analysis like that suggested for (103). But I see no reason at the moment to consider cases like (103) genuine counterexamples to the initial absolutivity condition.

6. CONCLUSIONS

6.1 *Overlapping Arcs and 'Coreference'*

After some abstract background about pair networks, rules, etc., and some substantive remarks about indirect objects, direct objects and their relations, what I have chiefly tried to do in this paper is to support French Rules 2, 2a, 2b, and, in particular, the intial absolutivity condition.

If the arguments turn out to have some validity, and thus these French Rules are correct, some support will have been provided both for the view of rules I have advocated and for the view of sentences as pair networks. In particular, it is only the fact that in APG terms 'coreference' is represented by overlapping arcs that permits French Rule 2 to predict the possibility of EXI with 'coreferential' reflexive clauses in which the reflexive corresponds to an initial 2, although EXI is impossible with many other types of reflexives, including 'coreferential' reflexive clauses where the reflexive corresponds to a lower clause element or to an initial 3 of the main clause.

I think that the kind of case represented by French Rule 2, right or wrong, is one major sort that should be sought for in an attempt to provide 'syntactic' evidence for the overlapping arc conception of 'coreference'.

6.2. *Globality*

French Rules 2, 2a, 2b impose constraints on the class of potential ghost arc sponsors for the EXI construction in terms of arcs potentially distinct from those sponsors. If one attempted to mimic these constraints in some kind of *derivational* framework, one would inevitably thus be led to appeal to some kind of global devices, permitting direct access in a single rule to distinct levels of derivation, or indirect access via the coding of properties of earlier stages into later stages. None of this is either necessary or even sensible in APG terms. Reference to properties of different 'stages' is achieved naturally and directly with no extreme extensions of the character of rules[68] by allowing reference to arcs with different coordinates, as in the rules posited above for French. To a significant extent then, viewed from the APG perspective, much of the discussion of globality in derivational terms has involved pseudo-problems, although it is a real feature of natural languages that they involve constraints which refer at once to distinct levels.

6.3 *A Restriction on Local Successors*

As noted in footnote 54, the view that a nominal can, e.g., advance from 3 to 2 and then from 2 to 1, integral to the analysis in this study, is incompatible with a suggestion made by Lakoff (1977). We might interpret his proposals in our terms as claiming, inter alia, the existence of a restriction on parallel arcs related by the successor relation. More precisely, we might interpret his claim as saying in APG terms:

(105)   Local Successor(A, B) $\wedge$ Local Successor(C, D) $\wedge$ Local
         Successor(E, F) $\rightarrow$ Not(D = A) $\wedge$ Not(B = E)

Thus, under Lakoff's view, each nominal can participate in a maximum of *one* advancement/demotion per clause.

It is much harder to find evidence against (105) than one might assume. But I believe the analysis of EXI developed here yields such. In particular, this is true for a variety of French which permits EXI with either or both 'coreferential' reflexive clauses or initial I taking intransitive clauses. For the possibility of EXI with these clause types shows that the sponsor of the ghost arc defining an EXI construction is not only parallel to an initial absolutive arc but must itself be a 1 arc. This being the case, the possibility of EXI with ordinary and *se*-moyen passives, as in (48c, d), shows that (105) is incorrect. Consider (48c). There the nominal *des erreurs* heads an initial 2 arc, B, permitting the initial absolutivity condition for EXI to be met. But, since the generalization about EXI involves 1 arc sponsors of ghost arcs, B in (48) could not be the ghost sponsor. Since (48c) is a passive, B has a 1 arc local successor, C. This can both meet the initial absolutivity condition, since it is parallel to B, and sponsor the ghost arc, since it is a 1 arc. However, *des erreurs* is not the final 1, rather the dummy *il* is, so that C itself has an 8 arc local successor determining that *des erreurs* is a final chômeur and keeping (48c) consistent with the principle of stratal uniqueness. In short, if (48c) is correct, the constraint in (105) cannot be a sentence law or even a rule of French.

But every relevant aspect of (48c) seems well-motivated, since it amounts to little more than a translation into APG terms of the traditional view that examples like (48aii) are EXI variants of personal passive clauses, meaning that the possibility of the dummy as final 1 depends on the previous status of the initial 2 as a 1 (due to passivization). This view is consistent with the fact that the active corresponding to a passive on an initial 2 has, of course, no 'pseudo EXI' variant with the dummy manifesting as a 2:

(106)   *On l'a commis des erreurs.

Such examples would be expected if 2 arcs could sponsor stable (hence 2 arc) ghosts. On the other hand, if 2 arcs could sponsor 1 arc ghosts, one would predict falsely the existence of 'pseudo-EXI' variants of actives like (107a) of the form *(107b): that is, where *(107b) had the same meaning as (107a) and where *Il* is a dummy.

(107)   ˙a. On a commis des erreurs.
            one committed   errors
         b. *Il a commis des erreurs. ((107b) is well-formed only on an
            irrelevant reading 'He committed some errors.')

These facts support the view that EXI variants of passives like (48aii) involve a ghost 1 arc sponsored by a 1 arc, incompatible with principle (105).

6.4 *Grammatical Relations*

Chomsky (1964: 65) remarked as follows:

The primary motivation for the theory of transformational grammar lies in the fact that the significant grammatical functions and relations are expressed, in a natural way, only in underlying elementary Phrase-markers. For the present, the transformational model for generative grammar is unique in that it allows for the generation of structural information of a variety rich enough to account for facts of the kind discussed here and in §2, above – and, furthermore, to do so in many cases in a principled way thus reaching the higher level of explanatory adequacy – though it is by no means without its problems.

Assume that Chomsky's claim was correct in 1964 and thus that the theory of transformational grammar then was the only known way to

represent 'the significant grammatical functions and relations'. While
many linguists have currently apparently abandoned the belief that there
are such relations, I continue to agree with Chomsky's earlier position that
they are central to grammatical structure.

But, as I hope to argue more fully in other works, the APG framework is
superior in every way to transformational theories as a vehicle for
representing such relations. In the current paper, this is best brought out
perhaps by the way the underlying 3 relation plays a role in precluding a
wide array of otherwise expected EXI clauses in French. In particular, it is
shown by the way the overlapping arc ('node sharing') approach to so-
called 'coreference' provides the basis for an account of the possibility of
EXI clauses like (39b). This was possible only because the APG approach
permits, in a way no explicit transformational approach ever has, the
nominal bearing the initial subject relation to also bear the initial direct
object relation. It is precisely the latter 'significant grammatical function' in
Chomsky's terms which is crucial to an account of examples like (39b) via
the initial absolutivity condition. And yet no version of transformational
theory ever sketched by Chomsky over the last quarter century would
permit the required analysis. I think this case is typical of many which
would ultimately show that the very motivations taken by Chomsky in the
quote above (and in dozens of other contexts) to support transformational
grammar actually support the APG approach against any conceivable
version of transformational theory.

7. APPENDIX: COUNTEREXAMPLES AND A NEW FORMULATION

After completing sections 1–6 of this study, I became aware of Pollock
(1978), which cites as well-formed the following EXI example:

(108)   = Pollock's (146b)
           Il mange beaucoup de linguistes dans ce   restaurant.
           it eats   many   linguists in   this restaurant =
           'Many linguists eat in this restaurant'

Within the context of PID, there seems no way of construing such an
example except as falsifying the assumption of earlier sections (cf. (38)) that
EXI is systematically impossible for all varieties of French with unspecified
object clauses. This claim, taken from Ruwet (1972: 166), was supported by
examples like *(38b), repeated here:

(38)   b. Ruwet (1972: 166)
         *Il a mangé quelqu'un.

However, given the well-formedness of (108), together with PID, it seems that only *some* (even with the same verb) unspecified object clauses block EXI. Note that the difference between the 'extraposed' nominals in *(38b) and (108) is irrelevant since *quelqu'un* is a perfectly 'extraposable' nominal in other contexts. But since French Rule 2 above predicts that *no* unspecified object clause can permit EXI, (108) is incompatible with French Rule 2. Given that (108) is both a well-formed unspecified object clause and an EXI clause, it cannot be a necessary condition on the sponsor of a ghost arc in an EXI construction that it be parallel to an initial *absolutive* arc.

To complicate matters, however, (108) is not acceptable to all French speakers. While Pollock (personal communication: 9/8/79) has verified that (108) is well-formed for him, N. Ruwet (personal communication: 10/8/79) emphasizes that (108) is ill-formed for him. I see no alternative then but to view the acceptability of (108) as variable across variants of French. This does not really offer any solace for French Rule 2, however, since we want the essence of the rule for EXI to express general conditions which hold for all varieties of French.

Necessary, then, is an alternative to French Rule 2 having most of its consequences but which, unlike French Rule 2, is not in principle incompatible with examples like (108). An obvious alternative would weaken the requirement on the ghost arc sponsor with respect to the type of initial arc it must relate to. French Rule 2 requires the ghost sponsor to be parallel to an initially absolutive arc, that is, to an initial 2 arc, or an initial *intransitive* 1 arc. A natural weakening relevant for cases like (108) would lift the requirement that a relevant initial 1 arc be absolutive. The resulting condition is simply that the ghost sponsor be parallel to an initial 1 arc or 2 arc, that is, to *any* initial nuclear term arc. Cases like (108) would then no longer be blocked because the initially ergative 1 arc of the initially transitive clause in (108) is now a suitable EXI construction ghost sponsor. For it is parallel to an initial nuclear term arc, namely, itself.

The weakening just discussed retains many of the explanatory consequences inherent in French Rule 2. In particular, the revision maintains all implications relating to the need for the ghost sponsor to be parallel to an *initial* 1 arc or 2 arc. Thus the revision still properly blocks all cases where a ghost sponsor is parallel to *no* 1 arc or 2 arc at all, or parallel only to one which is not initial, e.g., *(55a). For in (55b) the ghost sponsor, C, is parallel to no initial nuclear term arc. In the same way, the proposed revision would, like French Rule 2, properly block other cases in which the condition of parallelhood to an initial nuclear term arc could not be met, e.g. *(63b), *(65b), *(67), *(70), *(72c), *(73b), *(74f) and *(75d). Just so, the revision would predict the failure of either type of 'raising' construction to 'feed' EXI in the main clause, for the same reasons, and hence correctly proscribe *(88d), *(92) and *(96).

However, at the same time, the proposed modification throws open the gates to many impossible EXI clauses. Nothing now blocks EXI with any arbitrary initially transitive clause and thus the grounds for, e.g. *(31b), *(32b), *(32d), *(33b), *(38b), *(85), and *(101b) are lost. Evidently then, if it is correct to weaken the condition on the initial arc to which an EXI construction ghost sponsor must be parallel, this weakening must be accompanied by some further condition of a different sort. Before turning to such a condition, consider briefly the formalization of the revised condition requiring a ghost sponsor to be parallel to an initial nuclear term arc.

One can, I believe, state this new condition in a slightly stronger form. The motivation for formulating the original absolutivity condition of French Rule 2 in terms of the concept *Parallel* was to account for the possibility of EXI with 'coreferential' reflexive clauses like (39b). However, if even initially ergative arcs are relevant, the possibility of EXI with 'coreferential' reflexive clauses can be attributed to the initial 1 arcs which such contain. Thus, my suggestion is that the initiality condition relevant for EXI is that the ghost sponsor be connected by the ancestral of the local successor relation (cf. footnote 2) to an initial nuclear term arc. This ancestral is the relation *R-Local Successor*. Now, there is an elegant way to build into the rule which will replace French Rule 2 the necessary concepts involving *R-Local Successor*.

Johnson and Postal (to appear) introduces (cf. definition 227 of Chapter 14) the concept Gr_x *Projection* as a property of an arc. An arc B·is a GR_x projection if and only if there is some arc, A, not necessarily distinct from B, such that A is both self-sponsoring (hence having the coordinate c_1) and a GR_x arc and B is related to A by *R-Local Successor*. Required here is essentially the identical notion, except that instead of a *property* of a single arc (B in the above discussion), one needs it to be a *relation* between B and A. More precisely:

(109) GR_x *Arc Projection*$(A, B) \leftrightarrow$
         GR_x arc(B) $\wedge$ Self-Sponsor(B) $\wedge$ R-Local Successor(A, B)

In these terms, *Nuclear Term Arc Projection*(A, B) is simply the special case of the notion in (109) where the value of the variable GR_x *arc* is fixed as *Nuclear Term arc*. Given this, what is now being proposed as the proper initiality condition on an EXI ghost arc sponsor, A, is:

(110) $(\exists C)$(Nuclear Term Arc Projection(A, C))

Given (110), the only 1 arcs which can sponsor EXI ghosts are those which are R-local successors of initial nuclear term arcs (Recall that *R-Local Successor*, like all ancestrals, is reflexive. Thus an arc is its own R-local successor although no arc is its own (local) successor).

We turn to the question of adding some condition to (110) to account for the fact that by no means all clauses satisfying (110) are suitable EXI clauses. In particular, a condition must eliminate most transitive initial 1s as possible EXI nominals, but somehow not necessarily eliminate those of cases like (108) nor, interestingly, those of 'coreferential' reflexive clauses like (39b). I will propose a hypothesis as to the nature of this condition. To state this, it is convenient to have a term for an arc instantiating the variable C in condition (110). That is, for a given EXI ghost sponsor A, it is useful to have a name for the initial arc, C, of which A must, according to (110) be an R-local successor. Informally, I will say that C is the *EXI basis* of A.

Given this, my hypothesis about the condition which supplements (110) is based on the following idea. When the EXI basis of a ghost sponsor is ergative at any stratum, that EXI basis must be parallel to a 2 arc. It is immediately clear how this condition will block EXI in ordinary transitive clauses. For in these, the EXI basis is the ghost sponsor itself, which is parallel to no 2 arc. The same idea explains why 'coreferential' reflexive clauses like (39) can permit EXI. Because, given the APG parallel arc approach to so-called 'coreference', the initial 1 arc in such clauses is parallel to an (initial) 2 arc (cf. (42b)). At the same time, it is clear how the proposed condition that the EXI basis be parallel to a 2 arc will permit EXI in general with intransitive clauses, whose I arcs will in general fail to be ergative at any stratum and thus will be suitable for EXI constructions if they satisfy (110). The same considerations hold for *non-reflexive* passive clauses (like that in (48c)), whose non-initial 1 arcs will also not be ergative at any stratum and which will satisfy (110) if their 2 arc predecessors are self-sponsoring. In the case of *reflexive* passive clauses like that represented in (48d), the non-initial 1 arc due to passivization will always be ergative in its first stratum, but will satisfy the proposed secondary condition by virtue of being parallel to the 2 arc of which it is a local successor. So far so good.

It remains to be shown, however, how this view of the supplementary condition accounts for (i) the well-formedness of examples like (108) in some varieties of French; (ii) the difference in well-formedness of (108) in different variants of French and (iii) the contrast between unspecified object clauses like (108) and those like *(38b). Recall that (46) above displays two different a priori possible structures for French unspecified object clauses. Assuming French Rule 2, it was unnecessary to find evidence distinguishing them, since either structure interacted with that rule to predict the impossibility of EXI with such clauses. Given (110) though, one can posit that those unspecified object clauses like (108) which are compatible with EXI are so because they are antipassive structures like (46b). On the contrary, unspecified object clauses which are incompatible with EXI, like (38b), can be hypothesized to have structures like (46a), in which the EXI basis is parallel to no 2 arc. Observe that in the antipassive structure (46b), the EXI basis, A, *is* parallel to a 2 arc. The antipassive hypothesis about clauses like (108) thus brings out a similarity within the class of initially transitive clauses between EXI with cases like (108) and EXI with 'coreferential' reflexive clauses. Namely, in these types, exceptionally for initially transitive clauses, an ergative EXI basis is parallel to a 2 arc.

Moreover, the antipassivization approach to (108) has the virtue of offering the proper flexibility to handle the varying acceptability of (108) in differing versions of French. We can say that all these versions have the same conditions on EXI, but that they (in particular, Pollock's and Ruwet's French) differ in the conditions under which antipassivization is possible. Since Ruwet's type of French apparently permits EXI with *no* unspecified object clauses, we can assume this variant of French does not permit antipassivization with such clauses, which leaves all of them failing to satisfy the supplementary condition. In the variant of French illustrated by Pollock's idiolect, however, antipassivization is permitted with a proper subset of unspecified object clauses, although we are not in a position to characterize this subset at the moment.

At this point, one might assume that the consequent of the proper replacement for French Rule 2 should be:

(111) $(\exists C)$(Nuclear Term Arc Projection$(A, C) \wedge$
         $(\text{Ergative}(C, c_1(a)) \rightarrow$
         $(\exists D)(2 \text{ arc}(D) \wedge \text{Parallel}(A, D))))$

(111) may be correct. However, it encounters a problem with cases of the sort referred to as reflexive antipassive clauses in Section 5.2. A glance at the

antipassive analysis of one such clause proposed in (80) above shows that, under such a treatment, these clauses satisfy (111). Despite this, they are incompatible with EXI, which is unexplained if (111) is correct. Since one virtue of French Rule 2 was to block EXI with clauses like (80), the lack of this consequence suggests that (111) is not altogether correct.

Unfortunately, predicting the ill-formedness of EXI with cases like (80) leads to a rather difficult area, one really beyond the scope of this discussion. Nonetheless, I would like briefly to indicate a possible approach to this question.

If, as I assume, examples like (108) are well-formed only because the clauses involve antipassivization, then this would also permit EXI in cases like (80). It may be necessary to conclude that cases like (80) are *not* antipassive clauses (of any subtype). An alternative hypothesis is that the proper structure for (79a) is then not (80) but:

(112)

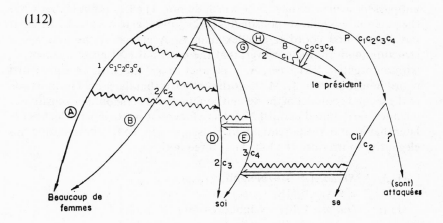

(112) is partially similar to the reflexive antipassive structure in (80). However, it contrasts in potentially important ways. In particular, (80) involves D, a *copy arc* in the sense of Johnson and Postal (to appear), that is, a replacer arc sponsored by a successor/predecessor pair which replaces and hence erases the *predecessor*. However, (112) involves a replacer arc, D, sponsored by a successor/predecessor pair which replaces and hence erases the *successor*. Suppose one refers to an arc like D in (112) as an *anticopy* arc. Such arcs were considered impossible in Johnson and Postal (to appear). They are inconsistent with several laws of that work, including PN laws 2

and 20 as well as Theorem 113 of Chapter 11. The latter is not a good basis for rejecting (112) as an analysis of (79a). For other evidence, some from Blackfoot (see Frantz (1979)) and some from Tzotzil (see Aissen, to appear b) has independently suggested that anticopy arcs do exist and thus that the assumption underlying Theorem 113 and the laws mentioned must be modified.

I will thus assume that (112) is viable. (112) now contrasts with antipassive structures like (46b). However, this contrast is so far useless for predicting the ill-formedness of EXI with clauses like (80). For (112) satisfies (111) as much as (46b) does, B in (112) being a 2 arc parallel to the initially ergative potential EXI basis A. My idea is that the second conjunct of the second conjunct of (111) must be slightly strengthened so that a potential EXI ghost sponsor whose EXI basis is an ergative arc is required not only to be parallel to a 2 arc but to *a special kind of* 2 *arc*. This will permit the rule to distinguish antipassive structures like (46b), which 'feed' EXI, from non-antipassive structures like (112), which do not. The key point is that while the potential EXI ghost sponsor A is (112) is parallel to a 2 arc, B, the latter has a later first coordinate index than A. A glance at the antipassive structure (46b) shows, however, that the potential EXI ghost sponsor, C, with an ergative EXI basis, A, is parallel to a 2 arc with an earlier first coordinate index than C. My hypothesis then is that the *proper* formulation of the second conjunct of the second conjunct of (111) should be sensitive to whether the required parallel 2 arc has a first coordinate index which is not later than that of the potential EXI ghost sponsor. To facilitate stating this elegantly, I introduce the following three notions:

(113) $Predate(A, B) \leftrightarrow Neighbor(A, B) \wedge$
         $c_k \alpha(A) \wedge c_j \beta(B) \wedge k \leqq j$

(114) $Outlast(A, B) \leftrightarrow Neighbor(A, B) \wedge$
         $\alpha c_k(A) \wedge \beta c_j(B) \wedge k > j$

(115) $GR_x \; Representative(A, B) \leftrightarrow Parallel(A, B) \wedge$
         $GR_x \; arc(B) \wedge Predate(B, A) \wedge Outlast(A, B)$

The term defined in (113) is to be read as 'A predates B'. Despite the asymmetrical implications of the term, A also predates B if they are neighbors and have the *same* first coordinate index. On the contrary, A outlasts B only if they are neighbors and A's last coordinate index is greater than B's.

The notion defined in (115) permits rules to reference the concept 2 *Representative(A, B)* introduced in (115), where the variable $GR_x \; arc$ is fixed as 2 *arc*. I then propose (116) as the proper replacement for French Rule 2:

(116)   French Rule 4
        Tail 1–1 Local Sponsor(a, A, B) ∧ Ghost(B) ∧
        Not(Head Labelled(Cl, A)) →
        (∃C)(Nuclear Term Arc Projection(A, C) ∧
        (Ergative(C, c_k(a)) → (∃D)(2 Representative(A, D))))

> "If a 1 arc, A, with tail node a and whose head node is not a
> clause node locally sponsors a ghost 1 arc, B, then there exists an
> arc, C, of which A is a nuclear term arc projection, and, if C is
> ergative at any stratum of a, then there exists an arc, D, of which
> A is a 2 representative."

The antecedent of French Rule 4 is, of course, the same as that of French
Rule 2. What this rule says, more informally, is that a 1 arc can be the
sponsor of an EXI ghost arc only if it is the remote local successor of an
initial (that is, self-sponsoring) nuclear term arc (its EXI basis) and only
where, if that EXI basis is ergative at any stratum, A is parallel to a 2 arc
whose first coordinate index is not greater than A's.

French Rule 4 predicts facts like *(82), under the assumption of structures
for these along the lines of (112), because the potential ghost sponsor in such
structures will not be a 2 representative. This follows because in (112),
although A is parallel to the 2 arc, B, A is not a 2 representative of B since B's
first coordinate index is greater than A's. On the contrary, French Rule 4
properly allows EXI with clauses like (108), on the assumption that these
have antipassive structures like (46b). For in (46b), the potential ghost
sponsor, C, is a 2 representative of B.[69]

Interestingly, French Rule 4 properly allows EXI with 'coreferential'
reflexive clauses having structures like (42b). For in these initially transitive
(ergative) clauses, the potential EXI ghost sponsor is a 2 representative.
Thus, in (42b), A is a 2 representative of B. It is now the notion 2
Representative which captures the similarity between antipassive clauses
and 'coreferential' reflexive clauses and which permits these, but not
structures like (112), to satisfy French Rule 4.

One difference between French Rule 4 and (111) has not been discussed.
In (111), the ergativity condition refers just to the first (c_1) stratum of the
EXI basis, while in French Rule 4, this has been generalized (via the
coordinate index variable k) to refer to the ergativity of the EXI basis at *any*
stratum. So far, no cases have been cited which differentiate these
formulations. Logically, such cases certainly could exist. French Rule 4
excludes as a potential ghost sponsor an initially absolutive 1 arc which is
ergative at a later stratum, while (111) was not incompatible with that. In
this respect, French Rule 4 contrasts as well with French Rule 2, which also

does not preclude cases where an initially absolutive 1 arc is ergative in a later stratum and yet sponsors an EXI ghost arc.

Examples relevant to distinguishing (111) and French Rule 4 do exist. One class of such cases would be initially intransitive clauses in which some oblique nominal advances to 2, making the initially absolutive 1 arc a later stratum ergative arc. French Rule 4 predicts that any such case must be incompatible with EXI in the absence of still later antipassivization. A natural potential source of such examples would be, e.g., single morphological verbs which are traditionally described as occurring intransitively with a locative complement or as transitives with a direct object of the locative sort. An example is *habiter* 'to reside'. Thus one finds such pairs of essential paraphrases as:

> (117)   a. Beaucoup d'avocats   habitent   à   Paris.
>   many   lawyers   live   in Paris
>   b. Beacoup d'avocats habitent Paris.

If cases like (117b) are analyzed with the nominal *Paris* as an initial locative which subsequently advances to 2 and which hence heads a 2 arc whose first coordinate is c_2, the 1 arc in (117b) would be initially absolutive, but ergative at a later stratum (the c_2 stratum). French Rule 4, unlike either (111) or French Rule 2, would then predict the incompatibility of EXI with such clauses, although it would not block EXI with those like (117a). And, as indicated to me by M. Gross, the facts support French Rule 4 here. For (117b) is like ordinary *initially* transitive clauses in being incompatible with EXI:[70]

> (118)   a. Il habite beaucoup d'avocats à Paris.
>   b. *Il habite beaucoup d'avocats Paris.
>   c. *Il habite Paris beaucoup d'avocats.

It might be argued that (118) does not really support French Rule 4 since the facts would follows also from French Rule 2 under the hypothesis that *habiter* has a dual analysis as an initially transitive verb and as an initially intransitive verb. This hypothesis would make *habiter* irrelevant to the question of whether ergativity at non-initial strata renders a 1 arc unsuitable as an EXI ghost sponsor. Such a dual analysis would, of course, be incompatible with PID, given the equivalence of (117a, b). Moreover, interestingly, there is straightforward evidence against such a dual analysis, this evidence then supporting both PID and French Rule 4.

As observed to me by M. Gross, with certain choices of nominals, the transitive *habiter* permits passives. If these clauses were genuinely *initially* transitive, one would predict the possibility of EXI with these passives. But this is impossible, just as with the passives based on *obéir*, etc., discussed earlier:

(119) a. Beacoup de petites villes françaises sont habitées par des
          many   small cities french   are inhabited by
          immigrants.
          immigrants
       b. *Il est habité beaucoup de petites villes françaises par des
          immigrants.

The impossibility of *(119b) follows from the requirement that the ghost sponsor be a nuclear term arc projection under the view that transitive *habiter* clauses involve locative to 2 advancement. For in these terms, the 1 arc provided by passivization is not a local successor of any *initial* 2 arc but only of a non-initial 2 arc which is a local successor of an initial locative arc. But the violation in *(119b) would be unexplained if *habiter* could occur in initially transitive clauses. I conclude that transitive clauses with *habiter* do involve locative to 2 advancement as PID predicts and thus that non-initially ergative 1 arcs are indeed blocked as EXI ghost sponsors, as the maximally general formulation of the ergativity condition in French Rule 4 claims.

While obviously this matter requires extensive testing with a variety of distinct verbs which can be argued to involve initially absolutive arcs which are later stratum ergative, my suspicion is that no clause which is transitive at later strata due to advancement will. permit EXI (without anti-passivization).

I have introduced French Rule 4 as a replacement for French Rule 2 chiefly to account for the possibility, in some varieties of French, of the combination of EXI with certain unspecified object clauses like (108), cited by Pollock (1978). I have then observed how French Rule 4 makes additional predictions with respect to clauses like those in (117). There is another potential domain where French Rule 4 may be superior to our original description. It has been observed that, for one class of speakers,[71] EXI is possible with 'coreferential' reflexive clauses. However, we have not previously pointed out that a French surface form which is interpretable as a 'coreferential' reflexive clause is normally also interpretable as a 'reciprocal' clause if it has a plural 1. Hence the following is ambiguous:

(120)   Beaucoup de femmes se sont tuées hier   soir.
        many   women self are   yesterday evening =

>   (i) 'Many women killed themselves yesterday evening', or:
>   (ii) 'Many women killed each other yesterday evening'

We have said nothing about the question of the compatibility of EXI with these different readings.

It appears though that, in many cases, even speakers who permit EXI with such clauses on 'coreferential' readings do not permit EXI with the 'reciprocal' readings. Hence Y.-C. Morin points out to me that (121) is unambiguous:

> (121)   Il s'est tué beaucoup d'hommes.
>   (i) 'Many men killed themselves'
>   (ii) *'Many men killed each other'

On the other hand, one cannot conclude that EXI is uniformly incompatible with 'reciprocal' interpretations. French has some verbs, including *entretuer*, morphologically related to that in (121), which seem only to occur in clauses with 'reciprocal' interpretations. But, as again observed to me by Morin, despite (121), the following example having only a 'reciprocal' interpretation is perfectly well-formed:

> (122)   Il s'est entretué beaucoup d'hommes.
>   'Many men killed each other'

The question arises, therefore, how a grammar of French can predict these facts and what bearing they have on the validity of French Rule 4 and its superiority to, e.g., French Rule 2. While I have not really been able to study this question, it is notable that unlike French Rule 2, French Rule 4 is compatible with a straightforward hypothesis which accounts for the facts about the interaction of EXI and 'reciprocal' interpretations just cited.

It follows from the meaning of 'reciprocal' clauses and, in particular, from their semantic contrast with 'coreferential' reflexive clauses that they will *not* have structures containing initial parallel 1 and 2 arcs, this structure characterizing 'coreferential' reflexive clauses. Therefore, the possibility of EXI in cases like (122) can be due only to one of two different factors, given French Rule 4. Either *entretuer* occurs in initially intransitive clauses, or in initially transitive clauses involving later stratum antipassivization. The former assumption is incompatible with PID given the essential equivalence of (121) on the relevant reading and (122). For *tuer* is evidently an *initially* transitive verb, and therefore, under PID, *entretuer* must be also. The possibility of EXI in (122) must then be attributed to antipassivization, just as for Pollock's (108). One can then simply describe the contrast between (121) and (122) with respect to EXI by stating that anti-passivization linked to 'reciprocal' structures in French is possible with *entretuer* but not with *tuer*. Conceivably, there is a broader generalization here, namely, if it turns out that EXI is systematically possible with 'reciprocal' verbs of the form *entre* + $stem_x$ but not with those of the form $stem_{x,}$. The grammar could then incorporate the generalization that 'reciporcal'-linked antipassivization in French is limited to clauses based on complex verbs with the prefix *entre*.

The 'reciprocal' cases, in particular (121), show that the possibility of EXI with 'coreferential' reflexive clauses is by no means solely attributable to the superficial intransitive-looking character of these clauses.[72] For the same superficial form occurs with 'reciprocal' interpretations and yet does *not* then permit EXI.

We have just discussed conditions which would differentiate the possibility of antipassivization with different types of 'reciprocal' clauses. Obviously, a differentiation is also necessary in the case of unspecified object clauses, to account for the contrast between e.g., *(38b) and (108) for those speakers who accept the latter. Some rule in this idiolect must guarantee that the former has a structure like (46a) and the latter one like (46b).[73] In this case, since both involve the same morphological verb, the dimensions of relevance seemingly must involve semantic factors, probably related to tense and aspect.[74]

In formulating French Rule 4, I have ignored the possibility that some properties of the EXI construction described therein might be con-sequences of grammatical laws. In particular, if it were lawful that *all* ghost arcs are sponsored by R-local successors of nuclear term arcs, it would not be necessary to specify this in French Rule 4. One would then expect to find that those properties of the French EXI construction which led to the nuclear term are projection condition would be typical of all constructions involving dummies in all languages.

While this possibility deserves study, there is some reason to doubt that such a strong law can be maintained. In particular, certain facts from French noted by Ruwet (1975: 116–121) cited in footnote 17 of Chapter 10 of Johnson and Postal (to appear) as falsifying a distinct potential law about ghost arcs (namely, that all ghost sponsors are self-sponsoring) also seem incompatible with the current proposal. Conceivably though, the proposal could be weakened in some way, perhaps only referring to 'non-clausal extraposition' dummies, since the facts attested by Ruwet involve clausal extraposition. That is, possibly the following potential law is viable:

(123)   Local Sponsor (A, B) $\wedge$ Ghost(B) $\wedge$
          Not (Head Labelled (Cl, A)) $\rightarrow$
          (($\exists$C)(Nuclear Term Arc Projection(A, C))

If something like (123) is valid, then, of course, much of French Rule 4 need not be stated in French grammar since it would be a theorem of grammatical theory and hence true of French (as of all languages) without any special statement. This discussion illustrates the general point that many grammatical truths about a particular language which seem to have to be taken as axioms (rules) of that language may later turn out to be theorems of axioms (laws) of grammatical theory. It is thus always reasonable and important to attempt to derive particular rules or their component conjuncts as theorems from some laws. But, of course, in many cases this will not be possible.

IBM Thomas J. Watson Research Center
Yorktown Heights

NOTES

[1] The present study would have been impossible without extremely generous help of a number of French speakers over some period of time. I would particularly like to express my deep appreciation to Gilles Fauconnier of the University of Paris VIII, Maurice Gross of the University of Paris VII, Vania Joloboff of the University of Grenoble, Yves-Charles Morin of the University of Montreal and Nicols Ruwet of the University of Paris VII for sharing some of their intuitions with me. None of them is, however, responsible for all of the judgements in this paper, still less are they to be blamed for any errors of fact or interpretation.

I must also express my great debt to Richard Kayne for the insights into French grammar I have obtained from his many writings on this topic, which have also proved basic to the present study.

I have some hope that the judgements cited in this work express properly the facts not only for those I consulted but for a wide range of French speakers. This hope is to a certain extent supported by citations and generalizations from the literature. Nonetheless, the hypotheses about French expressed here can and should be tested much more widely and I would be extremely pleased if this study were to stimulate such research on the part of French-speaking linguists.

I would also like to thank Judith Aissen, David Johnson, David Perlmutter, Warren Plath and Geoffrey Pullum for helpful comments on earlier versions of this study.

[2] An arc B is a *successor* of an arc, A, if and only if (i) A and B are distinct; (ii) A sponsors B; and (iii) A and B overlap, that is, they share the same *head* (node). If, in addition, A and B are neighbors, that is, share the same *tail* (node), then B is a *local* successor of A. In these cases, A is a (local) *predecessor* of B. For further details see Johnson and Postal (to appear).

[3] Roughly, we say that a nominal N *advances from* GR_x to GR_y when N is the head of a pair of arcs A, B, such that B is the local successor of A and the R-sign of A is GR_x the R-sign of B is

GR_y and GR_y outranks GR_x. If the ranking is reversed, we say that N *demotes* to GR_y from GR_x. The relevant ranking of R-signs is 1 outranks 2 outranks 3 outranks 8 or Oblique (= Instrumental, Benefactive, etc.).

[4] There has been considerable discussion in transformational terms about whether a nominal like *Joanne* in (1b) is a direct object or an indirect object (cf. Chomsky (1977: 157–8), Fiengo and Lasnik (1976: 185), Lightfoot (1976: 283)). There is no right answer since the question is wrongly posed to ignore what I claim is the right possibility, namely, that it is both. It is to me quite odd that it has proved so difficult for transformationalists to apply the same logic to this kind of case that has been more standardly applied to e.g., English passives. Given (i):

(i)   Joanne was tickled by Godzilla.

there was, at least at one time, widespread agreement that *Joanne* was both superficial subject and non-superficial direct object. What is necessary inter alia then is a framework which permits elements to bear more than one relation and to have these relations stratified into levels. Once one has this, the indirect object/direct object cases can be seen to be exactly parallel to passives, irrelevant questions of productivity aside.

[5] Examples like:

(i)   I showed to Bill *the tiny humanoid creature with the purple feet.*
(ii)   *What* did you show to Bill?

are not inconsistent with these ordering claims because the italicized nominals, although heads of 2 arcs in their respective pair networks, are not heads of *surface* 2 arcs, but of arcs representing distinct relations, claimed in Johnson and Postal (to appear, Chapter 7) to be members of a set of Overlay relations. Thus the heavy nominal in (i) is claimed to head an OW arc representing the overweight relation. This arc is a (foreign) successor of the 2 arc also headed by that nominal.

[6] One problem for this view consists of *converse* predicates like *buy/sell, left/right*, etc. It is unclear to me how to integrate these properly into the view being sketched. Perlmutter (this volume) also notes certain problems with the PID.

[7] But much of the rest of this paper is devoted to showing certain limitations on this constraint.

[8] The acceptability of examples like (10b) for different speakers is complicated by the alternative choices for marking what is, in current terms, the 2 chômeur determined by the advancement of the 3 to 2. In addition to the markers *d'* and *avec* in (10), one French speaker I consulted preferred *en*, although accepting *avec*, while rejecting *d'*. Several others also rejected *d'*, but did not like *avec* either. Nonetheless, the pattern in (10b) with *d'* is cited in standard French dictionaries (cf. Mansion (1940: 275)). Much further work would be necessary to determine the distribution of the general pattern in (10b) as opposed to limitations on the choice of chômeur markers.

[9] Blinkenberg (1960: 262) lists eleven verbs besides *fournir* which occur in both patterns like that in (10), that is, in patterns describable in current terms as involving the advancement of a 3 of 2.

[10] Morphologically, the preposition *à* combines with the plural definite article *les* to yield *aux*, with the singular definite article *le* to yield *au*. No analysis of this is offered here.

[11] These facts are described (in a very early transformational framework) in my doctoral thesis, published as Postal (1979).

[12] The technical notion necessary is apparently that of *output* 3, where an output 3 is a

nominal heading an *output* 3 arc, that is, one with no local eraser. A local eraser of an arc A is an arc B which (i) erases A and (ii) is a neighbor of A, that is, which shares its tail node with B.

[13] Unspecified nominals which are 3s are invisible, and I would claim the relevant 3 arcs self-erase, rather than have 2 arc local successors. This makes them final stratum 3 arcs but not output 3 arcs. Unlike the 3s which advance to 2 then, these do not determine object agreement (which is triggered by final stratum 2s).

[14] The word order in (17a) has the 3 preceding the 2 for the irrelevant reason that constituent-internal clauses are unacceptable in English.

[15] Some French speakers permit a superficial 2 with *pardonner*. But none seem to treat (*dés*)*obéir* in this way. We will thus stick to the latter two, which are of greater interest for present purposes.

[16] The dimension distinguishing personal from impersonal passive clauses can be precisely characterized in APG terms. Cf. the text below.

[17] We restrict attention here to *obéir* and related verbs with human complements. These verbs also take non-human complements designating orders, instructions, etc. Cf. footnotes 53.

[18] Of course, this terminology is transformational and not to be taken literally. In APG terms, there is nothing which could be called extraposition in the sense of a nominal with one 'position' taking on another 'position'. Also, we are not interested in cases, sometimes found with the same verbs, where *clauses* are 'extraposed'.

[19] The notion 'indefinite' here is vague, informal and inaccurate. For example, Ruwet (1975: 127) shows that this nominal can be cataphoric, and definite nominals in this construction are not lacking in the literature. We are not concerned here with these constraints, which are roughly analogous to those on post-verbal nominals with the dummy *there* in English.

[20] French permits two different prepositions with passive chômeurs, *de* and *par*. While the conditions on the choice of these need not concern us, some speakers have a distinct preference for *de* with (*dés*)*obéir*. Further, some speakers do not seem to accept personal passives with (*dés*)*obéir* with the *de/par* phrase absent. These restrictions seem independent of, and irrelevant to, any of the issues in this study.

[21] Morin (1977: 35) remarks as follows:

> Le verbe *obéir*, qui n'a pas de COD peut cependant entrer dans une construction SN-*par*, comme le montre l'exemple (i).
>
> (i)   (a) Jean sait faire [ses enfants obéir à soi]
>   (b) Jean sait se$_2$ faire [t_1 obéir t_2 par ses enfants$_1$]
>
> Cependant la construction SN-φ est impossible dans les mêmes conditions, comme le montre (ii).
>
> (ii)   *Jean sait se$_2$ faire [t_1 obéir t_2 ses enfants$_1$]
>
> Ce qui montre bein que les constructions SN-φ et SN-*par* sont bien en distribution complémentaire partout.
>
> Notons que Kayne *injustement* exclut *obéir* des constructions SN-*par*. C'est un fait que ce verbe ne peut pas rentrer dans une telle construction lorsque le COI de *obéir* n'est pas un réfléchi coréférentiel au subject du verbe *faire*, e.g., (iii). Mias il semble qu'il s'agisse là d'une condition sémantique. On observe les mêmes restrictions avec le verbe *respecter*, par exemple, qui lui possède un COD, cf. (iv).

(iii)   (a) Jean sait faire [ses enfants obéir à André]
       (b) *Jean sait faire obéir André par ses enfants
(iv)   (a) Jean sait se faire respecter par ses enfants
       (b) *Jean sait faire respecter André par ses enfants

Morin's terms 'COD' and 'COI' are roughly equivalent extensionally to our '2' and '3'. Morin's (i) gives rise to the example *Jean sait se faire obéir par ses enfants* 'John knows how to get himself obeyed by his children.' The parallelism between Morin's (iiib) and (ivb) indicates that the constraint on *obéir* as complement to *faire* is independent of any hypothetical adjectival status.

[22] Y.-C. Morin verifies that examples like (i) are ill-formed:

(i)   *Ça l'a rendu obéi de ses enfants.
          that him made obeyed by his children

And although he points out that not all indisputable adjectives can occur with *rendre*, there is still an argument against the adjectival character of *obéir*, etc., passives. For if these are passives, the properties in (i) follow directly, while if they are adjectives, some unknown constraint not necessarily of any generality must be invoked to block (i).

[23] Although *earlier* is not introduced as a technical term in Johnson and Postal (to appear), it is easily definable formally in that framework. One would say, roughly, that node a is an earlier GR_x of node b than it is a GR_y of node b if and only if a is the head of a GR_x arc (A) and a GR_y arc (B) both with tail b and the *first* coordinate index of A is less than the *first* coordinate index of B.

[24] I will not give the definition here (cf. Def. 153 in Chapter 10 of Johnson and Postal (to appear)). The basic idea is that a ghost arc is an arc with one of the nominal R-signs (1, 2, 3, etc.) with a single non-overlapping sponsor.

[25] For discussion, (cf. Perlmutter (1978), Perlmutter and Postal (to appear b, to appear c), Postal (to appear)).

[26] A brief idea of the potential power of this view is provided by Mohawk (cf. Postal (1979)). Recall that with transitive verbs, initial 2s generally permit incorporation. However, unusually, Mohawk also permits incorporation with the 1s of *some* intransitive verbs. If we claim that these verbs are a sub-set of those which take initial 2s, then the simple generalization needed for transitive cases carries over to the intransitive ones. Otherwise, as in Postal (1979), one needs an unrelated division of intransitive into two sets, a division ad hoc to Mohawk. The unaccusative hypothesis suggests to the contrary, that the intransitives which permit incorporation in Mohawk should be of the same set semantically as verbs which behave as unaccusatives in other languages, e.g., in never allowing impersonal passives (cf. Perlmutter (1978), Perlmutter and Postal (to appear b, to appear c), Postal (to appear)).

[27] If the initial 2 fails to advance to 1, and no other element advances to 1, a violation ensues of the earlier relational grammar law requiring every final stratum of a basic clause to contain a 1 arc. Cf. Perlmutter and Postal (to appear a), Johnson and Postal (to appear, PN Law 44).

[28] In fact, traditionally no distinction is usually drawn between EXI variants of personal passive clauses, clausal extraposition variants of personal passive clauses and genuine impersonal passive clauses. Cf. Grevisse (1969: 557), Gross (1975: 99).

Kayne and Pollock (1978) observe that in certain contexts, including subjunctive complements, the dummy of impersonal passive clauses can be invisible, so that one finds both (ia, b):

(i)   a. = Kayne and Pollock's (46a)
                     Je veux qu'il soit procédé au réexamen de cette question.
                     I want that it be proceeded to the reexamination of this problem
                 b. = Kayne and Pollock's (42a)
                     Je veux que soit procédé au réexamen de cette question.
                     I want that be proceeded to the reexamination of this problem
                     I want this problem to be reexamined.

They also note that in the same environments, a variety of other dummy nominals, including
that of EXI constructions (cf. (iid)), cannot be invisible:

(ii)   = Kayne and Pollock's (47–50)
                 a. Je veux qu'il pleuve.
                     I want that it rain
                     I want it to rain.
                 b. *Je veux que pleuve.
                     I want that rain
                 c. Je veux qu'il vienne 35 personnes.
                     I want that it come 35 people
                     I want 35 people to come.
                 d. *Je veux que vienne 35 personnes.
                     I want that come 35 people

    In APG terms, it seems that such invisibility of pronominal elements is to be accounted for by
permitting certain arcs to self-erase (that is, in the terms of Section 1 of this paper, failing to
block self-erasure for certain arcs). In the French cases of interest here, what is involved then is
the possibility of the self-erasure of certain ghost arcs or their 1 arc local successors in a class of
contexts we can abbreviate as K. Significantly then, one can easily distinguish well-formed
cases of such self-ensure as in (i) from ill-formed cases like those in (ii), especially EXI cases like
(iic), by assuming the relevant rule refers to the distinction between stable and unstable ghost
arcs. That is, the only 1 arcs headed by dummies which can self-erase in K are those local
successors of *un*stable ghost arcs, hence those of impersonal passives but not, inter alia, those of
EXI constructions like (iic). The distinction noted by Kayne and Pollock thus provides some
support for the distinction between stable and unstable ghost arcs.
[29] The reasons why neither non-reflexive accusative cliticization nor 'extraction' 'feed' the
EXI construction are briefly gone over in Section 5.1.
[30] Some of the first category permit this:

(i)   Kayne (1975: 379)
                 Il lui   est venu une idée.
                 it to him/her came   an idea = '(S)he got an idea'

Cf. Section 5.5.
[31] Ruwet (1972: Chapter 3) provides a detailed account of many differences between inherent
or neuter reflexives and *se moyen* reflexives.
[32] Roughly (for a precise account, cf. Johnson and Postal (to appear: Chapter 8)), final stratum
transitive clauses contrast with final stratum intransitive clauses in complements in clause
union construction, of which the *faire* construction is an instance as follows. If the

complement is final stratum intransitive, its final 1 is the head of an upstairs foreign successor 2 arc. If the complement is final stratum transitive, its final 2 is the head of an upstairs foreign successor 2 arc, its final 1 the head of an upstairs foreign successor 3 arc. In French, one then finds contrasts like:

(i) a. Marie a fait sortir l'enfant / (*à l'enfant).
          Marie had   go out the child   = 'Marie had the child go out'
     b. Marie a fait manger du pain (*l'enfant)/à l'enfant
                    eat   bread   = 'Marie had the child eat bread.'

Thus the complement 1 of a transitive clause shows up upstairs as a 3. By this criterion, passive clauses, unspecified object clauses, and simple 'coreferential' reflexive clauses are all final stratum intransitive:

(ii)   a. Le capitaine a fait détruire la   maison /(*à la maison) par les soldats.
             the captain   had   destroy the house   by the soldiers
             = 'The captain had the house destroyed by the soldiers.'
        b. Marie a fait manger Claude / (*à Claude).

(on the reading where *Claude* is initial 1 of the complement; (iib) also means 'Marie had unspecified eat Claude' on which reading it involves, I think, a passive complement with invisible initial 1)

          'Marie had Claude eat'
       c. Marie a fait se   tuer Jacques /(*à Jacques).
                 self kill   = 'Marie had Jacques kill himself'

[33] Thus:

(i)   Marie a fait parler Claude à   Gilles.
        Marie had   speak Claude to Gilles   = 'Marie had Claude speak to Gilles.'

However, the situation is complicated by the fact, briefly noted in Kayne (1975: 276, footnote 4) and stressed in Morin (1977), that many speakers permit variants of (i) in which *Claude* is marked with *à*, or, better, where the complement 1 manifests as a dative clitic on the main verb. These examples cause problems for most of the analyses of these constructions which have been suggested, including that assumed here.

[34] Ruwet (1972: 21, 166–7) and Kayne (1975: 331) have considered the possibility of accounting for certain features of EXI constructions as consequences of Emonds' conception of structure preservation (see Emonds 1976 for a recent exposition) combined with the view that there is a structure preserving transformation of NP extraposition. Kayne (to appear) citing Hériau (1976), which I have not seen, gives examples which he takes to preclude such an analysis, even in transformational terms.

    Moreover, a survey of the rest of this paper will show that the restrictions accounted for by the structure preservation approach follow from the constraint argued for here. But the latter constraint has a wide range of other apparently correct consequences which do not follow from a notion of structure preservation, and is thus to be preferred on this ground.

[35] Such reflexive clauses must be distinguished from many other types of reflexives includig *se* moyen reflexives and neuter reflexives. For another type, cf. Section 5.2.

There is evidently a dialect split with respect to the possibility of EXI with 'coreferential' reflexive clauses. Martin (1970: 380) rejects this possibility outright and V. Joloboff also did not accept them. Alternative descriptions of these several dialects are given below.
[36] As discussed in Postal (1976). Cf. footnote 32 (iic).
[37] Kayne (1975: 381) gives such striking contrasts as:

(i)   Il s'est dénoncé   trois mille   hommes ce mois-ci.
           it self denounced three thousand men   this month

(ii)   *Il $\left\{ \begin{array}{l} \text{nous} \\ \text{les} \end{array} \right\}$ a dénoncés trois mille hommes ce mois-ci.

           $\left\{ \begin{array}{l} \text{us} \\ \text{them} \end{array} \right\}$

[38] This is the APG reconstruction and elaboration of an idea which has previously surfaced in both stratificational and transformational linguistics.Cf. Postal and Pullum (1978, fn. 10) for references.
[39] E, which self-erases and is thus not a surface arc, is present under the assumption inherent in PID that a fixed predicate like 'offer' always takes a fixed number (in fact, three) of arguments of a fixed type. The logic of this assumption is rather parallel to that appealed to by Dowty, who writes in a different framework (David R. Dowty, 'Dative "Movement" and Thomason's Extensions of Montague Grammar,' in Steven Davis and Marianne Mithun (eds.), *Linguistics, Philosophy and Montague Grammar*, The University of Texas Press, pp. 202–03. Copyright © 1979 by the University of Texas Press):

> An analogous problem arises with certain *to*-datives that do allow dative shift but do not allow dative passive (at least for some speakers): these are verbs that describe the propelling of an object through space in a particular way, such as *pitch, toss, throw, roll, slide, hurl, sail, etc.* Thus everyone accepts *Mary tossed John the apple*, but few accept (*) *John was tossed the apple* (*by Mary*). Under the rules given so far, the grammaticality of the first sentence ought to imply the grammaticality of the second.
> I think that a clue to the correct analysis of this class (whatever that analysis may be) is that the *to*-phrases with these verbs (like *for*-phrases) are adverbial modifiers and do not represent the third argument of a three-place predicate. Whereas any true three-place verb entails the existence of a recipient even when that recipient is not mentioned. *cf. John awarded the prize* above). I believe it can be true that John tossed (pitched, rolled, etc.) the ball without it being true that there was someone to whom John tossed (etc.) the ball. (Note that it is the entailment of an intended *recipient* (typically animate) of the direct object, that is relevant here, not just the entailment of an intended *goal*; dative shifted verbs are inevitably interpreted as having an intended recipient, as witnessed by the anomaly of *John tossed the fence the ball* vis-a-vis *John tossed the ball to the fence*, or the familiar fact that *John took his pet alligator to the zoo* is ambiguous, but *John took the zoo his pet alligator* is not.) Of the *to*-datives listed in the appendices in Green (1974), those that turn out to be two-place rather than three-place verbs by the entailment test are almost exactly the ones for which Green marks the dative passive as unacceptable in her judgment, and I doubt that this correlation can be accident.l. Thus *John tossed Mary the ball* should definitely not have an analysis parallel to *John gave Mary the book* (lest the undesirable passive be produced), but one in which *Mary* is an adverbial modifiers rather than the direct object.

In current terms, incidentally, the difference between *toss* and, e.g., *give*, would be that *give* takes an initial 3, while *toss* takes an initial directional which subsequently advances to 3. The variant of English which does not permit passives of the type *Melvin was tossed, rolled, slid the apple* would then have a rule of roughly the form in (i):

(i)   3-Directional Local Successor(A, B) ∧ R-Local Successor(C, A) →
                Not (1 arc(C))

       "If A is a 3 arc local successor of a directional arc B and C is a remote local successor of A, then C is not a 1 arc."

The failure of a directional like *the fence* to show up as a 2 with these verbs noted by Dowty, e.g.,

(ii)   a. I rolled the ball to $\left\{ \begin{array}{c} \text{John} \\ \text{the fence} \end{array} \right\}$

        b. I rolled $\left\{ \begin{array}{c} \text{John} \\ *\text{the fence} \end{array} \right\}$ the ball.

could be represented by a condition saying that directional to 3 advancement with these verbs (possibly with all verbs in English) is possible only when the nominal heading the directional arc is 'animate' (i.e., designates a mind-possessing object).

[40] Although formulated in essentially derivational and transformational terms, the discussion in Cole and Sridhar (1977) claims in effect that the relevant laws must be rejected. But although they present some difficult data, I do not think they justify such a rejection. The matter deserves a more thorough discussion than is possible here. But one should mention one of their two cases, which concerns Hebrew causative constructions. This is worth discussing because it is related to our earlier discussion of limitations on the advancement of 3s to 2.

If I understand Cole and Sridhar properly, they reject the claim that a transitive clause union complement lawfully has its final 1 manifest as an upstairs 3 because, although there are, in Hebrew, causative constructions which even superficially satisfy this claim, there are others which could only be made compatible with it by assuming that 3s advance to 2 in causatives. Cole and Sridhar reject such an analysis just because there seem to be *no other cases* in Herbew where 3s advance to 2. But, as the earlier discussion should have made clear, there is no reason to object to a language having a rule which says that 3s can advance to 2 only with a single verb, e.g., the causative verb, any more than there can be an a priori objection to a language like French, which has this kind of advancement for only a few dozen verbs at best. Cole and Sridhar give no reason to believe that a better description of Hebrew is obtained by abandoning the laws of relevance as opposed to maintaining them while positing a highly ad hoc constraint on advancement of 3s to 2.

Cole and Sridhar in effect consider the latter possibility, but reject it, not on substantive linguistic grounds, but on methodological ones, claiming (1977: 705, footnote) that 'this position is not in keeping with sound linguistic methodology'. They then go on to state that the position they reject, and which I advocate, would be 'denuding linguistics of its empiricial basis'.

But this methodological claim is not only not supported by these authors, it is unsupportable and false. It is trivial to find possible factual consequences of the kind of ad hoc rule postulation which these authors claim must be methodologically banned as empty. Suppose, for example, that Hebrew had some rule which was sensitive, in something like the way French EXI is argued to be, to the difference between 2s that head arcs which are local successors of 3 arcs and others. Then the analysis I advocate for Hebrew, and that which Cole and Sridhar try to convince us must be abandoned *on methodological grounds*, would make different predictions with respect to the behavior of the superficial 2s whose earlier 3hood is in doubt.

Below I argue that the French verb *munir* occurs in clauses which have properties much like those needed to account for Hebrew causatives in a way consistent with the laws Cole and Sridhar reject. In particular, I argue that *munir* occurs in clauses which must involve advancement of the 3 to 2, even though *munir* clauses never occur with superficial 3s. And while advancement of 3s to 2 is not as limited in French as in Hebrew, it is hardly productive. Thus the validity of the analysis of *munir* clauses already would show that Cole and Sridhar's methodological objections cannot stand.

While these remarks fail, of course, to show that my proposal about Hebrew is correct and theirs incorrect, they do indicate that there can be no methodological objection of the sort they raise to the proposal to ad hoc 3 advancement. And Cole and Sridhar fail to offer any substantive grounds for preferring their position. I would conclude that since my proposal maintains otherwise (as even they admit) highly desirable laws which theirs must reject, the advancement proposal is to be adopted unless some factual grounds can be discovered which support its rejection.

[41] The invisibility of the relevant nominal would be consistent with the final stratum transitivity of (40b) if the final stratum 2 arc either self-erased or had a foreign eraser. For, as shown by Theorems 44 and 45 in Johnson and Postal (to appear, Chapter 6), either of these conditions guarantees that the erased arc is a final stratum arc.

[42] On the other hand, as illustrated in (46b) below, antipassivization is still possibility the correct analysis for the final intransitivity of unspecified object clauses. For reasons discussed in Johnson and Postal (to appear, Chapter 9), a demotion to 3 analysis is not possible in these cases in any language.

[43] In APG terms, there are two distinct issues to be kept clear here. First, some rule must guarantee that the full range of relevant reflexive 2s demote to 3. Second, if, as seems probable, no other 2s demote to 3 in French, some other rule must guarantee this.

The rule guaranteeing the first constraint is not hard to state, given a definition of the notion *reflexive arc*. This is not defined in Johnson and Postal (to appear). But, making use of concepts introduced there, one could introduce a relevant notion as follows:

(i)   Definition
           Reflexive arc$(A) \leftrightarrow (\exists B)$(Anaphoric arc(B) $\wedge$ R-successor(A, B) $\wedge$
           (Seconds (C, B) $\rightarrow$ Neighbor (A, C)))

           "A is a reflexive arc if and only if there is an anaphoric arc B of which A is an ancestral successor and if C seconds B then A is a neighbor of C"

Seconds and *Anaphoric arc* are introduced in Johnson and Postal (to appear, Chapter 11). The prefix *R*-designates the ordinary ancestral of the relation which follows it. Thus, informally, a reflexive arc A is an arc ancestrally connected by the successor relation to an anaphoric arc B, where A is a neighbor of the arc which seconded B. *Seconds* is a relation which holds between that one of the two sponsors of a replacer arc (all anaphoric arcs are replacers) which is *not* a facsimile of the replacer. Thus in (40b), C is a replacer seconded by A. Since C is an anaphoric arc and since it is a neighbor of B, it is a reflexive arc.

Given (i), a rule demanding that all French reflexive 2s demote to 3 can be given simply as:

(ii)   French Rule for Reflexive Demotion
        Reflexive arc(A) ∧ 2 arc(A) → (∃B)(3–2 Local Successor(B, A))
        "If A is a reflexive arc and a 2 arc, there exists a 3 arc B which is a local successor of A"

[44] In relational grammar (cf. Perlmutter and Postal (1977, to appear a)) this principle was stipulated as a law. In Johnson and Postal (to appear), it is shown how, under certain assumptions, the result follows as a theorem. But these assumptions are themselves unsettled, and it may be right to return to taking the condition as a law.

[45] When a wider class of French facts is considered, it may be necessary to amend this in such a way that only demotion 3 chômeurs would fail to determine dative clitics, while advancement 3 chômeurs would allow this. Demotion 3 chômeurs are those resulting from the demotion of a 1 or 2 to a 3, with an earlier 3 then demoting to a demotion 3 chômeur. Advancement 3 chômeurs are those resulting from the advancement of, e.g., a dead nominal (cf. Johnson and Postal (to appear, Chapter 8)) to 3, with an earlier 3 then demoting to an advancement 3 chômeur. One reason for thinking that the latter type of chômeurs do determine dative clitics arises from unusual, ignored or wrongly rejected (cf. Martinon (1927: 287), footnote 5)) sentences like (i), cited in Morin (1977, 1978):

(i)   Elle me leur   en   a fait donner deux.
       she me them of them had give   two   = 'She had me give two of them to them.'

Here *me* and *leur* are both dative clitics. My tentative view is that this is possible, despite the injunctions of traditional French grammars, because both the complement 1 and complement 3 are 3s of the upstairs clause, a different strata. Schematically, the situation is this. The downstairs 1 is assigned as upstairs 3, the downstairs 2 as upstairs 2, the downstairs 3 as upstairs dead. This yields the third stratum upstairs. But then the dead advances to 3, with the 3 demoting to an (advancement) 3 chômeur. The conditions permitting or requiring the advancement of deads to 3 require intensive study. But if this analysis is correct, it follows that 3 chômeurs cannot always preclude dative clitization.

[46] This does not mean there are not exceptional cases, which follow so far from no known constraints. Thus, M. Gross points out that a verb like *aimer* 'to like, love' does not permit EXI variants of its passives.

[47] Therefore, although (25c) involves advancement of a 2 to 1, it is *not* a passive clause. The condition defining passivization is more easily stated in terms of the concept *overrun*, introduced in Johnson and Postal (to appear). Roughly, one arc, A, overruns another, B, if and only if A and B are facsimiles and the first coordinate index of A is + 1 of the last coordinate index of B. In these terms, a passive clause is one in which:

(i)   (∃A)(∃B)(∃C)(1–2 Local Successor(A, B) ∧ Overrun(A, C))

[48] This is the simplest situation and that assumed in the rule in (ii) of footnote 43.

[49] Observe that G in (48d) is a reflexive arc by the definition in (i) of footnote 43 and thus falls under the rule in (ii) of that footnote.

[50] Y.-C. Morin has pointed out to me that the passive-like construction in (i) permits EXI

variants under certain conditions, as shown by (ii):

(i)   De grand malheurs   sont à craindre.
           great   misfortunes are   to be feared
(ii)   Il est à craindre de grands malheurs.

This suggests that this construction should have a passive analysis.
[51] On the other hand, Obenauer (1976: 26) records the following judgements:

(i)   *?Il a travaillé trois plombiers ici.
           it worked   three plumbers here.

(ii)   *?Il a chanté deux frères   de Paulette.
           it sang   two brothers of Paulette.

[52] One difference is that (47) would apparently preclude EXI for indirect transitive clauses while (52) would allow it. But cf. Section 5.5.
[53] Although (dés)obéir occurs with both human and non-human complements, we have so far restricted attention only to the former. Non-human complements also raise interesting problems for an account of EXI. In particular, the interaction of passivization and EXI with these non-human complements seems to be quite parallel to that found with human complements:

(i)   a. On a obéi à beaucoup d'ordres.
              one obeyed to many   orders = 'One obeyed many orders.'
           b. Beaucoup d'ordres ont été obéis   (par/de les soldats). (de + les = des)
              many   orders were obeyed by   the soldiers
           c. *Il a été obéi beaucoup d'ordres (par/de les soldats). (de + les = des)

That is, given previous remarks, the non-human nominals with these verbs behave with respect to EXI as if they are *not* initial 2s. This raises problems at this point basically for PID. For it is not clear how this should be made concrete with respect to verbs meaning 'order' to guarantee that the non-human nominals with *obéir* would *not* be initial 2s. Of course, if it were simply a matter of assigning some initial relations to these nominals ad hoc, there would be little problem in assigning them some initial relation distinct from 2.
[54] I am assuming that French does *not* allow the direct advancement of 3s to 1, that is, that it has the rule:

(i)   1-GR$_x$ Local Successor(A, B) → Not(3 arc(B))
           "If A is a 1 arc local successor of an arc B, then B is not a 3 arc".

In effect, this means that when the earlier 3 of *obéir*, etc., shows up as a later 1, it must be via an intermediate stage of 2hood.
   This view is incompatible with the claim made in effect in some unpublished work by G. Lakoff and in Lakoff (1977). Cf. Section 6.3.
[55] That is, nothing a priori determines that these French verbs are not like English *telephone*, which, given PID, must be a verb which takes a 3, requires it to advance to 2 when the initial 2 is unspecified, but which is not incompatible with the 3 being a final 2.
[56] The situation is more complex. M. Gross informs me that even examples like (57), which contain features maximally compatible with the *se moyen* construction, are at best only 'sort of acceptable'. Without these, *obéir*, etc., are impossible in *se* moyen clauses. Gross indicates that

examples like (57) really belong to a variety of non-standard French usually referred to as 'popular French'. Consequently, the interaction of *se moyen*, verbs like *obéir* and EXI can really only be studied for genuine speakers of that language variety.

[57] Making use of the ancestral relation of the relation *Local Successor*, indicated by *R-Local Successor*, a simpler version of the consequent of (61) can be given as:

(i) $(\exists C)(\text{Absolute }(C, c_1(a)) \wedge \text{R-Local Successor}(A, C))$

[58] For questions of the choice of chômeur marking in such cases, cf. footnote 8.

[59] Alone among the French speakers whose opinions on such sentences I have been able to obtain, M. Gross did not report a relatively clear distinction between pairs like (63a, b) (and also (74d, f)) below. That is, examples like (63b, 74f) seemed only strained to him. I have no explanation of these judgements at the moment.

[60] Arcs C, D and E in (68) indicate a curious interaction between the assumption that *munir* is a verb requiring (certain) of its 3 arcs to have 2 arc local successors and the assumption, formalized in footnote 43, that reflexive 2 arcs in French have 3 arc local successors. These assumptions combine to yield the 'black and forth' situation in (68).

We have not made precise the constraints which determine the existence of D in (68). I believe the natural way to state these is as follows. First, since we are assuming *munir* requires certain instances of the advancement of 3s to 2, it follows that *munir* permits this. Once can account for this by adding *munir* to the list of stems in the set of French Rule 1 in (11b). This permits D. Something is then necessary to indicate that a *munir* clause without the analogue of D would be ill-formed. Given other constraints, both universal and particular to French, including that in footnote 54(i), I would assume the proper constraint would block output 3 arcs with *munir*. However, E in (68), which is an output 3 arc (that is, one with no *local* eraser), shows that a restriction is necessary. This is required by the assumption that reflexive 2s demote to 3, and may indicate that assumption is incorrect.

Without going that far, we can accommodate (68) to the reflexive demotion rule in footnote 43, by giving a constraint for *munir* of the form:

(i)   3 arc(A) $\wedge$ Tail Output 3 arc(a, A) $\wedge$ V-Stemmed(a, *mun*(ir)) →
        $(\exists B)(3$–2 Local Successor(A, B)))

"If A is an output 3 arc with tail node *a* and *a* is v-stemmed *mun*, then there is a 2 arc B of which A is the local successor."

This then allows output 3 arcs in *munir* clauses only in cases like (68), that is, only where the output 3 arc in question is the local successor of a 2 arc. Given (i), there could not be a variant of (68) in which C had no local successor and showed up as an output 3 arc, since C is not the local successor of any 2 arc.

[61] The nature of the underlying predicate represented by x in (84) need not concern us here. Some speculations on this score are given in Johnson and Postal (to appear, Chapter 7).

[62] Fauconnier (1974: 209–210) takes facts like (88) to be an argument for the cyclicity of the transformation Extraposition relevant to (89a), since post-cyclical application of the rule would not account for differences like (88d) vs. (89b). In APG terms, however, cyclicity makes no sense. It is noteworthy, therefore, that the facts in question are direct consequences of the initial absolutivity condition which, as we have seen, is motivated by, and accounts for, a host of facts for which appeal of cyclicity would be irrelevant.

[63] One cannot test EXI with *se* moyen variants of examples like (91a) because, as observed by Ruwet (1972: 113), *se* moyen is not possible in these 'raising' cases.

[64] Actually, one of those French speakers I consulted, V. Joloboff, seemed at one point to accept some EXI variants analogous to (92), but only with certain complement adjectives. I do not understand these reactions and this matter obviously deserves much further investigation.

[65] As observed by Aissen (1979), the following interaction of EXI with 'coreferential' pronouns support the initiality part of the absolutivity condition even under the APG view that the indefine nominal would head a complement clause 1 arc as well as a main clause 1 arc:

(i)   a. Quelques hommes ont dit qu'ils avaient été arrêtés.
              A few men said that they had been arrested.
           b. *Il a dit quelques hommes qu'ils avaient été arrêtés.

The point is that even though *quelques hommes* in (ib) heads an initial absolutive arc in the complement, this does not suffice to satisfy French Rule 2, which requires that the initial absolutive arc be a neighbor of the ghost arc defining the EXI clause itself, in (ib), the main clause. And in the main clause, *quelques hommes* heads only an initial ergative arc, since the *dit* clause is initially transitive, with the whole complement clause as initial 2.

[66] As argued in Perlmutter (1978), Perlmutter and Postal (to appear b, to appear c), Johnson and Postal (to appear) and Postal (to appear), a key claim connected with initial unaccusativity is that no such clause can have an impersonal passive variant (more generally, any passive variant, thus nothing like an English pseudo-passive, also possible with some intransitives). Hence taking a clause like that in (99) to be unaccusative claims that it cannot enter into the marginal French impersonal passive construction.

[67] Of course, it is irrelevant if some French speakers accept (101b) on a reading 'He/it makes/has many things laugh', which has nothing to do with EXI.

[68] Actually, as discussed in detail in Johnson and Postal (to appear, especially Chapter 14), certain phenomena which would be global in derivational terms require the use of ancestrals of certain APG relations, and thus an extension of the class of terms required for rule statements. However, it is easy to restrict this kind of extension, simply by limiting the class of such ancestrally defined terms which can appear in APG rules.

[69] Observe that the 2 representative condition properly predicts that A in (46b) is not a possible ghost arc sponsor.

[70] While rejecting *(118b), N. Ruwet informs me that he finds (118c) relatively acceptable. I can finds no explanation for this judgement, which appears as an anomaly in the framework developed here unless one appeals to antipassivization. Even this, however, would offer no insight into the différence Ruwet finds between (118b, c).

[71] Earlier, distinct rules were provided for varieties of French which, e.g., did not permit EXI in 'coreferential' reflexive clauses, e.g., French Rule 2a vs. French Rule 2. The same dialectal contrasts can be characterized with French Rule 4 as a starting basis. Necessary would be a less general version of the notion GR_x *Representative* (A, B) in (115) in which the conjunct *Local Successor* (A, B) replaces *Parallel* (A, B). Suppose one refers to this slightly different notion as *Strong* GR_x *Representative* (A, B). Then if one utilizes this notion in a rule otherwise like French Rule 4, the grammar maintains most consequences previously discussed but does not permit EXI with 'coreferential' reflexive clauses.

[72] This point is already made by the fact, reiterated in footnote 71, that certain French speakers also reject EXI with 'coreferential' interpretations of superficial reflexive clauses.

[73] The assumption that some French unspecified object clauses do *not* involve anti-

passivization requires a major modification in the treatment of the behavior of these clauses as complements in the *faire* construction, mentioned in footnote 32. While no discussion of this is possible here, other evidence points in the same direction, indicating that the 'intransitive' behavior of certain French clauses must be analyzed in terms of advancement of a 3 to 2 in the main clause rather than in terms of detransitivization in the complement.

[74] The relevant condition seems to have something to do with 'habituality' but is obscure. In particular, it is not simply that EXI in these cases is incompatible with past tense. As J.-Y. Pollock has verified, alongside *(38b) and (108), one finds the well-formed past tense example:

(i)   Il n'a jamais mangé autant de linguistes dans ce restaurant.
         it has never eaten as many linguists in this restaurant

REFERENCES

Aissen, J. (1979) Formal comments given at Brown University Conference on the Nature of Syntactic Representation, Providence, Rhode Island.

Aissen, J. (to appear a) 'Indirect Object Advancement in Tzotzil,' in Perlmutter (ed.) (to appear a).

Aissen, J. (to appear b) 'Possessor Ascension in Tzotzil,' in L. Martin (ed.), *Studies in Mayan Linguistics*.

Authier, J. (1972) *Étude sur les formes passives du français*, Documentation et Recherche en Linguistique Allemande Contemporaine – Vincennes, Papier No. 1, Université de Paris VIII.

Blinkenberg, A. (1960) *Le Problème de la transitivité en français moderne*, Munksgaard, Copenhagen.

Boons, J.-P., A. Guillet, and C. Leclère (1973) *La Structure des phrases simples en français*. I: *Les verbes intransitifs* Laboratoire d'Automatique, Documentaire et Linguistique, C.N.R.S., Paris.

Chomsky, N. (1964) *Current Issues in Linguistic Theory*, Mouton and Co., The Hague.

Chomsky, N. (1977) *Language and Responsibility*, Pantheon Books, New York.

Cole, P. and S. W. Sridhar (1977) 'Clause Union and Relational Grammar: Evidence from Hebrew and Kannada,' *Linguistic Inquiry* 8, 700–713.

Dowty, D. (1979) 'Dative "Movement" and Thomason's Extensions of Montague Grammar', in S. Davis and M. Mithun (eds.), *Linguistics, Philosophy and Montague Grammar*, University of Texas Press, Austin.

Emonds, J. E. (1976) *A Transformational Approach to English Syntax*, Academic Press, New York.

Fauconnier, G. (1974) *La Coréférence: syntaxe ou sémantique*, Seuil, Paris.

Fiengo, R. and H. Lasnik (1976) 'Some Issues in the Theory of Transformations,' *Linguistic Inquiry* 7, 182–192.

Frantz, D. G. (1979) 'Multiple dependency in Blackfoot,' *Proceedings of the Fifth Annual Meeting of the Berkeley Linguistic Society*, University of Califormia, Berkeley.

Gaatone, P. (1970) 'La transformation impersonnelle en français,' *Le Français moderne* 38, 389–411.

Grevisse, M. (1969) *Le Bon Usage*, Editions J. Duculot, Gembloux.

Gross, M. (1975) *Méthodes en syntaxe*, Hermann, Paris.

Harris, A. (1976) *Grammatical Relations in Modern Georgain*, unpublished Doctoral Dissertation, Harvard University, Cambridge, Mass.

Harris, A. (to appear a) 'Inversion as a Rule of Universal Grammar: Georgian Evidence,' in Perlmutter (ed.) (to appear b).

Harris, A. (to appear b.) *Georgian Syntax: A Study in Relational Grammar.*

Hériau, M. (1976) *Le verbe impersonnel en français moderne.* Thèse de Doctorat d'état,Universite de Haute-Bretagne, Rennes.

Johnson, D. E. and P. M. Postal (to appear) *Arc Pair Grammar.* Princeton University Press, Princeton, New Jersey.

Kayne, R. (1975) *French Syntax*, MIT Press, Cambridge, Mass.

Kayne, R. (to appear) 'Rightward NP Movement in French and English.'

Kayne, R, and J.-Y. Pollock (1978) 'Stylistic Inversion, Successive Cyclicity, and Move NP in French, *Linguistic Inquiry* 9, 595–622.

Lakoff, G. (1977) 'Linguistic Gestalts,' in W. A. Beach, et. al., eds., *Papers from the Thirteenth Regional Meeting, Chicago Linguistic Society*, Chicago.

Lightfoot, D. (1976) The Theoretical Implications of Subject Raising. *Foundations of Language* 14, 257–376.

Mansion, J. E. (1940) *Mansion's Shorter French and English Dictionary*, D. C. Heath and Co., Boston.

Martin, R. (1970) 'La Transformation impersonnelle,' *Revue de linguistique romane* 34.

Martinon, P. (1927) *Comment on parle en français*, Librairie Larousse, Paris.

Morin, Y. C. (1977) 'Une réanalyse des constructions en *faire*,' unpublished paper, Université de Montreal.

Morin, Y. C. (1978) 'Interprétation des pronoms et des réfléchis en français,' *Syntaxe et semantique du Français, Cahier de Linguistique* 9, Montreal.

Obenauer, H.-G. (1976) *Etudes de syntaxe interrogative du français*, Max Niemeyer Verlag, Tübingen.

Perlmutter, D. M. (1971) *Deep and Surface Structure Constraints in Syntax*, Holt, Rinehart and Winston, New York.

Perlmutter, D. M. (1978) 'Impersonal Passives and the Unaccusative Hypothesis,' in *Proceedings of the Fourth Annual Meeting of the Berkeley Linguistics Society.*

Perlmutter, D. M. (1979) 'Working 1s and Inversion in Italian, Japanese and Quechua,' in *Proceedings of the Fifth Annual Meeting of the Berkeley Linguistics Society.*

Perlmutter, D. M. (to appear a) 'Evidence for Inversion in Russian and Kannada,' in Perlmutter (ed.), (to appear b).

Perlmutter, D. M. (to appear b) *Studies in Relational Grammar.*

Perlmutter, D. M. and P. M. Postal (1977) 'Toward a Universal Characterization of Passivization,' in *Proceedings of the Third Annual Meeting of the Berkeley Linguistic Society.*

Perlmutter, D. M. and P. M. Postal (to appear a) 'Some Proposed Laws of Basic Clause Structure,' in Perlmutter (ed.) (to appear b).

Perlmutter, D. M. and P. M. Postal (to appear b) 'The 1-Advancement Exclusiveness Law,' in Perlmutter (ed.) (to appear b).

Perlmutter, D. M. and P. M. Postal (to appear c). 'Impersonal Passives and Some Relational Laws,' in Perlmutter (ed.) (to appear b).

Pollock, J.-Y. (1978) 'Trace theory and French syntax,' in S. J. Keyser (ed.) *Recent Transformational Studies in European Languages*, MIT Press, Cambridge, Massachusetts.

Postal, Paul M. (1976) 'Antipassive in French,' in J. A. Kegl, D. Nash and A. Zaenen (eds). *Proceedings of the Seventh Annual Meeting of the Northeastern Linguistic Society*, Cambridge, Mass. Also in *Lingvisticae Investigationes* 1, 333–374 (1977), and in Perlmutter (ed.) (to appear, b).

Postal, Paul M. (1979) *Some Syntactic Rules in Mohawk*, Garland, New York.

Postal Paul M. (to appear) 'The Unaccusative Hypothesis.'

Postal, P. M. and G. K. Pullum (1978) 'Traces and the description of English complementizer contraction', *Linguistic Inquiry* 9, 1–29.

Ruwet. W. (1968) *Introduction à la grammaire générative*. Plon, Paris.

Ruwet, W. (1972) *Théorie syntaxique et syntaxe du français*, Seuil, Paris.

Ruwet, W. (1975) 'Montée du sujet et extraposition,' *Le Français moderne* 43, 98–133.

IVAN A. SAG

A SEMANTIC THEORY OF "NP-MOVEMENT" DEPENDENCIES*

0. INTRODUCTION

The various complex dependencies found in English sentences containing infinitival complements have provided some of the most compelling arguments for transformational grammar (TG) (for a survey of such arguments, see Postal (1974), Soames and Perlmutter (1979)). As a consequence, these dependencies also provide a testing ground for current alternatives to TG. Few linguists would take seriously a theory of grammar which did not address the fundamental problems of English grammar that were dealt with within the framework of "standard" transformational grammar (STG) (Chomsky (1965), Rosenbaum (1967)) by such rules as *There*-Insertion, *It*-Extraposition, Passive, Subject-Subject Raising, and Subject-Object Raising.[1]

In this paper, I will consider certain data which have been thought to provide fundamental arguments against traditional phrase structure grammars and essential evidence for transformational grammars which include the rules just mentioned. An examination of current transformational analyses of these data, however, reveals an extensive appeal to filtering devices of various sorts. It will be suggested that syntactic filtering can be eliminated in favor of a single *semantic coherence principle*. Once such a principle is adopted, I show that the familiar complex dependencies just alluded to can all be predicted within a theory of grammar that countenances no transformational rules. The theory I suggest is a version of the theory of context-free phrase structure grammars developed by Gerald Gazdar (this volume), augmented by the semantic coherence principle just mentioned. Such a theory, by eliminating syntactic filtering devices and an entire class of supposed linguistic rules (transformations), constitutes a significant step forward in approaching the fundamental goal of constraining the class of grammars cognized by language users.

P. Jacobson and G. K. Pullum (eds.), The Nature of Syntactic Representation, 427–466.
Copyright © 1982 by D. Reidel Publishing Company.

1. AN OVERVIEW OF NP-VP DEPENDENCIES

The dependencies I wish to consider in this paper are the following. In a certain class of non-complex English structures (which I will refer to loosely as *simplex structures*), one observes dependencies between the subject NP and the following VP. VP's are of (at least) three types in English: (1) those which require a referring expression (by which I mean to include quantified NP's, e.g. *all women*) as their simplex-subject; (2) those which require (so-called "existential") *there* as their simplex-subject, and (3) those which require (so-called "dummy") *it* as their simplex-subject. These observations are illustrated in examples (1)–(3).

(1) { (a) Sandy Smith   }
     { (b) *There   }   walks to school.
     { (c) *It[2]   }

(2) { (a) There   }   { a pig roasted every year.   }
     { (b) *It   }   is { a riot developing somewhere.   }
     { (c) *Sandy Smith }   { nothing in Reno.   }
                                  { nobody prouder than Kim.   }

(3) { (a) It   }
     { (b) *Sandy Smith }   is obvious that Kim is angry.
     { (c) *There   }

Systematically, these dependencies also hold, on the surface, over any number of verbals (verbs or adjectives) of a certain class ("A-Raising" verbals in the terminology of Postal (1974)), which includes *seem*, *appear*, (be) *likely*, *continue*, etc. (4)–(9) illustrate this point.

(4) { (a) Sandy Smith   }
     { (b) *There   }   is likely to walk to school.
     { (c) *It   }

(5) { (a) There   }
     { (b) *It   }   is likely to be
     { (c) *Sandy Smith }

                             { a pig roasted every year.   }
                             { a riot developing somewhere.   }
                             { nothing in Reno.   }
                             { nobody prouder than Kim.   }

(6) { (a) It   }
     { (b) *Sandy Smith }   is likely to be obvious that Kim is
     { (c) *There   }   angry.

(7) $\left\{\begin{array}{ll}\text{(a)} & \text{Sandy Smith} \\ \text{(b)} & \text{*There} \\ \text{(c)} & \text{*It}\end{array}\right\}$ is likely to continue to walk to school.

(8) $\left\{\begin{array}{ll}\text{(a)} & \text{There} \\ \text{(b)} & \text{*It} \\ \text{(c)} & \text{*Sandy Smith}\end{array}\right\}$ is likely to continue to be

$\left\{\begin{array}{l}\text{a pig roasted every year.} \\ \text{a riot developing somewhere.} \\ \text{nothing in Reno.} \\ \text{nobody prouder than Kim.}\end{array}\right\}$

(9) $\left\{\begin{array}{ll}\text{(a)} & \text{It} \\ \text{(b)} & \text{*Sandy Smith} \\ \text{(c)} & \text{*There}\end{array}\right\}$ is likely to continue to be obvious that Kim is angry.

These same dependencies hold, of course, between NP's and VP's which follow members of other verb classes, such as *believe* and *expect*, as shown in (10)–(12).

(10)   Everyone believes $\left\{\begin{array}{ll}\text{(a)} & \text{Sandy Smith} \\ \text{(b)} & \text{*there} \\ \text{(c)} & \text{*it}\end{array}\right\}$ to walk to school.

(11)   Everyone believes $\left\{\begin{array}{ll}\text{(a)} & \text{there} \\ \text{(b)} & \text{*it} \\ \text{(c)} & \text{*Sandy Smith}\end{array}\right\}$ to be

$\left\{\begin{array}{l}\text{a pig roasted every year.} \\ \text{a riot developing somewhere.} \\ \text{nothing in Reno.} \\ \text{nobody prouder than Kim.}\end{array}\right\}$

(12)   Everyone believes $\left\{\begin{array}{ll}\text{(a)} & \text{it} \\ \text{(b)} & \text{*Sandy Smith} \\ \text{(c)} & \text{*there}\end{array}\right\}$ to be obvious that Kim is angry.

And similarly, in the passive analogues of (10)–(12) we find that the dependencies hold between the surface subject and the embedded infinitival VP over (any number of) the appropriate passive verb forms:

(13) $\left\{\begin{array}{ll}\text{(a)} & \text{Sandy Smith} \\ \text{(b)} & \text{*There} \\ \text{(c)} & \text{*It}\end{array}\right\}$ is believed to walk to school (?by everyone).

(14) $\left\{\begin{array}{l}\text{(a) There}\\\text{(b) *It}\\\text{(c) *Sandy Smith}\end{array}\right\}$ is believed to be
$\left\{\begin{array}{l}\text{a pig roasted every year}\\\text{a riot developing somewhere}\\\text{nothing in Reno.}\\\text{nobody prouder than Kim}\end{array}\right\}$ (by everyone)

(15) $\left\{\begin{array}{l}\text{(a) It}\\\text{(b) *Sandy Smith}\\\text{(c) *There}\end{array}\right\}$ is believed to be obvious that Kim is angry (??by everyone).

Simple phrase structure grammars (PSG's) provide no obvious explanation for discontinuous dependencies of the sort just illustrated. Assuming that referring expressions and the dummies *there* and *it* are all NP's, as their behavior in inverted questions, tags, and the like appears to indicate, any attempt to generate these examples directly by PS-rules such as the ones in (16) encounters difficulties.

(16)   (a) $S \rightarrow NP \quad VP$

(b) $VP \rightarrow V \left(\left\{\begin{array}{l}(XP)^*\\\overline{VP}\\\overline{S}\\VP_{passive}\end{array}\right\}\right)$

(c) $VP_{passive} \rightarrow V_{passive}\left(\left\{\begin{array}{l}XP\\\overline{VP}\end{array}\right\}\right)\ldots$

(d) $\overline{VP} \rightarrow to\ VP$

(e) $AP \rightarrow A\left(\left\{\begin{array}{l}\overline{S}\\VP\end{array}\right\}\right)$

(f) $\overline{S} \rightarrow COMP\ S$

(g) $NP \rightarrow \left\{\begin{array}{l}N\\PRO\end{array}\right\}$

The problem, quite simply, is that such PSG's allow all the examples in (1)–(15) to be generated. Nothing guarantees that the NP and VP in those examples expand in accordance with the observed dependencies.

The facts of (1)–(15) follow, however, from an appropriate transformational description of English that includes, *inter alia*, raising transformations or their equivalent. There is no one place in the transformational literature (that I am aware of) where all of these facts are assessed and offered as evidence against PSG's, yet the observed dependencies are of just the sort that were cited in the early transformational literature as evidence against non-transformational theories.[3] Furthermore, the facts of (1)–(15) are well-known, and hence I believe it is fair to conclude that, implicitly at least, they constitute part of the fundamental motivation for raising and passive transformations in particular, and for transformational grammar in general.

The remaining evidence for raising transformations is provided by idioms whose parts may be "displaced" in a fashion that is partially predictable by such transformations. The patterning of the following examples is exactly like (1)–(15) above.

(17) The FBI $\begin{Bmatrix} \text{(a)} & \text{kept} \\ \text{(b)} & \text{*held} \end{Bmatrix}$ (close) tabs on Kim.

(18) (Close) tabs were $\begin{Bmatrix} \text{(a)} & \text{kept} \\ \text{(b)} & \text{*held} \end{Bmatrix}$ on Kim (by the FBI).

(19) (Close) tabs are likely to have been $\begin{Bmatrix} \text{(a)} & \text{kept} \\ \text{(b)} & \text{*held} \end{Bmatrix}$ on Kim (by the FBI).

(20) Everyone expected (close) tabs to have been $\begin{Bmatrix} \text{(a)} & \text{kept} \\ \text{(b)} & \text{*held} \end{Bmatrix}$ on Kim (?by the FBI).

(21) ?(Close) tabs were expected (??by everyone) to have been $\begin{Bmatrix} \text{(a)} & \text{kept} \\ \text{(b)} & \text{*held} \end{Bmatrix}$ on Kim (??by the FBI).

The nature of the transformational account of all these dependencies is sketched in the next section.

2. "STANDARD THEORY" ACCOUNTS

Within STG, or one version of it at least, the dependencies discussed in section 1 are accounted for in roughly the following way. *There* and *it* are introduced only by transformations, the rules of *There*-Insertion and *It*-

Extraposition respectively. Hence, of (22) (a–c), only (22) (a) is a possible
deep structure.

(22)

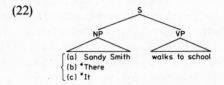

Trees of this sort do not meet the structural condition of either *There*-
Insertion or *It*-Extraposition. Hence no derivation from such a structure
will produce (1)(b) or (1)(c). The dependency in (1) is thus accounted for.

   The verb phrases of (2) are assumed to have the form indicated in (23)
(a)–(c).[4]

(23)   (a)

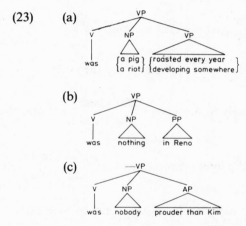

        (b)

        (c)

The verb *be* is not subcategorized for the environments illustrated in (23),
hence these VP's are not possible deep structure VP's Rather, they are
produced as the output of *There*-Insertion, which maps trees like (24) into
ones like (25).

(24)

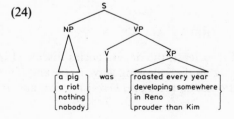

(25)

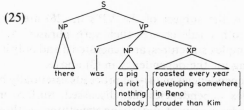

Since this transformation inserts *there* and requires the presence of *be* or another member of a restricted class of verbs, two facts follow immediately: (1) the VP's in (23) are generated when *there* is the subject of the simplex S, and (2) (assuming no other origin is possible for such VP's or for *there*) nothing except *there* is generated as the subject of the VP's in (23) in simplex sentences. The dependency in (2) is thus accounted for.

Similarly, the VP's in (26) are not possible deep structure VP's because of subcategorization restrictions (other verbals, e.g. *think*, *happy*, may appear in such configurations in deep structure).

(26)   (a)

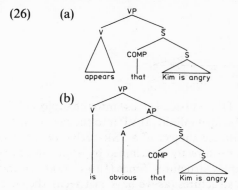

         (b)

Hence examples like (3) (b) are ungenerable. VP's like those in (26) arise only through application of *It*-Extraposition, which maps trees like (27) into ones like (28).

(27)

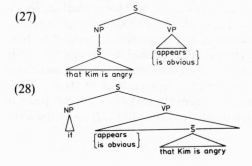

(28)

Simplex sentences where *it* is the subject of the VP's in (26) are thus generated. Furthermore, no other rule creates such verb phrases. As a result, such verb phrases (in simplex structures) are generated if and only if *it* is the subject, thus accounting for the dependency in (3) above.

The STG account of the dependencies in (4)–(6) proceeds essentially by reducing them to the simplex dependencies just discussed. Surface infinitives are assumed to derive from clausal underlying structures, i.e. those containing embedded S's (or S̄'s). In particular, the rule of Subject-Subject Raising (SSR) maps structures like (29) into ones like (30).

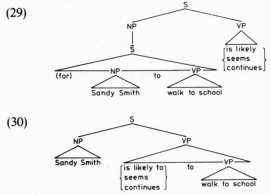

(29)

(30)

Since SSR makes the subject of the embeded clause into the subject of the matrix clause and raises the embedded infinitival VP into the matrix VP, it follows that what can be the surface subject of a SSR-verbal (when it is followed by an infinitive of type x is directly determined by what can be the subject of a VP of type x in simplex structures. Since (1)(b, c), (2)(b, c), and (3)(b, c) are blocked as simplex structures (as we have just seen), they can never be generated as the sentential subject in structures like (29). Hence there are never any inputs to SSR of a sort that would give rise to the ungrammatical examples in (4)–(6). The derivation of (4)(a) has just been illustrated, that of (5)(a) involves application of *There*-Insertion in the embedded clause with subsequent application of SSR, and (6)(a) is derived similarly by downstairs application of *It*-Extraposition followed by SSR.

The dependencies in (4)–(6) are thus all explained by a single rule: SSR. Moreover the account extends to multiple embeddings: the dependencies of (7)–(9) are also a function of the simplex dependencies in (1)–(3). These examples derive from underlying structures like (31) which are mapped into ones like (32) which are in turn mapped into ones like (33) (both the SSR).

(31)

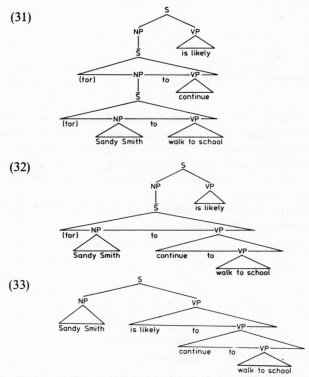

(32)

(33)

In this way the only NP's which may become surface subjects of *is likely to continue* to VP$_x$ are those which may be subjects of VP$_x$ in simplex structures. By assuming SSR and the existence of deep structures like (31), the dependencies of (7)–(9) (and similar examples with deeper embeddings) are directly accounted for.

In like fashion, the dependencies of (10)–(12) are reduced to the simplex dependencies of (1)–(3) by assuming a transformation of Subject-Object Raising (SOR). SOR maps trees like (34) into ones like (35).

(34)

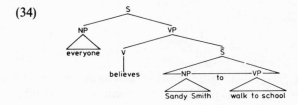

(35)

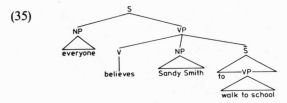

In order for an NP to become the direct object of *believe* in the matrix clause, it must first be a subject of the embedded clause. Thus assuming that no other rules produce structures like (35) containing verbs of the *believe* class, it follows that VP's of the form $[_{VP}[_V$ believe$]$ NP$_x$ to VP$_y]$ are derivable if and only if, modulo tense differences, $[_S$NP$_x$ VP$_y]$ is a well-formed simplex structure.

(10)(a) is derived in the fashion just sketched. The examples of (11)(a) are derived from structures like the following.

(36)

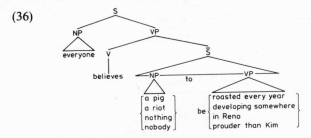

Application of *There*-Insertion in the embedded clause creates structures wherein *there* is the subject of the embedded clause. These may then undergo SOR to produce the examples of (11)(a). Similarly, (12)(a) is derived from (37) by application of (1) *It*-Extraposition in the embedded clause and (2) SOR.

(37)

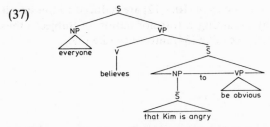

Therefore, assuming no other rules create structures of the form $[_{VP}[_V$ believe$]$ NP to VP$]$. (10)(a)–(12)(a) are generated, but (10)(b,c)–

(12)(b, c) are not, for the latter would have to derive from structures whose embedded clause was (1)(b, c)–(3)(b, c), which, as we have seen, are ungenerable.

Structures produced by SOR, e.g. (35), satisfy the structural condition of the Passive transformation. Passive applied to (35) yields (38).

(38)

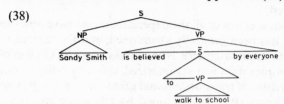

Assuming the Passive transformation is the only rule which creates structures of this form, the observed dependencies ((13)–(15)) are again reduced to those of simplex structures. A sentence of the form: $[_S NP_x$ is believed to VP_y (by everyone)] is derivable only if the corresponding sentence of the form $[_S$ everyone believes NP_x to $VP_y]$ is derivable. But as we have just seen, the latter is derivable only if $[_S NP_x VP_y]$ is a well-formed simplex structure. Hence the facts of (13)–(15) are also explained straightforwardly. The observed dependencies ultimately reduce to the dependencies of (1)–(3), which are explained in STG.

Finally, the complex dependencies of idioms follow the pattern of the examples just discussed and are explained in essentially the same fashion within STG. Whatever device is adopted for assigning idiomatic interpretations to certain configurations of lexical items functions with respect to underlying syntactic structures, guaranteeing for example that (39)(a) but not (39)(b) is assigned an idiomatic interpretation.

(39)

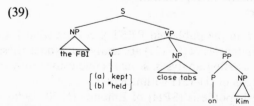

The STG account of idioms in fact guarantees that (39)(b) is not a possible deep structure. $[_{VP} [_V keep] [_{NP} (close) tabs] [_{PP} [_P on] [_{NP}]]]$ is listed in the lexicon, but *tabs* per se is not.

From this it follows that (17) (a) but not (17)(b) is a well-formed simplex structure. From the assumption that there is a Passive transformation which operates structures like (39) it also follows that (18)(a) but not (18)(b) is a wellformed simplex structure. Once this is explained, the contrasts of (19)–(21) also follow, for the well-formedness facts of these constructions, as we have seen, reduce to the question of simplex well-formedness. Hence, the dependencies of (17)–(21) are all explained in just the same way as those we have already considered.

STG thus provides an account of all the dependencies we have observed so far. STG, however, has been generally abandoned, and the reasons for this are too numerous to summarize here. Nonetheless, given STG's success in dealing with the complex data just summarized, it is surprising to note that within current versions of transformational grammar, e.g. the Revised Extended Standard Theory (REST) developed by Chomsky and others (Chomsky (1973, 1975, 1977, 1980), Chomsky and Lasnik (1977)), little attempt has been made to provide detailed and explicit alternative analyses of these fundamental facts of English syntax.

3. NP-VP DEPENDENCIES IN THE REVISED EXTENDED STANDARD THEORY (REST)

REST, as developed recently by Chomsky and others, is a theory which countenances the following classes of rules, *inter alia*, within sentence grammar.

(40)   (a) Phrase structure rules
          (b) Exactly one transformational rule: "move-α"
          (c) Local or "minor movement" rules
          (d) Stylistic rules
          (e) Rules of semantic interpretation
          (f) Surface filters

There is no single discussion in the published REST literature (that I am aware of) where all the dependencies of (1)–(21) are analyzed. Nonetheless, extrapolating from various existing analyses, several conclusions may be drawn concerning the analysis of (1)–(21) within REST.

The structure preserving hypothesis (SPH) of Emonds (1970, 1976) is assumed. Two principles go hand in hand with SPH: (1) lexical insertion is optional and (2) any derivations producing surface structures containing nodes which remained empty throughout the syntactic derivation, i.e. nodes filled neither by deep structure lexical insertion nor by the application of transformations (or local rules), are deemed ungrammatical by a general filtering convention. Thus, accepting SPH, all the following examples are generated by the syntactic rules, but are ruled deviant by the general filter operating at the level of surface structure.

(41)   (a) *Kim store.
        (b) *to the
        (c) *has the to
        (d) *The kids proved.
        (e) *They put into the box.

The well-formedness of simplex NP-VP sentences is thus a function of the phrase structure rules, strict subcategorization restrictions, and the general filtering convention just mentioned.

Simplex *there*-sentences illustrate a further filtering device within REST. Following Chomsky (1980), *there* is introduced by a local rule which simply inserts *there* onto an appropriate empty node. Sentences containing *there* must undergo the semantic rule of *there*-interpretation (Milsark (1974)) which assigns to surface structures like (42) logical forms like (43).

(42) $[_S [_{NP_i}$ there$]$ is $NP_i ...]$ ("there is a book on the table")

(43)   (there is $NP_i)_x [_S [_{NP_i} x] ...]$("(there is a book)$_x [_S x$ on the table])

The only structures to which this rule can apply, presumably, are those whose subject NP has been moved (by "move-α") into the appropriate position within VP. Chomsky provides no further details regarding this analysis, yet the intention is clear: *there*-interpretation will be formulated in such a way that it applies to structures like (2)(a), but not to ones like (1)(b) or (3)(c). Surface structures containing *there* which do not undergo *there*-interpretation are assigned no logical form (assuming no other rules interpret *there*), and structures which cannot be interpreted are ruled deviant by the following logical well-formedness condition.

(44)   *Logical Well-Formedness Condition*(LWFC).
        A syntactic structure Σ is grammatical with respect to a grammar G only if G assigns to Σ a representation LF, which is a *sentence* of the language of "logical forms".

LWFC is a further general filtering condition, some version of which is assumed in all recent work within REST.

Simplex sentences derived by *It*-Extraposition in STG may be similarly derived within REST (Emonds (1976), Baltin (1978)), if the movement of S̄ is viewed as a specific case of "move-α". Alternatively, extraposed clauses are generated *in situ*, in which case the deviance of (3)(b) is dealt with by subcategorization restrictions, LWFC, or both. Dummy *it* presumably cannot be interpreted as a referring expression or quantifier, hence (1)(c) is also to be ruled deviant by LWFC.

The general character of the STG account of raising constructions is preserved in REST. The deviance of the complex cases is a function of the deviance of the relevant simplex structures. The specifics of the REST account however are slightly different. SSR and Passive are viewed as two specific instances of "move-α" (move NP), and the dependencies discussed in section 1 above are a rather complex theorem of the grammar and the assumed conventions.

An A-Raising verbal like *likely* is subcategorized as [+ Δ ... ____ S̄], or perhaps [+ Δ ... ____ S], thus ensuring that its deep structure subject is empty. If it remains empty throughout the syntactic derivation, the resulting surface structure is filtered by the general filtering convention. If on the other hand the subject of the embedded clause replaces the empty matrix subject (by application of "move-α"), then the result is a well-formed surface structure of the form shown in (45). (Here $[_{NP_i} e]$ is the trace left by the movement rule.)

(45) $[_S[_{NP_i}$ Sandy Smith] is likely $[_S[_{NP_i} e]$ to walk to school]]$

Various constraints and conventions interact to ensure that only the embedded subject can be affected by "move-α" in such derivations.[5]

As in STG, the dependency in question is reduced to a simplex dependency. An NP_x is generated in the environment:___(be) Vbl. to VP_y (where Vbl. is an A-Raising verbal) just in case $NP_x VP_y$ is a well-formed simplex structure (modulo tense differences). Thus presuming REST provides an account of the simplex dependencies, through the interaction of the phrase structure rules, subcategorization restrictions, the general filtering convention, LWFC, and various further constraints on the functioning of rules, the dependencies of (4)–(9) above follow from the assumption of "move-α".[6]

REST countenances no rule of SOR. Rather, verbs like *believe* and *expect* simply subcategorize a following S (or S̄ with ∅ complementizer). The relevant, deep structures are indistinguishable from the resulting surface structures, i.e. no relevant syntactic rules apply. The structures in question are of the form shown in (46)(a).

(46)   (a)

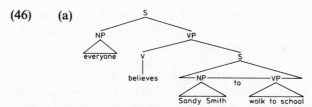

On this theory, the dependencies of (10)–(12) *are* simplex sentence dependencies, and the relevant facts follow without appeal to any further syntactic rules.

Structure similar to (46), *viz.* those like (47), are the basis for examples like (13)–(15).

(46)   (b)

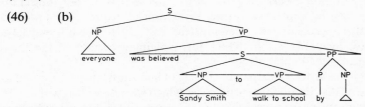

First the matrix subject is moved into the *by*-phrase by "move-α" (here performing the operation of the rule of Agent-Postposing in previous theories), leaving an empty subject NP. "Move-α" again applies, this time preposing the subject of the embedded clause making it the new matrix subject. The resulting structure is the one in (47), where $[_{NP_i} e]$ is the trace left behind by the second application of "move-α".

(47)

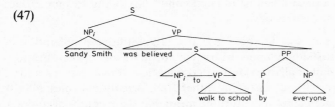

Various constraints on rule application prevent any element inside the embedded clause other than the subject from becoming the matrix subject.

Thus the dependency of (13)–(15) again reduces to a simplex dependency. Assuming no other rules create structures like (47) without violating some rule, constraint or filter assumed within REST, it follows that sentences of the form: NP_x *was believed to* VP_y *(by* NP) are generated only if $NP_x VP_y$ is a well-formed simplex structure, *modulo* differences of tense.[7]

Finally the idiom dependencies of (17)–(21) can be explained within REST in at least two distinct ways. Assuming that idiom dependencies are fixed at the level of deep structure, just as they were in STG, the behavior of idioms in simplex structures is accounted for immediately. Since the complex dependencies reduce to simplex dependencies, as we have seen, it also follows that the complex dependencies of (17)–(21) are explained.

Alternatively, the complex dependencies of derived structures may be dealt with, at least partially, by interpretive filtering. Extending the analysis of Fiengo (1977, 57), passive VP's in structures like (47) must be interpreted as properties of the matrix subject. Assuming that a VP such as: *were believed to have been kept on Kim* (*by the FBI*) is interpreted as a property, this interpretation process may be constructed so that the only object this property may be applied to is (the denotation of) (*close*) *tabs*. I will not explore this approach further here. Instead I simply note that it may be an alternative available within REST for explaining certain of the idiom dependencies in complex structures.

To summarize, REST employs a variety of filtering devices to account for the complex distributional dependencies which were described within STG solely by means of the interaction of the appropriately-formulated phrase structure rules, subcategorization restrictions and transformations. As we have seen, the REST filtering devices include the following.

(48)   (a) LWFC
          (b) general filtering condition on surface structures containing
              never-filled empty nodes
          (c) surface filters (stipulated conditions ruling certain surface
              structures deviant)

What I would now like to show is that this unintuitive proliferation of filtering devices is simply unnecessary. An adequate and "generalization-capturing" account of all the complex dependencies summarized in section 1 can be provided without assuming either transformational rules, (48)(b), or (48)(c). By generalization-capturing I mean that the accounts of complex and simplex dependencies will be unified as they are in transformational theories. An important advantage of such a theory, as I will show, is that it allows all relevant generalizations to be expressed while at the same time constraining the class of rules hypothesized to be cognized by language users. Furthermore, it does so without the introduction of otherwise unmotivated devices.

4. NON-TRANSFORMATIONAL THEORIES AND SEMANTIC FILTERING

Recent work by several scholars (Bresnan (1978), Brame (1976, 1978), Gazdar (this volume, 1980)) and much other work still in progress is motivated essentially by this same goal. Of the recent attempts to develop explanatory alternatives to transformational grammar that I am aware of, none to date has addressed the question of how the full range of complex dependencies discussed in section 1 is to be analyzed. Although the ideas I will present in the remainder of this paper were originally developed in an attempt to refine a quasi-transformational theory of the sort presented in Bresnan (1978), the general framework I will assume is Gazdar's, which I regard as extremely promising in the light of certain recent research (Gazdar 1981; Gazdar, this volume; Gazdar and Sag, to appear; Gazdar, Pullum and Sag, ms). I assume familiarity with Gazdar's proposals and notational conventions as set out in his contribution to this volume.

The key problem is how to deal with sentences containing dummy *it* and *there*. One solution investigated by Gazdar in unpublished work involved handling dummies with a mechanism essentially like the one used for syntactic concord: the feature system. The first step is the introduction of terminal symbol features [*it*] and [*there*]. VP's requiring *there* and *it* as (simplex) subjects are analyzed by rules like (49) and (50) respectively:

(49) $\langle 49, [_{VP} \text{ V NP PP}], \lambda\mathscr{P}[\mathscr{P} = \text{NP}' \wedge \text{PP}'(\mathscr{P})]\rangle$
       $\quad\quad\quad {}_{[there]}$

where $V_{49}^{*} = \{be\}$

(50) $\langle 50, [_{VP} \text{ V S}],\ldots\rangle$ where $V_{50}^{*} = \{seem,\ldots\}$
       $\quad\quad\quad {}_{[it]}$

(Since categories are analyzed as bundles of syntactic features (Chomsky (1970), Bresnan (1976)), adding [*there*] and [*it*] as syntactic features is no extension of the theoretical apparatus.)

The basic rule for simplex sentences is given as (51), and (52) is the rule expanding NP's as the appropriate dummy element, *it* or *there*.

(51) $\langle 51, [_{S} \text{ NP VP}], \text{VP}' (\text{NP}')\rangle$
       $\quad\quad\quad {}_{[\delta]}\ \ {}_{[\delta]}$

(52) $\langle 52, [_{NP} \delta], \delta'\rangle$, where $\delta\in\{it, there\}$
       $\quad\quad\quad {}_{[\delta]}$

δ ranges over (sets of) syntactic features, hence rule (51) guarantees that in simplex sentences, $\underset{[there]}{NP}$ is the only possible subject of $\underset{[there]}{VP}$, $\underset{[it]}{NP}$ the only possible subject of $\underset{[it]}{VP}$, etc. In this way the only simplex sentences analyzed by the grammar are those which are in accord with the dependencies observed with respect to (1)–(3) above.

Infinitive phrases ($\overline{VP}$'s) inherit the syntactic features of the VP's they directly dominate, in accordance with the following rule.

(53) $\langle 53, [\underset{[\delta]}{\overline{VP}}\ to\ \underset{[\delta]}{VP}], VP' \rangle$

Similarly, A-Raising verbals are introduced by rules such as (54), which guarantee that the matrix VP inherits the syntactic features of the $\overline{VP}$ which in turn inherits those of the embedded VP.

(54) $\langle 54, [_{VP}\ \underset{[\delta]}{V}\ \underset{[\delta]}{\overline{VP}}], \lambda\mathscr{P}V'([\widehat{\ }\overline{VP}'(\mathscr{P})]) \rangle$

$V_{54}^{*} = \{happen, tend, \ldots\}$

As a result, structures of the form: NP_x *happens (tends, seems . . .)* to VP_y are analyzed only if $NP_x\ VP_y$ is a well-formed simplex structure (*modulo* tense differences). The fundamental dependency regarding (4)–(9) is a direct consequence of the grammar.[8]

Likewise, the SOR dependencies are a consequence of the following rule.

(55) $\langle 55, [_{VP}\ \underset{[\delta]}{V}\ NP\ \underset{[\delta]}{\overline{VP}}], V'([\widehat{\ }\overline{VP}'\ (NP')]) \rangle$

$V_{55}^{*} = \{believe, expect \ldots\}$

Again the dependency observed earlier follows directly: structures of the form: *NP believes (expects)* NP_x *to* VP_y are analyzed only if $NP_x\ VP_y$ is a well-formed simplex structure, *modulo* tense differences.

The "raised-passivized" dependencies of (13)–(15) follow from the passive metarule, which creates rules like (56) as the passive analogue of (55).

(56) $\langle 56, [_{VP}\ \underset{\substack{[PASS] \\ \delta}}{}\ \underset{[PASS]}{V}\ \underset{[\delta]}{\overline{VP}}\ \underset{[by]}{(PP)}], \lambda\mathscr{P}V'([\widehat{\ }\overline{VP}'(\mathscr{P}))(PP')]) \rangle$

The grammar thus ensures that structures like (13)–(15) are analyzed only if the matrix subject and the embedded infinitive agree with respect to the syntactic features *there* and *it*. The observed dependency follows immediately. The account extends to dependencies which are observable in structures of arbitrary complexity.

There are at least three defects of the proposal just outlined. First, the translation offered for VP's simply won't work. Second, the appeal to the
[there]
syntactic features [*there*] and [*it*] could be accused of being an ad hoc proposal which fails to explain the fact that the syntactic dependencies correlate with the function-argument structure. Third, no account is given of how the parallel dependencies of "idom chunks" (the observations of (17)–(21)) are to be analyzed. Of these defects, I regard the last two as the most serious.

The proposal for the semantic analysis of *there* sentences fails to generalize to the full range of indefinite NP's. (57), for example, is assigned the following logical analysis.

(57)   There is nothing in Reno.

(58) $[\lambda \mathscr{P}[\mathscr{P} = \lambda P \sim \exists x P(x) \wedge \text{in}' (\text{Reno}')(\mathscr{P})]](\lambda Q \exists y Q(y))$

   $\equiv \lambda Q \exists y Q(y) = \lambda P \sim \exists x P(x) \wedge \text{in}' (\text{Reno}')(\lambda Q \exists y Q(y))$

Here $\lambda Q \exists y Q(y)$ is the translation of *there*: the set of properties some entity has. (58) is simply a contradiction from which it follows that the set of properties that some entity has is the set of properties no entity has. Clearly a different semantic analysis must be provided.

More importantly, the introduction of δ-"matching" conditions within rules is unprincipled in that it treats the observed dependencies essentially as an arbitrary fact. Given the logical analysis Gazdar assumes, which I believe captures an important aspect of the semantic structure of English sentences, the δ-matching dependency holds ultimately between a VP and an NP only if they are in a function-argument relation in the semantic structure.

This is particularly clear in the case of rules (51) and (55), where the third component of the rule states the function-argument relation directly. In the case of the A-Raising rules, e.g. (54), one must undo one λ-abstraction to see the function-argument dependency. A structure whose form is (59) is translated as in (60), which is equivalent to (61) by λ-conversion.

(59) $[_S \text{ NP } [_{VP} \text{ V } \overline{\text{VP}}]]$
          $_{[\delta]} \quad _{[\delta]} \quad _{[\delta]}$

(60) $[\lambda \mathscr{P} V'(\mathbb{C} \overline{VP}'(P))](NP')$

(61) $V'(\mathbb{C} \overline{VP}' \ (NP'))$

The feature proposal outlined above would leave this correlation completely unexplained. It would be just as possible within this analysis to introduce δ-matching conditions on the rules introducing "EQUI" verbals, so that * *There hopes to be a riot* was predicted to be grammatical. The complex dependencies and the simplex dependencies, I will argue, should both follow from the nature of the function-argument structure.

Finally, consider the problem of how the complex "idiom chunk" dependencies are to be analyzed. Idioms are assumed to be introduced by rules such as (62).

(62) $\langle 62, [_{VP} [_V keep][_{NP} tabs][_{PP}[_P on]NP]], \ldots \rangle$

It is mysterious how the passive metarule is to apply to (62) to produce an appropriate passive rule which ensures the appropriate passive morphology. Even if we assume that problem can be dealt with, however, we end up with the following rule at best.

(63) $63, [_{VP} [_V \ kept][_{PP}[_P on]NP] \ (PP)], \ldots$
          $_{[PASS]} \ _{[PASS]} \qquad\qquad\qquad _{[by]}$

This allows passive VP's like *were kept on him by the FBI* to be analyzed, but provides no mechanism for guaranteeing that the simplex subject of such VP's must be (*close*) *tabs*. Moreover, since not even the simplex dependencies are accounted for, none of the complex dependencies of (17)–(21) are explained either.

Note further that the system sketched above, which purports to eliminate semantic filtering of any kind, really allows only one way of approaching the problem at hand, *viz.* the introduction of further syntactic features. Passive VP's such as *were kept on Kim* (*by the FBI*) would somehow have to be coded with the feature [*tabs*], which would then be inherited by the appropriate dominating categories in the same fashion as the [*there*] and [*it*] features. This solution, though possible, involves an incredible multiplication of the syntactic categories of the language and has no independent motivation whatsoever.

The last two defects of the this system, it seems to me, are related.

Furthermore, taken together, they are quite suggestive of a modification which would allow all the dependencies discussed in section 1 to be accommodated within a non-transformational theory. This modification will make use of a filtering device much like LWFC.

With the success of STG in dealing with the dependencies of (1)–(15) and (17)–(21) in purely syntactic terms, we are accustomed to thinking of these dependencies in purely syntactic terms. What I would like to explore here is the possibility that this is a fundamental error. It is possible to view the dependencies in question entirely as function-argument dependencies in the semantic analysis.

The behavior of idioms is particularly suggestive in this regard. Note that the only idioms whose parts may undergo the processes of passive and raising, however analyzed, are those which are intuitively semi-compositional. Whereas an idom like *keep tabs on* has pieces each of which contributes to the interpretation of the idiom as a whole, other locutions such as *kick the bucket, trip the light fantastic* seem rather to be unanalyzable. *Tabs* has roughly the sense of *Surveillance*, and the sense of *keep* is perhaps the very same as the sense of *keep* in *keep a record of*, etc. Nothing can be said of *kick the bucket* except that it means 'die'. Correlating with this fairly precisely is the fact that *tabs*, but not *the bucket*, occurs in "passive" and "raising" structures, as is well known.

While idiomaticity remains somewhat mysterious and no currently-available theory provides a wholly adequate account thereof, it should be noted that similar contrasts manifest themselves with regard to nominal modification. *Close tabs, very close tabs, unfair advantage, extremely unfair advantage* are all possible, yet *the bucket* resists such modification, except perhaps in *kick the proverbial bucket*. The correlation between semantic semi-compositionality, modifiability, and the ability to occur in "passive" and "raising" structures is unexplained in all theories I am aware of.

This shortcoming, I suggest, is due to the universally held belief that the dependencies we have been discussing are syntactic in nature. Suppose, however, that the complex dependencies of section 1 and the dependencies among semi-compositional idiom chunks (by which I mean, e.g. the fact that *keep, tabs* and *on* depend on each other's presence) are both essentially semantic in nature. Oversimplifying somewhat, the latter might amount to the following. The idiomatic *keep* denotes a partial function which is defined only on the intension of *tabs*, and perhaps on several other objects which are the intensions of the other idiom chunks with which *keep* can combine. The intension of *tabs* is peculiar in that it is outside the domain of other functions which are the denotations of transitive verbs or other more complex expressions.

On this theory, *keep tabs on* would find a denotation in any model, but *hold tabs on* would not, since the intension of *tabs* is outside the domain of the function *hold* denotes. Idiomatic competence would then involve knowing certain facts about idiomatic senses and restrictions on the domains of denotational functions.

Since the semantics of passive verb phrases simply involves the creation of new functions, directly determined by the denotational functions of corresponding active VP's (these are represented by means of the λ-operator), it follows that the denotations of passive verb phrases preserve these restrictions. Thus, say, if *keep on Kim* denotes a function defined only on the intension of *tabs*, the denotation of *were kept on Kim* is a function defined only on that same intension. Hence *tabs were kept on Kim* has a denotation in any model, yet **strings were kept on Kim* and **tabs were held on Kim* do not. The deviance of the last two examples then reduces to the fact that the functions which the passive VP's denote are not defined on their arguments, the NP-intensions provided by the subject NP's. These examples are ruled semantically deviant. For further discussion and justification of this approach to the analysis of idioms, see Nunberg, Sag, and Wasow (in preparation).

This theory predicts the fact that *the bucket was kicked by Kim* has no idomatic interpretation by analyzing non-compositional idioms in an entirely different fashion. Following Gazdar, *kick the bucket* is simply introduced by a rule which assigns it roughly the sense of *die*. Its semantic analysis is thus entirely non-compositional. Since no part of *kick the bucket* denotes a function of the relevant sort (a transitive verb denotation), it can no more passivize than *die* can.

This appeal to *functional deviance* can be extended to deal with the full range of dependencies of section 1. In essence, this program amounts to reanalyzing all such dependencies as cases of function-argument mismatch. In addition, I will entertain the possibility that certain of the deviances in question result from the verb phrase denotation being a function of the wrong type entirely to take as argument the denotation of the NP that it is provided with by the rules of semantic composition.

I will couch my discussion in terms of a typed logical language of the sort developed by Montague (1973, 1974). Hence certain of my proposals concerning functional deviance will involve claims of the following form:

(64) (a) The translation of a given NP (NP') in a given syntactic structure is a logical expression of type a.

(b) The translation of a given VP(VP') in the same structure is a logical expression of type $\langle b, c \rangle$, (b ≠ a).

(c) The principles of semantic composition, given by the rules of translation (the third component of rules) require a logical translation containing an expression of the form: VP (NP').

(d) But since b ≠ a, VP' (NP') is not a well-formed expression of the logical language (since the syntactic rules of the logical language recognize expressions of the form $\varphi((\psi)$ only if ψ is of type α and φ is of type $\langle \alpha, \beta \rangle$, for some α and β.)

(e) Thus there is no sentence of the logical language associated with the structure in question by the principles of semantic composition.

(f) Hence, the structure is ruled deviant by the grammar.

Several comments are in order here. First, the reliance on the *syntax* of the logical language is convenient, but inessential. My central claims are to be construed in terms of whether or not the function which is the denotation ultimately associated with a given VP of English includes in its domain the object which is the denotation associated with a given NP of English. Because I employ a typed logical language of a familiar sort wherein the syntactic type of an expression and its denotational type are directly correlated, it appears that I am making use of a filtering condition indistinct from LWFC (see above). As emphasized by Montague (1973), however, the logical language is merely a convenience. Direct interpretation of the syntactic structures, along the lines suggested by Montague (1970) would not significantly alter the character of the analyses I offer here. I will therefore refer to the principle implicitly invoked in (64) as the Semantic Coherence Principle (SCP), although I will continue to discuss things in terms of "type mismatches" in the logic for the sake of perspicuity. SCP functions essentially as a filtering device, the only such device I will assume in reanalyzing the dependencies of section 1. Hence, in addition to achieving the wholly desirable goal of eliminating transformational rules entirely, the theory I present avoids the proliferation of filtering devices in (48)(a).

The analysis I will put forth thus employs semantic filtering, similar in effect to the semantic filtering employed within REST (though far more constrained), without multiplying syntactic features in the way Gazdar suggests. As many details of the semantics of *there* and *it* constructions in English are not fully understood, any analysis I provide will not be wholly adequate. I make certain assumptions for the sake of precision, revision of which would not alter the essential character of the overall account of the dependencies. I return to the question of semantic filtering in the final section.

5. A NON-TRANSFORMATIONAL THEORY OF "NP-MOVEMENT" DEPENDENCIES

The fundamental idea put forward here is that *all* the dependencies of (1)–(15) are logical (semantic) in nature, rather than syntactic. For convenience and ease of presentation I assume that the logical properties of English sentences are to be characterized by specifying a translation procedure from syntactic structures of English into a typed language of intensional logic of the sort developed by Montague (1973). I will provide relevant details of this procedure adopting the general format introduced by Gazdar (this volume). Modifications of various sorts are possible, both with respect to the logical language (henceforth $\mathscr{L}$) in general and with respect to the particular translation rules I propose, without essentially altering the overall character of the theory I present.

I make no use of the types $\langle s, e \rangle, \langle s, \langle\!\langle s, e \rangle, t \rangle\!\rangle$ or $\langle s, \langle e, t \rangle\rangle$. Instead I will work in terms of such types as $e, \langle e, t \rangle, \langle s, \langle\!\langle e, t \rangle, t \rangle\!\rangle$, etc. "Purely extensional" predicates, which are distinct from the $\mathscr{L}$-translations of the corresponding English verbs, are those like the ones in (65).

(65)   (a) walk$'_*$, of type $\langle e, t \rangle$
        (b) love$'_{**}$, of type $\langle e, \langle e, t \rangle\rangle$
        (c) give$'_{***}$, of type $\langle e, \langle e, \langle e, t \rangle\rangle\rangle$
        (d) man$'_*$, of type $\langle e, t \rangle$

For convenience, I will treat all common nouns as purely extensional.

Following Montague (1973) (*modulo* the differences just noted), I treat quantified NP's, proper names, and definite NP's as functors on one-place predicates. These *basic NP's* translate into $\mathscr{L}$-expressions of type $\langle s, \langle\!\langle e, t \rangle, t \rangle\!\rangle$, as shown in (66).

(66)   (a) every man $\Rightarrow \hat{P}\forall x[\text{man}'_*(x) \to P(x)]$
        (b) Sandy $\Rightarrow \hat{P}P(s)$
        (c) Kim $\Rightarrow \hat{P}P(k)$
        (d) A woman $\Rightarrow \hat{P}\exists x[\text{woman}'_*(x) \wedge P(x)]$
        (e) nothing $\Rightarrow \hat{P} \sim \exists x[P(x)]$

Following Thomason (1976a, b) and Gazdar, intransitive verbs denote functions from basic NP-denotations to truth values; that is intransitive verbs translate into $\mathscr{L}$-expressions of type $\langle\langle s, \langle\langle e, t\rangle, t\rangle\rangle, t\rangle$, which I abbreviate as $\langle \text{NP}', t \rangle$. Thus walk', run', and whistle' are all expressions of this type.

Similarly, transitive verb translations, love', kiss', etc., are of type $\langle \text{NP}', \langle \text{NP}', t\rangle\rangle$, i.e. they denote functions from NP-denotations to intransitive verb denotations. Ditransitive verbs are dealt with in like manner, give' being of type $\langle \text{NP}', \langle \text{NP}', \langle \text{NP}', t\rangle\rangle\rangle$. Predicate adjectives are treated here in the same fashion as intransitive verbs, with copular *be* not contributing to the semantic interpretation:

(67) $\langle 67, [_{AP} A], A' \rangle$, where $A^*_{67} = \{\text{happy, angry...}\}$

(68) $\langle 68, [_{VP} V \; XP], XP' \rangle$, where $V^*_{68} = \{\text{be}\}$
    [N.B. XP here abbreviates $\{\text{NP, PP, AP}\}$]

Extensional first-order reducibility is guaranteed by the following meaning postulates.

(69)   (a) $\exists P \forall \mathscr{P} \,\Box\,[\delta(\mathscr{P}) \leftrightarrow \mathscr{P}\{\hat{x}P(x)\}]$
        where δ translates any intransitive verb.
    (b) $\exists M \forall \mathscr{P} \forall \mathscr{Q} \,\Box\,[\delta(\mathscr{Q})(\mathscr{P}) \leftrightarrow \mathscr{P}\{\hat{x}[\check{\,}M](\mathscr{Q})(x)\}]$
        where δ translates any transitive verb.
    (c) $\exists N \forall \mathscr{P} \forall x \,\Box\,[\delta_*(\mathscr{P})(x) \leftrightarrow \mathscr{P}\{\hat{y}[\check{\,}N](y)(x)\}]$
        where $\delta_* = \lambda\mathscr{R}\lambda z\delta(\mathscr{R})(\hat{P}P(z))$, δ translating any transitive verb except *seek*, *conceive*, etc. N.B. – the existence of δ_* is guaranteed by (69)(b)

This incomplete list of meaning postulates is inspired by a suggestion of Partee's (Partee (1975, 289)). The intent is that expressions containing walk reduce to ones containing walk$'_*$, those containing find' or seek' reduce to ones containing find$'_*$, or seek$'_*$, and that those containing find$'_*$ reduce to ones containing find$'_{**}$. I will provide one example of such a reduction in a moment.

Simplex sentences containing basic NP's are analyzed by means of the
following rules. For the sake of perspicuity, I omit all discussion of tense.

(70) $\langle 70, [_s \text{ NP} \quad \text{VP}], \text{VP}'(\text{NP}')\rangle$

(71) $\langle 71, [_{vp} \text{ V}], \text{V}'\rangle$, where $\text{V}^*_{71} = \{\text{walk, run} \ldots\}$

(72) $\langle 72, [_{vp} \text{ V NP}], \text{V}'(\text{NP}')\rangle$, where $\text{V}^*_{72} = \{\text{love, find, seek} \ldots\}$

(73) illustrates the analysis of a simplex sentence whose subject and object
are basic NP's.

(73)
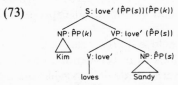

The extensional first-order reducibility of the resulting $\mathscr{L}$-sentence is
illustrated by the following derivation (further details of such derivations
may be found in Partee (1975).

(74)   (a) $\text{love}' \, (\hat{P}P(s))(\hat{P}P(k))$ (translation rules)

        (b) $[\hat{P}P(k)]\{\hat{x} \, \text{love}'_*(\hat{P}P(s))(x)\}$ (meaning postulate (69)(b))

        (c) $[\check{}\hat{P}P(k)](\hat{x} \, \text{love}'_*(\hat{P}P(s))(x))$ (definition of $\{\}$-notation)

        (d) $[\lambda PP(k)](\hat{x} \, \text{love}'_*(\hat{P}P(s))(x))$ (definition of $\hat{}$-notation, $\check{}$-cancellation

        (e) $[\hat{x} \, \text{love}'_* \, (\hat{P}P(s))(x)](k)$ (λ-conversion)

        (f) $[\lambda x \, \text{love}'_* \, (\hat{P}P(s))(x)](k)$ ($\hat{}$-notation)

        (g) $\text{love}'_* \, (\hat{P}P(s))(k)$ (λ-conversion)

        (h) $[\hat{P}P(s)]\{\hat{y} \, \text{love}'_{**}(y)(k)\}$ (meaning postulate (69)(c))

        (i) $[\hat{y} \, \text{love}'_{**}(y)(k)](s)$ ($\hat{}$-notation, $\check{}$-cancellation, λ-conversion)

        (j) $\text{love}'_{**}(s)(k)$ ($\hat{}$-notation, λ-conversion)

From (74)(k) the observed semantic properties of *Kim loves Sandy*,
substitutivity of identicals, existential import, etc., follow directly.

The essence of the analysis of *there* and *it* is to treat them as identity
function, which it seems to me reflects the fundamental observation which
inspired the treatment they received in STG, namely the observation that
they fail to contribute substantively, to the semantic interpretation of
sentences. Let us take dummy *it* first. I translate *it* according to the
following rule.

(75) $\langle 75, [_{NP}\ it], I_P\rangle$
          [PRO]

Here I_P is the identity function on propositions (of type $\langle\langle s,t\rangle, \langle s,t\rangle\rangle$) which may be thought of simply as λpp.

Extraposed clauses are analyzed by rules such as the following.

(76) $\langle 76, [_{VP}\ V\ \bar{S}], \lambda sV'(s(\bar{S}'))\rangle$,

          where $V_{76}^* = \{$seem, appear,...$\}$

(77) $\langle 77, [_{AP}\ A\ \bar{S}], \lambda sA'(s(\bar{S}'))\rangle$,

          where $A_{77}^* = \{$obvious, likely,....$\}$

(78) $\langle 78, [_{\bar{S}}\ that\ S], [\hat{S}']\rangle$

The s-variable in rules (76) and (77) are of type $\langle\langle s,t\rangle, \langle s,t\rangle\rangle$. Seem', obvious' and the like are assumed to be $\mathscr{L}$-expressions of type $\langle\langle s,t\rangle, t\rangle^9$. These rules analyze trees like the following one.

(80)

The resulting $\mathscr{L}$-translation for this sentence reduces to (81) by λ-conversion and application of the identity function.

(81)   obvious' $([\hat{\ }angry'\ (\hat{P}P(k))])$

This in turn reduces to (82) in the fashion of (74):

(82)   obvious' $([\hat{\ }angry'_*(k)])$

Such representations provide an appropriate account of the semantic properties of simplex sentences like (80).[10]

The treatment of *there*-sentences is similar, but somewhat more complicated because there are at least four types of VP's which may take *there* as their simplex subject. Let us consider first the analysis of simple copular sentences containing PP's, which are in general (except for case-marking prepositions, *to*, *by*, etc.) analyzed according to the following rule.

(83) $\langle 83, [_{PP} \text{ P NP}], \text{P}'(\text{NP}')\rangle$, where $\text{P}^*_{83} = \{\text{in, on, under}...\}$

Prepositions are here analyzed essentially as transitive verbs, e.g. in' is of type $\langle \text{NP}', \langle \text{NP}', t\rangle\rangle$.

By (83) and (68), we analyze structures such as (84).

(84)

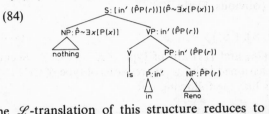

The $\mathscr{L}$-translation of this structure reduces to (85), which reflects its semantic properties appropriately.

(85) $\sim \exists x[\text{in}_{**}(r)(x)]$

Now *there*, like *it* will be translated as an identity function, but one of a different type, namely I_N – the identity function on NP-denotations. I_N is of type $\langle \text{NP}', \text{NP}'\rangle$ and may be thought of simply as $\lambda \mathscr{P}\mathscr{P}$. *There* is introduced by the following rule.

(86) $\langle 86, [_{NP \atop [PRO]} \text{ there}], I_N\rangle$

To create rules for the VP's which require *there* as their simplex-subject, I introduce the following metarule (*n* is a variable of type $\langle \text{NP}', \text{NP}'\rangle$).

(87) $\langle i, [_{VP} \text{ V } \alpha], \text{T}\rangle \Rightarrow$
          $\langle i, [_{VP} \text{ V NP } \alpha], \lambda n\text{T}(n(\text{NP}'))\rangle$,
          where $\text{V}^*_i = \{\text{be, arise}, ...\}$ and $\alpha = \text{PP, AP, or VP}$

This metarule applies to one instantiation of (68) to create the following rule.

(88) $\langle 68, [_{VP} \text{ V NP PP}], \lambda n\text{PP}'(n(\text{NP}'))\rangle$
          $\text{V}^*_{68} = \{\text{be, arise}...\}$

With this rule we now have an analysis of trees like the following.

(89)

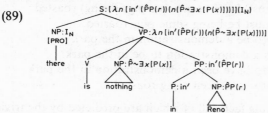

The $\mathscr{L}$-translation of this structure reduces by λ-conversion to (90), and (90) reduces to (85) which, it will be recalled, is the reduced $\mathscr{L}$-translation of *Nothing is in Reno*.

(90) $[in' \, (\hat{P}P(r))](I_N(\hat{P} \sim \exists x[P(x)]))$

The proposed analysis thus correctly predicts the truth conditional equivalence of (84) and (89).

Further refinements are possible. It may be possible to deal with the definiteness restriction on existential *there*-sentences by limiting the domain of I_N, i.e. defining it as an identity function only on certain NP-denotations. Alternatively, a modification of the *there*-analysis to incorporate the semantic distinction proposed by Milsark (1974, 1977) may also be workable, though I will not explore these possibilities here.

Further support for this mode of analysis is provided by the fact that the "leftmost-*be* restriction" (Milsark (1974)) can be accommodated in the following way. Assuming progressive participles, but not gerund or gerundive *ing* forms, are marked with the feature [PRP] (see Gazdar, Pullum and Sag ms.) for further discussion), the metarule (87) may be modified so as to affect only rules expanding VP's that are [− PRP]. This modification, taken together with whatever device is assumed to block passivization of copular *be* (some such device is necessary in any analysis), predicts precisely the following data.

(90)   (a) *There is being no one polite.
         (b) There is no one being polite.
         (c) There has been a riot in this park.
         (d) Kim resented there being no guard on duty.
         (e) There being no one in the waiting room, I'm leaving.
         (f) There must have been a riot in this park.
(91)   (a) There was a pig roasted.
         (b) *There is being a pig roasted.

(c) There is a pig being roasted.
(d) There (must) have been some pigs (being) roasted.
(e) *There must be being some pigs roasted.

(92)   (a) There is to be a demonstration in the park.
(b) *There is a demonstration to be in the park.
(c) There is to have been a demonstration in the park.
(d) There is to have been a pig roasted.

These seemingly perplexing facts, all of which are predicted by the trivial modification just suggested, are not accounted for within any transformational analysis that I am familiar with.

Another problem case for previous theories is the existence of examples like (93), which (compare (94)) have no grammatical source in an STG account (hence requiring some new device to make the *There*-Insertion transformation obligatory in this one case).

(93)   There is a Sanata Claus.
(94)   *A Santa Claus is.

These are analysed in the present framework by the following rule.

(95) $\langle 95, [_{\text{VP}} \text{ V } \text{NP}], \lambda n \text{V}'(n(\text{NP}'))\rangle$,

where $\text{V}^*_{94} = \{\text{be}\}$

This assumes that the *be* of V^*_{95} ("existential" *be*) translates as exist'. There is no rule that will analyze (94).

Several peculiarities of simplex *there*-sentences which have resisted analysis within TG of any variety are dealt with straightforwardly in the analysis I have just sketched. The essential regularity of the construction is expressed by the metarule (87) and no ad hoc devices need be introduced.

The intended account of the dependencies of (1)–(3) should by now be clear. Basic NP's, dummy *there* and dummy *it* translate into $\mathcal{L}$-expressions of three different types, as summarized in (96).

(96)   (a) Basic NP's.
$every\ man \Rightarrow \hat{P}\forall x[\text{man}'_*(x) \rightarrow P(x)]$ all $\mathcal{L}$-expressions of
$Sandy \Rightarrow \hat{P}P(s)$ type:
$nothing \Rightarrow \hat{P} \sim \exists x[P(x)]$ $\langle s, \langle\langle e,t\rangle, t\rangle\rangle$
(b) $there \Rightarrow \text{I}_{\text{N}}$ of type $\langle\text{NP}',\text{NP}'\rangle$
(c) $it \Rightarrow \text{I}_{\text{P}}$ of type $\langle\langle s,t\rangle, \langle s,t\rangle\rangle$

Simplex VP's are also of three translation types:

(97)   (a) Basic VP's

$\left.\begin{array}{l} walks \Rightarrow \text{walk}' \\ loves\ Kim \Rightarrow \text{love}'\ (\hat{P}P(k)) \end{array}\right\}$ all $\mathscr{L}$-expressions of type: $\langle \text{NP}', t \rangle$

(b) *There*-VP's

is nothing in Reno $\Rightarrow \lambda n[\text{in}'(\hat{P}P(r))$ of type: $(n(\hat{P} \sim \exists x[P(x)]))]$ $\langle\langle\, \text{NP}', \text{NP}' \rangle, t \rangle$

(c) *it*-VP's

is obvious that Kim is angry $\Rightarrow \lambda s$ of type $\langle\langle\langle s, t \rangle,$ obvious' $(s([\hat{\ }\text{angry}'(\hat{P}P(k))]))$ $\langle s, t \rangle\rangle, t \rangle$

Each VP-translation (VP') is an $\mathscr{L}$-expression of the type $\langle \alpha, t \rangle$, for some α, and each NP' is of type α, for some α. The translations for simplex sentences are given by the translation rule: VP' (NP') and this results in a sentence of $\mathscr{L}$ (an expression of type t) whenever VP' is of type $\langle \alpha, t \rangle$ and NP' is of type α, for some α. The translation of (1) (a)–(3) (a) thus proceeds as desired.

If however, in a sentence of NP-VP form, VP' is of type $\langle \alpha, t \rangle$ and NP' is of type β, where $\alpha \neq \beta$, then VP' (NP') is not an expression of $\mathscr{L}$ (because the syntactic rules of $\mathscr{L}$ define no such expressions). Thus any attempt to translate a structure consisting of a basic VP and a *there*- or *it*-subject, a *there*-VP and a basic NP or *it*-subject, or an *it*-VP and a basic NP or *there*-subject will fail. But these are precisely the ill-formed examples of *(1)(b–c)–*(3)(b–c). The grammar must assign a coherent sentence translation. When it cannot, the structure in question is ruled "functionally" deviant by SCP, the principle mentioned at the end of the previous section. The translation rules I have given, together with SCP, thus provide an account of the simplex dependencies of (1)–(3).

This analysis of the simplex dependencies immediately extends to the SOR cases ((10)–(12)). We adopt the following two rules (only slightly modified from (53) and (55) above, and basically as proposed by Gazdar), which have as a consequence that the infinitive phrase translation takes the object NP-translation as argument.[11]

(98) $\langle 98, [_{\overline{\text{VP}}}\ to\ \text{VP}],\ \text{VP}' \rangle$
(99) $\langle 99, [_{\text{VP}}\ \text{V NP}\ \overline{\text{VP}}],\ \text{V}'([\overline{\text{VP}}'(\text{NP}')]) \rangle$,
        where $V^*_{99} = \{\text{believe, expect} \dots\}$

The dependencies of (10)–(12) are thus explained in terms of SCP in exactly the same way as (1)–(3) were dealt with. (10)(b, c)–(12)(b, c) are functionally deviant.

To accommodate the dependencies of (4)–(9), I analyze A-Raising verbals in terms of rules whose third element is a translation rule schema. In rules such as the following, which are closely related to Gazdar's (see (54) above) and to the analysis assumed by Dowty (1978), α ranges over variables of any type (although the only types utilized here are the three translation types of NP's).

(100) $\langle 100, [_{VP} \; V \; \overline{VP}], \lambda\alpha V'([^\frown \overline{VP}'(\alpha)])\rangle$,

where $V^*_{100} = \{\text{tend, happen}\ldots\}$

(101) $\langle 101, [_{VP} \; V \; \underset{[TO]}{(PP)} \; \overline{VP}], \lambda\alpha V'(PP')([^\frown \overline{VP}'(\alpha)])\rangle$,

where $V^*_{101} = \{\text{seem, appear}\ldots\}$

(102) $\langle 102, [_{AP} \; A \; \overline{VP}]. \lambda\alpha A'([^\frown \overline{VP}'(\alpha)])\rangle$,

where $A^*_{102} = \{\text{likely},\ldots\}$

Since in any given structure the translation-type of a given embedded infinitive phrase $(\overline{VP}')$ is unique, it follows that only one instantiation of α results in a well-formed $\mathcal{L}$-expression. The schemata of (100)–(102), together with SCP, guarantee that the functional dependencies of embedded $\overline{VP}$'s are inherited by the immediately dominating nodes. That is, we have VP's containing A-Raising verbals which are also of exactly three types.

(103)   (a) Basic VP's
             is likely to walk $\Rightarrow \lambda\mathscr{P}$ likely' $([^\frown \text{walk}'(\mathscr{P})])$; of type $\langle NP', t\rangle$
        (b) There-VP's
             is likely to be nothing in Reno
             λo likely' $([^\frown [\lambda n[\text{in}'(\hat{P}P(r))(n(\hat{P} \sim \exists x[P(x)]))]](o)])$;
             of type $\langle\!\langle NP', NP'\rangle, t\rangle$
        (c) it-VP's
             is likely to be obvious that Kim is angry
             λt likely' $([^\frown [\lambda s \text{ obvious}' (s([^\frown \text{angry}' (\hat{P}P(k))]))]](t)])$;
             of type $\langle\!\langle\!\langle s, t\rangle, \langle s, t\rangle\!\rangle, t\rangle$[12]

The dependencies of (4)–(9) are thus analyzed in quite the same fashion as the simplex dependencies. A VP-translation of a given type can take as argument only one type of NP-translation.[13]

It should be noted that the introduction of translation schemata is motivated on independent grounds. As is frequently noted, words like *even* and *only* operate on expressions of various kinds: NP's, VP's, AP's, V's, P's, and others, whose logical analysis is uncontroversially diverse. Thus any rule for translating phrases containing *even* or *only* must make some part of the translation vary systematically with another, which is all that a rule schema of the sort I have introduced involves.

Turning to the "raised-passivized" dependencies of (13)–(15), it is evident that they are all predicted by a version of the passive metarule quite like Gazdar's:

(104) $\langle i, [_{VP \atop [-PAS]} V\ NP\ X], T \rangle \Rightarrow$

$\langle i, [_{VP \atop [+PAS]} V\ (PP) \atop [by] \ X], \lambda\alpha T'(PP') \rangle,$

where $T' = T_\alpha^{NP'}$, i.e. the result for uniformly substituting α for NP' in T.[14]

(104) applies to rule (99) to yield the following CSR.

(105) $\langle 99, [_{VP \atop [+PAS]} V\ (PP) \atop [by] \ \overline{VP}], \lambda\alpha V'([^\wedge \overline{VP}'(\alpha)])(PP') \rangle,$

where $V_{99}^* = \{believe, expect...\}$

Passive *be* subcategorizes [+ PAS] VP's (see Gazdar, Pullum, and Sag(ms.) for further details). Hence, trees like the following are analyzed.

(106)

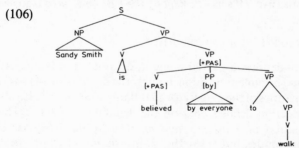

Because the embedded infinitive phrase translates as an expression of type $\langle NP', t \rangle$, (105) provides only one functionally-coherent translation of $VP_{[+PAS]}$. and hence of the highest VP (since *be* does not contribute to the translation). That translation is given in (107).

(107)   *is believed by everyone to walk*

$\lambda \mathscr{P}$ believe' $([\hat{\ } \text{walk}'(\mathscr{P})])(\hat{P}\forall x[\text{person}'_*(x) \to P(x)])$

This $\mathscr{L}$-expression is also of type $\langle NP', t \rangle$. Hence, when it is applied to a *basic* NP-translation, a sentence-translation is produced. The sentence translation of (106) reduces to (108), exactly as desired.

(108) $\forall x[\text{person}'_*(x) \to \text{believe}'_*([\hat{\ } \text{walk}'_*(s)])(x)]$

If the subject of (106) were dummy *there* or dummy *it*, however, the translation of (107) could not apply to the translation of the subject NP. Thus the dependency of (13) is also explained as a matter of functional deviance. Moreover, the account extends to (14) and (15), whose embedded VP's are a *there*-VP and an *it*-VP, respectively. The translation schema of (105) and SCP predict the observed dependencies.

The treatment of (semi-compositional) idioms fits into the present framework, although certain details remain to be worked out. If the dependency between *keep*, *tabs*, and *on* is a semantic one, each of these expressions has an $\mathscr{L}$-translation, denoting a function with drastic domain restrictions, as noted earlier. Thus the rule in (109) may undergo the passive metarule to yield (110).

(109) $\langle 109, [_{VP} \text{ V NP PP}], V'(PP')(NP') \rangle$

(110) $\langle 110, [_{VP} \text{ V (PP) PP}], \lambda \alpha V'(PP')(\alpha)(PP') \rangle$
         [+PAS]   [by]   [by]

(110) in turn allows passive VP's like *be kept by the FBI on Kim* to translate as (111).

(111) $\lambda \mathscr{P}\text{keep}'(\text{on}'(\hat{P}P(k)))(\mathscr{P})$ (the FBI')

Assuming that keep' denotes a partial function defined on only one NP-intension at its second argument position, namely the denotation of tabs', it follows from the semantics of the λ operator that the expression in (111) also denotes a partial function defined only on the denotation of tabs'. Thus (112), the $\mathscr{L}$-translation of *Tabs are kept on Kim by the FBI*, has an interpretation in any model, but (113), the $\mathscr{L}$-translation of *Observations are kept on Kim by the FBI* does not.

(112) $[\lambda \mathscr{P} \text{keep}'(\text{on}'(\hat{P}P(k)))(\mathscr{P})(\text{the FBI}')](\text{tabs}')$

(113) $[\lambda \mathscr{P} \text{keep}'(\text{on}'(\hat{P}P(k)))(\mathscr{P})(\text{the FBI}')]$ (observations')

The result of this kind of semantic dependency is that idiom chunks like *tabs* may appear in syntactic structures only if the functional structure guarantees that the denotation of the idiom chunk is provided as the argument of the denotational function of the expression upon which it depends, e.g. *keep on* (NP). In the case of VP-idioms, this will happen only if the rules introducing semi-compositional idioms are input to the passive metarule and the structures which arise from these rules are embedded within the appropriate structures whose translation passes dependencies along. As we have seen, there are four constructions where the functional dependencies are passed along by the translation process: simplex sentences, SSR-constructions, SOR-constructions, and "raised-passive" constructions. The dependencies of (17)–(21) are thus all reanalyzed as semantic dependencies.

Assuming that other idioms are handled in the semantics, e.g. (114).

(114)   The cat is out of the bag.

the very same dependencies follow immediately. That is, if the idiomatic *be out of the bag* always denotes a function defined only on the idiomatic denotation of *the cat*, all of the following examples are analyzed (on the idiomatic reading).

(115)   (a) The cat is likely to be out of the bag.
          (b) Kim believed the cat to be out of the bag.
          (c) The cat was believed to be out of the bag.

Moreover, EQUI-constructions, which I have not discussed here at all, involve no translation schemata, but rather are analyzed by such rules as (116).

(116) $\langle 116, [_{\text{VP}} \text{ V } \overline{\text{VP}}], \lambda \mathscr{P} \mathscr{P} \{ \hat{x} \text{ V}'(\hat{\ } \overline{\text{VP}}'(\hat{P}P(x)))(\hat{P}P(x)) \} \rangle$,

where $\text{V}^*_{116} = \{ \text{want, try} \ldots \}$

Here the infinitive phrase translation is not applied to the matrix subject translation at any stage of the reduction, but rather is applied to $\hat{P}P(x)$, which must be of type $\langle s, \langle\langle e, t \rangle, t \rangle\rangle$, i.e. the translation type of *basic* NP's. Thus on the theory presented here, all of the following examples are ruled semantically deviant.

(117)   (a) *The cat wants to be out of the bag. (idiomatic reading)
          (b) *Tabs wanted to be kept on Kim by the FBI.
          (c) *It wanted to be obvious that Kim left.

$$\text{(d) *There wanted to be} \begin{cases} \text{a pig roasted every year.} \\ \text{a riot developing somewhere.} \\ \text{nothing in Reno.} \\ \text{nobody prouder than Kim.} \end{cases}$$

These are central facts which any serious alternative to STG must explain.[15]

Finally, it should be noted that certain semantic facts, which as far as I can see are entirely problematic for most current theories, follow immediately from the analysis I have suggested. As was noted first, I believe, by Julius Moravcsik, sentences like (118) have a de dicto reading.

(118)   A unicorn is likely to be in the park.

That is, on one reading (118) does not entail (119).

(119)   There is a unicorn.

The translation for (118) produced by our rules is (120) (again ignoring details of the translation of definite descriptions).

(120) $[\lambda \mathscr{P} \text{ likely}'(\hat{}[\text{in}' \text{ (the park}')]$
          $(\mathscr{P}))](\hat{P}\exists x[\text{unicorn}'_{*}(x) \wedge P(x)])$

This in turn reduces to (121).

(121) $\text{likely}'([\hat{}\exists x[\text{unicorn}'_{*}(x) \wedge \text{in}'_{**}(\text{the park}')(x)]])$

Since the existential quantifier is inside the scope of likely', (119) does not follow from (121), correctly accounting for the observed semantic fact.

The same in fact is true of the translations produced for examples like those in (122).

(122)   (a) Kim believes a unicorn to be in the park.
          (b) A unicorn was believed to be in the park.

In short, the semantic analysis sketched here correctly associates with each such sentence a de dicto translation, thus avoiding the crucial shortcoming (noted by Montague himself) in the framework outlined in Montague (1973)[16]

Finally, it should be observed that examples like (123) also have a de dicto reading (I owe this example to Emmon Bach).

(123)   A good man is hard to find.

By analyzing the *tough*-construction by means of rules like the following, such facts are predicted to the letter.[17]

(124) $\langle 124, [_{AP}$ A (PP) $\overline{VP}/NP],$
                           [for]

$\lambda \mathscr{P} PP'\{\hat{x}A'(\hat{P}P(x))(\hat{~}\overline{VP}/NP'(\hat{P}P(x)))\} \rangle$

where $A^*_{124} = \{easy, tough....\}$

I take it as evident that an adequate semantic analysis of English must predict all the facts just cited.

CONCLUSION

In this paper, I have offered a reanalysis of various fundamental facts of English grammar. The complex dependencies summarized in section 1, standardly dealt with in TG by syntactic transformations have been dealt with by a phrase structure grammar and a single principle of semantic coherence. The account offered here is preferable to current transformational theories in that it does without transformational rules entirely, and eliminates otherwise unmotivated filtering devices (see section 3). The class of possible grammars available within a theory of the sort outlined here, and in Gazdar (this volume) is drastically constrained, yet the observed generalizations are expressed without the addition of otherwise unmotivated devices.

I conclude with two remarks concerning filtering. First, the semantic coherence principle developed here need not be viewed as "applying" to the output of the grammar. If it should prove to be desirable to do so, the type dependencies can be guaranteed locally by adding further conditions on rules.

This is illustrated for the relevant rules in (125).

(125)   (a) $\langle 70, [_S$ NP VP], VP'(NP')$\rangle$

          NP' is of type $a \supset$ VP' is of type $\langle a, t \rangle$

          (b) $\langle 99, [_{VP}$ V NP $\overline{VP}],$ V'([$\hat{~}\overline{VP}'(NP')$])$\rangle$,
          where $V^*_{99} = \{believe, expect...\}$
          NP' is of type $a \supset$ VP' is of type $\langle a, t \rangle$

          (c) $\langle 100, [_{VP}$ V $\overline{VP}], \lambda \alpha V'([\hat{~}\overline{VP}'(\alpha)])\rangle$
          where $V^*_{100} = \{tend, happen...\}$
          VP' is of type $\langle a, t \rangle \supset \alpha$ is of type a

Second, if it should prove to be desirable to eliminate filtering devices altogether,[18] one could do so simply by retaining the syntactic features proposed by Gazdar, together with the logical reanalysis I have sketched here. An approach of that sort, which seems ad hoc from a syntactic point of view, as I have noted, would nonetheless provide an adequate account of the dependencies in section 1 including the idiom chunk dependencies, without any appeal to filtering.

Finally, though there are several places where the analysis I have suggested admittedly lacks independent motivation (particularly in the semantic analysis of the *there* construction). I have provided a comprehensive and precise account of the facts motivating cyclical movement transformations in STG. Furthermore I am aware of no successful analyses of comparable detail in any transformational or non-transformational framework (except STG). It is only when such analyses are provided that theories can be judged.

Stanford University

NOTES

* Various versions of the present paper were presented at Stanford University, The University of Washington, The University of Wisconsin at Madison, The University of Texas at Austin and Sussex University. I would like to thank the following people for helpful discussions: Jon Barwise, Mike Brame, Robin Cooper, David Dowty, Gerald Gazdar, Jorge Hankamer, James Higginbotham, Jerry Morgan, Fritz Newmeyer, Barbara Partee, Stanley Peters, Geoffrey Pullum, Robert Stalnaker, Tom Wasow, and Steve Weisler. The research reported here was conducted while I was an Andrew Mellon Fellow at Stanford University.
[1] The names for these rules vary somewhat from author to author. I use essentially the terminology of Soames and Perlmutter (1979).
[2] "It walks to school" is of course grammatical if *it* is a referring personal pronoun, which it is not in the examples I am considering.
[3] For a critical summary of the literature citing such dependencies as evidence for the inadequacy of phrase structure grammars, see Gazdar and Pullum (ms.).
[4] For arguments in favor of surface structures of roughly this form, see Milsark*(1974).
[5] For a discussion of these constraints and conventions, see Chomsky (1973, 1975, 1977, 1980).
[6] Many problems of detail have never been actually worked in REST (to my knowledge). Note for instance that the *there*-interpretation analysis assumed by Chomsky (1980), i.e. Milsark's (see (42)–(43) above) works only for simplex structures. If some further rule of interpretation is assumed to "feed" the rule interpreting the structure in (42) as (43) in the A Raising cases, then that rule would necessarily do just what "move NP" does, but in reverse. I presume that such obvious redundancy is an intolerable consequence. Though I see no other possible solution to this problem within REST, I leave its further investigation to others.
[7] The interpretation of *there* in examples like (14) (a) encounters the same difficulties in REST as that noted earlier (note 6).

[8] I have used the rule in (54) as an illustration rather than the similar rule which analyzes AP's whose head is *likely*, etc. in order to avoid unnecessary complication of exposition. For further details see Gazdar (this volume).

[9] I omit here discussion of the irrelevant modifications required in order to accommodate optional indirect objects.

[10] This is not quite true of course, as the notion of proposition assumed here, i.e. functions from indices to truth values, is not fine-grained enough to distinguish among logical truths or contradictions.

[11] More precisely, the denotation of the infinitive phrase translation (in any model) is a function which takes the denotation of the object NP-translation as argument.

[12] Here o and n are variables of type $\langle NP', NP' \rangle$; t and s are variables of type $\langle\langle s, t \rangle, \langle s, t \rangle\rangle$.

[13] More precisely, a VP-translation of a given sort has as its denotation (in any model) a function which can take as argument only one type of NP-translation denotation.

[14] For a different treatment of passives by metarule, see Gazdar and Sag (1981).

[15] I have not discussed related facts, concerning *persuade, force* and the like, which receive a similar account.

[16] I assume *de re* readings are to be produced by augmenting the semantic translation algorithm with something very close to the "storage mechanism" suggested by Cooper (1975, 1979). An initial step in this direction is taken by Sag and Weisler (1979).

[17] This proposal assumes that traces translate as variables ranging over (intensional) NP-denotations. It is intended that $\mathscr{P}$ occurs freely in $\overline{VP}/NP'$.

[18] As far as I am aware, no arguments for or against the desirability of this have ever been given.

REFERENCES

Baltin, M. R. (1978) *Toward a Theory of Movement Rules*, Doctoral Dissertation, MIT.

Brame, M. K. (1976) *Conjectures and Refutations in Syntax and Semantics.* New York: North-Holland.

Brame, M. K. (1978) *Base Generated Syntax*, Seattle: Noit Amrofer.

Bresnan, J. W. (1978) 'Toward a Realistic Model of Transformational Grammar,' in M. Halle, J. Bresnan, and G. A. Miller (eds.), *Linguistic Theory and Psychological Reality*, Cambridge: MIT Press.

Chomsky, N. (1965) *Aspects of the Theory of Syntax*, Cambridge: MIT Press.

Chomsky, N. (1973) 'Conditions on Transformations,' in *Eassy on Form and Interpretation*, New York: North Holland, 81–160.

Chomsky, N. (1975) *Reflections on Language*, New York: Pantheon.

Chomsky, N. (1977) 'On *wh*-Movement,' in Culicover et al. (eds.), *Formal Syntax*, New York: Academic Press.

Chomsky, N. (1980) 'On Binding', *Linguistic Inquiry* 11, 1–46.

Chomsky, N., and H. Lasnik (1978) 'Filters and Control', *Linguistic Inquiry* 8, 425–504.

Cooper, R. (1975) *Montague's Semantic Theory and Transformational Syntax*, Doctoral Dissertation, University of Massachusetts, Amherst.

Cooper, R. (1978) 'A Fragment of English with Questions and Relatives', unpublished manuscript, University of Wisconsin; Madison, Wisconsin.

Dowty, D. R. (1978) 'Lexically Governed Transformations as Lexical Rules in a Montague Grammar', *Linguistic Inquiry* **9**, 393–426.

Emonds, J. (1976) *A Transformational Approach to English Syntax: Root, Structure-preserving and Local Transformations*, New York: Academic Press.

Fiengo, R. W. (1977) 'On Trace Theory', *Linguistic Inquiry* **8**, 35–62.

Gazdar, G. J. M. (1980) 'Unbounded Dependencies and Coordinate Structures', *Linguistic Inquiry* **11**.

Gazdar, G. J. M. (this volume) 'Phrase Structure Grammar'.

Gazdar, G. J. M., and G. K. Pullum (ms.) 'Natural Languages and Context-free Languages', unpublished, Stanford University.

Gazdar, G. J. M., G. K. Pullum and I. A. Sag (ms.) 'A Phrase Structure Grammar for the English Auxiliary System'.

Gazdar, G. J. M., and I. A. Sag (1981) 'Passives and Reflexives in Phrase Structure Grammar', in proceedings of the Third Amsterdam Colloquium on Formal Methods in the Study of Language.

Milsark, G. (1974) *Existential Sentences in English*, Doctoral Dissertation, M.I.T.

Milsark, G. (1977) 'Toward an Explanation of Certain Peculiarities of the Existential Construction in English', *Linguistic Analysis* **3**, 1–29.

Montague, R. (1970) 'Pragmatics and Intensional Logic', in Montague (1974).

Montague, R. (1973) 'The Proper Treatment of Quantification in Ordinary English', in Montague (1974).

Montague, R. (1974) *Formal Philosophy* (ed. R. Thomason), New Haven: Yale University Press.

Nunberg, G., I. A. Sag, and T. Wasow (in preparation) 'The Semantic Compositionality of Phrasal Idioms,' Stanford University.

Partee, B. H. (1975) 'Montague Grammar and Transformational Grammar', *Linguistic Inquiry* **6**.

Postal, P. M. (1974) *On Raising*, Cambridge, Mass.: MIT Press.

Rosenbaum, P. S. (1967) *The Grammar of English Predicate Complement Constructions*, Cambridge Mass.: MIT Press.

Sag, I. A., and S. Weisler (1979) 'Temporal Connectives and Logical Form', in Proceedings of the 5th Annual Meeting of the Berkeley Linguistic Society.

Soames, S., and D. M. Perlmutter (1979) *Syntactic Argumentation and the Structure of English*, Berkeley: University of California Press.

INDEX

SYNTHESE LANGUAGE LIBRARY

Texts and Studies in Linguistics and Philosophy

Managing Editors:

JAAKKO HINTIKKA (Florida State University)
STANLEY PETERS (The University of Texas at Austin)

Editors:

EMMON BACH (University of Massachusetts at Amherst), JOAN BRESNAN
(Massachusetts Institute of Technology), JOHN LYONS (University of Sussex),
JULIUS M. E. MORAVCSIK (Stanford University), PATRICK SUPPES (Stanford
University), DANA SCOTT (Oxford University).

1. Henry Hiż (ed.), *Questions.* 1978.
2. William S. Cooper, *Foundations of Logico-Linguistics. A Unified Theory of Information, Language, and Logic.* 1978.
3. Avishai Margalit (ed.), *Meaning and Use.* 1979.
4. F. Guenthner and S. J. Schmidt (eds.), *Formal Semantics and Pragmatics for Natural Languages.* 1978.
5. Esa Saarinen (ed.), *Game-Theoretical Semantics.* 1978.
6. F. J. Pelletier (ed.), *Mass Terms: Some Philosophical Problems.* 1979.
7. David R. Dowty, *Word Meaning and Montague Grammar. The Semantics of Verbs and Times in Generative Semantics and in Montague's PTQ.* 1979.
8. Alice F. Freed, *The Semantics of English Aspectual Complementation.* 1979.
9. James McCloskey, *Transformational Syntax and Model Theoretic Semantics: A Case Study in Modern Irish.* 1979.
10. John R. Searle, Ferenc Kiefer, and Manfred Bierwisch (eds.), *Speech Act Theory and Pragmatics.* 1980.
11. David R. Dowty, Robert E. Wall, and Stanley Peters, *Introduction to Montague Semantics.* 1981.
12. Frank Heny (ed.), *Ambiguities in Intensional Contexts.* 1981.
13. Wolfgang Klein and Willem Levelt (eds.), *Crossing the Boundaries in Linguistics: Studies Presented to Manfred Bierwisch.* 1981.
14. Zellig S. Harris, *Papers on Syntax*, edited by Henry Hiż. 1981.
15. Pauline Jacobson and Geoffrey K. Pullum (eds.), *The Nature of Syntactic Representation.* 1982.